UNITED NATIONS STUDIES

Number 10

FIELD ADMINISTRATION

IN THE

UNITED NATIONS SYSTEM

Carnegie Endowment for International Peace
United Nations Studies
ISBN 0-313-20320-2 UNSS

1. The Budget of the United Nations, 1947, *ISBN 0-313-20328-8 BUNN*

2. Coordination of Economic and Social Activities, 1948, *ISBN 0-313-20329-6 CESA*

3. Consultation Between the United Nations and Non-Governmental Organizations, 1949, *ISBN 0-313-20330-X COUN*

4. The United Nations Secretariat, 1950, *ISBN 0-313-20331-8 UNNS UNNS*

5. Voting and the Handling of Disputes in the Security Council, 1950, *by Eduardo Jiménez de Aréchaga, ISBN 0-313-20332-6 ARVH*

6. The International Court of Justice: Its Role in the Maintenance of International Peace and Security, 1951, *by Oliver James Lissitzyn, ISBN 0-313-20333-4 LICJ*

7. The Political Role of the General Assembly, 1951, *by Henry Field Haviland, ISBN 0-313-20334-2 HAPG*

8. Latin America in the United Nations, 1956, *by John A. Houston, ISBN 0-313-20335-0 HOLU*

9. The General Assembly of the United Nations, A Study of Procedure and Practice, 1964, *by Sydney Dawson Bailey, ISBN 0-313-20336-9 BAGA*

10. Field Administration in the United Nations System: The Conduct of International Economic and Social Programs, 1961, *by Walter Rice Sharp, ISBN 0-313-20337-7 SHFA*

11. The Secretariat of the United Nations, 1964, *by Sydney Dawson Bailey, ISBN 0-313-20338-5 BASU*

FIELD ADMINISTRATION
in the
UNITED NATIONS SYSTEM

The Conduct of
International Economic and Social Programmes

By
WALTER R. SHARP
Professor of Political Science
Yale University

Published under the auspices of
THE CARNEGIE ENDOWMENT FOR INTERNATIONAL PEACE

GREENWOOD PRESS, PUBLISHERS
WESTPORT, CONNECTICUT

Library of Congress Cataloging in Publication Data

Sharp, Walter Rice, 1896-
Field administration in the United Nations system.

Reprint of the ed. published by Stevens, London, which was issued as no. 10 of United Nations studies.
Includes bibliographical references.
1. United Nations--Technical assistance. 2. United Nations--Officials and employees. I. Title. II. Series: United Nations studies ; no. 10.
[JX1977.8.T4S52 1978 341.7'59 78-2807
ISBN 0-313-20337-7

Reprinted in 1978 by Greenwood Press, Inc.
51 Riverside Avenue, Westport, CT. 06880

Printed in the United States of America

10 9 8 7 6 5 4 3 2 1

CONTENTS

PART TWO

HEADQUARTERS-FIELD RELATIONSHIPS

PART THREE

THE PROGRAMME PROCESS

APPENDIX

MAPS

TABLES

FOREWORD

> United Nations technicians are working with nearly all ministries. They are training policemen and soldiers and have taken the country's telecommunications in hand. . . . In such areas as finance, government administration and health services, the United Nations technicians are making surveys of the Congo's need.

So read a dispatch in *The New York Times* in late July 1960.*

What the United Nations has been called upon to do in the Congo under such dramatic circumstances differed only in degree from what it has been doing and will for many years continue to do in the newly independent states of Asia and Africa and also in Latin America. Several agencies are performing a myriad of tasks in many countries. The machinery is necessarily complex and problems of efficient administration constantly arise.

The Carnegie Endowment has been interested in international administration for a long time. It has devoted several of its publications to surveys of technical assistance operations in one country or region and has initiated a number of meetings and conferences to discuss the many factors involved in assisting development projects and the new problems of international administration. Believing that the time was ripe for a comprehensive survey of field organization in the United Nations system, the Endowment was happy to co-operate with the Rockefeller Foundation and Yale University to sponsor this study by Dr. Walter Sharp.

Dr. Sharp has examined in depth for the first time the way in which the aid programmes of the United Nations system are managed. He has focused upon questions of efficiency and has suggested methods to improve operations. He has also stressed the importance of co-ordinating United Nations operations with the administration of aid from all sources—private, national, international—so that 'admittedly inadequate technical and capital resources can be pooled for maximum impact on world economic and social growth.' This is a

* *The New York Times*, 26 July 1960.

'complex problem,' Dr. Sharp observes, 'as much administrative as economic or financial.'

Based on extensive first-hand research covering a period of four years, the volume presents original data derived from hundreds of interviews and observations in Latin America, the Middle East, South Asia, and the Pacific, as well as at the headquarters of the United Nations, the World Health Organization, the International Labour Organisation, the Food and Agriculture Organization, Unesco, the International Civil Aviation Organization, the International Bank for Reconstruction and Development, and the International Monetary Fund.

Dr. Sharp's main concern is with the administrative process—how it is affected by cultural and institutional relationships, staff multinationalism, time-space factors, and the loose-jointed framework of the United Nations system itself. Yet he does not overlook the role of national and bloc politics in conditioning the operational environment in which international officials and technicians work.

The author brings to this study his own experience as a former staff member of FAO, WHO, and Unesco. During 1954–55 he was Technical Co-Director of the Cairo Institute of Public Administration, jointly sponsored by the United Nations Technical Assistance Administration and the Government of Egypt. Dr. Sharp has also held senior staff positions with the Department of State and UNRRA, and in 1952 served as administrative consultant for the United States Mutual Security Agency in Indo-China. At present, he is Professor of Political Science and Director of Graduate Studies in International Relations at Yale University.

Joseph E. Johnson
President
Carnegie Endowment for International Peace

ACKNOWLEDGMENTS

It is a very pleasant duty to record my personal gratitude to the hundreds of persons who generously contributed of their time and thought to this study at various stages of its preparation.* My principal debt is to those headquarters and field officials and experts of the United Nations and specialized agencies who freely permitted me to bombard them with questions, discreet and otherwise, and whose ideas in many instances found their way into the text of the present volume—without direct attribution of source. For obvious reasons these individuals must with few exceptions remain anonymous. I do wish, however, to convey my special thanks to Laurence Michelmore and Bruce Stedman, both at the time senior officers of the TAB secretariat in New York, for their long-suffering patience with my persistent queries over a period of three years and, in particular, for their kindness in alerting TAB Resident Representatives in Latin America, the Middle East, and Asia concerning my field trips to these areas.

I should like also to express sincere appreciation to my 'advance critics'—the nearly fifty officials and others who took the time to examine the draft manuscript in detail, to note errors of fact or interpretation, to indicate significant omissions, and to submit constructive suggestions. Whatever value the study may have in its final form owes much to their comments.

It is in order to acknowledge with thanks permission to reproduce the following official materials:

from the World Health Organization, the two maps entitled *WHO Regional Offices and the Areas They Serve* and *Network of Epidemiological Radio-telegraphic Communications*; from the International Civil Aviation Organization, the map showing *ICAO Air Navigation Regions*; and from the Technical Assistance Board secretariat, the diagram indicating the *Procedure for Planning and Developing the Programme*.

* I deeply regret that circumstances made it impossible to arrange to continue through subsequent stages of the study the collaboration of Professor H. Paul Castleberry of Washington State University, who, while Fulbright Scholar in Egypt, ably assisted me in assembling a portion of the initial field data on which the study is based.

The study received financial support from Yale University, the Rockefeller Foundation, and the Carnegie Endowment for International Peace. To each of these institutions I am grateful for substantial assistance without which the basic research could not have been brought to completion.

To Miss Anne Winslow and her staff associates at the Carnegie Endowment go my heartfelt thanks for penetrating criticism, meticulous editorial labour, making arrangements for meetings with United Nations Secretariat personnel, and the preparation of the index.

Finally, I am indebted to my indefatigable secretary, Miss Ruth Davis, for handling so superbly the clerical and allied operations involved in manuscript production.

It is perhaps unnecessary to add that responsibility for all expressions of fact and opinion in this volume rests exclusively with the author in his private capacity. The study does not purport to reflect the official views of any United Nations organization or of any Member government.

WALTER R. SHARP

New Haven
June, 1960

ABBREVIATIONS

ACC	Administrative Committee on Co-ordination
ASFEC	Arab States Fundamental Education Centre—Egypt
BMS	Bureau of Relations with Member States (of Unesco)
BTAO	Bureau of Technical Assistance Operations (United Nations)
CCAQ	Consultative Committee on Administrative Questions
CD	*Corps diplomatique*
CREFAL	*Centro Regional de Educación Fundamental para América Latina* (Fundamental Education Centre for Latin America)—Mexico
ECA	Economic Commission for Africa
ECAFE	Economic Commission for Asia and the Far East
ECE	Economic Commission for Europe
ECLA	Economic Commission for Latin America
ECOSOC	Economic and Social Council (United Nations)
EPTA	Expanded Programme of Technical Assistance
ESA	Department of Economic and Social Affairs (United Nations)
FAO	Food and Agriculture Organization of the United Nations)
FOA	Foreign Operations Administration (United States)
GA	General Assembly (United Nations)
IAEA	International Atomic Energy Agency
IA/ECOSOC	Inter-American Economic and Social Council
IBRD	International Bank for Reconstruction and Development
ICA	International Co-operation Administration (United States)
ICAO	International Civil Aviation Organization
ICSAB	International Civil Service Advisory Board
IDA	International Development Association
IFC	International Finance Corporation
ILO	International Labour Organization
IMCO	International Maritime Consultative Organization
IMF	International Monetary Fund
IRO	International Refugee Organisation
ITU	International Telecommunications Union
MSA	Mutual Security Agency (United States)
NGO	Non-Governmental Organization

OAS	Organization of American States
OEEC	Organization for European Economic Co-operation
OPA	Office of Public Administration (under UN Secretary-General)
OPEX	Division of Operational, Executive, and Administrative Personnel
OPI	Office of Public Information (United Nations—formerly Department of Public Information)
PAHO	Pan American Health Organization (since 1958)
PASB	Pan American Sanitary Bureau
PASO	Pan American Sanitary Organization (to 1958)
PAU	Pan American Union
RTAR	Resident Technical Assistance Representative (TAB)
SF	Special Fund (United Nations)
SUNFED	Special United Nations Fund for Economic Development)
TA	Technical Assistance
TAA	Technical Assistance Administration (United Nations—succeeded by BTAO in 1958)
TAB	Technical Assistance Board
TARS	Technical Assistance Recruitment Services (United Nations)
TVA	Tennessee Valley Authority
UN	United Nations
Unesco	United Nations Educational, Scientific, and Cultural Organization
UNHCR	United Nations High Commissioner for Refugees
UNIC	United Nations Information Centre
UNICEF	United Nations Children's Fund (formerly United Nations International Children's Emergency Fund)
UNKRA	United Nations Korean Reconstruction Agency
UNREF	United Nations Refugee Fund
UNRRA	United Nations Relief and Rehabilitation Administration
UNRWA	United Nations Relief and Works Agency for Palestine Refugees
UPU	Universal Postal Union
USOM	United States Operations Mission (ICA)
WHA	World Health Assembly
WHO	World Health Organization
WMO	World Meteorological Organization

INTRODUCTION

I

THE CONTEXT

The year 1960 marked the tenth anniversary of the birth of the United Nations Expanded Programme of Technical Assistance. The preceding decade witnessed a proliferation of field activities of comparable intent under the auspices of the United Nations and the major specialized agencies. The implementation of these interlocking programmes has involved successive measures of administrative improvisation, innovation, and adaptation. For many facets of this programme planning and operation new paths have had to be charted or old ones 'retreaded'. Precedents directly relevant to the administration of global programmes under an inter-governmental system as complicated as that of the United Nations are not numerous.

The study that follows attempts to analyse and interpret *in depth* this decade of experience with international administration. The literature on international administration, until very recently, has given little attention to its 'field' aspects if only because, prior to World War II, they were virtually non-existent. To the writer's knowledge, the present study represents the first effort to examine across-the-board the interplay of centrifugal and centripetal forces within the United Nations family of agencies as they have affected the administration of economic and social programmes.

At the outset, it is essential that the dimensions of the study be classified—so that the reader may understand, in particular, what it does *not* undertake to do. While the study had to concern itself to some extent with the processes of central policy-making, in order to provide orientation for an understanding of headquarters-field relationships, it does not pretend to consider critically the substantive rationale of United Nations technical assistance. To do so would have carried us beyond the dimensions of an administrative analysis. Nor does the study cover United Nations field operations in the domain of 'peace and security,' trusteeship, human rights, the care of refugees, or emergency relief.[1] Drawing the boundary lines so as to exclude these significant features of administration away-from-headquarters was necessary primarily because of limitations of time and money for field research. Apart from this practical consideration, it could be argued that an analysis focused on continuing economic and social activities offers a more suitable basis for valid generalizations than if the foregoing disparate types of field action were also dealt with.

Viewed affirmatively, the objectives of the study may be summarized as follows:

1. to describe and classify the forms of field organization evolved by the United Nations and the major specialized agencies for the conduct of economic, social, and technical programmes, including relevant aspects of public information;

2. to identify the assumptions and forces underlying (*a*) the expansion of field machinery and (*b*) trends towards 'decentralization' in programme planning and administration;

3. to assess the effectiveness of field staffing policies developed by the United Nations and associated organizations;

4. to examine the adequacy of communication networks and logistical support for field missions both within and between agencies;

5. to analyse the process by which substantive programmes are planned, co-ordinated, carried out, and evaluated as to impact; and finally,

6. to suggest constructive proposals for the improvement of United Nations programme operations in the light of a decade of experience.

Within UN organizational circles these are all 'live' questions. During recent years governing organs and secretariats alike have become increasingly concerned over the implications of expanding and criss-crossing programme operations as to administrative costs and effectiveness. At UN, WHO, FAO, ILO, Unesco and ICAO headquarters,[2] there has been active

[2] The official names of all organizations mentioned in this study and their abbreviated titles are listed on pp. xiii–xiv.

[1] Accordingly, such operations as the following are not included:
Office of the U.N. High Commissioner for Refugees
U.N. Relief and Works Agency for Palestine Refugees
U.N. Korean Reconstruction Agency
U.N. Truce Supervisory Organization in Palestine
U.N. Emergency Force

discussion, for example, of the pros and cons of territorial 'decentralization,' or 'deconcentration,' or 'devolution,' of programme administration. These terms tend to be employed inter-changeably to connote the delegation of administrative decision-making, in varying degree, from headquarters to field offices, whether at the country or regional level. Only in WHO does one find regional decentralization of programme-formulation (as well as administration) by constitutional sanction; but trends in this general sense may be detected not only within the United Nations itself (*e.g.*, through its regional economic commissions) but in FAO, ILO, and ICAO by means of legislative or administrative directive. The 'country programming' scheme initiated by the Technical Assistance Committee of the Economic and Social Council in 1954 for the Expanded Programme represents a clear-cut example of the devolution of programme making and implementation down to the national level—a scheme that has had its ardent defenders and persistent critics ever since.

Other phases of programme administration are under current scrutiny. These include the feasibility of 'rationalizing' organization field structures by inter-agency agreement; the complex of problems relating to the selection, compensation, assignment, rotation, and tenure of field personnel; ways and means of inducing recipient governments (*a*) to live up to project obligations more effectively and (*b*) to undertake follow up action after their termination; and the development of criteria for evaluating the impact of different types of programme operations. The establishment, in 1958, of a United Nations Special Fund for the provision of longer-range technical assistance than has been typical of the Expanded Programme perhaps adds to the timeliness of an appraisal of methods and procedures thus far devised for operating a wide variety of country and regional projects.

U.N. Military Observer Group in India and Pakistan
Visiting Missions to Trust Territories

Since the study is focused primarily on technical assistance types of action, the reader should be warned that the field functions of the International Bank for Reconstruction and Development and the International Monetary Fund are dealt with only in so far as (*a*) they are similar in character to technical assistance or (*b*) they relate to the follow-up of technical assistance projects under the auspices of other UN organizations. It should also be noted that at the time this study was under way, the new International Atomic Energy Agency (established in 1958) was just beginning to organize its field activities.

Barring a nuclear catastrophe, the United Nations system is likely to be utilized increasingly as a framework through which the world's knowledge, skills, and resources can be shared for the general welfare. The accomplishment of this crucial task will require all the administrative wisdom that can be brought to bear on it. Should the present study make a modest contribution to this end, it will have served its purpose.

Research Methods and Materials

The writer's approach to his subject is that of a student of international relations and, more particularly, of public administration. The focus of the study is the administrative process, broadly defined to include the political decision-process as it affects the conditions of programme administration. As a pioneer survey of a highly complex set of institutional relationships, the study is perforce largely descriptive in character. Its judgments are necessarily tentative—and qualitative—in view of the conditions under which the research was carried out. The time period covered was too short for many firm generalizations. Available official data, moreover, were such as not to make it possible to develop quantitative comparisons of agency practices.

To some extent the study reflects the author's own experience as a former staff member of FAO, WHO, and Unesco, and more recently (1954–55), as the head of a UN-sponsored technical assistance team in Egypt. It was then that the idea of undertaking such an inquiry originated. During the next three years most of the relevant—and massive—documentary sources were analysed, while consultations were held with a substantial number of officials at organization headquarters in New York, Washington, Montreal, Geneva, Paris, and Rome. By this time the design of the study had taken tentative shape.

The next stage involved the preparation of sets of questions as a basis for interviewing four categories of persons in the field: (1) the staffs of country and regional offices; (2) a sample of field project personnel; (3) host country officials; and (4) representatives of non-United Nations programmes at the country level (*e.g.*, U.S. Point Four, the Organization of American States, Colombo Plan, and the Ford Foundation). Two field trips were arranged: one to Latin America during the summer of 1957, and the second to Europe, the Middle East, South Asia, and the Pacific from August 1958 to March 1959.

In all, fourteen under-developed countries were covered, as follows:

Latin America	*Middle East*	*Asia and the Pacific*
Mexico	United Arab Republic	Pakistan
Panama	Lebanon	India
Peru	Iran	Thailand
Chile		Philippines
Argentina		
Uruguay		
Brazil		

These countries range from tiny places like Panama and Lebanon to such huge areas as Brazil and India. The sample includes countries of 'medium' as well as 'low' development—with annual United Nations technical aid programmes varying in value from less than $200,000 to well over $2 million. The selection of countries was in part dictated by the desire to observe situations where a cluster of organization offices operate at the same centre (*e.g.*, Mexico City, Santiago, Rio de Janeiro, Cairo, New Delhi, and Bangkok). Nearly eighty field offices, including regional as well as country-level offices, were visited in the fourteen countries.

During the data-gathering process approximately 350 individuals were interviewed. About a fifth of them were interviewed several times, spanning periods of a few days to as much as four years (in the case of certain headquarters officials). Roughly one-third of the persons interviewed consisted of field office staff members; one-fourth, of central secretariat personnel; another fourth, of field project personnel; while the remaining sixth included host government officials, non-United Nations programme field representatives, and delegates to organization meetings. In a few countries it proved possible to hold off-the-record discussions with project personnel in a group setting. As far as time allowed an effort was made to visit project sites outside national capitals.

The main body of the research underlying the study was completed by the mid-summer of 1959. Accordingly, much of the factual data derived from official annual reports dates from 1958 and earlier years. During the preparation of the manuscript, an effort was made to take account of significant changes of policy and procedure through the spring of 1960, though this was not always possible with respect to internal specialized agency developments. The regrettably long time-lag between completion of the draft manuscript and publication was in large part the result of unavoidable delays in receiving comments on the manuscript from busy international officials around the world —comments which in many instances were exceedingly perceptive and helpful.

For the most part the interviews were conducted with the understanding that the information thus conveyed would not be identified as to source. Only under this condition would it have been possible to elicit the frank—at times even indiscreet—expressions of opinion and attitude that constitute perhaps the most revealing data in the study. Some use was also made of private memoranda prepared by agency staffs in response to the investigator's request—memoranda to which no direct reference could be made in the printed volume.

In approaching the subject-matter of the study, the author's assumption was that there is no inherent reason why international organizations cannot plan and manage overseas field programmes as effectively and as economically as can national governments. This assumption was the product of his own personal observation, operational experience, and reflection over a considerable period of years. As a student of public administration, however, he was particularly interested in discovering how and to what extent differences in the composition and *milieu* of international bureaucracies, in comparison with national, affect operational methods, procedures, and relations with clientele. As regards internal housekeeping services, such differences are negligible; so also with the more formalistic aspects of organizational machinery. But when it comes to human relations problems of administration, we enter 'the realm of "cross-culturism," of tensions produced by conflicting patterns of social behaviour, of communication barriers arising partly from linguistic, semantic, and ideological factors and partly from the impact of the time-space factor.'[3] Here are significant differences.

Furthermore, the United Nations system, in contrast to a stably organized national government, consists of a congeries of quasi-autonomous agencies bound together only loosely by freely consented but weakly sanctioned agreement and inter-secretariat consultation. In terms of the system as a whole, international officials receive their basic policy directives from a multiplicity of assemblies, conferences, councils, and boards—directives that are sometimes vague, ambiguous, or conflicting. This organizational pluralism has led on the one side to the separate budgeting of separate agency field programmes, and on the other to the emergence of EPTA and, most recently, the Special Fund, as operations financed by special voluntary contributions. Budgetary payments could be—and still are—made in different national currencies, thus creating an intricate problem of currency management.

Within this multi-agency context, effective field action has called for the development of a wide variety of co-ordinative and co-operative arrangements. Under what conditions have they worked well—or poorly? How has their operation been influenced by multi-nationalism on the staff side, or by communication tangles between headquarters and the field? Here again are questions that relate to special characteristics of UN system administration.

It is not contended that the present study provides any precise measure of the impact of international differentials in the administrative equation. To make any such measurement—if this is feasible at all—would require the application of intensive 'case analysis' techniques. This was not possible in a general survey type of inquiry. The query 'how' could be answered much more easily than 'to what extent'.

Throughout, the author has done his best to arrive at objective assessments. Where the evidence is thin or inconclusive, the generalizations are qualified accordingly. Where there is criticism of administrative planning or method, it is intended as constructive criticism—with full appreciation of the hard realities confronting the responsible official. Where suggestions for

[3] Quoted from the author's article, 'The Study of International Administration', in *World Politics* (Oct. 1958).

future policy or action are ventured, they have been formulated with due regard for their political feasibility.

With these introductory observations, the author consigns the results of his labours to the tender mercies of the reader—whether he be student, investigator, policy-maker, or operator.

PART ONE

FIELD ORGANIZATION AND STAFFING PATTERNS

2

THE EMERGENCE OF FIELD ACTIVITIES WITHIN THE UN FRAMEWORK

International administration involving sustained field operations is a very recent phenomenon. Indeed, administration under inter-governmental auspices, even in the most restricted sense, is scarcely a century old. Virtually all existing (let alone defunct) inter-governmental agencies have come into being since the 1850s. Prior to World War I, such institutions consisted, for the most part, of the so-called administrative unions set up by treaty in such technical fields as postal and telecommunications, inland transport, health, copyrights and trade marks, weights and measures, and world-mapping.[1] Their administrative apparatus typically took the form of miniature central secretariats (usually known as bureaux) whose functions were confined to clearing-house activities, research, reporting, publication, the servicing of meetings of supervisory boards and conferences, and, in the case of the river commissions, the exercise of minor regulatory powers. In no instance did any such agency develop what today would be considered a 'field establishment.'

During the pre-1914 period, the only example of a multi-purpose international organization was the Union of American Republics (now the Organization of American States), for which the Pan American Union served as administrative headquarters. The activities of the PAU outside Washington, however, were limited to the staffing of inter-American conferences held at various Latin American capitals. Within the loose framework of the embryonic inter-American system the Pan American Sanitary Bureau, dating from 1902, had responsibility for administering various international sanitary conventions to which the American Republics were parties. As early as 1906, the PASB was authorized to establish in each of these Republics 'Sanitary Information Committees composed of three medical or

[1] The best general analysis of the administrative unions is contained in Norman Hill's *International Administration* (New York: McGraw-Hill, 1931).

sanitary authorities which, under the direction of the International Sanitary Bureau (as it was then called), in Washington, were to collect and exchange data relative to public health.'[2] A branch office of the Bureau was organized in Montevideo to serve as a regional centre for the countries located south of the equator. Gradually, the PASB began to provide sporadic advisory services to the national health administrations of Latin America by sending out technical consultants on temporary field missions—a practice faintly foreshadowing the far-flung technical assistance operations of the later World Health Organization.

PRECEDENTS FROM THE INTER-WAR PERIOD

The establishment of the League of Nations and its affiliate, the International Labour Organisation, marked the first attempt to institutionalize economic and social co-operation on a world-wide scale. Article 23 of the League Covenant, *inter alia*, recognized the obligation of Member States 'to secure and maintain fair and humane conditions of labour' for their peoples; to 'entrust the League with the general supervision over the execution of agreements with regard to the traffic in women and children, and the traffic in opium and other dangerous drugs'; 'to secure and maintain freedom of communications and transit and equitable treatment for the commerce of all Members of the League'; and, finally, 'to take steps in matters of international concern for the prevention and control of disease.' On the other hand, the Covenant itself did not provide for any special League machinery for the implementation of these obligations.[3] Both the League and ILO were based, so far as economics was concerned, on the general acceptance of 'liberal capitalism,' and they reflected an essentially restrictive view of the scope of economic action through international instrumentalities. In accordance with this view, the economic relations of national

[2] Miguel E. Bustamente, *The Pan American Sanitary Bureau: Half a Century of Health Activities, 1902–1954*, Misc. Pub. No. 23 (Washington: Pan American Sanitary Bureau, 1955), p. 5.

[3] Article 24 of the Covenant provided that international bureaux already established by treaties should be placed under the League's direction 'if the parties to such treaties consent.' In fact, only five so agreed: the International Commission for Air Navigation, the International Hydrographic Bureau, the Central Office for the Control of Liquor Traffic in Africa, the International Bureau of Assistance to Foreigners, and the International Exhibitions Bureau.

states might appropriately be co-ordinated, restrained, or regulated by freely consented treaty agreements for which the League Secretariat (and the International Labour Office) could usefully serve as stimulus, as planner, or in certain respects as an administrative mechanism; but it was not assumed by the founders of these two institutions that they would concern themselves with national policies involving 'state interventionism in economic affairs—even less with the promotion of programmes of aid to Member States for their economic and social betterment. In 1919 the 'welfare' state had hardly appeared on the horizon, while the revolution of the underdeveloped nations was yet to come.

Within this context what took place was the pragmatic emergence of a congeries of so-called 'technical organizations' attached to the League Secretariat. In various ways these organizations, functioning administratively as semi-autonomous sections of the Secretariat, were governed by a committee structure created partly by the League Assembly, partly by the Council, and partly by outside agreement. The largest of these groups was the Economic and Financial Organization; the others included the Communications and Transit, Health, Drug Control, and Social Questions Organizations.

During the earlier years of the League, their work consisted primarily of research, pre-legislative drafting, and the preparation of agenda documentation for specialized conferences and committee meetings convened directly or indirectly under League auspices. Such activities could be, and in fact were, conducted within or from the Geneva headquarters. Even so, the League was almost immediately drawn into limited field operations as a result of three urgent situations: (1) the alarming spread of epidemic disease in Eastern Europe after World War I; (2) the need of resettling thousands of war refugees; and (3) the precarious economic condition of a number of the smaller war-devastated countries. Basically, the League's interventions into all three of these situations, representing responses to international emergencies, were expected to be of temporary duration only. Even so, the League's successful anti-epidemics campaign during the early 1920s paved the way for the establishment of a permanent office at Singapore (with a sub-office at Melbourne) to collect and disseminate by telegraph and radio intelligence reports on the incidence of epidemics throughout the Far East. Set up originally as the 'Eastern Bureau' of the League's Health Organization, this office continues to function today as a field arm of WHO.[4] The League Health Organization later convened a number of regional conferences of health administrators, especially in Eastern Asia and the Pacific, and, with financial support from the Rockefeller Foundation, organized study tours abroad for national health officials.[5]

The League's efforts on behalf of refugees, originally directed by Dr. Fridtjof Nansen, were destined to continue, in one form or another, down to and through most of World War II. 'The business of refugee settlement,' notes the League's historian, 'was never finished.'[6] For some years its High Commissioner for Refugees, in addition to utilizing a small staff in Geneva, maintained resident representatives in fifteen countries who, however, 'were usually government officials and in only a secondary degree agents of the League.'[7] The League's functions in the refugee field were eventually taken over on a greatly expanded scale, first by the United Nations Relief and Rehabilitation Administration, and then, in 1948, by the International Refugee Organization established by the UN General Assembly. In effect, IRO continued the displaced persons operations of UNRRA.

The contribution of the League to the financial reconstruction of certain Central and Eastern European nations, begun in 1922 and continued through the ensuing decade, foreshadowed in some ways the techniques employed years later by the International Bank for Reconstruction and Development.[8] The League's Financial Committee drew up a code of principles to govern 'sound economic and financial administration,' and

[4] For an authoritative official account of the evolution of international public health agencies and activities (including those of WHO), see *The First Ten Years of the World Health Organization* (Geneva: WHO, 1958).

[5] The League Health Organization also co-operated closely with the International Office for Public Health (dating from 1907), with headquarters in Paris. This Office utilized, for regional informational purposes, the Eastern Bureau at Singapore, the Pan Arab Health Bureau at Alexandria, and the Pan American Sanitary Bureau at Washington. Robert Berkov, *The World Health Organization: A Study in International Decentralized Administration* (Geneva: Droz, 1957), pp. 43–44.

[6] F. P. Walters, *A History of the League of Nations* (London, New York: Oxford University Press, 1952), Vol. I, p. 187.

[7] *Ibid.*, p. 189.

[8] The standard work on the League's economic and financial activities is Martin Hill's *The Economic and Financial Organization of the League of Nations* (Washington: Carnegie Endowment for International Peace, 1946).

helped to mobilize capital funds from major creditor governments and the European money markets. The terms and conditions of the reconstruction loans thus made available were supervised by resident commissioners appointed by the League Council, with the consent of the borrowing governments concerned. These 'field' representatives of the League also acted as general financial advisers for the latter during the period of the reconstruction loans.

As the League built up its administrative resources, Member governments in a number of cases appealed to it for what would in current UN language be termed technical assistance. This usually took the form of providing experts to conduct on-the-spot surveys of railway reorganization, currency reform, health problems, and the like. The most notable instance of this type of co-operation was the large-scale scheme of assistance undertaken at the request of the Chinese Government during the 1930s. To co-ordinate this undertaking the head of the League's Health Section was detailed to China as its Technical Agent. The China programme included aid not only in developing better health services and combatting epidemics, but in road construction, agriculture, education, and the training of Chinese students in various technical fields. The League's work in China was beginning to show promising results when its progress was tragically disrupted by the Sino-Japanese war.

Although the League Secretariat, with the aid of expert committees, conducted a number of valuable inquiries into the international aspects of such problems as slavery, housing, child welfare, and nutrition, none of these endeavours led to any projection of the League's administrative framework beyond Geneva. Senior Secretariat officials went on tour to various Member countries from time to time, but the purposes of such missions covered political and diplomatic as well as technical matters. The League also convened a number of regional conferences on rural life, narcotic drugs, and traffic in women and children.

The nearest approach to anything like a permanent field establishment is to be found in the cluster of small 'branch' offices set up by the League's Information Section at a number of major national capitals. In addition, so-called 'correspondents' were appointed for several of the lesser countries. Such outposts provided 'public relations' channels with Member governments but little else. 'Taken as a whole,' concludes Egon Ranshofen-Wertheimer, 'these external activities of the League never constituted a major feature of the administration. They were reluctantly initiated; their growth and evolution was somewhat haphazard. In contrast to the ILO, they were never considered an important element in the mechanism of the League.'[9]

The International Labour Organization, under the dynamic leadership of its first Director, Albert Thomas, recognized from the outset the value of establishing direct liaison with its tripartite constituency around the world—governments, workers' organizations, and employers' organizations. Thomas ardently believed the Geneva Office should 'have "*in all important centres*" a correspondent or a branch office.'[10] Accordingly, the ILO, as early as 1920, initiated the appointment of permanent correspondents in its Member States of 'chief industrial importance'. A decade later not only had the number of correspondents more than doubled but those in the eight major countries had become heads of small 'branch' offices. These field officials (and their staffs), being nationals of the host country, in effect served two masters—the ILO and the host country, and thus cost the Organization's budget comparatively little. While they never quite developed the full role envisaged by Thomas, they helped to popularize the ILO 'at home,' prodded governments to answer Geneva's questionnaires, maintained liaison with national labour publics, and prepared reports on local economic and social conditions. As we shall see later, this system of branch offices and national correspondents is a distinct part of the network of field offices now operated by ILO.

Although the work of the International Labour Office at Geneva, during the inter-war period, consisted primarily of research and the drafting of international labour standards for incorporation into labour conventions and recommendations, the Office soon found itself called upon by governments of the less-developed countries for advice and assistance—in drafting national legislation to implement the provisions of the inter-

[9] *The International Secretariat* (Washington: Carnegie Endowment for International Peace, 1945), p. 189.
[10] E. J. Phelan, *Yes and Albert Thomas* (London: Cresset Press, 1936), p. 41.

national conventions, and in the designing of national administrative machinery for their application. 'In all these cases advisory services were provided by the detachment or special assignment of regular members of the staff of the Office.'[11]

Another significant development, destined to bring regional influences into ILO's programme-making, was the inauguration, in 1936, of the practice of holding periodic conferences of representatives of regional groupings of Member countries. This innovation, which started in Latin America, was gradually extended, after World War II, to Asia, the Middle East, and Europe. During the 1930s, the ILO also began convening regional technical meetings on such subjects as vocational training, labour statistics, labour law administration, and social security. The role played by both types of regional gatherings, in generating new ideas for ILO's work, and later in stimulating technical assistance proposals, will be considered in a subsequent chapter.[12]

While the experience of the League and the ILO between wars contains useful precedents which later were to affect arrangements for the economic and social activities of the UN system, negatively as well as positively, the administration of both the League and the early ILO remained highly centralized. Such activities as they carried on in the field were tightly controlled by headquarters. In no case was there any delegation of policy or operational authority to country missions or to such modest field offices as were set up. The functions of the latter were almost entirely restricted to liaison and information-gathering. Moreover, field operations of whatever kind were conducted on an exceedingly small scale in terms of monetary expenditure, staff personnel, and machinery. They tended to be sporadic and were often undertaken in response to crisis situations. Continuing field programmes did not materialize partly because neither organization had sufficient budgetary resources to undertake them, even more because the pre-war conception of international co-operation in furtherance of economic and social goals did not embrace the sustained provision of aids and services to national governments. The League and the ILO undeniably did important pioneering but they

[11] UN Doc. A/3142, 10 July 1956.
[12] See pp. 324–327.

hardly deserve recognition as 'prototypes' of United Nations field administration.

UNRRA as Prototype

It was the catastrophic havoc wrought by World War II that led to the emergence of the first large-scale 'field operating' organizations under inter-governmental management. One of these organizations was the United Nations Relief and Rehabilitation Administration, created in 1943 while the war was still going on, and the other was the International Refugee Organization, set up by the United Nations General Assembly five years later. Neither of these agencies was destined to be permanent (though they had not completed their tasks when they were terminated); yet each had an experience which was substantially drawn upon later by United Nations and specialized agency administrators, some of whom had served on the staffs of one or both of the temporary organizations.

It is beyond the scope of this study to describe in detail the organizational structure of UNRRA or IRO.[13] Suffice it to note here that both agencies developed elaborate field machinery for the conduct of their relief and refugee operations. In the case of UNRRA, the 'principle of regionalism was adopted in the fields of both policy-making and administration.'[14] There were, for example, policy committees of the central UNRRA Council for Europe and for the Far East, each consisting of representatives of the Member countries in the region concerned. A regional office was established in London to which, after some initial confusion, considerable operational discretion was delegated by Washington. Decentralization evolved, interestingly enough, in proportion as the executive control at headquarters grew stronger and came to recognize the advantage of deconcentrating the complex business of procurement and distribution of supplies to UNRRA's clientele—the derelicts of the war. Full delegation to London of the power to supervise UNRRA's missions in the receiving countries of Europe and

[13] The most comprehensive account of UNRRA is by George Woodridge, *et al.*, under the title, *UNRRA: The History of the United Nations Relief and Rehabilitation Administration* (New York: Columbia Univ. Press, 1950), three vols. The comments on UNRRA's administration made here are drawn mainly from this invaluable study.

[14] Berkov, *op. cit.*, p. 47.

the Near East, however, was not fully worked out for nearly two years. Nor for various reasons was any regional office ever set up in the Far East, although the UNRRA mission to China functioned in effect as an area office. Other area offices were located at Cairo (for the Middle East) and at Sydney (for the South-west Pacific). There was also a decentralized and specialized organization for displaced persons in Germany as well as in other parts of Europe and the Far East. In all, UNRRA employed nearly 13,000 persons on its international staff—scattered over three continents—or about ten times as many as the League and the pre-war ILO combined had at their peak. During the five years of its life, UNRRA's expenditures aggregated almost $4 billion.

Headquarters-field relationships in UNRRA gave rise to a number of difficulties some of which, as we shall discover later, were to plague UN system administrators. One of these was the tendency, especially during the first years of the organization, for separate administrative units to initiate their own orders both at headquarters and at the European office, causing annoying confusion which was only gradually cleared up. As late as 1946, a basic 'field manual' was issued by headquarters without consulting the London office. Conflicting directives resulted when the latter office was bypassed and certain sections of the manual were sent directly to European country missions. Field inspection by headquarters officials was not frequent enough and often proved to be too hurried for maximum effectiveness. Hastily improvised reporting and accounting procedures on a decentralized basis had to be replaced by a system that concentrated responsibility in a controller, the role of London as a regional accounting office being discontinued and mission accounts being routed directly to headquarters. As regards staffing policies, a jurisdictional struggle developed between the Personnel Division and the Bureaux of Areas and Supplies which was eventually resolved by the Director-General in favour of the former Division. Yet headquarters and London often found themselves in conflict with regard to the determination of personnel practices.

Notwithstanding such difficulties, UNRRA, once it got over its growing pains, managed to handle its vast and complex operations with generally admitted efficiency. The agency was conceived and began its activities during and in the wake of global war, and as a civilian organization endeavouring to function in an atmosphere geographically and psychologically dominated by the military, it was confronted with untold difficulties in terms of communications, transportation, and shipping. This contributed in part to the delay in establishing adequate regional machinery. Its pattern of regional decentralization may have exerted some influence on the system of regional committees and regional offices later created by WHO, which, incidentally, inherited by transfer the health functions of UNRRA on the latter's termination. Responsibility for 'residual relief problems,' moreover, was assumed by the United Nations International Children's Emergency Fund and the short-lived International Refugee Organization, to which reference was made above.[15] UNRRA's experience left its mark on the field administrative structure of both of these agencies, the first of which, UNICEF, although established initially on a year-to-year basis, was accorded permanent status by the United Nations General Assembly in 1953.

Categories of UN System Field Operations

From the standpoint of the present study, the League of Nations and the United Nations system contrast sharply in terms of their functions and administrative apparatus relating to international economic and social co-operation. The League Covenant took no direct cognizance of the economic or sociological forces that lie behind international tension and conflict. Nor did it envisage any direct action by the League aimed at economic development or social welfare *per se*. During the turbulent period following the League's birth, not only had the world suffered from recurring wars, culminating in the global upheaval of 1939–45, but it had felt the shattering repercussions of the Great Depression and had witnessed the widespread adoption of 'welfare economics' by many countries, capitalist as well as socialist. National economic planning, involving far-reaching intervention by the State into economic affairs, was on the way to becoming a fairly general feature of domestic public

[15] The standard treatise on IRO is Louise W. Holborn's *The International Refugee Organization of the United Nations, Its History and Work, 1946–1952* (London: Oxford Univ. Press, 1956).

policy. Moreover, the victory of the Allies in the Second World War let loose a chain reaction which was to lead to the movement of non-Western peoples for political independence and, concomitantly, to a concerted drive by them for rapid industrialization.

This transformation of the context of international relations set the stage for a far wider system of organized co-operation than the old League had provided. Even the League, ironically enough, was on the point of revamping and strengthening its own economic and social machinery when the war came. The recommendations of the Bruce Committee, submitted in 1939, called for the creation of a new Central Committee for Social and Economic Questions to supervise and co-ordinate the League's growing non-political activities.[16] It is to these recommendations that 'the essential pattern' for the United Nations Economic and Social Council may be traced.

The United Nations Charter, and even more the constitutions of the specialized agencies created from 1944 onward, reflect the impact of all these new ideas and forces. Chapter IX of the Charter pledges states to take 'joint and separate action in co-operation with the Organization' for the promotion of 'higher standards of living, full employment, and conditions of economic and social progress and development'; as well as for 'solutions of international economic, social, health, and related problems,' including 'international cultural and educational co-operation.' At the San Francisco Conference, the smaller States succeeded in making the Economic and Social Council one of the 'principal' organs of the new Organization and in broadening the purposes of co-operation outside the 'peace and security' field. ECOSOC was given a dual responsibility: (1) to initiate studies, make reports, and formulate recommendations for action, and (2) to co-ordinate the activities of the specialized agencies brought into agreement with the United Nations.[17]

For the implementation of the UN's sweepingly broad economic and social mandate, there is no direct evidence from the San Francisco debates that extensive operational programmes, to be conducted by the UN itself, were envisaged, although

[16] For the official text of these recommendations, see *The Development of International Co-operation in Economic and Social Affairs: Report of the Special Committee*, Special Supplement to the Monthly Summary of the League of Nations (Geneva: August 1939).

[17] By Articles 62–63 of the Charter.

such a possibility was not ignored. During the discussion of 'regional arrangements' relating to the maintenance of international peace and security, consideration was given to the advisability of extending such arrangements to include economic and social matters, but it was decided not to recognize (in the text of the Charter) the regional approach to such problems.[18] On the other hand, ECOSOC's permissive authority to 'set up commissions in economic and social fields' did not preclude the establishment of commissions on a regional basis. Such action was taken in 1947-48, when the three economic commissions for Europe, for Asia and the Far East, and for Latin America, respectively, were created, and, more recently in 1958, the Commission for Africa.

The point to be stressed here is that Chapters IX and X of the Charter were couched in sufficiently general terms to allow ECOSOC, with the approval of the General Assembly, to institute programmes of technical aid to Member States and to devise arrangements for their implementation by field action. Thus the UN, through a series of resolutions dating from 1948, proceeded to initiate modest programmes of assistance in the fields of social welfare, economic development, public administration, and human rights—under its own auspices[19]—even before the inauguration in 1950 of the Expanded Programme of Technical Assistance, in which most of the specialized agencies as well as the United Nations have since participated.

Going further than the UN Charter, the constitutional instruments of the major specialized agencies clearly authorize, and in some cases make mandatory, activities of an operational character. Thus the WHO Constitution states that the Organization *shall* 'assist Governments, upon request, in strengthening health services'; and, again, *shall* 'furnish appropriate technical assistance and, in emergencies, necessary aid' (Chapter II). Acting under this mandate, WHO lost no time in instituting a substantial programme of assistance to national health administrations, in organizing field campaigns for the control of communicable diseases, and in sponsoring various kinds

[18] Leland M. Goodrich and Edvard Hambro, *Charter of the United Nations: Commentary and Documents* (2nd and rev. ed., Boston: World Peace Foundation, 1949), p. 311.

[19] Notably by GA Resolutions 260 (III), 418 (V), 723 (VIII), 926 (X), and 1256 (XIII). The provision of advisory social welfare services represented the UN's first venture into direct technical assistance.

of arrangements for training health administrators, sanitary engineers, nurses, and laboratory technicians. All these activities, financed out of WHO's regular budget, were well under way before the advent of EPTA and have steadily expanded since then.[20] Significantly, the WHO Constitution contains a special chapter on 'Regional Arrangements' (Chapter XI) which obligates the World Health Assembly to 'define the geographical areas in which it is desirable to establish a regional organization,' sets forth the conditions under which regional committees and regional offices *may* be established, and enumerates their substantive and administrative functions, respectively. These provisions form the basis for WHO's decentralized framework of field operations.

The Constitution of the Food and Agriculture Organization similarly stipulates that one of its functions shall be 'to furnish such technical assistance as governments may request' and 'to organize, in co-operation with the governments concerned, such missions as may be needed to assist them to fulfil' their obligations under the Constitution (Article I). Permissive authority is granted to the Organization under Article VI to establish 'technical and regional standing committees,' and to convene 'technical, regional, or other special conferences'; while Article X provides that 'there shall be such regional offices as the Director-General with the approval of the (FAO) Conference may decide.'

Although FAO, unlike WHO, did not during its formative years develop any continuing programme of direct technical aid to governments, agricultural survey missions were sent to Greece, Thailand, Poland, and Venezuela, and various regional commissions were created on a permanent basis to deal with the technical aspects of rice production, forestry, fisheries, and the control of foot-and-mouth disease.[21] By 1948, moreover,

[20] In addition to funds provided directly by WHO, the Pan American Health Organization has its own budget for international health work in the Western Hemisphere, and a large number of governments (notably that of the United States) make special contributions for specific aspects of WHO's and PAHO's activities (*e.g.*, for a world-wide malaria eradication campaign). Serving as the WHO Regional Office for the Americas, the Pan American Sanitary Bureau in Washington administers both its regional share of WHO's budgetary allocations for the Americas and the annual appropriations made by PAHO.

[21] See, for a vividly written popular survey of FAO'S work, Gove Hambidge, *The Story of FAO* (New York: Van Nostrand, 1955). A somewhat more analytical (and semi-official) account is presented in *So Bold an Aim: Ten Years of International Co-operation Toward Freedom from Want* (Rome: FAO, 1955).

regional offices were in operation in the Near East and the Far East and others (in Latin America and Africa) were added later. Since the inauguration of EPTA, FAO has utilized these regional units to facilitate the execution of its technical assistance work under the Expanded Programme.

The Constitution of the United Nations Educational, Scientific and Cultural Organization employs less explicit language than the WHO and FAO Constitutions with respect to field activities. In Article I (listing Unesco's functions), however, there is repeated reference to 'collaboration' with Member States for 'the development of educational activities' and the advancement of the related goals of the Organization. In addition to Unesco's role in EPTA this collaboration has taken a variety of forms, including the dispatch of educational missions, the conduct of country surveys, the sponsorship of national and regional training centres, the award of fellowships, aid in teaching the natural and social sciences, the provision of advisory services to national institutions, and the establishment of a number of regional 'field science co-operation' offices.[22] In 1956, the Unesco General Conference authorized a new programme of 'Aid to Member States' (later renamed the 'Participation' Programme) which is financed from regular budget funds. This programme makes possible the provision of educational, scientific, and cultural assistance in certain defined areas to Member governments on request, not excluding those of advanced countries, thus supplementing the kinds of aid available from Unesco under EPTA. Another action by the 1956 Conference was to authorize the Director-General to undertake a ten-year 'major' project for the extension of primary education in Latin America—a regional undertaking now being co-ordinated largely by the staff of the organization's Western Hemisphere office at Havana.

In 1946, the Constitution of ILO was amended so as to take account of the 'Declaration concerning the Aims and Purposes'

[22] The Institute of Intellectual Co-operation (with headquarters in Paris), affiliated with the League, may be regarded, in part, as the prototype of Unesco. For a comprehensive survey of the evolution of Unesco's organization and programme, see Walter H. C. Laves and Charles A. Thomson, *UNESCO: Purpose, Progress, Prospects* (Bloomington: Indiana Univ. Press, 1957). Earlier treatments of Unesco include Theodore Besterman's *UNESCO: Peace in the Minds of Men* (New York: Praeger, 1951), and Charles S. Ascher's illuminating study of *Program-Making in Unesco: 1946–1951* (Chicago: Public Administration Service, 1951).

of the organization adopted at Philadelphia two years earlier. This Declaration recognizes the 'solemn obligation' of ILO 'to further among the nations of the world programmes which will achieve' an impressive array of economic and social goals some of which, by implication at least, call for expanded action by the organization over and beyond its regular research and legislative work. Since World War II, ILO has in consequence initiated modest operational programmes in such fields as workers' education and vocational training and has greatly amplified its earlier structure of field offices—all in addition to its active participation in EPTA.

Turning to the domain of transport and communications, both the International Civil Aviation Organization and the International Telecommunication Union engage in technical assistance now on a restricted scale. By the 1944 Convention for International Civil Aviation, ICAO is charged, among other things, to 'encourage the development of airways, airports, and air navigation facilities for international civil aviation,' with a view to furthering its 'safe and orderly growth.'[23] To this end the organization has divided the world into a number of 'air navigation regions.' It has also set up regional offices the main function of which, as we shall note later, is to 'monitor' the application by Member governments of regional plans for the provision of air navigation facilities and services to international civil aviation. In addition, with EPTA funds, ICAO has, since 1951, given technical assistance to almost all branches of civil aviation and has established and helped to operate national and regional centres for training aeronautical staffs for national aviation services.

The traditional constitutional functions of ITU did not include the provision of technical aid to national telegraph, telephone, and radio services. But it has been allotted a small share of EPTA funds for projects of this character, the administrative responsibility for which, until 1960, was assumed by the Technical Assistance Administration (since 1958 Bureau of Technical Assistance Operations) of the United Nations. ITU has not found it necessary to set up any field machinery of its

[23] The forerunner of ICAO was the International Commission for Air Navigation (dating from 1919), whose former headquarters are now occupied by the Paris regional office of ICAO. ITU stems from the International Telegraphic Bureau, founded in 1868.

own. Currently, there is, however, a movement of ideas within the Union for amendment of its rules so as to permit the provision of technical assistance in the EPTA sense out of the Union's regular budget.[24]

Closely related to the ITU functionally, the World Meteorological Organization, which came into being as a UN specialized agency only in 1951, has a comparatively minor share of EPTA funds at its disposal. Like the ITU, its technical assistance operations are administered by BTAO on its behalf. These operations are concerned chiefly with aiding new states to set up, and others to improve the standards of, their weather information services, which contribute to economic development through safer communications and transport and more productive agriculture. The WMO Convention of 1947 provides a constitutional justification for such operations in the sense that they also contribute to a more adequate interchange of meteorological data. To facilitate WMO's work, the Convention groups the Member States into 'regional associations' on a continental basis. These groups hold periodic meetings to promote the application of WMO resolutions in the region and to supplement these resolutions by informal regional agreements. While the organization does not maintain field offices, the President of each regional association is consulted with reference to technical assistance projects in his region and kept *au courant* of their progress.

The foregoing 'bird's-eye' account of the origins and variety of field operations in the UN system covers those agencies which, along with the United Nations itself, participate directly in the Expanded Programme of Technical Assistance.[25] In all, the 'regular' programmes of aid provided by them constitute perhaps one-quarter of the aggregate UN system expenditure for technical assistance (including UNICEF). The other three-fourths is financed out of EPTA and other special resources. To a considerable extent, as will be explained later, the two

[24] *Annual Report of the Technical Assistance Board for 1957*, ECOSOC Official Records (ECOSOC, O.R.): 26th Sess., 1958, Suppl. No. 5, p. 56.

[25] The International Atomic Energy Agency (with headquarters in Vienna), which came into being in 1958, also participates in EPTA now, as well as provides various forms of 'atomic assistance' to Member governments from its own 'operational' budget. The basic legislation for EPTA is conveniently summarized in *An Explanatory Booklet: the Expanded Programme of Technical Assistance for Economic Development for Under-Developed Countries* (New York: TAB, United Nations, 1958).

categories of field programmes are administered together, and it is not uncommon for projects under one programme to be transferred to the other for reasons of financial convenience. Sometimes a given project will be charged in part against regular budget funds and in part against the EPTA special account. However, the rules governing the selection of projects to be undertaken are not necessarily the same: allocations of EPTA funds are subject to the criteria laid down by ECOSOC while in many cases different criteria may obtain for allocations from an agency's regular or special funds.

It is EPTA that has been primarily responsible for the spread of continuing operational activities around the globe—into Latin America, the Middle East, Asia, and Africa. Indeed, it is not too much to say that the impact of EPTA converted certain of the specialized agencies from essentially reporting and debating societies into 'service' institutions and, in effect, vitalized their work.[26]

There are two other members of the UN family of agencies—the International Bank for Reconstruction and Development and the International Monetary Fund—that have a more independent status *vis-à-vis* the United Nations than do the others.[27] For one thing, the membership of the Bank and Fund does not coincide with that of the UN, an important difference since the services of both institutions are limited to their members, who are also the subscribers of the capital resources of both agencies. For another, unlike the UN, the voting powers in the Bank and Fund are proportionate to capital subscriptions. Neither the Bank nor the Fund takes any direct part in the operations of EPTA although they both send staff observers to the meetings of TAB. At the same time, each of the two institutions performs important functions of an operational and technical character for its Members. This is particularly true of the Bank, whose

[26] In this context, Gunnar Myrdal's observation is worth quoting: 'Technical assistance has not only given the international organizations a new and important purpose and function; by sending experts to those countries that most needed their advice, they have drawn these same countries into active co-operation, at least in technical matters.' *An International Economy* (New York: Harper, 1956), p. 219.

[27] As does also the Bank's affiliate, the International Finance Corporation, established in 1956 to further economic development 'by investing—without government guarantee—in productive private enterprise in association with private investors who can provide competent management.' For administrative purposes the IFC utilizes the machinery and services of the Bank. The former agency may possibly send out consultants to the field for short periods but it is not likely to set up field missions or offices on its own.

primary *raison d'être* is to make loans to 'sound' economic undertakings, under government guarantee, for reconstruction or developmental purposes. During the first two years of the Bank, all of its loans were granted to European countries to help rebuild their war-torn economies, but since 1949 the Bank's lending has been primarily for development purposes in the less developed of its Member countries and territories.

In conjunction with its general functions, the Bank has conducted, in almost a score of countries, comprehensive surveys of their national economies by teams of technologists and economists—often in co-operation with FAO. Before entering into formal negotiations for loans, the Bank normally has a field report on the soundness of the loan project made by a staff group. Also, during the life of active loans, the Bank's headquarters sends out 'end-use' technical missions to assess the progress of the undertakings being assisted. On occasion, moreover, members of the Washington staff are assigned as 'resident representatives' of the Bank in various countries. The functions of some of these representatives are limited to gathering information and maintaining liaison with the host government; others have served, on request, as advisers to governments on economic development and fiscal policy. A technical assistance advisory staff has also been furnished to numerous countries on a temporary basis without any immediate reference to the lending process. In several instances, the Bank has helped governments organize national 'development banks.' The Bank, on the other hand, has not developed any considerable field office structure. In New York it operates a small 'marketing' office, while in Paris there is a small office which houses the Bank's Special Representative in Europe, and also combines marketing and information activities with such European regional institutions as the Organization for European Economic Co-operation and the Common Market.[28]

The International Monetary Fund, in carrying out its constitutional mandate 'to promote international monetary co-operation' and 'exchange stability,' maintains constant consultation with Member governments by means of informal field missions on a confidential basis. The Fund has also found it

[28] For some years the Bank operated an office in Beirut but it is now closed. There is also a small joint office with IFC in London.

useful to make available technical advice to governments on such matters as statistical procedures, central banking policy, and exchange controls, including the training of personnel to administer national financial programmes. In part, such assistance is provided by short-term field missions, in part, more recently, by 'continuing' country advisers for periods of one to two years. For some time IMF also maintained three regional offices (in Paris, Cairo, and Bombay) to follow as closely as possible significant economic developments in each region. But experience showed that this function might more effectively be performed by travelling staff teams, with the result that only the Paris office is now in operation. Like the Paris office of the Bank, it provides a close link with various European regional agencies and monetary blocs, in addition to disseminating information about the Fund's policies. These are all experimental devices designed to facilitate consultation and collaboration with Member governments.

Mention was made earlier in this chapter of the establishment by the General Assembly of UNICEF—at first in 1946 on a year-to-year, and then in 1953, on a permanent, basis. UNICEF is not in the legal sense a specialized agency: it serves rather as a semi-autonomous 'subsidiary' arm of the United Nations for the support of certain objectives coming within the provinces of the UN Department of Economic and Social Affairs, of WHO, and of FAO. As in the case of EPTA, UNICEF's financial resources are derived wholly from voluntary contributions by Member States outside the regular UN budget. It was set up originally to 'utilize some of the residual funds of UNRRA for work that, with the anticipated termination of the agency, threatened to come to a stop.'[29] Until the early 1950s UNICEF confined its operations largely to supplying needy children, nursing mothers, and pregnant women in war-stricken Europe with dried skim milk, clothing, and drugs; as well as transport and equipment for the mass immunization of millions of children against tuberculosis. Since then, UNICEF has shifted its main attention to under-developed countries where, in conformity with technical advice from WHO and FAO, it provides supplies and equipment for milk plants and penicillin factories, and for

[29] Robert E. Asher, *et al.*, *The United Nations and Economic and Social Co-operation* (Washington: The Brookings Institution, 1957), p. 58.

national child welfare, maternal health, and welfare services. Currently it is venturing into the field of nutrition and community development. UNICEF utilizes technical personnel provided by certain specialized agencies (WHO and FAO) and to a more limited extent by the UN Bureau of Social Affairs. In effect, UNICEF supplements the limited 'welfare' assistance available directly from the United Nations and the specialized agencies. It 'represents the second largest action programme of the United Nations, and it shares with the Expanded Programme of Technical Assistance the honour of being the most popular programme of the United Nations.' [30]

For the conduct of its activities UNICEF has developed a field structure similar in certain respects to that of UNRRA. This structure embraces a hierarchy of regional, area, country, and liaison offices. As will be indicated later, these offices work in close co-operation with the field offices of WHO and FAO, as well as with the Resident Representatives of TAB. Procurement of supplies and equipment is controlled at UNICEF headquarters but actually takes place all over the world, wherever government contributions can be converted into usable materials. The Paris regional office serves as an important subsidiary procurement centre and there is a sub-office in Australia for this purpose. In many countries UNICEF buys through government purchasing departments.

The latest in the long series of moves by the United Nations into field service operations was the creation in 1958 of the Special Fund.[31] Representing a compromise between the viewpoint of Member States advocating for years the establishment of a Special United Nations Fund for Economic Development, and the position of other Member States which for various reasons favoured the postponement of such action, the new Special Fund is designed to assist longer-term and larger projects than EPTA can manage, with the object of facilitating 'new capital investment of all types by creating conditions which will make such investments either feasible or more effective.'[32] It is anticipated that such projects will take the form mainly of comprehensive surveys of natural resources and of aid in

[30] *Ibid.*, p. 370.
[31] GA Resolution 1240 (XIII), 14 Oct. 1958.
[32] *The United Nations Special Fund: An Explanatory Paper by the Managing Director* (New York: SF/1, 1 Jan. 1959), p. 1.

inaugurating permanent training centres—both nationally and regionally—in such fields as public administration, statistics, technology, and agricultural and industrial research. For the time being at least, the new Special Fund, like EPTA, will be financed from voluntary annual contributions by national governments.

The Special Fund is administered by a Managing Director assisted by a small headquarters staff. For administrative services, a Joint Division (with TAB) is drawn upon. The Managing Director utilizes the field representatives of TAB as his channels with governments applying for aid from the Special Fund. For other services he is expected to rely on the existing facilities of the United Nations and the specialized agencies, upon which the execution of approved projects will be devolved 'whenever possible.' The Director, however, is authorized in his discretion to contract for the services of other agencies, private firms, or individual experts in cases where the services of the UN and specialized agencies are 'wholly or partly unavailable or inadequate.' In order to relate the management of the Special Fund's activities with those of EPTA as closely as possible, the Managing Director has the right to participate in meetings of TAB without vote. For general policy guidance on administration and operations, a Governing Council, elected by ECOSOC, will serve as the Fund's inter-governmental organ.

Administratively, the set-up of this new instrumentality is unique among UN system operational programme arrangements in that no field bureaucracy of its own—at least not at the outset—is contemplated. If, however, the Special Fund's resources should rapidly expand it is not unlikely that the country-level machinery of TAB may be obliged to enlarge its staff and other facilities (in certain countries at any rate) in order to handle the additional work load. This point is discussed in the final chapter.

A background survey of field operations would not be complete without calling attention to the Information Centres which have been set up by the UN Office (formerly Department) of Public Information in some twenty-seven national capitals around the world.[33] While these Centres have no administrative or

[33] For a critical survey of the organization and work of the UN Information Centres, see the *Report of the Committee of Experts on United Nations Public Information*, UN Doc. A/3298, 20 Sept. 1958.

substantive responsibility in connection with economic and social programmes, they are expected to co-operate with agency field officials by providing facilities for appropriate local and regional publicity for programme achievements. Such facilities include press releases, the holding of press conferences, the preparation of radio broadcasts, and the distribution of pamphlets, posters, charts, films and filmstrips, and photographic materials. As staff resources permit, the Information Centres also endeavour to promote teaching about the United Nations and the specialized agencies in schools and universities and to encourage the formation and strengthening of various non-governmental groups in support of the UN's work. How effectively these 'public relations' tasks are performed will be discussed later in this study.[34]

In 1959, the coverage of the UN Information Centres extended to seventy-one Member States, two non-member states, and several non-self-governing territories. Except in a few instances, each Centre is responsible for a regional grouping of countries adjacent to the host nation. In addition, two of the major specialized agencies—WHO and FAO—maintain field informational services of their own, while within the secretariats of three of the UN regional economic commissions (at Bangkok, Santiago, and Addis Ababa), there are informational units which absorb the functions of separate UN Centres.

Indices of the Growth of Field Operations

The increasing importance of non-political field activities in the United Nations system may be seen in quantitative terms by examining available budgetary and personnel information. From 1951 through 1960, as shown in Table 1, the regular annual budgets of the United Nations and the specialized agencies (not counting IBRD, IFC or IMF) steadily expanded from $78.6 million to $126.9 million, or by about 61 per cent. In large measure this expansion was due to increasing allocations of funds to economic and social functions requiring field administration—a trend that was accentuated by the admission of more than a score of new Members, many of which consist of recently independent and economically under-developed countries. It is

[34] See pp. 464–474.

significant to note, in this connection, that the budgets of the functional agencies as a whole increased during this period by as much as 117 per cent., in contrast to only 29 per cent. for the United Nations. The budget of WHO, where the largest technical assistance programme is to be found, was close to three times as large in 1960 as a decade earlier. Even in the case of the UN, the greatest single increase was for the work of its regional economic commissions and its special technical programmes.

The annual outlays of EPTA rose from $22 million in 1952 (its first year of full operation) to $32 million in 1958,[35] and contributions were received from eighty-six governments for this latter year—as against only fifty-four at the outset. Yet this relatively modest expansion of financial resources was not sufficient, by any means, to take care of all of the meritorious requests for aid presented by governments, in part, to be sure, because country allocations have recently had to be spread among a substantially larger number of countries and territories —well over one hundred by 1958. By the end of 1959 the aggregate amount of aid given under the auspices of EPTA since its advent was expected to approximate $235 million.

The over-all picture for a single recent year (1958) is shown in Table 2. During that year the aggregate budgetary allocations for all purposes and from all sources, made by he UN, UNICEF, and the seven specialized agencies then participating in EPTA, amounted to $176 million. Of this grand total, it is roughly estimated that $85 million, or almost 50 per cent., was earmarked for the administrative and substantive costs of economic, social, and technical activities carried on away from UN and agency headquarters. This estimate is decidedly on the conservative side since there are various expenditures of a mixed headquarters-field character which are not segregated in agency budgets. Nor was it possible to measure in monetary terms how much time was spent by headquarters personnel in administrative and substantive bureaux on the budgeting, staffing, planning, and back-stopping of field programmes.

Among the specialized agencies the allocations for field activities ranged from 13 per cent. for ITU up to 62 per cent.

[35] Statistical data on EPTA presented here are derived from the annual reports of TAB to the Technical Assistance Committee of ECOSOC, and the *Technical Assistance Newsletter* for June-July 1959 and for January 1960 (issued periodically by the UN Office of Public Information in collaboration with the secretariat of TAB).

for FAO and 80 per cent. for WHO—the two institutions with the most extensive field programmes and field machinery. The relatively low percentage for the United Nations is explained by the fact that it is a multi-purpose organization embracing political, diplomatic, 'peace and security,' trusteeship, and other functions. Even so, of the UN's total expenditure on economic and social matters alone (roughly $26 million, including EPTA funds), at least 50 per cent. was absorbed by the regional economic commissions and operational programme costs.

Another way of quantifying the scope of field activities is to compare the size of staffs on field assignments with the total number of persons on UN and agency payrolls during a recent typical year. Such a comparison is presented in Table 3. In constructing this table certain difficulties were encountered. Accessible data, for example, did not permit any accurate differentiation of staff stationed at field offices concerned only with economic and social matters from staff on other kinds of non-project field assignments (*e.g.*, at the United Nations Information Centres or serving on various field missions relating to peace and security). Short-term consultants engaged to do specific jobs, whether at headquarters or in the field, were not included. On the other hand, the table covers all regular staff whether on fixed-term, indefinite, or permanent contract, together with all technical assistance experts regardless of the source from which they are paid.

What these enumerations reveal is that almost half of the nearly 14,000 individuals on UN and agency payrolls during 1958 had field assignments of one kind or another (though not all for the full year). The different organizational units, in terms of the proportion of staff on duty away from headquarters, scale downward from WHO to FAO to the smallest technical agencies (WMO, ITU, and UPU).

Still a further index is the increase in the number of field experts recruited annually for EPTA since its inception in 1950. For the first financial period (July 1950 to June 1951) only 765 experts were appointed. From then on there was a fairly steady increase up to around 2,400 for the year 1958. In all, more than 8,000 individual experts were recruited over the entire period. This sizable army of 'shirt-sleeve diplomats' (as Jonathan Bingham has picturesquely called them) has represented over sixty different nationalities. By 1958 as many as one-fourth of them, significantly, were being provided by the less developed countries.

Added to the formidable tasks of recruiting, paying and supervising these thousands of project experts (including those financed out of the agency regular budgets) were various operations involved in managing large-scale, world-wide fellowship programmes. During the period indicated above, more than 14,000 men and women received awards of fellowships and trainee grants for study abroad on EPTA stipends, with about three-fifths that number under regular agency programmes. These awards were made to nationals of 137 different countries and territories around the globe. For the year 1958, WHO accounted for over 40 per cent., and the UN for about 20 per cent., of the total number of grantees, the remaining agencies following in this order: Unesco, ILO, FAO, ICAO, and WMO.

Underlying Forces and Assumptions

By way of summarization, the emergence and spread of non-political field activities within the over-all framework of the United Nations system may be attributed to the following interlocking features:

1. Initially, there was the legacy of the League, the early ILO, and UNRRA which set patterns for field action designed by headquarters secretariats and frequently implemented through regional or country-level field machinery or both. The pre-existence of such regional functional units as the Pan American and the Pan Arab Sanitary Bureaux provided compelling precedents for the decentralized regional structure of WHO.

2. It was early recognized by the UN itself that for the treatment of basic economic problems significant regional differences called for special arrangements. This view led to the creation of the regional economic commissions, each with its own regional secretariat. Similar assumptions in FAO, ILO, and ICAO circles lay behind a gradual trend towards the deconcentration of field programme execution in one form or another.

3. The inauguration of EPTA in 1950, under the United States Point Four impetus, markedly altered the balance of forces

TABLE 1

REGULAR BUDGET EXPENDITURES: UN, THE SPECIALIZED AGENCIES, AND IAEA*
(in U.S. dollars—figures rounded to 000s)

Organization	1951	1954	1956	1958	1960 [a]	*Per cent Increase* 1960 *over* 1951	
United Nations	48,628,000	48,510,000	50,508,000	62,506,000	61,863,000	29	
ILO	5,835,000	6,755,000	7,291,000	8,023,000	9,617,000	66	
FAO	4,581,000	5,500,000	6,398,000	7,868,000	10,790,000	135	
Unesco	7,989,000	9,019,000	11,437,000	12,316,000	13,779,000	73	
WHO [b]	6,259,000	8,135,000	9,983,000	13,961,000	16,919,000	174	
ICAO	3,172,000	3,087,000	3,348,000	3,999,000	4,578,000	48	117
ITU	1,643,000	1,327,000	1,685,000	1,890,000	1,964,000	19	
UPU	354,000	435,000	441,000	452,000	661,000	87	
WMO	186,000	327,000	371,000	441,000	655,000	252	
IMCO [c]	—	—	—	—	256,000	—	
IAEA [d]	—	—	—	3,868,000	5,843,000	—	
Grand Total	78,647,000	83,095,000	91,462,000	115,324,000	126,925,000	61	

**Sources:* UN Docs. A/2921, A/4032, and A/4170 (Reports of the Advisory Committee to the UN General Assembly).

(*a*) The totals for 1960 are appropriations or estimates—not actual expenditures.
(*b*) The WHO totals do not include appropriations under the regular budget of PAHO, which for 1960 amounted to over $4 million.
(*c*) IMCO (International Maritime Consultative Organization) did not come into being until 1959.
(*d*) IAEA, established in 1958, has, in addition to its 'regular' budget, a so-called 'operational' budget financed mainly by voluntary contributions and an allocation from EPTA. For 1960 this was estimated at $2.39 million.

in programme-making towards the provision of direct aids and services to Member governments, with proportionately less attention to world priorities. This shift caused certain organizations, notably the UN, Unesco, and ILO, to make from their regular budgets larger allocations for special operational programmes, major projects, and the like.

4. Lending strength to these developments was an insistent drive by the less developed countries, as they grew in voting strength, for additional assistance in the form not only of advisory services, demonstration projects, and training facilities, but also of supplies, equipment, and capital resources (*e.g.*, low-interest, long-term loans, and direct grants for the financing of non-self-liquidating development undertakings). This drive was marked by the prolonged debates in ECOSOC over the SUNFED issue—debates which, in substantial measure, were responsible for the establishment of the International Finance Corporation in 1956 and of the Special Fund two years later—as well as for the expansion of the capital stock of the World Bank during 1958–59. The projected International Development Association, slated to go into effect in 1960, will add a further capital-financing agency to the UN family.

5. As the moves for larger aid programmes gained momentum, the argument was advanced that there should be closer and more continuous contact by agency administrators with governments and peoples on the spot. This attitude prompted the governments of newly created States to seek the location of field offices on their territories, and led various 'host' countries to urge the expansion of the functions and staffs of field offices already operating in their capitals.

The cumulative impact of all these forces and assumptions enhanced the prestige value of operational programmes in the annual over-all competition for budget appropriations. Accordingly, in the aggregate, proportionately more money, more persons, and more machinery tended to be provided for such programmes.

The administrative implications of the thrust of continuing action to the far reaches of the world community (apart from the Sino-Soviet orbit) will be analysed in succeeding chapters of this study. Suffice it to remark here that the management of such

TABLE 2

ESTIMATED AGGREGATE ALLOCATIONS FOR FIELD OPERATIONS DURING THE YEAR 1958*
BY THE U.N., THE SPECIALIZED AGENCIES, EPTA, AND UNICEF
(in $ U.S., rounded figures)

Organization	*Estimated Funds (all sources)*	*Allocations from Regular Budgets involving Field Operations*	*Allocations from EPTA (Category I Approved Projects plus administrative costs)*	*Allocations for Field Programmes from other sources*	*Percentage for Field Operations (all sources)*
United Nations	67,611,000 [a]	7,507,000 [b]	6,530,000		19
ILO	11,299,000	935,000 [c]	3,226,000		37
FAO	16,870,000	1,894,000 [d]	8,085,000	490,000 [e]	62
Unesco	16,856,000	1,505,000 [f]	4,532,000		36
WHO	29,426,000 [g]	8,535,000	5,462,000	9,614,000 [g]	80
ICAO	6,241,000	850,000 [h]	1,240,000		33
ITU	2,481,000		324,000		13
WMO	828,000		346,000		41
TAB	1,990,000 [i]		1,990,000		100
UNICEF	22,607,000			22,607,000 [j]	100
Grand Totals	176,409,000	21,226,000	31,735,000	32,711,000 [k]	49

**Sources*: The totals and percentages in this Table were derived from UN and special agency annual budget documents; *The Report of TAB for 1958*, UN Doc. A/4032; and information supplied by the UNICEF secretariat.

NOTES ON TABLE 2

(*a*) The UN does not include special voluntary contributions made by governments for UNRWA or the UN Refugee Fund administered under the High Commissioner for Refugees—aggregating about $50 million for the year 1958. Including the new Special Fund, the aggregate funds available to the UN system as a whole, for the year 1960, were estimated by the Advisory Committee of the General Assembly at $235 million (assuming the same voluntary contributions as for 1959). UN Doc. A/4170.

(*b*) This figure does not cover the costs of the UN Geneva office (apart from ECE), the UN Information Centres, or miscellaneous field trips by the staff of the Department of Economic and Social Affairs; nor any field activities relating to refugee, diplomatic, security, or trusteeship functions.

(*c*) This total includes the expenses of ILO's 'field' and 'branch' offices, its 'national correspondents,' and various 'operational' activities, but not regional conferences.

(*d*) This figure covers expenditures for FAO's regional offices, outposted technical personnel, the meetings of regional conferences and commissions, and miscellaneous field missions.

(*e*) This represents a rough estimate of contributions from Member governments for special purposes.

(*f*) This total includes outlays for experts on mission, the administrative costs of the Field Science Co-operation Offices and the Havana regional office, and the costs of regular budget fellowships. The figure is probably too low since many Unesco officials are concerned with technical assistance in ways not shown in the budget breakdown.

(*g*) These totals include the Special Malaria Eradication Account, appropriations by PAHO, and special contributions from Member governments. UNICEF's contributions to joint WHO-UNICEF projects are included under UNICEF (see below).

(*h*) This total covers the costs of regional air navigation meetings, the operational expenses of regional offices, and an approximation of the costs of regional office staffs.

(*i*) This allocation is for TAB's central secretariat and field offices.

(*j*) About 5 per cent. of this total was allocated for the central management of UNICEF's world-wide field operations.

(*k*) In addition, IBRD, in the fiscal year 1958, expended $639,000 on technical assistance to Member governments (*Thirteenth Annual Report*, 1957–58). The dollar totals for similar assistance provided by IMF are not given in the Fund's Annual Reports since it is not possible to isolate the technical assistance phase of the Fund's consultation missions from their 'exchange restriction' aspects.

multi-national, geographically dispersed operations has been complicated by the complex, cumbersome structural framework within which UN and agency administrators are obliged to work. Not only is there no central legislative authority for the system as a whole, but the administrative headquarters of the quasi-autonomous organizational entities comprising it are scattered in nine different cities divided by the Atlantic Ocean. Although the specialized agencies are tied to the UN by limited agreements 'to co-operate,' each retains substantial 'sovereignty' within its own constitutional province, which, in several cases, over-laps that of other agencies. Each agency, moreover, developed its own administrative practices more or less independently over the earlier years, with varying degrees of delegation to field units whose hierarchical patterns have tended to evolve in unplanned fashion—'like Topsy'—and which, in some instances, criss-cross the regional jurisdictions of related agencies.

The system can work—and it does work surprisingly well under the circumstances—only to the extent that the various

TABLE 3

Geographic Dispersion of UN System Personnel for the Year 1958*

Organization	*Total Number (a) of Posts (all budgetary sources)*	*Established Posts (b) at Central Headquarters*	*Staff (c) stationed at Field Offices*	*Field Project (d) Experts (all sources)*	*Percentage of Total Personnel on Field Assignments*
United Nations	5,078	2,842	1,556	680	44
ILO	1,304	804	167	333	39
FAO	2,016	1,088	206	722	46
Unesco	1,524	968	116	440	36
WHO	2,461	554	644 (e)	1,263 (f)	77
ICAO	587	390	65	132	34
ITU	244	220		24	10
WMO	92	62		30	33
UPU	35	35			0
TAB	229	45	184		80
UNICEF	373	141	232 (g)		62
Grand Totals (h)	13,943	7,149	3,170	3,624	49

* *Sources*: The totals and percentages in this Table were derived from the following: *Information Annex III to UN Budget Estimates for the Financial Year 1958*, A/3600/Add. 1; *Nineteenth Report of the Advisory Committee on Administrative and Budgetary Questions to the General Assembly at Its Fourteenth Session*, A/4257; *WHO Official Records*, No. 89; *Report of TAB for 1958*, *op. cit.*, Annex VIII; PASO *Proposed Programme and Budget Estimates*, 1958, Official Docs. No. 21, July, 1957; and UNICEF Docs. E/ICEF/L.1056 and E/ICEF/R.526.

(*a*) The Table covers both internationally and locally recruited staff. It does not, however, include personnel employed on a temporary basis by UNRWA, UNKRA, or UN field 'security' missions.
(*b*) These totals, in the case of ILO, FAO, Unesco, and WHO, include administrative posts financed out of EPTA funds.
(*c*) The totals in this column include, for the UN, the staffs of its Geneva office and of the Information Centres; and for certain specialized agencies, the small staffs of liaison offices maintained at UN headquarters—as well as the staffs of all permanent 'field' offices of the UN and the various agencies.
(*d*) Included under 'Field Project Experts' are WHO's 'area representatives,' FAO's 'country representatives,' and Unesco's country 'chiefs of mission.'
(*e*) This figure includes 57 WHO and 177 PASB personnel stationed at Washington, which serves both as WHO's Regional Office for the Americas and as the headquarters office for PASB, and 84 personnel assigned to PASB's 'zone' offices in Latin America.
(*f*) This total includes 268 experts financed by PASB's own budget.
(*g*) This total does not include locally recruited personnel financed by host governments.
(*h*) These 'Grand Totals' do not cover the staffs of the IBRD, IFC, or IMF, only very few of whom are stationed away from headquarters on a continuing basis.

secretariats will it to work: by continuous staff consultation; by the adoption of increasingly similar rules and regulations; through the common guidance provided by the Administrative Committee on Co-ordination and, under its nominal aegis, the Technical Assistance Board, aided by a cluster of sub-committees and working parties for specific purposes; and, not least, by inter-agency participation in important field projects. Even so, the heavy work load resulting from the growing network of field offices and operational programmes has produced considerable strain, multiplying paperwork and often tangling the communications process. That the standards of field administration have by now reached relatively high levels of effectiveness is a tribute to the devotion, intelligence, and ingenuity of responsible international officials both at headquarters and at field centres.

3

DELIMITATION AND USES OF REGIONAL AREAS

The United Nations and its affiliated agencies consist of associations of sovereign States for specified purposes. This fact necessarily is the point of departure for understanding the patterns of field organization that have emerged within the system. It is individual Member States, or groups of Member States, that constitute the ultimate targets of all UN operational programmes and projects. Not only is this so, but the execution of these programmes depends upon the consent of the governments concerned; unlike similar programmes conducted by national governments, they cannot be imposed upon their clientele by legal fiat. It follows therefore that the Member State must be the primary areal unit in so far as programme administration involves continuing action at the territorial base of the UN pyramid.

This statement, to be sure, requires some qualification. Certain Member States still exercise political control over dependent territories detached geographically from their metropolitan areas. As a result, it has become necessary to associate the metropolitan Powers with arrangements for administering projects relating to their non-self-governing territories. While most UN field offices are located within the metropolitan confines of Member States, almost invariably at their national capitals, a few small offices have been set up within dependent territories (*e.g.*, in the Far East, Africa, and the Caribbean).

States belonging to the UN family of agencies vary tremendously both in population and in area. Not counting Communist China, their populational spread ranges from nearly 400 million (for India) down to 160,000 (for Iceland)—the former country having 2,400 times as many people as the latter. The variation in territorial area is even wider—the U.S.S.R. (the most expansive Member State) being 2,800 times as large as tiny Luxembourg.

These figures are cited to illustrate the difficulties involved in constructing field machinery that will realistically correlate area with function. As Arthur Macmahon has noted,

> the administration of international affairs is a fruitful laboratory in which to observe the perplexities that cluster in the problem of reconciling function and area. Here the emphasis is heavily geographical; areal divisions are of the essence. This would be true even if nation-states were not legally sovereign. Yet in the modern world international relations are increasingly functional in content. The diversified activities within nations are reflected globally in subject-matter specialities that ramify across geographical boundaries. There is increasing need, therefore, for the careful provision that will harmonize the two sets of factors.[1]

Since the UN system, however, is far from constituting a world government, this harmonization cannot be complete—indeed it is rarely so even for the field establishments of national administrations. Such regional areas as have been delineated by various UN agencies have perforce had to conform to national boundaries, however artificial they may be from the functional standpoint. Typically, these areas are composed of groupings of contiguous States, though there are some exceptions to geographic contiguity in connection with the grouping of 'island' States or territories.

Regionalism for UN System Administration

Regionalism in the administration of a world-wide co-operative system may be utilized with several objects in view. Regional offices, for example, may be set up merely as field outposts of central headquarters—for liaison, information-gathering, or public relations, covering an area larger than that of the host State. Budgetary economy is not infrequently the reason for establishing regional in lieu of separate country offices (*e.g.*, most of the UN Information Centres). A second object may be to deconcentrate from the centre to regional units varying degrees of administrative supervision over field programmes that relate functionally to a group of States. This is now broadly characteristic of the regional offices of WHO, FAO, ILO, and UNICEF. Still a further reason for regionalism may be to interject policy as well as administrative controls between

[1] 'Function and Area in the Administration of International Affairs,' *New Horizons in Public Administration* (University: Univ. of Alabama Press, 1945), p. 119.

headquarters and country-level operations. In this context regionalism tends to have a decentralizing effect, as illustrated by the WHO regional structure, and, to a lesser extent, by that of FAO. A fourth goal of regionalism, whether explicitly recognized or not, may be to unify or integrate more closely the relations of States within a diversified region by providing a regional forum and staff for the consideration of regional problems and for the stimulation and planning of regional operational projects. This last observation would apply more or less to the roles of the UN regional economic commissions (and their secretariats), especially in Latin America, in Asia and the Far East, and in Africa.

All four of these purposes are exemplified by the congeries of regional arrangements currently concerned with the conduct of UN economic and social activities. A given arrangement may serve more than one objective. In proportion as it has a decentralizing purpose, it is likely also to contribute to the other objectives enumerated above.

Given the necessity of using States as the components of international regional areas, the question arises as to the criteria that may be applied to determine the size and the boundary lines of the areas. Theoretically, it is possible to conceive of a series of objective criteria that might appropriately be taken into account. These criteria include (1) such geographic factors as climate (*e.g.*, arid zones), river valleys (*e.g.*, the Nile or Mekong River), and topography (*e.g.*, mountain barriers); (2) cultural cohesion—in terms of a common language, history, religion or ideology, or similarity of political institutions; (3) distinctive economic features (*e.g.*, stage of industrial development, tropical agriculture, sources of mineral resources, and the like); and (4) various technical and welfare considerations (*e.g.*, common air transport needs, incidence of endemic disease, pest control, or illiteracy). On a different level of generalization, administrative geography is of special relevance to the delimitation of regions (*e.g.*, volume of work, intra-regional communications and transport facilities, convenience for field operators and co-operating national government officials, the existence of suitable sites for regional offices, and working relations with the regional authorities of similar agencies).[2]

[2] For a penetrating analysis of this whole problem as seen from the American national

The first difficulty encountered in trying to apply such objective criteria to regional construction is that no one of them is ordinarily adequate if taken alone. In the second place, geographic, cultural, or economic unity seldom coincides with national frontiers. Illiteracy and poverty tend to be associated together but without regard for political boundary lines. This is even truer of health conditions. Other illustrations come easily to mind. The point here, as Fesler has aptly observed, is that 'agencies often go astray in their efforts to discover natural physical, economic, or social areas bearing upon their functional responsibilities.'[3] It may be easy to identify the central core of a functional-regional complex, but its outer reaches do not often coincide with existing political boundaries. Seldom are there clear functional guide-lines for an administrative region. In actuality, the size, shape, and number of field regions are usually the result of compromises involving diverse factors and pressures, many of which have a decidedly political complexion. Such has notably been the experience of the UN family of agencies. As we shall see, the UN agencies have tended, for various reasons, to set up field regions that are much larger in territorial extent than those serving most national administrations. Concomitantly, UN field regions, being international, are marked on the whole by far greater cultural and linguistic diversity than is typically the case with intra-national administration.

Influences Affecting the Composition of Regional Areas

The San Francisco Conference of 1945 abandoned the attempt, advocated notably by Egypt, to include in the UN Charter a formula defining regional groupings of states for the maintenance of peace and security, 'as well as for . . . *the development of their economic and cultural relations*' (italics added). This proposal was 'rejected on the ground that while "it clearly defined obvious legitimate and eligible factors for a regional arrangement," it probably failed to cover all the situations which might be covered by regional arrangements.'[4] Similarly, in respect of the

framework, see James W. Fesler's *Area and Administration* (University: Univ. of Alabama Press, 1949), Chaps. I–III.

[3] *Ibid.*, p. 59.

[4] Goodrich and Hambro, *Charter of the United Nations: Commentary and Documents*, *op. cit.*, p. 310.

constitutions of the major specialized agencies, the delineation of 'regions' was left to subsequent action by the sovereign policy organ of the agency concerned.

Existing regional structures within the United Nations and its related functional institutions have for the most part evolved gradually over the years—as need appeared to require. Except for WHO and ICAO, no over-all design for regionalism was formulated at the outset (though UNICEF came close to doing so). Not only this, but despite repeated exhortations from ECOSOC and the Administrative Committee on Co-ordination that there should be inter-agency consultation and, as far as possible, agreement as to location of regional offices, each agency tended to act in accordance with its own particular functional requirements as they were influenced by political bargaining. While complete identity of agency regional boundaries could not in any event have been expected, or even justified, the over-all result was sets of regional areas that cut across one another spatially to a far greater extent than called for on purely functional grounds.

The UN regional economic commissions

The ramifications of this problem may be illustrated by examining the way in which the composition of regional areas was arrived at by specific agencies and for specific programmes. As regards the UN regional economic commissions, the establishment of the first two—ECE and ECAFE—was dictated largely by 'the recognized need to give effective aid to the countries devastated by war.'[5] Action to this end was taken by ECOSOC in 1947.[6] The following year, on the proposal of various Latin American delegations (but with only lukewarm support from the United States), the Council extended its regional commission pattern by authorizing the creation of a Commission for Latin America.[7] In the meantime, there developed within ECOSOC a movement for the establishment of a commission for the Middle East. Failing agreement as to its areal dimensions, however, a decision was postponed

[5] UN Doc. E/3052. 6 Feb. 1958. This document summarizes developments leading to the establishment of ECE, ECAFE, and ECLA.
[6] By ECOSOC Resolution 36 (IV) for ECE, and 37 (IV) for ECAFE.
[7] By ECOSOC Resolution 106 (VI).

indefinitely.[8] The idea of adding a commission for Africa was raised in the Council as early as 1947, and from time to time until 1957, when the establishment of such a commission (ECA) was approved.[9] The driving force behind the move for both ECLA and ECA, neither of which concerned areas still devastated by war, was the conviction that the economic development of these two regions could be materially assisted thereby.

The Council gave special consideration to the geographic scope and membership of each regional commission at the time it was established. For ECLA this presented no serious problem, Latin America being a well-defined geographic (as well as political) area. The United States was included as a member of the Commission partly because of its intimate historic relations with Latin America but, more importantly, because it was recognized as the main source of economic aid to the countries south of the Rio Grande. The United Kingdom, France, and the Netherlands were admitted as Powers responsible for dependent territories in Central and South America and the Caribbean.

Full-fledged membership in ECE was restricted initially to European countries then belonging to the United Nations, in addition to the United States.[10] Other countries in Europe were granted 'consultative status' and later, upon their admission to the UN, full membership. Although not a UN Member, the Federal Republic of Germany was also admitted to ECE by ECOSOC in 1955. Switzerland is the only European country participating in a consultative status. The inclusion of the United States could be legally justified (in 1947) by its interests as an occupying Power in Germany, but the major consideration was the desire of the European States to associate it as closely as possible with ECE's role in the economic reconstruction of the European Continent.

[8] In this connection, a sub-committee of ECOSOC struggled with the problem of how to weight geographic, historical, cultural, economic, and social factors in determining whether such 'marginal' political units as Greece, Libya, Ethiopia, and Pakistan should be included in the 'Middle East.' See *United Nations Bulletin* (15 May 1948), p. 421.

[9] By GA Resolution 1155 (XII).

[10] Turkey, although consisting partially of territory located in Asia, was considered as 'European' for this purpose. Under Art. 11 of the terms of reference of ECE (as well as the other commissions) any UN Member may on request be granted consultative status. In ECE, for example, Australia, Brazil, Canada, India, Israel, and the U.A.R. (among others) have participated on this basis.

The determination of ECAFE's membership was complicated by two questions: (1) How far 'westward' should 'Asia and the Far East' extend? and (2) What should be done about the large number of territories within this vast area which either were independent States still outside the United Nations, or were dependencies of UN Members? The first question was settled without much difficulty by including India as the 'western-most' original Member of the Commission and, upon partition, Pakistan along with her. The limits of ECAFE's western 'frontier' were pushed further westward with the admission of Iran at her own request in 1958.[11]

The second question proved more troublesome. In general, the solution gradually arrived at was to accord 'associate' membership (with limited voting rights) to non-UN States and dependent territories and to change their status to full membership when they became Members of the United Nations.[12] By this process the ECAFE 'region' eventually took the shape of a broad arc extending from Japan through South-east Asia to the eastern boundaries of Turkey and Iraq. Located outside this arc were seven States—the United States, the U.S.S.R., the United Kingdom, France, the Netherlands, Australia, and New Zealand—which, for reasons of propinquity or alleged or actual interests, were also included in ECAFE's membership. By 1958 ECAFE consisted of twenty-three full-fledged and two associate members.[13]

When it came to deciding upon the territorial scope of the recently created African Commission, the Council was faced with a relatively simple task in that, even more clearly than in the case of Latin America, there was a distinct land area to deal with. The decision was to include 'the whole continent of Africa, Madagascar and other African islands.'[14] Over the question of Commission membership, however, a sharp political controversy arose. Most of the African States wanted both the Soviet Union and the United States as Commission members. But the metropolitan Powers feared that to include the Russians might

[11] This action clearly extended ECAFE's membership into what is conventionally thought of as the 'Middle East.'

[12] By exception, the Republics of Korea and of Viet-Nam, although blocked from admission to the UN, were accorded full ECAFE membership in 1954.

[13] UN Doc. E/3052, 6 Feb. 1958, provides full details regarding the evolution of ECAFE's geographic scope and membership.

[14] ECOSOC Resolution 671 (XXV), 29 April 1958.

open the door to their using the Commission to further the spread of Communist influence in Africa. After some manœuvring, the United States was persuaded to oppose membership for any State (including itself) which did not have direct governmental responsibilities in Africa. This shift of position, while resented by the U.S.S.R., produced a majority vote for the restriction of original membership to the nine independent African States (ten with Guinea by 1959) and the six Powers with responsibility for administering non-self-governing territories in Africa. Following the pattern previously set for ECAFE, the Council's enabling resolution further provided (1) for the admission as associate members of such territories on presentation of their application by the Member State responsible for their international relations, and (2) for eligibility to full membership for territories achieving independence and thereafter admission to the United Nations.

The aggregate composition of the four regional commissions now embraces the entire membership of the UN (plus a few non-member States) except for Canada, Israel, and certain Arab nations. With the establishment of a commission covering all of Africa, the inclusion of Turkey in ECE, and the admission of Afghanistan and Iran to ECAFE, there are only a few countries in the Middle East which do not belong to some regional commission. It is not unlikely that Israel may sometime elect to join ECE, and that ECOSOC will give its authorization; while Syria, as part of the newly constituted United Arab Republic, by a curious anomaly, already falls within the province of the African commission even though it is situated on the mainland of Asia. The continuing Israeli-Arab impasse, further complicated by sharpening divisions among the Arab States themselves since the reorientation of Iraq's ideological position, prevents sufficient regional cohesion for a workable co-operative arrangement in this troubled area. If it was not possible a decade ago to devise a generally acceptable formula defining the 'Middle East,' the present outlook is even less favourable for any sort of regional agreement.

The first three regional commissions were set up originally on an experimental basis. Within a few years, however, their usefulness had become so fully recognized that the Council accorded them permanent status in 1951, and similar status seven

MAP I WHO REGIONAL OFFICES AND THE AREAS THEY SERVE

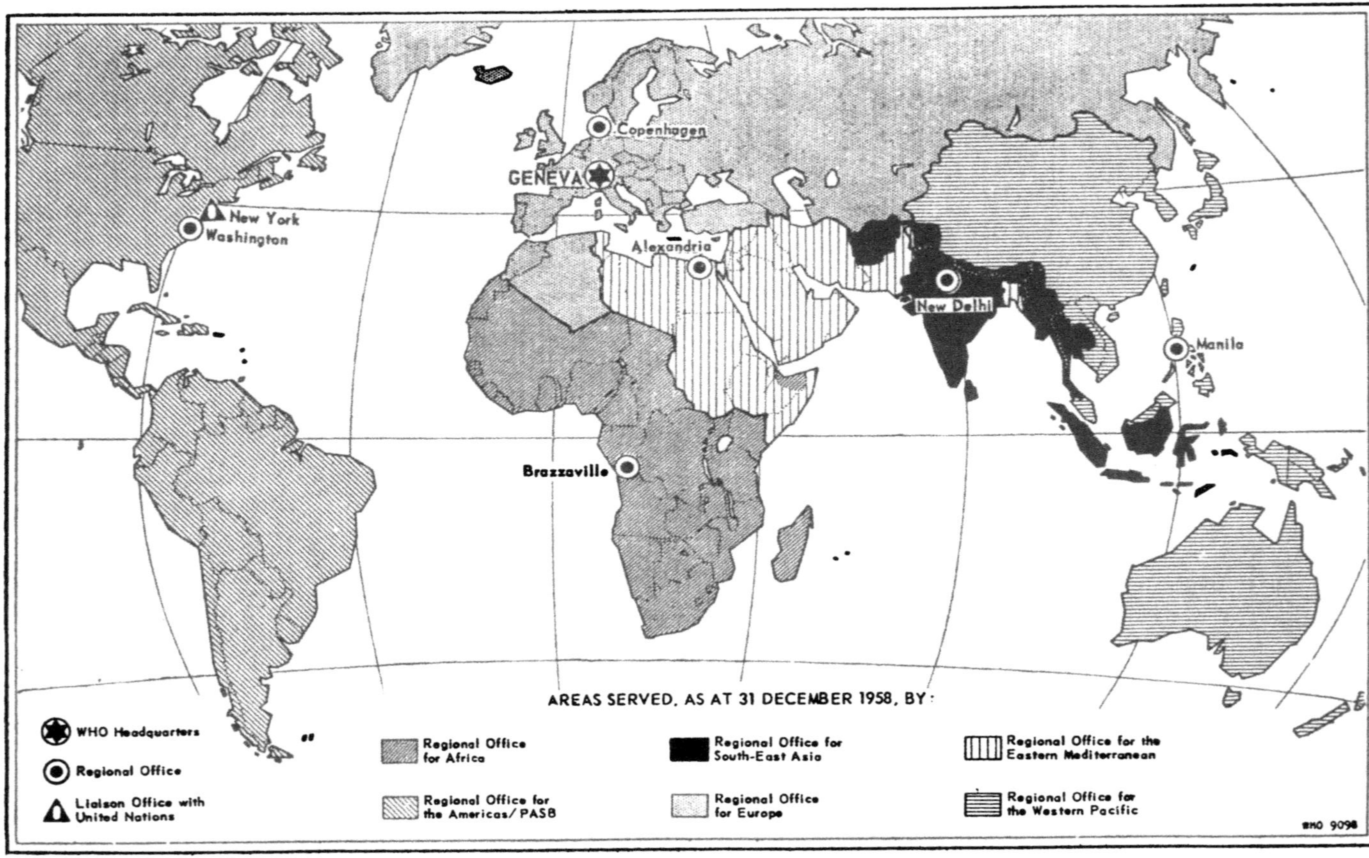

years later for the African Commission. Together with their regional secretariats the commissions represent the only important example of geographic decentralization within the UN proper. The consideration that led to the location of the regional secretariats at Geneva, Bangkok, Santiago, and Addis Ababa, respectively, will be examined in the next chapter.[15]

WHO's regional areas

As already indicated, the WHO Constitution stipulates that the World Health Assembly 'shall from time to time define the geographical areas in which it is desirable to establish a regional organization.' At the first session of the WHA (1948) there was considerable debate over whether the delineation of a complete network of regional areas should be worked out immediately or on a stage-by-stage basis. The former view finally prevailed and the Assembly proceeded to divide the world into six broad regions for WHO purposes (see Map 1).[16] In doing this, some attention was given to such factors as 'the standard of health in the countries to be included in the areas; the existence of any foci of epidemics in such countries; how far the countries concerned had succeeded in overcoming the effects on health of the war; and the efficiency of existing health administrations and their ability to deal with their problems.'[17] Even so, it did not prove possible to construct any composite formula incorporating these criteria. Three of the proposed six regions —Europe, the Americas, and Africa—followed essentially continental lines (the northern boundary of the Africa region being fixed as the Sahara). The other three were denominated the Eastern Mediterranean, South-east Asia, and the Western Pacific regions, respectively. The Assembly 'delegated to the Executive Board (of WHO) full authority to set up regional organizations within the areas delineated as soon as the consent of a majority of Members situated in such areas was obtained.'[18]

In its original delineation of regions, the Health Assembly

[15] See pp. 87–88, 91–92.
[16] Berkov, *The World Health Organization, op. cit.*, pp. 62-65. Some WHO officials are of the opinion that such action was premature.
[17] *The First Ten Years of the World Health Organization* (Geneva: WHO, 1958), p. 76.
[18] 'Organizational Study on Regionalization,' in WHO, Official Records (O.R.): No. 46, Jan.-Feb. 1953, p. 162.

did not employ a uniform method. The American and European regions were 'defined as including the whole of the continents concerned; on the other hand, the definition of the Africa region was based partly on the selection of political frontiers and partly on that of purely geographical frontiers.'[19] Only for the Eastern Mediterranean, South-east Asia, and the Western Pacific areas were the States and territories composing them actually enumerated. During succeeding years, various States falling outside this enumeration, along with a substantial number of new Member States, were assigned to regions by the Assembly. Still other States were transferred from one region to another on their own request. These assignments and transfers, in some instances, gave rise to prolonged argument. For example, to what region should Tunisia and Morocco be assigned—Africa, the Eastern Mediterranean or Europe? Assignment to Africa had little support. A strong bloc of delegates favoured the Eastern Mediterranean on grounds of 'community of religion, language and customs, as well as the similarity in epidemiological conditions between North Africa and the Eastern Mediterranean basin.'[20] Equally insistent claims for assignment to the European region were advanced by those who stressed the geographical separation of Tunisia and Morocco from Central Africa by the Sahara, and from the Eastern Mediterranean by the Libyan desert; the intensity of passenger and commercial traffic between the two territories and Europe; and the similarity of health conditions with the countries of southern Europe. The latter arguments carried the day and both territories were placed in the European region. When, however, Tunisia gained independence and became a full-fledged Member of WHO in 1956, she asked to be shifted to the Eastern Mediterranean region and the request was granted. In another case, Indonesia sought (and was granted) transfer from the Western Pacific to the South-east Asia region reportedly because she preferred to be in a region containing other Moslem countries.

This *ad hoc* procedure of assigning and shifting States to regions led to an attempt in 1953 to draw up 'rules and criteria' to govern future decisions. The Director-General solicited by

[19] *Ibid.*, p. 248.
[20] *Chronicle of the World Health Organization* (August 1952), p. 178.

mail the views of all Member States on the matter. Their replies overwhelmingly indicated that the desires of each sovereign government should be given first priority. The Executive Board of WHO then submitted recommendations to this general effect, while adding that such factors as geographical position, similarity of health problems, economic situation, and administrative considerations should be taken into account by each government concerned.[21] The Health Assembly, avoiding any direct stand on the Board's proposal, decided that 'the establishment of rules and criteria . . . shall be deferred until the results of the studies undertaken by the United Nations and other specialized agencies have become known.'[22] If any such studies were ever completed, the results have not come to light.

This decision by the WHA left WHO practice exactly as it was. Without prejudice to the 'sovereignty' question, the Assembly proceeded 'to make a number of provisional assignments covering territories responsibility for whose external relations was vested in certain Member States.'[23]

The dilemma posed by allowing individual States to determine their regional identifications on grounds largely irrelevant to health was highlighted by the stubborn refusal of the Arab States to participate with Israel in the Eastern Mediterranean Regional Committee of WHO. Israel had been assigned without objection to this region in 1948, and her delegation had attended two meetings of the Committee along with representatives from the Arab States. But in 1951, as the relations between Israel and her Arab neighbours worsened, the latter suddenly announced that they would no longer sit at any regional committee if the Israelis were present. As a result of this situation it was not possible to convene the meeting of the Regional Committee for the Eastern Mediterranean in 1951, 1952, and 1953. As a makeshift procedure, the World Health Assembly, in 1953, expressed the wish that the Committee should provisionally carry out its duties through two subcommittees, the constitution of which would be fixed in accordance with the wishes of the countries concerned. Despite the

[21] Ex. Bd. Resolution 11.R.51, 2 Feb. 1953.
[22] By WHA Resolution 6.45, 22 May 1953.
[23] *The First Ten Years . . ., op. cit.*, p. 83.

preference expressed by the Health Assembly, the meetings of the two sub-committees could not be convened. Accordingly, the 1954 WHA decided that the Regional Committee concerned should provisionally carry out its duties by being divided into two sub-committees and adopted a set of rules for this purpose. In 1955 Sub-Committee A only, which included all the States in the region with the exception of Israel, could be convened, and this situation prevailed also in 1956 and 1957. In 1958 and 1959 it was possible fully to implement the decision taken by the WHA in convening the meetings of both Sub-committees A and B, Sub-committee A including the Arab States and certain other Member States in the region, whereas Israel and still other Member States in the region attended Sub-committee B. The up-shot of these persistent intra-regional political tensions, for which WHO was in no way to blame, was that programme and budgetary operations in the region were made more difficult. The internal crisis that threatened for a time to paralyse WHO activities in the Eastern Mediterranean prompted Turkey, in 1952, to ask to be transferred provisionally to the European region—a transfer that eventually became permanent.

Some reference to certain anomalies in the composition of the region of the Americas is now in order. By the agreement concluded between WHO and the Pan American Sanitary Organization in 1949, the latter's Bureau at Washington was recognized as the regional office for WHO in the Western Hemisphere.[24] Membership on the Directing Council of PASO, however, had been restricted to 'the American Republics,' a provision that ruled out Canada. In order to make Canada eligible to join, the PASO Constitution was altered so as to entitle 'all self-governing nations of the Western Hemisphere' to membership. It was further provided that membership be extended to countries (outside the American region) which had dependencies in the Americas (*i.e.*, the United Kingdom, France, and the Netherlands). To date, the Government of Canada has not seen fit to accept membership in PASO (re-named, in 1958, Pan American Health Organization[25]) and accordingly has been represented on its Directing Council

[24] The full text of this agreement is contained in *Basic Documents of the World Health Organization* (9th ed., Geneva: 1958).
[25] Resolution XXVI of the Fifteenth Pan American Sanitary Conference, 2 Oct. 1958.

(which also serves as the WHO regional committee) only by observers.[26] Conversely, Columbia, although a member of PASO, did not ratify the WHO Constitution until 1959 and therefore in the meantime could not participate formally in the PASO Directing Council when it was functioning as WHO's regional committee.

To facilitate field operations in Latin America, the region of the Americas has been subdivided by PAHO into six 'zones,' covering the following areas: (1) Venezuela-Caribbean dependent territories; (2) Mexico-Cuba-Haiti-Dominican Republic; (3) Central America-Panama; (4) Western South America (including Bolivia); (5) Brazil; and (6) Southern South America (including Paraguay). To each zone office considerable authority over field programme-making and implementation has been delegated. In large measure the rationale governing the size of the zones was an attempt to achieve as even a distribution of work as possible among the six offices in relation to available communication and transport facilities. This 'sub-regional' decentralization means that for the Americas WHO in effect operates through three levels of field areas—regional, zonal, and country.

One further aspect of the WHO operational system remains to be noted. This has to do with arrangements for disseminating epidemiological information. Under the International Sanitary Regulations, WHO is responsible for collecting and distributing to the national health administrations up-to-date information 'on the appearance, presence, and termination of quarantinable diseases.' Such information is 'collated by the four WHO quarantine and information services at Geneva, Singapore, Washington, D.C., and Alexandria.'[27] Dissemination is effected both by air mail and by a network of radio-telegraphic stations, as indicated on Map 2. While the globe is not divided into fixed spatial regions for this purpose, the four information centres span substantially the following areas: Washington-Latin America; Geneva-Europe and Africa; Alexandria-the Middle East; and Singapore-the Indian Ocean, South-east Asia, and the Western Pacific.

[26] According to Berkov (*op. cit.*, p. 140), it is believed in WHO circles that Canada's decision not to join may have been due partly to the fact that it does not belong to the Organization of American States, and partly, perhaps, because it did not wish to assume any additional financial obligation resulting from PAHO's scale of regular budgetary assessments.

[27] *The First Ten Years . . ., op. cit.*, p. 262.

MAP 2 WHO NETWORK OF EPIDEMIOLOGICAL RADIO-TELEGRAPHIC COMMUNICATIONS

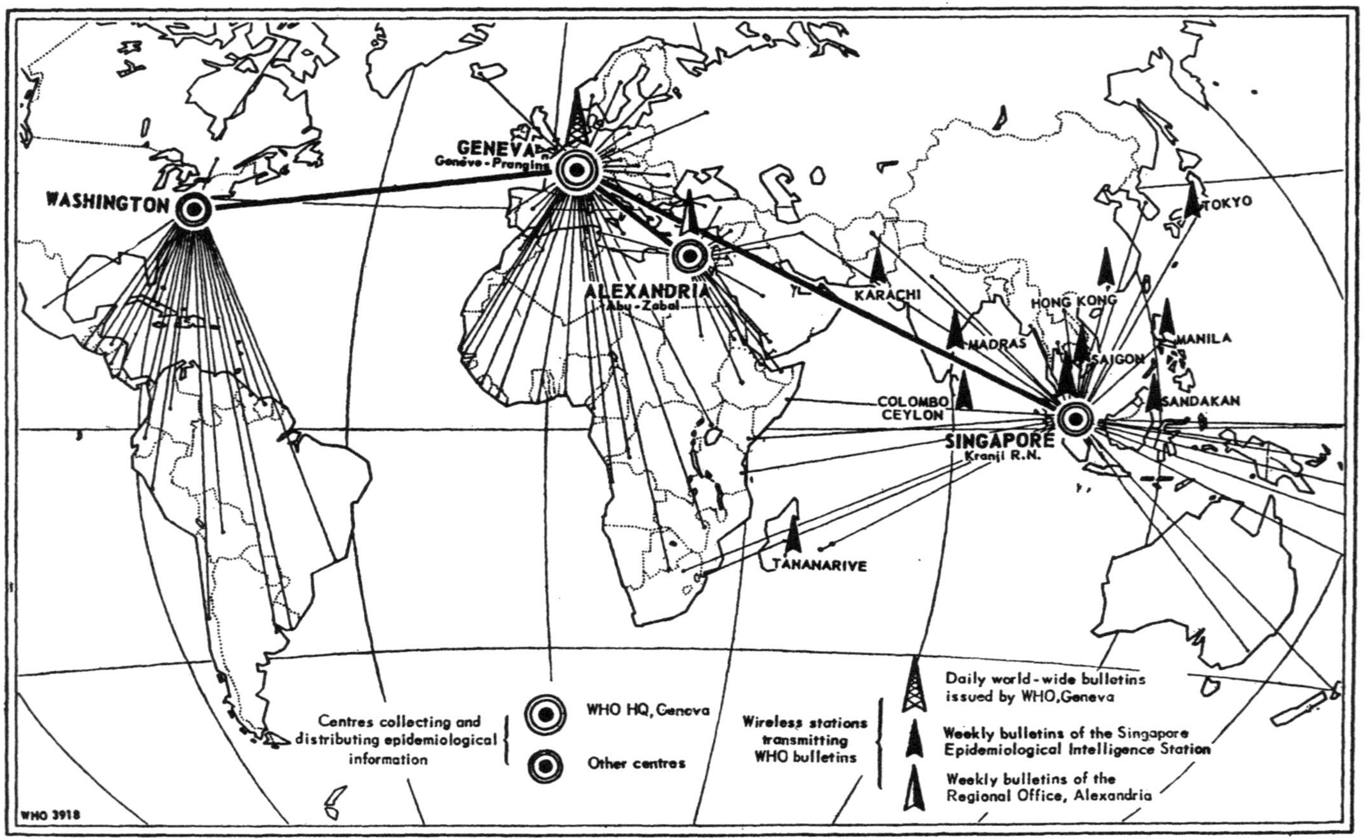

ICAO's air navigation regions

WHO was the only specialized agency to develop from the start a world-wide pattern of multi-purpose field regions on a genuinely decentralized model. For all the other agencies, administrative regionalism has to date served more limited objectives. ICAO's scheme of air navigation regions, like the WHO pattern, was designed *in toto* at the outset of the organization, but in contrast to WHO's structure, its province was initially restricted to only one of ICAO's major functions; nor did it involve the delegation of substantive authority to regional levels.

Under its Convention, ICAO has the duty of adopting and amending from time to time international standards, recommended practices, and procedures in a number of subjects, to the end that the contracting States, which by the Convention undertake to collaborate in order to attain uniformity, shall have a model. Included among these subjects are those which together are broadly called 'air navigation services.' These are aeronautical communications, radio aids to navigation, air traffic services, aeronautical meterology, aerodromes, and search and rescue. These services, taken together, enable aircraft to be navigated with safety and regularity and to be guarded against the risk of collision and other dangers. At the inception of ICAO it was recognized that in addition to standards, recommended practices, and procedures, which are for compliance by all contracting States, agreements would be needed on the facilities and services to be supplied. It would be necessary to agree, for example, on the sites and area of cover of radio aids to navigation, on the sites and the nature of the service to be rendered by air traffic units and meterological offices, on the site and capacity of aerodromes to be used by international aircraft, and so on.

Accordingly, the ICAO Council, which is empowered to 'create subordinate air transport commissions on a regional or other basis and define groups of states or airlines with or through which it may deal to facilitate the carrying out of the aims of this Convention,' created a number of air navigation regions, and began to hold a series of regional air navigation meetings, one for each region.[28] The first—for the North Atlantic region—was held in February 1946. An ICAO region consists of a group of contracting States which have in common a distinctive set of conditions of aircraft operation, some of the States because they are situated in the region in which these conditions obtain, and the rest because their international airlines fly through the region. Thus every contracting State is a member of the air navigation region within whose boundaries it is situated. It is also a member of any region through which its aircraft fly.

The concept by which a region was first delineated was a set of common air navigation problems. Thus the boundaries of such regions were not easy to define closely. These boundaries, though drawn upon maps to give a general representation of the relation of regions to one another, have not been adhered to strictly where, for example, the development of the pattern of air routes has suggested the invitation to a meeting of a State previously considered outside the region. In fact, the whole regional organization of States has remained flexible, so as to respond to shifts and changes in the world's air routes. Moreover, the boundaries of regions overlap in recognition of the fact that some States on account of their position have to deal with flying in more than one region. For example, a State on the eastern seaboard of a continent will be concerned both with the oceanic flying to the east and the continental flying to the west.

At first there were ten regions, but in 1952 the number was reduced to eight by amalgamation. These eight regions now are: North Atlantic; Pacific; European-Mediterranean; Middle East; South-east Asia; Caribbean; South American-South Atlantic; and Africa-Indian Ocean. The first two are oceanic regions, of which the members by geography are the States bordering the oceans; the next four are largely continental; and the last two are partly continental and partly oceanic, though the amount of oceanic flying in the African-Indian Ocean region and the South American/South Atlantic region is relatively small. Finally, parts of the U.S.S.R. (a non-contracting State) and China were not 'included in the regions for political reasons,

[28] See Jacob Schenkman, *The International Civil Aviation Organization* (Geneva: Droz, 1955), pp. 229–48.

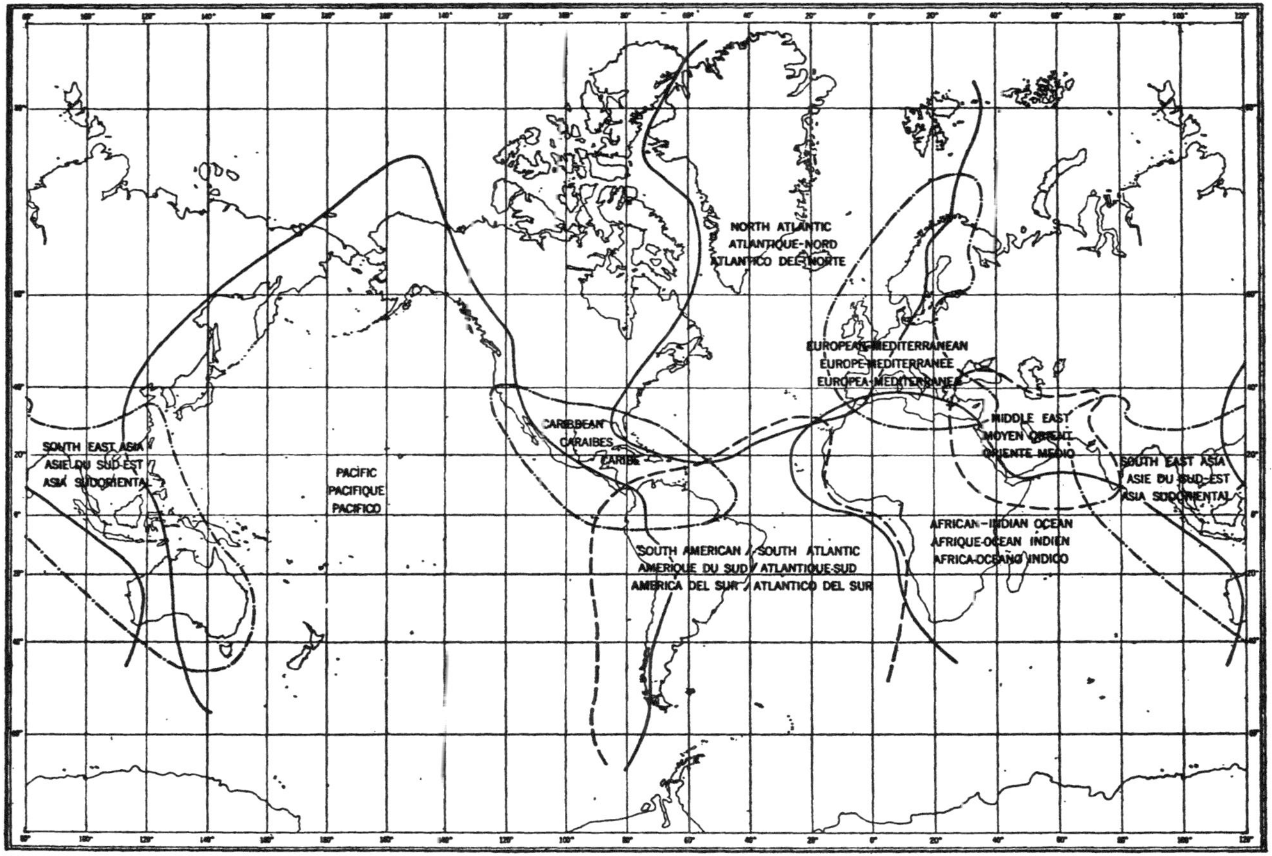
NORTH ATLANTIC
ATLANTIQUE-NORD
ATLANTICO DEL NORTE
EUROPEAN-MEDITERRANEAN
EUROPE-MEDITERRANEE
EUROPEA-MEDITERRANEA
MIDDLE EAST
MOYEN ORIENT
ORIENTE MEDIO
SOUTH EAST ASIA
ASIE DU SUD-EST
ASIA SUDORIENTAL
CARIBBEAN
CARAIBES
CARIBE
PACIFIC
PACIFIQUE
PACIFICO
SOUTH AMERICAN / SOUTH ATLANTIC
AMERIQUE DU SUD / ATLANTIQUE-SUD
AMERICA DEL SUR / ATLANTICO DEL SUR
AFRICAN–INDIAN OCEAN
AFRIQUE-OCEAN INDIEN
AFRICA-OCEANO INDICO
SOUTH EAST ASIA
ASIE DU SUD-EST
ASIA SUDORIENTAL

and much of North America was similarly omitted as it was not considered advantageous to bring the bilateral co-ordination between Canada and the United States under ICAO's aegis. Map 3 shows the overlapping boundary lines of the eight navigation regions.

At a regional air navigation meeting, the air routes to be exploited are drawn up. Then a complete plan is made for the facilities and services needed to enable aircraft to navigate with safety along these routes. If the conditions of the region call for the use of procedures not necessary on a world-wide basis, these are drawn up and are published as 'regional supplementary procedures.' The number of these is, however, relatively small. The resulting network of services is known as 'the regional plan,' which is published for the use of all concerned. States of the region are expected to fulfil the obligations which the plan imposes upon them under the general obligation, included in the Convention, to provide services for international air navigation as far as practicable. Where States are unable to fulfil their obligations, other means of providing the services may be invoked; for example, joint financing by other interested governments. To promote the fulfilment of a regional plan, to obtain agreement upon changes made necessary during the interval between successive meetings, and to keep all States concerned fully informed upon progress in the fulfilment of the plan are the primary tasks of the ICAO regional offices.

At first it was planned to establish a regional office in each air navigation region. For various reasons, including the desire to avoid the proliferation of correspondence between a State that is a member of several regions and the different regional offices, it was decided to accredit regional offices to groups of States solely by relation to geography. The offices are as follows:

Site	*Accredited to*
Mexico City	States of Central and North America and the Caribbean
Lima	South America and Panama
Paris	Europe and certain African States and territories

Site	*Accredited to*
Cairo	Middle East and certain African States and territories
Bangkok	States of Asia and Australasia

Each office is responsible for the affairs of the air navigation regions which primarily concern the States to which it is accredited. Thus, for example, the Paris office is responsible for the plans for the European-Mediterranean and North Atlantic regions; the Bangkok office for the plans of the South-east Asia and Pacific regions. The ICAO regional offices, by correspondence between themselves, maintain the necessary liaison in respect of States which are members of regions with whose affairs offices other than those accredited to the States are charged. The States to which each office is accredited form a complete geographical group. For example, the Lima office is accredited to all South American States and to Panama. The only region in which the territories and States to which regional offices are accredited do not form clearly defined groups is the African region, where the sharing of responsibility between the offices in Cairo and Paris has been determined in accordance with the office accredited to the mother country of dependent territories. It is normal for a regional office to be responsible for the implementation of the plans in two regions.

Increasingly, as experience reveals how similar the needs and conditions of adjacent regions are becoming, the practice is to hold joint regional air navigation meetings. Thus, in 1959, a joint meeting for the Middle East and South-east Asia regions took place in Rome.[29] Member States may participate in regional meetings in accordance with the following rules: territorial location in the region; actual or probable operation of airlines in the region; or contribution to facilities for international air transport within the region.[30]

On the whole, given its limited functional scope, ICAO's regional structure appears to work in a reasonably satisfactory manner. In the near future, as jet traffic expands via the North

[29] The FAO headquarters building in Rome was used for this meeting apparently because there were no offers from countries within either region to contribute towards the costs of the meeting.

[30] Schenkman, *op. cit.*, pp. 235–40.

Pole, and especially if the Soviet Union should join ICAO, a polar region may possibly be created. Certain minor difficulties have arisen in the Middle East region as a result of the Arab-Israeli impasse. Correspondence between the Cairo office and the Israeli authorities, for instance, has had to be routed by way of the Paris office since there is no direct communication between the U.A.R. and Israel. The Arab countries do not officially admit the existence of Israel aircraft because they still refuse to recognize Israel as a sovereign State. Israel participated in the 1950 air navigation meeting held within the region. Since then the issue of its participation along with Arab delegations has not arisen by reason of the fact that no subsequent meeting has taken place there. In 1958, however, Israel was represented at the Rome meeting.

The regional structure of FAO

As suggested in the preceding chapter, FAO's regional structure has had a bit-by-bit pragmatic development. The Quebec Conference of 1945 (at which the FAO Constitution was adopted) recommended the setting up of regional offices. As a first step in this direction, Member governments were requested by the FAO Conference of 1946 to establish 'national FAO committees' (which now exist in fifty-three of the seventy-seven Members). It was assumed that such committees would have much to say 'regarding the need for a regional office in their areas and the kinds of service it should be prepared to render if they wish to have one.'[31] In the meantime, the idea of developing a network of 'agricultural attachés' at the country level was toyed with and then abandoned. Instead, the Director-General was authorized to appoint 'temporary regional advisers' in Europe, Egypt, India, and China. In 1947, the Conference instructed him to prepare plans 'whereby offices may be established *in each principal region*, and more especially in Latin America, Europe, the Near East, and Asia' (italics added).[32] A review of discussions in the Conference and at subsequent sessions of the FAO Council does not show that much attention was ever given to systematic

[31] *First Annual Report of the Director-General to the FAO Conference* (Washington: 1946), p. 10.

[32] *Report of the Third Session of the FAO Conference* (Geneva: 1947), p. 42.

methods for determining the geographic boundaries of 'each principal region.' The assumption appears to have been that these would follow the wishes of the 'core' governments located in each continental or other major geographic area as designated by the Conference.[33]

By 1948, a fairly definite pattern of regional organization emerged. Regional representatives of the Director-General, had by that time been appointed for Europe, for the Near East, and for Asia and the Far East, with provisional offices at Rome, Cairo, and Bangkok, respectively. To these offices was assigned the responsibility for maintaining liaison with, and providing technical advice to, Member States within the three regions. Arrangements for the Latin American region were delayed for a year or so because of difficulty in reaching agreement on the location of regional offices there. For the time being, a regional officer for Latin America was stationed at FAO headquarters in Washington, while 'zone' officers were assigned provisionally to Mexico City, Rio de Janeiro, and Santiago. Effective lobbying by the Latin American bloc in the Conference eventually led to the definite division of the region into three zones, each with its field office, as follows: (1) Mexico-Central America-Caribbean; (2) Eastern South America; and (3) Western South America. By 1952 Rio was designated as the principal regional office, together with two zonal offices at Santiago and Mexico City. Four years later, for reasons that will be explained later, the principal office was transferred to Santiago, the Rio office being down-graded to zonal status.[34]

With the removal of FAO headquarters from Washington to Rome in 1951, the European office disappeared as such (though Europe is still recognized as a region for certain purposes), and an office for North America was established in Washington to maintain contact with the United States and Canadian Governments on agricultural problems.

No further change was made in FAO's regional structure until

[33] See, in this connection, the 'Statement of the U.S. Delegation Concerning FAO Regional Offices,' FAO Doc. CL 2/36, 8 April 1948.

[34] In addition to considerations of geographic propinquity, the boundaries of the zones within South America were fixed with some regard for similarity of types of agriculture. Thus the territorial coverage of the Rio sub-office (since 1956) has included Argentina, Brazil, Venezuela, Paraguay, and Uruguay—the majority of them countries with essentially tropical agriculture. Use of the term 'zone' appears to have been a tactic to sell the idea of having more than one office in Latin America—on the assumption that staff costs would be less for zonal 'sub-offices' than for full-fledged 'regional' offices.

1957. Then Africa had begun to take on great importance as an area for FAO technical assistance activities. Moreover, the decision of ECOSOC to establish a regional commission for Africa underlined the increasing attention being given in United Nations circles to pressing problems of African economic development. Accordingly, the Director-General of FAO was moved to recommend that Africa should formally be recognized as an additional FAO region and that an African regional office be set up. The 1957 FAO Conference approved his recommendation,[35] and he shortly afterward convened a consultative meeting of representatives of African States and territories to give him guidance on where the new regional office (or offices) should be situated. While admitting 'the diversity' of African conditions, the delegates to this meeting

> agreed fully that certain major problems are common to a number of African countries . . . [and] stressed the necessity of FAO activities being orientated regionally in so far as possible, it being understood that the word 'regional' should in many cases in Africa be applied not to the entire continent but to the large natural zones which are similar in their climate, their soils, their vegetation and their economic and social characteristics.[36]

It was consequently proposed that the new regional organization should include three field offices, one serving that part of the continent north of the Sahara not included in the jurisdiction of the Near East regional office at Cairo, and the other two serving the area south of the Sahara, which would be divided into western and south-eastern zones. The exact boundary line between the two areas south of Sahara was referred to the Director-General for administrative determination in the light of 'relevant factors.'

Once the new African regional structure is in full swing, FAO will have blanketed all of the 'principal' economically underdeveloped areas of the globe (except for the mainland of China) under its permanent field establishment.[37] This establishment is currently in process of being strengthened as to staff and other resources, and of being given increasing operational authority

[35] FAO Doc. C57/SR-II/7, 16 Nov. 1957.
[36] FAO Doc. CL/29/14, 30 May 1958.
[37] It should be added that this establishment now also includes permanent 'country representatives' (formerly called 'chiefs of mission') in some forty countries where there are substantial technical assistance operations.

(though by no means as much as in WHO's case).[38] The present Director-General is reported to favour expanding the number of regional offices and limiting the territorial coverage of each to about six countries on an average. Budgetary limitations, however, are likely to prevent any such proliferation in the immediate future even though it is generally recognized that the jurisdictional area of the Far Eastern office, in particular, is too vast for effective supervision of field activities.

Although FAO, in contrast to its sister agency in the health field, does not have a structure of permanent regional committees with prescribed constitutional functions, it early began the practice of holding 'pre-Conference' regional meetings of senior national agricultural officials to review the FAO programme and to make suggestions for future policy and action in terms of regional office staffs. In addition, the organization has set up a variety of semi-autonomous technical bodies with a more or less fixed regional composition. Among these are fisheries councils for the Mediterranean, the Indo-Pacific area, and Latin America; regional forestry commissions for Europe, Asia, the Near East, and Latin America; and the International Rice Commission, which, while not restricted in membership to Far Eastern countries, operates primarily as a regional body. There is also a European Commission for the Control of Foot-and-Mouth-Disease and, more recently in 1956, a European Committee on Agriculture was set up. While none of these subsidiary bodies has a secretariat of its own, the preparation of agenda and arrangements for meetings is a responsibility of one or more technical officers 'outposted' to the appropriate regional office of the Organization.[39] Meetings are held every year or so in accordance with need and available funds. The delegates consist typically of directors of functional services in national ministries of agriculture.

ILO's field establishment

As was indicated in Chapter 1, the International Labour Organisation evolved a network of national correspondents and branch

[38] The Director-General's proposals to this effect are elaborated in FAO Doc. C 57/5, 11 March 1957.

[39] Except for the European Commissions, which are serviced by the Rome secretariat.

offices as far back as the pre-World War II period. As the membership and activities of the organization have expanded since then, this network has been correspondingly enlarged. All of these field outposts, it is to be noted, have a single country focus. Following World War II, ILO 'set on foot a special operational manpower programme covering employment service organization, vocational guidance and training, and migration.'[40] With a view to studying and reporting on manpower conditions in different areas, regional *manpower* offices were established in Asia in 1949, in Latin America in 1950, and in the Middle East in 1952, the European region being handled by the Geneva headquarters. This programme received a major impetus in 1950 by a grant of $1 million to ILO from the Organization for European Economic Co-operation.[41] The main object of this grant was to enable ILO to facilitate overseas emigration from European countries. To this end migration field missions were established in Austria, Italy, and West Germany on a temporary basis. With the exhaustion of the OEEC grant two years later, the Governing Body of the ILO approved appropriations for a modest continuation of migration work.

Concurrently (in 1950), the UN Expanded Programme of Technical Assistance inaugurated its operations, and the ILO authorities decided gradually to convert the three manpower offices (at Bangalore, São Paulo, and Istanbul) into *general* field offices. This conversion was completed by early 1954. Since then, their principal activity has been to aid in planning, negotiating, and executing ILO technical assistance projects within their respective areas.

The territorial scope of the ILO field offices has been determined primarily by technical assistance needs. The geographic coverage of the Asian office extends from Pakistan on the west all the way to Japan on the east (coinciding roughly with that of FAO's Far Eastern Office at Bangkok). The Near and Middle Eastern office (as it is called) covers most of the Arab States, Israel, Iran, Turkey and Greece—a grouping, interestingly enough, that extends substantially beyond what is ordinarily meant by the Near (or Middle) East. In 1954, Latin America

[40] ILO Doc. G.B. 138/T.A./D. 1/2 (1952).
[41] This money came in fact from the European Co-operation Administration of the United States Government.

was divided into two field regions—one for South America and the other for Mexico, Central America, and the Caribbean, with an additional field office at Mexico City for the latter area.[42] This action stemmed in part from the increasingly heavy concentration of ILO technical assistance work (notably the large Andean Indian regional project) in South America and partly, because it became difficult to take care of the programme to the north from a single office located as far away as Lima.

In 1958, ILO joined FAO in taking cognizance of the rapid emergence of Africa as an area requiring international technical aid, by setting up a further ILO field office at Lagos (in Nigeria). Its geographic coverage will presumably include all of Africa south of the Sahara. Sudan and Somalia have also been assigned to the new African office. Tunisia and Morocco are handled directly from Geneva, while Libya remains within the purview of the Istanbul office.

During recent years the ILO secretariat has devoted serious study to ways of rationalizing the Organization's cumbersome field structure. As it now stands, there is unavoidably considerable duplication in the activities of the 'branch' and the general field offices. The fact that the former (where located within a recognized field region) are not formally subordinate to the field office of the region tends to cause some confusion. Yet when it was recently suggested by the Geneva secretariat that such branch offices be made responsible hierarchically to the field office of the region concerned, objections were feared from certain 'host' governments to having the branch offices down-graded in status (or possibly discontinued in certain instances).[43] All of which again under-scores the impact of national psychologies on well-meaning efforts of UN system administrators to streamline organizational machinery.

Unesco's fragmentary regional apparatus

By comparison with those of WHO, FAO, or ILO, the multifarious field operations of Unesco are conducted primarily from

[42] The São Paulo office, for reasons to be explained later (see pp. 90), was shifted to Rio and later to Lima.

[43] This information is based on the author's interviews with ILO headquarters officials. As of early 1960, the whole question of ILO's field establishment was still under consideration.

agency headquarters. The only continuing regional machinery Unesco has thus far devised consists of four small 'field science co-operation' offices (mentioned in the preceding chapter) and an equally modest Western Hemisphere office (at Havana), the activities of which were, at any rate until 1956, so vaguely defined and so meagrely supported as to mean little. Within the Unesco secretariat there was not for several years much enthusiasm for any generalized regional structure accompanied by operational decentralization. In some measure, no doubt, this lack of interest in geographic decentralization may be traced to the fact that a large part of Unesco's work is contracted out to non-governmental groups, national and international, resulting in what amounts to functional decentralization.

The Unesco field science co-operation offices were reportedly the brain-child of the first Director of the Department of Natural Sciences. In any event, the first Unesco General Conference (1946) was persuaded to authorize the Director-General to establish a series of offices which would be concerned chiefly with developing direct contacts with scientific personnel and furthering the exchange of scientific information in regions where the state of science training, teaching, and research is relatively backward. On the basis of this authorization, the terms of which have been substantially repeated by succeeding annual Conferences, such offices were set up at Cairo for the Middle East (1947); at Montevideo for Latin America (1947); at New Delhi for South Asia (1948); and at Shanghai for South-east Asia (1949). The Communist conquest of the Chinese mainland led to the transfer of the Shanghai office first to Hong Kong then to Manila, and finally to Djakarta (by 1953), where it has since operated.[44]

In 1950, the Unesco Social Sciences Department, deciding to get into the regional game, proposed that the terms of reference of the Middle Eastern and South Asian offices be extended to include social as well as natural sciences. This extension was authorized by the General Conference, and the following year the Director-General was empowered to station social science staff at the other two offices as well. In actual fact, however, this latter authorization was never acted upon.

[44] As one secretariat official remarked to the author, the vicissitudes of this office were like those of a political refugee.

Moreover, the assignment of a social science officer to New Delhi was soon discontinued, leaving only Cairo as a regional outpost for the social sciences until 1960, when a social science officer was assigned to the secretariat of ECA at Addis Ababa.

The functions of the regional offices in the science fields are still limited substantially to liaison, informational activities, and the facilitation of regional training seminars for scientists. To extend their terms of reference 'across Unesco's board' (including technical assistance) would, as one official put it to the writer, involve 'adoption of the principle of regional administration,' concerning the wisdom of which he had great scepticism.[45] Nevertheless, the Executive Board at its May 1958 session requested the Director-General to submit to the 1960 General Conference a report on the advisability of broadening the functions of the field science co-operation offices to 'programme responsibility for other chapters of the programme,'[46] and support within secretariat circles for such a step now appears to be growing.

Curiously enough, Unesco was lured early in its life into setting up a fifth field office, for the Western Hemisphere—designed ostensibly to strengthen liaison with Member governments and to help co-ordinate the activities of Unesco National Commissions in the region. It is an open secret that this action, taken at the 1948 session of the General Conference, stemmed from vigorous lobbying by various Latin American delegations. Not only this, but the decision to locate the new office in Havana, a city decidedly on the periphery of the region, was due mainly to an offer from the Cuban Government to provide free office space and an annual contribution of $10,000 towards the expenses of the office. For some years (after its opening in 1950) no specific tasks were assigned to the Havana office and it was often referred to in secretariat gossip as 'a joke.'[47] It was commonly believed that Director-General Luther H. Evans personally favoured the liquidation of the Havana office, but in

[45] Unesco has attached great importance not only to the development of its National Commissions but also to the sponsorship of permanent regional training and research centres, the operation and financing of which will eventually be assumed *in toto* by the participating governments.

[46] Unesco Doc. 50/EX/33, 22 May 1958.

[47] See Unesco Doc. 44 EX/48, 22 June 1956, for an evaluation of the work done by the Havana office on the basis of replies to a questionnaire circulated to Member States in the Western Hemisphere.

the face of strong political opposition from Latin American countries it was decided in 1956 to undertake to vitalize its existence by giving it responsibility for co-ordinating the new Unesco ten-year project for the extension of primary education in Latin America.[48]

Unesco's regional machinery presents some peculiar features. First of all, it has taken shape largely in piecemeal, unplanned fashion—as a consequence of pressures reflecting power relationships within the Paris secretariat on the one hand, and successful log-rolling by groups of Member States in the General Conference on the other. Thus one finds a duality of offices for one region—Latin America—but not for the others. Secondly, the functions of none of the regional offices extend, except incidentally and sporadically, to Unesco's field operations under EPTA or, for that matter, under its own 'Participation' programme. As we shall see in Chapter 6, Unesco's role in both of these programmes is controlled almost entirely from Paris. Finally, the geographic coverage of the Cairo, New Delhi, and Djakarta offices has been delimited on a kind of *ad hoc* basis by the central secretariat—which means in effect the Department of Natural Sciences. Within the purview of the Cairo office are at present the Arab States, plus Turkey, Iran, and Ethiopia. Originally, New Delhi was assigned an area that included only India, Burma, Ceylon, and Nepal; but after the Suez Canal crisis of 1956 Pakistan was shifted from the Cairo to the New Delhi office, and, two years later, Afghanistan as well (the latter action apparently with a view to easing the pressure of work in the former office). The rest of Asia, along with the Western Pacific, has fallen to the lot of Djakarta.

For a time the Cairo office maintained a small 'branch' at Istanbul as a kind of postbox for communication with Israel. While this arrangement was soon discontinued, the problem of handling Israel relations has recently become, if anything, more troublesome than before the events of 1956. The Egyptian Government has objected even to the listing of Israel publications in science bibliographies prepared by the Cairo office. The upshot of this whole tangled situation is that communication with Israel is currently being handled directly from Paris.

[48] For further information as to how this project is being administered, see pp. 331–332.

UNICEF's field structure

In Chapter 2, brief reference was made to the hierarchy of field offices developed by UNICEF in connection with the conduct of its country project operations. The contours of this field machinery have, by and large, been determined in accordance with administrative and programme requirements; probably no UN agency has been less subject to political pressures in this respect. Furthermore, UNICEF has tended to adjust its field structure to trends in volume of operations with considerably more flexibility than has been true of most specialized agencies.

Three UNICEF regional offices, now located at Paris, Bangkok, and New York, are responsible for planning and co-ordinating functions within three main operating regions, as follows: Africa-Europe; Asia; and Latin America.[49] A fourth office (at Beirut) served at first as a branch of the Paris regional office but was later designated as an 'area' office, reporting directly to the New York headquarters, largely because Paris had become a communications bottleneck. In most respects, however, Beirut operates as if it were a 'regional' office.

Below the level of, and administratively responsible to, each regional office are several 'area' and 'country' offices, the number of which depends on the relative dimensions of project operations within individual countries, or groups of contiguous countries, in the region. In addition, UNICEF has assigned 'liaison' officers to certain countries where the size of its operations is too small to justify the cost of maintaining a full-fledged local office.

By way of illustration, the huge Asian region, where UNICEF ministers to the needs of 'Half the World's Children,'[50] has two area offices (one for India-Afghanistan-Nepal and the other taking care of Thailand, Malaya, Singapore, North Borneo, and Netherlands New Guinea), and five offices on a single country basis. On the other hand, the Africa-Europe region includes five area offices (all in Africa, where most of the programme is) and only one country office (for Turkey). The pattern varies from region to region.

[49] Initially, the Latin American regional office was located at Lima. It was moved in 1956 to New York primarily in order to take advantage of superior air communication channels with various points of South America.

[50] This is the title of S. M. Keeny's vivid portrayal of UNICEF's work in Asia (New York: Association Press, 1957). Mr. Keeny has been the director of UNICEF's Bangkok office since its establishment in 1948.

Field Organization and Staffing Patterns

The composition of each of UNICEF's administrative regions consists of all those States and dependent territories (within each region) to which project funds are allocated. Since the three main regions tend to coincide with recognized cartographic areas, no controversy has arisen over the assignment of countries to this or that region (as in WHO). For the Beirut office the situation is somewhat different. Its territorial coverage now embraces all of the Arab countries receiving UNICEF aid, as well as Iran, Israel, Ethiopia, Italian Somaliland, British Somaliland, the Aden Protectorate, and Aden Colony. As regards Israel, a special arrangement has been worked out whereby the Beirut office is allowed to utilize the transport facilities of the UN Truce Supervision Organization for movements across 'no man's land' (in Jerusalem) into Israel territory. The Jordanians are aware of this procedure but have raised no objection to it. Children's needs, at least, appear to take precedence over clashing political interests.

Currently there is a growing opinion within the UNICEF field bureaucracy that the number of administrative echelons in the field should be reduced. Certain country directors interviewed by the writer went so far as to contend that the regional offices might be abolished without loss of operational effectiveness.[51] Those who advance this radical view (not widely shared at headquarters) would strengthen and delegate more authority to the area and country offices. On the other hand, some thought is now being given to the advisability of dividing the far-flung Asian region into two parts, and raising the status of the New Delhi area office to that of a regional office. Any such move would have the advantage of bringing UNICEF's regional pattern in Asia and the western Pacific into somewhat closer conformity to that of WHO, with which UNICEF has continuing co-operative relationships.[52]

[51] According to one UNICEF official with both headquarters and field experience, the procurement functions of the Paris office could easily be farmed out to commercial channels. This office, in his view, represents 'a whacking waste of funds,' its nearest operational programme being a thousand miles from Paris. On the whole, however, the need for regional offices is taken a good deal more seriously at headquarters than it was a few years ago.

[52] On the other hand, UNICEF's relations with the WHO regional office would not be greatly simplified if Bangkok retained jurisdiction over countries under the two WHO regional offices involved (at New Delhi and Manila).

TAB's field machinery

The field structure contrived to facilitate the conduct of the Expanded Programme of Technical Assistance differs from any of the arrangements thus far described in two significant respects: (1) it has an inter-agency base, and (2) it serves a particular programme rather than the agencies that participate in the programme. The Technical Assistance Board, as early as 1951, decided to appoint Resident Technical Assistance Representatives (RTARs) to those countries where EPTA operations were of sufficient size to require 'co-ordination' at the country level. Accordingly, RTARs were appointed at the outset for only nine countries on an experimental basis. Initially, TAB tried out various formulae governing their status *vis-à-vis* the United Nations and the participating agencies. By 1952, however, it was decided to apply a uniform procedure to all appointments. All Resident Representatives are now appointed by the Executive Chairman of TAB 'in agreement with' it, and are administratively responsible to the Board through the Chairman.

The adoption by ECOSOC in 1954 of a revised country programming formula (to be explained in Chapter 9) strengthened the case for appointing as many field representatives as budgetarily feasible. With a view to holding down administrative costs, TAB has resorted to the device of designating 'liaison officers' or 'correspondents' for countries where project operations are quite small. Largely for the same reason it has, in a few instances, given the RTAR responsibility for handling regional groupings of countries or territories or both. For some years the RTAR based in Mexico City covered Central America as well as Mexico. Similarly, a regional office was set up in Bangkok for EPTA operations extending from Thailand to and including Cambodia, Laos, Republic of Viet-Nam, Malaya, Hongkong, Singapore, Republic of Korea, and Japan. During 1958, however, the territorial coverage of both the Mexico City and the Bangkok office was reduced—in the former case by detaching Central America and in the latter by detaching Cambodia, Laos, and Viet-Nam. Small regional offices were established in San Salvador and in Phom-Penh, respectively, for the two latter areas.

In all, as of 1959, there were thirty-five TAB field offices covering operations in over fifty countries and territories which in the aggregate accounted for more than 90 per cent. of the entire Expanded Programme.[53] In addition, TAB correspondents were serving in ten other countries, such correspondents usually being designated from among the field experts of a specialized agency. In Damascus a 'sub-office' of the Cairo office had been established by reason of the joining of Syria with Egypt in the newly created United Arab Republic. In effect, the U.A.R. office in Cairo has during recent years served as a regional office—with added responsibility for Saudi Arabia and Yemen. Pakistan resembles the Egyptian-Syrian situation in that it is territorially separated into two distinct provinces—West and East Pakistan—by a distance of a thousand miles. In the opinion of one RTAR formerly stationed at Karachi, a convincing case could be made for the establishment of a sub-office in Dacca.

Reporting to the Administrative Review Group of TAC in 1957, the Executive Chairman of TAB referred to pressures from various governments to open new field offices in their capitals.[54] This statement provoked an expression of concern over the increase in administrative and operational expenditures arising chiefly from the expansion of TAB field office staffs. In this connection, 'the possibility of regrouping the functions of field offices by geographic and economic regions' was mentioned. It is fairly generally agreed in TAB circles, however, that neither the regional office concept nor the device of TAB correspondents, provides as satisfactory a means of supervising EPTA field activities as does the RTAR with terms of reference limited to a single country. The added responsibilities now devolving upon the RTAR in connection with the new Special Fund's operations lends weight to this view.

[53] UN Doc. E/TAC/79, 27 Oct. 1958. Six additional TAB offices were scheduled to be set up during 1960.

[54] UN Doc. E/3055, Annex II, 6 Dec. 1957.

The Regional Mosaic and Inter-Agency Co-operation

Table 4 purports to show (as of 1959) the over-all pattern of administrative regions recognized by the United Nations and those agencies with extensive field operations.

Several observations are suggested by this table, which is necessarily an over-simplified presentation. First, the more under-developed a geographic region is in the economic sense, the more extensively it appears to be used for purposes of field administration. Thus the Middle East constitutes an operational area for all organizations but the UN itself, while the vast Asia-Far East complex of land and water not only is utilized by every agency, but in two instances (WHO and Unesco) it is divided into two separate field regions. Africa, particularly south of the Sahara, will doubtless soon be in the same category. By contrast, Europe and North America serve as distinct regions to a much lesser extent—the former only for the UN, WHO, and FAO, and the latter for FAO alone. This situation is attributable not only to the fact that the North Atlantic (Western Europe, United States, Canada) is economically the most advanced area of the globe (and therefore least in the market for UN economic and technical assistance), but also to the fact that the headquarters of all UN organizations are located within this general area. It is further to be noted that the UN Geneva office, which provides physical premises for ECE (as well as for WHO), is *de facto* a projection of UN headquarters from New York across the Atlantic. WHO is the only agency now maintaining a distinct regional office for Europe itself (at Copenhagen), while the only regional office serving North America as such is the Washington office of FAO.

In the second place, as already pointed out, the composition, especially of the *non*-Western administrative regions, in terms of 'assigned' or 'accredited' States, tends to vary from agency to agency for two reasons: (1) differences in agency membership or in programme incidence (*e.g.*, UNICEF), and (2) deviations in the outer boundaries of regions, or sub-regional zones, as the case may be. Hence, in such marginal belts as those demarcating the Middle East from Europe on the one side, and from South Asia on the other, a State may find itself in regions with different geographic foci as regards aggregate agency operations.

TABLE 4

PATTERN OF ADMINISTRATIVE REGIONS

Regions	*UN*	*WHO*	*FAO*	*ILO*	*Unesco*	*ICAO*	*UNICEF*
The Americas	X (excl. Canada)	X (6 zones)	N. America S. America (2 zones)	Mexico Central America S. America	Latin America Western Hemisphere	N. Atlantic Caribbean S. America S. Atlantic	Latin America only
Europe	X (incl. U.S.)	X	X (no reg. office)			incl. Mediterranean	incl. Africa
Near (Middle) East		X	X	X	X	X	Beirut 'area'
Asia-Far East	X (incl. U.S. U.S.S.R.)	S.E. Asia Western Pacific	X (incl. one zone)	X	S. Asia S.E. Asia	S.E. Asia Pacific Ocean	X
Africa	X	X	X (2 zones)	X		incl. Indian Ocean	incl. Europe
Number of 'main' regions	4	6 (incl. 6 zones)	6 (incl. 5 zones)	5	4	8	4 (incl. Beirut area)
Number of regional offices	4	6 (incl. 6 zones)	9 (incl. zones)	5	5	5	4 (incl. Beirut)

Pakistan, for example, belongs to the Middle East regions of WHO and ICAO but to the Asia-Far East regions of the UN, FAO, ILO, and UNICEF; while Turkey is included in the European regions of the UN, WHO, FAO, and UNICEF but in the Middle East regions of ILO and Unesco. The newly created States of North Africa (Tunisia and Morocco) are somewhat similarly divided as between Europe, the Middle East, and Africa in their regional identifications. Comparable situations result from discrepancies in the WHO 'zonal' and the FAO 'zonal' boundaries in Latin America.

Thirdly, to stress again a point made repeatedly earlier in this chapter, agency regional patterns likewise vary in terms both of their functional scope and of the degree to which operational or substantive authority is devolved upon regional offices (and regional inter-governmental bodies).[55]

These regional divergencies have in some cases given rise to administrative complications. Increasingly, the field programmes undertaken under UN auspices have called for inter-agency co-ordination as to programme planning and inter-agency participation in important field projects, some of them restricted to individual countries and others conducted on a regional basis. This is particularly true of projects financed exclusively or partly by EPTA funds.

As far back as 1953, the WHO Executive Board took cognizance of the difficulties caused by the difference in agency regional schemes: 'This difference between the regional arrangements of WHO and various devices of other agencies,' the Board noted, 'considerably complicates the procedure for liaison with those agencies on field programmes and projects. Only with UNICEF is there a standard agreed procedure. . . . More often, however, the arrangements for joint work with other agencies have tended to be empirical and to be made *ad hoc* in each case.'[56] The Director-General expressed the opinion that WHO should take the initiative in trying to obtain agreement with other UN agencies for more nearly co-terminous regions, and in so doing, to indicate its willingness to alter its own regional boundaries 'if necessary in the interest of co-ordination.' The Board agreed with this proposal. While acknowledging

[55] See Chap. 8 for a detailed consideration of regional decentralization.
[56] WHO, O.R. No. 46, Jan-Feb. 1953, p. 164.

also that 'there should be a greater degree of uniformity of practice as regards decentralization by the United Nations and the specialized agencies,' it nevertheless went on to stress the belief that 'the advantages all lie with a system of decentralized authority.'[57] So far as the writer was able to ascertain, nothing ever came of any negotiations WHO may have initiated, through ACC or otherwise, on these matters.

In succeeding chapters of this study, we shall have occasion to illustrate concretely some of the operational complexities arising from the mosaic of regions, zones, and areas, in some cases layer upon layer, that now features the administrative map of the UN system. In particular, we shall see how agency particularism has in several instances blocked half-hearted efforts to co-ordinate the locaton of the field offices of related agencies.

[57] Berkov, *op. cit.*, p. 128.

4

FIELD OFFICE NETWORKS

Classification of Field Offices

If it is not inappropriate to describe the pattern of UN system field *areas* as a mosaic, its multi-agency congeries of field *offices* may perhaps with equal justification be termed a maze. As of mid-1959, the number of established offices at all levels approximated 250.[1] These offices were located in eighty-three cities, distributed geographically as follows:

The Americas	21	Asia-Far East	17
Europe	19	Africa	13
Middle East	13		

Included in these totals were seventeen central headquarters offices covering the UN itself, twelve specialized agencies, UNICEF, TAB, the Special Fund, and the recently created International Atomic Energy Agency—dispersed among nine different cities in North America and Europe. Also included were thirty-two offices maintained by three UN subsidiary relief and refugee agencies (UNRWA, UNHCR, UNKRA), with which this study does not directly deal. Within the totals, in addition, were small 'liaison' offices set up by four of the specialized agencies and IAEA at UN headquarters in New York. Subtracting these fifty-four offices from the grand total still leaves close to 200 offices serving economic, social, cultural, and technical programmes *away from headquarters*.[2] It is with the inter-relations of these networks of field offices that the present chapter is primarily concerned.

[1] The statistics cited in this chapter relative to field office locations are derived from compilations made for the ACC by the UN Secretariat, together with the *Advisory Committee on Administrative and Budgetary Questions Tenth Report to the General Assembly at Its Fourteenth Session*, UN Doc. A/4170, 1959.

[2] In addition, various UN special missions (*e.g.*, the UN Truce Supervision Organization in Palestine, the UN Emergency Force, and others) have small administrative offices at some thirty different places.

By region and major organization these offices were distributed as follows:[3]

TABLE 5

DISTRIBUTION OF FIELD OFFICES BY REGION AND ORGANIZATION

Region	*UN*	*WHO*	*FAO*	*ILO*	*Unesco*	*ICAO*	*UNICEF*	*TAB*
The Americas	11	8	4	6	2	2	8	13
Europe	14	3	0	6	0	1	5	3
Middle East	3	3	1	1	1	1	8	9
Asia-Far East	8	13	3	3	2	1	12	9
Africa	3	4	2	1	0	0	6	7
Total number of offices	39	31	10	17	5	5	39	41

In interpreting this table, two points should be kept in mind. First, certain agencies (UN, WHO, and UNICEF) have more than one office at the same location. At Geneva, for example, there is the large UN European office (essentially a projection of UN headquarters for servicing meetings and to which certain central secretariat units are now attached), and along with it the ECE secretariat and an Information Centre. At Santiago de Chile are located the ECLA secretariat, an Information Centre, and a small 'outposted' unit of the UN Bureau of Social Affairs. For WHO, at New Delhi, there is an 'area' office as well as the South-east Asia 'regional' office; while UNICEF maintains an 'area' along with a 'regional' office both at Paris and Bangkok. Further instances of the doubling of offices in the same city could be given.

Second, the term 'office' requires definition. As here employed, it refers to a permanent field unit with a locale of its own and an administrative budget financed largely (if not entirely) from organizational funds. There are various operational arrangements at the country level that do not fully satisfy this definition, whether because of their lack of permanence, or of a distinct office locale, or of a special expense budget provided

[3] The following agencies maintain no field offices: ITU, WMO, UPU, IMCO, IFC (except jointly with IBRD in New York and Paris), and IAEA. The tabulation given here does not include the offices of IBRD advisers in various countries or the Paris regional office of IMF.

by the agency concerned. Among such arrangements are the so-called ILO 'national correspondents,' the FAO 'country representatives,' Unesco 'chiefs of mission,' TAB 'correspondents' (in a few countries with minimal EPTA activities), and a considerable number of large-scale technical assistance missions (*e.g.*, training and research centres on a relatively long-term basis. None of these arrangements was included in the preceding enumeration.

The ILO national correspondents, for example, are invariably nationals of the host country, most of them being part-time appointees drawn from the national ministry of labour or some cognate ministry. They have very little clerical staff, the costs of which are often borne in large part by the host government. Their functions, moreover, are limited almost entirely to liaison and information. While the FAO country representatives aid in negotiating and supervising country technical assistance projects, their office accommodations consist typically of a room or two located in the national ministry of agriculture and some of them have virtually no clerical staff. The Unesco chief of mission is ordinarily designated as such by reason of being a member of a country technical assistance mission, usually in the educational field. The mission chief in effect wears two hats: one as educational adviser to the host government and the other as quasi-supervisor (or co-ordinator) of Unesco's over-all technical assistance activities in the country. Many of these men lack office facilities of their own and some have to draw upon the RTAR's office for assistance in typing letters and reports.[4] The 'office' status of the TAB correspondents is similarly ambiguous.

By now the reader will probably have realized that the terminology employed by different agencies to identify similar types of field offices is neither uniform nor always consistent. The lack of uniformity springs from the fact (as previously indicated) that the field structure of each agency has been built brick by brick, over differing time sequences, in terms of its own particular needs, predilections, and administrative vocabularies. For example, in ILO, regional offices are designated as 'field' offices, while the terms 'area' and 'branch' are used in

[4] The roles played by these FAO and Unesco field officials *vis-à-vis* EPTA country programming are discussed more fully in Chapter 9.

various ways by different organizations. Indeed, in the case of UNICEF, the term 'area' is employed in two different senses, its Beirut 'area' office having quite a different status from any of the other so-called area offices. WHO/PASB's American 'sub-regional' units are called 'zone' offices while comparable (though smaller) WHO multi-country offices in Africa and the Western Pacific are designated as offices of 'area representatives.' Sometimes the term 'area' applies to an office covering a group of countries; at other times (*e.g.*, in the South-east Asia region) only one country.

Such terminological anomalies, to be sure, do not present any serious problem to the administrator once he has become familiar with official nomenclature. To some extent, however, they reflect significant differences in the hierarchical relationships of field offices in cognate agencies. As we shall see later in this study, such differences have at times given rise to operational complications.

As of mid-1959, the various hierarchical patterns (including *all* categories of field offices) are shown below:

Regional offices—responsible to central headquarters

1 UN European office (Geneva)
4 UN regional economic commission secretariats
16 UN Information Centres
6 WHO regional offices
1 WHO Epidemiological Intelligence Station (Singapore)
5 FAO regional offices
5 ILO 'field' offices
4 Unesco 'field science co-operation' offices
1 Unesco office for the Western Hemisphere (Havana)
5 ICAO regional offices
1 ICAO Technical Assistance Representative (Beirut)
3 UNICEF regional offices
1 UNICEF 'area' office (Beirut)
4 TAB regional offices
1 IBRD-IFC office
1 IMF regional office
4 UN Bureau of Social Affairs 'outposted' units
1 European office of TARS (Paris)

Sub-regional, zonal and area offices (covering two or more countries)—responsible to a regional office but in some cases reporting also to central headquarters

1 ECLA 'sub-office' (Mexico City)
6 WHO offices of 'area representatives' (Africa, Western Pacific)
6 WHO-PASB 'zone' offices (Latin America)
4 FAO 'zone' offices (Latin America, Africa, Asia)
10 UNICEF 'area' offices (in various regions)
1 UN Bureau of Social Affairs 'outposted' unit (Mexico City)

Single country offices—responsible to central headquarters

11 UN Information Centres
12 ILO 'branch' offices
33 ILO 'national correspondents'
29 Unesco country 'chiefs of mission'
35 TAB-RTAR and 'liaison' offices
10 TAB 'correspondents'
1 IBRD-IFC 'marketing' office (New York)

Single country offices—responsible to a regional office

6 WHO offices of 'area representatives' (South-east Asia)
38 FAO 'country representatives'
25 UNICEF 'country' and 'liaison' offices (in various regions)
1 ECLA office (Washington)

Sub-country offices—responsible to a country office

1 UNICEF office (Dacca—in Pakistan)
1 TAB office (Damascus—in the United Arab Republic)

As we shall see in a later chapter, the operation of these interlocking field office networks has necessitated the development of elaborate procedures for communication, reporting, and consultation. The allocation of responsibility for decision-making to functionally related offices is not without ambiguity and at times the lines of communication tend to get tangled.

Factors Governing the Location of Field Offices

The geographic location of field offices has been influenced in large measure by the same factors that have determined the number and the boundaries of field areas. The two processes are necessarily closely related. In Chapter 3 examples were given of the reasons why certain regional offices were placed where they were. Reference was also made to the early concern of ECOSOC and the ACC that, so far as feasible, the location of regional offices of UN agencies should be 'co-ordinated,' that is, placed in the same city. Indeed, this subject has been on the agenda of almost every meeting of ACC since its establishment in 1947. Shortly thereafter, ECOSOC adopted a resolution calling for 'full consultation as far in advance as possible, through the ACC, on the establishment of new regional or branch offices' by Members of the United Nations family.[5] Moreover, under the terms of the formal agreements concluded between the UN and the specialized agencies, most of the latter undertook, as far as practicable, to locate any regional or branch office they might set up in close 'association' with such offices as the UN itself might later establish.

In fact, however, the obligation to consult in advance of decisions as to the location of field offices has been given little more than lip service. With certain exceptions (as noted below), consultation with the ACC has usually meant the reporting of the intention to choose a particular location or, more often than not, the announcement of a decision already taken by an agency's governing body for what it held to be good and sufficient reasons. ACC typically has 'taken note' of these *faits accomplis*, without being able to modify the decisions. In part, ACC's reluctance to do so has stemmed from the fact that particular field office patterns were already well crystallized before it got under way as an active inter-agency co-ordinative mechanism. More importantly, refusal to take a stronger line with individual agencies may be explained by the political psychology of agency relations: as the chief administrative officer of his agency, each member of the ACC ordinarily feels under obligation to yield to the 'sovereign' desires of the other agencies.

The various factors influencing agency governing bodies

[5] ECOSOC Resolution 259 (IX), 9 Aug. 1949.

(or directors-general when so authorized) in locating regional and area offices are enumerated below:

(1) Political pressures accompanied in many instances by material inducements from 'host' governments in terms of rent-free office quarters, contributions towards administrative costs, favourable 'privileges and immunities,' etc.
(2) Use of pre-existing international office centres (*e.g.*, the Palais des Nations in Geneva; the PASB in Washington; the Pan-Arab Sanitary Bureau at Alexandria; the International Commission for Air Navigation at Paris).
(3) Proximity to the regional offices of related agencies or to continuing major regional projects.
(4) Favourable communication and transport facilities and good accessibility to the outer reaches of the region.
(5) Budgetary considerations (in relation to volume of programme operations, pay scales for local staff, costs of materials and equipment, etc.).
(6) Favourable climatic and housing conditions for office staffs.

Much as in the case of regional area delineations, these factors have operated in differing combinations in each agency and thus have led to such decisions as the choice of a high-cost or poor climatic location for political or other reasons. This has been true not only with respect to original locations but also to transfers of offices to other places after their establishment.

How these forces have actually worked may best be understood by examining certain concrete situations (in addition to those cited in the preceding chapter). The office of ECAFE, originally set up at Shanghai, was shortly thereafter transferred to Bangkok instead of to Bangalore (the other city under consideration) because the former city is more centrally located within ECAFE's far-flung region, has superior air communications, and is the capital of a small country. On the other hand, the climate of Bangkok is much less agreeable than at a 'hill station' like Bangalore and also has certain disadvantages as to working conditions, such as shortage of water, poor drainage, and lack of educational facilities—all of which, to be sure, may be remedied in time.

Santiago was selected as the site for ECLA's main office

despite the more central location of Caracas (also considered) midway between New York and Buenos Aires, largely as a result of effective lobbying by the Chilean Government—plus widespread opposition to the then dictatorial régime in Venezuela and, incidentally, to the sky-high prices in Caracas. Some years later, in 1951, ECLA decided to set up a sub-office in Mexico City primarily so that its Secretariat might devote closer attention to the Central American Economic Project that ECLA had fathered.[6] The Mexican Government generously offered 'to place at the disposal of the ECLA office in Mexico all the necessary facilities.'[7] A further factor affecting the selection of Mexico City rather than one of the small capitals in Central America itself was the fear that the latter would provoke 'jealousies' in which ECLA might become involved; while by operating from Mexico City it was hoped that a more objective perspective on the integration project might be ensured.

By contrast with ECAFE and ECLA, the two largest non-western offices of WHO were located in the dominant country of the region concerned—Egypt for the Eastern Mediterranean and India for South-east Asia. The wisdom of these choices, both of which were influenced by political considerations, has since been questioned. But the availability of an attractive building (the former headquarters of the Pan-Arab Sanitary Bureau) in Alexandria made that city a natural choice, while a somewhat less commodious structure (a former Maharajah's palace) in New Delhi was offered by the Indian Government.

In 1951, the Western Pacific office of WHO, set up at first in Hong Kong, was transferred to Manila for a number of reasons: the crowded conditions in Hong Kong (resulting from the influx of refugees from Communist China), the uncertainty of Hong Kong's future as a Western-controlled territory, and various inducements from the Philippine Government. Yet Manila is one of the highest-cost cities in the Far East and has a most depressing climate.

The selection of a site for WHO's African office posed in some respects the most difficult problem of any of its regional offices.

[6] ECLA also maintains a small office in Washington for direct liaison with the United States Government and the Pan American Union.

[7] ECLA Resolution 30 (IV), 16 June 1951. A secondary consideration influencing this decision was the prospect of reducing travel costs for staff participating in the Central American Project.

'In view of the size of the region,' as Berkov has noted, 'it was desirable to have (regional) headquarters as near as possible to the center of the region. A location in the Union of South Africa was unacceptable to those countries represented by Negroes. . . . Since it was generally admitted that racial discrimination was virtually nonexistent in the French colonies, the Regional Committee finally selected Brazzaville, in French Equatorial Africa.'[8] This choice, however, did not prove to be a very happy one: living costs were exorbitant there and living conditions were difficult. At one time the transfer of the office back to Geneva (where it had initially operated), or to another African centre, was considered. Eventually, however, the French Government made available a new air-conditioned building on the outskirts of the city, together with good housing arrangements for the staff. Accordingly, no further suggestion of shifting the office was made.

WHO is the only specialized agency, with its central headquarters in Europe, that maintains a separate regional office for that continent. At the outset the impetus for such a move came largely from Eastern European countries desirous of obtaining direct assistance from WHO in rebuilding their war-devastated health services. These countries, however, soon ceased to participate actively in WHO and opposition developed to setting up a separate European office on grounds of economy. Temporarily, therefore, the office was maintained in Geneva—in effect as a part of the central secretariat. Those member countries that favoured a separate office eventually gained the day and its establishment was approved by the WHA in 1954. This action precipitated a flood of offers of facilities from Austria (Vienna), from France (Nice), from West Germany, and from Denmark (Copenhagen). The Danish capital won over its rivals by a single vote. The selection of a Danish-speaking centre has led to some difficulty in recruiting local staff competent in English or French—a point not considered in the voting.

The choice of Cairo and Bangkok as sites for FAO's main offices, for the Near East and Asia respectively, resulted from a combination of political pressures, local inducements, and technical considerations. But the transfer of FAO's principal Latin American office from Rio to Santiago in 1956 calls for

[8] *The World Health Organization . . .*, *op. cit.*, p. 119.

special comment. This decision was taken for several reasons: first, and most important, in order to be able to maintain closer relations with ECLA; second, because the Chilean Government was prepared to offer a rent-free building and to conclude a generous agreement for staff privileges and immunities; and finally, on account of certain difficulties FAO had experienced in connection with the operation of its Rio office (*e.g.*, the necessity of having to change dollars for Brazilian currency at the official rate and suffering a loss thereby, and of being obliged to use the Portuguese language for its publications and correspondence). The Government of Brazil reportedly manœuvred to block the transfer, while Mexico tried to persuade the 1955 FAO Conference to revert to its original plan of having three 'co-ordinate' offices in Latin America—at Rio, Santiago, and Mexico City, respectively. But the Chilean Government lobbied so adroitly with other Latin American delegations that the Conference instructed the Director-General to ascertain their wishes and decide accordingly. His decision was for Santiago, which had the effect of down-grading Rio to the status of a 'zone' office and leaving the Mexico City office as it was.

In South America, ILO's 'field' office was initially placed in São Paulo and then was moved to Rio. In 1954, the Rio office was transferred to Lima partly because the Government of Brazil not only wanted the office run too much like a 'national' office but had failed to live up to certain promises relating to staff privileges and immunities. But the principal reasons favouring the Peruvian capital were its somewhat better air communications with other parts of South America, its proximity to the Andean Indian programme, and the fact that the ICAO regional office was located there.[9]

It is interesting to note that among the specialized agencies only WHO and ILO now operate a regional office in a city *not* the capital of the host country—WHO in Alexandria (for reasons already explained) and ILO in Istanbul and Bangalore. The selection of Istanbul over Ankara apparently was because of its superior communications and urban amenities. The desire to escape possible 'domination' by a host government may have

[9] In 1959, incidentally, ILO, at the request of the Soviet Union, opened a new 'branch' office in Moscow. As of then, the only other UN system field office in the Soviet capital was the UN Information Centre.

been a secondary factor. At the same time, the choice of Istanbul has not facilitated close contact with the Turkish national ministries.

On the whole, the location of ICAO's regional offices has been determined by technical rather than political desiderata, *i.e.*, convenience and accessibility in terms of monitoring regional air navigation plans. When, however, it was decided in 1957 to move the North American-Caribbean office southward from Montreal, so as to be in closer touch with problems in the Caribbean area, two cities are reported to have competed as sites for the office—Miami and Mexico City. The latter won out chiefly because it was felt desirable to have a Spanish-speaking location, not to mention Mexico's offer of spacious office premises at a nominal rental, with free utilities as well, and the pleasant climate of the Mexican capital.[10]

As indicated in the preceding chapter, the year 1958 witnessed major extensions of regional organization into Africa—involving decisions as to the most suitable location for the ECA secretariat, for a regional office of ILO, and for one regional and two zone offices of FAO. At first glance, the virtually simultaneous incidence of moves by the UN and these two specialized agencies might seem to have afforded unusual opportunity for joint consultation and perhaps agreement on common locations for two or more of the new offices, or, for one or two of them with the WHO Brazzaville office, or possibly with the TAB country office set up at Accra a year earlier.[11] There were some informal discussions between the officials of FAO and of the UN Department of Economic and Social Affairs concerning appropriate ECA and FAO office sites (though apparently none by ILO with either group). But in the end the pattern of independent action, for various reasons, prevailed, and the new offices were all located at separate sites.

In effect, ECOSOC's decision to establish ECA at Addis Ababa precluded any chance of inducing either ILO or FAO to locate its regional office there. ECOSOC's action was a political compromise. The Council had before it invitations from five African Governments: from Ghana on behalf of Accra; from

[10] There was a subsidiary political point also, namely, the reluctance of the Caribbean States to having the office located in any of the dependent territories in the area.

[11] TAB (1959) maintained RTARs at Tripoli, Rabat, and Tunis. Also, there were UN Information Centres at Cairo, Accra, and Monrovia.

Morocco on behalf of Tangier; from Egypt on behalf of Cairo; from the Sudan on behalf of Khartoum; and from Ethiopia on behalf of Addis Ababa. The African members of the Council did not relish Tangier in view of its extreme northerly situation and its former 'international' status, while the notoriously hot climate of Khartoum brought the latter place little support. Difficulty in reaching a consensus prompted a proposal to postpone the decision for a time, but this was refused by the non-African delegates for fear that to delay further might favour Cairo, to which they were opposed for political reasons despite its obviously superior air communications and local facilities. The Council then proceeded to a secret ballot which Addis Ababa won by a divided vote.[12]

The selection of the Ethiopian capital evoked private expressions of regret by certain UN officials, some of whom were said to be 'quite happy' for FAO and ILO to go ahead with the selection of other sites. Even though blessed by a fine climate, Addis Ababa is located off at a corner of the African Continent and is not easily accessible. Neither FAO nor ILO considered it a suitable location for their new offices in relation to their expanding technical assistance activities in Africa.

The FAO Director-General, after taking account of suggestions from the 'consultative' meeting of African representatives (to which reference was made in Chapter 3), concluded that the principal FAO office should be located in the western part of the continent and that Accra would be the best site by reason of its relatively good communications with Rome and the other zones and the agricultural importance of the surrounding tropical forest belt for future African economic development. The FAO Council subsequently approved this decision and further decided that the zone office for North Africa should be located at Rabat (in Morocco), leaving the question of the site for the second zone office to the 1959 session of the Conference.[13]

As noted in the preceding chapter, ILO compared the relative advantages of Accra and Lagos (Nigeria) before deciding where to place its new 'field' office. Like FAO, it felt on the whole that the western coastal area would be preferable to an eastern

[12] The vote was as follows: Addis Ababa, 11; Tangier, 3; Cairo, 2; Accra, 1; and Khartoum, 1. UN Doc. E/SR.1021, 7 May 1958.

[13] The Conference further postponed a decision. FAO has set up a liaison unit with the ECA secretariat in Addis Ababa.

location. After consulting with the ILO Governing Body, the Director-General chose Lagos instead of Accra.[13a] To some extent the rationale of the ILO action may have been a desire to enhance the prestige of Nigeria, slated for independence in 1960 and likely to become a leader among the new nations of Africa. In both Accra and Lagos the meagre housing and other facilities present a serious problem. In connection with the rapid expansion of UN system activities in Africa, the Advisory Committee on Administrative and Budgetary Questions, reporting to the 1958 session of the UN General Assembly, significantly expressed the hope that, 'despite the different location of the various offices, the secretariats of the United Nations and the specialized agencies will constantly strive to achieve the closest co-operation in their work in Africa.'[14] This statement epitomizes the failure of the formula of inter-agency consultation to achieve the results anticipated a decade ago for the 'co-ordination' of field office locations.

So far as the rival claims of would-be hosts for regional offices are concerned, it is in order to point out that the governments of under-developed countries tend to regard such offices as symbols of prestige.[15] For countries whose international payments are chronically out of balance, the hard currency expenditures of UN agency offices and their staffs (including field experts routed through the offices) constitute a further reason for seeking to have UN offices on their territory. Once offices are established, moreover, it is hard to liquidate them because of political resistances. Not only this, but certain host governments have been known to press for the enlargement of field office staffs and functions.[15a]

Inter-Office Administrative Relations at Field Centres

Notwithstanding the obstacles referred to above, there is substantial field office concentration in certain cities. Table 6 is designed to show (as of mid-1959) the clustering of offices at eleven principal centres:

[13a] Notwithstanding the decision of FAO to locate its regional office in Accra and the recent establishment of a TAB country office there also.

[14] UN Doc. A/4032, 5 Dec. 1958.

[15] Partly for this reason and partly because of the Arab communications blockade, the Government of Israel proposed at the 1957 Conference of FAO that a field office be set up in Israel, suggesting that its cost might be met by reducing the budgetary allotment for the North American office at Washington.

[15a] *e.g.*, the Government of the U.A.R. in respect of the FAO Cairo office.

TABLE 6

FIELD OFFICES AT PRINCIPAL CENTRES

Centre	*Total Office staff (approx.)*	*Headquarters Office*	*Regional Offices*	*Sub-regional, Area or Zone Offices*	*Country, Branch or Liaison Offices*	*Total Number of Offices and Units*
Geneva	2,200	WHO, ILO, ITU, WMO, UNHCR	UN, ECE, UNIC, BTAO		UNICEF, FAO, TAB	12
Washington	1,200	IBRD, IMF, IFC	WHO-PASB, FAO		UNIC, ILO, ECLA, BTAO	9
Rome	1,170	FAO			UNIC, ILO, UNHCR	4
Paris	1,150	Unesco	UNIC, TARS, UNICEF, IBRD, IMF, ICAO	UNICEF	ILO, UNHCR, WHO	11

Bangkok	440		ECAFE, UNIC, FAO, ICAO, UNICEF, TAB, Soc. Aff.	UNICEF, WHO	IBRD (adviser)	10
New Delhi	290		WHO, UNIC, Unesco	UNICEF, FAO, WHO	ILO, TAB, IBRD (adviser)	9
Santiago de Chile	210		ECLA, FAO, UNIC, Soc. Aff.		TAB UNICEF	6
Manila	180		WHO		TAB, UNIC, UNICEF	4
Mexico City	150		UNIC, ILO, ICAO	WHO-PASB, FAO, ECLA, Soc. Aff.	TAB	8
Cairo	110		FAO, ICAO, UNIC, TAB, Unesco		ILO, UNICEF, UNHCR, UNRWA	9
Lima	105		ILO, ICAO	WHO-PASB, UNICEF	TAB, IBRD (adviser)	6

There are eleven other centres of lesser importance in terms of total where three to six offices are located: Accra, Addis Ababa, Bogotá, Buenos Aires, Copenhagen, Djakarta, Karachi, London, Rio de Janeiro, Sydney, and Teheran. A twelfth city, Beirut, which is the headquarters for UNRWA and the site of four small regional and country offices, has a large concentration of staff (1,900), most of whom, however, are engaged in refugee operations. Of the seven *non*-headquarters cities included among the eleven principal centres, the four with the greatest concentration of staff are the site either of a regional commission secretariat or of a large WHO regional office.

In considering the administrative role of major field offices, it should be remembered that a constant flow of technical assistance experts, staff visitors from agency headquarters, and temporary consultants pass through, and in some cases spend considerable time at, the UN regional commission offices, the regional offices of the specialized agencies, and the major TAB country offices. All of which involves arrangements for travel, salary and allowance payments, consultation, local interviews, briefing, de-briefing, and the like. These operations add markedly to the work loads of the field office concerned and necessitate continuing administrative contacts with related offices at a given centre.

Both the ACC and the GA Advisory Committee on Administrative and Budgetary Questions have long been concerned with the administrative inter-relations of field offices situated in the same locality. This concern has been focused on the desirability of achieving the most efficient use of staff personnel and resources (1) by avoiding unnecessary duplication of administrative and technical services and (2) by sharing or pooling such services as far as this may be found to be feasible. From time to time, ACC has conducted studies on the co-ordination of office services at some of the larger centres, such as Geneva, Washington, Bangkok, Cairo, New Delhi, and Beirut.[16] In 1953, moreover, TAC requested TAB to undertake inquiries as to possible common services between field offices dealing with technical assistance matters. Since then, joint studies have been initiated by ACC and TAB on the feasibility of using common facilities and services in Mexico City, Manila, Djakarta,

[16] *Fifteenth Report of ACC*, UN Doc. E/2512, 26 Oct. 1953.

and Karachi. More recently, the Advisory Committee, reporting on the UN budget for 1958, recommended that the responsibility for the rental and operation of premises and equipment, and incidentally of communications and other common services, at field offices, should be centralized. The Committee went on to observe that

the potential economies to be achieved through the concentration of premises (including, where feasible, the premises of specialized agencies) and services should lend weight to an appeal to the interested Member States to assist the United Nations in obtaining the most favourable terms. This grouping of offices should, where possible, include those of the specialized agencies situated in the same area.[17]

Following on the Committee's recommendation, the Secretary-General of the United Nations instructed the UN Office of General Services to seek ways of stimulating the development of common inter-agency services in centres where a group of offices exists. This Office proceeded to conduct a survey of agency premises and working relationships at various places around the world. The UN's strategy, according to the Director, would be to offer inducements of various kinds to the specialized agencies if they will agree to consolidate their offices with those of UN organizations where it proves possible to find a building of adequate dimensions, or, lacking this, to arrange for the pooling of such operations as local procurement, local transport, the recruitment of local staff, the handling of accounts and of travel arrangements, and possibly typing and mimeographing services.

Progress in this direction has been decidedly spotty. As already intimated, many of the agencies, as a *quid pro quo* for locating an office in a particular country, made good bargains with the host government, entitling them to rent-free quarters and various perquisites. They are naturally reluctant to surrender such benefits for arrangements with the UN that might turn out in the end to cost them more money. Apart from this financial factor, there is the desire of certain influential office directors to retain separate office identifications (mail address, plaque at the front entrance, the agency's flag fluttering in the breeze, etc.)—for prestige purposes. Also, such agencies

[17] *Advisory Committee on Administrative and Budgetary Questions Fifth Report to the Twelfth Session of the General Assembly*, UN Doc. A/3624, 1957, para. 154.

as ILO and FAO often wish to keep their offices either within or near to the national ministry with which they have close working relations.

Even so, by 1959, there was considerable sharing of office premises in several major centres, as illustrated in Table 7.[18]

TABLE 7

LOCATION OF OFFICE PREMISES AT MAJOR CENTRES

Centre	*Organizations sharing office premises*	*Organizations with offices in separate buildings*
Geneva	Palais des Nations: UN-ECE-UNIC-UNHCR-WHO FAO-liaison unit	ILO, ITU, WMO
Paris	Unesco-UNIC IBRD-IMF-IFC UNHCR-TARS	ICAO, ILO, UNICEF, WHO, UNHCR
Rome	FAO-UNIC (by 1960)	ILO, UNHCR
Santiago	ECLA-UNIC-UN Soc. Aff. unit.	TAB, FAO
Mexico City	ECLA-UNIC-TAB-FAO-UN Soc. Aff. unit	ILO, ICAO, WHO-PASB
Bangkok	ECAFE-UNIC-ICAO-UN Soc. Aff. unit	TAB, FAO, UNICEF, WHO
Manila	In new WHO building: WHO-UNIC-TAB-UNICEF	None
Beirut	In the 'Unesco compound': UNRWA-UNICEF-TAB-UNIC	UN Soc. Aff. unit

At Cairo, the TAB and FAO offices are housed in the same building (along with a number of local commercial offices and residential apartments). UNRWA and UNHCR share adjoining space at another address. The others have separate premises, all but ICAO being concentrated in the same district within fairly close walking distance of each other. At Rangoon, a

[18] Information concerning office premises and inter-agency administrative arrangements presented in the following pages is based on personal observations and interviews by the author at sixteen field centres during the period 1955–59, supplemented by a draft report of the Secretary-General to the ACC on 'Consolidation of Premises at Overseas Offices', dated 13 May 1959 (in part reproduced in *The Advisory Committee . . . Tenth Report . . .*, UN Doc. A/4170, *op. cit.*).

relatively minor field centre, all agency offices (TAB, UNICEF, UNIC, WHO) have quarters in a bungalow provided rent-free by the Burmese Government. It is to be noted, however, that the premises of most of the TAB country offices over the world are separate from those of any other agency offices that happen to be located at the same place.

At twenty-two major centres (not counting New York or Geneva) the situation regarding office accommodations (as of 1959) was as follows:

Status	*No. of offices*
Organizations owning their own office premises	6
Number of organizations located in buildings owned by another organization	9
Premises provided free of charge by the host government	54
A percentage of the rent paid by the host government	4
Rent paid by the occupying organization	60

During recent years, plans for the construction of new quarters for the largest agency office at certain centres have led to negotiations between the agency concerned and the authorities of other agencies with a view to allocating space to the latter organizations. These negotiations, except in two instances, have thus far had only limited success for a variety of reasons.

With a view to illustrating the practical difficulties of effecting such arrangements, let us first take the situation at Paris. When the Unesco Director-General asked the other agencies with offices in the French capital whether they would be interested in having accommodation in Unesco's new quarters on the Place de Fontenoy, the reactions ranged from 'no interest' to a mild affirmative. IBRD and IMF made it clear that they would prefer to remain by themselves. ICAO expressed a distinct interest but said it would need an entire floor, which the Unesco Conference felt was out of the question in view of the needs of Unesco's growing staff and of the permanent national delegations in Paris.[19] Initially, UNICEF's response was negative since at the time it still enjoyed only temporary status. After it was made permanent its attitude changed, but by then it was too late

[19] Subsequently ICAO was reported to be planning a new building of its own.

to revise Unesco's building plans. Eventually only the UN Information Centre moved into the 'Annex' at Unesco's new headquarters, which it now shares with permanent national delegations and various non-governmental organizations associated with Unesco. At present the Unesco secretariat not only completely fills the main building but a number of small units have to be housed in the Annex. However, there is plenty of ground for additional construction in the future if desired.[20]

At Geneva, where WHO has long since outgrown its limited quarters in the Palais des Nations, plans are under way for the construction of a new headquarters building. Some of WHO's offices have already overflowed into a nearby building financed by private enterprise. Both ITU and WMO likewise contemplate new headquarters buildings notwithstanding an offer by the UN in 1955 to add a new wing to the Palais des Nations for their occupancy—at a rental of only a dollar per year—the construction costs to be reimbursed to the UN without interest over a fifty-year period.[21] But the Government of Geneva offered more attractive inducements and the governing councils of these two agencies indicated a strong preference for separate premises. The *pros* and *cons* of a joint building were debated with the conclusion that 'only minimal advantages' would be gained therefrom. Consequently, there are to be two separate structures, located in the new 'International Centre' project now being developed in an expansive park area adjoining the Palais des Nations grounds. This Centre is expected to comprise not only several international office buildings but a *Maison des Conferences* as well, all embellished by fountains and flower beds.

In Latin America, there have been efforts at two centres to provide common office quarters for the UN and the other agencies. In 1957, the Government of Chile generously offered a plot of land on the outskirts of Santiago for the construction of a UN centre building. This proposal was warmly approved by ECLA and the 1957 General Assembly on condition that satisfactory financing arrangements could be worked out. A year

[20] Unesco's new headquarters are situated on land leased for ninety-nine years at a token rental from the French Government, which has also provided an interest-free loan to finance construction.

[21] GA Resolution 982 (X), 16 Dec. 1955.

later the Secretary-General was authorized by the Assembly to proceed with the preparation of plans on the understanding that building costs would be financed out of the UN regular budget in annual instalments over a four-year period.[22] This action may constitute an important precedent for similar arrangements for inter-agency regional headquarters at other centres. The new buildings at Santiago, when completed, will presumably house the local offices of TAB, FAO, and UNICEF in addition to ECLA and UNIC.

The situation in Mexico City was somewhat different. For some years the Mexican Government had provided rent-free quarters for ECLA and FAO offices there. TAB, UNICEF, and UNIC also had offices in this building but on a rent-paying basis. If there had been adequate space, ICAO and PASB would have been prepared to move their offices into the building, though ILO appeared to prefer to remain in its 'downtown' location at a lower rental. In the summer of 1957 the ECLA building suffered serious damage from an earthquake. A move was then initiated to locate all of the UN family (except possibly PASB) in the building after it was repaired. Unfortunately, it soon became apparent that the necessary reinforcement of the structure would reduce satisfactory space on the lower floors below the requirements of the various agencies. An attempt was subsequently made to find another suitable building that would be large enough, but without success. Consequently, ILO, ICAO, and PASB planned to continue for the time being at their existing locations.

In 1955, the Government of Egypt informally indicated its willingness to set aside a plot of ground across the street from its Foreign Ministry for a common UN office building. This land was to have been leased to the UN at a nominal figure. All of the agencies in Cairo, and WHO at Alexandria, reportedly looked with favour on this proposal. WHO, as the agency with the largest staff in Egypt, was designated to undertake negotiations with the Egyptian authorities. Unfortunately, financing difficulties and the ensuing unsettled political situation in Egypt

[22] GA Resolution 1273 (XIII), 14 Nov. 1958. This resolution also instructed the Secretary-General to negotiate with the governments of States members of ECLA with a view to their making reimbursable interest-free advances to the UN to meet cash requirements for construction. By 1959 the estimated cost of the building had increased from $850,000 to $1,550,000.

combined to kill the idea for the present.[23] WHO subsequently obtained a new lease on its regional quarters in Alexandria and hence lost interest in participating in combined premises in Cairo.

At two centres, in Asia and the Far East, WHO has plans for new buildings to house its regional offices. These plans were undertaken in conformity with a request from the ACC (1955) that WHO assume responsibility, 'on behalf of the United Nations and interested specialized agencies,' with a view to providing consolidated office quarters.[24] At Manila, negotiations with the Philippine Government, which began as early as 1954, resulted in an agreement three years later whereby the government offered free use of a spacious tract of land in the centre of the city and a peso contribution amounting to approximately half of the estimated cost of the building. Other countries and territories in the WHO region have made voluntary contributions towards the cost of the structure. In the meantime WHO had asked the other agencies with offices in Manila whether they would be interested in occupying space in the WHO building. The replies were all affirmative. In order to allow for future expansion of WHO's regional staff, the 1958 Health Assembly, on recommendation by the Director-General, from within the funds already authorized, voted a supplementary allocation sufficient to cover the costs of an additional floor (to be constructed before the roof stage was reached).

The new building was formally opened in February 1959. Although housing TAB, UNICEF, and UNIC, the building is officially designated as WHO's regional headquarters and has a conspicuous WHO sign on its roof, with small plaques identifying the other offices at the ground-floor entrance.[25] Arrangements were made with the various agencies for sharing maintenance costs, including air-conditioning operations. While this imposing edifice will probably be more expensive to operate than the overcrowded, old-style quarters previously utilized by the four

[23] In November 1958, there was an unverified report of a scheme for the UN and other agencies to lease office space in a new skyscraper to be built by an insurance company at another location in the city.

[24] See *The Work of WHO for 1955*, WHO, O.R.: No. 67, March 1956.

[25] There was apparently some scepticism in TAB circles as to the wisdom of locating the TAB Manila office in a building to be known as the regional headquarters of a specialized agency; but the RTAR in Manila took the view that the official designation was of little consequence since all the UN organizations were working for common objectives. On a tourist map of Manila seen by the writer the area where the new WHO building is located was indicated as 'United Nations Park.'

offices, anticipated economies from pooled services and equipment will to some extent offset the increased operating expense. However, the most substantial benefits may be expected to come from improved working conditions for office and project personnel, which will significantly contribute to staff efficiency and morale.

Negotiations between WHO and the Indian Government for a modern WHO office building in New Delhi were still (at the time of writing) at the blue-print stage.[26] The Indian Government had generously agreed to provide an acre of ground and to construct a six-story, air-conditioned building which it would allow WHO to occupy at a nominal rental. This agreement was consequential to the original offer of India in 1948 to act as host to the WHO South-east Asia regional office. In this case it seems that WHO was not disposed to raise the question of space for TAB and the other agencies for fear this might prejudice the chance of a favourable arrangement. The TAB Resident Representative, however, reportedly asked UN headquarters to take up the matter with India's permanent delegation in New York—as well as with WHO headquarters. Preliminary *démarches* were also said to have been undertaken with the Government of India concerning the possibility of its helping to finance a separate office building for the other agencies in case adequate accommodations could not be provided in the new WHO regional premises. It was later decided by WHO that there would be no room for any other agency in the proposed new building.

At Bangkok, ECAFE and ICAO now share the occupancy of a rent-free building originally constructed by the Thai Government for the accommodation of national delegations to ECAFE meetings, on account of the then-extreme shortage of local hotel space. After the hotel situation had improved, the bedrooms in this building were converted into offices and ECAFE moved into the structure, except for one wing which had been promised to ICAO as an inducement for the transfer of its office

[26] Working conditions for WHO staff in Patiala House (formerly a Maharajah's palace) had become almost intolerable as a result of the expansion of programme operations in South-east Asia: desk facilities were glaringly inadequate; there was no place where field experts could prepare reports; piles of documents had overflowed into the corridors and on the floors; and part of the staff was labouring in an outside tent despite New Delhi's torrid summer climate. As a palliative, WHO urged UNICEF, which occupied one wing of the structure, to find other quarters. It succeeded in doing so early in 1959.

from Melbourne to Bangkok. At one time, the TAB Resident Representative sought permission to occupy the top floor of the building (which certain Thai private groups were then using), but it was decided to provide for additional committee rooms in lieu of additional office space. It would still be quite feasible to add a wing for the other agencies if the wooden shacks on the area adjacent to it were torn down. Even so, there is some indication that certain agencies may be disinclined to move their offices into the building (even if it were expanded) for fear of being 'swallowed up' by ECAFE's larger-scale operations. The offices of all the UN system agencies operating in Bangkok are provided free of charge by the Thai Government.

From the foregoing review of efforts to achieve inter-agency office consolidation at various centres, it is clear that the problem is a complex one. Agency objections based on a desire to retain separate office identity, questions of prestige, financing obstacles, lack of suitable building sites, and a shortage of available rental properties—all these factors, in one way or another, have tended to retard, if not to block altogether, plans for common office quarters.[27] To quote from the Secretary-General's draft report:

> In most cities, where offices have already been established, the combination of rented, rent-free and partially rent-free space now occupied by the international organizations presents such a complicated pattern that unless the host Government provides major assistance no practical solution to the problem can be anticipated.

Where office consolidation would clearly involve increased outlays for rent and other items, it is hard to make a case for it purely on grounds of anticipated operating economies.[28]

In reality, the case for common office premises would appear to rest rather more on the provision of facilities for better administration than on financial grounds. Also, the concentration of field offices in a common building would undoubtedly make it less confusing and more convenient for host government officials to conduct their day-to-day business with 'the United

[27] In some instances an agency may be disinclined to give up a particularly convenient or agreeable location (as, for example, the FAO office in Rio on the edge of a beautiful botanical garden where it is quiet and there is ample parking space—though far from the centre of the city).

[28] At the time of writing (early 1960), local inter-secretariat groups, set up by the UN Office of General Services at ACC's request, were exploring the possibilities of office consolidation at Paris, Bangkok, Djakarta, Lima, Buenos Aires, Karachi, and Rio (the last two places in view of the imminent removal of the national capital to an interior city). These groups were to submit recommendations to ACC.

Nations galaxy' of organizations than by having their local offices dispersed all over town, as is now often the case.[29] 'An imposing combined headquarters, flying the UN flag, should also help to focus public attention on the UN as an instrument of "united" action for the welfare' of the country and region.[30] Such a centre would serve as a physical symbol of the UN in action 'at the grass roots' and thus have considerable prestige value. Over and beyond this, the location of agency offices in the same premises would facilitate the informal face-to-face contacts of staff personnel that are so essential to effective inter-agency programme co-ordination. Further consideration will be given to this point in the final chapter of this study.[31]

Although inter-agency office consolidation is still spotty and fragmentary, a certain amount of sharing (or pooling) of administrative services has developed in a number of centres. Where two or more agencies occupy the same premises, the costs of building management (including messenger, receptionist and telephone service), duplicating services, local transport, the operation of a staff cafeteria, etc., are shared in one degree or another by the tenant agencies. Even in these circumstances, however, it has been difficult to persuade certain agencies to participate in a common typing pool, partly because such an arrangement is frequently considered to be less convenient than the maintenance of separate clerical staffs, partly also, it would seem in some places, because of the 'individualism' of locally recruited typists who want to be identified with a single agency. In a few instances, as at Mexico City and Beirut, the administrative officer of a major agency performs accounting service for one or more of the smaller agency offices in the same locale. In this connection, UN headquarters reportedly is considering making available at field centres an administrative officer for those specialized agencies willing to co-operate in respect of procurement, space arrangements, and the handling of accounts. At Geneva, a common printing arrangement between the UN European office and WHO, in effect for some years, was terminated in 1957 by reason of the fact that the latter agency found it

[29] See Harland Cleveland, 'The Fits and Starts of Foreign Aid,' *The Reporter* (16 April 1959), for examples of the growing number of foreign national and multilateral agencies with which various Asian Governments now have concurrent foreign aid business.

[30] The quotation is from the writer's article on 'The United Nations System in Egypt,' *International Organization* (May 1956).

[31] See pp. 538–541.

to be more economical to contract for its own printing since, *inter alia*, only one proof-reading would be necessary (the UN had always insisted on doing, and charging for, a completely separate proof-reading operation). WHO, however, does utilize the UN office postal, communications, documents distribution services, and conference facilities. Except for the last-named facilities, it is expected that when WHO has its own building these services will be performed separately.

At certain of the more important centres, where some or all of the agency offices have separate locations, there are inter-agency agreements for the provision of common services. Thus, for example, a common medical benefits service is administered by Unesco in Paris, by WHO in Geneva, and by ECLA in Mexico City, the participating agencies sharing the costs. There is a common purchasing service at Geneva for the UN, WHO, ILO, ITU, and WMO. The pouch service of the principal agency at a given centre is often shared by one or more of the lesser agency offices whose volume of traffic does not justify a separate pouch. Cost-of-living surveys to determine the basis for 'post adjustment' allowances are now normally conducted by a designated agency for the entire group—usually the agency with the best-equipped statistical staff (*e.g.*, ILO in Geneva, Unesco in Paris, ECLA in Santiago, ECAFE in Bangkok, and WHO in Alexandria, in New Delhi, and in Manila). Country TAB offices frequently handle local currency payments of salaries and allowances for the technical assistance experts of various specialized agencies at their request.

The need of continuing consultation on administrative matters has led to the establishment of standing committees at a number of centres. The initiative for such arrangements has ordinarily come either from the principal agency office or from the local TAB Representative. It is customary to rotate the meeting place and the chairmanship of these committees among the participating agencies. Inter-agency committees exist at Geneva, Cairo, Mexico City, New Delhi, Bangkok, Manila, and a few less important places. At Geneva, for example, there is a Committee on Local Problems to deal with the Swiss authorities on such questions as privileges and immunities, the importation of motor-cars, customs clearance, and military service for locally recruited

Swiss personnel. The UN European Office provides secretarial staff for the Committee.

Most of the inter-agency committees at non-headquarters cities tend to restrict their agenda to two types of business: (1) exchange of information regarding forthcoming events and visits of headquarters 'top-brass,' and (2) recruitment, pay and allowances, and import privileges for office staffs.[32] Here and there some consideration has been given to the development of co-operative procedures for local staff recruitment, and it is not uncommon for the largest agency office to aid the smaller ones in finding suitable candidates for secretarial posts. Some progress has also been made towards agreement on standardized grading schemes and conditions of service for local staff groups.

While the device of an inter-agency consultative committee is undoubtedly useful in terms of promoting mutual acquaintance and the exchange of ideas on common administrative problems, most of the routine items with which such committees deal could probably be handled equally well by the circulation of memoranda, or by delegation to the administrative unit of one of the major offices. Periodic committee meetings are regarded by certain agencies as a waste of time. Consequently, at some centres, they are held only 'as necessary.' In countries where technical assistance operations are sizable, TAB Representatives have endeavoured to broaden the scope of committee discussion from essentially 'trade-union' concerns to include substantive problems. But most of these efforts, largely because of indifference on the part of agency participants, have proved relatively unsuccessful.

On the other hand, in connection with local celebrations of UN Day and of Human Rights Day, inter-agency co-operation has produced impressive results in a number of centres. Where this has happened it has been due to sustained preparatory work by the Director of the UN Information Centre, in close collaboration with the RTAR and the heads of agency missions. Also, there are instances where meetings of an inter-agency advisory

[32] The writer was invited to attend a meeting of the Cairo committee in November 1958. On the agenda of the meeting were the following items (in the order here stated): announcements of forthcoming meetings; cost-of-living in Egypt; import privileges for UN personnel; Tenth Anniversary of the Declaration of Human Rights; increments for messengers; payment of premiums on international air tickets for non-resident personnel; the celebration of UN Day; miscellaneous reports from agency representatives; and *per diem* rates for local chauffeurs.

committee have led to a greater mutual understanding of the work of the various agencies, especially when one item on the agenda is set aside for the presentation of a detailed account of one agency's activities by its representative on the committee. If properly planned, such meetings can cultivate a better sense of teamwork among the members of field missions.

One minor problem arising from the plurality of independent offices at major field centres has to do with the hierarchical status of office directors. In matters of protocol and official representation on ceremonial occasions, it is not always clear to the national foreign ministry how the different UN office heads should be ranked. The Director of the UN Information Centre has at times behaved as if he were the 'official representative' of the UN Secretary-General since he is usually the only office head with direct appointment from him.[33] At the more important centres, however, the UNIC Director is in fact inferior in grade to one or more of his colleagues (*e.g.*, the TAB Resident Representative or the head of a specialized agency regional office). Where two office Directors are equivalent in rank, the situation may be a bit confused. Hierarchically, the Executive Secretaries of the UN regional commissions, being at the same grade level as Under-Secretaries at UN headquarters, out-rank all their local colleagues except at Geneva, where the Director of the UN European office has equivalent rank status and also acts as the senior representative of the Secretary-General for protocol purposes. At Santiago, the Executive Secretary of ECLA, reportedly not caring for 'public relations' functions, has asked the RTAR, though of lower rank, to make the principal speech and do the other formalities on ceremonial occasions.

In respect of the hierarchical relations of field office heads, the question of who is entitled to fly the UN flag on his official car has occasionally given rise to minor resentments, especially when one director is accorded this privilege and another with the same or higher rank is not. This, of course, is not a serious matter since most officials are broad-minded enough to adjust to the situation good humouredly. But it is symptomatic of problems inherent in the lack of any officially recognized country

[33] At one major centre the UNIC Director, shortly after arrival for duty, reportedly ruffled the feathers of the other office directors by calling a meeting as 'representative of the Secretary-General' and introducing subject-matter in which he obviously was not competent.

representative for the *ensemble* of UN organizations operating locally.[34]

'Privileges and Immunities' for Field Staffs

No office of any UN organization may be established on the territory of a Member State without its consent. In turn, the presumption is that the host country will grant appropriate privileges, immunities, and facilities for the effective functioning of the office and its staff. This *quid pro quo* is not always easily translated into a mutually satisfactory agreement. Negotiations have often been long and tedious. Even when a formal agreement is successfully concluded, its provisions may not be fully implemented by national foreign ministries, immigration authorities, or customs services; or disputes may arise as to their interpretation. Where, as is frequently the case, the scope of such agreements, or their administration, varies significantly as between agencies operating in a given country, a sense of being discriminated against may develop among the office and project personnel of agencies receiving less favourable treatment than the others. Here the chief bone of contention usually turns out to be whether, how often, or to what extent field staffs may import duty-free such items as motor-cars, household equipment, certain types of drugs and preserved foodstuffs, tobacco, and alcoholic beverages.

All but a few of the States belonging to the UN have acceded to the Convention on Privileges and Immunities of the United Nations, drawn up by the General Assembly in 1946. Considerably fewer States, however, have ratified the companion Convention relating to the Specialized Agencies prepared the following year. These two general Conventions, while fairly explicit as to such matters as the inviolability of headquarters premises and of official documents, communications facilities, immunity from legal process, and exemptions from taxation, did not—and indeed could not then—spell out the obligations of Member States relative to field offices or to technical assistance projects operating within their territories. Such obligations were subsequently covered in special bilateral agreements between each agency and the host country concerned. As noted earlier in this chapter,

[34] For the author's proposals concerning this problem, see pp. 537–541.

many of these agreements provide for contributions by the host government towards the operating expenses of field offices, including in some cases rent-free occupancy of office premises.

Inasmuch as field offices were set up at different times by different organizations in different countries, each of them proceeded to bargain as best it could for facilities and privileges. Where firm commitments were received in advance from the future host country, an agency was likely to obtain more favourable treatment than if it went ahead and opened its office on the basis of vague promises, some of which might never be carried out or, at best, be put into effect only after protracted discussion. This is one reason why WHO, for example, was able to make somewhat more liberal arrangements for its regional offices than were some of its sister agencies. Similarly, FAO and ICAO succeeded in getting from the Government of Thailand generous treatment from the outset, while ECAFE encountered long delays in negotiating an acceptable agreement with that country. Other examples of this state of affairs will be indicated shortly.

When the Expanded Programme of Technical Assistance was inaugurated, 'basic' agreements were originally concluded with most recipient governments. Under these 'umbrella' agreements, supplementary agreements were entered into between individual agencies and governments covering specific projects. In 1954, TAB decided to draw up a 'revised standard' agreement in the hope that formal supplementary project agreements might be dispensed with in the future. This revised agreement was used as the norm for re-negotiating the original basic agreements. Under the new procedure, arrangements for projects are covered by informal exchanges of letters between the recipient government and the agency (or agencies) involved.

By 1959, the Revised Standard Agreement had been accepted by some forty-two countries including most of those with substantial technical assistance programmes. Even so, a number of important countries in this category still had not acceded to the agreement, to wit: Brazil, Iraq, Lebanon, Libya, Mexico, Thailand, and the United Arab Republic. TAB has also prepared a 'model' letter covering the appointment of each RTAR. This letter, in effect, serves as his 'credentials' to the government to which he is assigned, setting forth his functions, enumerating the facilities and services to be provided for him by the government, and expressing the hope that appropriate privileges and immunities will be extended to him and his staff.

The provisions of the Revised Standard Agreement describe the various forms that technical assistance may take in the signatory country, the process by which field experts are selected, their relations with the recipient government, as well as the respective administrative and financial obligations of the donor organization and the government. Further, the Agreement stipulates that the recipient government 'shall apply to the Organisation(s), their property, funds and assets, and to their officials, including technical assistance experts, the provisions of the Convention on the Privileges and Immunities of the United Nations and the Convention on the Privileges and Immunities of the Specialized Agencies.'[35] Finally, it is laid down that each organization, its experts and other officials 'shall have the benefit of the most favourable legal rate of conversion of currency'—a provision of particular relevance to countries with multiple currency systems.

To summarize: technical assistance personnel enjoy privileges and immunities the content of which may vary depending on what international conventions or agreements a government has accepted, as well as any special arrangement it may make in so far as the latter does not conflict with, or restrict the scope of, the applicable convention or agreement. Any privileges that may be granted over and beyond its provisions are extended 'as a matter of courtesy and not of right.' Such extensions have occasionally resulted from personal appeals by the TAB Representative to the chief of protocol of the foreign ministry or other national authority. Concessions obtained in this manner would appear to vary with the kind of approach used by the RTAR: this calls for a subtle blend of tact, patience, and firmness.

The web of conventions, agreements, and administrative practices encompassing the status of field offices, their staffs, and members of technical assistance missions produces widely divergent country situations. Both as to granting privileges and facilities and in administering agreed obligations, the attitudes of governments range from liberal to equivocal to

[35] Article V of the Agreement. The full text is contained in the *TAB Field Manual* (as revised to 1959).

restrictive, depending on national susceptibilities, domestic politics, and bureaucratic behaviour. A change of régime, or the replacement of one governing *élite* by another, may markedly affect the approach to the rights of international organizations operating on a sovereign State's soil.

The kinds of administrative and psychological issues that arise from these differential situations may be seen concretely by reference to a sample of thirteen countries where the writer had the opportunity of discussing the matter with UN and national officials. This sample includes countries of varying importance distributed through Latin America, the Middle East, South Asia, and the Far East.

The countries in the sample, which will not be identified by name,[36] tend to fall into two fairly distinct categories: (1) five countries whose treatment of the UN agencies has on the whole been consistently fair and generous; and (2) the remaining eight where there have been persistent delays, snags, or difficulties, or where agency treatment has been either deliberately or unintentionally discriminatory.

In category (1), all five countries have acceded to the Revised Standard Agreement covering EPTA and have made special agreements providing liberal facilities to most (if not all) local agency offices. Office heads are accorded full diplomatic status, ordinarily with the right to use CD (or UN) plates on their official cars.[37] Office and project personnel are allowed to import free of duty private motor-cars every two or three years, and reasonable amounts of foodstuffs, tobacco, and liquor while on duty in the country. In tropical areas this privilege extends to such household appliances as refrigerators and air-conditioners. In one case, where only the RTAR himself may import foodstuffs, liquor, and tobacco, he has contrived to set up a small commissary where technical assistance experts may draw in modest quantities from his own supplies. For a time, in another country, EPTA experts were getting limited quotas of duty-free liquor while other personnel working for the same agency

[36] To identify them might be embarrassing to informants whose private observations to the writer form the basis of much of what follows relating to this subject.

[37] In one country, however, the TAB Representative got diplomatic status much later than the director of a large regional office and then only after establishing friendly relations with the chief of protocol. In this same country all international personnel are permitted to use UN designations on their personal cars.

were not; but this discrimination was later removed and the privilege extended to all international personnel. In most cases UN officials (and to some extent field experts also) are entitled to purchase tax-free gasolene—a much prized right in view of its high cost and the poor public transit facilities.

In category (2), the picture is much more blurred. Country A (one of the worst cases) has not yet accepted the United Nations (or Specialized Agency) Convention on Privileges and Immunities, or the Revised Standard Agreement covering EPTA. During the earlier years of UN activity in the country foreign office officials are reported to have been decidedly unsympathetic towards the Organization. Recently a somewhat more favourable attitude has manifested itself. Yet it has not proved possible to negotiate formal site agreements covering the largest UN or TAB office. While three specialized agencies managed to do this, the draft agreements have been stalled in the national legislature for years and therefore lack legal validity. In the opinion of most UN officials, the resultant state of affairs is unsatisfactory all round. The host government purports to apply the relevant 'privileges and immunities' article of the United Nations and Specialized Agency Conventions 'in accordance with international law and custom,' but its administrative interpretation of the article tends to be erratic if not arbitrary, leading to unequal treatment of different agencies. This situation has provoked friction and resentment. For instance, one senior official was denied, for some time, the right to import an official car; when he got the right he was permitted to use only ordinary licence plates on it. If, to cite a hypothetical possibility, it were claimed by this host government that there was a political trouble-maker on a UN agency staff, and its premises and archives were searched by the local police, there would be no legal ground for complaint by the United Nations.

In some respects the situation in Country B has been equally exasperating. Here domestic political 'in-fighting' has exacerbated national sensitivities. Among the older foreign service officials an anti-foreign complex is markedly noticeable. In consequence, there have been serious road-blocks in negotiating formal agreements—let alone in getting them ratified by the national legislature. The status of most UN offices is still governed by an informal exchange of letters. Clearance of the personal baggage of incoming UN personnel has been a chronic headache. A Unesco Jeep, for example, was held up for three months, while it has taken as long as six months to get private motor-cars through the labyrinth of customs formalities. UN officials sometimes have had their trunks opened at the customs despite their special status. The UN agencies, moreover, have been required to use the official (overvalued) exchange rate for converting staff salaries from dollars into local currency. What with rampant inflation and a galloping black market for such currency, this meant (in 1957) a reduction of the purchasing power of their salaries by 20 to 25 per cent. below what they feel it should be. As one UN field official remarked to the writer, 'the treatment of UN personnel in this country has been outrageous. The UN should reduce its technical assistance programme unless the situation is corrected.'

In Country C, political instability (until quite recently), combined with bureaucratic inertia, has retarded the conclusion of office site agreements. It took from four to six years to negotiate agreements for three specialized agency offices. Only two years were necessary for a fourth office, thanks, apparently, to the intervention of its deputy director (a national of the country) with his friends in the foreign ministry. The government of this country had still not accepted the Revised Standard Agreement for EPTA, nor was there any formal agreement governing the status either of the TAB office or of the UN Information Centre.

Among the anomalies of this tangled situation are the following: technical assistance experts do not receive free import privileges as regards liquor or tobacco in contrast to other personnel (often associated with them in the same office) who enjoy this right.[38] The Director of the UNIC has been accorded diplomatic status but not the right to import duty-free liquor despite his recurring 'hospitality' obligations *vis-à-vis* visiting dignitaries and the local newspaper fraternity. Some officials have been able to import refrigerators, washing machines, radios, etc., free of customs duty, while others have had to pay duty on certain of these items depending on the whim of customs

[38] Some years ago the visiting auditor of one agency discovered that the locally recruited staff of a field office was being allowed to buy duty-free cigarettes from the office commissary—a privilege denied to internationally-recruited technical assistance experts. This practice, bordering almost on a scandal, was ordered discontinued.

inspectors or their ignorance of regulations. For several years one specialized agency had considerable difficulty even in getting its official publications into the country for similar reasons. On the other hand, another agency, with a firm host country agreement, has received liberal treatment on all counts. A third agency, though failing to conclude a formal agreement, has been especially favoured—again reportedly by reason of the local political connections of its Deputy Director (a national of the host country).

In Country D, the first agency on the scene succeeded in making relatively liberal arrangements with the host government. Both the Director and the Deputy Director of the regional office of this agency have diplomatic status and unlimited free import privileges, while the rest of its staff receive limited privileges. At one time, the government considered reducing these privileges but the office director, a former high official in the national administration, successfully resisted any such 'unilateral' action by pointing out that it would violate the terms of the agency's agreement with the government.

Although a party to the Revised Standard Agreement covering EPTA, this government has been notoriously sticky with respect to granting free import rights to EPTA personnel. Long and tortuous negotiations were necessary before a reasonably satisfactory TAB site agreement could be concluded. Even now, neither the TAB Representative nor the WHO regional Director or his deputy is allowed to have CD plates on his official car. Nor does the site agreement authorize the purchase of tax-free gasolene by office staff or field experts, although the practice now is for EPTA personnel to buy gasolene with government-provided funds. Import restrictions in this tropical country have made it very difficult for resident UN personnel, regardless of agency, to import, until recently, except at black market rates, Western products obtainable locally (if at all) only at terrifically high prices, such as baby food, vitamins, facial tissues, drugs, and cosmetics. Refusal of the right (except for chiefs of mission) to import liquor free of duty has been a burning issue in view of the high local price of whisky. The importation of personal and household effects without duty is allowed only within a four months' period after the date of arrival for duty. Nor are motor cars regarded as falling within the definition of personal and household effects. Recently, the government has agreed to pay the duty on imported cars but the owners must either re-export them or repay the government the duty if they are sold in the country.

Country E has on the whole pursued a more generous policy towards such matters. Even so, its treatment of individual agencies has varied in important particulars. There are formal site agreements covering three of the regional offices located in its capital but not covering the other two. All of these agreements were concluded only after several years of tough negotiation, the national bureaucracy reportedly being fearful of taking formal decisions.[39] The other two regional offices, although having no formal host country agreements, have been accorded privileges and facilities roughly comparable to those enjoyed by the three with agreements. By and large, the administrative application of agreements is more liberal than a strict interpretation of their provisions might appear to require. Substantial concessions have been granted by the Protocol Department of the Foreign Ministry following various *démarches* by agency officials. The *de facto* arrangements now include, *inter alia*, diplomatic status for the heads of all major offices and, for staff personnel, the duty-free importation of household effects (within six months after arrival), liquor and tobacco for official entertaining, and foodstuffs from a nearby free port (four times a year). Tax-free gasolene is also available to all international staff personnel.

So far as the three remaining countries in our sample are concerned, it would be possible to cite minor deviations from the patterns outlined above. But the illustrations already given are broadly representative of the kinds of problems that UN organizations have encountered in trying to obtain appropriate conditions for the operation of their field offices and field personnel. While the over-all situation has substantially improved in most countries during recent years, the morale of field staffs still suffers not so much from inherently bad treatment as from the fact that certain groups are treated less advantageously

[39] The head of one of the principal offices is reported to have put CD plates on his official car without authorization. The plates were discovered but he continued using them for some years simply by not registering the car. As a result, the Foreign Office 'got its back up.' This may have helped to obstruct the negotiation of a site agreement by his successor.

than other foreigners doing similar work in the same country, including national foreign services and other international agency staffs. In this connection, there is understandable resentment among staff personnel with families in being allowed to import food and drugs in no larger quantities than their 'single' colleagues. A further cause for complaint is that such 'free' medical service as recipient governments agree to provide to UN technical assistance experts is often woefully inadequate, nor does it cover their dependents.[40]

One may deplore the abuse of commissary privileges by the embassy staffs of certain wealthy countries, and it is not intended here to argue that comparable privileges be extended to the international staffs of UN organizations. Yet there is a strong case for equality of privileges as among these staffs, all the more in that they become involved in situations where reciprocal hospitality is part of their normal functions. If they do not have minimum privileges in this respect, or lack privileges which their opposite numbers in the UN family enjoy, a heavy drain may be placed on their personal income.

One reason why UN organizations have been unable to obtain more satisfactory privileges and immunities for their field staffs is that each organization has conducted separate negotiations with host governments—in lieu of presenting a united front. Given the different times at which field offices and field programmes were set up in most countries, this was perhaps inevitable. One wonders if the time has not come for the UN family of agencies to undertake to conclude 'comprehensive' country agreements, as nearly as possible with uniform provisions for all offices and personnel functioning in a given country.[41] In the opinion of many operating officials, moreover, the UN could take a firmer position with host governments which either will not assume, or fail to implement effectively, appropriate obligations as to the status of UN field personnel and the provision of local facilities for technical assistance projects. Is it really true, as sometimes suggested, that the donor of a large bilateral aid programme,

[40] In this context, one group of technical assistance experts in a Middle Eastern country, whom the writer met privately, referred to themselves as 'the step-children' of their organization—in comparison with headquarters staff. Realistic information on 'privileges and immunities,' they felt, should be included in each post report and be stressed in the initial briefing of field experts—in order to avoid false expectations.

[41] Except, of course, for formal diplomatic status, which obviously would have to be graded according to official rank.

such as the United States, is in a position to apply stronger sanctions against backsliding governments than is a world organization with a less extensive multilateral programme?[42] The fact is, the United Nations and its associated agencies have never ventured to act jointly *vis-à-vis* recipient governments that fail to live up to their obligations. A diplomatically conveyed warning that programme operations might be curtailed, or that a field office might be moved to another country, should in some cases have a marked effect if made in the name of ACC through the UN Secretary-General. A resolution by ECOSOC instructing the ACC to formulate 'model' provisions for over-all country agreements might also be a useful means of prodding governments to accord more satisfactory arrangements across the board.

[42] According to reliable report, a certain Asian country threatened some time ago to 'down-grade' the privileges and immunities of resident American Point Four technicians; whereupon the United States Government entered a vigorous protest and the host government desisted.

5

THE HUMAN ELEMENT

'Good administration,' as the present writer once observed in another context, 'is a composite of effective organization, adequate material facilities, and qualified personnel.'[1] Even poorly devised machinery may be made to work if it is manned with well-trained, intelligent, imaginative, and devoted staffs. On the other hand, the best-planned organization may produce unsatisfactory results if it is operated by mediocre or disgruntled people.

This truism applies with special force to the field programmes of an international administration for two reasons. First, its staffs must necessarily be drawn from many different cultures, a wide variety of linguistic and educational backgrounds, and an extraordinary diversity of professional experience. Secondly, its operational milieu is equally multi-cultural, consisting as it does of a multiplicity of national government bureaucracies, local institutions, and private groups. These two sets of complicated relationships create difficult problems of communication and adjustment. To quote Dr. Brock Chisholm, the distinguished former Director-General of WHO:

> Organization is still only an instrument; people, with all their emotional problems and distortions, have to use the instrument sensibly in the service of goals which are sufficiently common to all of them. Loyalty to any one culturally determined way of using the instrument can, and often does, get in the way of such sensible use.[2]

This is by way of introducing the subject of the present chapter—the tasks involved in recruiting, assigning, and managing the several thousands of persons who staff field offices and operate field projects for the UN family of agencies.[3] In terms of professional identification these field staffs include both 'generalists,' and 'specialists,' the latter group, to be sure, vastly

[1] *National Administration and International Administration: A Comparative Survey of Fourteen Countries* (Brussels: Unesco-IIAS, 1951), p. 61.

[2] From a personal letter to the writer dated 8 April 1957.

[3] This chapter does not pretend to treat exhaustively the subject of personnel selection for international service—a subject on which there is a rapidly growing literature.

outnumbering the former; teams of experts headed by a chief and individual technicians working by themselves; persons selected from within the organization and those recruited directly from the outside for specific field assignments. Included in these various categories, moreover, are personnel compensated from *regular* budgets and those paid out of *special* programme funds, notably EPTA. Not infrequently the staff of a field office or of a major field project will include personnel financed from regular as well as special budgets. To round out this complex picture: a few of these field staffs enjoy permanent tenure; slightly over half are on intermediate term appointments (one to five years), while the rest have short-term contracts of a few months to a year (which, however, are in numerous instances renewed for additional periods).

Although standards of selection and conditions of service for staff personnel are now governed to a substantial extent by inter-agency agreement, the responsibility for personnel recruitment and management still rests with each autonomous agency. This is so despite the fact that the formal agreements covering the relations of the specialized agencies with the United Nations recognize the desirability of developing a 'unified' international civil service. There is no international civil service bureau or commission with authority over the UN and its affiliated agencies.[4] Consequently, as might be expected, the different organizations have developed recruitment processes that vary considerably, depending on their particular organizational patterns and subject-matter concerns. At the same time, all agencies have faced—and indeed continue to face—certain common problems when it comes to discovering, attracting, and retaining suitably equipped personnel for myriad field assignments around the globe.

[4] The International Civil Service Advisory Board, set up in 1949, has made some useful studies of international personnel problems; but this Board, as its name implies, has only advisory functions. The Consultative Committee on Administrative Questions, functioning under the aegis of ACC, has been an important mechanism for the development of inter-agency agreement as to recruitment, compensation, and grading practices. The achievement of such agreement has been made more difficult by the fear of agencies of having 'legislative' measures imposed upon them. Further progress towards uniformity presupposes mutual confidence and co-operation.

The Recruitment Process

With the exception of WHO, the appointment of all *internationally* recruited personnel, whether for field offices or for field missions, is subject to approval by agency headquarters. This category of staff includes the higher administrative, supervisory, and professional (technical) grades, in addition to translators and interpreters where necessary (*e.g.*, for the secretariats of the UN regional commissions). *Locally* recruited field office staffs, on the other hand, are normally appointed by the director of the office concerned. Within this group are secretaries (often bilingual), junior accountants, typists, file clerks, messengers, duplicating machine operators, telephone operators, receptionists, chauffeurs, and custodial employees—as need dictates.

WHO's recruitment system deviates from the norm by being partially decentralized to the regional level. The directors of its regional offices, according to the WHO Constitution, were to be appointed by the Executive Board 'in agreement with the regional committee.'[5] This provision represented a compromise between those who favoured appointment by the Director-General in consultation with the Board and the regional committee, and those who wanted to lodge the appointing power in the Director-General subject to the approval of the Board alone. In actual practice, however, the Board has exercised no initiative in regard to such appointments, invariably confirming the single nominee submitted to it by the regional committee. In several instances, significantly, the nominees have been members of the Executive Board or of the regional committee. Although they owe their nominations to the regional committee, the regional directors are responsible to the Director-General as 'the chief technical and administrative officer of the Organization.' This dual relationship, while it has apparently caused no serious difficulty thus far, is viewed by some Member governments of WHO as potentially conducive to strained relations between the Director-General and the regional office heads.[6]

[5] Article 52.

[6] In 1957, the Government of New Zealand proposed that the selection process for regional directors be changed by affording the Director-General an opportunity to submit a recommendation to the Executive Board, with his reasons. The Board would then make the nomination and refer it to the regional committee concerned for confirmation. Under such a procedure the initiative would rest squarely with the Board (WHO, O.R., No. 76, Jan. 1957). In large part, WHO's regional directors to date have been

However this may be, the first Director-General, being a firm believer in the principle of regional decentralization, readily delegated to the regional directors the power to select personnel within the following broad limits. Regional selection committees, set up in each regional office, may make selections for *project* posts up to and including grade P-4, irrespective of the origin of the candidate and without confirmation from headquarters. For regional *office* posts these committees may select up to and including P-3, except for unit heads at this grade, for which they must obtain approval from Geneva. P-4 posts in regional offices are filled by the Senior Staff Selection Committee at headquarters. For those posts for which selections are made at the regional level, headquarters tries to keep the regions supplied with a reservoir of suitable candidates, to be considered along with those available from within the region.

The personnel unit of each regional office processes all staff appointments. While it has no machinery of its own for the interviewing of candidates in the region, considerable interviewing is carried on by the staff of the personnel unit, technical officers, area representatives, and project personnel. So far as vacancies in senior regional office staff are concerned, all applications are received at headquarters. Notice of such vacancies is circulated to all UN agencies, whose staffs, other things being equal, are given preference. After thirty days, the *dossiers* on eligible applicants are sent to the regional office director, who nominates his first, second, and possibly third choice for the post to headquarters, which then decides.

As regards the recruitment of senior technicians for field project assignments, most of the candidates are in fact provided by the technical divisions at headquarters (though occasionally the regional office may also make suggestions) by reason of their cumulative professional contacts with major recruitment sources (*e.g.*, public health services, medical and nursing schools, and research institutes). Headquarters thus acts as a clearinghouse for candidates and makes the final selection; but it seldom does this without consulting the regional director. The vast majority of senior professional experts are recruited from outside

quasi-political appointees—for five-year, renewable terms—most of them highly capable men. The working relations between Geneva and the first Director of the Washington office (who is in fact chosen by the Directing Council of PAHO) were anything but smooth.

the region to which they are assigned since it is considered desirable to inject advanced methods and techniques into the areas where public health standards are backward. Even so, and particularly with respect to experts of intermediate grade, the choices of certain regional directors, so it is claimed by some officials at Geneva, are not infrequently influenced by local 'health politics.' As this somewhat involved, decentralized control over recruitment works out in practice, virtually no field staff, regardless of grade, is appointed against the strong objection of the regional director concerned; in effect, he has the final word.

Although all the other organizations have a much more centralized recruitment system than WHO, only the UN itself has thus far developed any continuing field machinery for the scouting of talent or the appraisal of candidates by interview and confidential inquiry; and even the UN machinery is far from adequate to meet its recruitment requirements in non-western areas. Budgetary limitations have prevented the UN Office of Personnel from employing professional interviewing teams except in Europe and North America. This machinery is administered by what is known at headquarters as the Technical Assistance Recruitment Services, whose staff (as of 1959) consisted of a total of twenty-six persons, of whom only twelve were in the professional category.[7] A small recruitment office is maintained in Paris as a base from which three or four field recruitment men rove about Europe as necessary. These field teams work in conjunction with National Technical Assistance Committees set up by some twenty European governments.[8] As far as possible, each applicant is interviewed by two different persons either in Paris or wherever convenient. Some attention, in the interviewing process, is said to be given to family attitudes and the candidate's home environment. The UN field team endeavours to contact references and other persons acquainted with his qualifications. The interviewers, however, are for the most part not 'personnel technicians' selected

[7] This title is a misnomer; actually about sixty per cent. of the work of TARS relates to personnel services for experts after appointment.

[8] The British, Dutch, and Scandinavian committees are considered to be the most effective. Included among the other committees are four in Communist countries: the U.S.S.R., Poland, Czechoslovakia, and Yugoslavia. Israel also has an active committee. These committees have an important voice in regard to their governments' financial contribution to EPTA.

specifically for this purpose but 'bright young men trained on the job.'[9]

Each year from 60 to 65 per cent. of the experts recruited for UN technical assistance come from countries with National Committees. In North America, from which 25 per cent. more are drawn, there are no national recruitment committees as such, but some assistance in finding candidates is provided by a State Department 'liaison officer' at Washington and by the Canadian Technical Co-operation Office in Ottawa. Periodic field trips across the United States and into Canada are made by two personnel officers from UN headquarters, not only for interviewing but to establish contacts with universities, research institutes, and other sources of recruitment.

In TARS at New York a roster of potential applicants has been built up over the years. This consisted (as of late 1959) of slightly more than 5,000 coded cards containing information about persons in North America and some 9,000 additional cards for the rest of the world except Europe, the European roster being kept at the Paris office. An attempt is made to keep this personnel information up to date by inserting factual material from field team reports and other sources. Now that TARS is recruiting for Special Fund as well as EPTA projects its task has an additional dimension. Ordinarily, according to the Deputy Director of TARS, it is necessary to write or talk to at least three and more likely as many as six or seven potential candidates in order to get a panel of two or three available well-qualified experts to present to a recipient government. In some cases, where highly specialized experience and foreign language requirements are involved, from thirty to fifty different individuals may have to be approached.

For the other parts of the world—Latin America, Asia and Africa—the UN depends for personnel information on such sources as the RTARs, the UNIC staffs, and the secretariats of the regional economic commissions. Although the bulk of appointments to technical assistance posts still comes from Western Europe and North America, the number originating from non-western areas is steadily increasing. It is particularly

[9] This policy seems to reflect a feeling that the technique of interviewing applicants of different nationalities for technical assistance posts calls for special aptitudes not necessarily possessed by men who have come up through national civil services. Attached to the Paris office of TARS is a Russian who assists in recruiting in Eastern Europe.

in such areas that evaluation of educational attainments and previous professional experience is most difficult. Yet the interviewing of candidates from these areas is not nearly so adequate or systematic as in Western Europe and North America. The UN Recruitment Services would welcome the establishment of a national recruitment committee system in the less developed countries, but so far this has not seemed feasible.[10]

Before a candidate can be processed for submission to the government to which he is to be assigned, agreement must be reached, after consultation, as between the UN Department of Economic and Social Affairs, including BTAO, and the Recruitment Services. In the case of substantive fields such as geology, petroleum engineering, and rural welfare, for which the Economic (or Social) Affairs Bureau has no competent specialist on its staff, TARS seeks technical advice from outside sources so far as possible.

A word is in order here concerning the way in which the professional staffs (economists, statisticians, demographers, and industry specialists) of the UN regional commissions are recruited. The initiative in proposing outside candidates for such posts is ordinarily taken by the Executive Secretary, though on occasion the UN Department of Economic and Social Affairs may suggest names. Also, now and then, this Department may detail one of its professional members for service with a commission secretariat. The professional staffs of the regional commissions are drawn mainly from the region concerned, with a view to tapping the enthusiasm and dynamism of regional specialists for economic development research and planning. All nominations for appointment for a period of a year or more are reviewed by the Appointment and Promotion Board, comprised of seven secretariat officials of different nationalities and located at UN headquarters. This Board considers nominations seriously and does not by any means always agree with proposals of the Department of Economic and Social Affairs. The Secretary-General almost always accepts the Board's recommendations.

Within the limits of their staff resources for recruitment

[10] In New Delhi the writer was reliably informed that the Indian Government was becoming concerned over the 'haphazard' way in which Indian experts had been recruited for EPTA posts in other countries. The idea of setting up some central recruitment clearance machinery was then under consideration (December 1958).

purposes, the specialized agencies (as well as UNICEF) attempt to interview at least once most candidates for field assignments. In the case of applicants from remote regions, however, it is sometimes necessary to rely on paper credentials, including written recommendations—with no opportunity to check their validity by reference to independent sources of judgment. The staffs of an agency's technical services will have personal knowledge of a good many candidates, or can get direct appraisals on them from members of the professional 'fraternities' around the world—through previous connections with universities and private organizations in the educational, welfare, scientific, technical, and cultural domains.

Although the terms of reference of the National Technical Assistance Committees in Europe cover specialized agency as well as UN recruitment, some of the agencies appear to make comparatively little use of these aids to recruitment. WHO, for example, does not use the committees because the Executive Board has decided that such procedure would not be consistent with WHO's methods of recruitment. Unesco, on the other hand, regularly uses the committees, or the Unesco national commissions, or specific ministries or institutes, as each government prefers. In July 1959, at a two-day meeting of the European committees held in Geneva, all the specialized agencies were represented. This meeting, to be followed by another in 1960, produced a fruitful exchange of ideas on the whole recruitment process for technical assistance, its difficulties, and possible improvements.

A definite effort to strengthen the headquarters personnel units of most UN agencies has taken place in recent years. In 1958, for example, the ILO Personnel Office staff was enlarged and moved up the headquarters hierarchy, primarily in view of the expanding field programme requirements of that organization.[11] This Office is now responsible for the recruitment, processing, and management of all ILO personnel for headquarters, field office, and EPTA assignments. Its present set-up notably includes a research and development division which is expected to make continuing analyses of personnel practices and problems not only in regard to ILO but other agencies as

[11] Formerly a special unit within the Personnel Office handled the recruitment of EPTA experts.

well. To an increasing extent, as convenient, candidates for EPTA posts are interviewed at field or branch offices. At London, Paris, Bonn, Ottawa, and Washington, the latter offices endeavour, so far as their facilities permit, to stimulate applications from qualified specialists for EPTA projects in the major industrialized nations of the West.[12] Notwithstanding its tripartite constituency, the ILO has apparently not found it expedient to use employers' and workers' organizations as channels for the recruitment of management engineers or trade union specialists, preferring to deal rather with national committees, or ministries of labour, commerce, and industry for such purposes.

In FAO, the expansion of field activities of various kinds has prompted the Director-General to concentrate responsibility for all staff recruitment in a strengthened Personnel Branch. Most of the candidates for EPTA assignments are suggested by the subject-matter divisions, the Personnel Branch doing the formal processing of appointments. In a few countries, also, FAO National Committees are of some aid in locating available applicants.

In certain respects, Unesco's recruitment problem is more complex than that of its sister agencies. The reason for this is Unesco's extraordinarily wide range of subject-matter interests, embracing the natural and social sciences, all levels of education, mass communications, museum and library management, and specialists in various historical, philosophical, and cultural fields. For recruitment (as well as other) purposes these myriad activities involve continuing contacts with universities, research institutions, national education authorities, press and radio services, and literally hundreds of private scientific and professional associations both at the national and the international level. To complicate matters still further, Unesco, as we have already noted, maintains four different types of field operations—under EPTA, the Special Fund, and the Participation and Major Projects programmes, respectively.

Until 1956, EPTA matters were administered by a separate Technical Assistance Department in the Paris secretariat, recruitment, however, being handled by a small special unit in the

[12] At Washington, the Division of International Affairs of the U.S. Department of Labor helps the ILO office to spot suitable candidates.

Personnel Division. Subsequently, recruitment operations for all personnel, field as well as headquarters, were concentrated in the Bureau of Personnel and Management, with a view to 'reconciling the conditions of service under different programmes.'[13] This Bureau, which has since lost its management functions, is now divided into four divisions, dealing with field staff, headquarters staff, standards and classification, and training and welfare, respectively. The Bureau's classified roster, maintained up to date, contains files on some 3,000 candidates.

Although this reorganization is clearly an improvement over previous arrangements, Unesco's recruitment operations are still inadequately staffed. As quoted in the *Unesco House News* of 7 February 1958, one experienced technical assistance expert (subsequently appointed TAB Resident Representative for Central America) observed that 'in Unesco House a relatively small number of people deal with the many-sided problem of recruitment, involving correspondence with candidates, appointment of experts, contact with the different recruitment sources, etc.' In his opinion, greater budgetary provision should be made for regular visits to existing recruitment sources and the cultivation of new sources in Latin America and the Middle and Far East, many of which are as yet untapped. This testimony was corroborated by a high official concerned with technical assistance matters who admitted to the writer that the screening of candidates was still largely a paper operation, based on sketchy *curricula vitae* and not enough field interviewing, although, for recruitment in Europe, a part-time consultant with wide experience in personnel selection does the best he can with the very limited resources at his disposal. Some aid in spotting suitable applications is provided by the more active Unesco National Commissions, while the Unesco Liaison Office at UN headquarters tries the best it can, with its woefully meagre staff facilities, to assist in locating American candidates for field posts, some of whom can be interviewed in New York. In non-western areas the Unesco Chiefs of Mission help in the search for candidates.

Unesco relies to a substantial extent on the advertisement of staff vacancies. Its programme departments also propose candidates of their own. Once there is agreement on a panel of

[13] For a trenchant criticism of Unesco's earlier organization for personnel administration, see the *Report of the Management Survey Committee*, Unesco Doc. 50 EX/27 (1957).

names (in order of preference), the Personnel Bureau communicates with the first choice, and so on, in order to discover who is available and interested. When an applicant's reply is favourable, the field administration unit in the Personnel Bureau prepares his contract and assumes responsibility for all subsequent arrangements, such as travel, pay and allowances, and extensions of appointment.

So far as ICAO is concerned, field recruitment is a comparatively simple matter. The professional staffs of its five regional offices consist partly of men previously recruited for duty in the Montreal secretariat, and partly of men recruited principally for duty in a specific office because of their knowledge of the area and its problems. For the recruitment of experts for technical assistance missions, the Technical Assistance Bureau at headquarters keeps close contact with national civil aviation departments, especially in North America and Western Europe, where most of the available aviation technicians are to be found. Advertising of vacancies in the professional aviation journals is also said to have brought results. The regional offices play no direct part in recruitment operations. By and large, in view of its highly specialized requirements, ICAO has experienced little difficulty in attracting competent experts from government aviation services. On the other hand, few of the major private airlines have been inclined to permit their best men to take leaves of absence for service with ICAO.

For its field operations, UNICEF draws men from many different employment fields. As heads of field offices it requires individuals of some stature and experience, having the ability to negotiate with technical experts without being experts themselves. Such persons are recruited by special search; among them are ex-ministers of economics and ex-Resident Representatives. At the junior level, UNICEF has developed a 'trainee' arrangement by which P-1 and P-2 recruits serve at headquarters for several months and then go to the field for further orientation. The UN Bureau of Personnel, TAB field offices, and UNICEF's own field offices are all used in locating candidates for these posts. Trainees who show promise are assured of a permanent career following a one- to two-year indoctrination period. It is most exceptional for UNICEF to hire anyone on the basis merely of paper credentials.

SPECIAL RECRUITMENT PROBLEMS

Over and beyond the limitations of recruitment machinery and procedures described above, specific recruitment difficulties are encountered by virtually all of the larger agencies. Among these are (1) the impact of unrealistic job descriptions for technical assistance; (2) shortages of available talent in important professional areas; and (3) delays in the acceptance of experts for appointment. Each of these problems calls for special comment.

Unrealistic job descriptions

There has been a noticeable tendency on the part of national government authorities to formulate project requests in vague or unduly sweeping terms. Or, as noted in a recent TAB Report, job descriptions are frequently 'inadequate, leading to correspondence back and forth; [or] at times they are over-elaborate to the point of being unrealistic, asking for a combination of qualities rare, if not impossible, to find in one individual.'[14] One senior recruitment officer characterized some of the job specifications received by his organization as positively 'weird.' Even after examination by the substantive bureaux, he went on to say, they were often still so unsatisfactory as to make it difficult to discover suitable candidates or, when discovered, to induce them to accept job offers. The personnel units of a number of other agencies report similar experiences. TARS is now preparing a 'style manual' for use by RTARs and headquarters, with specimen job descriptions in a variety of fields. It has also been proposed that a 'standard' *curriculum vitae* be developed for general use by employing agencies.

The responsibility for unrealistic job descriptions rests not only with the requesting governments but also in some measure with agency negotiators eager to 'sell' them impressive projects. Where careful reconnaissance surveys of a country's needs in a specific sector are carried out—and this is becoming increasingly the practice in certain agencies—more manageable project requests are likely to emerge. The point is that many governments of the less-developed countries need to be taught how to draw up their proposals with due regard for the practical possi-

[14] *Annual Report of the Technical Assistance Board for 1957*, ECOSOC, O.R.: 26th Sess., 1958, Suppl. No. 5, p. 80.

bilities of finding experts with appropriate technical competence for their implementation. As TAB has pointed out, this is of course a 'remediable' problem that governments and donor agencies working together should eventually be able to solve. In this connection, the new Special Fund has decided to allocate funds for the specific purpose of helping governments to put project requests into better shape.

Shortages of available talent

Even at best, suitable talent for technical assistance assignments remains in short supply for a variety of professional fields. For a time following the inauguration of EPTA the availability of qualified specialists seemed slowly to be on the increase as the requirements of governments for administrative and technical personnel after World War II became less urgent. But the steadily rising cost of living since the Korean war, accompanied by substantial salary increases for industrial, civil service, and even academic personnel in the more advanced countries, has tended to reduce the attractiveness of overseas employment with UN agencies. During this recent period salary and allowance scales, prevalent in the UN system, even after taking account of income tax exemption, have not kept pace with improving compensation rates for comparable domestic employment, especially in North America and north-western Europe.[15]

To be sure, individuals are motivated to go into international service for other than purely materialistic considerations. Missionary zeal, the challenge of pioneering work, the chance to travel abroad and to become acquainted with exotic cultures and peoples, at times, even, a desire to escape from some difficult situation at home—all these may in one way or another influence decisions to accept overseas assignments.[16] But for most professional persons with growing families the financial factor is likely to be important if not decisive. And it is especially in the age ranges from thirty to fifty years that this factor is apt to be

[15] During the period 1956–58, for example, 30 per cent. of the UN field experts recruited were at the two top salary levels; for 1959, it was necessary to raise these levels to 45 per cent. Yet, according to TARS, the calibre of appointees was no higher—if as high.

[16] See the *Report of the Salary Review Committee* of the UN General Assembly, UN Doc. A/3209, 1956, pp. 13–14, for a brief discussion of non-financial factors affecting recruitment and retention of international staff. The International Civil Service Advisory Board recently undertook a special study of how such factors operate.

given the greatest weight. Also, a good many qualified individuals may be deterred from accepting overseas employment by the offer of short-term contracts—of a few months up to a year—in connection with field projects which, on any realistic calculation, would appear to require longer periods for effective implementation.

Virtually every appointing officer with whom the writer discussed this problem during 1958–59 complained of how difficult it was becoming to obtain the services of competent experts in certain key fields where technical skills are concentrated in a few advanced countries. Thus, for example, the UN is now finding it almost impossible to recruit industrial management, engineering, and technological specialists from the United States, Canada, or north-western Europe. Even ECE is facing serious competiton for economists from such European regional organizations as OEEC, the Coal and Steel Community, and the Common Market, which are able to out-bid it by offering better salaries, higher staff grades, and in some cases the lure of lower living costs and better housing conditions (*e.g.*, in Brussels and Luxembourg).

For ECLA and ECAFE, the reservoir of regional specialists is so limited that they have found it necessary to appoint senior economists from countries outside their respective regions. ECLA has experienced difficulty in attracting (or retaining on its staff) outstanding economists from such countries as Brazil, Colombia, Mexico, and Venezuela (let alone the United States), where big private firms tend to lure them away as high-priced consultants. In Asia and the Far East, good economists for ECAFE's staff are now available only in India and Japan, and a few from Pakistan and the Philippines. This situation has led to the temporary 'secondment' of a considerable number of specialists from national government departments, most of these seconded officials being men about to retire, or who have retired at fifty-five or sixty years of age. Short-term consultants are also being utilized increasingly—often, to be sure, with excellent results.

WHO reports comparable difficulty in getting sanitary engineers, health educators, professors of medicine, and maternity and child welfare experts. In FAO, outstanding agricultural economists and agricultural extension specialists from the

United States are now almost impossible to obtain, while ILO is having considerable trouble in locating competent vocational training experts. Although Unesco's recruitment problem in this respect has been less acute, in view of the relatively smaller differential between academic salary levels in most countries and its own pay scales, it is now able to attract only two types of Americans—men in their thirties or over sixty.

So far as the United States is concerned, nearly every UN agency finds itself in competition with ICA and the major private foundations in the quest to find top-flight personnel for overseas service. To the writer's knowledge the over-all compensation (including substantial housing allowances, educational grants, air-conditioners, and private cars) received by overseas experts on private United States foundation contracts is, in certain Asian countries, from 30 to 50 per cent. higher than for comparable UN field personnel. The difference between the status of ICA and UN agency personnel as to pay and allowances is only slightly less marked.

For assignments in the Middle East and Asia, there was for a time a large corps of ex-colonial administrators (British, French, and Dutch) upon which the UN agencies could draw; but this reservoir of admirably experienced talent is now beginning to dry up.

The problem of overseas recruitment has been aggravated by a further factor, namely, the tendency of 'medium-developed' countries to insist upon 'senior' experts with well-established (if not international) reputations. Such countries, it should be remembered, may already have substantial numbers of technicians and administrators with a broad general education, many of them having been trained in Britain, Europe, or the United States. It is frequently with this group of officials that foreign advisers are associated during their assignments in the country. In many instances, only mature international experts with impressive professional experience and attainments are in a position to 'tell off' senior national officials when the latter put forward impracticable ideas for the conduct of a project. In such relationships the question of status becomes very important.

Furthermore, even in the least developed areas, governments which have only recently become independent often seek as a matter of national pride 'the best' that the older and more advanced countries have to offer. Many officials in these new states do not yet appreciate how much better suited to their needs less eminent, relatively young experts might be than older, physically less vigorous, and more 'set-in-their-ways' individuals. Although considerable progress is now being made by RTARs and agency representatives towards convincing these inexperienced governments to accept specialists in the intermediate age ranges, or recruited from areas less highly developed than North America or Western Europe, the problem has by no means been completely solved. Since no UN agency can force a government to take an expert it does not want, it is increasingly necessary to tap the supply of 'retired' civil servants and professors for technical assistance assignments.[17] Many such persons, lured from retirement while still in vigorous health, have done remarkably well on short-term assignments.

Recently the Dutch Government inaugurated an interesting experiment bearing upon this problem. Under this scheme a limited number of 'junior' but basically well-trained Dutch nationals have been made available to work with UN technical assistance teams, alongside senior specialists. In 1959, the Government of the German Federal Republic initiated a similar scheme. When acceptable to the agency and the recipient government concerned, such persons are given the title of 'associate expert,' their government, however, paying their salaries and various auxiliary allowances. In a few cases associate experts, after experience in the field, have been taken on agency payrolls as full-fledged experts. Although experience with these arrangements is still too limited for any generalized conclusion, further extension of the idea would appear to offer promising possibilities.[18]

Delays in the arrival of experts

A further aspect of field recruitment that causes considerable difficulty is the time frequently required to get candidates accepted for appointment after their nomination to governments.

[17] In this connection, one of Unesco's personnel officers remarked to the writer that Unesco might well utilize university professors on sabbatical leave much more often than it actually does.

[18] Opinion among the UN agencies as to the administrative desirability of further extension seems to be mixed. In TAB circles there is said to be a growing feeling that the agencies should not be required to defray the additional administrative costs involved in the use of junior experts.

'In sixteen out of thirty-eight countries' where an analysis was made, reported TAB for the year 1957, 'the average time taken to decide on the nominations exceeded one month; and often it was much longer, extending to several months. The consequences were at times awkward—rather than wait indefinitely, some of the candidates ended by accepting employment elsewhere.'[19] Long delays between the interviewing of candidates and the final decision on their candidacies tend to dry up sources of recruitment. Many such delays are the result of sheer bureaucratic inertia—or poor inter-ministerial communication. When, as in some cases, a government decides to reject a nominee, the selection process has to begin all over again. Or, when, as sometimes happens, a panel of names is submitted to a government and the candidates are so advised, failure to be accepted may 'sour' qualified talent on UN technical assistance work in the future. This situation, fortunately, is now showing signs of improvement—thanks in large measure to strenuous efforts by the RTAR to expedite action by recipient governments.[20] It might be helped further if deadlines were given governments for the acceptance (or rejection) of nominees.[21]

In connection with this matter, it should be noted that the period required for the 'security' clearance of United States experts has contributed to the unavailability of candidates who have to make arrangements for leaves of absence from their jobs well in advance of appointment. During the height of the wave of 'McCarthyism' in the United States a few years ago, government clearance customarily took from four to eight or nine months. Recently, however, United States clearance procedures have been speeded up and this problem is now less serious.

The Nationality Factor in Field Staffing

The question of nationality affects the selection and assignment of field personnel in a number of ways. This problem may for

[19] *Loc. cit.*

[20] The writer heard of an amusing case (in Latin America) of a Minister of Agriculture who refused to accept an American agricultural extension specialist because the Minister did not like U.S. techniques; whereupon the FAO solved the problem by recruiting a Greek expert trained at the Cornell College of Agriculture!

[21] BTAO has advised governments that no more than two weeks should be taken for the consideration of nominees.

convenience be considered under three headings: (1) selection policies of the UN regional commission secretariats; (2) practices followed by the specialized agencies; and (3) trends in the geographic distribution of EPTA personnel.

Regional commission secretariats

As noted earlier, there has been a marked tendency to staff these secretariats from the region concerned. Basically, this policy is designed to provide professional specialists familiar with the conditions and problems of the region. In the case of ECE, aside from a few Americans and an occasional Canadian or Australian, the internationally recruited staff consists almost entirely of Europeans (including British). Even in selecting Europeans, however, the Executive Secretary is obliged to pay some attention to 'geographic distribution' within the UN Secretariat as a whole. For some years the British have been above their 'quota,' while the Russians were decidedly below theirs. More recently (1959) the latter group has increased to a point close to its quota (about eight out of a total of seventy-six professionals). How to utilize the Russians has created something of a problem. It has proved difficult to use them on economic policy research because of their rigid ideological orientation. Soviet statisticians and specialists in specific industries (*e.g.*, steel) have apparently adapted themselves more easily to the requirements of objective analysis. Nearly all of the Russians speak English and thus present no serious problem on that score.

As regards ECLA and ECAFE, a somewhat larger proportion of professional staff personnel is drawn from countries outside their respective regions. There has reportedly been some pressure on the Executive Secretary of ECLA to achieve as wide a geographic distribution as possible of staff recruited from the Latin American countries. From the beginning, the Deputy Executive Secretary of this Commission, interestingly enough, has been a national of the United States. The staffing policy of ECAFE may be characterized as an attempt to maintain a proper balance between Asians and a high degree of technical competence—a policy that has necessarily involved the appointment of a number of senior economists from the advanced countries of the West.[22]

It is anticipated that for some time the new African Commission will obtain most of its professional staff by detail from the UN Department of Economic and Social Affairs. But as trained African personnel is developed the region will be expected to provide an increasing proportion of ECA's staff needs.

In the Fifth Committee of the General Assembly, each year brings forth complaints that the staffs of the various economic commissions are not sufficiently recruited from within the regions concerned. Presumably for propaganda reasons the Soviet bloc usually spearheads such criticisms.[23]

Field office staffs

Agency practices differ as to the advisability or not of assigning nationals of host countries as directors of field offices. Although the appointment of non-nationals is accepted as a principle, numerous exceptions to the rule have been made for political and other reasons. The heads of three of WHO's regional offices—at Washington, Alexandria, and New Delhi—were for years nationals of the United States, Egypt, and India, respectively. When, as in these three cases, the office is located in the major country of the region, there may be some advantage in such appointments so far as enlisting co-operation and support from the host government is concerned. On the other hand, as Charles Ascher has pointed out, 'one can envisage situations that may produce conflicting pressures and great strain upon a man thus chosen.'[24] This pattern was departed from recently with the appointment of a Chilean Director at Washington and of an Iranian at Alexandria. On balance, it would seem that the most desirable arrangement would be to appoint able, broad-

[22] Alexander Loveday, in his *Reflections on International Administration* (London: Oxford Univ. Press, 1956, p. 12), makes this observation: 'Relatively few Asiatics are willing to make international service outside Asia a life career, a fact which creates inequality in the roles that different nationalities can play in international affairs. Asiatics are today the most unfavourably placed, though with the development of regional offices their situation has improved.' This state of affairs may have been true during League of Nations days, but it is not borne out by UN experience.

[23] See, for example, the statement of the Soviet delegate to the Fifth Committee during the twelfth session of the Assembly (630th meeting, 28 Nov. 1957). It should be remembered that many of the regional appointees from Asia have, in fact, been trained in the West—a fact that also may annoy Communist representatives.

[24] 'Current Problems in the World Health Organization's Program,' *International Organization* (Feb. 1952).

gauged men who know the region well but are not nationals of the host country.[25] Where several different UN agencies happen to be represented by host country nationals (as currently in New Delhi) the case for appointing non-nationals is even stronger.

FAO's practice in this regard more or less parallels that of WHO. Here again the principle of not using host country nationals is given lip service by the agency. Yet political pressures have led to the assignment of two Egyptians as successive directors of the Cairo office and of a Mexican to the Mexico City office. In the former case there was perhaps a special advantage in having as first regional director a man who had been Minister of Agriculture in a leading Arab country and who was widely known and respected throughout the Arab world; while the second appointee, also formerly Egyptian Minister of Agriculture, is said to be equally well regarded regionally. What with the increasingly apparent division of the Arab States politically, however, it is not impossible that certain Arab Governments may come to resent the 'monopolistic' hold of Egypt (now the U.A.R.) on the FAO Cairo office.

So far as the Washington office of FAO is concerned, the successive appointment of two Americans as directors can be justified on special grounds, namely, the role of that office as a liaison unit with the U.S. Department of Agriculture, within whose building it is physically located. One of the best jobs as FAO regional representative has reportedly been done at the Bangkok office by a man chosen from outside the region but with long and first-hand acquaintance with its problems previous to his appointment.

With only two or three exceptions, FAO's 'country representatives' are not citizens of the host country. Although a host country national may in some instances have local contacts helpful to him in negotiating technical assistance agreements, for this very reason his objectivity in evaluating project requests may be suspect.[26]

[25] While the heads of the WHO-PAHO 'zone' offices in Latin America are drawn from the Americas, they are never citizens of the host country. From 40 to 60 per cent. of the staffs of these offices are Latin Americans.

[26] In one Asian country a senior member of the TAB office staff characterized as 'a scandal' the assignment of a host country national as FAO country representative. This particular appointee admitted to the writer that in view of his former position with the Ministry of Food and Agriculture he could not press his government 'too hard' to follow up on project recommendations.

ILO adheres fairly consistently to the principle of not using host country nationals to head its field offices. Most of the field office directorships are filled by men with previous experience at ILO headquarters rather than by appointment from outside the organization. Neither the director nor his deputy (with one exception) has ever been a local national.[27] On the other hand, the entire staff of ILO's branch offices is invariably chosen from the administrative services of the host government since such offices are regarded as 'diplomatic outposts' for liaison with the host government and with employers' and workers' organizations in the country.

ICAO follows the practice of spreading regional office professional staffs in terms of nationality. With a single exception (at Paris), no director has been a national of the host country. In making such appointments, preference tends to be given to men with headquarters experience. In a few instances pressures from host governments have led to the appointment of their nationals to technical positions at field offices (*e.g.*, communications experts). Such appointees would appear to be of limited utility; it cannot be easy for an ICAO technician to make objective recommendations regarding the aeronautical administration of his own country, perhaps involving criticism of his former employer.

In UNICEF the heads of field offices are rarely nationals of the host country. In recruiting field office staffs, however, UNICEF has had difficulty in finding competent non-English-speaking personnel. As of 1958, nearly 80 per cent. of its field staffs were drawn from English-speaking countries—a situation said to be resented by some Latin American and Asian Governments. Since then, there has been some increase in non-English-speaking field staff.

For directors of the UN Information Centres, the policy has been not to use host country nationals. In nearly every case, however, the deputy director (if any) is deliberately so chosen.

Finally, nationality as such has played no direct part in the assignment of TAB Resident Representatives. It is the fixed rule of TAB never to appoint host country nationals to these posts, but to choose the best qualified man available regardless

[27] The exception was that of a Deputy Director at Bangalore where considerations of a personal character broke down the rule.

of the country from which he comes as long as he is politically acceptable to the host country. At the same time, some consideration has been given to cultural and linguistic backgrounds. Thus, for example, most of the RTARs who have served in Latin America have come from Latin nations—France, Spain and those of Latin America itself. As of mid-1958, slightly over half of the entire group of RTARs originated from English-speaking countries. This was natural, not only because all of them are technologically advanced countries but also in view of the fact that English is the *lingua franca* of much of the Middle East, Asia, and Africa.[28] A substantial number of RTARs are at home in more than one language.

Field project personnel

Within this category of personnel, as distinguished from the staffs of field offices, the nationality spread has over the years included nearly eighty different countries. Since the inception of EPTA, a conscious effort has been made to broaden the geographic composition of its corps of field experts. Despite the difficulties noted earlier, this effort has had considerable success. During the year 1958, for example, of some 2,400 EPTA experts on duty, the distribution by regional areas of origin was as follows:[29]

Region	*Number of Experts*	*Per Cent. of the Total*
Europe	1,411	58
North America (U.S. and Canada)	379	16
Asia and Far East..	273	11
Latin America	228	9
Middle East	114	5
Africa	11	Less than 1

The United Kingdom provided the largest single group of experts (398), with the United States (287), France (237), the Netherlands (144), and India (109) following in order. Nearly

[28] The rule against appointing host country nationals also holds for deputy and assistant Resident Representatives for the limited number of countries where such appointments are made. It is worth noting that, in one instance, strong objection was raised by a particular government against the appointment of one of its nationals (who happened to be a political refugee) as RTAR in a neighbouring country; as a result the appointment was withdrawn.

[29] *Annual Report of the TAB for 1958*, ECOSOC, O.R.: 28th Sess., 1959, Suppl. No. 5, p. 22. Among the total were eleven 'stateless' persons and a few experts not residing in the country of origin at the time of their recruitment.

a fourth of the grand total came from the economically less-developed areas. While EPTA obviously could not be expected to adhere to fixed nationality quotas in recruiting experts (as are the UN and the specialized agencies for their regular staffs under the geographic distribution rule), representatives of Soviet bloc and Asian countries, in TAC discussions, are prone to call attention to what they allege to be 'under-representation' so far as the distribution of experts is concerned.

The attitudes of certain governments with respect to the nationality (or religion) of experts have had to be taken into account in making field assignments. It is well known, for example, that the U.A.R. not only will not take Jewish experts but is reluctant to accept men who, though not Jews, have previously worked in Israel. The Government of Brazil has shown some unwillingness to approve experts hailing from other Latin American countries; while Thailand was for a time not inclined to welcome Japanese. The acceptance of Soviet specialists (some forty in 1958) has thus far been limited to such 'neutral' Asian countries as India, Burma, and Afghanistan, and to the United Arab Republic and Yugoslavia. By far the largest group of Soviet experts was concentrated on two Indian projects: a Statistical Education Centre at Calcutta and an Institute of Technology at Bombay. Although the head of each Soviet team reportedly could speak English, he was assisted by a Russian translator-interpreter paid in part by TAB as a special charge against the project. Among other Soviet bloc countries, Poland and Czechoslovakia have provided a few experts for substantially the same group of countries. It is not without significance that most of the experts from Communist countries thus far have been technologists, engineers, statisticians, and medical officers; educators, economists, and public administrators were apparently in slight demand.

Personality and Adjustment

Fully as important as technical competence or nationality in the selection and assignment process for field service is the question whether the appointees possess personality traits that will facilitate their adjustment to what the anthropologists call 'cultural shock.' This point is officially recognized by the

TAB Manual of Personnel Policies and Procedures, which states that 'project personnel shall be chosen not only for their technical competence, but also for their sympathetic understanding of the cultural backgrounds and specific needs of the countries to be assisted and for their capacity to adapt methods of work to local conditions, social and material.'[30]

It is in the implementation of this policy that difficulties arise. An assessment of a candidate's personality structure is admittedly difficult to make at the recruitment stage, even when appropriate tests and interviewing techniques can be employed. As we have already noted, the facilities for field interviewing leave a good deal to be desired in most agencies with sizable technical assistance programmes; while no aptitude testing has been tried out either by the UN or any of the specialized agencies. In many cases reliance has had to be placed on formal credentials, written recommendations, and other indirect information sources. Such information may, and frequently does, provide a reasonably good basis for evaluating technical qualifications and experience; but it may be worth little in terms of predicting a candidate's ability to work harmoniously with persons of different nationality and cultural backgrounds, or to withstand the stress and strain that often accompany technical assistance operations. Both physical and emotional factors are closely associated with adaptability. There also seems to be some correlation, as suggested by certain studies of the behaviour of overseas personnel of national governments, between 'home ties,' or between the attitudes of accompanying wives and children, *and* a field expert's capacity for sustained co-operative effort in cross-cultural situations.[31]

On the whole, it is only fair to say, more emphasis is now being put on 'depth' interviewing and the tapping of environmental data on candidates than was the case some years ago. The TARS staff, having interviewed some 20,000 candidates for

[30] Article 211, UN Doc. TAB/CM/782, 31 Aug. 1957, reproduced from ECOSOC Resolution 222A (IX), the basic legislation for EPTA.

[31] For a penetrating discussion of this problem, see Mottram Torre, 'Personality Adjustment in Overseas Service,' in *The Art of Overseasmanship*, eds. Harlan Cleveland and Gerard J. Mangone (Syracuse Univ. Press, 1957), pp. 83–95. For the role of wives, Harlan Cleveland's article entitled 'The Pretty Americans: How Wives Behave Overseas' (*Harper's*, March 1959), is revealing, at least so far as one nationality group is concerned. How far his findings would apply to overseas wives from less affluent societies is an interesting speculation. According to report, the behaviour of wives either 'makes or breaks' U.S. Point Four technicians in about 80 per cent. of the cases.

technical assistance posts during the past decade, feels that this experience enables it to judge with considerable accuracy the kinds of individuals most likely to be successful on field assignments. Where field personnel are on relatively long-term or permanent contracts, the termination of appointments for unsatisfactory performance might afford an index of really serious failure. But for experts appointed initially for periods of a year or less no such drastic action is likely to be taken short of flagrant misbehaviour, such as dishonesty or alcoholism, or a general nervous breakdown. In rare instances experts have had to be withdrawn for reasons of this sort.

At the request of TARS, the TAB Resident Representative submits a confidential report on the performance of each UN expert at the end of his assignment, covering such items as his ability to deal easily and effectively with government officials, his appreciation of the country's problems, and his capacity to present ideas to local groups in such a way as to enlist their interest and support. The value of these reports varies (1) with the extent of the RTAR's personal contact with the expert in question (which may be very slight in large countries like Brazil, Pakistan, India, or Indonesia, where experts are widely scattered), and (2) with the disposition of the RTAR to make a careful, objective appraisal of an expert. According to recruitment officers at UN headquarters, the RTAR's report, far from being taken lightly, is used to help determine whether an expert is suitable for another assignment. In doubtful situations TARS may write a second time to the RTAR for fuller information on the expert's personality traits. There have been cases where, despite an adverse report from the RTAR, an expert has been assigned to another country and, in a fresh environment, has proved to be an outstandingly effective operator.

In ILO, under its staff regulations, the technical divisions at Geneva provide annual evaluations of field experts within their subject-matter competence in order to justify (or not) the granting of salary increments to persons continuing beyond a single year. For such evaluations a simple guide-line form has been devised, calling (1) for a description of duties and (2) for a narrative account of performance (conditions, efficiency, integrity). The sources of information for these appraisals are the expert's own reports, field mission reports, and visits of headquarters staff to the field. Some of the technical divisions, so it appears, tend to regard this chore as 'a bit of a nuisance.' Since, according to regulations, every staff member is permitted to see his performance report, and indeed must sign it, there understandably is considerable reluctance to comment freely on his shortcomings. One official of ILO volunteered to the writer the comment that it was becoming more and more difficult to get suitable men 'on the personality side,' several ILO field specialists having recently 'gone sour.' ILO's chief problem, this official added, was how to find men of emotional stability, mature judgment, and the ability to negotiate.

In WHO, a number of cases have been reported where medical scientists, of acknowledged competence, have had difficulty in communicating their methods to members of an international team with different cultural origins from their own. Perceptive officials of both FAO and Unesco made the observation to the writer that first-rate technicians as such were relatively easy to find, in contrast with broad-gauged, adaptable persons possessing qualities of patience, tact, and understanding. To cite a further bit of testimony: one TAB Resident Representative with long experience in Asia gave it as his opinion that the EPTA experts he had worked with were on the whole professionally qualified for their jobs—some of them perhaps overqualified—but that 'personality misfits' were still being recruited.

What has just been said may perhaps convey an exaggerated notion of the extent to which the field corps serving the UN family of agencies lack that elusive something which the sociologists call 'cultural empathy'—the ability to project one's personality so as to understand problems as they are seen by persons of other cultures. It is the writer's impression that proportionately fewer cases of difficult cultural adjustment are to be found among UN field personnel than among their counterparts in the U.S. Point Four programme. While this impression cannot be supported by statistical evidence, it stands to reason that the multinational composition of UN field staffs should include a greater percentage of individuals closely related by cultural background to the areas where they are assigned than would be true of uninational groups drawn exclusively from a single country (such as the U.S.) whose technological development is in many respects the highest in the world. By the same token, UN field personnel tend to have superior language skills and a larger proportion of their number (than in the case of Point Four) have probably had previous foreign and international experience relevant to technical assistance work. For all these reasons multilateral staff groups tend to 'merge' more easily with the local community.

Even so, there clearly is room for improvement in UN agency selection procedures. Positive recruitment campaigns need to be carried out on a sustained basis, while experimentation with more thorough investigative techniques would be likely to pay rich dividends.

Conditions of Field Service

The morale of staff on field duty is conditioned by a variety of factors. One aspect of the problem was considered in our discussion of privileges and immunities in the preceding chapter. At this point it is proposed to examine other conditions of service that affect morale. Of primary importance is the character of the pay and allowance system for internationally recruited personnel serving on assignments for different agencies and different programmes. A secondary phase of the problem is concerned with the treatment of field staff, with respect to promotion, home leave, and similar matters, in comparison with that accorded to staff at headquarters. Finally, there is the question of pay rates and related benefits for field office staffs recruited locally.

Pay and allowances

The task of developing a compensation structure that will provide equitable treatment for international staff on field assignments involving similar professional skills and responsibilities is an extraordinarily complex one. This complexity derives partly from differences in staff grading standards and salary levels within different agencies, and partly from variations in cost of living at different duty stations.

Although the UN family of agencies has gradually over the years managed to reach agreement on substantially uniform patterns of personnel regulations for regular staff, there are still noticeable discrepancies with respect to position classification and employment tenure. To a certain extent this of course is inevitable. For various categories of highly specialized personnel employed by only one agency (*e.g.*, sanitary engineers and agronomists) the employing agency has to determine for itself, taking account of the 'market,' what salary level to offer. In its technical assistance programme, for example, 'FAO tries to strike a balance between the earning power of a particular expert in his home country and the need to avoid too large discrepancies between the salaries of the various members of a single FAO mission.'[32] In ILO, technical personnel assigned to field posts, whether detailed from headquarters or recruited from the outside, are as a rule started at a higher salary level than the prevalent rate for similar work at headquarters. If and when a regular staff member is transferred back to Geneva, he reverts to his former salary, with any increments he may have earned.

In the case of certain types of field staff, similar specialists are employed by more than one agency (*e.g.*, budget officers, accountants, economists, statisticians, librarians, teachers, physical and social scientists, public administration experts, and the like). In so far as unjustifiable differences in grading standards exist for such personnel, staff morale may be affected adversely. On the other hand, common grading standards should 'materially assist the proper functioning of a common salary system . . . and facilitate the recruitment of staffs drawn from virtually all the nations of the world in many different programmes . . . [and] equally, they will facilitate the placement and transfer of staff from organisation to organisation.'[33]

Recently the second problem mentioned above has been given intensive consideration. Here a fundamental question to be decided is where the geographic base of a common salary system should be located for the purpose of applying cost-of-living differentials. Prior to 1956, New York, as UN headquarters, served as the base. But New York had become such a high-cost area that the consolidation of existing cost-of-living allowances there into new base salary scales would have meant that 'minus' differentials would have had to be applied to most other duty stations. Faced with this dilemma, the Salary Review Committee set up by the UN General Assembly in 1955

[32] Arthur T. Mosher, *Technical Co-operation in Latin-American Agriculture* (Univ. of Chicago Press, Copyright 1957 by the Univ. of Chicago), p. 232.
[33] *Preliminary Report of the International Civil Service Advisory Board on Common Grading Standards*, UN Doc. CO-ORD/CIVIL SERVICE/8, 1958.

decided that there would be some advantage in selecting Geneva as the base for a new scheme of 'post adjustments,' as the Committee called them.

The system then in operation left much to be desired on other counts. Different methods were being used by different agencies to adjust staff pay to variations in living costs at different duty stations. The United Nations, for example, applied differentials for this purpose based on gross salaries and limited them to a fixed ceiling. WHO, on the other hand, applied its differentials to net salaries without any set ceiling. Among other anomalies the status of EPTA personnel differed significantly from that of regular agency staffs in terms of auxiliary benefits received while on field assignments.

The Salary Review Committee, in its report to the 1956 General Assembly, proposed an elaborate set of recommendations intended to reconcile the conditions of service for all field staffs.[34] In approving the Committee's report, the General Assembly urged the specialized agencies to conform as far as possible to the principles adopted for UN personnel.

The basic principles governing the Salary Review Committee's recommendations were (1) that all internationally recruited staff serving on field assignments should be provided with approximately equivalent living standards per staff grade, and (2) that there should be equal treatment of all such staff as regards pensionable salary irrespective of duty station. Accordingly, the Committee proposed the adoption of a schedule of non-pensionable 'post-adjustments' which would be related to the staff member's grade, net salary, and family status. For the determination of the amounts of such adjustments, plus or minus, the cost of living at Geneva in 1956 was taken as the base. The original plan was to place Geneva in class 1, stations with higher living costs being classed as 2, 3, 4, or 5 (up to a maximum of 30 per cent.), and those with lower costs being scaled downward similarly by letter classifications (A, B, C, D, E, etc.). When, however, the General Assembly was persuaded to raise the status of New York from class 4 (as originally intended) to class 5, dissatisfaction at Geneva prompted the World Health Assembly to raise its status to class 2 so far as WHO staff was concerned. This, in turn, led to the shift of

[34] *Op. cit.*

the staffs of the UN and other agencies with offices in Geneva up to the same level. This state of affairs threw the plan slightly out of gear and gave rise to certain technical complications in adjusting the status of other duty stations.

In connection with the proposed post adjustment system, the Salary Review Committee considered whether there should be special allowances for 'hardship' areas but finally decided that any such arrangement would be 'virtually unworkable." Instead, it was suggested that the problem of hardship posts be solved 'by non-salary methods, mainly by an enlightened personnel policy which limits tours of duty involving climatic or similar hardships, and by appropriate modification of rules relating to hours of work, leave, and similar conditions of service.'[35]

Since 1958 the salary and allowance status of all field personnel, including EPTA as well as regular staff, has been virtually the same except for tenure and pension rights. In addition to base salary (as adjusted up or down for cost of living), all field staff are now entitled to (1) an *assignment* allowance (if assigned to a duty station for one but less than five years), which is higher for staff with dependants than for single persons; (2) a *dependency* allowance similarly adjusted; (3) *education* grants (if there are children in school under specified conditions); (4) an *installation* grant (equal to fifteen or to thirty days' subsistence allowance depending on the staff member's family status), provided his assignment to a new duty station is expected to be of one year's duration or more. For project personnel on short-term appointment (*i.e.*, for less than a year) a *daily subsistence* allowance (in lieu of installation grant and assignment allowance) is paid for the duration of the period of service in a given area. The amount of this allowance is set so as to cover a reasonable standard of board and lodging plus such incidental expenses as tips.

With respect to pension rights, only staff on indeterminate or fixed-term appointments totalling at least five years are eligible to participate fully in the Joint Staff Pension Fund, to which the UN and most of the specialized agencies belong. All other staff, including EPTA personnel, on appointments of at least one but less than five years are now entitled to receive on the termination of their employment what is called a 'service

[35] *Ibid.*, p. 26.

benefit,' equivalent to 8 per cent. per annum of the final base salary outside the established country of residence and to 4 per cent. per annum during service within it. As 'associate' participants in the Pension Fund, such persons are also entitled to disability and death benefits (but not to retirement annuities). Social security provisions still vary somewhat from agency to agency: certain of them have group life insurance schemes and others provide various types of medical insurance plans. As indicated earlier, however, medical expenses incurred by project personnel in the field are supposed to be covered by the recipient government—actually under conditions of widely ranging adequacy.

Although it is generally recognized that the new 'co-ordinated' system of pay, allowances, and benefits represents a distinct improvement in terms of ironing out discrepancies and providing more equitable treatment for comparable categories of field personnel, the inauguration of the system provoked considerable complaint from field staff, especially those stationed at centres outside Europe and North America. At a number of duty stations the post adjustment scheme was introduced during a period of rapidly rising prices and the claim was made that the local inter-agency machinery was too cumbersome and not adequately staffed to assess equitably changes in the cost of living affecting staff. Cultural differences in the patterns of expenditure of an international staff make this a tricky operation at best. In certain other areas, with a *minus* post adjustment classification, the new pay system brought about an actual reduction in the total emoluments to which staff were entitled, with a decidedly unfortunate effect on their morale.

The post adjustment scheme, it is feared, may have a bad psychological impact on recruitment. No candidate, observed one experienced personnel officer to the writer, relishes being told that he will have *x* per cent. of his salary deducted, particularly if he comes from a high-cost country where he will have continuing obligations to meet, such as insurance, real estate taxes, and school costs for his children. In at least one organization, the practice now is to give newly appointed experts additional salary increments to compensate for *minus* adjustments. A recent review of salaries and allowances conducted by the Director-General of WHO comments on this problem in the following terms:

> In many cases these [minus areas] are areas which are less attractive, generally speaking, to prospective staff and therefore the most difficult in terms of recruitment. The Organization finds itself in the somewhat anomalous situation of inviting scientific personnel to serve in isolated posts where the amenities of life are restricted, and as an inducement, it offers a reduction in salary from that which would be paid in a more attractive location. Equally, the prospect of a reduction in basic salary on transfer to such a duty area is a severe deterrent to the rotation of staff which is essential to the maintenance of an effective and well-rounded staff.[36]

This state of affairs had led in 1957 to a decision by the Directing Council of the PAHO not to apply minus differentials to PASB staff at its zone offices in Latin America, thus producing a situation in their favour as compared with WHO staff stationed at the same offices. Early in 1959 the WHO Executive Board decided to suspend minus post adjustments for all WHO field staff and also to instruct the Director-General to consult with his colleagues in ACC with a view to their 'definitive elimination.'[37]

A second source of growing dissatisfaction is with the inadequacy of the pensionable portion of the total take-home pay received by internationally recruited staff. The basic salaries of UN and specialized agency personnel in the professional categories have not been increased for several years. During the ensuing period prices have steadily risen nearly everywhere in the world. Instead of facing squarely the problem of basic salary revision, most agency governing bodies have resorted to the expedient of a series of non-pensionable supplementary allowances, apparently on the shaky assumption that the general inflationary trend could be halted—if not reversed. In 1956, however, the General Assembly asked the Secretary-General, in conjunction with the executive heads of the specialized agencies, to review the whole question of 'pensionable remuneration' of staff. A small expert committee, set up for this purpose and working in co-operation with the Joint Staff Pension Board, noted in its report that professional staff subject to overseas assignment had in effect been treated less generously than 'general service' staff (most of whom are locally recruited for duty at one place only), in that the latter had received salary

[36] WHO, O.R.: No. 91, Jan.-Feb. 1959, p. 76.

[37] *Ibid.*, p. 10. Meanwhile, the ICSAB recommended that an expert committee be established by ACC to advise on ways of improving the statistical methodology involved in administering post adjustment schemes. At the time of writing, only a preliminary report of this Committee had been issued (CO-ORD./R.293, 14 April 1959). Among other problems considered in the report is that of how to relate post adjustments to price changes brought about by monetary devaluation.

increases estimated at 15 per cent. in two years, which were 'automatically incorporated in their pensionable remuneration,' whereas the former had not benefited at all in this regard. The committee went on to recommend a uniform increase of 10 per cent. in pensionable remuneration for professioanl staff at all duty stations.[38] The Pension Board, on the other hand, proposed an increase of only 5 per cent. Pending a comprehensive study of the financial situation of the Pension Fund, which everybody advocated, the Board also proposed a supplement amounting to 10 per cent. of the benefits to persons receiving retirement or disability payments.

When these two reports were considered by ACC, its members unanimously supported a 5 per cent. increase in pensionable remuneration but divided on the second proposal of the Pension Board. Those agency heads who opposed this latter proposal did so for fear its adoption might prejudice the results of the comprehensive survey of the Fund. At its 1958 session the General Assembly authorized a 5 per cent. increase in pensionable pay together with a 5 per cent. increase in pension benefits (in lieu of 10), as of the beginning of 1959, pending consideration of a new survey group's recommendations at its 1960 session.[39] By way of stressing the urgency of a general upward revision of basic salaries, the Executive Board of WHO shortly thereafter adopted a resolution requesting the Director-General to pursue this question with ACC in the hope of securing 'a co-ordinated recommendation' from that body.[40] So the matter rested at the time these lines were written.

The foregoing account of recent efforts to arrive at uniform and equitable standards of compensation and related benefits for UN system staff underscores the continuing complexity of the problem—a complexity compounded by the fact that individual agencies in the UN family may, if they wish, still take unilateral decisions on salary matters and staff grading. The present complicated structure of pay and allowances, moreover, adds greatly to the paper-work of recruitment offices. During the year 1958, for instance, some 1,500 different personnel actions were taken by the UN Technical Assistance Recruitment

[38] UN Doc. A/C.5/760, 3 Nov. 1958.
[39] GA Resolution 1310 (XIII), 10 Dec. 1958.
[40] WHO, O.R.: No. 91, Jan.-Feb. 1959.

Services, the majority of which had nothing to do with recruitment but dealt with salary and allowance payments, currency matters, and the like.[41] If it could somehow be contrived, a more simplified compensation system that would make it possible to cite a total *net* figure to applicants might not only facilitate recruitment but give rise to fewer complaints from staff during their tour of duty in the field. As things now stand, it is often not clear to them from agency personnel regulations precisely what they are entitled to and how they should go about getting what is due them in case of dispute.

Other questions affecting staff morale

There are certain other aspects of personnel policy that impinge upon the morale of staff stationed away from headquarters. It is perhaps natural that overseas staffs should be inclined to regard themselves as 'the forgotten children' of their organization. This attitude is quite noticeable with regard to the promotion of career personnel at field offices. At the UN regional commission secretariats, for instance, the writer discovered a fairly widespread feeling among younger professional staff members that they were not receiving fair consideration for promotion at UN headquarters, where all final promotion decisions are made. This feeling was accentuated by the adoption in 1957 of new promotional procedures according to which the Appointment and Promotion Board in New York reviews annually all cases 'across the board,' irrespective of the unit or office to which staff members happen to be assigned.[42] Under the previous arrangement, the Executive Secretary of each regional commission submitted promotional recommendations which were considered separately; under the revised plan such recommendations are lumped into the total staff list (by grade) for evaluation. The Board recommends to the Secretary-General such staff members it considers should be promoted immediately and places on a promotion register other cases, at each grade, deemed to be deserving of early promotion as vacancies arise.

The results of the first across-the-board review were so disappointing to younger economists, especially in ECE and

[41] Information supplied to the writer by courtesy of the Deputy Director of TARS.
[42] Further details are contained in the UN Information Circular (UN Doc. ST/ADM/SER.AO437, 17 Oct. 1957).

ECAFE, as to provoke considerable reaction against the new system. This group, containing a number of very able men, was also said to believe too much stress was being placed on seniority in determining promotions.[43] Senior administrative officers at Geneva and Bangkok observed that the cases of commission staff up for promotion should have more vigorous advocacy at headquarters—that they all too often had 'no friend in court.'

In the writer's opinion, these views probably tend to exaggerate the situation. While it is admittedly true that the UN Promotion Board does not conduct field investigations of its own, this being regarded as 'too time-consuming and expensive,' the Board appears to be aware of the psychological attitudes of overseas staff. It now asks each field office head to evaluate his staff eligible for promotion, with a priority listing. Whenever a field office director happens to be at headquarters he is invited to appear before the Board and discuss his staff priorities. It is also current policy to include in the Board's membership one or two persons with previous field experience. It is reported on reliable authority that the Board, in certain recent cases, deliberately gave a slight edge to field over headquarters staff in recommending promotions. On the other hand, the Board has not deemed it advisable to grant 'extra points' for field service as such. If this were done, it might (1) help to reduce the sense of unfair treatment among field staff, and (2) make field assignments less unattractive to headquarters staff and thus facilitate staff rotation—a special point to which we shall shortly turn.

From all accounts, field promotion procedures in the specialized agencies and TAB appear to have caused less dissatisfaction. At the same time one finds some complaint over the rigid way in which staff and financial regulations are applied to project personnel by headquarters. The conditions governing home leave, for example, allow a greater degree of flexibility for headquarters staff on permanent appointment than for field experts whose continuity of assignment is uncertain. As noted in Chapter 3, moreover, field project staffs keenly resent the lack of a housing allowance in areas where rents are exorbitantly

[43] During 1958, ECE lost three first-rate younger economists (two of them to European regional organizations) partly because of their failure to be promoted.

high. At some centres outlays for rent absorb a disproportionate part of their salaries, in contrast to foreign embassy and U.S. Point Four staffs, and private foundation personnel, many of whom receive allowances sufficient to cover the rent of suitable houses for a family of two or three children. A minor cause of irritation in many areas has been the inadequacy of hospitality grants allowed to the heads of field offices, some of whom find it necessary to dig down into their own pockets to meet the costs of official entertaining even on a modest scale. More numerous are complaints of administrative delays in the payment of salary and allowances and in processing travel arrangements, the reasons for which will be discussed in a subsequent chapter.[44]

Locally recruited staffs of field offices

The bulk of the routine clerical and manual work at field offices is performed by persons recruited from the local area. In addition, at many of the larger offices, bilingual (even trilingual) secretaries and junior accountants are similarly recruited. Since 1949, the basis for establishing salary and wage scales for these staffs has been the best prevailing conditions of employment for comparable jobs in the local area, although, for manual workers, wage rates are in some places governed by local trade-union agreements. As noted earlier in this study, periodic surveys, ordinarily conducted by the principal agency office, are used to determine levels of pay and their adjustment. For such surveys, the better paying foreign embassies and international business firms provide the standard to be approximated.

In most places this system has proved reasonably satisfactory. A number of difficulties, however, have been encountered in applying it. For instance, it is not easy to make exact comparisons between UN and outside jobs (except for secretarial posts); private business firms may use grading patterns differing from those in effect at UN field offices; the compilation of data on the pay scales of private employers is frequently a time-consuming and tedious task; and the best prevailing local pay rates do not always keep in line with rapidly changing prices. Where there has been rampant inflation it has at times been necessary to increase local pay scales almost month by month. At Geneva, a

[44] See pp. 249–252.

non-pensionable cost-of-living allowance of 5 per cent. was added to existing pay rates in 1952 by all organizations but WHO, which, however, revised its pensionable scales so as 'to give an approximately similar result.'[45] More recently, a new survey of outside rates was conducted at Geneva as a basis for a general revision of local salary scales.[46] The Consultative Committee on Administrative Questions of ACC has considered the advisability of substituting for the existing 'best prevailing rates' formula the cost-of-living index used for post adjustments for internationally recruited staff, but it felt on the whole that the present system is preferable.

Local staff on indefinite appointment are eligible to join the UN Pension Fund and they enjoy other benefits appropriate to their 'stationary' employment base, such as children's allowances, social security, and medical benefits. At a few posts, such as Manila, it has been necessary to hire secretaries from outside the area (*e.g.*, from Hong Kong) in order to obtain satisfactory language competence.[47] Such appointees, although receiving the same base pay as other staff in the 'general service' categories at their grade, are paid a 'non resident's' allowance to compensate for expatriation expenses and are entitled to education grants for children and to home leave privileges.

While at most field offices it is not hard to recruit local clerical staff, their ability to handle written English often leaves much to be desired. Once hired, they tend to stay on indefinitely—thanks to the relatively attractive pay scales. On the whole the turnover of local staff is quite low.

At the larger regional offices there are fairly active staff associations, organized on the same pattern as those at agency headquarters. In Asia the leadership for these associations usually comes from westerners in the professional categories—a situation sometimes resented by the Asians. These staff associations are concerned primarily with the improvement of working conditions and staff welfare (*e.g.*, office lighting, cafeteria arrangements, recreational facilities, and housing). At the WHO regional office in New Delhi the staff association (at the time of

[45] *Report of the Salary Review Committee*, *op. cit.*, p. 22.
[46] For an account of the problem of local staff pay adjustments at Paris, see Unesco Doc. 10C/34, Part II, 14 Aug. 1958.
[47] In 1959, at Teheran, the big oil companies were paying bilingual secretaries the equivalent of $200–$300 a month—reportedly quite out of reach of the TAB office pay scale.

the writer's visit in December 1958) had just conducted a survey of housing conditions for the Indian staff.

Not infrequently local staff members in the 'general service' category stand up well in comparison with internationally recruited staff. It is possible for such persons to be proposed for promotion to a junior professional grade. Unless, however, they are willing to accept assignments at other field posts or at headquarters, the UN Promotion Board is not inclined to recommend such promotions. Both budgetary and geographic considerations may be involved. If there were any real prospect of promotion, even on a limited scale and for exceptionally qualified local staff, it would mean a considerable boost in their morale.

Staff Tenure and Rotation

At various points during the preceding discussion of personnel policies pertaining to field staff, reference was made to problems of assignment tenure and rotation. These two problems are inter-related. In the case of project personnel on short-term appointments, for example, the greater the possibility of rotation from one field mission to another, the better the prospect of relatively long periods of duty, thereby providing some of the elements of a career service. From another point of view, the rotation of staff between headquarters and the field, or from one field assignment to another, may serve as an important means of improving understanding and communication, both vertically and laterally, through the organization. Let us now examine (1) agency policies governing the assignment of staff to field offices and (2) trends within field programmes relating to the duration of service for project personnel.

Field office staffs

Agency practices with respect to the appointment of field office staffs tend to set fairly definite limits to the length of service at a given office. These limits vary depending on whether it is a 'hardship' post, whether the staff member takes his family with him to the field, and the operational nature of the assignment. The duration of field office assignments in most agencies ranges from around two to five years, though there are exceptions both below and above these limits.

Virtually all agencies have in recent years given their official blessing to the desirability of achieving as much rotation of staff as possible between headquarters and the field, while in certain agencies rotation from one field office to another is even more stressed.[48] Yet the extent of rotation in practice is markedly less than official policy might imply. The reasons why are made clear below.

In the United Nations, the general rule is to limit the assignment of headquarters staff to the regional economic commission secretariats, the Information Centres, and the TAB field offices to periods of two to four years. Regional appointments (*e.g.*, of Asians to ECAFE) do not come under this rule and are made for longer, sometimes indefinite, periods. According to current UN staff regulations, 'each staff member must be prepared, as a basic duty, to undertake field assignments as required by the needs' of the Organization.[49] In deciding individual cases, however, due consideration is given to such factors as previous field service, compelling personal or family circumstances, and advice from the Health Service. If a man takes dependents with him, the minimum period of assignment is ordinarily two years; if, on the other hand, he has no dependents, or they are not permitted to accompany the staff member, it is usually one year. Among the professional staff of the Department of Economic and Social Affairs there is some tendency to regard assignment to overseas offices (Geneva excepted) as disadvantageous from the career standpoint, such appointments often being viewed as 'life in exile.' Even so, not counting the *World Economic Survey* staff, from 50 to 60 per cent. of the professional personnel of the Department (as of early 1959) had had field experience of some type or other (much of it, however, on temporary field missions).

On the other hand, there was until quite recently comparatively little interchange of staff between headquarters and the regional economic commission secretariats, let alone from one such secretariat to another. The flow, such as it was, tended to be one-way: from New York to Geneva or Bangkok or Santiago. Since 1956, however, administrative officers have been detailed from headquarters for tours of duty with ECLA and ECAFE.

[48] Typical official exhortations for more staff rotation are contained in the *Report of the Salary Review Committee*, *op. cit.*, pp. 13–14; and in GA Resolution 1294 (XII), 5 Dec. 1958.
[49] UN Doc. ST/SGB/114, 14 Nov. 1958.

There has also been a number of transfers from ECE to help strengthen the research staffs of ECAFE, ECLA, and the new African Commission. In the converse sense, a few of ECAFE's younger professional staff reportedly were to be assigned during 1959 to headquarters for two-year periods, after which they would be expected to return—presumably enriched by the experience. All of the regional commission secretariats would welcome more staff interchange but practical difficulties have thus far militated against extensive rotation.

It is now generally agreed that the directors of the UN Information Centres have been allowed to remain too long at a given post—sometimes for as much as five or six years. The desirability of their having more frequent contacts with OPI at headquarters was emphasized as far back as 1955 by a Survey Group set up by the Secretary-General to assess the needs of UN overseas offices. Three years later the Expert Committee on Public Information appointed by the General Assembly strongly advocated a policy of frequent rotation for UNIC directors.[50] This Committee was unfavourably impressed by the fact that almost none of the senior headquarters officers had had any field experience. Partly as a result of such criticisms, OPI inaugurated, during 1956–57, a series of two-way transfers between headquarters and the field centres as a policy designed not only to prevent its field staffs from going stale on the job, but to give its central press and radio personnel an opportunity to become intimately acquainted with information problems 'at the grass roots.'

In WHO, tours of duty for administrative and professional staff at regional offices average three to four years. This average covers the so-called 'regional advisers' assigned to such offices on fixed-term contracts. Health and morale problems are taken into account in deciding whether the initial terms of regional office personnel should be extended. Many of the technical staff are in fact on loan from national health services for limited periods. If already on permanent contract, area representatives are usually assigned for indefinite periods. Reluctance of WHO's central staff to accept field assignments reportedly is dying out although some of the 'old hands' still find Geneva 'too comfortable' a place to live in to want to leave it. Some of

[50] UN Doc. A/3928, 20 Sept. 1958.

the headquarters professionals are said to regard themselves as 'superior' to their counterparts at field offices, many of whom hold lower grades. Although WHO staff regulations now make all regular staff subject to assignment anywhere, it has been found to be disruptive of morale to force an individual to accept field duty against his will. Nevertheless, according to information supplied by the WHO Personnel Division, nearly 40 per cent. of the professional staffs at headquarters (as of October 1958) had had some kind of field experience with the organization.[51]

The interchange of technical personnel among WHO regional offices has been vigorously encouraged during recent years but with only modest success. Apart from language and cultural factors, as Berkov has noted, it has not been easy to persuade able specialists to shift their base to another region on account of health or family considerations.[52] Further, the decentralized system of regional appointments, which in effect gives a regional director the right to veto a candidate from another region when proposed by headquarters, does not always facilitate inter-regional transfers.

As regards supervisory administrative and financial staff for regional offices, WHO inaugurated some years ago a somewhat unique rotational scheme. The increase in field programme activities, and the consequent enlargement of regional office work-loads, led to the view that the organization should develop a well-trained administrative 'cadre' immediately available for service at regional offices as needed. In order to permit an uninterrupted rotational movement, 'floater' posts were established at headquarters for administrative, budget, personnel, and supply officers.[53] Assignment at a given regional office is limited to four to six years for such officers, following which they normally are sent back to Geneva for 'refresher' experience. This system involves periodic shifts of administrative personnel from one regional office to another. During pressure periods, or during absence of administrative officers on home leave, temporary assistance can be provided by drawing upon experienced rotational staff from headquarters. This is believed to be a

[51] This percentage is exclusive of the group previously called 'Central Technical Services,' the staff of which has functions which differ considerably from those related to field programmes.
[52] *The World Health Organization* . . ., *op. cit.*, pp. 122–25.
[53] WHO, O.R.: No. 81, Dec. 1957, p. 63.

more economical arrangement than increasing the permanent establishments of the administrative and financial units of the regional offices. Speaking before the 1958 World Health Assembly, the Assistant Director-General in charge of administration was able to report that 'the small beginnings of rotating staff among different offices of the Organization have proved their worth and it is the Director-General's belief that this policy should be energetically pursued.'[54]

FAO and ILO policies relating to the assignment of professional staff to field offices appear to be less well-formulated than in the case of WHO. Since their field office staffs are much smaller, the potential dimensions of inter-office rotation are decidedly narrower than in the Health Organization. In FAO, there is an increasing degree of transfer of staff between headquarters and the field, and occasional transfers between regions (*e.g.*, of statistical officers) take place. FAO has developed the system of 'outposting' technical personnel from its substantive divisions at headquarters for tours of duty with regional offices. On the termination of such an assignment, the outposted officer usually returns to Rome for a considerable period.

In ILO, headquarters staff are ordinarily assigned to field offices for periods of three to five years. Personnel recruited from the outside for field office posts frequently serve as much as five years before being moved—or terminated if on fixed-term contracts. It is believed that several years' service is desirable for maximum usefulness in terms of human relations and knowledge of the region. As far as possible, ILO attempts to rotate staff between field offices, with intervals at Geneva. As of late 1958, slightly over 10 per cent. of ILO's upper administrative and professional staff on duty at headquarters had held field assignments.

In ICAO, there is no established policy governing the tenure of assignments of headquarters staff to regional offices. The Paris office, for example, has had the same director ever since its establishment, while at Cairo the first director stayed for ten years. During the earlier period of ICAO the staffs of its regional offices tended to remain stable. More recently, some shifts have taken place, the ICAO Council having declared in favour of more rotation a few years ago. One or two deputy

[54] WHO, O.R.: No. 87, Dec. 1958, p. 287.

directors have been promoted to the post of director at other offices. But most inter-office staff transfers appear to have been accidental rather than the result of any set policy. It takes a long time for aviation specialists to learn the regional peculiarities affecting ICAO's air navigation plans.

As for Unesco's field science co-operation offices, suffice it to say that, as in ICAO, there has been no consistent assignment or rotational policy. A director of the New Delhi office, who joined Unesco in 1949, had been moved from Shanghai to Manila to Djakarta, and from 1954 to 1959 was posted at New Delhi; then he was transferred to headquarters. No other case parallels this one. At Montevideo, a Spaniard was office director from 1949 until 1955, when he was succeeded by a Chilean, recruited from outside the organization, who served until 1959. The chiefs of mission who supervise Unesco's field programme operations in various countries have, with few exceptions, fixed-term contracts (of one to two years) since they are on project assignments. Occasionally, however, permanent headquarters officers are appointed chiefs of mission. Only a few chiefs of mission, as already noted, actually have offices of their own. Many of them actually serve in the same country as long as four or five years.

Finally, a word about UNICEF. Here again, lip service is officially paid to field rotation as a goal; but, as in the other agencies, not nearly as much has occurred as the headquarters high command would like. It is not uncommon for UNICEF field operators, whether stationed at area or country offices, to remain for seven or eight years at the same place. Many staff members have not changed location since 1950, with the consequence, according to one experienced headquarters official, that there is considerable 'beefing,' and some of the older men reportedly are going stale on their jobs. But, added this informant half-seriously, why shift them to other locations where the climate is just as bad? A good number of the younger staff look upon UNICEF as a career and apparently do not mind protracted spells of duty within a given area. Even so, a sustained effort is now being made to circulate more personnel among country and area duty stations. At best, however, the amount of rotation will probably not be great because of the language problem, the necessity of recruiting westerners for assignments in non-western areas, and the need of persons with extended experience in specific areas.

To summarize: it seems clear that for a variety of operational considerations there are definite limits beyond which the rotation of field office staffs, however desirable in principle, is not likely to extend. This generalization applies more or less to all UN organizations with field office structures. At the same time, the potentialities of staff rotation are now beginning to be recognized and there is a discernible trend in this direction.

Field project personnel

When it comes to determining appropriate terms of appointment for personnel assigned to field projects, the problem is much more complicated than for field office staffs. For one thing, as we have already seen, there is a multiplicity of field programmes financed from different sources and including an almost infinite variety of projects—country, regional and inter-regional; advisory, demonstrational, training, and quasi-operational; of fixed (short) terms and of indefinite duration. Secondly, the duration of many of the larger projects cannot be estimated initially with any certainty. In the third place, and most importantly, the hazards of annual voluntary financing under which EPTA is obliged to operate have made it exceedingly difficult to offer experts contracts of more than one year irrespective of the probable length of the project concerned. Within the UN family only WHO, as a matter of policy, offers two-year contracts initially.

Under existing staff regulations, regular staff of the UN, as well as most of the functional agencies, may be detailed, or seconded, to field projects under any programme for short terms of less than one year, or on intermediate-term status of one but less than five years, or on what is called long-term status for five years or more. In principle, these rules are also applicable to experts recruited for and paid by EPTA. In practice, however, comparatively few initial project appointments (except in WHO) extend beyond one year; indeed, a substantial number are for periods of a few months only.

There is general recognition that such a restrictive appointments policy has had two unfortunate effects. On the one hand, it has acted as an obstacle to the attraction and retention of suitably qualified experts in certain subject-matter fields; on the other, it has frequently made it difficult, if not impossible, to plan field projects intelligently. Except for very narrow-gauged advisory or survey types of undertakings, it is seldom realistic to gear projects rigidly to fixed monthly or annual calendars in advance; the time required to bring projects to full fruition may actually vary from a few weeks or months to several years.[55] Because of delays in the arrival of experts or in the procurement of supplies, or both, or other local operational difficulties, adjustments in the time-span of existing projects are often necessary.

What actually happens in the case of many projects is that the short-term contracts of on-the-job experts are if possible renewed, or new experts have to be engaged, or both. In proportion as new personnel is introduced into a going project, at frequent intervals, lost motion and lack of continuity in project direction may result. To be sure, the infusion of some fresh blood into a project team may be desirable but unless substantial overlap in the membership of a project mission can be assured the chances of successful implementation may be prejudiced or, at best, unduly delayed. This point is relevant to one-man projects as well—all the more because few foreign experts are able to orientate themselves effectively in the local cultural, political or administrative environment short of several weeks or even months, particularly if they have had no previous trans-cultural experience.

A computation made by the TAB secretariat showed that 40 per cent. of EPTA experts in thirty-eight countries at the end of a typical year (1957) had served for less than twelve months, 30 per cent. for one to two years, 16 per cent. for two to three years, and 14 per cent. for over three years.[56] A not inconsiderable number had been on duty for as long as four, five, or even six years.

In the case of Unesco, to cite the experience of a major specialized agency, the trend towards periods of field service beyond one year is even more pronounced. Of a total of 246 experts in the field at the beginning of 1959, including not only EPTA personnel but also experts serving Unesco's major

[55] As will be explained more fully in Chap. 9, TAC, in 1959, authorized the planning of EPTA projects on a two-year basis—as an 'experiment.'
[56] *Annual Report of the TAB for 1957, op. cit.*, p. 80.

project and participation programmes, only 7 per cent. were on short-term assignments of less than one year, 27 per cent. had served one year (subject to renewal), 53 per cent. had been on duty two to five years, while as many as 13 per cent. had more than five years' continuous service in the field.[57] With few exceptions, it has been Unesco's practice not to offer initial appointments for more than one year, though it intends in the future to make as many two-year appointments as possible to experts financed from its regular budget.

In WHO, initial contracts for field project staff both on regular budget and EPTA funds are, in most cases, limited to two years, extendable for two years more. Since 1957, however, WHO's policy has been moving towards the granting of career service status up to 75 per cent. of the established posts in the organization. In line with this policy a considerable number of project staff have been given five-year contracts and a few accorded permanent career status.

Since none of the other specialized agencies has extensive operational programmes financed from regular budget funds, most of their field experts are governed by EPTA appointment conditions. This means, as already noted, that few initial contracts of more than a year or two can be offered. Even so, the actual distribution of experts by periods of continuous service—in FAO, ILO, and ICAO, for example—roughly parallels the distribution for EPTA field personnel as a whole.

On questioning recipient governments in 1957–58, the RTARs found that there was a strong preference on their part for the initial appointment of experts for a minimum of two years for most assignments, while for projects of a long-term nature, such as a comprehensive natural resources survey or a training institute, assignments of three, four, or even five years were considered desirable. In this connection, there seemed to be some relation between the stage of economic development a recipient country had reached (including the availability of local counterparts) and the length of experts' assignments.[58]

Whether this be so or not, there is evidence to indicate that the tenure uncertainties of field service have had a disturbing

[57] Information supplied to the author by courtesy of Unesco's Personnel Division.

[58] *Annual Report of the TAB for 1957*, *op. cit.*, pp. 79–80. In passing, it should be noted that agencies recruiting experts for Special Fund projects will be able to offer appointments for the duration of the project, which could be for as long as three to five years.

effect on the morale of able experts on the job. All too often they are left in doubt until near the end of their appointments whether their contracts are to be renewed. Legally, separation must be assumed in the absence of any official notice to renew. Whether because the government cannot make up its mind or because of bureaucratic slowness in completing the country programming process, the decision to request the expert to remain another year may, and sometimes does, reach him after he has arranged to sell (or transport to his home base) household effects and motor-car, or, what may be even more serious, after he has made definite plans to resume his former employment or accept a new position.

One expert (then in his sixth year of service) recounted to the writer how he had sold his refrigerator and other appliances, at a financial loss, wound up his personal and family affairs, and returned home three times (without home leave privileges). At one stage he had actually gone to agency headquarters for 'debriefing' and the preparation of his final report; after a month's trip came an urgent appeal to resume his field post; at considerable personal inconvenience he did so because he was challenged by the job. Another expert, from a different agency, had had his first annual contract extended for six months, following which he was repatriated to the United States—only to be offered a longer-term contract if he would return once again to the project he had helped to organize; and he, too, went back. Several other examples of this type of situation came to the writer's attention.

In some instances, of course, experienced field experts are lost in the shuffle simply because they cannot arrange at the eleventh hour to stay on—or to return later. At best, such uncertainties tend to reduce the interest and enthusiasm of able field staff—a state of mind they doubtless convey to colleagues back home who may at some time be offered similar posts with some UN field programme; at worst, when tenure is disrupted completely, the situation is wasteful of time and money to the employing agency and detrimental to the progressive development of the project concerned. As one experienced chief of mission thoughtfully observed, the expert is asked to take all the risks while the organization takes none. In his view, an expert should never be left in doubt about his contractual status less than one month ahead, preferably two months. If renewal is granted in the light of the best available information, and the post subsequently is abolished (which would rarely happen), the organization should be able to take care of the expert's salary for a limited period by drawing upon savings made in some other project.

During recent years there has been much discussion in EPTA circles concerning the feasibility of establishing a small career nuclear staff as a basis for recruiting better-qualified experts and of rotating them from one field area to another and, to some extent, to and from headquarters. In 1956, TAB took a cautious step in this direction. It was then agreed that the agencies participating in EPTA might at their option grant to carefully chosen, well-qualified experts, for whom there was likely to be a continuing need, a new type of contract called a 'programme appointment,' which would provide security of tenure for the duration of EPTA itself. The number of such appointments was limited at the outset to 5 per cent. of the experts then on the payroll of the organization.

By the end of 1957, between thirty and forty programme appointments in all had been made by four agencies: FAO, TAA, Unesco, and ICAO. A fifth agency reported it was considering the grant of regular career status to selected experts. One other agency, however, stated that it preferred not to change its practice of making fixed-term appointments only. In connection with what may appear at first glance to be a very timid policy as regards programme appointments, three points should be kept in mind: (1) a large number of experts, for reasons explained earlier, are simply not interested in making a professional career in technical assistance work; (2) other experts that might be so motivated do not relish the prospect of having to move their children from one overseas area to another because of school problems; and (3) for highly specialized personnel the possibility of finding a succession of project assignments for which they would be suitable is at best limited. Among the subject-matter fields with which the UN itself is concerned, for example, career appointments are said to be feasible for economics, public administration, and social welfare, but seldom for the engineering profession. On the whole, such major specialized agencies as ILO, FAO, and Unesco are probably the best situated to handle hiatuses between field projects—by utilizing project personnel on short-term assignments at headquarters, either in their substantive divisions or in the overhead administration of field programmes. Such a policy is already being applied as regards experts on fixed-term contracts.

For an effective implementation of the new programme appointment policy, the most rigorous scrutiny of the qualifications, performance, and personality traits of eligible experts clearly will be necessary. The point has been made by certain observers that the criteria of selection to date may not always have been as objective as one would hope. As an experienced TAB Resident Representative remarked to the writer, special precaution will need to be taken against granting indefinite appointment status to the type of expert who becomes enamoured of a 'cosy situation' and manœuvres adroitly to have his project continued year after year. Such 'characters,' in the view of one agency personnel officer, sometimes tend to become too intimately identified with the viewpoint of the counterpart officials with whom they find 'fraternization' pleasant.

All things considered, however, a good case can be made for increasing the proportion of fixed-term contracts covering periods of two to three years. As noted above, some of the most successful experts have actually served this long (or even longer) on the basis of the successive renewal of annual contracts. Here again, the risk to the employing agency would appear to be minimal since the number of cases where the post in question would not be continued, or another assignment could not be found elsewhere, are likely to be very few indeed. Any indemnities payable in the event of termination of appointment prior to the expiration of the expert's contract might be appropriately regarded as a legitimate charge on the over-all programme in view of the dividends in better recruitment and staff morale to be anticipated therefrom.

In this context, it is highly doubtful whether the potentialities of rotating competent field staff from one project to another have as yet been fully tapped. Where this has been done (*e.g.*, by moving an expert from a fundamental education centre or a public administration institute in one area to a similar undertaking in another) the utilization of accumulated experience has contributed significantly to the development of the second project.

It is only fair to say that most of the agencies are now making a special effort to encourage the rotation of project staff between countries; in a limited number of instances this has involved the transfer of experts from one agency to another.

A related aspect of this problem is the desirability of providing project experience to a larger number of permanent headquarters staff than is now the case. In certain agencies, a distressingly large number of persons responsible for 'back-stopping' functions at headquarters have had little or no project experience and their understanding of the working conditions of project personnel thus often lacks reality. A realistic undertaking can seldom be gained from short, hurried visits to field missions. Conversely, it would appear particularly useful for country chiefs of missions and project team leaders to have had previous experience at agency headquarters as far as practicable. Nor should a permanent staff member at headquarters be obliged to go on 'secondment' to EPTA without full assurance that his future employment status will in no way be prejudiced thereby.[59] It should be made clear that he may return to headquarters after a reasonable period on field duty, whenever a suitable vacancy occurs. In some agencies, project assignments of headquarters staff tend to be made chiefly in connection with some necessary reduction of established posts, transfers to the field seeming to be the only way for the organization to retain the services of experienced personnel. Such a policy scarcely enhances the prestige value of field employment.

SELECTED FIELD PERSONNEL PROFILES

In concluding this chapter, it is proposed to present the findings of an analysis of biographical data relating to four samples of senior field officials with a view to illustrating concretely types of educational and professional backgrounds, kinds and range of experience in trans-cultural situations, and the extent to which *de facto* careers may be emerging in international field service.

[59] According to the *TAB Manual of Personnel Policies and Procedures*, *op. cit.* (Article 101), 'Regular staff members of participating organizations shall, on being detailed, seconded or transferred to posts paid from the Special Account, retain such rights and benefits as shall be determined by that organization.' This provision obviously leaves a loophole through which an organization may, if it is so disposed, guarantee something less than full 'rights and benefits' to such staff members. It should be noted that WHO has a policy of staff rotation involving projects, regional offices, and headquarters.

The four samples include (1) FAO regional directors and deputy-directors; (2) ILO 'field' office directors; (3) UNICEF regional, area, and country office heads; and (4) TAB Resident Representatives.[60] Even though the time periods and samples covered are too limited for firm statistical inferences, some indication of significant trends may perhaps be gained from the analysis that follows. In presenting the results, we shall proceed from the two smallest samples (FAO and ILO) to the intermediate-sized group (UNICEF), and finally, to the largest sample (the RTARs).

FAO regional office directors

Here our sample consists of the nine individuals who, by the end of 1958, had held, or were currently holding, assignments as director or deputy director of FAO's six regional offices.[61] The age at which they were appointed to these posts ranged from forty to sixty-one, the average being about fifty years. Five of the nine men had had previous experience at FAO headquarters ranging from six months to ten years; eight had served in national ministries of agriculture in various capacities (including that of minister in two cases); one had spent many years in rural reconstruction work in the Far East; one had been engaged in overseas forestry activities in his government's colonial service as well as privately; while another had served for two years with the U.S. Institute of Inter-American Affairs and a year on an UNRRA field mission. Seven of the nine had had advanced training in some branch of agricultural science; one was primarily an agricultural economist; and the ninth had been an editor and writer with extended service as the senior public information officer in the U.S. Department of Agriculture. Six of the nine had had substantial previous experience in some kind of trans-cultural situation. The total number of years of prior service per person on assignments relevant to FAO's work ranged from seven to twenty-one years, the average being sixteen years. As of the end of 1958, these nine men had served as FAO regional directors (or deputy directors) for periods of one to ten years, with an average of three and one-half years. None,

[60] The author is indebted to the headquarters personnel units of FAO, ILO, and UNICEF, and the TAB secretariat, for assembling the factual information on which the analyses presented in the following pages are based.

[61] Deputy directors, as noted earlier, head what are known in FAO terminology as 'zone' offices.

however, had been transferred from one regional office to another. In the group were three Americans, two Egyptians, one Frenchman, one Burmese, one Mexican, and one Costa Rican, the three Latin nationals having been stationed at Latin American offices.

From this analysis it is clear that the primary requirement in the selection of men for these key field posts was that they should have had extensive professional experience relevant to FAO's tasks. In two instances political considerations probably were also given some weight. As a new specialized agency in its field, FAO was not able to draw upon any predecessor organization for senior staff, such as was done by the UN, or in a somewhat different sense by ILO's utilization of some of its own experienced headquarters personnel. While it is too soon to tell whether FAO's field office directorships will tend eventually to fall within recognized career avenues, by selection primarily from inside the organization and frequent interchange between headquarters and the field, there are signs that organization policy will evolve in this direction.[62]

ILO field office directors

The ILO sample includes twelve persons who, as of the end of 1958, had served, or were serving, as directors of ILO's four field offices at São Paulo-Rio-Lima, Istanbul, Bangalore, and Mexico City.[63] In age range at the time of first appointment as field office director, this group was somewhat younger than its FAO counterpart, the range being from thirty to fifty-one, with forty-two years as the average. Three-fourths of the group had had previous experience at ILO headquarters in fairly senior posts, ranging from one to eighteen years. Two others had been exposed to foreign environments from two to four years, while only one had neither ILO nor other trans-cultural experience. The aggregate period served in international settings varied from none to twenty-two years, the average being six years. The formal educational backgrounds of the group varied widely: all had the bachelor's degree or equivalent, while half held higher degrees. Major fields of training included law, economics, business administration, agriculture, mathematics, and the classics. Only four persons had served prior to their

[62] Towards the close of 1958 it was announced that one FAO regional director was to be transferred to Rome to head up FAO's central public information division.

[63] The location of one field office was moved successively from São Paulo to Rio to Lima.

appointment to ILO in national labour ministries; among the rest were practising attorneys, professors, an aircraft designer, and a chief of the Manpower Division at SCAP during the Allied occupation of Japan. In the group there were four Americans, three Frenchmen, and one each of the following nationalities: British, Swiss, Canadian, Brazilian, and Bolivian.

Distinctly more rotation of assignment characterizes the ILO than the FAO sample. The average period of field office service was only two years, the range being from six months to four years. At one office there had been four successive directors; at two others, three directors; and at the fourth, two directors. On the other hand, three of the twelve men had been transferred from one office to another, while three returned to ILO headquarters at the expiration of their field assignments.[64] By way of generalization, it may be said that the post of ILO field office director is coming to be viewed increasingly as a step in the career ladder for professional staff on permanent status, though appointment to this post will doubtless continue to be made from outside the organization in some instances.

UNICEF field office directors

The UNICEF sample was composed of twenty-two persons (two of them being women) who, at the middle of 1958, were on assignment as regional, area, and country office heads.[65] Their ages at the time of first appointment to a UNICEF field post averaged forty, the range extending from thirty-two to fifty-five years—slightly younger than either the FAO or ILO group. Only one of them had had previous experience at UNICEF headquarters, all of the rest being recruited from the outside. Four, however, had served on UNRRA field missions for substantial periods (including one person with some IRO experience as well); two others were drawn from WHO's field staff, thus making six persons in all with prior international field service. Educationally, the UNICEF sample spans a wide diversity of subject-matter fields, sociology and social work accounting for about a third of the cases, with law and medicine

[64] Early in 1959 another field office director was shifted from Istanbul to the newly established African office at Lagos (Nigeria), while the post at Istanbul was assigned to the *chef de cabinet* of the ILO Director-General.

[65] In addition, UNICEF maintains a number of small liaison offices, handled for the most part by non-UNICEF personnel, and a few special overseas offices for supply or other purposes—none of which is included in the sample.

next in order. At least four of the group appear from the available data not to have gone beyond the secondary school; a few others reported 'certificates' or 'diplomas' that are difficult to evaluate; the rest were all holders of bachelor's or higher degrees, including four with doctor's degrees. Prior to joining UNICEF their principal professional experience was distributed as follows: social service and relief activities, 17; public health, 3; and one each in national diplomatic and colonial service.

Of the twenty-two cases, as many as sixteen had had previous experience in some kind of trans-cultural situation ranging from one to twenty-one years, the average being six years. Overseas assignments with the Red Cross accounted for the three longest periods of such experience, the next in order being with the Friends Service Committee. It is interesting to note that most of this cross-cultural experience (aside from prior international organization work) was with voluntary (non-governmental) agencies. The group included persons of eleven different nationalities: American, 5; Swiss, 4; British, 3; Indian, 3; and one each of Canadian, Belgian, French, Swedish, Dutch, Danish, and Colombian nationality.

The aggregate length of their field assignments with UNICEF extended from one to eleven years, the average being about seven. This was substantially longer than was the case with their FAO or ILO colleagues. Moreover, fifteen of the twenty-two persons had been rotated, often by promotion, from one field office to another, seven having served at two offices, five at three different offices, two at four offices, and one at as many as five offices. On the other hand, there were seven cases of continuous service of six to nine years at the same office—3 in Asia, 2 in Africa, and 2 in Latin America.

These statistics on tenure of service support the point made earlier with respect to UNICEF field staffs in general, namely, that there is a pronounced tendency in UNICEF for its professional and administrative personnel to regard overseas service as a career, *de facto*, if not in a formal sense. Resignations of field directors have been comparatively rare and the general policy is to retain them as long as they wish to stay with the organization. The strong sense of dedication to UNICEF's humanitarian goals that characterizes most of the group has played a not unimportant part in encouraging longevity of service.

Resident technical assistance representatives

The position of the RTARs in the overseas framework of the UN system, as has already been noted, differs from that of the foregoing categories of field officials in that the former represent not a single organization but a programme in which the UN, seven specialized agencies, and now the IAEA, participate. The evolving functional role of the RTAR will be described in detail in a later chapter.[66] It is enough to say here that the task of recruiting for the post of RTAR has in some ways been a more difficult one than for field office directorships of the functional agencies. This is because a successful RTAR must not only have an intelligent layman's understanding of the major subject-matter specialities involved in EPTA, but in addition must possess qualities of diplomacy, tact, and judgment if he is to become an effective field 'co-ordinator' of a country programme as a whole. Further, he must be able to create a favourable local climate for UN technical assistance, and in order to win the respect and co-operation of widely diversified groups of agency experts he should have a distinct edge over them in terms of general knowledge of the recipient country (or region), its political and administrative institutions, and its development problems and needs. This is a large order.

Accordingly, TAB and its Executive Chairman have had to cast their net widely in order to find individuals that reasonably measure up to the exacting requirements of so unique a position. The recruitment process has necessarily involved a good deal of trial-and-error. For the fifty-four persons who, by the end of 1958, had held or were then holding, assignments as RTARs, the average age at initial appointment was forty-eight, the youngest being thirty-two and the oldest in their middle-sixties.[67] In terms of major professional identification, the group was drawn from the ranks of civil servants, international, national, and local; the university world; private business and banking; law, journalism, and engineering—roughly in descending order of frequency.[68] From the standpoint of formal education, the members of the group were distributed as follows:

[66] See pp. 376–379.

[67] This sample does not include persons who held assignments as 'acting,' assistant, or deputy representatives, or as 'liaison' officers or 'correspondents,' and were not advanced to the post of Resident Representative during the period covered.

[68] There were also a few cases where the principal professional experience had been in national politics, the judiciary, or the military.

bachelor's degree or equivalent	6
master's degree or equivalent	27
doctor's degree	10
law degree (LL.B.)	5
professional 'diploma'	3
military academy	1
no university degree or diploma	2

It will be noted that three-fourths of the total had had professional training beyond the bachelor's degree.

The group included persons of twenty-two different nationalities, approximately three-fourths of whom came from the economically advanced countries and the rest from the less developed nations. In the former category were 12 of American nationality, 8 British, 5 French, 4 Canadian, 4 Swedish, 2 Belgian, and one each of Dutch, Swiss Norwegian, Australian, and New Zealand nationality. The latter category included 3 Venezuelans, 2 Ecuadorians, and one Pole, Yugoslav, Chilean, Mexican, Indian, Pakistani, Iranian, Egyptian, and Filipino. For the most part the RTARs from the less developed countries were appointed more recently than the others.

About two-thirds of the total sample had had previous experience with international organizations, while four persons had held overseas assignments with voluntary agencies. In all, forty-six of the fifty-four had had trans-cultural service of some kind or other, as shown below:

Type of Employment	*Number of Cases*	*Length of Service in Years*	
		Range	*Average*
National government service:			
diplomatic	7	1 to 30	11
colonial	7	9 to 27	18
overseas economic	9	1 to 8	4
Voluntary agencies (overseas) ..	4	2 to 12	7
International organizations ..	34	1 to 34	7

Certain individuals who were employed in two or more of the above categories are listed more than once in the table. The aggregate number of years of trans-cultural experience of all kinds averaged eleven years for the forty-six individuals concerned.

A breakdown of the cases with international organization experience shows that there were as many as fourteen persons who had served on the staffs of organizations pre-dating the UN system: 3 with the League of Nations, 5 with the pre-war ILO, 9 with UNRRA, and 3 with minor agencies, four of this group having been employed by two or more organizations. Two of the ex-Leaguers were veterans of sixteen and twenty-five years' experience, respectively. Eleven of the fourteen persons in the pre-UN category subsequently accepted positions with the UN or a specialized agency where they were working at the time of appointment as RTAR.

For the total of thirty-one persons who had had service with the UN family of agencies prior to their appointment as RTARs, the distribution of employment by organizational units was as follows:

Organizational Unit	*Number of Cases*
TAB headquarters secretariat	7
UN Technical Assistance Administration (headquarters or field) ..	4
Regional economic commission secretariats	3
UN Department of Economic and Social Affairs (headquarters) ..	3
Office of Public Information	2
UN Department of Trusteeship and Non-Self-Governing Territories	2
Food and Agriculture Organization	4
Unesco	3
International Labour Organisation	3
Miscellaneous UN field missions	8

Here, again, there were a number of persons who had had assignments with more than one agency or unit. During the earlier years of TAB's operations, a considerable number of the RTARs were 'seconded' from specialized agencies, most of them later being transferred to TAB.

It has been TAB's policy normally to limit the initial appointments of its RTARs to one or two years. During the earlier years of EPTA, this policy was dictated partly by the experimental nature of the programme and partly by the uncertainties of the voluntary annual pledging system. Nor would it then have been easy to persuade many men to take on such appointments for longer periods. Even though the programme has now become a well-established operation, with good prospects of indefinite continuance, the practice of offering short-term contracts still holds in most instances.

Even so, almost half of the RTARs appointed to the end of

1958 had served for more than two years, as indicated below, by renewal of their appointments.[69]

Total Period of Service	*Number of RTARs*
one year or less	10
two years	18
three years	6
four years	7
five years	6
six years	8

In most of the cases of service beyond two years, inter-country transfers were involved. Thus, eleven RTARs had been stationed in two countries (or regions) while six others had had assignments in as many as three. There were only five instances of as long as four years in the same area, the optimum assignment at any one place being considered to be about three years. In eight cases, persons originally appointed as 'liaison' officers for countries with small programmes, or as assistant or deputy or 'acting' representatives in areas with large programmes, were promoted to full-fledged RTARs either at the same field office or by transfer to another.

After termination of their tours of field duty, four of the most experienced RTARs received senior assignments at UN headquarters, one as Director of the Bureau of Economic Affairs; one as Special Assistant to the Executive Chairman of TAB, then as Director of the Programme Division of TAA, and still later as Director of the Bureau of Operations of the Special Fund; and two as Directors in the Department of Trusteeship and Non-Self-Governing Territories (one of whom subsequently joined the secretariat of the newly created International Atomic Energy Agency). In one case, a man was moved from UN headquarters to the field as TAB Regional Representative and then served two years in the TAA Programme Division, after which he was sent out to the field on a second assignment.

What general observations are suggested by this detailed comparison of the case histories of fifty-four RTARs? First, as EPTA has developed, there would appear to have been a steady progression towards a quasi-career concept with respect

[69] The trend towards longer periods of service was actually greater than these figures would imply for two reasons: (1) the establishment of RTAR posts had been gradual over the years, the number, for example, having increased from only 16 in 1952 to 33 in 1958; and (2) a good many of the RTARs on duty at the end of 1958 will undoubtedly serve for additional periods.

to this key field post. Second, there is little doubt that its drawing power is substantially greater now than it was, say, five or six years ago. It is the writer's distinct impression, based on private discussions with some twenty RTARs, that the challenge of the job tends to grow with length of service. Third, the unique experience gained therefrom has been such as to enrich the equipment of many of the occupants of the post for top-level administrative assignments in international civil service generally. This is not to assume, of course, that every RTAR has been an outstanding success; on the contrary, an appreciable number are recognized as having failed to cope effectively with the frustrations inherent in a situation where authority is not commensurate with responsibility. On the whole, however, the batting average has been high. As we shall see later, much of the improvement in technical assistance programming and administration during recent years may be attributed to the persuasiveness, ingenuity, and innovating abilities of the better Resident Representatives.

PART TWO

HEADQUARTERS-FIELD RELATIONSHIPS

6

FIELD DELEGATION AND CENTRAL CONTROL

In Part I of this study our chief concern was to describe the development of field machinery and field staffing arrangements in response to the expansion of operational activities which, in varying degree, has characterized the UN family of agencies over the past decade or so. The resultant interlocking network of field offices, as we have seen, serves generally as an instrument for the spatial projection of headquarters authority with a view to facilitating the implementation of centrally established policies and programmes; in part, also, notably in the case of the UN regional economic commissions, WHO, and TAB, it has been intended to decentralize—or at least deconcentrate—field programme-making and co-ordination. We come now, in Part II, to a consideration of the procedures that govern headquarters-field relations within this general framework. On the one hand, administrative procedures are necessary to define the conditions and forms of field delegation, both substantively and operationally; and on the other, to prescribe the type and extent of central control exercised over delegated functions. In a still broader sense, the working relationships of central and field staffs involve a variety of communication and logistical devices—briefing, back-stopping services, reporting, supervision, inspection, interchange of experience, and the like—which we shall examine in the next chapter. The programme process as a whole will be analysed and evaluated in Part III of our study.

Conditions and Forms of Delegation to Field Units

WHO's regional committees and regional offices

As noted earlier, the delegation of functions to field units may take one or more forms in the same agency or programme. Thus, for example, the functions of WHO's regional committees and regional offices are broadly indicated in its Constitution. The concrete application of these Constitutional provisions, however, has required 'legislative' action—by the Executive

Board and the World Health Assembly—as well as the issuance of administrative and budgetary directives by the Director-General on his own initiative. For a full understanding of the working of WHO's regionally decentralized system it is necessary to examine all three of these inter-related methods of implementing territorial devolution.

The annual reports of the Director-General of WHO frequently contain enumerations of functions that constitute the exclusive prerogative of headquarters; of those for which Geneva and the regional offices share responsibility; and of those which are handled primarily in the regions. Similarly, and in fuller detail, the annual budget document delineates the functions of regional offices in connection with the allocation of funds to regional programmes and field operational expenses.[1] The WHO Executive Board has from time to time conducted studies on 'regionalization' which set forth its rationale in a more systematic manner, including composite statements of the respective functions of regional office directors and area representatives and descriptions of the typical set-up of regional offices.[2] Notwithstanding, some confusion still exists 'regarding the relative responsibilities of headquarters and the regions.'[3] Each regional office, moreover, has been allowed to develop pragmatically its own internal structure in terms of regional conditions and the dimensions of regional programmes.

UN regional economic commissions

With respect to the UN regional economic commissions, ECOSOC, as the 'legislative' creator, has specified their terms of reference in a series of formal resolutions.[4] When the new Commission for Africa was established in 1958, a spirited debate ensued in the Council as to whether its purview should include 'social' as well as 'economic' development. As a compromise, the approved terms of reference authorize the Commission to 'initiate and participate in measures for facilitating concerted action for the economic development of Africa, including the

[1] See, in this connection, the Executive Board's *Report on the Proposed Programme and Budget for 1959*, WHO, O.R.: No. 84, Part II, Jan. 1958.
[2] Notably in the *Organizational Study on Regionalization*, WHO, OR.: No. 46, Jan.-Feb. 1953.
[3] Robert Berkov, *The World Health Organization . . ., op. cit.*, p. 86.
[4] For the text of the resolutions on ECE, ECAFE, and ECLA, see the Annex to UN Doc. E/3052, 6 Feb. 1958.

social aspects of such development' [italics added].[5] The formal mandates of the older commissions have since been broadened along the same lines. The terms of reference of the African Commission also make mandatory the establishment of appropriate liaison and co-operation with the other regional commissions, thus giving legislative sanction to practices that had already been evolving in the inter-relations of ECE, ECAFE, and ECLA.

Within their formal terms of reference, the regional commissions have substantial latitude to develop policy recommendations and to initiate studies and projects of particular interest to the governments of their respective regions. While they are all subject to policy directives from ECOSOC, these are ordinarily couched in flexible terms. As one Executive Secretary picturesquely expressed it to the writer, the regional commissions are like 'teenagers' and ECOSOC does not dare to impose rigid rules for fear of arousing resentment among their Member governments. The Executive Secretaries of the commissions receive from time to time policy directives from the Secretary-General, usually by way of the Under-Secretary for Economic and Social Affairs at UN headquarters; but, here again, the tendency is to allow them fairly wide discretion in carrying out the instructions they get from the commissions. Also, the annual budget estimates prepared by each Executive Secretary for regional secretariat operations, while subject to formal approval by the UN Controller and incorporated into the overall UN budget, is seldom modified appreciably by the Secretary-General before submission to the General Assembly. In theory, the Executive Secretaries are administratively responsible to the Secretary-General, but in fact they can make basic operational decisions within the terms of their budgets and the guidance they receive from the commissions, which constitute their immediate 'legislative' organs. There is of course voluminous reporting on formal policy matters to the head of the Department of Economic and Social Affairs at headquarters, and on technical and research problems directly to the appropriate technical official in the Bureau of Economic Affairs. But the technical staff of this Bureau is too small to provide 'country desk' officers as in a national foreign office.

[5] ECOSOC Resolution 671 (XXI), 2 May 1958.

In the case of ECAFE and ECLA, there was reportedly some tendency on the part of ESA, during the early years, to step across the line of guidance and try to establish an order of priority for their activities. This happened perhaps because the problems of these two commissions were more difficult than those of ECE, while their staffs were less experienced. On the whole, however, their Executive Secretaries, as able and vigorous personalities, have not hesitated to exercise strong leadership at the regional level. It is relevant further to remember that the evolution towards increasing regional 'autonomy' has been affected by the impact of the cold war on UN deliberations. In ECOSOC, even more in the Second Committee of the General Assembly, policy deadlocks between rival power blocs have frequently occurred; whereas within the regions there is more emphasis on immediate practical problems on which general agreement is possible. At the meetings of the regional commissions the Great Powers often take a different approach and have a different focus from that displayed in ECOSOC and the Assembly.

UN European Office

In passing, mention should be made of the unique status of the UN European Office at Geneva. Originally this office was primarily a servicing unit for the flow of conferences and meetings held in the Palais des Nations. Gradually, however, various substantive units were physically attached to the Office by administrative order of the Secretary-General. By 1959, these included the UN Information Service; the Division of Narcotic Drugs (previously located in ESA at New York); the Bureau of Missing Persons and Declaration of Death; a small BTAO advisory and briefing office; a TAB liaison unit; the Office of the UN High Commissioner for Refugees; and an outposted unit of the UN Bureau of Social Affairs. From the beginning, moreover, the ECE Secretariat has had its locale in the Palais des Nations. Since all of these offices and units had to have locally recruited staff and needed various common housekeeping services, it was decided to confer on the Director of the European Office authority to co-ordinate their administrative requirements. Instructions to this effect were issued by the Secretary-General in 1957. A year later the original terms of reference of the European Office were revised and incorporated in a new edition of the Headquarters Services Administrative Manual, which now contains a complete description of the organization, functions, and activities of the Office, in addition to ECE and the other associated units. This entire process of delegation was initiated and put into effect by administrative action of the Director of the European Office and subject to budgetary sanction by the General Assembly. Except for ECE, the substantive functions of the European Office 'are in every sense headquarters activities of world-wide scope, the responsible secretariat being located, however, for historical or practical reasons, at Geneva instead of at New York.'[6] In other words, ECE again excepted, it is not a regional office with general responsibility for UN activities on the continent of Europe but rather an overseas branch of UN headquarters.

The Expanded Programme of Technical Assistance

The third area where there is substantial decentralization of programme making is in the Expanded Programme of Technical Assistance. Here ECOSOC, acting on recommendations from the Technical Assistance Committee, approves the procedures that govern country (and regional) programming, largely, to be sure, on the basis of proposals submitted to TAC by the Technical Assistance Board. This legislation on programming is translated into operational terms by periodic directives drafted by the TAB secretariat which, after approval by TAB, are circulated to the headquarters of each participating organization and to the TAB Resident Representatives at the country (or regional) level. As noted earlier, each RTAR, on assignment to a given country, receives a letter specifying his duties and functions. In conjunction with the programme procedural directives, this provides in effect a delegation of authority for him to act within the limits of his assignment. On administrative and financial matters, the Executive Chairman of TAB, in conformity with such instructions as are laid by TAC or TAB or both, may and does devolve upon the RTARs limited discretionary powers. These powers, together with communications procedures, have been codified in a voluminous TAB

[6] UN Doc. A/3049, 28 Nov. 1955.

'field manual.' The working relations of the RTARs with field representatives of the specialized agencies, as defined by TAB, are spelled out in a special administrative circular issued by its secretariat for their information and guidance.[7]

In those agencies employing more centralized patterns of control over field activities, such as FAO, ILO, Unesco, and ICAO, the delegation process is lodged, to a considerably greater extent, in their executive heads, subject always to general guidance from their executive boards and general conferences. During the earlier years, the terms of reference for field offices in most of these agencies were couched in general if not deliberately vague terms. As operational experience was gained, however, the functions of regional and other field units were made increasingly explicit. Eventually each agency developed a field (or administrative) manual in which is set forth in detail the administrative and budgetary status of its principal field offices. In some instances, this development has tended to produce considerable annoyance, if not frustration, on the part of regional office staffs who dislike being circumscribed by a web of minute procedures which are sometimes difficult to interpret and which may not always fit the conditions prevalent in their region. Even so, as we shall see later, the authority of the country representatives in FAO was not until quite recently defined with sufficient clarity, the consequence being that their relations with the upper levels of the FAO field hierarchy were left in a state of uncertainty. Somewhat similarly, the country chiefs of missions in Unesco have often been in doubt as to the precise extent of their operational authority.

The Director-General of FAO proposed in 1957 that the operational functions of its regional offices should be substantially expanded. These proposals were of such magnitude that he felt impelled to seek their approval by the Conference of the organization before putting them into effect administratively.[8] The changes suggested by the Director-General involved, *inter alia* (1) the preparation by the regional directors, for consideration by headquarters, of regional work programmes, due account being taken of recommendations made by regional

[7] UN Doc. TAB/CM/FIELD/110, 2 Aug. 1956.

[8] These proposals are described in the *Programme of Work and Budget for 1958 and 1959*, FAO Doc. C57/5, 11 March 1957.

conferences to be held in the off-Conference years (the FAO Conference meets biennially); and (2) the outposting to the regional offices of additional technical personnel which would in the future be under the full administrative control of the regional director concerned. During the debate in the Conference on these proposals, certain delegations were apprehensive lest they might lead to 'an undesirable degree of decentralization.' Upon assurance by the Director-General that his proposals, far from being designed to 'decentralize' the Organization, were intended simply to strengthen 'its peripheral activities,' the Conference approved them, but with the admonition that he should 'keep this consideration of the balance between the authority of Headquarters and of the regions under constant review.'[9] The new arrangements would appear none the less to make it possible for the regional office directors to exert considerably greater influence on FAO programme formulation in regional terms than hitherto. How their increased powers in this regard are working out in practice will be examined in Chapter 8.

Before concluding this brief survey of the forms of field delegation, attention should be called to the tendency of headquarters technical bureaux in various agencies to resist the expansion of field office functions and staffs. During the earlier years, this was quite noticeable in the WHO secretariat, where, as Berkov has observed, 'the process of decentralization has had the effect of converting many line supervisors into staff . . . advisers without power of decision.'[10] Although the geographic devolution of decision-making authority has not gone nearly so far in FAO or ILO as in WHO, comparable psychological reactions may be seen in these two agencies as well. In FAO, for instance, a marked distrust of regionalization has persisted from the beginning—a fear that this might produce a congeries of 'little regional FAO's' and undermine the central authority of the organization. On the whole, the FAO technical divisions have been opposed to scattering their professional personnel thinly around the globe because they feel that this would inevitably weaken their staff resources for essential research and clearing-house functions and for the effective back-stopping of

[9] *Report of the Ninth Session of the FAO Conference*, Nov. 1957, para. 357.

[10] *Op. cit.*, p. 104; see also Charles S. Ascher, 'Current Problems in the World Health Organization,' *International Organization* (Feb. 1952).

field project operations. In the International Labour Office, few of the technical bureaux appear to have been in favour of assigning large technical staffs to field offices for similar reasons. The Programme Departments at Unesco headquarters have for the most part reacted adversely to proposals for decentralizing programme operations. In ICAO, the Air Navigation Bureau is reported to have been lukewarm towards the idea of broadening the functions of its regional offices to include air transport and technical assistance matters.

When, in 1955, the UN Secretary-General suggested that small staff units of the Technical Assistance Administration might advantageously be outposted to the secretariats of ECLA and ECAFE, considerable opposition developed in the Programme Division of TAA, largely on the ground that this move could not help but weaken TAA's headquarters staff for effective programme control. There also lurked the fear that the proposed outposting arrangement might lead to the acquisition by the regional commission secretariats of 'too much' influence over UN technical assistance programming in the Latin American and Asian regions.

The announced objective of the Secretary-General's proposal was to associate TAA's field programme operations directly with the substantive divisions of ECLA and ECAFE so as to take fuller advantage of their expertise in such fields as industrial development, natural resources, transport, power, and the like. Since this proposal not only was controversial from the administrative point of view but had certain budgetary implications as well, it was submitted to the 1955 General Assembly for consideration.[11] During the discussion in the Fifth Committee, objections were raised by various governments to what seemed to them to be an unwise move towards a partial 'decentralization' of TAA's functions. The Advisory Committee had previously expressed misgivings partly on this score and partly because it was afraid that the arrangement might cause 'delays in the formulation and approval of requests and in the recruitment and servicing of experts.'[12] Accordingly, the Advisory Committee had recommended that consideration of the proposal be post-

[11] See UN Doc. A/3041, 23 Nov. 1955, for the text of the proposal, which was derived in large part from recommendations made by a Secretariat Survey Group appointed by the Secretary-General to examine the operation of UN overseas offices.

[12] UN Doc. A/3050, 2 Dec. 1955.

poned for a year in order to enable governments to examine it more closely and to allow ECOSOC time to study its substantive implications. In the Fifth Committee, the Secretary-General protested that his proposal was in no way 'connected with the philosophy of decentralization,' but was simply part of an overall plan, the purpose of which was 'to serve more effectively the under-developed areas of the world.'[13] The upshot of the debate was that the Secretary-General was authorized to implement the proposal only 'on a trial basis and in a single region'—Latin America.

The arrangement was continued from year to year until 1959, when it was liquidated despite strong support for it from the Department of Economic and Social Affairs. As will be explained in the next chapter, the apprehensions that it would involve serious administrative complications would seem to have been well founded.

By contrast, a companion proposal to station staff units of the UN Bureau of Social Affairs at various overseas points stemmed directly from the initiative of the Bureau's Director. A first step in this direction was taken by the Director in 1948 when a Social Welfare Adviser was detailed to Santiago (ECLA), to Bangkok (ECAFE), to Beirut (for liaison with UNICEF's work in the Middle East), and to Geneva (UN European Office) to help organize the Advisory Social Welfare Services part of the UN programme of assistance under its regular budget. After the inauguration of EPTA, the functions of these advisers were extended to TAA projects in the social development field (*e.g.*, social welfare training seminars, housing, community development, demography). In 1954 the Director of the Bureau suggested to the Secretary-General that the overseas detachment of such personnel be carried further by the permanent establishment of small social affairs units at the secretariats of the regional commissions. This plan was recommended in his report to the 1955 Assembly referred to above. Although the Assembly refrained from giving the plan its unqualified blessing, the Secretary-General proceeded to implement those aspects of it that required no immediate increase in budgetary appropriations.

When this action came up for discussion in ECOSOC the following summer (1956), the United States representative

[13] GA Official Records (O.R.): 10th Sess., 5th Committee, 524th Mtg., 6 Dec. 1955.

expressed concern lest the establishment of the social affairs units, if they were to become 'integral parts' of the ECLA and ECAFE secretariats, might start a trend towards transforming the regional commissions into 'miniature Economic and Social Councils.' In his view, it was essential that social affairs personnel detached from headquarters should 'receive their instructions direct from Headquarters.'[14] In replying to this statement, the Under-Secretary for Economic and Social Affairs gave assurance that the UN Secretariat had never intended that the arrangement should imply any delegation of responsibilities and that the power of decision with regard to the work programmes of the new units would rest with headquarters. This assurance, however, did not fully satisfy either the United States or certain other delegations, which were fearful that difficulties might arise from the 'divided authority' that would be exercised over the new units—by UN headquarters on the one hand and by the Executive Secretaries of the regional commissions on the other. The Council consequently requested the Secretary-General to prepare for the General Assembly a report on the results of the experience gained in the outposting of headquarters personnel to regional commission offices.[15] The 1956 Assembly agreed to provide additional budgetary allotments to finance the overseas social affairs units during 1957 and they have continued to operate on an experimental basis since then.[16] The unit at Geneva, it should be noted, is attached to the UN European Office rather than to ECE since the latter has not been much concerned with social development matters.

The outposting of staff personnel from TAA and the Bureau of Social Affairs, in the manner just described, represented a compromise between clear-cut decentralization of function and full retention of control by central headquarters. In both instances, as we shall see later, there were serious administrative problems arising from the resultant system of 'dual supervision.' By and large, the members of ECOSOC and of the Assembly representing the major 'donor' countries have taken a cautious

[14] UN Doc. E/AC.24/SR.144, 2 Aug. 1956.
[15] ECOSOC Resolution 630 B (XXII), 9 Aug. 1956.
[16] The new Commission for Africa is to have a Social Affairs Section in its Research Division. There is also a regional Social Affairs Office at Beirut which, completely under headquarters control, provides advisory services to Middle Eastern governments in building up their social programme and works in close co-operation with the RTARs in the region.

stand on what seems to them to be a potentially dangerous trend towards decentralization—a trend that might from their point of view undesirably inflate the role of the regional commissions. On the other hand, the 'receiving' countries have tended to favour moves that appear to shift the operational balance of the UN in economic and social programming towards the less developed regions.

These two cases illustrate how clashing forces may influence the administrative framework of a world organization. Also, they reflect a good deal of confusion among both secretariat officials and government delegates as to the real difference between 'decentralization' of substantive authority and 'deconcentration' of administrative action. We shall revert to this problem when we consider the programme process for the UN system as a whole.

Headquarters Organization for Field Programme Supervision

Regardless of the degree to which field programme operations are deconcentrated geographically, central headquarters has to be adapted to the maintenance of continuing supervision over, and communication with, such operations. It is beyond the purview of this study to analyse the internal structure of headquarters organization in any complete sense. In what follows attention will be centred chiefly on two problems that have plagued the UN and all of the associated agencies to a greater or lesser extent: (1) how to organize headquarters so as to provide effective 'integration' of control over *all* types of field programmes with which a particular agency is engaged, and (2) how to channel communication on programme and administrative matters between headquarters and field units, including project missions. While the arrangements evolved for handling these two problems vary considerably from agency to agency, a distinct trend towards similarity of organizational patterns may be discerned.

UN headquarters

Prior to the inception of EPTA, the administration of the limited programmes of technical assistance being carried out under the regular UN budget was handled by the then Departments of Economic and Social Affairs, respectively, with such assistance as necessary from the finance and personnel divisions of the Secretariat. When the Expanded Programme came into being, an inter-departmental committee on technical assistance was set up by the Secretary-General to recommend arrangements for administering the new programme. If there had at that time been a single Department of Economic and Social Affairs (as was later established), the chances are that the UN's share of EPTA would have been placed under its supervision. Largely because of jurisdictional tensions between the two substantive departments, the idea of establishing a separate operational unit to administer all technical assistance prevailed. In this connection, the advantages of separating operations from research, analysis, and substantive back-stopping functions were stressed by many officials in the Secretariat.

Accordingly, the Technical Assistance Administration was set up in July 1950 under a Director-General.[17] To this new unit was given responsibility for providing services and facilities for field projects and for the organization of field missions and the processing of technical assistance fellowships. By 1952 the internal organization of TAA consisted of two main divisions—one on Programme and one on Public Administration—together with an administrative and a fellowships placement office. The Programme Division was staffed on an area basis, with three sections covering Asia; Europe, the Middle East, and Africa; and Latin America. The creation of a separate Division to handle Public Administration activities may be explained primarily by the fact that the province of the two subject-matter Departments (of Economic and of Social Affairs) did not include this field. The Public Administration Division was therefore made responsible not only for the operational aspects of technical assistance projects but also for planning and support services in the substantive sense.[18] Later, in 1957, the

[17] Secretary-General's Bulletin 32/Rev. 7, 31 July 1950. The anomalous title of 'Director-General' for the head of TAA was apparently used in order that he might have hierarchical equivalence with the then assistant secretaries-general. See Walter R. Sharp, *International Technical Assistance* (Chicago: Public Administration Service, 1952), pp. 64–65, for a fuller account of the reasons for establishing TAA as a separate unit.

[18] For an excellent analysis of its earlier development, see H. L. Keenleyside, 'Administrative Problems of the United Nations Technical Assistance Administration,' *Public Administration* (Autumn 1955). Dr. Keenleyside served as Director-General of TAA until 1958.

operational functions of the Public Administration Division were transferred to the Programme Division, reducing the former essentially to a planning and technical advisory unit with a role somewhat analogous to that of the merged Department of Economic and Social Affairs.[19] This change reflected an effort to concentrate all operational actions in a single division of TAA.

TAA and the substantive Departments co-operating with it attempted to cover an enormous range of technical assistance fields, including not only economic development, social welfare, and publication, but 'every sphere of activity not specifically or inferentially covered by one of the Specialized Agencies.'[20] This broad responsibility placed a heavy load on the TAA staff, in particular that of the Programme Division. It is this Division that, *inter alia*, serves as the channel of communication with field experts and field missions on programme operational matters. Communications from the field relating to purely administrative matters (*e.g.*, salary payments, leave arrangements, and orders of supplies and equipment) were passed along as appropriate to the recruitment, finance, or purchasing units of the Secretariat for action. It was to the Programme Division that reports from experts were addressed.

With a view to achieving a closer integration of the research, planning, and operational aspects of the totality of UN's activities in the economic and social fields, the Secretary-General, in 1958, effected an organizational 'merger' of TAA and the Department of Economic and Social Affairs. The Advisory Committee had for some years argued in favour of such a consolidation on administrative and financial grounds. In his report to the Fifth Committee of the Assembly, the Secretary-General echoed this view by expressing the belief that

> in a unified Department there would be a considerable lightening of the administrative machinery, a reduction in the volume of correspondence and in the time required to attend meetings as well as a simplification of the work. Above all, central direction would make it possible to organize the optimum use of staff in both areas, including the increased use of substantive staff in field assignments.[21]

Whether such consequences will ensue from the merger remains to be seen. Within the 'unified' Department technical

[19] This merger took place in 1955.
[20] Keenleyside, *op. cit.*
[21] UN Doc. A/C.5/752, 16 Oct. 1958.

assistance operations (as distinct from research and planning) would continue to be handled by 'a clearly identifiable entity' (in the Secretary-General's language), to be known as the Bureau of Technical Assistance Operations (TAA renamed BTAO), under a 'Commissioner' with the rank of Under-Secretary. For the time being, the Public Administration Division of the old TAA was to function as an independent unit—as the Office for Public Administration—outside the Department, under the direction of a senior officer reporting directly to Secretary-General Dag Hammarskjold. This seemingly anomalous arrangement reportedly conformed to his desire to keep a firm hand on the initial development of his new scheme for the 'Division of Operational, Executive, and Administrative Personnel,' for which the Office of Public Administration was to have policy responsibility, including the evaluation of requests from governments for this type of aid.[22] In December 1959, however, this office was incorporated into ESA under the old designation of 'Division.'

In principle, the consolidation of TAA with the Department of Economic and Social Affairs had much to commend it. The relations between certain of the functional units of the Department and the geographic units of TAA had at times been strained, each group resenting what it alleged to be encroachments upon its proper domain by the other. Whether BTAO will be content to serve merely as an executive arm for ESA, or will seek a policy-making role as well, will probably depend upon the kind of working relations that develop between the head of ESA and the new Commissioner for Technical Assistance. If these relations are characterized by mutual trust and a determined will to co-operate, the merger should bring about a distinct improvement in headquarters organization affecting technical assistance. At best, even with optimum utilization of professional personnel, it is doubtful if any over-all reduction of staff will result from the consolidation. One of the real problems has been the inadequacy of professional staff for substantive support and operational services. The Bureau of

[22] OPEX, a new type of technical assistance, is designed to make available to governments of under-developed countries senior administrative experts who will be under their administrative direction for specified periods, the UN supplementing as necessary the salaries of such experts so as to make it possible to attract highly qualified candidates. The new scheme was formally approved by the General Assembly by Resolution 1256 (XII), 14 Nov. 1958.

Economic Affairs, in particular, needs additional high-grade technical specialists in various fields, while the Programme Division of the former TAA has been staffed too thinly, and too much with relatively inexperienced personnel, to handle with dispatch its operational relations with the TAB field offices and project missions.

Since the merger of 1958, responsibility for providing administrative support services in respect of field projects has devolved upon the Field Operations Service of the UN Office of General Services—a unit experienced in this sort of operation by reason of having handled the administrative aspects of UN political missions in the field for some years. Henceforth, it will form the sole channel of communication with technical assistance field experts on purely administrative matters, including payroll questions and the application of personnel rules. In effect, though not in name, this unit has absorbed the former Central Administrative Section of TAA. In order to expedite decisions on budgetary and financial control activities, the Chief of BTAO's Fiscal Control Section has been transferred to the Office of the UN Controller to whom, subject to general supervision by the Director of BTAO, he is directly responsible. These changes are designed to 'streamline' administrative procedures at UN headquarters relating to field programme operations.

On the project side, three programme sections, with geographic jurisdictions corresponding to old TAA sections, are to organize 'substantive support of technical assistance activities in collaboration with the other units of the Department [ESA].'[23] With a view to tailoring the dimensions of project operations more realistically to the professional resources of ESA, BTAO now endeavours to limit itself to seven principal functional areas, as follows:

industrial development
non-agricultural natural resources (*e.g.*, water)
inland transport
public administration
fiscal advisory services (not provided by IBRD or IMF)
statistical organization
social welfare

[23] UN Doc. ST/SGB/122/Amend. 3, 16 Dec. 1959.

For certain of these areas the boundaries are subject to agreement with the specialized agency (or agencies) concerned (*e.g.*, with ILO for industrial development and with Unesco for public administration). A serious effort now appears to be under way to relate basic ESA research on economic and social development needs to country and regional programming through technical assistance. In this connection, ESA is drawing increasingly on the special knowledge of the regional commission secretariats.

The WHO pattern

In some respects the question of an appropriate central structure for field programme control in WHO has involved less serious difficulties than at UN headquarters. The reason for this is obvious, namely, the extensive decentralization of programme operations to the regional offices, Geneva mainly providing general policy guidance, programme co-ordination, and over-all budgetary control. Concurrent with the inauguration of EPTA, WHO arrangements were put into effect for integrating its operations with those of the regular programmes, the total dimensions of which, as indicated in Chapter 2, are substantially larger than those of the Expanded Programme. Also, WHO (with PAHO) has available additional extra-budgetary resources to provide advisory services to governments, including, notably, the world-wide malaria eradication programme.

During the early years of EPTA, there was a small unit for liaison with TAB and other participating organizations and co-ordination within WHO itself of activities under the new programme. This unit was eventually moved up to the Office of the Director-General and its staff somewhat increased as EPTA developed. In 1955 the unit was combined with the Office of External Relations and given a new designation—the Division of Technical Assistance and External Relations, under the Deputy Director-General. In the opinion of officials on the management side, the old unit had tended to 'stick its fingers' into substantive and financial matters instead of confining itself to liaison and co-ordination work. The new combined office was intended to deal primarily with the formal relations of WHO with other organizations and with Member governments, 'Technical Assistance' being retained in its title for 'political reasons.'

In 1957, following a review of the work in the Office of the Director-General, this Division was abolished and its functions relating to technical assistance were transferred to a new Office of Programme Co-ordination in the Department of Advisory Services, which then included all the functional divisions concerned with field programmes. In addition to essential liaison duties, this Office now assembles for the Director-General all programme proposals submitted by the subject-matter divisions and from the regional directors as well, after examination for duplication and costing by the Division of Budget and Finance.[24] Any necessary correspondence with the regional directors regarding changes in their proposals (*e.g.*, in case they exceed the tentative target set by the Director-General for the regional programme) is routed through this Office. It also serves as the channel of communication with the RTARs and with the TAB secretariat in New York in respect of such matters as the transfer of EPTA projects from one priority category to another. The Office maintains a 'Central Project Inventory' which includes a record of operational agreements, WHO obligations and expenditures, the status of project personnel and of supplies and equipment, and a summary of reports by project leaders. In addition, the Office is responsible for developing the guide-lines of an adequate field reporting system.

It should be kept in mind, so far as WHO is concerned, that the vast bulk of field programme-making and implementation is the responsibility of the regional offices. It is at the regional level that field projects are formulated and initially approved, most field experts appointed and briefed, and their periodic reports received and examined.

FAO's central control structure

Field programme control within FAO's headquarters has evolved through a series of stages towards an elaborate set of integrating services located in the Director-General's office.

[24] During 1959 the WHO Director-General put into effect an across-the-board reorganization of the two headquarters substantive departments (of Central Technical Services and of Advisory Services) with a view to further integration of programming. See WHO, O.R: No. 89, Dec. 1958, pp. 22–47, for details.

Headquarters-Field Relationships

During the earlier years of the organization the planning of regular programme activities, which then involved field administration only to a minor extent, was done largely in piecemeal fashion—through the five Technical Divisions that dealt with agriculture, fisheries, forestry, nutrition, and economics. Relations with FAO's regional offices, at that time functioning on a skeleton basis, were directly channelled partly through the Director-General's office and partly through these divisions. With the advent of EPTA, a small central unit was established in the front office to handle relations with TAB and recipient governments. A separate unit was also set up in each Technical Division for the supervision of its EPTA activities and liaison with the central unit. Substantive support services were provided by these Divisions. The central unit was in charge of briefing arrangements for experts and administered the headquarters aspects of FAO's fellowship programme, while the Personnel Branch handled the processing of field staff appointments.

In 1956 this structure was altered by establishing in the Director-General's office a Programme and Budgetary Service, into which the central EPTA unit was absorbed. 'In line with the objectives of programme integration, more systematic programming and budgeting, and relieving technical officers of administrative details,' Programme Co-ordination Services were also installed in the various Technical Divisions.[25] At the same time, the divisional technical assistance units were abolished, with a view to underlining the 'direct relationship between the regular continuing work of a technical division and its technical assistance activities.'[26] A new Field Liaison Service also became a part of the enlarged staff apparatus of the front office. This Service was made the channel for communication between headquarters and the regional and country representatives on all programme matters, including fellowships. The over-all responsibilities for programme co-ordination and the costing of projects were lodged in the Programme and Budgetary Service.

During 1958–59 concentration of programme planning and execution within the office of the Director-General were carried a step further. The Programme and Budgetary Service was placed under the direction of an officer of higher rank and given

[25] *The Work of FAO, 1956–1957: Report of the Director-General*, FAO Doc. 57/6/3848, p. 83.
[26] *Third Report of the Advisory Committee on Administrative and Budgetary Questions*, UN Doc. A/3598, 9 July 1957.

a considerably larger staff. Its internal organization, moreover, was differentiated by setting up within it seven distinct 'branches' for: (1) programme formulation and co-ordination, (2) programme research and evaluation, (3) programme liaison, (4) field operations liaison, (5) training and fellowships, (6) budget, and (7) international agency liaison.[27] Two of these branches were concerned particularly with field programme operations. The Programme Liaison Branch became the co-ordinating unit (*a*) for programme activities involving more than one subject-matter division of the organization, and (*b*) for the work of the FAO regional conferences, the European Commission on Agriculture, joint survey missions (in which other UN agencies participate), and projects under the new UN Special Fund. Further, this Branch was to provide 'a central focal point' for technical and programme matters with the regional offices. The Field Operations Liaison Branch (in effect the old Field Liaison Service renamed) was delegated responsibility for assisting the technical divisions in the field aspects of programming and supervising technical assistance projects on a day-to-day basis. In this connection, it would continue to serve as the channel for communication with the FAO country representatives and field experts. Under the new scheme, regional office directors were to report to the head of the over-all Programme and Budgetary Service, acting on behalf of the Director-General.

The FAO Council, at its twenty-ninth session in the autumn of 1958, approved the reorganization plan without important change.[28] At first glance, the overhead staff apparatus would appear to be somewhat top-heavy and it may require some careful internal 'co-ordinating' if it is to function expeditiously, and not as a headquarters bottleneck, in dealing with matters referred to it from the field. This problem is complicated by what is called in FAO circles the 'godfather' system whereby field experts are back-stopped directly by their counterparts in the headquarters technical divisions. What effect the concentration of stronger control over field operations in the Director-General's office will have on the working of this system is not entirely clear.[29] In

[27] For a detailed acconut of this reorganization scheme, which involved the technical divisions as well, see FAO Doc. CL.29/18, 10 Aug. 1958.

[28] FAO Resolution No. 8/29.

[29] Headquarters 'godfathers' will probably continue to be used to provide technical back-stopping, but they will no longer act, as some did earlier, on administrative matters.

its broad aspects, however, the new FAO plan represents an extensive effort to integrate the formulation and execution of all of FAO's field activities regardless of kind or source of financing.

ILO's headquarters framework for field control

'By trial and error,' to use the expression of one ILO official, the International Labour Office has endeavoured in recent years to integrate its traditional research and standard-setting functions with the newer operational programmes, including both EPTA and undertakings financed from its regular budget. As in FAO, this process has gone through a number of steps. The resultant control pattern, however, is significantly different in certain respects from that of FAO.

At the time EPTA was established, an Assistant Director-General was 'made responsible for all of the operational activities of the Organization.'[30] At the working level a special unit, known at first as the Advisory Missions Section, was set up. Shortly thereafter, this unit was re-designated the Technical Assistance Division. While essentially a servicing unit, it tended in fact to take on various substantive aspects of the new Programme, such as project formulation and development, drawing only to a slight extent on the technical divisions for help. Indeed, for two or three years the traditional and operational activities of ILO 'followed virtually separate courses.'[31] The Director-General reportedly felt that the Office was becoming 'two shops' under one roof, the technical divisions being operationally 'isolated' from EPTA developments. With the shift of emphasis in ILO from research and legislative work to field activities, and from Europe to Latin America and Asia, it seemed desirable to mesh the two sides of ILO's work so that EPTA might benefit from the reservoir of professional knowledge in the technical divisions and, conversely, so that their traditional functions might be enriched by the findings and recommendations of technical assistance missions. Accordingly the technical divisions of the Office were 'progressively drawn into the operations of the technical assistance programme as regards technical advice on projects, establishment of job

[30] *Report of the Advisory Committee on 'Administrative and Budgetary Co-ordination between the United Nations and the International Labour Organization with Particular Reference to the Working of the Expanded Programme of Technical Assistance,'* UN Doc. A/3142, 10 July 1956.
[31] ILO Doc. G.B. 138/T.A./D.1/2, Feb.-March 1958.

descriptions, selection of experts, and advice to the experts during the execution of projects.'[32]

This evolution took place concurrently with the expansion (in 1954) of the province of ILO's 'field' offices (originally confined to the 'manpower' programme) to include representation of the central Office *as a whole* for operational purposes. Instead, however, of placing their supervision under the Technical Assistance Division, the pre-existing External Services Division was given this task, apparently because it was already administering the network of branch offices and national correspondents, although, as noted earlier, they had little or nothing to do with technical assistance matters. It was gradually recognized that constant liaison between these two divisions was essential; nor was the co-existence of two distinct channels of communication conducive to expeditious field supervision. Thus, in 1957, the two divisions were consolidated into a single Field Services Division. Unlike the FAO pattern, however, the new Division (or for that matter its predecessor units) is not attached to the Director-General's office but operates under the general supervision of a designated Assistant Director-General, who reports up the line to the Deputy Director-General. This arrangement conforms to the ILO practice of distributing over-all supervisory responsibilities for all of the internal units of the secretariat among several assistant directors-general, the front office consisting of only a few special assistants to the Director-General, the legal counsellor, and a small research and analysis unit.

The enlarged Field Services Division now performs four types of functions: (1) It maintains liaison with all services carried on outside of ILO headquarters, including the issuance of field instructions and the receipt and circulation within the secretariat of reports from such services and from all overseas offices. (2) The Division is a principal channel of communication between the ILO field offices and the technical, administrative and finance divisions at headquarters, and it handles the relations of the RTARs with respect to EPTA problems. (3) It is in charge of the administration of fellowships and worker grants. And (4) it co-ordinates the evaluation of operational projects done by the

[32] *Report of the Advisory Committee on 'Administrative and Budgetary Co-ordination between the United Nations and the International Labour Organisation . . .,' op. cit.*

technical divisions. In a general sense, the Division co-ordinates the operation of ILO's field programme as a whole, including project allocations and fund transfers. It also provides secretariat services for the Programme Board (see below).

To advise the Director-General on major policy questions, the planning of operational activities, the approval of specific projects, and the evaluation of programme results, an Operational Planning Board was set up in 1954 consisting of the Deputy Director-General (as chairman), the Assistant Directors-General, and the Treasurer. Staff services for this top-level Board were provided at first by the Technical Assistance Division and later by the Field Services Division. In 1958 this Board was amalgamated with a previously established Research Planning Board and is now known simply as the Programme Board. According to various operating officials with whom the writer discussed the problem, the Board has worked well when faced with basic policy questions but less satisfactorily when obliged to consider specific projects (under ILO's regular budget) because its members not only are too busy with other matters but often lack the technical competence to render informed judgments. Although the Director-General does not sit with the Board, he is said to study seriously its recommendations. All final decisions as to field projects are made by him.

Broadly speaking, ILO's central structure for field programme control appears to have shaken down into an orderly, well-integrated set of staff arrangements. Their tasks, to be sure, are somewhat less formidable than those facing the UN, WHO, or FAO in that ILO's total field programme operations have decidedly smaller dimensions.

The complex situation in Unesco

The problem of achieving co-ordinated control over Unesco's field programme operations has been complicated by two special factors: (1) the extraordinarily wide subject-matter scope and diversified character of these operations, and (2) centrifugal tendencies within the Paris secretariat arising from its essentially 'university faculty' type of organization. In addition to EPTA, Unesco, as noted in an earlier chapter, is now engaged in three other fairly distinct categories of field activities: its regular programme of training and research seminars, survey missions, and fellowships; its so-called 'major projects' extending over periods of several years; and its Participation (formerly Aid-to-Member States) Programme. While all four of these forms of activity have some relation to economic and social development goals, only EPTA is planned on a 'country' basis, the others consisting of projects selected, in theory at least, in terms of world-wide functional priorities. The establishment in the secretariat at the outset of 'programme' departments, dealing with Education, the Natural Sciences, the Social Sciences, Cultural Activities (the humanities), and Mass Communication (journalism), tended to compartmentalize programme making along the lines of recognized university disciplines. This tendency was accentuated by pressures exerted by outside professional groups with which the secretariat had close contact, and which are ordinarily represented on national delegations to the General Conference. In this context, it was not uncommon for members of the programme departments of the secretariat to join forces with their professional counterparts (unofficially and largely behind the scenes, to be sure) during Conference sessions, with a view to enlisting support for their 'pet' programme proposals.[33]

In an effort to bring programme proposals into some kind of ordered pattern, the Director-General, in 1948, appointed an Executive Officer for Programme whose task, as top-level 'co-ordinator' in his office, was to ride herd over the programme departments. While considerable progress was made during the ensuing years towards agreement on over-all priorities in the construction of Unesco's work programme, the execution of projects requiring field action was left in the hands of each programme department concerned, with such assistance as needed from budget, personnel, and various housekeeping units in the secretariat. There was one exception to this: fellowships sponsored by Unesco were administered by a separate Exchange of Persons Service reporting directly to the Director-General.

In 1950, a Technical Assistance Unit was created to supervise Unesco's participation in EPTA. As operations within the expanded programme got under way, this Unit was 'graduated' in 1951 into a Service, and the following year it became a full-

[33] For a perceptive analysis of the impact of these 'log-rolling' operations on Unesco's programme during the earlier years, see Charles S. Ascher, *Program-Making in Unesco, 1946–1951, op. cit.*

fledged Department, with a director on the same hierarchical level as the directors of the other Programme Departments. In 1953, the Technical Assistance Department was reorganized, in order to handle the growing needs of EPTA, into an 'administrative' division and a 'programme' division—the latter being subdivided into four sections covering the major areas of the world receiving Unesco technical assistance.[34] Although the TA Department drew to a limited extent upon the subject-matter departments for technical advice, its terms of reference permitted it to keep under its wing virtually all aspects of EPTA operation, including the preparation of contracts for field experts, the provision of administrative support services for field missions, and the review of progress reports from the field. On the other hand, it had nothing whatever to do with regular programme matters, which still remained with the subject-matter departments.

This bifurcation of responsibility for programme planning and execution prompted Director-General Evans, in 1957, to establish a new Bureau of Relations with Member States within which would be concentrated over-all responsibility (1) for conducting Unesco's relations with Member governments and National Commissions and (2) for the administration of all field programmes. During his field tours the Director-General reportedly had been struck by the lack of co-ordination between EPTA matters and the other manifold contacts of Unesco with Member governments, frequently involving political and diplomatic considerations. The programme departments, it appeared to him, could all too easily 'get out of line' and make commitments that might prove embarrassing. In his view, the need for some kind of stronger central control had become imperative.

The new Bureau represented in effect a merger of the Technical Assistance Department and of a small Division of Relations with Governments and National Commissions that had formed a part of his own office for some years.[35] The internal organization of

[34] *Report of the Advisory Committee on 'Administrative and Budgetary Co-ordination between the United Nations and UNESCO with Particular Reference to the Working of the Expanded Programme of Technical Assistance*, UN Doc. A/3166, 22 Aug. 1956, p. 14.

[35] In this connection, it is interesting to note that the *Report of the Management Survey Committee* (Unesco Doc. 50 EX/27, 1957, p. 35) urged that Unesco's relations with other international organizations also be channelled through BMS in order to promote a more 'multilateral conception' of Unesco's activities. The Director-General, however, decided against this for fear it would 'overload' BMS. See Unesco Administrative Memorandum ADM.A/86, dated 4 Feb. 1957, for a description of BMS's organization and functions as of then. During 1959 it was reorganized in certain minor particulars.

BMS followed roughly the same pattern as that of the former TA Department, but its professional staff was substantially expanded. This Bureau now performs not only co-ordinating and management functions with reference to all field programmes, but serves as the principal communication channel with TAB field offices (which handle various administrative operations for Unesco projects at the country level); with technical assistance missions; with national and regional training and research centres sponsored by Unesco; with national ministries and Unesco national commissions; and with permanent national delegations at Unesco headquarters.

For programme co-ordination and management, BMS operates by means of five 'area' units, the geographic competence of which is distributed as follows: Arab-speaking countries; Asia; Europe; English-speaking countries and Africa; and Latin America. In view of the fact that Unesco (aside from its Havana office) has no permanent field machinery with direct responsibility for programme operations, the administrative load carried by BMS at headquarters is an unusually heavy one—all the more in that Unesco's regular and Participation programmes span advanced as well as under-developed countries.

On an average, about two-thirds of the time of the professional staffs of the BMS area units (totalling some fifteen persons) is spent on EPTA matters. They prepare country and regional project submissions for TAB and, on approval, see to it that funds are obligated for their execution. In this task they are assisted by the Administrative Division of BMS, which is responsible for the planning of field programmes from the budgetary point of view. This latter Division also prepares draft project allotments, processes obligating documents, and authorizes the purchase and shipment of project supplies.

The programme departments not only provide technical advice but implement approved projects, including any necessary changes during the course of their operation. The tendency since 1957 has been to shift decisions to the programme departments on substantive matters; for example, they may correspond directly with field missions, a copy of each letter, however, being sent to BMS.

The procedures governing the content of the Participation programme differ substantially from those used for EPTA country programming. In the former case, the General Conference specifies by resolution, directed to each programme department, the subject-matter fields on which programme projects should concentrate. In large part these resolutions are based on proposals made by the departments themselves and incorporated in the Programme and Budget document that goes to the Conference. Requests from governments under this programme may be submitted at any time; all Member States are eligible to make requests and there are no 'country' targets. Action on requests is not in terms of priorities that may be proposed by requesting governments, and they may find that one of their relatively low-level projects is approved as against another of higher priority. This sometimes causes misunderstanding.

Since each programme department seeks as large a share of available programme funds as possible, under its Conference resolution, some inter-departmental log-rolling inevitably results. In principle, each project is considered on its merits, the criteria of selection including geographic distribution, the technical soundness of the project, and its probable 'multiplier effect.' Project requests, which for the 1957–58 biennium exceeded budgetary resources by about four to one, are screened by an inter-departmental committee chaired by the Director-General.[36] From this point on, BMS assumes responsibility, in collaboration with the programme departments, for project management in much the same manner as for EPTA projects.

This complex structure of programme planning and execution initially had a mixed reception in Unesco House. In the opinion of various officials on the administrative side, it brought about a considerable improvement in programme integration, and it clearly provided a better total picture of field operations. Notwithstanding, the staff of BMS complained of having too much paper-work to do and of not being able to handle with dispatch its voluminous correspondence with governments and TAB field offices. Nor did it consider its double responsibility for programme management and for handling political and diplomatic relationships with governments an altogether happy arrangement. As one BMS area officer remarked, it was neces-

[36] By the end of 1958, 116 projects involving eighty-eight experts, had been completed under Unesco's Participation programme. *Annual Report of the TAB for 1958*, ECOSCC, O.R.: 28th Sess., 1959, Suppl. No. 5, p. 188.

sary to be 'a jack of all trades.' It is perhaps natural that some jealousy and friction should have arisen between BMS and the programme departments, each feeling that its jurisdiction should not be encroached upon by the other, and that the boundaries could be more carefully defined. During the writer's visit to Unesco in the fall of 1958, a typical observation made by programme department heads was that BMS could only be either a 'rubber stamp' or a 'bottleneck,' with its staff buried in masses of paper it was too busy to read or digest. In reality, remarked one programme director, it was a bit of both. Another official characterized BMS as a 'white elephant' moving with elephantine slowness on matters calling for prompt action. There was also some feeling that many of the professional personnel of BMS lacked sufficient familiarity with the substantive aspects of programme projects to act intelligently on their administration. BMS, so it was charged, tended to stick its fingers into matters for which it was not competent. To this charge BMS retorted, with some justification, that the programme departments themselves were not adequately staffed for programme back-stopping in certain subject-matter fields and that it therefore was at times obliged to act on its own.[37]

Commenting on the situation towards the end of 1957, the Management Survey Committee admitted that the new set-up had led to 'some measure of confusion' between BMS and the programme departments, given 'the interdependence of programme . . . and management responsibilities.' 'The Departments,' in the Committee's view, 'are not equipped to be the sole managers' of all types of programmes; complete concentration of control in them would raise more problems than it would settle.[38]

According to reliable information received from Paris by the writer, the attitude of the directors of the programme departments towards BMS grew markedly more favourable during 1959. This appears to reflect a more efficient and expeditious handling of operations by the Bureau as a result of some two years' experience.

[37] A senior member of the Bureau of Personnel called the writer's attention to a stack of papers just received from BMS, with the request that Personnel 'pressure' the programme departments to take action on them without delay—the Personnel Bureau thus being caught in the middle.

[38] *Report of the Management Survey Committee*, *op. cit.*, p. 25.

Headquarters-Field Relationships

On balance, however, there would seem to be no easy way to simplify Unesco's central machinery for field operations control so long as it is responsible for a multiplicity of over-lapping world-wide programmes, each with a special objective and different financial base. The streamlining of secretariat procedures for registering and circulating incoming correspondence, together with a reduction in the number of controls now exercised at various levels over outgoing mail, might help to speed up staff decisions.[39] Even so, some topheaviness, and lack of operational cohesiveness, in Unesco's headquarters bureaucracy is perhaps inevitable due to the nature of its far-flung and disparate spheres of action.

ICAO's control arrangements

The status of ICAO, with regard to the problems we are here considering, contrasts sharply with that of all of the major UN agencies. ICAO is an institution that operates within a well-defined and relatively narrow technical sphere. Under its regular budget it carries on a variety of activities designed to promote 'the orderly growth of safe, efficient and economical international civil aviation.'[40] While these activities are geared to world-wide priorities and needs, they have involved, as indicated in an earlier chapter, some regional differentiation in terms of recommended air-safety plans adapted to the conditions of major geographical areas. It will be recalled that for the purposes of 'monitoring' these plans a number of regional offices were established at the outset. These offices are responsible to the Air Navigation Bureau through the Regional Affairs Section of this Bureau. In the technical sense their terms of reference are contained in the ICAO Technical Manual as revised from time to time by the regional Air Navigation meetings. Gradually, the regional offices have been asked to perform, on behalf of headquarters, certain incidental tasks relating to air transport, legal and administrative matters and, indeed, during recent years, technical assistance; but they still function essentially as overseas extensions of the Air Navigation Bureau.

[39] *Ibid.*, pp. 47–48.
[40] *Report of the Advisory Committee on 'Administrative and Budgetary Co-ordination between the United Nations and the International Civil Aviation Organization with Particular Reference to the Working of the Expanded Programme of Technical Assistance,'* UN Doc. A/3861, 20 Aug. 1958, p. 11.

The Montreal secretariat, in addition to this Bureau, consists of an Air Transport Bureau, a Legal Bureau, a Bureau of Administration and Services, and, since 1950, a Technical Assistance Bureau for the administration of ICAO's relatively restricted role in EPTA. In comparison with such agencies as WHO, FAO, ILO, and Unesco, ICAO has a neat and tidy organizational structure which has remained remarkably stable over the years.

ICAO's regular programme activities are planned in terms of a work programme over a three-year period. This programme, in draft form, is established by the ICAO Council on the basis of the recommendations of the Secretary-General and is submitted for approval to the Assembly at its triennial session (the Assembly meets in intervening years for administrative business only).

ICAO differs from other specialized agencies in the volume of technical regulatory and procedural material that arises from meetings of its Air Navigation Commission, Air Transport Committee, Regional Air Navigation meetings, and other international bodies, which must be reviewed and approved by the Council. In so far as policy matters are concerned, the implementation of the programme is the responsibility of the Council and, for some matters, of its permanent President. Subject to the policy directives of the Assembly and Council, the Secretary-General implements the programme of the organization, administers the budget and acts as 'the chief executive officer' of the organization.

When EPTA came into the picture, its administration was devolved upon the Secretary-General under authority delegated by the Council to its permanent President. To carry out this responsibility, the Secretary-General set up a Technical Assistance Bureau to which virtually all aspects of EPTA management were sub-delegated. This Bureau, for example, prepares the drafts of all EPTA field projects (consisting chiefly of national and regional training centres), recruits technical specialists, provides necessary central administrative services, acts as the channel for communication to and from the field and generally supervises the work of the technical assistance missions.

From this brief survey of ICAO's headquarters structure, it

will be recognized that its regular programme and EPTA are administered quite independently. There are, moreover, two distinct lines of communication from the field—one from the regional offices to the Air Navigation Bureau and the other from the TA field missions to the TA Bureau. Only incidentally and informally are the regional offices used to facilitate technical assistance operations at the field level. As we shall see later, this situation sometimes gives rise to confusion and it is clearly not the most economical way to utilize ICAO's regional machinery. Eventually, as ICAO's activities expand in the jet age, it would seem desirable to separate the regional offices from the Air Navigation Bureau and give them authority to represent ICAO in the field 'across the board.' If this were done, the two existing units at headquarters having to do with field relations—the Regional Affairs Division of the Air Navigation Bureau and the TA Bureau—might advantageously be consolidated into a 'Directorate of Field Services,' with integrated responsibility for headquarters supervision over all field activities. At the moment, any such proposal would be likely to encounter stiff resistance from both of the principal parties concerned, each wishing to cling to its present jurisdiction. Yet the forces for integration within ICAO circles are growing in strength and it will probably be only a matter of time before some such change is seriously contemplated.

The UNICEF operational system

UNICEF has developed what is generally regarded as an effective method of implementing its programme, which is entirely of a 'field' character. There is thus no problem of integrating differently based programmes as in the UN and most of the specialized agencies. Programme making in UNICEF may be said to be selectively centralized, by which is meant that the degree of delegation to the field may vary from one regional office to another or from one type of programme operation to another. If an operation is a new one or is unusually complex, the reins are at first tightly held by headquarters and then gradually relaxed. Procedurally, delegation is defined in the letter appointing the regional director, but this is largely a formality and his authority may subsequently be altered as circumstances dictate by informal directives from headquarters.

The programme budget of UNICEF consists in effect of a three-year forecast revised annually for purposes of appropriation estimates. Money is allocated by the UNICEF Executive Board (which meets semi-annually) not to countries but to projects. Appropriations do not lapse at the end of the fiscal year but continue for the duration of the project concerned.

Under this flexible scheme, authority may be and is delegated to regional offices, with the assistance of the area and country offices under their jurisdiction, to negotiate draft project agreements with governments. Such agreements are transmitted to the Programme Division at New York headquarters. Before each meeting of the Executive Board a staff 'working group on programme' evaluates these proposals and makes recommendations thereon up the line to the Executive Director, who in turn approves them for submission to the Board. The Board seldom rejects his recommendations but often makes suggestions as to desirable future trends in UNICEF's over-all activities. After formal action by the Board, the Programme Division authorizes the Supply Division to undertake the necessary procurement. This Division is responsible for the purchase, warehousing, and shipping of all equipment and supplies for approved projects, drawing up specifications, arranging for competitive bidding from interested firms, and preparing contracts and purchase orders.[41]

The Programme Division exercises broad supervisory and servicing functions with respect to project execution. For this purpose it is organized on an area basis, with three sections for Europe and Africa, Asia, and the Eastern Mediterranean, corresponding to the coverage of the Paris, Bangkok, and Beirut offices. For Latin America, as indicated earlier, the regional office was moved to headquarters some years ago and there is thus no 'area desk' for the Americas in the Programme Division. The staffs of the area units do the run-of-the-mill work for the Division. They constitute the channel for correspondence on programme operations with the regional offices (including Beirut), and they circulate periodic reports from the

[41] As noted earlier, authority to make certain types of purchases in the European area has been delegated to the Paris regional office. UNICEF also maintains small offices in London, Copenhagen, and Sydney for liaison with governments regarding procurement, contributions, and private fund-raising.

regional directors to other divisions in the secretariat. Although the Personnel Bureau handles the formal aspects of staff recruitment and administers salary, allowance and leave regulations, the Programme Division is consulted whenever a proposed field appointment relates to programme execution. On urgent supply matters, area and country offices may communicate directly with the Supply Division, but the Programme Division is kept *au courant*. The latter Division may review operating plans for projects, delegating to field offices as it deems appropriate authority to approve such plans without clearance by headquarters. In all its programme-making work, it should be added, the Programme Division keeps in close touch with the technical advisers of WHO, FAO, and the UN Bureau of Social Affairs assigned to UNICEF headquarters.

To sum up: there are three main reasons why UNICEF has been able to develop a comparatively efficient form of programme making and execution. First, it has managed to escape from the strait jacket of the yearly calendar with regard to programme formulation and money allocations. Over the years it has wisely built up a substantial backlog of funds by not immediately earmarking all of the annual contributions received from governments and other sources. This has made it possible to do forward planning with reasonable assurance that enough money would be available to finance its projected programme over a period of years.

A second reason for UNICEF's success may be attributed to the fact that its top command has kept under constant surveillance the operational relationships between headquarters and the field units. Instead of allowing these relationships to crystallize into a rigid procedural mould, headquarters adjusts them as need requires by simple, informal administrative directive. In the third place, UNICEF's personnel problem has been relatively easy to handle in view of the relatively small size of its administrative and operational staffs.[42] With regard to the technical aspects of project planning and operation, it relies on WHO, FAO, and to some extent on BTAO and the UN Bureau of Social Affairs, for advice and personnel. Moreover, the comparatively low turnover in UNICEF's compact bureaucracy

[42] For 1959, UNICEF's total establishment included only 175 professional and 251 general service posts. UN Doc. E/ICEF/L.1230, 8 June 1959.

has facilitated the evolution of smooth-working operational mechanisms.

TAB's headquarters secretariat

At UN headquarters the Technical Assistance Board has a permanent staff of approximately fifty persons, divided fairly evenly between the professional and general service categories, for general supervision over the inter-agency Expanded Programme. This secretariat consists of three units: (1) the Office of the Executive Chairman of TAB, (2) an Administrative Division, and (3) a Programme Division. The first unit assists the Chairman in exercising control over the TAB field offices, in maintaining liaison with participating agencies and governments, and in handling questions of financial policy affecting EPTA. The second unit provides for both headquarters and field offices services relating to personnel and budget administration, supply, transport, registry, and documentation. It is further responsible for the calculation and collection of amounts due from governments as 'local costs' of EPTA projects. Since the establishment of the Special Fund, this unit has also provided such central administrative services as are required for the Fund's operations.

The Programme Division of the TAB secretariat serves as the Executive Chairman's staff arm in connection with the formulation of country and regional target figures for programme planning purposes; processing and analysing programme requests submitted by individual governments; and consolidating such requests into the draft annual (now to be biennial) technical assistance programme for consideration by TAB and its subsequent submission to TAC for approval. Additional duties of this unit include preparing the sections of TAB's annual report dealing with programme operation and evaluation, and advising the Executive Chairman on how to act 'on urgent requests from governments for assistance to be financed from the Working Capital and Reserve Fund.' Further aspects of programme formulation and implementation, under TAB rules, will be discussed in Chapter 9.[43]

[43] This summary description of TAB's central secretariat is based partly on interviews with senior officers and partly on the Budget Estimates for 1959 contained in UN Doc. E/TAC/79, 27 Oct. 1958.

Central Financial and Management Controls over Field Operations

During the foregoing comparative survey of headquarters arrangements for field programme supervision, passing reference was made to the existence of various forms of control over the budgetary and management operations of field offices in those agencies maintaining permanent field machinery. It is now proposed to discuss briefly the nature, scope, and appropriateness of such controls.

At the outset it should be emphasized that no UN organization has found it either desirable or expedient to delegate to its field offices complete freedom as to financial expenditure, whether for staffing, supplies, travel, project outlays, or other purposes. Over-all fiscal accountability to the central legislative organ, and the necessity of controlling from one point the utilization of funds in different national currencies, has made it necessary to lay down detailed rules governing the allotment of moneys to field units, the extent to which headquarters approval must be obtained for the transfer of funds from one budget heading to another, and how actual expenditures are accounted for to headquarters. In general, the degree of discretion devolved upon field offices in these respects tends to vary with the size of office budgets, staffs, and volume of work. The same observation would hold with reference to the degree of central control exercised over the internal organizational structure of field offices; for example, the larger the office (as in WHO), the more leeway the director has to determine his office set-up, although he may feel all the more disposed to call upon headquarters for guidance in improving office methods and procedures.

The allotment process

Without exception field office directors prepare annual estimates of their office expense needs—apart from those items provided by the host government and, in the case of ILO and FAO, the salaries and other costs of headquarters staff assigned (or outposted) to such offices, which are paid from the budgetary appropriations of their respective headquarters divisions.[44] Field

[44] In FAO, the budgetary responsibilities of the main regional office for Latin America (at Santiago) and the two zone offices (at Rio and Mexico City) are divided. Each zone director submits to the regional director estimates relating to his office staff, maintenance,

office budget estimates are duly transmitted to the appropriate financial unit at headquarters for incorporation into the over-all draft budget of the agency. While the executive head may, and sometimes does, alter these estimates up or down (and of course they may be modified by the appropriating organ of the agency), they tend to become stabilized except when the operational responsibilities of an office are undergoing substantial change.

After approval of the budget by the assembly (or conference) of the agency, its executive head issues in writing, in terms of the relevant appropriation headings, allotments of funds for the ensuing year to the director of each field office. The latter then becomes responsible for assuring that obligations of funds are incurred only for the purposes indicated in the allotment and within the amounts specified. In most agencies the allotments are revised by headquarters two or three times during the year and adjustments made accordingly. Monthly (or quarterly) reports to headquarters showing the status of expenditures and obligations against allotments are required from the field offices of every agency.

Allotments are itemized by object of expenditure in all cases and, with few exceptions, the transfer of funds from one major item (*e.g.*, from supplies or hospitality to staff travel) may not be made without advance authorization by headquarters. While this usually is not difficult to obtain, it is sometimes delayed to the point of causing inconvenience in making local arrangements. In most cases local or regional staff travel schedules or both must be drawn up for periods of three months or longer in advance. Field office heads, however, ordinarily have authority to adjust such schedules within the limits of the total allotment for travel. In certain agencies (notably WHO), the regional director may on his own transfer minor items of operational expense within the 'general services' category (*e.g.*, office supplies, local transport, telephone, and printing), but for any major expenditure not provided in his budget he must always get headquarters approval.

---

supplies, and communication costs, which are then forwarded to Rome as separate estimates. For staff travel, on the other hand, the regional director submits an over-all estimate for all Latin America. Later, an allotment for travel is made to the regional office, which in turn sub-allots travel funds to each zone office as needed.

The general practice is to permit field offices to purchase locally supplies and materials needed for purely administrative purposes. This procedure not only obviates transport delays and customs clearance but makes it possible to utilize available local currency. Frequently, however, such items of office equipment as typewriters and adding machines may not be available locally and must be obtained from abroad. Operational (*i.e.*, project) supplies and equipment are generally procured through agency headquarters in order to take advantage of bulk-buying and to make use of the various national currencies that accrue to the agency. Such items, under EPTA rules, are limited to supplies and apparatus needed for setting up pilot projects or demonstrating new techniques, or for helping to equip training and research centres (*e.g.*, drugs, seeds, fertilizers, simple farm tools, laboratory equipment, books, technical documents, films, and audio-visual materials). During recent years expenditures for such items by all the participating agencies has averaged 9 to 11 per cent. of total project costs.[45] In a typical year purchases may be made from as many as fifty different countries.

It is customary in some agencies to permit project experts to make local purchases of small amounts of urgently needed supplies, and an imprest account is occasionally provided to cover such purchases, all of which must of course be accounted for.[46] In WHO, regional advisers assist in ascertaining medical supply requirements for field projects; the specifications are drawn up in the regional offices and forwarded to Geneva for action. In certain agencies project agreements do not always clearly stipulate supply ceilings and governments may ask for more than the project supply allotment calls for. In such cases the field office concerned has to cable headquarters for an additional allotment prior to initiating procurement operations, resulting in considerable delay. Various RTARs called the writer's attention to the

[45] Sometimes project equipment has been known to arrive at its destination with no experts to assemble it!

[46] In one agency, according to reliable report, a country mission chief in the Middle East sought permission to purchase Land-Rovers (jeeps) locally because of urgent need. Headquarters refused his request on account of the substantially higher costs, and the Land-Rovers were imported from Britain—after much delay. This was probably a case of bad planning; the order should have been placed much earlier. In another agency an expert cabled headquarters for permission to buy a tyre for his official car, but the Comptroller's ruling was negative and he was without the use of a car for field trips over a period of several weeks. Here was an emergency—not poor planning—yet the regulations were applied literally.

long lag between the placing of orders and the arrival and installation in the country of essential project equipment. With a view to speeding up this process, ILO, for example, has authorized its field offices to incur expenditure up to $100 at any one time provided the purpose is sound, there is urgency and conformity with TAB rules, and the expenditure is reported immediately to headquarters. In FAO, the Washington office is used for the procurement of supplies in the United States and Canada.

In WHO, where field programmes under the regular budget are drawn up on a regional basis, allotments are made to the regional offices covering each project separately. For continuing projects, money is allocated at the beginning of the fiscal year; for each new project, however, the regional director has to request headquarters to make an allotment when agreement is reached on the plan of operations. If there are savings on certain projects, the regional office may propose the transfer of funds to other projects or even to some new project not in the current budget, but all such proposals require headquarters approval. Under TAB regulations, limited transfers of funds from one EPTA project to another in the same country may be made by the agency headquarters concerned; transfers of funds from one country to another, however, must in addition be authorized by the Executive Chairman of TAB. The power to shift funds relating to regular programme projects was recently delegated by WHO headquarters to the Washington regional office, and in 1959 consideration was being given to delegating similar authority to all regional directors. This would permit any regional director to utilize all his savings in his own region, whereas at present Geneva may, if it wishes, transfer part of the savings to projects in other regions.

In WHO, there is some feeling that allotment controls over regional office expenditure are now too rigid. As might be expected, this view is encountered more frequently among regional than among central administrators. The former point to the annoying amount of correspondence and other paperwork involved in obtaining allotment changes from headquarters. In lieu of itemized allotments, it is argued, regional directors should be given a lump sum for administrative expenses, with maximum limits on the number of staff posts by grade. When a director feels it necessary to exceed such limits, headquarters would review the situation and decide. It is recognized that a bloc allotment system without limits would probably not be feasible since this would imply completely decentralized control over the manning table of regional offices and might lead to excessive deviations in the staffing structure of different offices.

Accounting and audit

Accounting for field programme expenditure is a complex process in the UN system for two reasons: (1) the existence of concurrent programmes financed from different budgetary sources, and (2) the necessity of utilizing a multiplicity of national currencies. Separate allotments, for example, have to be issued covering all expenditures under EPTA for accounting purposes. When it is remembered that the staffs of field offices are often paid partly out of regular budget funds and partly from the special EPTA account, and that the financing of numerous larger-scale projects may be similarly divided, the need of elaborate book-keeping arrangements is not surprising.

The accounting problem is further complicated by the fact that many of the national currencies in which EPTA (and even regular budget) contributions are made are not fully convertible. Although this situation has considerably improved during recent years, as late as 1959 only twenty-one countries made contributions in U.S. dollars convertible everywhere. Some forty-nine countries made no provision for the conversion of their contributions, while those of fifteen other countries were fully convertible in only two cases (Switzerland and the Netherlands), the rest being only partially convertible into sterling or dollars. The use of contributions from the Soviet bloc has caused particular difficulty.[47] The U.S.S.R. has

> refused to permit more than 25 per cent. of its contribution to be converted into other countries and then only for projects which it approves. . . . Much of the Soviet contribution can, as a matter of fact, be used only for supplies and equipment from the Iron Curtain countries since few Soviet experts come to the multilateral programs and no experts go to the Soviet.[48]

[47] See Robert Loring Allen, 'United Nations Technical Assistance: Soviet and East European Participation,' *International Organization* (Autumn 1957).

[48] Rowland Egger, 'Financing Technical Co-operation,' *The Annals* of the American Academy of Political and Social Science (May 1959).

As one means of easing the problem of how to use iron curtain currencies, TAB has set up 'special' projects for those countries willing to accept Soviet experts or equipment. Such arrangements frequently have involved what are in effect bilateral negotiations between the contributing and the receiving government. With a view to checking this tendency towards bilateralism in a multilateral programme, ECOSOC, in 1956, adopted a resolution which prohibits 'planning the expanded program so as to absorb any particular difficult currency.'[49]

There are other aspects of UN system field operations that tend to multiply the number of separate accounts that field offices have to keep. When a TAB office, for example, has responsibility for more than one country, it is obliged to maintain a separate programme account for each country. Also, TAB offices in many countries handle on request various local currency payments to experts or fellowship holders of certain specialized agencies. Unesco, for example, uses these offices for local payments arising out of its regular and Participation programme projects. Many of these operations require some additional accounting. Further, where a host government makes regular contributions towards the expense of a field office, a special accounting of expenditures from such contributions must be maintained in the currency of the country concerned.

Internal accounting arrangements in WHO have been fully decentralized to the regional offices. Funds of the organization are transferred to these offices from a primary account at Geneva and each regional director may set up such secondary accounts as he deems necessary. Detailed accounting and financial reporting procedures, however, are prescribed by headquarters in order to ensure uniformity in reporting. A somewhat similar arrangement obtains in UNICEF with respect to its regional offices.

All field offices with disbursement functions keep one or more imprest accounts as a cushion to cover day-to-day operational and emergency expenditure. This type of account is replenished periodically—usually each month—by headquarters so as to maintain a steady balance. For the UN regional commissions

[49] Allen, *op. cit.*, summarizing ECOSOC's Resolution 623 (XXII) of 9 Aug. 1956.

an imprest account is maintained in dollars at UN headquarters as well as locally in the currency of the host country. As indicated above, all agencies require monthly reports of expenditures with accompanying vouchers. The local currency portions of the salaries of internationally recruited field staff, in addition to all entitlements for local staff, are paid by the appropriate field office of the employing organization, while headquarters normally handles 'home' currency payments directly. Under TAB regulations, the local living costs of project experts are paid by the TAB country offices from funds advanced to TAB by recipient governments (in most countries) calculated on the basis of 50 per cent. of the subsistence allowance rate for each man-day spent by an expert in the country, the remainder being borne by the employing agency.[50] In case of serious hardship, TAB may grant exemptions to governments with respect to this charge for specified periods.

Internal audits of field office accounts in certain agencies include on-the-spot checks by visiting auditors from headquarters. WHO and UNICEF have gone even further and outposted an auditor from headquarters to various regional offices. In WHO this is now the practice as regards the Manila, Washington, and Lima offices.[51] The auditor at Manila handles the New Delhi regional accounts as well. The Chief of the Internal Audit Services at Geneva arranges to visit the Alexandria and Brazzaville office every year or so, while Copenhagen is audited directly from headquarters.

In FAO, regular visits are made by the head of its Internal Audit and Inspection Service at Rome to each regional and zone office every two years for on-the-spot reviews of regional accounts. During his tours he also attempts to cover the offices of the country representatives. To a limited extent this roving official looks into the administrative procedures of field offices but does not purport to conduct a thorough management audit. Similarly, internal auditors from the UN Controller's office at New York conduct field checks fairly regularly—at the UN European Office, the regional commission secretariats, the UN Information Centres, and the TAB country offices. By contrast,

[50] The annual reports of TAB list the relative amounts actually paid by governments and by the participating agencies for subsistence entitlements.

[51] This decentralization extends 'sub-regionally' in the Americas to the 'zone' offices of PASB—which is why an auditor has been stationed at Lima.

internal audits of field offices in ILO, Unesco, and ICAO are carried out for the most part at headquarters in connection with the general organizational audit.

For each organization a complete external audit is conducted annually in accordance with conditions laid down by its legislative organ. Auditors from various national governmental services are engaged for this purpose. These external auditors from time to time make spot checks at various overseas offices but do not visit the field periodically. Co-ordination of the external audits of the UN and the specialized agencies is provided through a Joint Panel of Auditors set up by the General Assembly. Separate audit reports covering EPTA accounts, after approval by the general conference of each participating agency, are transmitted to the Assembly for examination and final approval.[52]

It was not possible, within the scope of the present study, to make any intensive analysis of accounts and audit reports. All available evidence, however, would indicate that a high level of honesty and integrity in the handling of funds has characterized UN and specialized agency administration. Thus far no breath of scandal has touched their financial transactions. On the other hand, accounting procedures, although involved and time-consuming, would not appear to have contributed much, if anything, to the improvement of efficiency or economy in the management of field offices or of project operations. To this question we now turn our attention.

Review and inspection of field management

During the earlier years, such central control over the administrative management of field operations as was exercised by headquarters was limited to the normal budgetary process. As we have already indicated, headquarters finance services, in the course of approving draft budget estimates for field office expenses, review and adjust manning tables and the grading of internationally recruited staff. By and large, however, the internal organization of such offices has been left for determination by their respective directors, the latter also being authorized to classify all posts filled by local staff. In most of the agencies, there has been no attempt to impose any rigid or standard

[52] In accordance with GA Resolution 519 (VI), 12 Jan. 1952.

patterns upon field office administration.[53] WHO, in particular, has felt that each regional office should have 'the largest possible degree of flexibility in organizational arrangements in the interests of enabling each to be as responsive as possible to the specific needs of the region.'[54] This policy has resulted in a wide variation in the proportion of regional office staff to project staff in different regions, as well as in differing ratios of regional office expenditure to expenditure for field projects from one region to another. Notwithstanding the exercise of formal control over field office budgets by WHO headquarters, the political position of one or two regional directors has been so strong as to make it possible for them to indulge in a bit of 'empire-building' at the regional level—with the backing of the regional committee concerned.

In an effort to bring WHO regional office administration under closer and more continuous central surveillance, the practice of detailing administration and finance officers from Geneva to the regions was initiated a few years ago. As noted in Chapter 5, these officers are now rotated from one regional office to another, with intervening periods of duty at headquarters. A somewhat similar procedure has developed in the UN, where headquarters administrative officers are assigned to service with the regional commission secretariats. ILO also follows the practice of stationing central administrative staff at its principal field offices. While FAO does not do this, there are administrative officers in the regional offices (and attached to a few of the larger field missions) who, although administratively responsible to the regional or country representative concerned, look towards the Director of Administration at Rome for guidance.

A companion development has been the establishment in the central secretariats of two agencies—WHO and FAO—of

[53] One exception to this should be noted. Some years ago the General Assembly, desiring to restrict DPI (now OPI) expenditure, prescribed rigid staffing limits for the UN Information Centres in terms of a 'six-four-two' pattern. The largest Centres were arbitrarily limited to a staff of six persons, and the others to four or two persons, without regard to the amount of work to be done or the area to be covered. This restriction was removed in 1955 when the Secretary-General was given the right 'to make manning table adjustments between the centers and the Headquarters staff.' Waldo Chamberlin, 'Administrative Matters,' in Clyde Eagleton and Richard N. Swift, eds., *Annual Review of United Nations Affairs, 1955–1956* (New York Univ. Press, 1957), pp. 167–168.

[54] The quotation is from a statement made by the Assistant Director-General for Administration and Finance to the 1958 World Health Assembly, WHO Doc. A 11/AFL/18, 30 May 1958.

special units whose task is to conduct continuing analyses of administrative management procedures for the agency. While no comparable arrangement has yet been introduced into the UN Secretariat, the Office of the Controller has recently begun to give some attention to 'organization and methods' problems, largely as a result of recommendations made by the Advisory Committee on Administrative and Budgetary Questions.[55]

It was not until 1955 that the UN or any associated agency undertook to conduct on-the-spot surveys of overseas office operations. In that year, as noted earlier, the Secretary-General dispatched a Headquarters Survey Group to visit the European Office, the secretariats of the regional economic commissions, and the UN Information Centres, and to report on their administrative problems. Largely on the basis of this Group's proposals, various changes were made in the relationship of these field establishments to headquarters, as well as in their staffing and internal structures.[56] Some of these changes were referred to earlier in this chapter.

Concerned over the growing shift of emphasis to regional and country level units in UN's economic and social activities and public information work, the Advisory Committee subsequently pointed to the need of 'a continuous review and periodical inspections of all overseas offices and missions for the purpose of ensuring that they function efficiently and at a minimum cost.'[57] To this end it proposed the establishment of a small management unit in the UN controller's office. The Committee also urged that responsibility for the rental and operation of premises and equipment, and, incidentally, of communications and other common services at field offices should as far as possible be 'centralized' at UN headquarters. This latter proposal, as was noted in Chapter 4, led to a detailed report early in 1959 on the location of field offices, their facilities, and the progress being made towards the consolidation of premises and services. This report, however, was prepared, not by the Controller's Office, but by the Office of General Services

[55] In its *Fifth Report to the Twelfth Session of the General Assembly*, UN Doc. A/3624, 1957.

[56] See UN Doc. A/3041, 23 Nov. 1955, for the Secretary-General's comments on the Survey Group's recommendations; and A/3049, 28 Nov. 1955, for the Advisory Committee's reaction to his proposals.

[57] *Advisory Committee on Administrative and Budgetary Questions Fifth Report to the Twelfth Session of the General Assembly*, *op. cit.*

in view of the latter's direct responsibility for physical housekeeping operations in the Secretariat.

Within the former office, some progress towards the creation of 'a general management arm' had been made by the end of 1958. The Controller, speaking before the Fifth Committee of the 1958 Assembly, reported that 'there was already a small team of officials [in his Office] which had been dealing with review and inspection for several months and the Secretariat hoped ultimately to have a larger staff at its disposal for that purpose.'[58] Eventually it is anticipated that management review will include an attempt to develop common administrative standards for field units. The Administrative Management staff is now planning frequent personal inspections of the administrative affairs of the UN Information Centres, regional commission secretariats, and special political missions.

Among the specialized agencies only WHO has thus far undertaken on-the-spot 'organization and methods' studies of field offices. These studies, initiated in 1955, have been carried out by members of the staff of its central Administrative Management unit. In some instances requests for such studies have come from the regional director, but they have usually been stimulated by headquarters. By the end of 1958, management surveys, more or less comprehensive, had been made at Alexandria, Manila, Brazzaville, and New Delhi. When the Copenhagen office was opened, an Administrative Management official was sent to help the director set up his office organization. For the most part these various management surveys have dealt with such matters as the internal distribution of administrative duties and authority, classification of files, registry, record-keeping, and procurement. As a consequence, in several instances, improved procedures were introduced which are said to have produced considerable savings in time and clerical staff. While on-the-spot studies have been conducted sporadically in FAO the relatively small size of its field offices makes the need of such studies less important than in WHO. One survey has been conducted at Cairo and others are contemplated.[59]

In the fall of 1958 the Administrative Management division

[58] GA, O.R.: 13th Sess., 5th Committee, 659th Mtg., 16 Oct. 1958.

[59] The senior administrative officer at UNICEF headquarters spends a part of each year visiting field offices which (as in FAO) are for the most part too small to require detailed management surveys.

at WHO headquarters was reportedly contemplating studies of the administrative problems of project management and servicing. Supporting evidence from some of the regional office surveys had indicated that this constituted an important administrative need. So far, project arrangements have been in the hands of senior medical staff, the regional Administration and Finance division ordinarily not being allowed by the regional director to deal with project management. The aim of the contemplated studies would be to show how field projects might be got under way more expeditiously and be more efficiently operated. Such studies would involve consultations between the regional public health advisers and administrative personnel at the time project operational plans are drafted. Before actual initiation of a project, administrative staff would presumably go to the country concerned and aid in negotiations with governments as to facilities, supplies, transport, housing, and so forth. Such negotiations now often consume two to three weeks' time of project experts, who would doubtless welcome administrative help. If the WHO area representatives could be provided with more adequate secretarial and clerical assistance they might conceivably, after appropriate orientation, perform such services.

The development of strengthened administrative support for project operations would almost certainly require some additional staff both in the regional offices and at the country level. Whether WHO budgetary authorities can be convinced that the increased costs would be more than offset by improved project efficiency is at least doubtful. Nor is it likely to be easy to 'sell' the regional directors on the proposition that administrative specialists can do a better job than the 'medics' are now doing.

As suggested at the outset, the principal purpose of this chapter has been to describe the interplay of centrifugal and integrative trends affecting field programme supervision and execution. In tracing the evolving arrangements for field delegation and central control in various agencies, the focus has been mainly on the role and responsibility of their headquarters secretariats. In order to understand how these arrangements actually work, however, it is necessary to examine the process by which information and experience are communicated through the organization—vertically from headquarters to the field and from the field to headquarters—and laterally as between related field missions and with co-operating agencies. This process, of signal importance in multi-cultural administration, is the theme of the chapter that follows.

7

COMMUNICATION AND LOGISTICS

Communication in administration may be defined broadly as the process by which decisions, guidance, and information are transmitted through an organization and to the constituency it serves. Communication is a two-way operation, involving both a sender and a receiver. When it concerns headquarters-field relations it may, and often does, have a three-dimensional aspect, including lateral communication between various substantive and operational units at headquarters, and vertical communication between headquarters and field personnel. A primary purpose of such communication is to develop mutual understanding of programme goals and of the instrumentalities for implementing them. Considered from this point of view, communication channels may be said to play 'the dual role of providing the means by which the controllers control and for providing "feed back" filtering upward from subordinate [*i.e.*, field] levels.'[1]

The techniques of administrative communication are of many kinds. They may be formal or informal, primary or secondary. Formal communication embraces such devices as administrative manuals; the issuance of directives, orders and instructions; circulation of office memoranda; the use of standard forms (*e.g.*, for budgeting, accounting, clearances, applications, settlement of claims, and the like); and official reporting and correspondence. Informal communication, on the other hand, is built around 'the social relationships of the members of the organization.'[2] In this type of communication fact and rumour may be circulated by 'the grape-vine,' 'gossip,' or 'shop talk.' In many organizations rivalries among staff 'cliques' (sometimes taking

[1] J. A. Slesinger, *A Model for the Comparative Study of Public Bureaucracies* (Ann Arbor: Bureau of Government, Univ. of Michigan, 1957).

[2] The quoted passage is from Herbert Simon's *Administrative Behavior* (New York: Macmillan, 1947), Chap. VIII. Simon has done pioneering work on the role of communication in administration.

shape along national lines in UN agencies), in their quest for power or prestige, may produce conflicting or confusing information, often running counter to the official line.

Viewed from a somewhat different angle, communication channels may be classified as primary or secondary. In primary communication, information is ordinarily conveyed by direct, face-to-face contact, although a telephone conversation, when the connections are clear, may provide some of the same psychological values. Within an office, staff conferences, committees, and task forces constitute widely utilized methods of arriving at group decisions by face-to-face discussion. For the most part, communication between physically dispersed offices (or field missions) is necessarily indirect, or secondary, in that it requires the use of communication media—postal, telegraphic, and telephonic—for the flow of intelligence downward, upward, and laterally. Here the barrier of distance may to some extent be circumvented by frequent visits of staff to and from headquarters, the rotation of staff from office to office, and the interchange of experience by means of periodic conferences of related groups of central and field officials.

In this connection, it is relevant to consider how the delegation of programme administration to field units may affect communication. This is not an easy question to answer. Undoubtedly, as in WHO and EPTA, the geographic decentralization of programme-making facilitates informal communication with national governments, institutions, and population groups. At the same time, decentralization may increase the difficulty of developing effective communication between regional or country offices and headquarters, and possibly between different field areas. As a general proposition, it may perhaps be said that the more programme administration is decentralized, the more complex becomes the problem of communicating headquarters policy decisions to the field. On the other hand, 'delegation usually reduces the difficulty of communicating to the decision center information about the particular [field] situation in question.'[3]

[3] Herbert Simon, Donald W. Smithburg, and Victor A. Thompson, *Public Administration* (New York: Knopf, 1950), p. 239.

Special Conditions Affecting Communication in the UN System

Communication in international organizations is complicated by a number of special factors that are not present at all, or only to a much more limited degree, in most national administrations. The first of these factors, which is psychological, derives from the multi-cultural composition of the constituencies and the administrative staffs of inter-governmental agencies. Not only does this give rise to difficulties of language translation and interpretation as regards written documents, records, and correspondence, but large numbers—in some cases a majority—of the personnel in the policy control organs and the bureaucracies of an agency are obliged to employ in conference and staff work a spoken language different from their native tongue. For such persons significant shades of meaning are often lost.

Over and beyond this is the fact that public administrators, lawyers, and accountants are prone to develop specialized vocabularies of their own—'jargon' and 'gobbledegook' as it were—which are not easily understood by the layman or even, at times, by their counterparts from other cultures.[4] This tendency is to be found also among certain categories of technicians who serve on field missions (*e.g.*, educationists and social workers). For all these reasons areas of semantic confusion tend to be much more numerous in multi-national than in national administration.

A third differential is the time-space factor. Although this factor, to be sure, has to be coped with by the overseas services (diplomatic, consular, economic, informational) of national governments with world-wide interests, it involves certain special problems in the administration of international economic and social programmes. The shrinkage of the world in communication terms has of course made it technically possible to keep far-flung offices in much closer contact than before the days of inter-continental air mail and the overseas telephone. Even so, the mechanics of communication with offices off the beaten track, even more with field experts operating in isolated rural

[4] At a recent meeting of UNIC directors in Geneva, it turned out that one director thought that 'mass media' meant 'personal contacts with influential people' (as related to the writer by one of the participants).

areas, still leaves much to be desired.[5] The time it takes for air mail to go from Europe and North America to field centres in Asia, Africa south of the Sahara, various parts of the Middle East, and the southern part of South America currently ranges from four or five days to more than a week, while surface mail may take several weeks or even months.[6] The handling of air mail at many terminal points is exceedingly slow and inefficient—not alone, incidentally, in the so-called under-developed countries. In certain countries, moreover, national censorship not infrequently delays the dispatch of cables—as well as of letters sent outside the official pouch. When there is civil strife or a change of political régime in a country, local mail service may be disrupted for considerable periods. Letters sometimes get lost and never reach their destination.[7] In certain areas air mail has to be registered because otherwise the stamps may come loose or be pilfered by dishonest, impoverished postal employees.

Even so, air mail constitutes the principal method of field communication. Cables and telegrams must of course be used to a certain extent, but there are budgetary pressures in every agency to keep the outlays for this type of communication down to a minimum.[8] In the administration of technical assistance, for example, cables are resorted to chiefly to expedite decisions on the clearance of experts, the shipment of supplies, and travel arrangements, and to provide advice on the arrival and departure of experts. Frequently, also, according to the testimony of numerous field offices, cables are a necessary follow-up on air

[5] One reason why ECAFE, for example, has enjoyed more administrative freedom than ECE is probably because the former's location is much further away from UN headquarters.

[6] Some illustrative time periods required for mail from overseas offices to New York are indicated below:

Location of office	*Air mail*	*Surface mail*
Cairo	about 5 days	25 days to a month
Karachi	5 to 7 days	5 to 8 weeks
New Delhi	about 5 days	4 to 6 weeks
Teheran	6 to 10 days	3 to 5 months
Bangkok	7 to 10 days	6 to 10 weeks

From Santiago to Rome (FAO headquarters) surface mail sent by the FAO regional office takes about three weeks if the Andean railway is working and steamer connections are good; otherwise much longer. It takes three times as long for an air mail letter to go from Venezuela to Santiago than from Santiago to New York.

[7] It usually takes about eight days for a letter from Beirut to reach the designated office in Cairo, and vice versa, because of censorship delays. Letters from Cairo to Sudan and Ethiopia reportedly often fail to arrive at all.

[8] As well as from the UN Advisory Committee on Administrative and Budgetary Questions.

mail letters the replies to which are delayed at headquarters. One RTAR, in Latin America, related to the writer how he could have saved $200 in cable costs if TAA in New York had replied in time. Letters received at agency headquarters may pass from desk to desk without action. In certain field offices, it is fairly common practice to send a cable at the same time as a letter is dispatched in order to stimulate prompt action.

Use of the long-distance telephone for field communication is decidedly limited except for offices relatively close to headquarters (*e.g.*, Mexico and Central America in relation to New York and the Mediterranean in relation to Europe). There are three reasons for this. One is the high cost of overseas telephone messages, resulting in constant pleas for economy from central finance offices.[9] A second reason is that for many parts of the world the quality of long-distance telephone service is very poor—the connections being bad and the other end of the line often 'fading out.' Still more important, perhaps, is the difficulty of conducting informal discussions by telephone when one or both of the participants have to speak in a language other than their own—frequently with a marked accent. An official using 'Texan' English may even find it difficult to understand on the telephone another employing the 'Oxford' variety of the same language. Telephone conversations necessarily have to be hurried, and the man at the receiving end may not be mentally prepared to respond immediately to the sender's query. Telephonic communication thus has distinct limitations, given the poor service, the language problem, and the absence of facial impact—even if it were financially feasible to use it in other than crisis situations. Nor is it a substitute for face-to-face discussion.

Scheduled diplomatic air pouch services, usually two or three times a week, operate from UN and specialized agency headquarters to the principal field offices. The granting of

[9] In the UN, the overseas telephone is utilized primarily for 'peace and security' matters—comparatively little for economic and technical activities. One RTAR in Latin America told the writer how he had been officially 'scolded' for using the long-distance telephone too much—although, he observed, the telephone was really 'his salvation' when there was no answer to an air letter to UN headquarters calling for prompt action. In its report to the General Assembly on the 1958 UN budget estimates, the Advisory Committee, while recognizing that an appreciable reduction in outlays for long-distance telephone calls had been made at Headquarters, was not certain that 'equally stringent measures are applied at all other offices.' The Committee urged 'a similar application of the strict measures adopted at Headquarters.' UN Doc. A/3624.

diplomatic privileges to United Nations organizations by governments is 'a courtesy of trust,' granted on request (seldom denied). Only mail relating to the official business of the organization may be dispatched by pouch.[10] There is also regular air pouch service from field offices to headquarters (and occasionally to other field offices) when and as justified by the volume of traffic. As indicated in an earlier chapter, arrangements have been made at the more important field centres for the sharing of the pouch of one field office by others located at the same centre. Thus, for example, at New Delhi the WHO pouch to Geneva and New York is used by TAB, UNIC, and UNICEF. At Santiago the FAO regional office shares ECLA's pouch to New York, while at Beirut most of the local offices use the UNRWA pouch to headquarters and the UNICEF pouch to Cairo. At Karachi, the UNICEF 'area' office has its own semi-weekly pouch to the regional office at Bangkok. On the other hand, the UNICEF office at Lima discontinued some time ago its pouch to New York because the small volume of correspondence 'was not worth it.' In Cairo, the UNICEF 'country' office uses the UN pouch to New York and the Unesco pouch to Paris (for correspondence with the UNICEF regional office there). For communication with Beirut, this same office used a land pouch to Gaza and from there on the UN Truce Organization plane. Because of postal difficulties in Egypt the WHO office at Alexandria (during 1958 at least) was sharing the Beirut UNICEF pouch to New York. Arrangements vary from place to place as local needs and conditions dictate. When pouch service is shared, costs are apportioned among the agencies concerned according to volume of traffic. Traffic by pouch usually reaches its destination a day or two earlier than regular air mail since it does not have to be distributed by local postal authorities.

For bulky shipments of documents surface mail ordinarily must be employed for reasons of economy. This means that important official documents may not reach a field office (*e.g.*, to a remote place like Teheran) until months later. There is a good deal of complaint about this from field office directors in the Middle East and Asia.

[10] See the *Instructions Governing United Nations Diplomatic Mails and the Diplomatic Pouch Services*, UN Doc. ST/AI/124/Rev. 1, 24 Nov. 1958.

With a view (1) to reducing the costs of field communication and (2) to protecting itself against interruptions of traffic during international crises, the United Nations now operates a telecommunications network of its own. The establishment of such a network was approved by the General Assembly in 1948.[11] At first, lines were rented from the Radio Corporation of America and other commercial services but gradually the UN set up its own transmitters and operating personnel. The system grew bit by bit as the volume of traffic on 'peace and security' matters increased over the years. There are now eight major UN transmitters—in New York, Geneva, Pisa, Gaza, Jerusalem, Karachi, Bangkok, and Seoul—the establishment of each transmitter requiring the consent of the host government. The Telecommunications Centre in the UN Geneva Office is responsible, on behalf of headquarters, for administering radio frequencies, monitoring, and registration with the International Telecommunication Union. The system now connects New York with Geneva, and then on to Gaza and Jerusalem and various points east (Karachi, Bangkok, and Seoul). Messages are relayed by cable to nearby points not covered by the UN radio network (*e.g.*, from Seoul to Tokyo). Consideration has recently been given to the possibility of extending the network to South America but so far the volume of traffic with that continent is not deemed to be sufficient to warrant such action. Current facilities include a direct radio-teleprinter channel between New York and Geneva.

In Europe, Geneva is connected with London, Paris, Rome, and Bonn by 'telex,' which is rented like teletype. This service is similar to a teleprinter system, providing immediate connection and response. It is available to the specialized agencies with offices in Paris (Unesco, ICAO, IBRD, and IMF).

The UN radio network functions primarily for the UN Field Operations Service and such 'peace and security' missions as the Palestine Truce Supervision Organization, the Korean armistice command, the UN observers in Kashmir, and the UN Emergency Force in the Middle East. But it may be and is used for communication with the UN regional commission secretariats, the Information Centres, and the TAB field offices. Under regulations laid down by the 1952 plenipotentiary Conference of ITU,

[11] GA Resolution 240 (III), 18 Nov. 1948

however, its use by the specialized agencies is restricted to emergencies and to traffic directly relating to U.N. operations only.[12] These restrictions were imposed as a consequence of pressures exerted by various international radio cartels and national 'PTT' services which were afraid of losing traffic due to 'competition' from the UN family of agencies. Also, there was allegedly some fear that opening the door wide to the major specialized agencies might lead to requests to utilize the UN network from General Motors and other big private corporations operating overseas. Here, ironically enough, may be seen a not very edifying example of one member of the UN family—the ITU—limiting the use of an international service capable of benefiting its sister agencies largely as a result of opposition from commercial groups and national administrations. Within the limits set, the specialized agencies make comparatively little use of the UN telecommunications system, even for their UN business, since they must identify each message as being 'solely' for that purpose—which is an administrative nuisance.

Although the UN secretariat has not as yet made any systematic study of the costs of sending messages through the UN radio network by comparison with commercial channels, the savings are estimated at well over 50 per cent. Commercial rates per word are nearly 100 per cent. higher than the rates charged by the UN to the specialized agencies for such limited use as they make of the UN system. As the volume of traffic increases, the greater will be the gross savings. During the past few years the increase has been tremendous, particularly with the Middle East. For example, the volume going through Geneva in 1954 was only 200,000 words a month while by 1958 it had expanded to over 1,000,000 words.[13] If a UN telecommunications network spanning the entire world, and available to all UN agencies without restriction, could be established—this is the goal—the total savings would be even more impressive, in addition to providing the assurance of uninterrupted traffic during international crises.

[12] See Field Service General Instruction No. 310–3.

[13] Information supplied to the writer by courtesy of the head of the UN Telecommunications Centre at Geneva.

Briefing and Orientation of Field Staffs

Let us now shift our attention from the techniques and mechanisms of field communication to an analysis of its substantive content, adequacy, and effectiveness. For such an analysis it is appropriate to begin with the process by which field personnel are briefed for their assignments. As the term briefing itself implies, this process tends to be decidedly restricted in time and depth. Briefing arrangements, in the UN system, are mainly the responsibility of each employing agency. For the most part these arrangements have evolved in rather unplanned and unsystematic fashion. During the first few years of EPTA, little sustained thinking was devoted by the agency secretariats to the nature or importance of orienting experts for overseas service. Nor was the close relation of briefing to prior selection and training given the recognition it deserved.

In reality, briefing is, or should be, only the first stage of a continuous process of orientation and guidance throughout the duration of a field assignment. This is a highly complex problem, given the wide variety of nationalities, skills, and cultural situations involved in the conduct of global economic, social, and technical programmes. If, for example, it were possible to recruit ideally equipped experts in terms not merely of technical competence but of knowledge of the country of assignment and capacity to adjust to cultural shock, initial briefing might be reduced to a fairly simple operation consisting chiefly of the provision of factual information about the employing agency, its programme, and its administrative procedures. As revealed in our discussion of field staffing policies in Chapter 5, however, the vast majority of persons selected for technical assistance work do not possess anything approaching such ideal equipment. Many of them—possibly the majority—have had little previous experience in cross-cultural settings, or in adapting their professional skills to the value systems prevalent in underdeveloped areas. Still fewer have ever received any systematic training at home for international service.

For all these reasons initial orientation becomes a many-sided problem. Most newly appointed experts, when they arrive at agency headquarters or a field office, are strange to the *mores* of an inter-governmental organization. The kinds of information they need fall into four fairly distinct categories: (1) information concerning the role, set-up, and field programmes of the UN system in general, and of the employing agency in particular; (2) administrative information covering such matters as pay, allowances, rules governing travel, the shipment of personal effects, leaves-of-absence, reporting, purchase and accounting for supplies and equipment, and the working relations of the expert with the RTARs and the field representatives of his own and cognate agencies; (3) information bearing on the culture of the country of assignment and the kinds of difficulties and frustrations the expert is likely to encounter in carrying out his mission; and (4) information on the objectives and organization of his project, together with guidance as to how to communicate the skills and techniques required for its implementation, based as far as possible on previous successful (and unsuccessful) attempts to transmit such skills and techniques under similar circumstances. This is indeed a large order. Even now, after a decade of experience, no UN agency would claim to have solved the problem to its complete satisfaction.

As early as 1952, the Technical Assistance Board undertook a survey of the briefing arrangements then being used by the organizations participating in EPTA. To conduct this survey, the Board engaged Dr. Walter H. C. Laves, formerly Deputy Director-General of Unesco. The Laves Report, completed in September of that year, enumerated various deficiencies in agency briefing and made a number of constructive suggestions for its improvement.[14] TAB subsequently recommended to the agencies that they 'give due emphasis to briefing, if necessary by employing a briefing officer at the appropriate grade. The Board also arranged for a meeting of agency briefing officers, at which standard briefing "kits" were worked out,' and 'undertook to produce a uniform series of country reports' (on living conditions, for example). Concerning the most radical proposal in the Laves Report, namely, that four regional briefing centres be set up at Lima, Beirut, New Delhi, and Bangkok, the Board took no action; instead it decided as an experiment merely to appoint in 1953 to the staff of one RTAR 'a specialist qualified in anthropology or social science . . . to work out and apply, over a six-months' period, model orientation and briefing courses

[14] The text of the report is contained in UN Doc. TAB/R.203, 8 Sept. 1952.

for experts arriving in the country.' Nor did the Board, as the Laves Report had suggested, set up any central briefing service, each agency (including TAB for the staffs of its field offices) retaining primary responsibility for briefing arrangements both at headquarters and at the field level. The Board, however, did recommend that agencies with headquarters at Geneva 'should consider the possibility of pooling some of their resources for briefing and orientation, perhaps through the appointment of a common briefing officer.'[15]

Since 1953 considerable improvement in the briefing procedures of certain agencies has taken place, but the concrete follow-up on TAB's cautious recommendations has been disappointingly spotty. From time to time the Executive Chairman of TAB has sponsored inter-agency meetings to discuss briefing problems and more attention is now being given in briefing to the wider aspects of technical assistance and to information concerning the programmes of other UN agencies and the various bilateral schemes operating in the country concerned. But glaring weaknesses in agency briefing still persist.

What are the major weaknesses? First, in most agencies too little time is allowed for briefing at headquarters. The briefing period ranges from two or three days to a week or a little longer, the average being only four or five days. Among the reasons for this hurried procedure are (1) pressures from governments to get experts to the field as promptly as possible, especially those on appointments of a year or less, and (2) the tendency of busy headquarters staffs to regard briefing as 'an extra chore,' to be got through as quickly as possible. In most agencies the practice is for the personnel bureau to schedule a series of short interviews with such technical specialists as may be available at the time. Only a few agencies have a briefing officer as such. Where there is a field operations unit, it is usually responsible for supplying administrative and housekeeping information. Most agencies have prepared compact documents containing background information as a guide for experts in the field. For many countries there is also now available a so-called 'post report,' prepared under the auspices of the RTAR's office, in

[15] The foregoing quotations are from the *Fifth Report of the TAB*, ECOSOC, O.R.: 16th Sess., 1953, Suppl. No. 10 (E/2433), pp. 25–26.

which is summarized factual information on the history, climate, and geography of the country; on transportation and communications; on customs and currency regulations; on housing, food, and clothing costs and requirements, and on local recreational facilities. These post reports, while clearly useful, are not always kept up to date and the information provided, say, on the cost of living in inflationary economies may give the expert a completely false notion of what to expect.[16]

In the second place, the guidance provided on the substantive aspects of project operations is often spotty and seldom accurate. As one official frankly admitted to the writer, briefing is largely 'a matter of luck'—depending on what technical staff happen to be available and how disposed they are to talk at length with a newly recruited expert. During private talks by the writer with a substantial sample of technical assistance personnel in the field, this was the point mentioned most frequently. In many instances, it appears, there was not time to examine the file of field reports at headquarters relating to comparable projects or programmes—or in some cases the expert's attention may not even have been directed to the existence of such materials. Nor was there opportunity, except rarely, for group discussions with technical officers acquainted with the project and conditions in the country concerned. Films and audio-visual aids were apparently used but little to vivify the overseas activities of the UN family of nations. One is struck by the number of field experts who associate the UN in their minds with their inevitable frustrations and difficulties—instead of considering themselves the constructive emissaries of the world community. On the whole, information on administrative matters was reported to be reasonably adequate, but substantive briefing was characterized by a considerable number of experts 'as a farce.' A few said that they had had no such briefing at all as a result of the speed with which they were rushed through headquarters, or because it was too expensive to route them to headquarters or to a regional office on the way to their duty stations.

The tenor of the experts' testimony, to be sure, was not all on the critical side. One technician, for example, told how he had

[16] Some of these post reports are prepared by the wives of experts; others are based largely on reports issued by U.S. Embassies. In 1958 one TAB office in the Middle East was still using a report five years old.

been able to study relevant documents and reports in unhurried fashion, and then was asked to write a résumé of his assignment as he conceived it. This paper was reviewed and there was further staff consultation with a view to 'correcting his errors.' Another man (in a different agency) reported complete satisfaction with the reception given him at headquarters—he had read a collection of reports on related field projects and had had his job explained by two staff members who, as nationals of the duty country, knew local conditions intimately. This particular expert, incidentally, took shorthand notes on all his interviews, and was fortunate in being able to converse fluently in English, French and German. If space permitted, similarly favourable reactions from other experts could be cited. But they rather tended to be the exceptions.

The third and perhaps most striking defect in agency briefing appears to be a widespread neglect of the 'human relations' aspects of cross-cultural service. To quote from a discussion of this problem in another context: 'Either it has been assumed that most human beings will be able to communicate and relate to their new neighbours without assistance, or else the difficulties inherent in the new relationships were underestimated.'[17] Admittedly, how to provide really helpful guidance on ways of coping with anxieties and frustrations is a very difficult problem, requiring the application of modern psychological knowledge with which UN agency staffs ordinarily are not equipped. Not much systematic information has yet been assembled concerning the 'transformer' operations necessary to adapt the teaching techniques of one culture to the needs of another.[18] Much more than the language barrier is involved here. As the Laves Report suggested, this problem can probably be best dealt with at the regional (or country) level, where psychological theory and operational experience in related culture areas might, under skilful professional guidance, be joined.

All things considered, perhaps the most important value gained by most field experts from headquarters briefing is that

[17] *Working Abroad: A Discussion of Psychological Attitudes and Adaptation in New Situations*, Report No. 41 (New York: Group for the Advancement of Psychiatry, 1958), p. 515.

[18] In this connection, BTAO is now developing a new briefing concept designed to give to the incoming expert a sense of close relationship with previous project experience. Information explaining the application of UN techniques in the field (in reference to census-taking, budget classification, fiscal policies, and so forth) is made available to the new recruit.

they get something of the 'feel' of the secretariat—by meeting at least some of the staff with whom they will later be in communication when overseas. The ability to personalize headquarters-field relations can be a real satisfaction when emergencies arise.

In addition to briefing at headquarters, those UN agencies with field office establishments make use of them for the orientation of project personnel to the local environment. In cases where it is not possible to route new experts through headquarters, the only briefing they may get will be from the nearest regional (or country) office. In WHO, briefing is divided between Geneva and the regional offices, each dealing with certain aspects of the total process. To a somewhat less extent the ILO field offices are used for briefing purposes, while in FAO the 'outposted' technical personnel are helpful in this connection, as are some of the 'country representatives.'[19] In Unesco, country chiefs of mission, many of whom will have had four or five years of experience in the area, are depended upon to orient new members of a project team. In ICAO, experts coming from North America are almost always briefed at Montreal. When it is possible to send a new expert through a regional office this is done. In many cases briefing by chiefs of field missions is considered sufficient. Upon arrival for duty, technical assistance experts may draw upon the RTAR and his staff for general information concerning local conditions. Few RTARs, however, are equipped, or expected, to supply technical briefing. Especially in countries where there is no agency field office, or chief of mission, experts of the agency concerned have to depend on the TAB office for whatever on-the-spot orientation they get.

During recent years the substantive staffs of the regional economic commissions—at Geneva, Santiago and Bangkok—have been utilized increasingly to brief UN experts in such fields as industry, trade, power, transport, communications, and agriculture. For social welfare projects, the recently outposted UN Social Affairs units are similarly useful. These staffs, by reason of their continuing contacts in the region, are in a position to supply more realistic information about local situa-

[19] FAO experts from North America headed for duty in Latin America are ordinarily briefed at the Washington office rather than at Rome.

tions than are most of their counterparts at UN headquarters. Nor are they usually as busy as the latter. It should be added that BTAO has for many years maintained at Geneva a small branch unit of its own to provide initial administrative briefing for project personnel (as well as fellowship holders) who originate from, or are assigned to, European countries, and for whom a trip to New York headquarters would be too expensive and time-consuming.

Briefing arrangements for the TAB Resident Representatives themselves have substantially improved during recent years. The regular procedure now is for each new appointee to spend some time in the TAB central secretariat and then move from one agency headquarters to another for orientation. According to various RTARs questioned by the writer about this initial briefing, it would appear to be reasonably adequate for their purposes. Most of the agencies find it to their advantage to facilitate contacts between new RTARs and their programme and technical divisions. Appointment schedules in most cases are well organized, though one or two RTARs complained of having been 'run through too fast.' On the other hand, the briefing of RTARs when transferred to a new post is less adequate because of limitations of time and budget. Sometimes a specialized agency may have to be by-passed despite the desirability of renewing direct contact with all agency headquarters on reassignment. One of the unfortunate features of this process is that newly appointed RTARs usually are obliged to plunge actively into their country assignments without any time to feel out the situation. One knowledgeable RTAR said that he would favour a spell of three or four months in the field and then a return to agency headquarters for further briefing. This same official deplored the hiatuses that often exist between the departure of a RTAR and the arrival of his successor. While this sometimes cannot be helped, the advantage of providing some over-lap between the retiring and the incoming RTAR, as far as practicable, should offset whatever extra budgetary outlay may be involved.

Further improvements in the briefing and orientation process are clearly possible and desirable. In this connection, many of the suggestions made in the Laves Report of 1952, few of which were subsequently acted upon, are still relevant. But the realization of substantial improvement will require vigorous leadership not only from TAB but from agency executive heads as well. Moreover, it will involve some additional outlay of funds for specially trained briefing staff and the allowance of more time for actual briefing, both at headquarters and at the field level. Such extra costs, it is submitted, logically ought to be charged not to 'administrative' but to 'programme' expense, since the results should aid in improving the effectiveness of project operations. Furthermore there are substantial hidden costs in the time lost by badly briefed experts. It sometimes takes an expert several weeks in the field to gather the information necessary for him even to begin his work. More inter-agency co-operation on briefing—especially at such centres as Geneva, Santiago, Cairo, Beirut, New Delhi, and Bangkok—would help to reduce the costs per agency.

Among other things, better organization and use of available case materials needs to be encouraged. Some attention should be given to the orientation of experts' families—this is almost completely neglected at present. Intensive language instruction, especially for experts on assignments of longer than a year, might usefully be provided experimentally at one or two of the more important field centres. The preparation of a common syllabus on the UN system for field experts, as suggested in the Laves Report, could advantageously be sponsored by TAB. Greater use might also be made of informal seminars for orientation purposes.

TRAINING FOR CROSS-CULTURAL SERVICE

'The magnitude of the briefing and orientation process . . . derives essentially from a lag in the training of an entirely new kind of public servant to serve within the framework of technical assistance provided by the UN system.'[20] While better briefing should lessen the psychological insecurity of field experts and soften the difficulties of cultural adjustment, more effective preliminary training for overseas work, coupled with improved selection, would greatly reduce the dimensions of the problem. Comparatively little systematic attention has as yet been given

[20] The Laves Report, *op. cit.* See also, in this connection, Harlan Cleveland, 'The Real International World and the Academic Lag,' in the *Twenty-eighth Year-book of the National Council for the Social Studies* (New York: 1958).

to the training process—either by the UN operating agencies or in countries contributing large groups of experts.

The present study is neither the time nor the place to consider in detail how special training programmes for cross-cultural service might be devised. Suffice it to say that in at least two agencies operating overseas, and in several countries, some thought is now being devoted to this problem and a limited number of suggestive training experiments are under way. They can only be mentioned briefly here.

One of the most interesting experiments is the Overseas Interne Program recently instituted by the International Co-operation Administration of the United States Government. Under this scheme a limited number of junior officers with specialized academic and work experience are given preliminary orientation at Washington and then sent to the larger country missions for ten months' field training, followed by two years' probation. The aim of the programme is to develop a nuclear corps of young men and women who 'demonstrate a high potential for professional growth' and for whom the ICA expects to have 'a substantial and continuing need' over the years. Selected staff officers, after several years' experience in the field, are brought back for training at the graduate level on programme planning at American universities. Obviously, this type of programme would not be feasible for short-term technical assistance experts but it could be adapted to the needs of UN agencies in respect of regular staff serving in the field.

Among UN organizations, only WHO, to the writer's knowledge, has yet inaugurated a programme of refresher training for its permanent staff. From 1950 through 1958 with the aid of support from the Rockefeller and Kellogg Foundations, WHO was able to provide special leaves of absence, for a year of advanced study at universities and research institutes, to some thirty of its staff members. Among the group were several public health administrators and medical specialists who at the time were stationed at regional offices. Up to the present, staff members have had to apply for such leaves, but in the future the emphasis is to be reversed, and the Director-General may request certain officers to take special leave for advanced study 'in the interest of the Organization.' In the WHO regular budget for 1960 a modest allocation of funds for this purpose was provided.[21] Refresher training for long-term experts might properly be made a feature of personnel policy in other UN agencies.

The organization of special training for UN technical assistance experts on short-term appointment, whether under UN or national auspices, raises a number of practical problems. The irregular flow of newly appointed experts, plus the relatively limited number recruited within fixed periods from or for most countries, complicates the scheduling of short-course programmes. There is the related question of how much time experts on contracts of less than a year's duration can afford to spend on formal training activities. The Laves proposal for four regional briefing centres recognized that they would be useful primarily for the 'cultural orientation' of experts on assignments of a year or longer.

Such practical problems have had to be faced by two national training centres set up by the French and Indian Governments. The French Centre de Formation, inaugurated in Paris in 1957, is designed chiefly for personnel in the bilateral programme of assistance to French overseas territories, but international experts may also be admitted. Administered jointly by the Ministries of Foreign Affairs and Education, the Paris centre provides lectures and informal discussions on the economic and sociological problems of under-developed areas, the psychological implications of trans-cultural service, and the rationale of technical assistance. Each training round lasts from two to three months. While the availability of this centre has been called to the attention of RTARs and the agencies participating in EPTA by the Executive Chairman of TAB, no use had apparently been made of the centre by any UN agency down to the end of 1958. Without a marked change in TAB budgetary and appointment policies, the feasibility of such an arrangement for EPTA purposes is likely to remain extremely limited.

In New Delhi, a somewhat similar centre, supported financially by ICA and the Ford Foundation, was instituted by the Indian Government as early as 1954. Under the auspices of the Delhi School of Economics, this centre conducts seminars of two to four weeks for ICA and Ford Foundation staffs, and is open to a specified number of experts assigned to India by UN agencies

[21] WHO, O.R.: No. 91, Part I, Jan.-Feb. 1959, p. 78.

and the Colombo Plan, as well as to embassy staff. The seminars deal chiefly with Indian culture, history, economics, and social development. TAB took the position that it was for each agency to decide whether it could arrange to have any of its experts attend the Delhi centre—prior to undertaking active project duty. Meanwhile, it took a long time to get assurance from Indian Government ministries that they would have no objection to this procedure. By then, interest in the centre had begun to dwindle in UN circles. Presentation of subject-matter in the seminars reportedly tended to be prejudiced in favour of Indian national policies. In the opinion of one international official in New Delhi, the level of instruction was on the whole elementary—useful chiefly for 'the wives of American experts having their first overseas experience.' While this no doubt represents an extreme view, practical considerations have discouraged use of the Indian centre by UN organizations operating in India.[22]

Experimentation to date with training arrangements for field personnel clearly indicates the difficulties and pitfalls inherent in the development of practicable programmes. Although the problem is certainly not insurmountable, progress towards satisfactory solutions will doubtless involve much trial and error. The rate of progress will probably depend on the degree to which UN field programmes can be so planned to provide a substantial number of longer-term (if not career) appointments.

Support Services for Field Personnel

Closely related to briefing and orientation is the problem of continuing support services for field missions. This 'backstopping' function involves both headquarters and field office roles. Here our concern, to employ a military term, is with the 'logistics' of programme execution. Logistics is *par excellence* communication—of information, ideas, instructions—*plus* the provision of supporting services and facilities.

Generally considered, headquarters support of UN system

[22] In the United States, the Maxwell Graduate School of Syracuse University has recently initiated a special graduate programme, lasting eight months, for persons interested in overseas careers with U.S. government agencies, business firms, and voluntary organizations. This programme includes an inter-disciplinary seminar on geography, cultural anthropology, and comparative political-administrative processes; four weeks of intensive foreign language instruction; and four months' overseas study on a research-internship project.

field missions varies markedly in quality and scope from agency to agency and from area to area. 'Owing in part to an exaggerated respect for the freedom to improvise which the technician must certainly be given,' observes Philip M. Glick, 'some agencies virtually ignore their field missions.'[23] Others are prone to inundate them with a constant flow of materials—like 'manna from heaven'—some of which, to be sure, may be irrelevant and lie undigested or even unread. Similarly, the amount of support provided at the field level differs greatly, depending (1) on the adequacy of staff facilities in TAB country offices and (2) on the capacity of agency field offices (where available) to supply operational guidance to project personnel. Field experts working alone, often under rugged conditions and at great distances from the capital of the country, as, for example, in Brazil, India, and Pakistan, tend to develop an acute sense of isolation, some of them not seeing anybody from their own agency or from the TAB office for many months at a time.[24]

The amount of logistics per field expert in the UN system is decidedly less than that received at the country level by project technicians working for the U.S. Point Four programme. Indeed, in the opinion of some experienced observers, American project personnel are too elaborately 'nursed' by the lavishly equipped 'operations missions' maintained by the U.S. Government in each country where it runs an aid programme.[25]

However this may be, criticisms of UN agency back-stopping, from experts in the field, are too vigorous and too widespread to be ignored—even after discounting the 'complaint complex' which many field people tend to acquire.[26] So far as relations with headquarters are concerned, these criticisms fall into two distinct categories. The first has to do with technical aid and guidance, which frequently is alleged to be fragmentary or of little practical value; the second, with the way in which headquarters handles administrative problems affecting individual

[23] In his excellent study of *The Administration of Technical Assistance: Growth in the Americas* (Univ. of Chicago Press, 1957), p. 316.

[24] In India, for example, EPTA experts are scattered at more than twenty different locations, only about a quarter of them being stationed in or around New Delhi. In Nepal one TAA expert spent seven years doing a geological survey all by himself, moving from one valley to another, completely isolated.

[25] Most U.S. project personnel have modern office installations in the country mission, whereas EPTA experts, with relatively few exceptions, have to be content with more 'austere' facilities inside host country ministries or institutions.

[26] It is interesting, in this connection, how their attitude towards headquarters-field relationships may change when they are transferred to central staff posts.

field experts, the claim being that action is either exasperatingly slow or ambiguous, often requiring repeated follow-up inquiries.

In defence of agency headquarters, it is only fair to point out that governments have frequently been reluctant to provide the financing requisite for competent central leadership and guidance of field operations. In consequence, agencies often are not adequately staffed to cover all of the subject-matter areas represented by the extraordinarily wide gamut of project activity. This has notably been the case with the UN Department of Economic and Social Affairs and with Unesco, and to some extent with FAO.[27] Nor has sufficient effort been made by certain central technical staffs to assemble, analyse, and adapt available case materials for field use. A good deal of the documentation dispatched to field offices and field missions, in the form of instructions, bulletins, and informational memoranda, has only limited applicability to the actual problems with which they must cope. On the other hand, requests from the field for specific documents sometimes go unheeded. To cite a fairly typical example: one RTAR related to the writer how he had not been able to get any of the basic literature on 'economic development' through UN headquarters, his requests being answered by secretaries who merely pointed to the costs of such materials! The chief of a specialized agency field mission observed that except for the printed monthly bulletin of his organization, which was mailed to him regularly, he had to send in specific requests for the kinds of materials he urgently needed. Several field experts in a different agency significantly noted that the problems encountered in the least-developed countries were so 'elementary' as not to be comprehended by their professional counterparts at headquarters—unless they perchance had had personal experience in such places. Otherwise, how could they be expected to project their expertise 6,000 miles away—to areas about which they had only secondary knowledge?

In this connection, as intimated earlier, the headquarters field service units (or their equivalents), which now constitute the principal channel of communication to the field in most agencies, may become so 'procedure-minded' as to try to block informal

[27] Budgetary review bodies have been known to express the view that agency headquarters staffs for the guidance of field missions are too numerous, thus 'inflating' overhead administrative costs of field programmes.

communication between field personnel and senior technical officers at headquarters. One personnel expert stationed in a Latin American country, for instance, told how he had sent a letter to headquarters reporting that the President of the country supported the merit system 'only in principle'; whereupon there came a reply from some junior staff member 'congratulating him [the expert] on his progress.' Small wonder he felt a bit frustrated!

The real problem—and its solution is not easy—is how to channel materials so as not to snow under the local specialist with volumes of reading-matter—how to sift the wheat from the chaff. Certain of the substantive units of ESA are now building up careful selections of 'guidance' materials for project personnel. The Public Administration Division, for example, has developed evaluations of its own training institutes and of its experience with 'Organization and Methods' projects as aids to field teams initiating new assistance undertakings of similar character. With additional professional staff the Division could do much more of this sort of thing.

Within its subject-matter dimensions, the FAO 'godfather' arrangement, whereby field specialists are encouraged to communicate directly with designated technical officers at headquarters for professional advice, has worked well. Recently, as noted in an earlier chapter, the trend has been to restrict the role of the headquarter 'godfathers' somewhat by 'outposting' additional technical officers directly to regional offices, where they constitute 'the long arm' of Rome subject-matter divisions. Although their principal function is to advise national authorities in the region on agricultural policies and problems, they are frequently available to assist FAO technical assistance missions in project planning and operations. For specialized fields not covered by any of the outposted officers substantive backstopping still largely rests with the headquarters division staffs (*i.e.*, the godfathers). With a view to keeping its field offices currently informed of FAO programme activities, a monthly Progress Report containing factual summaries of each substantive division's work was, until quite recently, circulated to all regional directors. This procedure was abandoned apparently because the usefulness of the document did not justify the time required for its preparation. The present Director-General of

FAO has inaugurated the practice of sending to national Ministers of Agriculture a monthly letter, over his own signature, explaining significant developments in FAO policy. Copies of this letter are routed to each of the regional offices as well.

Visits by headquarters staff to the field are another means by which the sense of isolation felt by many agency experts may be minimized. Unfortunately, as we shall see later, such visits not only occur relatively infrequently but are often too hurried to have much constructive value. Under present conditions, such visits must as far as possible be co-ordinated with biennial home leave schedules.

Space will not permit extensive citation from the range of criticisms voiced by field experts as to how agency headquarters deal with their administrative and personal problems (*e.g.*, salary and allowance entitlements, travel for dependants, leave arrangements, hospitalization privileges, the termination and extension of contracts, the disposal of worn-out vehicles, and the like). In Chapter 5, attention was called to the adverse impact on staff morale of delayed and unclear action involving the interpretation of formal rules and regulations. There have been cases where experts with families have received no salary payments for months and have thus had to borrow money to tide themselves over a desperate situation. A considerable number of experts take delight in castigating headquarters for its 'incredible red tape' and its unimaginative, literal application of regulations to special field situations. One reportedly successful expert regaled the writer with a harrowing account of the difficulty he had encountered in trying to get a dollar advance to buy an imported car (he being from a soft-currency country). This request gave rise to correspondence '*ad nauseam*'—cables as well as letters—without satisfaction. During a visit of the agency head to the expert's duty station, the situation was explained to him and he agreed that the loan should be made—as a salary advance. The RTAR then wrote a letter to headquarters referring to this opinion and the money was immediately cabled to the expert. Although this was an unusual case, it goes to illustrate the disease of 'procedure-itis' that afflicts certain junior administrators at headquarters.[28] Experts left

[28] The other side of the picture is the fact that experts from soft currency countries have been known to use the 'dollar advance' request in an effort to evade currency restrictions. By getting dollars to buy cars they can then sell them for dollars when they leave.

with non-convertible currency at the termination of their missions sometimes find it difficult to dispose of it. In one agency field experts are instructed to write directly to a particular administrative official concerning personnel matters. When this official is absent from headquarters, such letters may lie unanswered until his return. The official concerned was frank enough to admit that this was 'a bad system.'

As an offset to the back-stopping limitations of central secretariats, agency field offices are being increasingly utilized for the provision of local support services to project missions in the region or country over which such offices have jurisdiction. On the substantive side, the overseas offices of WHO, FAO, and ILO play important communication roles in this respect. The WHO regional offices, supplemented by the system of 'area representatives,' are admirably equipped to give technical and operational guidance to WHO missions, both under EPTA and the other field programmes. The principal field offices of ILO provide considerable help to experts in smoothing out operational difficulties, though their technical staffs are not large enough to embrace the entire range of ILO project activity. Those ILO 'branch' offices located in under-developed countries are also able to adjust minor housekeeping problems for experts stationed in the country.

As for Unesco, it is the country 'chief of mission,' at any rate in those areas where the size of the field programme justifies the appointment of a mission chief, who does what he can to facilitate working arrangements for the experts under his wing. As Unesco's field programmes have expanded, however, the facilities at his disposal have not kept pace with the increased work load. He seldom has an office of his own and little or no clerical assistance or funds for travel around the country. Nor are the Unesco field science co-operation offices utilized as much as they might be—even in the natural science domain—to aid technical assistance experts. In one country visited by the author, the co-directors of a Unesco field project in education reported that there had been no mention in their briefing of the fact that such an office was located there; although they had been in the country for nearly a year, they had not yet even met the director of the local field science co-operation office.

It is the TAB country office, generally speaking, that now

performs the most important administrative back-stopping function at the field level. As suggested above, the scope of this function varies markedly from one TAB office to another. Nearly all RTARs complain of not being equipped with enough general service staff to handle the clerical and housekeeping needs of experts.[29] At the least, all TAB offices serve as a general 'post office' and for initial liaison with host country authorities and institutions. Over and beyond this, the RTARs and their staffs provide varying degrees of assistance to experts in getting baggage cleared through customs, in obtaining such official identification cards or permits as may be necessary, in locating housing accommodations, and in finding their way through the maze of formalities governing the purchase of motor-cars or the importation of household equipment.[30] In a few cases it has been possible to set aside a room or two (or at least a desk) in the TAB office where experts may work more or less in private—usually less—but office premises are ordinarily too cramped to permit of this luxury. A good many experts, failing to obtain satisfactory clerical assistance from the government departments to which they are attached, are obliged to type out letters and reports laboriously themselves.

In addition to providing such administrative services as mentioned above, most RTARs, after having served a year or longer in a country, are in a position to supply valuable information on local political and economic conditions; when things go wrong they act as 'trouble-shooters' for frustrated project teams. One of the RTAR's principal roles is to facilitate arrangements for project operation by bringing experts into touch with key officials and by prodding the host government to make available project 'counterparts' without unreasonable delay.

The RTAR may also perform what one may call a 'socializing' function with respect to the entire group of UN agency experts on duty in the country. A frequent device for this is the convening of periodic meetings of experts from the different agencies (or projects) in the TAB office, where common problems and difficulties are discussed and experience is exchanged.

[29] The total staff of the thirty-four RTAR offices in operation in 1959 averaged only seven per office.

[30] One of the most widespread causes of irritation among newly arrived experts is the lack of effective help in finding suitable housing. The present writer, from his own experience in Egypt as co-director of a TAA training project, can testify to this.

Such meetings provide a means of acquainting newly arrived experts with their colleagues. Wives are sometimes invited and tea or coffee may be served. One resourceful RTAR has held monthly meetings of experts at project sites, during which the project director describes its operation and invites questions from the group. Meetings of experts (sometimes in the form of cocktail parties) are also held to allow visiting 'top brass' from headquarters to explain significant new developments in the agency or programme concerned. For inter-agency projects, or functionally related projects being conducted by cognate agencies, informal group discussions under the sponsorship of the RTAR have been particularly valuable.[31] Yet there are still some RTARs, even if diminishing in number, who apparently attach little importance to such measures for the building of *esprit de corps* among project personnel—and their families. Without exception, experts testify to the need of more informal inter-project contacts within a country, if only to broaden their horizons and reduce the feeling of working in watertight compartments. At one centre, where a change of RTARs had recently taken place, the favourable impact of the new RTAR on staff morale was strikingly evident—in contrast to his predecessor, who was characterized by several experts 'as a total loss.' Obviously, much depends on the imagination, ingenuity, and vitality of the individual appointee to this key post.

FIELD INSPECTION PRACTICES

Interwoven with the provision of support services to field missions is the problem of project inspection. In addition to formal reporting (discussed below), on-the-spot inspection is indispensable if project operations are to be kept under effective surveillance and the mistakes made in one undertaking are not to be repeated in another.

The term 'inspection' is seldom employed in UN circles, perhaps because for many persons it has an unpleasantly negative connotation—implying 'a battle of wits between the inspector and the inspected.'[32] Nor have permanent field inspectorates,

[31] For example, some years ago in Cairo, the project staffs of the TAA-sponsored Institute of Public Administration and of the ILO-supported Vocational Training and Productivity Centre held joint meetings at the TAB office for the purpose of developing a glossary of terms, with their Arabic equivalents, in government and industrial management.

[32] V. O. Key, *The Administration of Federal Grants to States* (Chicago: Public Administration Service, 1937), p. 85.

such as are to be found in most national administrations, been developed by any of the major UN agencies. Instead, the typical practice is to utilize for the purposes of inspection both 'generalist' administrators and technical 'specialists' in conjunction with other staff functions. Staff field travel usually has more than one objective; for example, to acquaint Member government authorities with agency policies and programmes; to explore regional or country needs; to negotiate draft agreements for new aid projects; to represent the agency at conferences, meetings, and seminars en route; to help project teams over operational snags; and, more generally, to have a look at how field projects are progressing. This combination of objectives is necessary, partly because travel costs must be kept within limited budgetary allocations and partly to economize the use of staff time.

The process of project inspection involves in varying degree both headquarters and field office personnel. The more extensive an agency's field establishment is, the less important the inspectional role of central headquarters tends to be. Thus, in WHO, it is from the regional offices that most project inspection originates. This situation also obtains to a somewhat lesser extent in FAO. As for EPTA, the RTARs attempt to visit project sites as often as their travel budgets and other duties allow. Even so, the central secretariats of the UN, TAB, UNICEF, and all the specialized agencies undertake to make field inspections of their own—either periodically or on an *ad hoc* basis. Let us now look briefly at the comparative effectiveness of the two levels of inspection.

Regarding headquarters inspection, one general criticism emanates from field office and project personnel alike. This is that most visits from headquarters 'top brass' tend to be too short, hurried, or hectic to be of much value in terms of producing realistic judgments on operational problems. If, as is often the case, the visit lasts for only two or three days—frantic consultations between planes at airports are not unknown—the exigencies of protocol and official entertaining may absorb most of the visiting dignitary's time.[33] In this connection, also, the agency's local representative sometimes will arrange a heavy social schedule for the visiting official in advance. Even

[33] In a certain specialized agency one high-level official who spends about half of his time on field tours literally flies into and out of a country, sometimes remaining only a few hours. One field expert referred to this roving dignitary as his agency's 'sputnik'!

when there is time for a quick look at a few projects, he may get a distorted impression of the over-all situation. Nor, after lavish red-carpet treatment, is he psychologically disposed to refuse favours. There have been cases where top-level agency executives have made 'off-the-cuff' commitments to host government officials which the latter take seriously and which may later cause embarrassment to the RTAR or local representatives of the agency concerned. In one instance that came to the writer's attention, an agency's local representative received a cable the day before announcing the arrival of an agency executive. The latter held a press conference and proceeded on a round of official calls, apparently with no intention of meeting the resident technical assistance experts. When the desirability of so doing was suggested by the agency's representative, a cocktail party for them was hurriedly arranged at the leading hotel, but in such an atmosphere that no real discussion of their problems took place. On the other hand, there are instances where senior officials do remain long enough to examine the operation of important projects, even in the hinterland, in a leisurely manner. Such inspections not only can be instructive for the visiting official but may serve as useful 'morale-refreshers' for isolated project teams.

On-the-spot inspections by headquarters technical personnel are, by and large, less hurried and better planned. But even this level of inspection is regarded by many field people as insufficiently frequent. This is not so much because of any lack of willingness on the part of technical staff to undertake field travel as because it is exceedingly expensive and time-consuming to try to cover in their entirety all of the far-flung areas through which field projects are scattered. In Unesco, to cite one example, BMS 'area' officers make a field trip each spring but they are seldom able to visit by any means all of the sites where Unesco undertakings are in progress, especially those remote from national capitals. The travel of 'programme' department staff tends to be limited largely to participation in regional meetings and training seminars, with such incidental stops at other places as air scheduling may permit.[34] Unesco

[34] During 1957, 163 members of the Unesco headquarters staff were absent from Paris on official business, for all purposes including meetings, an average of twenty-seven days per person, at an aggregate cost of about $200,000. *Report of the Management Survey Committee*, Unesco Doc. 50 EX/27 (1957), Annex VII; Unesco Doc. 50/EX/5, Appendix I, 4 April 1958.

programme specialists from Paris do not often visit field projects.

While FAO seems to do somewhat better in this respect, the travel of headquarters technical personnel was until recently not always well planned in advance, with the result that there might be several arrivals in the same country simultaneously and long gaps between visits. In order to correct this situation, the Director-General, in 1957, made each regional representative responsible for planning and organizing visits of headquarters officials within his region, including their co-ordination as far as possible with the travel schedules of outposted technical personnel.[35]

In ILO, technical supervision of field projects appears to be handled effectively by the technical divisions at headquarters, with their long experience in research and standard-setting. In this connection, these divisions send members of their professional staffs out on mission as often as travel funds will allow. The ratio of technical staff available for this purpose to the number of field projects is considerably higher in ILO than in either Unesco or FAO. The head of the ILO Field Services Division also makes field trips from time to time.

The frequency of visits to project locations by the professional staff of agency field offices varies with (1) the size of the region (or country) that has to be covered, and (2) the number, distribution, and types of projects. In the aggregate, there is more regional level inspection in WHO than in any other specialized agency. At New Delhi, to take one example, fifteen or so 'regional advisers' in various subject-matter fields spend from a fourth to a third of their time travelling over the region—giving special attention to the newer (*e.g.*, community development) projects that require close supervision during their earlier stages.[36] The three public health administrators who supervise the work of these advisers go out to the field two to three weeks during each quarter—chiefly for 'trouble-shooting' at spots reported as peculiarly sticky by the regional advisers. Even so, in the opinion of the Director of the office, a more effective job of project supervision in such a vast area as South-east Asia

[35] FAO Doc. C/57/5, 11 March 1957.

[36] One regional adviser remarked that she had to spend half her time on routine clerical matters in the office which could be handled equally well by a competent secretary, the result being that she had too little time for project supervision in the field.

could be done if additional advisers were available.[37] This need was similarly stressed at the Alexandria and Manila offices. At the latter office one public health administrator deplored the fact that he had not been able to visit some of the island territories in the Western Pacific, where there are WHO projects, for nearly three years. Air transport schedules in that part of the world are such as to involve considerable loss of time en route. For the new malaria eradication programme WHO headquarters is now sending out special staff units to help initiate and supervise country project arrangements.

In ILO, about one-third of the time of field office staffs is devoted to the day-to-day implementation of projects. The tendency now is to staff such offices with men of broad administrative experience rather than with technicians. Consequently, the ILO field offices are not equipped to carry out much direct project supervision in the technical sense. A former director of the Bangalore office, later transferred back to Geneva, told the writer how he had spent seven to eight months a year in strenuous travel through South Asia, almost ruining his health, in order to maintain direct contact with project operations. His feeling was that ILO projects in the interior areas received too little attention from headquarters, but he admitted that a good job of technical supervision was done on the whole.

In Latin America, to move to a different part of the world, the FAO regional Director at Santiago reported, in 1957, that he was spending 50 to 75 per cent. of his time 'on the road,' his outposted officers doing about the same amount of travel on their own. Since the latter had to gear their travel schedules to the location of projects in their various specialities, it had not proved feasible for them to accompany him as a group—for a thorough going-over of country situations—as headquarters 'theory' envisaged. The head of the Rio zone office, with a larger geographical area to handle, managed to be away from his office about only one-fourth of the time, while the Mexico City head was able to make only one trip a year to countries other than Mexico itself. The main purpose served by the field tours of FAO regional representatives, much as with the

[37] As of mid-1958, there were some 150 project staff on duty in the WHO South-east Asia region serving projects in seven countries and two territories, with an aggregate budget of nearly $9 million.

WHO regional public health administrators, is to help resolve operational issues by injecting an outside point of view.

Most of the ICAO regional office heads complain that their travel funds are not large enough to permit as thorough coverage of their regions as they would like—in connection with the implementation of regional air navigation plans. Extra trips are frequently necessary to investigate reports on the deficiencies of airport communication services in various countries. During 1958, staff travel out of the ICAO Bangkok office aggregated 238 days, or an average of about forty days per man. As indicated earlier, the Technical Assistance Bureau at Montreal recently stationed at Beirut a field man whose principal task it is to inspect ICAO missions in the Middle East and South-east Asia and to perform other related work. In 1959 the travel budget for the Bureau was increased to provide for appointment of an Inspector of Training and a technical assistant.[38] The purpose of this action was to strengthen the service of inspection and supervision with a view to ensuring that the training given to personnel by ICAO technical assistance centres is kept 'uniformly up to ICAO standards.' So far as the writer could discover, this is the only instance to date where a UN agency has assigned staff officers exclusively for technical inspection work.

Within UNICEF's three-level framework, inspection of project operations is probably as thorough as in any UN organization. Not only do senior headquarters officials spend a lot of time in the field, but the regional directors travel extensively over their regions.[39] The head of the Paris office is out of the French capital about 60 per cent. of the year, 40 per cent. being used for visits to the area offices in Africa. The indefatigable Director of the Bangkok office makes two global trips each year—to and from the Executive Board meetings in New York—stopping en route at each area office for a careful assessment of its problems. On each area office staff, moreover, there are a number of field observers whose job is to cover country and liaison offices and the projects for which the latter are responsible. It is in order to note here that UNICEF has seemingly

[38] UN Doc. E/3191, Report of TAC, Annex II, 8 Dec. 1958.

[39] During 1957, for instance, the Executive Director of UNICEF took field trips on official business totalling six months and covering thirty-seven countries in Latin America, Europe, and the Middle East.

been less plagued by 'penny-pinching' policies regarding staff travel costs than have the UN and most of the specialized agencies.

The contribution made by the RTARs to EPTA project inspection consists mainly in smoothing out operational rather than technical difficulties. For travel within the country to which an RTAR is assigned, the host government normally pays transportation costs, TAB providing subsistence only. This makes it possible to stretch the modest TAB budget for staff travel further than would otherwise be the case. Notwithstanding, many RTARs are unable to visit the more remote projects in large countries as often as they would like. In Brazil, for instance, where projects are dispersed from the Amazon valley in the north to Rio Grande del Sul in the south, the RTAR (in 1957) reported that he tried to visit each project twice a year but did not always succeed. His travel outside Rio then amounted to about forty-five days a year, including fifteen days in the Amazon and north-eastern part of the country.

Where, as at Bangkok, the RTAR has responsibility for a far-flung regional grouping of countries, the problem is even more formidable. There the RTAR spends nearly six months a year in transit in an effort to get to each country twice. Frequent visits by him are particularly important for project missions that have no local back-stopping. In one country, the regional RTAR found on his first visit that the UN experts working there did not even know one another. Project supervision in Pakistan, as noted earlier, is complicated by the division of the country into two regions separated geographically by a thousand miles. A former RTAR at Karachi reports that he was able to inspect undertakings in East Pakistan only rarely, thus being obliged to handle them by 'remote control.' The administrative officer in the Karachi TAB office visited Dacca once during a three-year tour of duty—only to have TAB headquarters remonstrate against the cost of the trip.

As noted in Chapter 2, the International Bank sends out once a year 'end-use' missions to inspect the progress of current loan projects. These missions consist chiefly of engineers and technologists (*e.g.*, on highways or power). In certain countries, where the Bank maintains a Resident Representative, he may keep an eye on the way in which a particularly complex Bank-assisted enterprise is developing and report thereon to Washington.

The foregoing illustrations of field inspection conditions are perhaps sufficient to indicate the nature of the problem. While the over-all picture is still a mixed one, the quality of field supervision has distinctly improved in most agencies during recent years. That is not to say, however, that the situation could not be further improved. Field travel by headquarters staff, for example, could be more carefully planned in advance and better co-ordinated with the inspectional operations of field offices.

Another arrangement worth trying out might be to establish special 'inspectorates' for given subject-matter areas. 'Globe-trotting,' as C. W. Jenks once pointed out, may predispose one 'to superficial thinking unless the new impressions formed by rapid travel are sifted by a mind trained to assess their value by an intimate acquaintance with several contrasted cultures and social-economic backgrounds.'[40] While there is little evidence of 'junketing' for the fun of it among UN system officials—certainly not by technical personnel—their 'inspectional' activity, as we have seen, is often only one of several tasks en route; not infrequently, moreover, it is done by staff lacking the intimate knowledge of local conditions they should have. If, for example, permanent inspectional corps could be set up for such fields as public administration, industrial development, education, agriculture, health, or social welfare, it might be possible to mobilize 'expertise' more effectively for the complex job of field liaison and supervision. Such a corps, ideally, should consist of mature persons with a broad-gauged understanding of the subject-matter concerned. Between planned inspectional tours it should of course spend limited periods at headquarters for reporting and consultation. For such assignments, former TAB Resident Representatives with outstanding records and effective ex-directors of important field missions might be drawn upon. Field inspections under such arrangements might be organized in terms of culturally distinct regions, as, for example, Latin America, the Arab world, or ex-British Asia.

With a view to minimizing the negative implications of 'inspection,' some such title as 'field consultant' or 'field counsellor'

[40] 'Some Problems of an International Civil Service,' *Public Administration* (Spring 1943).

might appropriately be employed to identify the members of the corps. They should at all costs avoid acting like 'snoopers.' Their purpose should be fully as much to advise, help, and inject confidence as to inspect in the narrow sense. In this connection, as James W. Fesler has suggested, it might be advisable to let the field expert 'see the central inspector's report and submit his own comments on it.'[41]

The cumulative insights gained by such inspectional groups would probably be more meaningful than many of the disparate reports on hurried travel missions submitted by less well equipped staff personnel. In addition, they might be able to develop objective criteria for evaluating operational programmes in specific functional areas. A good case can be made for experimenting with such arrangements in selected substantive fields. There would of course still be need for field inspection by technical personnel, especially with respect to highly specialized and novel types of projects.

Inspection of field projects is above all a question of time and money. A corps of newly appointed inspectors would have to be borne on administrative costs. There would need to be agreement by TAC, TAB, and the participating agencies as to the necessary funds.

Irrespective of whether the establishment of permanent inspectorates should prove feasible there is little doubt that funds for staff travel need to be increased. This need is generally recognized by the executive heads of all UN organizations. Travel allocations have not kept pace with the expansion of field activities, or been adjusted to rising transportation costs during recent years. Because of this available travel funds are distinctly less adequate today than before the Korean war, when EPTA was inaugurated and world prices began their upward spiral.

The Secretary-General of the United Nations has repeatedly called attention to this situation in defending his annual budget estimates before the Fifth Committee of the General Assembly.

> My past five years' experience as Secretary-General [said Mr. Hammarskjold during the 1957 session of the Committee] has convinced me that, in this matter of official travel, we have as consistently as unwisely under-budgeted

[41] In Fritz Morstein Marx, ed., *Elements of Public Administration* (New York: Prentice-Hall, 1946), p. 282.

in terms of the Organization's real and essential needs. . . . Apart from the special provision for my own travel, two-thirds of the funds requested is assigned to travel of staff stationed away from headquarters on trips which have a very significant bearing upon the success of our programmes in the economic and social field in under-developed countries, and upon the progress of public understanding of what this Organization stands for. There are no junkets, I can assure you.[42]

The vigorous tone of this statement was undoubtedly influenced by the proposal made by the Advisory Committee for a 9 per cent. reduction in his estimates for staff travel—notwithstanding that they had deliberately been kept down to the figure for the preceding year. The Advisory Committee, as the watchdog of the UN treasury, has taken a consistently narrow view of the communication functions of staff travel. 'It is important,' the Committee observed in its report to the 1957 Assembly, 'to avoid creating an atmosphere where personal visits and contacts —whether by senior officials *or at the technical working level*—are preferred to other means of communication which would serve *equally well* the immediate ends in view' (italics added).[43]

A comparable economy complex may be detected in the attitudes of TAC (with reference to EPTA staff travel expenditure), and of the controlling organs of most of the specialized agencies. In 1956, for instance, an Administrative Review Group set up by TAC, spotting sizable differences between the agencies in regard to outlays for staff travel, was puzzled by the relatively higher level of travel costs in FAO. Apparently it did not occur to the Group that this might significantly be related to adequacy of field supervision. In Unesco, overhead administrative costs for EPTA have recently been kept down to the lowest level of any of the participating agencies—11 per cent. as against 15 per cent. for FAO (which has a programme three times as large). Yet it could hardly be claimed that on-the-spot guidance and inspection of field projects in Unesco has been as extensive as in FAO.[44]

[42] GA, O.R.: 12th Sess., 5th Committee, 720th Mtg., 15 Oct. 1957.

[43] UN Doc. A/3624.

[44] In spite of administrative costs being the lowest of any major agency, the Unesco General Conference and Executive Board have constantly demanded their reduction. Allocations for staff travel in Unesco were actually less for 1958 than for two years earlier, while the estimates for 1959 were even slightly lower. For 1958 aggregate outlays for staff travel on official business in the UN and the eight specialized agencies participating in EPTA were estimated at $2,213,000, or only a little over 2 per cent. of their regular budgets. *Information Annex III to Budget Estimates for the Financial Year 1958*, UN Doc. A/3600/Add.1.

One unfortunate aspect of inadequate appropriations for staff travel, as already noted, is that field inspection trips have to be geared as far as possible to home leave schedules. While no one would argue against combining home leave with such official business as can appropriately be handled en route, the consequence, when this practice is pushed too far, can be excessive gaps between field visits or the elimination of out-of-the-way stop-overs altogether—at the very places where project personnel are most isolated. The point is that few Member government delegates, in particular those representing treasuries and budget bureaux, appear to recognize that long-distance travel constitutes an extra cost factor in international administration.

Reporting from the Field

An essential part of the communications process in any organization with operational programmes is periodic reporting from its field units up the organizational hierarchy. Formal reporting supplements the more direct types of supervision described above. By its very nature it constitutes a device for 'remote control,' and is a basic requirement for effective relations between headquarters and the field.

Within the UN system reporting procedures are unavoidably more elaborate than in a typical national administration. There are several reasons why this should be so: (1) the loose, multi-agency structure of the system, involving lateral (as well as vertical) reporting for co-ordinative purposes; (2) the simultaneous operation of functionally overlapping programmes financed from different sources; (3) the existence of criss-crossing field office establishments with varying degrees of responsibility for programme execution; and (4) the necessity of having to account for programme effectiveness, and for the expenditure of programme funds, to a multiplicity of governing boards, councils, and conferences. Added to these factors are linguistic and semantic barriers which are conducive to highly detailed reporting formulae and which necessitate extra paperwork for editing and translation.

Field reporting in the UN framework embraces several categories of personnel: (1) the heads of field offices (including the RTARs); (2) the chiefs of various outposted units; (3) inspectional officials following the completion of travel missions; (4) field project leaders; and (5) individual project experts. Field reports may serve several different purposes. They may provide information on the operation, activities, and problems of field offices, helping headquarters to check on their efficiency and needs. In a more general sense, reports from such offices may supply a flow of useful information on political and economic trends in the region or country concerned—as they affect an agency's programme. Reports from project missions, depending on the stage at which they are made, may explain the plan of operations for new projects, describe the progress of continuing projects, or make recommendations for government action on an interim basis or at the termination of a project. Finally, the effectiveness of project operations and impact may to some extent be evaluated through the reporting process. These purposes often overlap and a given report may of course have more than one objective.

For testing the efficacy of reporting arrangements, a number of questions are relevant: How frequently should different types of reports be made? Do reporting 'guide-lines' set by headquarters ensure sufficient uniformity and objectivity to permit meaningful cross-comparisons of offices and projects? What uses are made of reports in terms of distribution within the agency or to governments, responses to the field, and operational and programme improvement? In what follows we shall briefly look at the reporting process from these three points of view, as illustrated by the practices of a number of agencies.

Frequency of reporting

Among UN organizations the frequency with which periodic reports are required varies considerably. The RTARs report quarterly, the third report each year now consisting of a detailed evaluation of EPTA operations in the country, and the other three dealing with political, economic, and social developments, in addition to anything significant that needs to be said concerning specific projects. ILO requires monthly reports from all of its field offices, as well as from the national correspondents. FAO headquarters follows a similar practice with regard to its regional offices, while the area representatives also report monthly to each regional office. WHO regional directors make short quarterly reports in addition to an elaborate annual report on WHO operations in the region, and the area representatives submit quarterly reports to the regional office. In ICAO, regional office heads report on a bi-monthly basis concerning technical and administrative matters and semi-annually on the deficiencies and progress of regional air navigation plans. The Executive Secretaries of the UN regional commissions make monthly activity reports of an essentially administrative character, together with substantive reports when some special development occurs.[45] In UNICEF, the Bangkok regional office submits monthly reports (the Director 'likes to write'!) while Paris reports at three-month intervals; the area and country offices likewise report quarterly to the regional office concerned, with copies to New York headquarters.

The periodicity of reporting by project staff ranges from a straight monthly basis in FAO to varying combinations of special, monthly, quarterly, and semi-annual reports in the other organizations. BTAO, for example, requires either a monthly or a quarterly report depending on the nature of the project assignment. ILO calls for an initial report on preliminary work plans, with progress reports every two months after the third month. In Unesco, experts on short-term assignments (of not more than two or three months) submit only one report—at the end of their mission; the others are expected to report at six-month intervals—on 30 June and at the end of the calendar year—the latter report being more comprehensive and dealing with solved and unsolved problems. In addition, a special report on project plans is required six weeks after an expert takes up his duties. Chiefs of mission also prepare six-month and annual reports covering their own activities and supplementing the reports from individual experts with a view to providing an over-all assessment of Unesco's activities in the country. WHO experts submit to the regional office monthly statistical summaries of project operations and somewhat longer descriptive reports each quarter. In ICAO, technical assistance missions report quarterly, the fourth quarterly report consisting of a review of the whole year's work.

[45] Also a detailed report on the work of each regional commission is made to ECOSOC annually.

Among field office and project staffs alike one encounters considerable grumbling over what they regard as 'excessive' progress reporting. In one agency, for example, a regional director remarked that he was so swamped with work that he did not always send in his monthly report to headquarters. In another agency a chief of mission made the point that regular reports might well be reduced to purely administrative documents, with substantive matters handled by correspondence as necessary. A distinguished RTAR observed that periodical reporting was not very meaningful for headquarters since operating conditions varied so much from country to country; in his opinion, the programme would probably be no better or no worse without the RTAR's activity report. A good many project experts are prone to complain of having to spend too much time 'punching out' a report each month—especially those without typing assistance. Another source of complaint relates to the 'double' reporting, in certain team projects, of the project leader and of individual members of the team. The necessity, in some agencies, of having to send copies of reports to two (or even three) sets of offices irks project experts as well as agency country representatives, one of them commenting on the 'bales of paperwork' resulting therefrom.

Various agencies have begun to recognize the desirability of 'streamlining' formal reporting requirements. In part this stems from the burden devolving upon headquarters staffs in reading, compiling, and digesting so many periodic reports. In numerous instances field officials, and experts as well, if one may judge from the length of their reports, appear to lack 'terminal facilities.' Hence, a discernible trend towards less frequent and shorter periodic reports, with more use of *ad hoc* reports at the discretion of the reporting officer. All in all, the special reports made by headquarters and regional personnel on field travel missions probably have more value for evaluative purposes than do regular reports.

Format and content of field reports

Concurrent with the tendency towards requiring fewer formal reports there has been a distinct effort to develop meaningful guide-lines for the form and content of field reports. The object of this effort is double: (1) to increase the comparability of reports on related matters and (2) to try as much as possible to reduce the element of subjectivity in descriptive reporting. It should not be surprising that more progress has been achieved towards the first than towards the second objective. In any administrative system, 'reports flowing upward in the organization . . . tend to be "sugar-coated." Information that will evoke a favourable reaction will be played up; the mistakes and the fumbles tend to be glossed over.'[46] The UN system is not immune to this psychology. If the difficulties of a field office, or of a field programme are stressed in reporting there is always the chance that it may be rated by headquarters as 'ineffective.' Accordingly, as Fesler has observed, 'few field officials will consciously report adversely on their own operations.'[47] While there may possibly be nationality differences in this regard, all UN agency personnel are human. This is merely to say that formal reports from the field clearly must be checked against other available sources of information, except perhaps for reports of a wholly statistical character.

Even so, prescribed guide-lines not only help to keep the content of reports within defined bounds but also facilitate their examination by the receivers. Without some more or less standard guide form, it is all too tempting for reporters to inject trivial and extraneous bits of information. Space will permit reference here to only a few examples of the kinds of reporting guide-lines now employed in UN organizations.

To take WHO first, the Administrative Manual stipulates that progress reports from project leaders should cover the following points, in the order named: definition of the project; objectives; methods, accomplishments to date; summary comparison of accomplishments with objectives; and difficulties. Assignment reports by individual experts follow roughly the same outline, as do the final evaluation reports on projects. According to the WHO Programme Evaluation Office at Geneva, the chief difficulty has been to get project personnel to relate their reports to planning for the future; but the general quality of WHO reporting appears to have improved considerably since the adoption of detailed reporting procedures.

[46] Simon, Smithburg, and Thompson, *Public Administration*, *op. cit.*, p. 240.
[47] In Morstein Marx, ed., *op. cit.*, p. 280.

In FAO, the check-list for monthly reports by regional directors includes the following: (1) developments on a regional scale of interest to FAO; (2) relations with governments and inter-governmental bodies; (3) FAO's activities in the region, with special reference to developments indicative of success or failure; (4) working relations with other agencies, UN and bilateral, including their field offices; (5) FAO publicity in the region; (6) programme progress, including activities of outposted officers, contacts with country representatives, project evaluations, and the work of FAO regional bodies, such as fisheries or forestry; and (7) administrative and financial matters as necessary. To some extent the range of topics to be covered overlaps with information submitted by other FAO personnel, but this may be justified with a view to getting an overall assessment of the regional situation from a higher-level official.

ILO has developed model report forms covering the tentative plan of work of experts, their subsequent progress reports, and their draft final reports, corresponding more or less to the same scheme as that of WHO. The Regional Office Manual of ICAO includes a suggested format for the monthly reports of regional office directors and also for reports on travel missions by regional office staff. The latter covers the object of the mission and its itinerary, a summary of contacts relating to ICAO air navigation, air transport, legal, technical assistance, and public information matters, and a statement of any action required by the regional office or by Montreal. ICAO technical assistance missions are instructed to report on progress as measured by the fulfilment of defined objectives contained in their annual work programmes. BTAO, in its Guide for Experts, contents itself with asking in general terms for a provisional outline of the proposed work programme and for subsequent reports on progress, including achievements and major operational difficulties.

Uses of field reports

The third test of any field reporting system is the uses to which reports are put. This question involves: (1) arrangements for circulation of reports through the organization and, in some cases, to governments and other outside bodies; (2) the action taken on reports requiring immediate attention; and (3) the utilization of technical reports for briefing purposes and over-all programme evaluation and accounting to policy organs.

As for (1), it is the practice in all organizations to route principal field reports through the headquarters set-up. Sometimes lengthy multi-purpose reports are reproduced in sections, only the relevant parts being sent to the interested substantive divisions. Also, as previously noted, in those agencies with field office establishments copies of project reports are sent to the regional or country office concerned or both as well as to headquarters. In WHO, for example, project reports usually receive more attention from regional advisory staffs than from the corresponding divisions at Geneva. In FAO, reports on project operations are routed through the Field Operations Liaison Branch to the technical 'godfathers' for such action as may be necessary. One team leader with whom the writer discussed FAO reporting procedures could not understand why members of his team should have to report through so many hierarchical levels—to him as project leader, to the country representative, to the regional office, and to headquarters. Prompt replies and useful comments, he said, were forthcoming from Rome, but the role of the regional office in this respect was by no means clear. The FAO country representative in Pakistan is obliged to send copies of his reports to two regional offices—at Cairo and Bangkok—since the government of that territorially divided country insists on maintaining connections with both offices.

At Unesco headquarters all project reports are addressed to BMS, whose Reports Unit, after registering them, circulates the relevant sections to the programme departments concerned for comment and action. Periodic reports from the field science co-operation offices, on the other hand, are addressed directly to the Regional Affairs unit of the Department of Natural Sciences (reports from the social science officer at Cairo going to the Social Science Department). In ICAO, regional office reports are made to the Air Navigation Bureau, which may then route such parts as are of interest to the Air Navigation, Legal, Administrative and Technical Assistance Bureaux. The latter Bureau receives all reports from ICAO's technical assistance missions and circulates them to all interested units at headquarters. Copies of such reports are sent by each chief of mission to the regional office accredited to the state concerned.

By and large, progress, as distinct from final, reports on field projects are not distributed to governments. In Unesco, by exception, project experts are encouraged to submit to host government authorities copies of informal progress reports. Also, when a programme department at Unesco headquarters thinks that a particular mission report would be of interest to other countries, it may agree to a wider circulation of the report after appropriate editing. But most agencies are averse to the distribution of progress reports to governments because they fear that such action might tend to discourage project experts from commenting frankly on controversial matters. In reality, however, regardless of how restrictive the distribution of reports may be, it is not feasible, in the UN system, to include in progress reports anything of a very confidential nature on host country attitudes or policies, since there always exists the possibility that some future official at headquarters (or in a regional office), of the same nationality, may run across the report in the files and privately pass along to his government critical observations that could be embarrassing.

In EPTA, the quarterly activity reports of RTARs are regularly circulated to BTAO and the substantive units of ESA at UN headquarters, to the participating specialized agencies, and to IBRD and IMF. The aggregate volume of these reports is so great that, according to various senior officials, they tend not to be used very much by the other agencies. All too often busy staff allow such reports to pile up unread. One RTAR, with previous experience at UN headquarters, complained that he did not really know to whom he was addressing his reports. Who, he queried, actually used them? In his opinion a clearer definition of report 'consumers' would be helpful. Nor did he see any reason why the RTAR's reports should not be made available to governments since they were primarily factual in nature. In theory, at least, this is not true of the annual evaluation report, the purpose of which will be examined when we consider programme evaluation in Chapter 11.[48]

[48] See pp. 496–499.

Concerning point (2), relative to staff action on project reports, we have already pointed out, in our discussion of support services, that agency effectiveness in dealing with communications from the field is a function (*a*) of the headquarters internal set-up and (*b*) of the adequacy of substantive units for the backstopping of field missions. As might be expected, the testimony of experts out in the field as to what happens to their reports varied from complete satisfaction to extreme irritation. It would be invidious to identify agencies in connection with this testimony, for significant variations occur within the same agency depending on the subject-matter category into which a project falls. In many instances, experts said that they uniformly got prompt, positive reactions and helpful replies to points raised in their reports; other experts observed that they received no comments at all—or only when a report arrived late at headquarters; some complained that replies often reached them too late—in some cases after a lapse of two or three months—to be of any practical value; while still others remarked that they got only *pro forma* acknowledgments of reports, which annoyed them no end.

To generalize: it would appear that the more fully headquarters programme officers are aware of conditions at an expert's duty station and of the nature of his project, the more likely they are to provide constructive suggestions to field personnel; otherwise, the tendency is to fall back on superficial generalities which, as one mission chief expressed it, 'look silly' out in the field. In his view, moreover, it was a mistake not to transmit to mission chiefs and team leaders critical comments by headquarters officers on the work of individual experts; if a chief of mission were advised of unfavourable assessments of the performance of project staff, he might at times be able to correct misunderstandings or help improve the situation by on-the-spot discussion. All of which of course buttresses the case for more rotation of technical personnel between headquarters and field duty.

As for point (3) above, relating to the value and limitations of field reports for other programme purposes, we called attention earlier in this chapter to the usefulness of mission reports as sources of information for the briefing of new experts. As such reports improve in quality, they might advantageously be drawn upon more than is at present the case; but for maximum utility the essentials need to be extracted, collated, and meaningfully classified, so that the incoming expert will not have to wade tediously through voluminous files for what he really needs. This is now being undertaken in certain agencies. The disposition of interim and final reports containing recommendations for host government action will be discussed in connection with the general problem of programme follow-up.[49]

Problems of 'Divided Supervision'

Earlier in this study reference was made to some of the operational complications that have arisen from the pulling-and-hauling of administrative and functional units at agency headquarters with respect to the control of field operations. There are in reality two lines of command running from the centre to the periphery of an agency, and the two sometimes tend to become entangled. 'Administrative' and 'technical' directives are equally authoritative and it is not easy to differentiate clearly between the two. In correspondence between project technicians and their opposite numbers at headquarters, scientific and operational matters may get 'mixed up,' or the project guidance provided by the centre may not always coincide with firmly held views of field office technical staffs. In most UN agencies this problem is now being adjusted reasonably well on a pragmatic basis, although some confusion and ambiguity still persist.

There are, however, a number of special situations where supervision over field units is shared by agency headquarters and a regional office of the same or a different organization. In such situations the possibility of stress and strain is very real and it has not always been averted.

The most important set of situations of this kind involve the UN regional commission secretariats. Associated with them in various ways are a cluster of staff units detached, or outposted, from UN and FAO headquarters. These units include UN Information Centres, UN Bureau of Social Affairs groups, FAO agricultural units, and, in the case of ECLA (until 1959), TAA outposted units. Supervision over these units is divided

[49] See pp. 474–477.

between the headquarters division and Executive Secretary concerned. In some cases, this scheme has worked well; in others there have been difficulties.

The joint FAO-regional commission units

Interestingly enough, probably the smoothest-working relationship has been that involving FAO and the regional commissions. In order to minimize duplication in regional agricultural analysis work, it was early agreed by means of 'memoranda of understanding' between the Director-General of FAO and each Executive Secretary, that FAO should detail to each regional commission secretariat a small technical staff group—to serve as the core of its 'Agricultural Division.' Jointly with their commission counterparts, these groups plan agricultural programmes for the commission to consider. Each agricultural division is headed by an FAO officer who, as it were, wears two hats. In his FAO capacity he is responsible to Rome on substantive matters; yet he must collaborate closely with the commission staff, and the work programmes of the division are subject to joint approval by the FAO Director-General and the Executive Secretary. The agricultural section of the annual regional economic survey issued by each commission secretariat is prepared by the division.[50] Its chief makes a monthly report on the joint programme to the appropriate functional division at Rome and a separate monthly activity report to the Executive Secretary. During the earlier years there was said to be some suspicion in FAO circles that such arrangements for inter-agency co-operation might result in FAO's being 'pushed around' by the commission secretariats; but this has gradually disappeared and there are now no serious disagreements. It is generally recognized that the joint arrangements have made possible a more efficient use of technical knowledge and staff, with avoidance of overlap.

Administratively, the FAO staff of the commission agricultural divisions remain on FAO's payroll. Their travel is controlled by Rome in accordance with plans prepared in advance by the functional division concerned (*e.g.*, Economics, Agriculture, Forestry, etc.). The budget of each detached unit covers

[50] Publications prepared by the FAO/ECAFE Agricultural Division appear under both the UN/ECAFE and the FAO imprint, the sales number depending on whether the main initiative came from FAO or from ECAFE.

office supplies and equipment as well as staff and travel costs. For various housekeeping services, however, the facilities of the commission secretariat are utilized. Each month a report on administrative matters is sent to the Division of Administration and Finance at Rome. FAO staff assigned to a commission secretariat may be transferred elsewhere on FAO initiative, but only after consultation with the Executive Secretary.

At Bangkok, the head of ECAFE's Agricultural Division also serves as a regional economist 'outposted' to the FAO regional office located in the same city. As such he may be called upon by the latter office for consultation on economic matters. Thus he actually wears three hats! His three-cornered status could easily result in conflicting pressures were it not for the excellent personal relations that have prevailed between FAO's regional director and ECAFE's head. A similar situation prevails at Santiago.

The overseas Social Affairs units

As noted in the preceding chapter, the UN Bureau of Social Affairs recently detailed small technical units to the secretariats of ECLA and ECAFE. These arrangements were designed (1) to help the commission staff deal more adequately with the social aspects of economic problems and (2) to provide direct advisory services to governments in the social domain. According to the rationale of the scheme, the detached Social Affairs units were to become 'integral parts' of the regional secretariats while remaining under substantive, or technical, control by the UN Bureau of Social Affairs in New York. From the standpoint of the latter, they were viewed as 'forward echelons' of headquarters, their budgets forming part of the Bureau's over-all budget.

The line of demarcation between 'administrative' and 'substantive,' however, turned out to be much less distinct in practice than in theory. The division of administrative and technical authority meant different things to officials with different administrative backgrounds. Under the original terms of the plan, for example, the work programmes of the detached units were to be prepared by the Executive Secretaries in accordance with basic policy directives laid down by ECOSOC and its Social Commission, subject to approval by the Under-Secretary for Economic and Social Affairs at UN headquarters. In the course of this operation, it was all too tempting for the Executive Secretary on the spot to insist upon a degree of control over the new units that amounted to administration *plus*—but plus *what* was not entirely clear. Instruction as to how each work programme was to be executed were to come from the Director of the Bureau of Social Affairs, and these instructions might, and on occasion apparently did, run counter to the views of the Executive Secretary.

One Executive Secretary, reportedly finding the dual control arrangement distasteful, sought an agreement in 'black and white' which would define and fortify his authority over the outposted unit. By contrast, another Executive Secretary apparently preferred a looser relationship. In this case, his senior staff are said at the outset to have resented the Bureau's control over the new unit; nor were they averse to making jokes about their Social Affairs associates which offended the sensitivities of the latter. Accordingly, the latter seemed to have developed a kind of 'inferiority complex' with regard to their professional colleagues in the regional secretariat and this did not make for easy day-to-day working relations. Gradually, however, the Social Affairs group was taken into 'the club' and invited to participate in weekly senior staff meetings. Even so, as of late 1958 there were still signs of some strain between the two groups.

These arrangements gave rise to complicated communication relationships. Functional specialists on the regional commission staffs, for example, could communicate with UN headquarters on demographic or community development matters *only* through the chief of the Social Affairs unit, and this indirect channelling of correspondence sometimes resulted in tangling the lines or in delaying action. All correspondence on substantive matters from the Social Affairs unit to the UN Bureau at New York was countersigned by the Executive Secretary, though he did not always read it. The Social Affairs units, for their part, tended to complain of receiving too many detailed directives, by letter and memorandum, from headquarters, and they would have liked more delegation of discretion. They were obliged, moreover, to do double reporting—a quarterly report to the director at the 'home' base and a monthly progress report to the Executive

Secretary for incorporation into his over-all report to the UN Department of Economic and Social Affairs—and this was looked upon as an unnecessary chore.

As part of their assignment, the outposted Social Affairs units help to brief BTAO experts in the social field and from time to time engage in trouble-shooting operations over the region when social welfare technical assistance projects go wrong. Accordingly, they find it necessary to correspond with TAB Resident Representatives on various matters, and copies of all important letters must be forwarded to BTAO in New York for its information or approval of whatever administrative action may be involved. In addition, the Social Affairs units may be called upon by UN headquarters to help arrange for the holding of regional seminars in which one or more specialized agencies participate; in this case the communication process may take on additional dimensions. In one situation that came to the writer's attention, preparations for a Latin American seminar on urbanization under UN-Unesco auspices were delayed for several weeks because of a snarl in transmitting proposals from the Santiago unit to Unesco *via* the Social Affairs Bureau in New York. Eventually, the Bureau authorized Santiago to write directly to the Unesco Social Science Department and the matter was adjusted. Here we have an interesting example of how differing degrees of decentralization of programme execution in two co-operating agencies may complicate communication between them.

Another illustration of how triangular communication lines can get crossed occurred in connection with plans for a social welfare training seminar held at Montevideo in 1957 under the joint sponsorship of ECLA and various specialized agencies. The chief of the Santiago Social Affairs unit, then being exceedingly busy, preferred not to attend this seminar—especially since it was to be directed by an able Latin American woman from his own staff. A telegram came from the RTAR at Montevideo urging him 'for prestige reasons' to come and make the opening speech. He then arranged to go for five days (the seminar was to last two weeks); whereupon another telegram arrived from Montevideo insisting that he remain for the entire period. In the meantime, his request to UN headquarters for travel authorization (since it was an *extra* trip not covered in advance travel plans) was not approved because the Bureau at New York had independently arranged to send to the seminar one of its senior staff—an equally able woman but with no knowledge of Spanish.

On the assumption that the outposting of Social Affairs staff offers important advantages from the standpoint of more effective programme planning and implementation in a given region, there would appear to be two ways of minimizing the confusion referred to in the preceding paragraphs. One possible solution would be to establish the outposted units on an independent basis so far as operational relations with the regional commission secretariats are concerned. In effect, this is the status of the European Social Affairs unit set up in Geneva during 1958. The terms of reference for this unit were drafted by its chief before he left New York for the new assignment. The unit maintains informal liaison with the ECE secretariat as to studies of European internal migration, social development, and the like; but it is substantively responsible only to the UN Bureau in New York—as an overseas arm of headquarters. For office facilities and housekeeping services it depends on the UN European Office. Without this latter arrangement, the administrative costs of operating such a small unit would be considerably higher.

An alternative—and seemingly more logical solution—would be to expand the mandates of all of the regional commissions to include social as well as economic development problems. As noted earlier, this was done for ECA when it was set up, and in its secretariat there is a Social Research section within its Research Division, along with a Community Development branch. The Social Affairs staff is thus completely integrated with the Commission secretariat, and the former does not communicate directly with the Bureau at UN headquarters. In 1959, ECOSOC broadened the terms of reference of ECLA and ECAFE so as to cover 'the social aspects of economic development' and 'the interrelationship of the economic and social factors,' corresponding with the mandate of ECA.[51] As a consequence, the Social Affairs units at Santiago and Bangkok seemed likely to be incorporated into the respective commission secretariats sooner or later. The Director of the Bureau of

[51] ECOSOC Resolution 723 (XXVIII), 17 July 1959.

Social Affairs, as of early 1960, characterized the general trend as devolution, both in the administrative and the substantive sense. The recent consolidation of BTAO with ESA at headquarters should facilitate this development.[52]

The TAA outposting experiment

In Chapter 6, brief reference was made to the conditions under which the Secretary-General, in 1955, was authorized by the General Assembly to outpost a small TAA staff unit to ECLA on a provisional basis. It will be recalled that this proposal not only was not greeted with much enthusiasm—except from certain Latin American Governments—but was privately opposed by certain senior TAA officials as an ill-defined arrangement that could only lead to administrative confusion. Experience with it since 1956 (when it was initiated) appears to have justified these misgivings.

Under the terms of the experiment, four officers from TAA's Programme Division were stationed at Santiago and two others at Mexico City, where ECLA maintains a sub-regional office. These officers *in toto* were to constitute the TAA Office for Latin America. They were to be the channel through which TAA matters would be referred to and from the regional commission. They were also to engage in direct consultation with governments in the Latin American region concerning their technical assistance needs and help them formulate project requests in collaboration with the RTARs. The ECLA secretariat was to be drawn upon for technical briefing and backstopping in those subject-matter fields covered by its staff.

On the whole, the TAA outposting arrangement seems to have contributed to improvement in EPTA programming and to have provided a source of useful advice to governments, most of which, for this very reason, favoured continuation of the experiment from year to year. Its difficulties were mainly administrative and procedural. The status of the outposted units *vis-à-vis* TAA headquarters, as prescribed by the latter,

[52] The outposted unit at Beirut is completely independent of any other field office. It is the only one of the five units that now receives both administrative and technical direction from New York. This unit (in 1958) was reportedly to be given premises in the re-located UNICEF area office there. As of mid-1959, there was a plan to outpost to New Delhi one member of the ECAFE Social Affairs unit, similar to the arrangement at Mexico City where an officer from the Santiago unit has been attached to the sub-office of ECLA.

hedged the former about with a network of restrictions and required headquarters clearance on so many routine matters as to impede action and multiply paperwork.[53] The outposted office, for example, lacked delegated authority to allocate funds to going TAA projects by utilizing savings from other projects. If a government proposed a new project during the financial year, this had first to be submitted to the RTAR, who then forwarded the request to the Santiago (or Mexico City) unit which in turn sent it to New York with its comments. New York's action on the request was transmitted back to the government by the same circuitous route. According to members of the Santiago staff (in 1957), it often took as long as twenty days to get headquarters approval of anything involving additional expenditure of funds—New York being a bottleneck.

Similar triangular communication channels were required for correspondence from and to project experts. Letters from them on routine matters (*e.g.*, leave-of-absence reports, travel claims, and so forth) were supposed to be addressed to the nearest outposted unit, which then had to process and forward them to New York.[54] The instructions relative to the submission of periodic progress reports on projects were so involved and so unclear that many experts mistakenly sent all three copies of these reports to Santiago (or Mexico City), instead of mailing one copy directly to New York.[55] With respect to orders for project supplies, it fell to Santiago to prepare specifications and send them to New York; but in case of delay in receiving an order, or if it was not accurately filled, the government concerned would first inquire of the RTAR, who then got in touch with Santiago, which would then have to follow up on the matter by cable to New York. Several RTARs remarked to the writer that they were never quite sure when they should route communications by way of Santiago or write directly to New York. Under the outposting scheme the Director of the Programme Division at New York normally communicated with

[53] The working relations between TAA New York and its Latin American office were spelled out in an administrative memorandum issued by TAA on 8 Oct. 1956, and subsequently modified in various particulars.

[54] In November 1957, however, this procedure was simplified and experts were instructed to correspond directly with the TAA Programme Division at New York on a long list of administrative matters.

[55] One copy was for the appropriate section of the ECLA secretariat for comment and a second for the outposted unit's files.

the RTARs only via Santiago. On the other hand, by a curious anomaly, the Public Administration Division of TAA could write directly to them. One RTAR, on the occasion of the writer's visit to his office, had just received a cable from New York asking for the government's reaction to certain regional projects; a day later a cable came from Santiago asking for the same information.

These are a few illustrations of how tangled were the relations between the outposted units and headquarters on the one hand, and with the RTARs and project experts on the other. From the field one almost wondered if TAA in New York was not deliberately trying to make the experiment as difficult to work as possible. In any event, the staffs of the outposted units found themselves so overloaded with clerical operations that they were having to work fifty to sixty hours a week. Since the outposting arrangement, under the General Assembly's budgetary authorization, was not supposed to add to the total administrative costs of TAA, the expenses of the Santiago and Mexico City units had to be taken out of headquarters funds. Yet the scheme also added considerably to the correspondence and secretarial staff required to handle it at headquarters as well. The administrative, recruiting, and financial aspects of TAA's operations, it is important to remember, were not decentralized. Each project, in the over-all operational sense, had to be 'looked after' from headquarters. Some duplication thus could not be avoided.

However, so far as the status of the TAA outposted unit with reference to ECLA was concerned, no serious problems arose. Unlike the Social Affairs unit, it was not considered as an integral part of the ECLA secretariat. While maintaining independence of action, it managed to develop friendly working relations with its ECLA associates without becoming a full-fledged member of the ECLA 'club.'[56] The annual budgetary allocation for the TAA office was 'notified' to the administrative officer of ECLA, who handled payments, the recruitment of local staff, travel arrangements, and the like for the unit (the same arrangement obtained at Mexico City through the ECLA administrative officer stationed there). Even so, there was some

[56] At Santiago, the TAA unit was at first located on the ninth floor of the ECLA building—like 'poor relations,' as one staff member wryly expressed it—but was later moved to more commodious premises a few blocks down the street. At Mexico City, however, the 'sub-unit' had quarters in the same building as the ECLA office.

indication that the top command of ECLA was casting about for ways of bringing the TAA unit more fully under its wing;[57] nor would such a development have been displeasing to the Latin American members of ECLA.

As noted in the preceding chapter, the TAA outposting experiment was liquidated during 1959. It had proved to be very expensive; it was not genuine decentralization. The basic alternative was either to move the entire TAA Programme Division to the regions or to keep it *in toto* at UN headquarters. But the regional decentralization of TAA programming, along WHO lines, would clearly not be acceptable in UN governing circles. Under a properly streamlined headquarters set-up, moreover, it should be possible to make just as effective use of the substantive staffs of ESA, both regionally and in New York, as under a decentralized arrangement. In this connection, as one thoughtful TAA official pointed out to the writer, two senior programme officers might be assigned to 'ride each regional circuit'—one to advise on the development of projects at the early stage and the other to aid in the negotiating phase. Whether such officers were officially based at New York or at Santiago (or Bangkok or Addis Ababa) would really not make much difference since they would in fact be dividing their time between headquarters and the region. Each could of course perform various inspectional functions en route.

Other examples of communication tangles

Where an agency, such as WHO, FAO, or UNICEF, maintains a three- (or four-) level pattern of offices, the hierarchical relations of field offices at different levels are not always clearly defined and some communication confusion may result. In FAO, for instance, the Rio and Mexico City zone offices are in principle subordinate to the Santiago regional office, although, for geographic coverage, Latin America is divided among them three ways. There is a single administrative budget for the three offices which is controlled by the regional representative at Santiago. The latter makes quarterly sub-allotments of funds to each of the other two offices and may, on his own initiative, shift moneys (*e.g.*, for staff travel) already sub-allotted from one

[57] By contrast, the Executive Secretary of ECAFE was reported to have characterized the TAA outposting scheme as 'a bastard arrangement,' and he would have none of it!

office to the other. The two zone offices are required to make a formal monthly report to Santiago but a copy also must be sent to FAO headquarters. Most of the correspondence of these two offices (aside from communication with governments and project missions) is actually with Rome and reports of all travel missions are sent directly there also—always with a copy to Santiago.[58] In short, the two zone offices are partly subordinate to and partly independent of Santiago. These cumbersome arrangements are conducive to some confusion, delay and extra paperwork.

In UNICEF, a somewhat similar type of situation prevails. The area offices, for example, regularly have to report and account for expenditures to the appropriate regional office. They find it necessary, however, to correspond frequently with New York headquarters about various matters, especially the shipment of supplies. In order to keep the regional office informed, copies of all important correspondence must be sent to the latter office. On occasion different solutions to an immediate problem will be proposed independently by New York and the regional director, and further correspondence by letter or cable may be required to clear up the situation. One experienced area officer, in commenting on these relationships, observed that there would be less paperwork and more expeditious action if he had no regional office to deal with—all the more because most basic decisions about programme were made at headquarters anyway.

Turning to ICAO, some confusion of responsibility seems to exist with regard to the implementation of technical assistance projects. In the Middle East and South Asia, this responsibility is divided among the Technical Assistance Bureau at Montreal, the field representative of this unit now stationed at Beirut, the technical assistance training missions (in countries where they are located), and occasionally the RTARs. The Director of one regional office told the writer that he was asking Montreal for clarification since most governments assumed that he, as ICAO's regional representative, had jurisdiction over technical assistance matters, which was not the case. Acting on this assumption,

[58] It is actually quicker for the Rio office to write to Rome than to send a letter by pouch to Santiago. The new zone office at New Delhi is in theory administratively responsible to the Bangkok regional office, but the former communicates directly with Rome on various matters.

national authorities often wrote to him about such matters and he was puzzled as to what course of action he should follow. He had recently requested Montreal to send him copies of letters concerning EPTA negotiations in his region but the reply was that this would be 'impractical.' When a certain government in the region had proposed the withdrawal of an expert for exceeding his terms of reference, the regional office was not informed by headquarters. If it had known about the situation, it might have been able to iron out the difficulty on the spot.

As noted earlier, ECLA maintains a sub-office at Mexico City. This office forms an integral part of the Santiago secretariat, its functions being delegated by the Executive Secretary and subject to review by him at any time. Its administrative funds, consisting of about 25 per cent. of the total ECLA budget, are sub-allotted from the Santiago office and its manning table is set by the latter. Monthly accounts of expenditures are submitted to Santiago, which passes them along to New York. The Mexico City office head may hire local staff and engage temporary consultants within the limits of his sub-allotment. While the principal channel of communication on policy and administration is with Santiago, his staff often write directly to their technical counterparts in ESA at New York in order to save time, always, however, with a copy to Santiago. Close working relations between the two offices have been facilitated by a considerable rotation of professional staff between them and frequent personal contacts at meetings of ECLA committees. Even so, the necessity of having to get Santiago's clearance on certain administrative matters, instead of dealing directly with New York, has caused annoying delays.

In various ways, the foregoing situations illustrate the kinds of confusion, or multiplication of procedural actions, that may occur from overlapping or unclear delegations of functions to field offices at different hierarchical levels. To be sure, most field administrators manage to contrive methods of minimizing such difficulties. Nevertheless, an intensive analysis of the operation of field structures, at least in some agencies, needs to be undertaken with a view to their further 'rationalization.' We shall return to this point at the end of the study.[59]

[59] See pp. 521–523, 537–542.

Pooling Field Experience

In concluding this chapter on communication and logistics, it seems appropriate to examine the extent to which the cumulative experience of administrators and technicians, within the UN system, is assembled, recorded, and utilized for the improvement of field programme operations. Certain aspects of the broad problem of pooling operational experience have already been dealt with—in our discussions of briefing, supervision, inspection, and staff rotation. There are, however, other devices which may be employed to promote the interchange of experience, vertically as well as laterally, through an organization. Among such devices are the following: (1) the convening of periodic meetings of field office directors for consultation among themselves and with central secretariat officials; (2) arrangements for the lateral exchange of information among field offices and among project experts in related subject-matter areas; and (3) the 'debriefing' of project personnel at the termination of their assignments in such a way as to capture the essence of their experience for maximum use in future briefing, programme planning, and project execution. Although there has been considerable experimentation along these lines in UN system field administration, the full potentialities of experience-pooling are yet to be realized.

Periodic meetings of field officers

In the United Nations, the Executive Secretaries of the regional commissions regularly meet together at Geneva during the summer session of ECOSOC. These meetings, held in private, provide an opportunity for them to engage in frank discussions of common problems. The Secretary-General is often able to participate in these meetings. During the earlier years, sizable staff contingents, headed by the Under-Secretary for Economic and Social Affairs, also sat in the meetings. More recently, smaller and more informal gatherings have been the practice. Agenda are said to be focused chiefly on administrative matters, not much attention being paid to high-level policy or economic conditions. The utility of such meetings, now that the various commissions interchange information regularly (see below), is perhaps less obvious than formerly.

On the other hand, the presence of the Executive Secretaries permits them to attend and participate in ECOSOC debates on economic development policy, and this has important values. In this connection, the problem of arranging the order of business in ECOSOC so as not to compel busy Executive Secretaries to remain in Geneva for a period of three weeks, or even longer, has come up. This problem provoked discussion at the spring session of ECOSOC in 1958, when arrangements for the summer agenda were being worked out. Members of the Council were unanimous in feeling that 'the participation of the Executive Secretaries . . . was the best way of achieving the co-ordination of the activities of the regional commissions,' and it was agreed that 'the Council should organize its work in such a way as to make it unnecessary for the Executive Secretaries to be present for an unduly long period.'[60]

Meetings of the directors of those UN Information Centres located in Europe and the Middle East have been held annually in Geneva in conjunction with the session of the Consultative Committee on Public Information (a subsidiary body of ACC). Senior members of the New York staff of OPI attend these meetings, which reportedly are more useful in terms of informal personal contacts than of any systematic discussion of field problems. The directors of the Centres in Asia and the Pacific used to be convened every two years in Bangkok for three or four days. This meeting was usually conducted by the Deputy Director of External Relations in OPI, who took home leave in that part of the world at such times. Meetings of the Latin American directors were formerly held at headquarters biennially but this was discontinued for reasons of expense. In the spring of 1959, all of the Information Centre heads were assembled at UN headquarters to participate in plans for reorganizing OPI in the light of recommendations made by the Committee of Experts of the General Assembly. This was the first time, incidentally, that many of the Centre directors had ever been back to headquarters since their initial assignment to field duty. The main criticism made by Centre directors concerning the earlier regional meetings was that they were not well planned in advance and were too brief. It is now hoped, budget permitting, to increase contact between the

[60] UN Doc. E/SR.1021, 7 May 1958.

Centres and headquarters by holding directors' meetings in New York every second year and by having a senior headquarters officer visit each centre at least once in two years —along with a more systematic rotation of senior centre personnel.[61]

Among the specialized agencies, it is the practice in WHO to have all regional office directors come to Geneva twice a year— in January for the Executive Board meeting on the budget, and in the spring for the annual session of the World Health Assembly. The Director-General and his deputies sit in these meetings where operational problems and difficulties are discussed and experience exchanged. During the Executive Board's discussion of the draft budget, the regional directors are available to give information on WHO's activities in their respective regions and to answer questions concerning proposed budgetary allocations to the regional office and its programme. The heads of the PASB zone offices in Latin America regularly attend the annual sessions of the Directing Council of PAHO for similar purposes. The senior professional staff of WHO's regional offices get to Geneva only at irregular and not very frequent intervals—ordinarily in connection with home leave. Such stop-overs in Geneva are usually too hurried to be of much value. It was suggested to the writer by several of these officers that they should be allowed to spend a longer period in Geneva (*not* to be counted as part of their home leave) for leisurely discussions with their headquarters counterparts as a kind of 'refresher' experience—or 'in-service training.' Instructions from Geneva, they contended, were often 'academic' because of lack of any 'real touch' with the field.

In FAO, meetings of regional office directors were convened at Rome during 1955 and 1956 to explain the new EPTA country programming procedures. This practice was discontinued by the present Director-General, presumably since most regional directors managed to come to Rome some time during the year for other business. In March 1957, however, the Director-General convened a special meeting of regional office heads in order to get their views on his proposals for strengthening FAO's regional machinery. During and after the biennial FAO

[61] See, for the reorganization of OPI, *Public Information Activities of the United Nations: Report of the Secretary-General*, UN Doc. A/4122, 16 June 1959.

Conferences the regional representatives get together informally; the deputies from the zone offices are also included.

Until recently, periodic meetings of ILO's field office directors were not held but in 1958 it was announced that henceforth they would convene in Geneva in January of each year for two weeks of 'concentrated' interchange of field experience.

Since 1950, biennial sessions of the directors of ICAO's regional offices have regularly been held at Montreal. These meetings, which are serious affairs, last from ten days to four weeks. Convened by the Air Navigation Bureau, they are in the nature of round-table conferences, some 80 per cent. of the time being devoted to air navigation business and the other 20 per cent. to air transport, technical assistance, and administrative items. Additionally, there is usually a day-long informal session between the regional office directors and the Air Navigation Commission, a technical body reporting to the Council and made up of twelve air navigation experts selected by the Council from among nominees of contracting States; the purpose of this is to give members of the Commission a first-hand picture of problems and progress in the air navigation field in the various regions. The chiefs of section in the Air Navigation Bureau and the Director of the Technical Assistance Bureau attend. There appears to be general agreement as to the value of such discussions. Further exchange of information takes place at the regional air navigation meetings, in which senior headquarters as well as regional staff participate.

Mention was made earlier of the practice in UNICEF of having the regional directors at Paris and Bangkok come to New York twice a year for the sessions of the Executive Board, during which future policies on programming and budgets are considered with their active participation. Meetings of area and country representatives are held from time to time at the regional office concerned. At Paris, the chiefs of the area offices convene every two years, but no such meeting has taken place at Bangkok since 1950, when, according to report, the regional Director 'did all the talking'—in the absence of any carefully planned advance agenda. Meetings of field representatives in Latin America are convened every year or so at various places by the Director of the Office for the Americas at New York headquarters. At Beirut, the policy of the area office is to bring nearby country representatives together as often as his budget will permit. In the opinion of most UNICEF personnel, more frequent meetings of field officials would be desirable but financial costs make this difficult.

We come now to the RTARs. During the first few years of EPTA, it was the policy of TAB to invite individual RTARs to participate in its meetings when they happened to be in New York on home leave or for 're-briefing' or other business. At nearly every meeting of the Board one or more RTARs would be present and be invited to give testimony on their country situations. Unfortunately, according to reliable report, certain RTARs took advantage of this opportunity to criticize in untactful terms the administration and procedures of various agencies with respect to EPTA. Such criticism was not appreciated by agency representatives on the Board. If, for example, an RTAR should refer to the 'over-selling' of projects by a given agency in his jurisdiction, this would be disturbing to the 'club atmosphere' that is said to characterize Board meetings. Apart from this, it was felt that the participation of RTARs in Board meetings tended to lengthen the sessions unduly. Consequently, the practice was discontinued some years ago, regrettably in the opinion of many RTARs.

In the meantime, the policy of convening regional meetings of RTARs was developed. In principle, these are held once a year, usually under the chairmanship of the Executive Chairman of TAB or one of his senior staff associates on tour in the region. During the winter of 1958, for example, such meetings took place at Athens, Cairo, New Delhi, and Bangkok, with a particular view to having an exchange of views on the new Special Fund and the contribution the RTARs might make to its operations. Similar meetings were held in Latin America, the Middle East and Asia during 1956 and 1957. Meetings of RTARs were to be held in all the major regions in the course of late 1959 and the first half of 1960. The business of such meetings ranges widely over a variety of matters—financial, administrative, public relations, fellowships, programme procedures, project evaluation, and the like. By general agreement they serve a very useful purpose, fully as much for TAB headquarters staff as for the RTARs themselves. But they are no substitute for direct contact with the Board itself. In lieu of this, consideration has been given to the desirability of holding a meeting of all RTARs at headquarters every two years, but this has not yet proved feasible.[62]

In an agency such as Unesco, which has no general regional office establishment, the country chiefs of mission feel peculiarly cut off from headquarters and from one another. For some years regional meetings of mission chiefs occasionally took place, but they have since apparently been abandoned. Direct contacts of chiefs of mission with headquarters programme specialists are few and far between. The former deplore the lack of opportunity to participate in the formulation of Unesco policies and procedures. In their view, mission staffs should be considered not only the 'hands' but the 'eyes and ears' of the organization along the operational front. Arrangements for fairly frequent and relaxed contacts with headquarters and with other technical assistance teams would contribute to a greater sense of loyalty to Unesco and its programme, and would act as a powerful morale booster. In contrast with Unesco, the general policy in WHO is to bring its area representatives to the nearest regional office for consultation once a year, while FAO pursues a similar practice with regard to its country representatives. But in Unesco there are no comparable field offices where country mission chiefs might foregather to talk over problems with one another and with outposted staff specialists.

Lateral exchanges of information

In this general context, there is clearly a need for more extensive interchange of information laterally among project experts working in similar subject-matter fields in different countries. The writer discovered a number of instances where a project team in one country had no knowledge of the vicissitudes of comparable undertakings in neighbouring areas. The circulation of digests of reports on related projects by agency headquarters to experts in the field might provide helpful insights as to what to avoid, or how to deal with knotty

[62] A number of RTARs deplored the lack of personal attention given them by TAB headquarters. A personal letter every four months or so from the Executive Chairman of TAB, said one, would help to remove the feeling of being 'a forgotten man.' During nearly five years in the field, this RTAR had received only one letter from the Executive Chairman, and there had been only three visits from TAB staff over this period. Recently, however, it has become the policy of the central secretariat of TAB to try to have each field office visited at least once a year.

problems, despite the fact that no two situations are ever quite the same.

At the regional office level, lateral exchange of information is currently developing in several agencies. For example, the UN regional commission secretariats now regularly exchange publications, secretariat studies, and relevant pre-publication memoranda. Recently a study on the overseas market for steel prepared by ECE was circulated to ECLA and ECAFE for their views, while an ECLA paper on the proposed common market for Latin America was sent to ECE for comment. In connection with such exchanges, the Regional Commissions Section of ESA in New York often serves as a clearing-house.[63] A senior specialist from the executive office of ECE was loaned to ECAFE for several weeks to help its secretariat prepare for a meeting on the Promotion of Intra-Regional Trade held in Bangkok during January 1959, thus making available the broad experience of ECE in trade promotion techniques.[64]

In WHO, the quarterly and annual reports of each regional director have for some time been circulated to the other directors. While there is not as yet complete reciprocity in the interchange of technical information, two offices (at New Delhi and Manila) exchange summary statements on completed projects and brief assessments on the status of continuing projects. The Washington office of FAO frequently supplies staff for FAO meetings held under the auspices of the Latin American regional offices and thus is able to keep in close touch with their needs. In ICAO, there is considerable interchange of information among various regional offices on an *ad hoc* basis. Also, meetings are held at intervals of a few weeks among the 'chiefs of sections' (at headquarters) dealing with the technical subjects of primary interest to regional offices, at which the status of current work projects and plans for future projects are discussed. Records of these discussions are sent to all regional offices on a routine basis. Furthermore, all documents and papers produced in headquarters

[63] The Chief of this Section is the 'eyes and ears' of the regional commissions at UN headquarters. It is his duty to call their attention to important official resolutions the implications of which are not readily apparent; to keep the commission secretariats on the right track legally and procedurally; and to serve as the principal channel of communication with them below the level of the Under-Secretary for Economic and Social Affairs.

[64] During this meeting, which the writer attended, the ECE secretariat official sat at the head table, alongside the Executive Secretary of ECAFE (who acted as chairman). The latter publicly thanked him for his 'invaluable assistance' to ECAFE.

are distributed to the regional offices, and the Regional Affairs Section at Montreal sends out a weekly list of the papers considered to be of greatest interest to a regional office. There is also a constant exchange of correspondence between regional offices and technical assistance missions.

The 'de-briefing' problem

The pooling of operational experience is, or should be, a cyclical process. From the standpoint of the individual expert, it may be said to begin with his initial briefing, followed by such backstopping service as he receives from headquarters and field office staffs during his tour of field duty. The cycle closes with his 'de-briefing' [horrible word!] at the conclusion of his assignment. This final operation, if properly organized, can be of immense value in terms of adding to the recorded store of 'inside' experience from which an agency can draw in building future programmes and in recruiting and orienting future technicians.

Until quite recently, few of the UN organizations appear to have recognized adequately the importance of de-briefing. For the most part it has consisted of hurried, unstructured interviews with busy staff members who view it as a chore to be handled as quickly as possible. There are currently some signs of improvement in certain agencies, as will be seen from the examples cited below.

In FAO, a series of standard questions to be put to each outgoing expert were being prepared in the fall of 1958. The replies to these questions are to be filed, country by country, in the Field Operations Liaison unit at headquarters. The same procedure will be employed in the Washington office for experts returning from Latin America. It is hoped that this information will provide a cumulative picture of recurring problems, difficulties, and trends.

For experts de-briefed at WHO headquarters a series of 'terminal interviews,' lasting two or three days, is scheduled with the technical and administrative divisions and the Programme Co-ordination office. In these interviews operational problems and difficulties, as well as weaknesses in the original briefing, are stressed. Each expert sees each member of a de-briefing committee of section chiefs. The information thus garnered is summarized in internal memoranda for future use in project planning and briefing. Those aspects of the information of a confidential character are filed without identification of the individual expert or of the government concerned. De-briefing also takes place at the regional office for all project staff at the termination of their assignments. This, however, has chiefly to do with the 'finalization' of project reports for submission to governments. A draft of the report, prepared in consultation with the expert's counterpart, is sent to the regional office two months in advance. During the de-briefing period, a final version is agreed to after clearance by the regional director with the government. The rest of the de-briefing period is taken up with various procedural matters relating to the termination of the expert's contract. Each expert is encouraged to provide a private, confidential report on his experience. In the case of project teams, the leader drafts the official report, attaching sections prepared by other team members.

At the International Labour Office, de-briefing operations may take as much as a week or even longer. The political aspects of de-briefing are handled by the Field Services Division, the administrative aspects by the Finance Division, the public relations side by the Public Information Division, and the technical phases by the appropriate technical divisions. The official project report, a preliminary draft of which will already have been prepared by the expert, is worked out in consultation with the technical division concerned, which is responsible for its contents. The final version is processed by the Field Services Division after approval by the Director-General. In some cases a returning expert may be asked to modify substantially or even to re-write his draft report before he departs from Geneva.

In Unesco, talks with the BMS staff and the relevant programme specialists are arranged for each outgoing expert, though without any attempt to standardize such interviews. In addition, the expert usually gives an oral *exposé* of his experience before a staff group. The substance of this discussion is recorded in a confidential memorandum for BMS files. This process ordinarily lasts from two to five days.

For most BTAO experts, de-briefing has been equally hurried. At the BTAO Geneva office, European experts spend a single day 'blowing off steam' with respect to their personal 'gripes' and administrative difficulties. A record of this is made in the form of personal notes to selected staff members at BTAO headquarters. According to one senior official in the Geneva office, so-called confidential memoranda sent to New York run the risk of being 'leaked' unless care is taken to conceal their identity. For experts de-briefed at New York, an inter-bureau committee in ESA conducts either individual or group interviews, depending on the availability of technical staff at the time. In the Public Administration Division each returning expert is now required to 'testify' at a staff meeting as to matters that cannot be put on paper. Early in 1959 BTAO headquarters was reported as contemplating the preparation of a check list of points to be covered in de-briefing interviews.

From this mixed picture of the manner in which de-briefing is handled, two tentative conclusions emerge: (1) more time should be allowed for this final exercise and (2) the process needs to be much more systematized than is now the case in most agencies. At a recent conference of National Technical Assistance Committees in Europe the suggestion was made that arrangements be worked out for returned experts to discuss their experience with newly appointed experts. Although it would be difficult to implement this excellent idea from a practical point of view, there seems little doubt that the possibilities of more effective utilization of field experience are far from having been exhausted in the UN family of agencies.[65] This fundamental problem of communication might advantageously be explored by a special inter-agency working group of operating officials and social science specialists.

[65] At the least, tape-recorded interviews with returned experts might be made available to their incoming colleagues.

PART THREE

THE PROGRAMME PROCESS

8

REGIONALISM IN FIELD PROGRAMMING

Parts I and II of this study were concerned mainly with the wherewithal of administration—machinery, manpower, materials, facilities, communication, and operational procedures. It is now proposed to shift attention to the products of these ways and means—the field programmes that emerge therefrom. How are these programmes formulated and co-ordinated within the UN family of agencies? By what methods are they implemented? How effectively are they co-ordinated with similar programmes (*a*) sponsored by other international organizations and (*b*) conducted by individual donor governments on a bilateral basis? To what extent do they lead to altered policies or administrative innovations by the governments that constitute their targets? How is their over-all impact evaluated? These are the principal questions with which Part III of our inquiry will attempt to deal.

At the outset of this analysis, it should be noted that the roles of agency governing organs and headquarters secretariats in the programme process will be considered primarily in order to clarify the impacts of regional and country-level machinery on the content and execution of *action* programmes. In the introductory section of this chapter, however, it may be useful to outline briefly the kinds of instrumentalities that have been evolved at the headquarters level with a view to determining programme priorities and to facilitating inter-agency co-operation in the conduct of approved programmes. We shall then proceed to examine the various degrees to which regionalism has influenced the content and administration of agency field programmes. The next chapter will view the problem in terms of programming at the country level—with special reference to the TAB formula.

Central Instrumentalities for Programme Co-ordination

As suggested earlier, the dispersal of programme functions among a cluster of quasi-autonomous agencies in the UN system has led over the years to a proliferation of mechanisms for inter-agency co-ordination. At the policy level, the Economic and Social Council, according to the rationale of the UN Charter, was to serve as the principal co-ordinating organ. Under the general authority of the General Assembly, ECOSOC *may* 'co-ordinate the activities of the specialized agencies through consultation with and recommendations to such agencies and through recommendations to the General Assembly and to the Members of the United Nations.' It *may* also enter into agreements with any or all of the agencies 'defining the terms on which the agency concerned shall be brought into relationship with the United Nations.'[1] But it has no power to issue binding orders to any of the agencies; it may only 'recommend' or 'request' that they follow certain lines of policy or action as to substantive programmes within their respective constitutional spheres. The governments belonging to the UN family of agencies have thus far established no authoritative centre for real co-ordination in the *legislative* sense. 'The Charter, the basic instruments of the specialized agencies, and the agreements linking them to the United Nations, establish a partnership, the success of which depends essentially on voluntary co-operation under the leadership of the United Nations.'[2]

The voluntary character of this partnership is emphasized in the agreements actually negotiated, like treaties, between the UN and the specialized agencies during the mid-1940s, and subsequently in the case of agencies established later.[3] Apart from provisions relating to financial, budgetary, and personnel questions, these agreements typically *authorize* the right of reciprocal representation at meetings and the right to propose agenda items; and *obligate* in general terms the exchange of information and publications, the consideration of recommendations made to a specialized agency by the General Assembly or ECOSOC, the consultation with the UN in regard to such recommendations, and the submission of reports to the UN.[4]

[1] Article 63 of the Charter.

[2] Robert E. Asher, *et al.*, *The United Nations and the Promotion of the General Welfare*, *op. cit.*, p. 81.

[3] For the official texts of these agreements, see *Agreements between the United Nations and the Specialized Agencies* (New York: United Nations, 1952).

[4] The agreements with the Bank and the Monetary Fund are specific in establishing the autonomous status of the two institutions *via-à-vis* the UN. These agreements begin by pointing out that the Bank and the Fund are agencies, not of the UN, but of their Member governments. In any conflict they serve the latter and not the former. This

In addition, the specialized agencies agreed to participate in any body or bodies which the Council might establish for the purpose of facilitating co-ordination.

With this object in view, ECOSOC in 1946 established the Administrative Committee on Co-ordination, to which reference has already been made. Although set up on the Council's initiative, this body is a standing inter-agency committee consisting of the Secretary-General (as chairman) and the executive heads of the specialized agencies (now including the IAEA as well). ACC was conceived of 'as the primary device at the inter-secretariat level' for assisting the Council in the discharge of its co-ordinative responsibilities under the Charter, and for the implementation of the UN-agency agreements. The Committee now ordinarily meets twice a year, and during recent years most of the agency heads have found it possible to attend regularly, which was not true earlier. Until about 1954, the ACC concerned itself largely with administrative, financial, and personnel matters. Since then, however, it has given increasing attention to problems of programme co-ordination and of inter-agency co-operation in the planning and conduct of projects at all levels —headquarters, regional, and country.

This shift of emphasis in ACC's work reflected a growing effort on the part of ECOSOC to bring about greater concentration in economic and social programme content by establishing over-all priorities as guides to agency programme planning. Hortatory resolutions to this general effect were adopted by the Council (as well as the General Assembly) as early as 1950, and at nearly every summer session since then.[5] High among the proposed priorities for programme action under regular budget financing was the economic and social development of the underdeveloped countries. Beginning in 1953 the Council went a step further and asked ACC to explore the possibilities of 'concerted action' by the UN and the specialized agencies in

is important because of the difference in membership and the weighted voting in each institution. These agreements, moreover, are supplemented by the records of the UN Negotiating Committee according to which the UN specifically agreed, as a matter of policy, not to make any recommendations to the Bank or the Fund on loans or loan policy. For a detailed discussion of the negotiation of the earlier UN-specialized agency agreements, see *Co-ordination of Economic and Social Activities* (New York: Carnegie Endowment for International Peace, 1948).

[5] Notably ECOSOC Resolutions 324 (XI), 451 (XIV), 496 (XVI), 627 (XXII), 664 and 665 (XXIV), and 693 (XXVI).

specific subject-matter fields. This approach envisaged full consultation by agency secretariats on programming 'at the earliest planning stages,' going beyond co-ordination after programme approval. In ACC's language, concerted action would be applicable only if a given programme were

> (*a*) sufficently complex to call for efforts from different directions; (*b*) sufficiently specific to allow a combination of efforts within a definite area; and (*c*) capable of a definition which the various parties concerned agree to accept as the framework of their joint efforts.[6]

Among the fields recently suggested by ECOSOC resolutions for such action are social welfare, community development, urbanization, industrialization, water resources, and the economic aspects of the use of atomic energy.

To return to the evolution of co-ordinative machinery: the ACC early decided to set up a number of subsidiary bodies to assist it in furthering programme co-ordination.[7] A Preparatory Committee of Deputies, designed to handle questions not requiring top-level decision, was established at the outset. From time to time, various *ad hoc* committees and working groups, composed of senior technical officers of the agencies concerned, were created for such overlapping fields as manpower, migration, housing, child welfare, fundamental education, and commodity problems. Reports from these groups were usually made to the Preparatory Committee, which took action, when required, on behalf of ACC. In 1954, ACC initiated arrangements for annual meetings (1) of senior representatives of ESA, ILO, WHO, FAO, and Unesco, to consider over-all programmes in the social field; and (2) of representatives of ESA, ECAFE, ECLA, FAO, Unesco, WHO, and WMO to promote co-operation on the development and utilization of water resources.[8] Concurrently, a Working Group on Community Development, which has since met annually, was set up to facilitate programme-planning in this somewhat amorphous domain, now involving UNICEF as well as the UN and four specialized agencies. In 1955, before

[6] *Twenty-second Report of the ACC*, UN Doc. E/3108, 13 May 1958, Annex I.

[7] Among these subsidiary bodies were the standing consultative Committees on Administrative Questions and on Public Information, which, however, had nothing directly to do with programme co-ordination.

[8] To serve as 'the focal point' at the secretariat level for concerted action in this field, a Water Resources Development Centre was established in the UN Secretariat in 1959, at the request of ECOSOC. UN Press Release EC/1962, 1 July 1959.

IAEA came into existence, a Sub-Committee on the Peaceful Uses of Atomic Energy was added with a view to promoting general co-ordination in this field. After the establishment of IAEA, it was decided to discontinue this body and to deal with the problem within ACC itself, of which IAEA had become a member.

Since 1954, ECOSOC has undertaken a more thorough scrutiny of the annual reports of the specialized agencies than had previously been the case. During the earlier years each report was considered separately and the Council usually contented itself by 'noting,' either with or without 'appreciation,' the individual reports. Under the new procedure the various reports are considered together, with the executive heads of the agencies taking part in the discussion. To aid the Council in conducting this annual review, ACC provides each year a document containing a 'General Review of the Development and Co-ordination of the Economic, Social, and Human Rights Activities of the United Nations and the Specialized Agencies as a Whole,' while the Secretary-General submits his own observations on the work programme of ECOSOC and its commissions in these fields. These annual discussions now form the basis for the resolutions on programme co-ordination and concerted action to which reference was made above.[9]

In addition to the co-ordinative machinery operating under the aegis of ECOSOC and ACC, the specialized agencies (as well as UNICEF) have, on their own initiative, concluded bilateral agreements providing for consultation in fields of common concern and, in a few cases, for an agreed division of labour.[10] Over and beyond the illustrations mentioned above, where for the most part it falls to the UN itself to exercise the initiative, there are various areas where functional overlaps of agency activity, or even contradictory policies, may easily develop. Loveday has observed:

> At one point or another the work of each international organization is liable to impinge upon that of another. Frequently it is far from obvious

[9] TAB, of course, serves as a co-ordinative organ of major importance. Its role in this regard will be considered in connection with country programming. See pp. 367–376.

[10] For the text of these agreements, see *Inter-Agency Agreements between Specialized Agencies and Other Inter-governmental Organizations* (New York: United Nations, 1953). During 1958, IAEA negotiated similar agreements with ILO, FAO, Unesco, WHO and WMO, and, in 1959, with ICAO.

to which organization an issue should be submitted as the body primarily concerned.[11]

With the object of minimizing duplication and utilizing limited agency resources as economically as possible, the major agencies have set up joint technical (or expert) committees in specific fields, such as, for example, nutrition (WHO-FAO); occupational health (ILO-WHO); and vocational education (ILO-Unesco). Both WHO and FAO have established joint policy committees with UNICEF to co-ordinate project activities in the field of maternal and child welfare. FAO and ECE maintain a joint Timber Committee.

Informal agreements, or memoranda of understanding, between cognate agencies, have in some cases delimited agency responsibilities in border-line areas (*e.g.*, between ICAO and WMO with regard to technical assistance in meteorology as applied to aviation). An interesting belated effort to reach an understanding on the respective functions of Unesco and the UN Public Administration Division in the field of public administration training resulted in a 'gentleman's agreement' by 1959. Inter-secretariat consultation at the planning as well as the operational stage has become an increasingly significant feature—in some ways more important than the use of formal machinery—of agency working relationships. Through such consultation arrangements for sharing research obligations, the collection and compilation of statistics, and the preparation of reports have been worked out.

The import of these developments for the present study will be evident from what follows in this chapter and the next. Suffice it to say here that the proliferation of *central* machinery, criteria, and processes for improved inter-agency co-operation has had a considerable influence on programme planning and execution at regional and country levels. As we shall see shortly, a number of important regional projects involving the participation of two or more agencies are either in progress or at an advanced planning stage. In such complex areas as community development, water control and utilization, industrialization, and urbanization, 'concerted' programmes are beginning to emerge, though at varying rates and with varying degrees of difficulty. 'The most remarkable thing,' observed the United States dele-

[11] *Reflections on International Administration*, *op. cit.*, p. 266.

gate to ECOSOC recently, 'is that all this has been achieved not by way of centralization, not by directives and orders, but by consultation and persuasion.'[12]

Even so, the actual picture remains more spotty than this designedly optimistic view might imply. While it is broadly true that agency programmes have 'gained in purpose, depth and strength,' and there are certainly fewer unilaterally conceived, *overlapping* projects than some years ago, inter-agency rivalries still persist. It is an open secret that the work of various co-ordinative bodies at the secretariat level continues to be hampered by internal tensions. Jurisdictional disputes as to which agency should have the *major* role in co-operative programmes are still by no means unknown.[13] Successive clearances up the hierarchy to ACC appear to be unavoidable, and operations often move with exasperating slowness. Partly because of this, ACC recently decided to review its own machinery and procedures.[14] Since, however, 'the co-ordinators are the same as the co-ordinated,' it is unlikely that any mere streamlining of machinery can change the basic situation very much. Vigorous assertions of agency 'rights' may still be expected and full harmonization of action will not be easy to achieve without some alteration of the constitutional framework of the UN system as a whole. What might be done short of this will be suggested in the conclusions of this study.[15]

The Role of Regional Bodies in Field Programming

With these introductory observations, we move to the central theme of this chapter, namely, the impacts of regionalism on economic and social programming. These impacts take diverse forms and are of varying significance. For convenience of

[12] Statement of Walter Kotschnig to ECOSOC, 11 July 1958, as reproduced in the U.S. Department of State *Bulletin* (1 Sept. 1958).

[13] As, for example, over the proposals for a programme of work in industrialization submitted by the Secretary-General to the twenty-first session of ECOSOC (1956), which had been prepared without consultation with the specialized agencies in order to save time. (See UN Doc. E/2832.) As a result, certain of the agencies were irritated no end and tried to get the proposals killed by having them referred to ACC for 'recommendation.'

[14] UN Doc. E/3108, 13 May 1958, Annex I, para. 5. ECOSOC, a year later, expressed the hope that ACC would not only continue this review but would also make 'a survey of the inter-agency structure of technical committees, working groups, and such bodies.' *Report of the Economic and Social Council*, UN Doc. A/4143, p. 68.

[15] See pp. 528–537. It is only fair to note that since the merger of the UN Departments of Economic and of Social Affairs, the co-ordination of policy and action through the ACC machinery has become noticeably more effective.

presentation, the programming situation in each major organization will be analysed separately. By using this approach it will be possible to make a rough comparison of the degree to which programme formulation has been regionally decentralized in the different agencies. In this context, the organization of a few of the more important regional and inter-regional projects of an inter-agency character will be described.

The UN regional commissions

As indicated earlier, the regional economic commissions are the only inter-governmental bodies within the United Nations proper, aside from its central governing organs, which perform programming functions in the economic and social field. Considered together, all these bodies represent, as it were, a mixed system of institutional centralization and decentralization. By their terms of reference, the regional commissions have been authorized by ECOSOC 'to initiate and participate in measures for facilitating concerted action' for the economic development of their respective regions. To this end, they may conduct or sponsor studies; collect, evaluate, and disseminate relevant information; make recommendations to Member governments and to the specialized agencies concerned; and submit for the Council's prior consideration any of their proposals that 'would have important effects on the economy of the world as a whole.' Each commission may, after discussion with any specialized agency functioning in the same general area and with the approval of the Council, 'establish such subsidiary bodies as it deems appropriate for facilitating the carrying out of its responsibilities.'[16]

Within the limits of their budgets, and subject to general policy and administrative supervision from UN headquarters, the commission secretariats engage in a wide range of functions. For 1959, the budgets of the three older commissions (ECE, ECAFE, and ECLA) aggregated nearly $6 million, or about one-tenth of the total regular budget of the United Nations. Although the internal structure of the three secretariats differs in nomenclature, they all include staff divisions for research and planning, for industrial development, for transport, and for

[16] The terms of reference of the different commissions vary in minor particulars. Here the essentials, for our purpose, where not quoted verbatim, are paraphrased.

agriculture, with various minor bureaux or sections as appropriate to the needs of each regional programme. The staff of each of these commissions now ranges close to 200 in size, of whom some seventy to eighty belong to the professional category.

Each commission has set up a battery of standing committees in such functional fields as trade, transport, agriculture, and natural resources.[17] Within the general committee set-up, sub-committees and working parties are created as necessary to deal with more limited matters.

During the first few years following the establishment of the commissions, the activities of their secretariats were principally of two types: (1) conducting research studies, making surveys, and preparing reports; and (2) arranging for and following up on special conferences, meetings, and seminars on regional problems, which were held at various places over the region. By way of illustration, such meetings have dealt with the improvement of government statistics in the economic field, techniques of census-taking, tax problems, flood control, inland transport, housing, and the like. At such gatherings, the secretariats of interested specialized agencies were often represented. From the meetings have come a flow of recommendations for further studies or policy action by governments. These recommendations are transmitted by the Executive Secretary to the appropriate commission committee or to the Commission itself.

Following the advent of EPTA, the work of the regional commissions took on a new aspect—the stimulation of technical assistance requests by individual governments and groups of governments. In a sense, the commissions were forerunners of EPTA. Once funds became available for the direct provision of advisory services to governments, it was natural that such regional bodies should play an increasing part in promoting and planning aid projects of particular concern to a region. In this connection, the TAB secretariat supplies for the information of each session of ECLA and ECAFE (and now of ECA as well) a summary of current EPTA activities in their respective regions. These changes have brought the commission secretariats into close relations with those of the specialized agencies and with BTAO. Not only have the secretariats at Bangkok and Santiago

[17] The committee structure of ECE is more elaborate than that of ECLA or ECAFE, including standing committees on electric power, coal, steel, timber, and (originally) manpower.

(to a lesser extent at Geneva), as noted earlier, become an important source of technical guidance for project experts in various economic fields, but they frequently have taken the initiative in proposing the establishment of joint working parties with one or more of the assisting agencies. Technical assistance funds, moreover, have been drawn upon to help finance technical conferences, workshops, and training seminars sponsored jointly by commission and agency secretariats.

Among myriad instances of these types of co-operative activity, only a few cases can be noted here.[18] ECE, for example, has co-operated with ILO on labour and manpower problems; with FAO (through the joint Agricultural Division referred to earlier and a Joint Timber Committee) on forest management problems and on the economic development of southern Europe (Italy, Greece, Yugoslavia, and Turkey); and with WHO and WMO on water pollution studies through an inter-agency working group. In addition to close co-operation with FAO on a wide range of problems, ECLA has had assistance from BTAO and WMO in conducting water resources surveys; from BTAO, FAO, Unesco, ILO, the Bank, and the Monetary Fund in operating the Central American Economic Integration Project (see below); from Unesco in organizing an investigation of the teaching of economics in Latin America; from BTAO in financing an annual training programme for young economists on development planning; and from BTAO, FAO, ILO, and IMF for a recent economic survey of Argentina. At its 1959 session, ECLA unanimously adopted a resolution setting up a committee of experts to draft an agreement for the establishment of a common market for Latin America. If and as this epoch-making proposal moves forward, the chances are that BTAO, FAO, and possibly IMF and IAEA will be drawn into its planning in one way or another.[19]

In view of the vastness of its regional coverage, ECAFE's activities in co-operation with BTAO and the specialized agencies have perhaps been even more extensive. ECAFE set up some years ago a Working Party on Economic Development and

[18] For fuller information, the reader may consult the annual reports of the commissions.

[19] By early 1960, the negotiations had resulted in the signing of a treaty for a free trade zone linking the following seven countries: Argentina, Brazil, Chile, Mexico, Paraguay, Peru, and Uruguay. *The New York Times*, 19 Feb. 1960. See also Galo Plaza, 'For A Regional Market in Latin America,' *Foreign Affairs* (July 1959).

Planning, which meets annually. In 1959, the first regional project in telecommunications within EPTA was begun under the joint sponsorship of ITU and ECAFE. Since 1952, it has sponsored a series of Conferences of Asian Statisticians at which representatives of certain specialized agencies have taken part.[20] With BTAO's backing, it has arranged study tours of Asian technicians in various fields. In collaboration with FAO, WMO, and various UN headquarters units, ECAFE publishes a Flood Control Series, providing governments with basic information on the effective use and control of water resources. On the initiative of the Population Commission of ECOSOC and the UN Statistical Office and with assistance from FAO, ECAFE ran a six-weeks regional training centre in Tokyo in 1958 for national census planners; this was to be followed by a series of teams of BTAO experts to advise individual governments on the setting up of national census training centres. Six countries in the ECAFE region were to hold censuses in 1960 and eleven more in 1961, some of them for the first time on anything like a scientific basis. And for what is potentially the most important project yet initiated by ECAFE—the development of the Lower Mekong River basin (see below)—it has utilized teams of experts provided by BTAO and FAO for preliminary technical surveys.[21]

In 1955, ECAFE's Highway Sub-Committee requested the secretariat to undertake studies on the improvement of road communication throughout southern Asia. The secretariat boldly proposed that the development of an international highway network (somewhat on the order of the Pan American Highway) should be considered.[22] In case such an ambitious undertaking should be approved by the commission, its technical planning may possibly involve the participation of BTAO and FAO.

Brief comment is in order here regarding the relations of the International Bank and Monetary Fund with the regional commissions. Both of these financial institutions are represented at most meetings of the commissions and of those of

[20] To aid in preparing for these conferences the UN Statistical Office at New York outposted to ECAFE two statistical experts from headquarters.

[21] For a summary of regional commission activities in the field of water resources development, see the Report of the Secretary-General, UN Doc. E/3071, 10 March 1958.

[22] See 'The Asian Highway—from caravan routes to modern roads,' *United Nations Review* (April 1959), for a colourful description of the probable route such a highway network would follow.

their committees dealing with problems of interest to IBRD or IMF. The Bank has made comparatively little use of ECLA's or ECAFE's economic studies since the latter tend to be of a somewhat theoretical character and are seldom geared to an investment programme. The regional commission secretariats, however, exchange information with the Bank's staff on technical matters and keep it informed of economic development projects arising from the work of commission committees that might need outside financing. The work of an economic survey mission sent by the Bank to Thailand in 1957–58 was materially assisted by advice and data supplied by ECAFE's staff, and there are frequent informal contacts between the Bank's representative in Bangkok and the Director of the Research and Planning Division of ECAFE. Some years ago the Bank asked ECLA to co-sponsor a study of electric power regulation in Latin America, and in 1959 a member of ECLA's secretariat participated in a power survey in Argentina conducted by the Bank.

The relations of the International Monetary Fund with the regional commission staffs are limited largely to the provision of data by the former on balances of payments and financial questions pertaining to each region. By the very nature of the Fund's functions, it does not have much contact with the operational activities of the commissions. As noted above, however, the Fund did participate in the recent ECLA-sponsored economic survey mission to Argentina by providing a monetary economist and certain background information.

To sum up, the role of the regional commissions and their staffs in programme planning has become a double one: (1) they conduct background studies and sponsor meetings, seminars, and workshops on special regional problems, both at the intergovernmental and the secretariat level, financed largely out of their own budgets but with increasing participation by other UN organizations; and (2) they act as catalytic agents *vis-à-vis* governments in the region with regard to using EPTA resources for projects to promote economic development regionally, as well as to serving individual country needs. The new African Commission wants to be regarded as the regional arm for the UN in Africa with respect to economic and social policies in general. As was indicated earlier, the scope of commission activity has recently broadened so as to cover the social aspects of development, in which the new social affairs units are now playing an important planning role. This activity is extending the purview of the commissions into such areas as community development, urbanization, social welfare, and demography.[23] In short, the regional commissions now tend to serve as intra-regional unifying forces—by providing a forum for the discussion of common development problems. Nationalisms have been noticeably tempered and often steered into constructive channels.

In determining their annual work programmes, the commissions are guided increasingly by the basic proposals of ECOSOC and ACC with regard to subject-matter priorities and concentration of effort on continuing problems of major importance and on projects 'promising practical results in the not-too-distant future.' In order to keep the costs of commission programmes within fairly stabilized budget allocations, the practice of farming out certain types of studies to universities and private research organizations is beginning to emerge. For similar reasons, various projects, during recent years, have been placed in a lower priority category, or deferred, or eliminated altogether. ECOSOC now engages in a much more careful review of regional programmes, during its annual examination of commission reports, than was the case in the early 1950s.[24] This operation has in turn had considerable influence on the focus of ECOSOC's recommendations as to UN system action in the economic and social domain. As the regional survey analyses done by the commission secretariats have improved in quality, the annual debates in ECOSOC on the world economic and social situation have given increasing attention to regional development problems.[25] Over-all programme orientation is in effect the product of a partnership between ECOSOC and its commissions, regional and functional, the former being the senior member, and the latter the junior members, of the partnership.

[23] The Secretary-General's Report on the *Relationship between the Work of the United Nations Regional Economic Commissions and the United Nations Programmes in the Social Field*, UN Doc. E/3250, 5 May 1959, gives further details.

[24] See, in this connection, the Secretary-General's *Observations on the Work Programmes of the Council in the Economic, Social, and Human Rights Fields*, UN Doc. E/3274, 12 June 1959, section V.

[25] The regional commission secretariats contribute to the preparation of the *World Economic Survey* issued annually by the UN Department of Economic and Social Affairs.

Regionalism in WHO's programme process

Of all the specialized agencies (the Bank excepted), WHO operates by far the largest field programme. Including expenditures under its regular budget, EPTA, its malaria eradication account, and appropriations made by PAHO for health work in the Americas, the outlay for programme activities around the globe in 1959 approximated $32 million. Of this total 13 per cent. was allocated for regional, area, and zone offices and 68 per cent. for programme activities in the field.[26] Nearly four-fifths of all staff personnel employed by WHO and PASB (including project experts) are stationed away from their respective headquarters (Geneva and Washington), about 20 per cent, being assigned to field offices and the other 60 per cent. to operational projects.

Functionally, WHO's over-all work programme embraces two main categories of activities: (1) permanent technical services of a world-wide character (*e.g.*, international quarantine, biological standardization, co-ordination of medical research); and (2) the provision of advisory seivices to governments and groups of governments. Broadly speaking, staff responsibility for the first category rests with the headquarters secretariat, while the second has been delegated to the regional offices.

As already suggested, the regional organizations in WHO's framework play a major role in the formulation of action programmes. In performing this function they are expected to observe the general principles, policies, and priorities established from time to time by the World Health Assembly.[27] For regular budget activities the programme cycle covers a three-year period; the 'planning' year, the 'approving' year, and the 'operating' year. Immediately after the annual spring session of the WHA, the Director-General issues to the regional directors instructions as to the preparation of programme proposals for the second succeeding year. 'The instructions include directives on programme trends and other policy considerations based on decisions of the [Executive] Board and the Health Assembly';

[26] These figures are from the *Proposed Programme and Budget Estimates for the Financial Year 1960*, WHO, O.R.: No. 89, Dec. 1958. The estimated total number of WHO-PASB staff for 1959 was 2,751, of whom 563 served at field offices and 1,627 on field projects.

[27] For a convenient summary of how WHO programme criteria have evolved, see *The First Ten Years of the World Health Organization*, *op. cit.*, pp. 112–15.

and they 'also indicate the tentative allocations of funds to each region' which the Director-General makes in accordance with certain principles set by the Board.[28] Although the Board has not deemed it feasible to 'establish firm criteria' governing such allocations, it has instructed the Director-General to give appropriate weight to advice from the regional directors and recommendations of the regional committees; availability of funds for national health work from outside sources other than WHO (*e.g.*, EPTA or bilateral aid programmes); and the capacity of governments to absorb further assistance.[29] In fact, the allocation of budgetary resources to regions is done largely on an *ad hoc* basis, with the increases slanted toward the 'newer' regions.

During the spring and summer of the planning year each regional director proceeds to plan the regional programme. While the process by which this is done varies from office to office, the procedures followed by the New Delhi office are fairly typical. In the light of information gained by the regional public health advisers and public health administrators, during their visits to governments in the region, each of them prepares initial programme proposals in his subject-matter domain. These proposals are then assembled and considered by a Programme Committee in the office consisting of the Director of Health Services and the three public health administrators over whom he has supervision. If the committee reaches agreement it is submitted to the regional director for approval; in case of disagreement it is up to him to resolve the issue. Once the proposals are approved they go to the Administration and Finance unit for costing, in accordance with detailed instructions from headquarters.

Next, a meeting of area representatives is held at the regional office during which the draft proposals are further discussed. Changes may be made at this meeting. In deciding on the final draft programme, consideration is given to the EPTA resources that will probably be available for health projects in the region. At this stage, national health authorities sometimes exert pressure to have specific projects placed on a high priority basis. Occasionally, the regional director may find it necessary

[28] WHO, O.R.: No. 92, Jan.-Feb. 1959, p. 13.
[29] WHO Docs. EB13/53 and EB13/R.23, in WHO, O.R.: No. 52, March 1954.

to reject 'diplomatically' certain project requests for which there is no money. Alternatively, such projects (provided they are technically sound) may be placed in a 'supplementary list' attached to the regional programme eventually sent to Geneva. The final decision on the draft programme is made by the regional director—after taking account of consultations with governments and, where appropriate, with other bilateral or international agencies providing health assistance in the region.

The approved draft programme and budget document is then transmitted to each government in the region and copies are forwarded to Geneva for review. Comments from governments are requested by mid-June. In the light of these comments, the document is finalized and sent to the members of the regional committee about the end of July.

The next phase of regional programme-planning takes place at the meeting of this committee in the autumn. Under the WHO Constitution, the regional committees are authorized to meet at any place they like, and they have tended to rotate their meetings among various cities in the region, thus adding to expense. The WHO Executive Board (as well as WHA), concerned over this, has gently reminded the committees that they should consider holding meetings from time to time at the site of the regional office, and has invited their attention to the desirability of asking host governments to share in the increased costs of meetings held elsewhere.[30]

The voting membership of each regional committee consists of the health ministers (or their deputies) representing WHO Member governments in the region. Representatives of 'associate' Members of WHO may participate in the discussions but have no vote. Over the years the continuity of committee personnel from one meeting to another has steadily increased. The committees now provide a useful training ground for delegates to the Executive Board and the WHA, many of whom have previously been active in regional committee work. The calibre of committee members, although differing from region to region, is said to have improved considerably since the earlier years. Most members now take their responsibilities seriously, whereas at the outset many of them did little or no 'home work' prior to the meeting, and some of them reportedly looked upon

[30] WHO Docs. EB13/R.28 (1953), WHA7.26 (1954), and WHA9.20 (1956).

appointment to the committee as an opportunity to engage in regional 'health politics'—if not merely to have an annual 'junket'.[31] It is customary for the Director-General, or some other senior officer from WHO headquarters, to attend regional committee meetings. Their educative value is coming to be recognized by Geneva and it is perhaps not an exaggeration to say that the more mature committees are now functioning as miniature regional 'parliaments' for the planning of improved national health services.

The agenda for regional committee meetings is prepared by the regional office. They include three principal items: discussion of the annual report of the director; review of the status of projects in the region; and, most important of all, consideration of the programme and budget proposed for the second following year. For the latter task some of the committees set up a special sub-committee at each session. Concerning programme and budget, the committees appear to have evolved through three stages. At first the tendency was to rubber-stamp the regional director's proposals, and few concrete recommendations emerged from the meetings. During the next stage, there was a good deal of general discussion accompanied by some 'log-rolling,' most members supporting each other's projects. More recently, the better committees have begun to subject the director's proposals to detailed scrutiny, with the result that various projects may be modified, some shifted to a different priority position, some deleted, and a few new proposals inserted.[32] If, as now and then happens, a government asks for a 'half-baked' or frivolous project which, for political reasons, the regional director has allowed to remain in the draft programme, the committee will usually spot it and ask that it be withdrawn.

The effectiveness of a regional committee depends to a large extent on how it is handled by the regional director. One director is said to have controlled his committee by skilful manœuvring. In another case, the director exerts strong

[31] One RTAR, who had recently attended a WHO regional committee session, observed to the writer that it operated like 'a closed club,' the members all agreeing that public health was 'the thing' and that health got too small a share of government budgets—with little appreciation of other equally urgent problems such as food supply or education.

[32] During the examination of PASB's annual budget by the Directing Council of PAHO, the heads of the 'zone' offices in Latin America defend their programme proposals in person.

leadership over his committee by the sheer force of his personality—stimulating it to tackle new problems. In still another, the director employs a more systematic technique of committee management. Each morning his senior staff meets for a post-mortem of the previous day's deliberations and to prepare plans for the coming day's work. For this purpose specific tasks are assigned to his technical and administrative aides.

The draft programmes, as endorsed by the respective regional committees, are sent to Geneva in October, with such comments on their technical and budgetary aspects as may be appropriate. After examination for duplication and costing by the Budget Division, the Programme Co-ordination office at headquarters assembles all programme proposals, including those submitted by the headquarters technical divisions, and puts them into proper form (with narrative justifications) for consideration by the top command. Many of the most significant items in WHO's general programme result from recommendations of *ad hoc* committees set up on a small informal basis with membership drawn from standing panels of experts. It is up to the Director-General to tailor the ensemble of programme proposals to fit his over-all budget. If, for example, a particular region exceeds the tentative target set for it, he may delete or defer certain items. Sometimes a regional director will be advised that a particular proposal is being transferred to the headquarters programme. Finally, the Director-General prepares his annual Programme and Budget document for submission to the Executive Board at its meeting in January. This terminates the planning phase of the programme cycle.

The Executive Board, aided by its Standing Committee on Administration and Finance, examines the budget more or less closely. In the course of this examination regional directors may be invited to explain orally how their respective regional programmes were formulated, and questions are often put to them by the Board. The Board also has before it the minutes of regional committee meetings. At this stage, however, substantial changes in the budget are rarely proposed since the Board tends to accept what the regional committees have already approved. The over-all programme and budget, with the Board's recommendations, is circulated by the Director-General to all Member governments for final consideration at the spring session of WHA, which seldom modifies the regional programmes appreciably. Its authorization of the budget for the ensuing year concludes the approving stage of the programme process.

The content of WHO's regional activities has gradually changed over the years. At first, as Berkov has noted, 'the regional program and budget represented merely a collection of individual country requests . . . based on priorities within the constituent countries.'[33] Beginning with the European committee, however, an attempt was made to correlate country requests with the goals of regional health development in general. This led to the emergence of an increasing number of projects of an inter-country character, chiefly in the form of regional seminars, training institutes, and study tours for health technicians.[34] The emphasis on regionally organized projects reflects the fact that the incidence of human disease ignores national boundaries. As a part of this evolution, various inter-regional undertakings have been stimulated by the regional offices. Thus, a training seminar held in one region may be attended by public health officials from other regions; or a conference on smallpox may be convened to improve and co-ordinate national control procedures in those parts of the South-east Asia, the eastern Mediterranean, and the western Pacific regions 'where the epidemiological situation is similar.'

At this point it is appropriate to note that the annual programme and budget document sent to the Health Assembly includes a summary of estimated WHO expenditures under the Expanded Programme of Technical Assistance. However, the country programme-planning cycle for EPTA, as we shall see in the next chapter, does not begin until April preceding the *operating* year—only a month or so before WHA's annual session. Nor does TAB know until several months later how much money will be pledged for EPTA financing during that year. Accordingly, the EPTA estimates presented in the WHO budget document have to be based on certain broad assumptions as to continuing and new projects for which WHO will be the executing agency.

Coming to the operating stage of WHO's field programmes,

[33] *The World Health Organization . . ., op. cit.*, p. 73.

[34] Annex 9 of *The First Ten Years of the World Health Organization, op. cit.*, gives a complete list of WHO technical meetings and seminars held to the end of 1957.

project allotments, as indicated in Chapter 6, are made to the regional offices at the beginning of the project year. As soon as these allotments are received, the regional advisers prepare 'plans of operation' for each project and request the regional Administration and Finance unit to proceed with the recruitment of experts (in consultation as necessary with WHO headquarters). Supply lists are drawn up and submitted to the Medical Supply unit of the regional office. During the course of the year, to take the procedure of the New Delhi office by way of illustration, weekly meetings of the Director of Health Services, the regional public health administrators, and the Administration and Finance officer are held at which the status of projects within a given specialization are carefully reviewed. When, for instance, a tuberculosis control project is up for review, the regional adviser in that field participates in the meeting and provides detailed information. Over a three-month period all current projects are examined in this manner. When savings on regular budget projects are indicated, the regional director (with headquarters approval) may transfer funds to other projects or activities (*e.g.*, supplies or fellowships).[35] Or, after consultation with the governments concerned, he may apply part or all of the savings to implement projects listed on the 'green sheets' at the end of the WHO annual budget document.[36] For each inter-country project a regional adviser is designated to convene an intra-office committee on a subject-matter basis to determine its scope and operating conditions. Roughly similar procedures for project review and supervision have been developed at the other regional offices.

Regional decentralization for programming has by now been accepted by most of the WHO headquarters staff as a desirable permanent feature of the organization. The double impact of relatively large regional staffs and of increasingly active regional committees has made it possible for WHO to maintain close relations with national health administrators. In line with the philosophy of Dr. Brock Chisholm, its first Director-General, WHO has deliberately sought to encourage wide initiative on

[35] Transfers from one EPTA project to another require the approval of the Executive Chairman of TAB.

[36] These 'green sheets' summarize technically sound 'additional' projects requested by governments which the Director-General was unable to include in the proposed budget without exceeding his over-all budget ceiling.

the part of the governments of the developing countries—so that they may 'learn by doing.' By taking part in the work of the regional committees, national health officials come to feel a fuller sense of belonging to the organization than if their participation were limited to its central organs. Moreover, the regional office, as Berkov has noted, has 'constituted a natural link between headquarters and national health administrations.'[37] It serves as a regional symbol of the principles and purposes of WHO.

Consequently, WHO's regular programme of work is probably more sensitively adapted to regional needs and conditions than that of other UN agencies. Regional variations are so important in the health field, observed one senior WHO official to the writer, that it would be highly unrealistic to determine field programmes 'by remote control from Geneva. The regional offices know best what can and cannot be done.' While this view is not shared by all of WHO's central professional staff, most of them would now agree that the pattern of regional decentralization has helped measurably to solidify the support of Member governments for the organization. Not only has regionalism appeared to have an educative effect in regard to local institutions, but it has stimulated national health ministries to co-operate on problems cutting across national boundaries. In this way the work of WHO in most of its regions can be, and usually is, better integrated intra-regionally than might otherwise be the case, even though the bulk of each regional programme still consists of 'country' projects. Notwithstanding, political log-rolling has not entirely disappeared from the deliberations of regional committees on programme formulation. Nor, except in the Americas, has regionalism yet produced any additional financial support for WHO's regional work from the governments of the respective regions, as envisaged by the WHO Constitution.[38]

Perhaps the most perplexing problem faced by WHO in connection with regionalism has been its relations with the Pan American Sanitary Bureau. As intimated earlier, the

[37] *Op. cit.*, p. 154.

[38] Among the functions of the regional committees (Article 50 f) is the right to 'recommend additional regional appropriations by Governments of the respective regions if the proportion of the central budget of the Organization allotted to that region is insufficient for the carrying out of the regional functions.'

availability of sizable independent resources to this regional Bureau has produced a situation where 'the tail can almost wag the dog.' The Bureau's Director is appointed by the Directing Council of the PAHO, the WHO Executive Board merely ratifying the action *pro forma*. For many years the Director of the Bureau appeared to run it as if it were an autonomous entity in a loose confederation with WHO.[39] Under these circumstances the degree of administrative, financial, and technical control exercised by WHO headquarters over the Bureau was tenuous indeed. There was no formal reporting by the Bureau Director to the Director-General, while the former official tended to look upon the PAHO Directing Council as his 'policy-control' organ—not in its capacity as the WHO Regional Committee but as a Pan American body. In Geneva's eyes, the Washington office seemed in certain respects to operate like a 'health bureau' of the United States Government, from which, incidentally, it received impressive financial support.

Some years ago the Director of PASB put into effect a series of measures designed to devolve upon his 'zone' offices in Latin America substantial powers of decision over personnel recruitment, payroll operations, and fellowship awards. Country programmes financed from WHO regular budget and PAHO funds are now formulated at the zone level, an initial major allotment of funds being made to the zone directors with authority to re-deploy them within broadly determined programme objectives. This stiff dose of 'sub-regional' decentralization was reportedly viewed by Geneva with considerable misgiving.

Although the *rapport* between Washington and Geneva has noticeably improved recently, it was perhaps with the PASB situation in view that the WHO Assistant Director-General for Administration reminded the 1958 session of the WHA that 'we must be keenly aware of the necessity to resist vigorously any tendency for WHO to become a mere federation of loosely-associated regional organizations.'[40]

The steady expansion of WHO's total budgetary resources during recent years has enabled it to maintain at Geneva a fairly adequate professional staff to handle the headquarters role

[39] Reliable report has it that this particular Director was wont to refer to the PASB as 'headquarters,' the WHO central office being in his mind merely 'Geneva.'

[40] WHO Doc. A 11/AFL/18, 30 May 1958.

of leadership in stimulating and co-ordinating research on a world-wide scale. WHO is currently entering new fields of research—on health statistics, trachoma, leprosy, cancer, heart disease, and radiation—which seem destined to become a conspicuous aspect of its central activities. During 1960, an intensified programme of medical research, to be financed in part by an increase of $500,000 in its regular budget, is to be inaugurated.[41] To promote this programme a special Division of Medical Research Planning has been set up within the office of the Director-General. The gravitational pull of these important additional functions should suffice to fortify headquarters against any undue centrifugal tendencies.

Growing regional influences in FAO programme-making

In contrast to WHO, FAO did not delegate programme-making functions to its regional establishment at the outset. Prior to the advent of EPTA, its overseas offices served primarily for informational and liaison purposes. During this early period the organization provided a limited amount of technical assistance to governments, largely by drawing upon residual UNRRA funds to which it fell heir, in the form of survey missions to countries whose agricultural services had been disrupted by World War II.[42] It also financed from its regular budget the establishment of a number of regional training centres and seminars to help groups of countries rebuild or improve their technical staffs in agriculture, forestry, fisheries, and nutrition. This action reflects a growing realization that, as in the health field, there are food and agricultural problems common to contiguous countries in the same climatic and geographic area. But the organization did not then, nor has it since, set up a programme of direct technical aid to individual governments as a part of its regular budget.

On the other hand, FAO began as early as 1948 to establish on a permanent basis various advisory technical bodies, most of which have a regional composition and deal with regional problems. Important among them are the International Rice Commission (1948); three fisheries councils for the Mediterranean,

[41] The United States Government has made a special contribution in support of this programme.

[42] See Gove Hambidge, *The Story of FAO*, *op. cit.*, Chap. 6, for an interesting summary of the Organization's early technical assistance activities.

the Indo-Pacific area, and Latin America (1949–51); four forestry commissions for the Asia-Pacific area, the Near East, Europe, and Latin America (1948–52); the European Commission on Agriculture (1949); and the European Commission for the Control of Foot-and-Mouth Disease (1954). In the main these subsidiary organizations were the result of recommendations made by the FAO Conference or Council (acting under permissive authority granted in Article VI of the Constitution), although the initiative usually came from the secretariat.[43] All of these bodies operate at the inter-governmental level and their members ordinarily consist of national directors of services in the functional field concerned. Those commissions dealing with Europe are serviced by the Rome secretariat and the others by technical officers outposted to regional offices (*e.g.*, at Bangkok for the International Rice Commission and the Asia-Pacific Fisheries Commission; at Santiago for the Latin American Forestry Commission). The agenda for their meetings, which take place every year or so, are drawn up by the appropriate technical division at Rome in consultation with the regionally outposted officers concerned, one of whom normally acts as executive secretary of the meeting.

For the purposes of the present study, the most significant feature of the work of these advisory bodies is the indirect influence they exert on the technical content of FAO's programme. From periodic interchanges of information and ideas among the participating national specialists concrete proposals for programme action, both generally and in regional terms, frequently emerge. These proposals (in the form of resolutions) are transmitted not only to Rome but also, more recently, to the FAO general regional meetings (see below), which are now held in the off-years between the biennial sessions of the FAO Conference. To assist in their work, some of the advisory commissions have set up working groups on specific problems, as, for example, the Working Groups on Rice Breeding and Fertilizers of the International Rice Commission. In addition, recommendations for 'concerted action' as to policies and

[43] There has been some confusion as to the legal status of certain of these subsidiary bodies. In some instances, the multilateral agreement device was used to establish permanent commissions entrusted with specific functional tasks falling within the constitutional terms of reference of FAO. The 1957 session of the FAO Conference recommended that the texts of such agreements should be brought into conformity with the provisions of the Constitution.

studies by governments in a region are often made by the advisory bodies, thus contributing to closer inter-governmental relationships in various subject-matter fields.

In 1948, FAO initiated the practice of holding regional meetings of a general character, called at first Pre-Conference Regional Meetings on Food and Agricultural Problems and Outlook. The original purpose of these meetings was to provide an opportunity (1) for an exchange of information at the top policy level on agricultural conditions, and (2) for developing a basis for a well-informed world review at the ensuing FAO Conference.

In 1955, the Director-General proposed that the role of such meetings (to be designated henceforth as Regional Conferences) should be expanded. Specifically, it was suggested that they should review the implementation of FAO's work in the region over the past two years and then discuss programmes and policies for the two years following the next session of FAO's General Conference,

> taking into account implications of the specialized conferences and sessions which have been held in the spheres of agriculture, economics and statistics, fisheries, forestry, and nutrition since the last Regional Conference. . . . Special attention would be paid to the co-ordination of technical aid programmes in the region, particularly the selection of regional projects and the organization of country group projects under [EPTA].[44]

The results of the deliberations of the Regional Conferences were to be reported as advice to the FAO Council through the Director-General.

Two years later, Director-General B. R. Sen (who took office in September 1956) went a step further. As a part of his scheme to strengthen FAO's regional organization, to which reference was made in Chapter 6, he proposed that responsibility for preparing the provisional agenda for the Regional Conferences should henceforth be delegated to the regional representative (this task had previously been handled directly from Rome), in collaboration with the outposted technical officers. The draft agenda, after approval by Rome, would become the basis for conference deliberations on a limited number of key issues. *Inter alia*, proposals from regional technical bodies involving

[44] FAO Doc. C55/49, Nov. 1955.

financial implications would be reviewed by the conference 'at the ministerial and administrative level.' The regional representative, moreover, would serve as its executive officer, assisted as need be by headquarters and regional office staff. Under this scheme, also, the meetings of technical groups in the region were to be planned in consultation with the regional representative, who would advise headquarters of the wishes of Member governments as to the scheduling of such meetings, the documentation for which would be provided jointly by headquarters and the regionally outposted technical officers. The plan further envisaged a substantial increase in the number of technicians to be outposted to the regional offices.[45]

The rationale of the Sen proposals was twofold: (1) to confer jointly upon the heads of the regional offices and the regional conferences a larger degree of regional programme advisory responsibility, and (2) to provide the regional offices with more adequate staff resources for their expanding liaison and supervisory tasks, covering both regular programme and EPTA activities. Although it is too early to form any firm judgment on how the plan is working, the reactions of the five regional representatives with whom the writer had opportunity to discuss the subject were generally favourable. One or two, however, feared that the scheme might result in weakening the technical division staffs at headquarters. The regional representatives attached particular importance to the enhanced role to be played by the regional conferences. In the past, these meetings had had little impact on programme planning because many governments followed the practice of sending to them technicians, or diplomats stationed in the host country, rather than higher-level policy representatives. This now appears to be changing. At the Tokyo Conference held in October 1958, for instance, four Ministers of Agriculture were present and the rest of the delegates were at the under-secretary level. The work papers reportedly were well prepared and the participants did not ask for 'fantastic' projects. Moreover, the Conference succeeded in reaching a consensus on future programme priorities.

As the regional conferences gain experience, they may become an important unifying force in such regions as Asia and the Near

[45] For fuller details as to the Sen proposals, see FAO Doc. C57/5, 11 March 1957.

East by promoting inter-governmental co-operation on basic problems like food supply and land reform.[46] Such a trend is now discernible. In the view of the FAO Director-General, the conferences held since 1956 have been the 'most successful' in the history of FAO, exhibiting 'down-to-earth realism' and giving impetus to the enforcement of FAO's regional structure. It is nevertheless to be remembered that they do not have the kind of constitutional status enjoyed by the WHO regional committees.

Furthermore, one procedural difficulty complicates the exercise of their programme advisory functions. Since FAO's budget is now on a biennial basis, it is necessary to formulate programme proposals some three years before the end of the period covered by the budget. While the Council may transfer funds between budget chapters for the second year of the biennium, there is little opportunity to make any substantial modifications during the two-year period. This long time-lag between preparation and implementation of the budget means that programme recommendations made by the regional conferences must necessarily be couched in rather general terms, as conditions may change in the meantime.

Despite this timing problem, regional conference proposals are valuable for indicating over-all programme content and focus (*e.g.*, the importance to be given country in comparison with regional projects, or to the provision of experts as against fellowships). Under the Sen scheme, the regional representatives, on the basis of these recommendations, and in the light of ideas provided by the FAO country representatives in the region, submit to Rome concrete proposals for incorporation in the regular work programme and budget, including types of activities to be suggested to governments for inclusion in their EPTA requests. At headquarters, these proposals are considered first by a Policy Advisory Committee composed of programme officers of the technical divisions and the Director of the Programme and Budgetary Service in the Director-General's office. Aside from recurrent work of a clearing-house

[46] Until recently, according to two regional representatives, it was hard to sell the regional approach to governments in these regions, what with their colonial background, nationalistic proclivities, and the lack of a tradition of working together. The Iranian Government, for example, did not relish being dovetailed with the Arab countries in the FAO Near East regional conference.

and research character, most of the headquarters programme-planning has been done within the technical divisions on a piecemeal basis. Director-General Sen, as noted in Chapter 6, is now giving increasing attention to the long-range projection of programme trends and priorities. With this in view a Programme and Policy Board, consisting of the Director-General, the Deputy Director-General, and the division directors, deals with major policy questions. The Budget Service 'prepares the detailed costing and financial estimates of the programme as it emerges' from the discussions of these two staff groups.[47]

After formal approval by the Director-General, the work programme and budget are put together in a single document for submission to the FAO Council. The latter relies on two committees—one on Programme and the other on Financial Control—to advise it on the substantive and administrative aspects of the proposed programme. At a summer meeting the full Council reviews the over-all programme in the light of the reports of these two committees. The programme and budget document, together with the Council's report, then goes before the biennial session of the FAO Conference in the fall for final review and approval.

The Programme and Budget document includes in an Annex a summary of expenditures on EPTA country and regional projects for the current and preceding years, but estimates for the ensuing budgetary biennium are not presented because information is not then available as to FAO's allocations from EPTA funds two years ahead. As in the case of WHO, the difference in the timetables of the regular programme and of EPTA make it difficult for FAO's governing organs to subject the latter to the same degree of scrutiny as the former receives. In view of the fact that FAO's EPTA-financed activities are larger in volume than those of any other patricipating organization, the financial implications of this situation have been a matter of some concern to the Advisory Committee of the UN General Assembly.[48]

[47] *Third Report of the Advisory Committee on Administrative and Budgetary Questions*, UN Doc. A/3598, 9 July 1957, para. 47.

[48] *Ibid.*, para. 53. For 1958, the total expenditure under FAO's regular budget and from EPTA allocations was approximately equal—at the level of $8·3 million each. FAO has from the outset consistently received the highest percentage of EPTA funds of any agency.

Since the introduction of the Sen proposals, the regional offices of FAO have been in a state of transition. Formerly, they were in effect advance outposts of headquarters and as such performed various duties related to the servicing of meetings and the operation of technical assistance projects. Now they have joint responsibility with headquarters for advising on regional programme-planning—translating the flow of ideas from regional conferences and technical meetings into proposals for consideration by Rome. The division of labour between them and Rome, however, is not very clearly defined and may give rise to some confusion. The regional office heads have become the senior field representatives of the Director-General for all of FAO's interests and activities in the region. They are now expected to cultivate the closest possible relations with national agricultural authorities and to exercise a large degree of personal initiative. In the Director-General's language, this arrangement is designed to 'provide a greater sense of regional identity within FAO's broad international framework . . . while avoiding the creation of a number of "little FAO's" '.[49]

Even so, the status and functions of FAO's regional offices still contrast markedly with those of WHO. For one thing, the professional staffs attached to the former are much smaller—even after taking into account the additional outposted officers promised under the Sen scheme.[50] Secondly, and again unlike what prevails in WHO, the FAO regional representatives have not been delegated authority to design projects in detail, to recruit project experts, or to transfer funds from project savings to other projects in the region. Decisions on all these important matters still rest with Rome. Nor, as in WHO, are tentative allocations from the FAO regular budget made to regions in advance of programme formulation. The over-all work programme is presented in the biennial budget along functional rather than regional lines. Accordingly, Chapter VI of the budget is divided into two parts, the Technical and the Economic Departments, each consisting of functional divisions (*e.g.*, fisheries, forestry, rural institutions, nutrition, commodities, economic

[49] The quotation is from Mr. Sen's monthly letter to national Ministers of Agriculture (No. 55, January 1957).

[50] Less than 8 per cent. of FAO's regular budget is absorbed by regional and country office expenses, as against 15 per cent. in WHO. For 1958, FAO regional office staffs (including outposted officers) ranged in size from about twenty at Bangkok and downward for the other offices.

analysis, and so on). These divisions embrace both headquarters and field activities and include numerous regional undertakings, such as technical meetings, seminars and study groups, as well as country projects, which are expected to be financed from future EPTA allocations.[51]

By way of summary: what appears to be taking place in FAO is a combination of programme-advisory decentralization in regional terms with the maintenance of strong headquarters control. So far as field programme execution is concerned, the balance is being tipped markedly towards the regional offices, the outposted technicians, and the country representatives.

Regional impacts on ILO programming

As indicated earlier in this study, ILO began, a quarter of a century ago, the practice of holding conferences on a regional basis to consider how the organization's work might be geared more effectively to regional needs. The initiative for such conferences stemmed from various governments in the principal regions. When the ILO Constitution was revised in 1946, the regional conference device was given special recognition by the insertion of an article authorizing the Governing Body to convene such regional conferences 'as may be desirable to promote the aims and purposes of the Organization.'[52] It was further stipulated that the 'powers, functions, and procedures of regional conferences shall be governed by rules drawn up by the Governing Body and submitted to the General Conference for confirmation.' Such rules were elaborated by the Governing Body in 1948 and amended at subsequent sessions.[53]

The decision to hold a regional conference is taken by the Governing Body itself, which also determines the agenda and indicates what governments shall be invited to nominate delegates. In conformity with ILO's tripartite system of representation, the membership of each regional conference includes two government delegates and one delegate each representing

[51] Technical assistance projects involving the provision of experts to individual governments are not financed out of FAO's regular budget. However, the regular budget does provide for a number of special fellowships mainly for research training.
[52] Article 38.
[53] See *Rules Covering the Powers, Functions, and Procedures of Regional Conferences Convened by the International Labour Organisation* (Geneva: 1956).

employer and worker organizations. The staff of the International Labour Office prepares the working documentation for the conference.

By 1958, six regional conferences had been held in Latin America (where they originated in 1936), four in Asia, and one in Europe. A 'preparatory' conference for the Near and Middle East (confined to government representatives) took place in 1947, but was not followed by any further conferences during 1958 or 1959. While regional conferences have become a permanent feature of the organization, no definite periodicity has been laid down for their sessions. During the period from 1936 to 1958, a conference was held in each of the two non-European regions about every three years (except for an interruption of some years because of World War II). In reviewing ILO's experience with regional conferences, a special Committee of the Governing Body, reporting in 1958, expressed doubt 'whether it is now necessary *in general* to hold sessions of a regional conference at shorter intervals than five years, which would mean about one conference a year.' The Committee pointed out that 'the staging of a session of a regional conference is a formidable undertaking—only less so than a session of the General Conference. It is costly. It imposes a heavy workload on the staff of the [Geneva] Office.' It was further noted by the Committee that the needs of one region might call for more frequent sessions than those of another.[54]

To each session of a regional conference the Governing Body normally sends a delegation from its own membership. The secretariat of the conference is provided by the Geneva office under the supervision of the Director-General, who personally participates in the discussions. While members of the staff of the ILO 'field' office in the region usually attend conference sessions, they have nothing to do with their preparation or follow-up, in contrast with the roles of the regional offices in WHO and FAO.[55] Decisions of a regional conference take the form of resolutions or reports addressed to the Governing Body, transmitted to it by the Director-General. In actual fact, most of the substantive resolutions adopted by the conferences are inspired by him or his staff. These resolutions consist of

[54] ILO Doc. G.B. 139/9/30, May-June 1958.

[55] The ILO 'branch' office at New Delhi aided in the material arrangements for the fourth session of the Asia Conference held there in November 1957.

(1) general recommendations as to ILO's programme orientation (*e.g.*, concerning 'freedom of association' for trade unions), and (2), at the field level, proposals for studies and action projects of special interest to the governments of the region. In this latter connection, it should be noted that the conclusions of various ILO technical committees and technical meetings, organized regionally, are often referred to the general regional conference for consideration.

The impact of regional conference recommendations on ILO programme planning has steadily grown, particularly since the advent of EPTA. The Governing Body usually accepts such recommendations without appreciable change in so far as budgetary resources make possible their implementation. In drafting ILO's over-all annual programme and budget, the Geneva Office, as indicated in Chapter 6, now attempts to integrate research and 'pre-legislative' functions with operational activities. In so doing, it takes into account reports from a battery of advisory committees, some of them standing committees with official tripartite membership and others consisting of experts appointed in their private capacity—for such fields as maritime labour, agriculture, industry, migration, social security, indigenous labour, and occupational health. As noted above, ILO's regular programme also provides from time to time for regional technical meetings, often in co-operation with cognate agencies, as, for example, a European Conference on Rural Life (with FAO), a Study Conference on Vocational and Technical Education for the Arab States (with Unesco), and a Technical Manpower Conference for Latin America. Some of these undertakings stem from proposals recommended by the general regional conferences.

From the foregoing it will be evident that ILO's field offices play little or no direct part in planning its programme. The earlier (branch) offices were established as liaison and diplomatic instruments while the later (field) offices were originally set up in connection with the special manpower programme. Even these offices have quite small staffs—only four or five professionals each. Various regional and functional groups adopt broad conclusions and emphasize the importance of certain aspects of ILO's activities. The actual content of each country programme, moreover, is reviewed by the field office directors with the technical divisions during the annual meetings at headquarters. But the field offices themselves are concerned chiefly with the supervision of country (and regional) project operations. They also help to negotiate project agreements with governments and to brief experts. But there is no inclination at ILO headquarters to allocate budgetary resources in terms of designated regions.

Actually, only a very minor percentage of ILO's regular budget is utilized for direct services to governments in the form of experts, supplies, or fellowships. For the most part, such activities are financed from EPTA funds.[56] The Governing Body, through its standing Technical Assistance Committee, keeps itself informed as to ILO developments under EPTA and, as we shall see later, has undertaken at times to evaluate selected EPTA projects. But 'neither the Governing Body nor the Conference is provided with proposals for a consolidated and integrated programme of work' which would enable the two bodies to examine each year ILO activities as a whole.[57] Here again, as in WHO and FAO, differing time schedules in the planning of the two types of programmes constitute an obstacle to over-all programme review.

Air navigation regionalism in ICAO

In Chapter 6, the functional character of ICAO and its headquarters structure were described in some detail. It will be remembered that this organization engages in two distinct but complementary types of activity involving technical assistance to Member governments. On the one hand, it supports from EPTA funds various resident technical assistance advisory missions and national and regional training centres—this phase of its field activities being planned and administered almost exclusively from headquarters. On the other hand, its regular budget work in the sphere of air navigation, which also entails technical advice to governments in connection with the execution of regional plans, is to a considerable extent decentralized

[56] For 1958, ILO's *regular* technical assistance programme approximated only $100,000 (out of a total budget of over $7 million), while its allocation from EPTA was nearly $3 million. *Annual Report of the TAB for 1958*, ECOSOC, O.R.: 28th Sess., 1959, Suppl. No. 5, pp. 17, 166. For 1959, the regular budget allocation for direct services to governments was increased to $164,000.

[57] *First Report of the Advisory Committee . . . to the Eleventh Session of the General Assembly*, UN Doc. A/3142, 10 July 1956, para. 43.

regionally, both at the planning and at the implementing stage.[58] Within this decentralized pattern, the role of the periodic regional air navigation meetings is of capital importance so far as 'legislative' planning is concerned. These meetings are governed by the ICAO Council on the recommendation of its Air Navigation Commission and are convened by authority of the Council. Full-scale meetings are held at intervals of three or four years for each air navigation region, or combination of regions, concerned. During the interval between full-scale meetings more informal meetings to deal with specific aspects of air navigation (*e.g.*, telecommunications, meteorology, jet operation requirements) frequently take place.[59] In 1958, a joint meeting with WMO was held in Geneva for the European region to make recommendations concerning the exchange of weather information between ground stations and its transmission to aircraft in flight.

Three categories of governments may participate in the full-scale regional meetings, as follows: (1) those territorially located in the region; (2) those located outside the region which provide aviational services (*e.g.*, a communications station) in the region; and (3) outside governments operating airlines through the region. Participating governments are ordinarily represented by senior officers in the specialized technical fields to be dealt with by the meeting, the Director-General of Civil Aviation often being present as chief of the delegation. The regional meetings, which usually last about a month, study regional plan requirements in detail. As new types of aircraft and equipment emerge, these plans need to be reviewed periodically. Proposals for amendment formulated at the regional meetings are transmitted to the regional offices for review and sent to governments in the region for comment. Next, they go to Montreal for detailed analysis by the Air Navigation Commission, which reports to the Council. Finally, the Council, which is a legislative as well as an executive organ, rejects, alters, or approves the proposals. As approved, they are incorporated into the Regional Plans and Regional Supple-

[58] Apart from these two kinds of field activity, ICAO administers 'joint support' arrangements for the North Atlantic Weather Stations and for air navigation services in Iceland, Greenland, and Greece.

[59] For a complete list of ICAO meetings of all kinds, held during the period from 1945 to 1957, see ICAO Doc. 7638/2, 21 Sept. 1957.

mentary Procedures which the Member States in the region are expected to carry out to the best of their ability.

Although the application of regional plans for air navigation facilities, as well as international standards and recommended practices for air safety, is primarily the task of individual governments, ICAO renders to them such assistance and encouragement as it can in the implementation of these requirements. It is the responsibility of the regional offices to provide this assistance by supplying information and by sending staff missions to countries in the region on short-term—usually less than a month—assignments. In addition, technical aid under EPTA is available for expert advice and the training of personnel 'on a larger scale and over longer periods than the resources of the regional offices permit.'[60] In this sense the latter form of assistance may be viewed 'as a logical extension of the regular programme.'

In the annual budget document of ICAO, however, estimates on EPTA project expenditure are not included. A report on EPTA activities is presented to the Council separately. The Advisory Committee of the UN General Assembly, reporting in 1958 on ICAO's programming and budgetary procedures, urged the Secretariat to provide for the Council a consolidated presentation of all elements of ICAO's activities, 'even though the listing of technical assistance projects may be provisional, pending preparation of final country programmes.' Such a procedure, in the Committee's opinion, would facilitate 'an over-all legislative review of at least the broad lines of the total programme of work.'[61]

Incipient regionalism in Unesco's programming

Among the major specialized agencies Unesco has by far the least extensive field establishment. Its permanent overseas structure, as we have seen, is limited to four tiny 'field science

[60] *ICAO Council's Budget Estimates, 1959, and Information Annex*, ICAO Doc. 7863, A11-AD/1, 20 March 1958, p. 9.

[61] The quotations are from the *Report of the Advisory Committee on 'Administrative and Budgetary Co-ordination between the United Nations and the ICAO with Particular Reference to the Working of the Expanded Programme of Technical Assistance,'* UN Doc. A/3861, 20 Aug. 1958, p. 20. The ICAO Assembly approves a general work programme for a three-year period, within which the Council establishes annual priorities covering the technical, economic, and legal aspects of ICAO's functions. The Assembly meets in full session triennially, with an 'administrative' session during each of the intervening years at which the organization's annual budget is authorized.

co-operation offices' and one small regional office for the Western Hemisphere at Havana.[62] None of these offices, as noted in Chapter 3, has any direct role in programme making. Unesco's diverse programmes, financed out of its regular budget, are planned by the Paris secretariat in consultation with (1) international non-governmental organizations in the domain of education, science and culture, many of them subsidized by Unesco; (2) a number of standing advisory committees for programme fields not covered by the NGOs; and (3) Unesco National Commissions, which now exist in seventy-eight of its eighty-one Member States. The NGOs are organized by subject-matter and have a more or less world-wide membership. The advisory committees are appointed by the Director-General either on his own initiative or as directed by the Executive Board of the General Conference.[63] Most of these committees are concerned with functional sectors of Unesco's programme, such as adult education, natural science research, and bibliography, only a few of them advising on specifically regional undertakings. The National Commissions (described more fully below) have been established in accordance with Article VII of the Unesco Constitution.

What this all adds up to is that regional groups as such do not materially affect the programme-making process. Unesco from this point of view operates within a more highly centralized framework than any of its sister agencies. On the other hand, among Unesco's multifarious field activities there are more regionally based undertakings in proportion to total expenditure than in any other agency. As was pointed out in Chapter 2, there has been, since 1956, a decided shift of emphasis, even in Unesco's regular work, towards the provision of aids to Member States (the so-called Participation programme). Concurrently, with a view towards concentration of programme focus, three 'major' projects, each of ten years' duration, were inaugurated. One of these long-range undertakings—on the extension of primary education in Latin America—calls for the stimulation

[62] In addition, as was indicated earlier in this study, there are Unesco 'chiefs of mission' in some twenty-nine countries, but they lack the status of established offices. The professional staff of each field science co-operation office consists of a director and one natural science programme specialist. At Havana (as of 1958), there were five professional officers.

[63] For full details relating to these committees, see *Policy as Regards the Composition and Functions of Advisory Committees*, Unesco Doc. 49 EX/14, 31 Oct. 1957.

and co-ordination of country and inter-country projects within a distinct cultural region. Another—on arid zone research—has regional implications.[64] Apart from these special activities involving field administration, Unesco's normal programme of work, as well as its operations under EPTA, is now shot through with meetings of experts, training seminars, courses, and institutes and scientific symposia, of a regional and inter-regional character.[65]

To aid in the designing and the supervision of some of the foregoing regional undertakings, special committees have been created. Examples of this include the Inter-governmental Committee on the Latin-American Primary Education project and regional advisory committees for two Fundamental Education Centres (to be described later) and for the Asian Research Centre on the Social Implications of Industrialization (at Calcutta, India). In connection with the administration of less extensive regional projects, in the natural sciences, the four field science co-operation offices are being increasingly utilized. It is through these offices that arrangements for the holding of regional meetings, symposia, and seminars are usually handled. To cite a few illustrations at random: the New Delhi office, in 1957, organized jointly with the Food and Agricultural Council of Pakistan a symposium on soil erosion problems at Karachi. That same year the Cairo office sponsored jointly with the Egyptian Desert Institute a regional training course on hydrology of the arid zones, while the Montevideo office convened at Rio de Janeiro a meeting of specialists on humid tropics research in Latin America. For the Unesco Social Science Department, the social science officer stationed at the Cairo office performs similar functions. Thus, in December 1957, he had charge of a regional round table held at Beirut on the 'Contribution of the Social Sciences to Economic Development in the Middle East.' Since 1957 the frequency of such arrangements appears to have increased. Ordinarily the Unesco headquarters staff is represented at regional technical meetings. It should be emphasized, however, that in most cases outside the natural science domain

[64] The third major project—for the 'Development of Mutual Appreciation of Eastern and Western Cultural Values'—spans the globe.

[65] The annual reports of the Director-General contain complete lists of all Unesco conferences, meetings, and seminars held during the preceding year. See also the *Proposed Programme and Budget for 1959–1960* (Paris: Unesco, 1958), Annex IV.

regional projects of temporary duration are both planned and arranged directly from Paris.

As an experiment, the Western Hemisphere office at Havana, in 1956, was delegated responsibility for co-ordinating the Latin American Primary Education project. In part, this step was intended as a means of revitalizing the work of this office, which had showed signs of becoming moribund.[66] With this in view, the professional staff of the office was strengthened by the appointment of a specialist in education and one in cultural relations. The former specialist, subsequently designated as the assistant director of the office, makes periodic visits to national capitals, helps to negotiate country agreements for teacher-training assistance, and arranges for regional meetings (such as the Regional Conference on Free and Compulsory Education in Latin America held at Lima).

In the opinion of certain officers at Paris, this whole project could just as easily be supervised from headquarters, if not from Unesco's liaison office at New York. Since the project involves the participation of several of Unesco's programme departments—Education, Social Sciences, Cultural Activities, and Mass Communications, in addition to its Exchange of Persons Service—the lines from Havana to Paris were said to get crossed at times, despite the efforts of BMS to keep them straight. In the course of his country visits, the Havana office co-ordinator reportedly had made informal technical assistance commitments without clearing with BMS as to country programme arrangements under EPTA. Significantly, Havana has not been given comparable responsibility with respect to projects under the Participation programme, which are managed directly from Paris. Nor does it appear to have anything to do with the supervision of EPTA projects. The Montevideo office, as we have seen, has still different functions—all of which is by way of suggesting once again that Unesco's field structure in the Western Hemisphere could stand overhauling.

Before we leave the role of regionalism in Unesco programming, reference should be made to the potential significance of the National Commissions for regional advisory purposes. These bodies are 'a unique feature; no other United Nations agency has a comparable arrangement formally linking citizen

[66] See p. 71.

groups with the work of the international organization.'[67] The membership of these Commissions varies somewhat from country to country, but usually it includes appointees from ministries of education and related government departments, as well as some representation of universities, academies, learned societies, and various professional and civic groups. The Unesco Constitution stipulates that the Commissions should act in an advisory capacity to 'their respective delegations to the [Unesco] General Conference,' and 'to their governments in matters relating to the Organization.' The Constitution further states that they 'shall function as agencies of liaison in all matters of interest' to Unesco—whether with the secretariat or within the Member State is not entirely clear. In any event, the practice of consulting the National Commissions about programme preparation was initiated by the secretariat early in the life of the organization. Also, as additional Commissions were established, some of them would be asked to perform tasks pertaining to the execution of Unesco's programme within the country concerned. To facilitate consultation the executive secretaries of many of the Commissions have been brought to Paris for direct contact with Unesco's central staff.[68] During sessions of the General Conference, Commission officers on hand as members of their national delegations have met together from time to time.

Beginning in 1950, the Unesco secretariat undertook to promote meetings of regional groups of Commissions—the two earliest meetings being held at Havana (for Latin America) and at Bangkok (for South Asia and the South Pacific). Since then, similar regional conferences have been convened on the initiative of the 'host' Commission, as at Tokyo (1956), for the Asian Commissions; at Aix-en-Provence (1956), and at Dubrovnik, Yugoslavia (1958), for the European Commissions; at Fez, Morocco (1957), for the Arab States Commissions; and at San José, Costa Rica (1958), for the Latin American Commissions. Smaller groups of Commissions (*e.g.*, the Scandinavian) have met occasionally, some of them in bilateral meetings (*e.g.*, Franco-German) to consider specific joint projects.

[67] Walter H. C. Laves and Charles A. Thomson, *UNESCO: Purpose, Progress, Prospects*, *op. cit.*, p. 315–327. This volume presents an excellent critical analysis of the development of the National Commissions.

[68] See *Policy as Regards Consultations with National Commissions*, Unesco Doc. 49 EX/13, 11 Oct. 1957.

What has been the value of such meetings? At the least, they have permitted regionally related commissions to work out methods of consultation among themselves. By facilitating personal contacts and generating an exchange of ideas, the meetings may also contribute to 'morale-building,' especially for Commissions in educationally retarded countries or in newly independent states.

With respect to programme matters, the value of regional meetings appears to be more potential than actual. Until quite recently, many of the resolutions adopted by them dealt with such things as urging governments to pay their Unesco budgetary assessments (*e.g.*, in Latin America), or recommending the adoption of Arabic as a Unesco working language (at the Morocco meeting). Concrete proposals as to programme are only beginning to materialize. In a few instances regional projects have been adumbrated for submission to the Conference. The project on the 'Mutual Appreciation of Eastern and Western Cultural Values' has given rise to the appointment of special regional committees to further its conduct. By and large the two European meetings have tended to be more constructive than the others.

The reason why this should be so is not hard to see. It is chiefly in Western Europe—and North America—where the most active commissions are to be found. In other areas, with few exceptions (*e.g.*, Japan, Turkey, Chile), they still exist largely on paper—or to enhance the political prestige of their members. As Laves and Thomson have pointed out, the National Commission concept originated primarily in 'countries with experience in political democracy.'[69] And it is primarily in such countries that it has been nourished. But nearly all of the Commissions suffer from lack of trained staff and funds for meetings and publications.[70]

The General Conference, at its 1954 and 1956 sessions,

[69] *Op. cit.*, p. 317. Laves and Thomson distinguish three types of Commissions: (1) the 'democratic' types, which include a wide representation of civic and professional groups, as in the United States; (2) the 'aristocratic' type, made up chiefly of members of the intellectual *élite*, as in the United Kingdom, France, and the Scandinavian countries; and (3) the 'bureaucratic' type, consisting almost exclusively of government officials, as in countries 'in process of rapid evolution, or where democratic institutions have not become securely established,' illustrated by most of the Commissions in Latin America, the Middle East, and Asia.

[70] The United States Commission, with a substantial budget and a secretariat provided by the Department of State, is by far the best equipped.

authorized the Director-General to study the structure, methods of work, and needs of the National Commissions.[71] As a consequence of these studies, provision has been made in recent Unesco annual budgets to assist Commissions, on request, by sending members of the secretariat on missions to the countries concerned, by furnishing technical and financial help to Commissions organizing regional conferences, and by aiding similarly Commissions that are in process of development. In this connection, the Unesco secretariat issued in 1956 a printed *Guide for National Commissions* which explains the roles they may usefully fulfil and indicates types of assistance they may request from the organization.

Summary

The foregoing survey of the programme-making process (apart from TAB), as it has evolved in the major specialized agencies, reveals a decided range of patterns. These patterns have been developed not so much according to any objective criteria as pragmatically. In general, a trend towards increasing impacts of regionalism on programme formulation, in one form or another, is noticeable. But the degrees and kinds of regional decentralization vary markedly from WHO at one end of the scale to Unesco at the other. FAO appears to be moving slowly towards something roughly equivalent to the WHO pattern, though without consciously intending to do so. ILO stands in a middle position, while only one sector of ICAO's programme—air navigation—is designed in regional terms. Regionalism in Unesco's programme-making is still largely of an incipient and fragmentary character, though it is currently growing. Factors peculiar to the historical background, philosophy, and functional province of each organization have strongly influenced all these developments.[72]

It is not suprising that the degree of regional impact on the programme process should be roughly correlated with the size of permanent field establishments. The more extensive the regional machinery, the more likely it is to impinge upon

[71] The findings are contained in Unesco Docs. 9C/PRG/21, 12 Sept. 1956, and 10C/8, 4 Aug. 1958.

[72] Strictly speaking, UNICEF (as noted in Chap. 6) does not formulate territorial 'programmes' whether on a regional or a country basis, but appropriates funds to independent 'projects' for their duration.

programme decisions at headquarters. There also seems to be a significant relationship between the size of regional technical staffs and the extent to which they participate in programme supervision in the field—the reasons for which are obvious. On the other hand, the total volume of field activities, measured in budgetary terms, is less closely related to regionalization as regards both programme planning and project supervision. Among the larger specialized agencies, Unesco, for example, stands third, after WHO and FAO, in volume of field operations but is at the bottom of the scale with respect to regional deconcentration of programme formulation and execution.[73]

Regional Projects: Design and Operation

It is now proposed to explore briefly some of the problems that arise in designing and implementing regional projects. The provision of technical assistance on a regional basis is one of the significant differences between the programmes of the UN system and of the United States and other bilateral aid programmes. To date, the United States ICA has seemingly been unable to develop effective activities requiring 'the concurrent action of several countries.'[74]

International organizations appear to have certain advantages over individual donor governments in carrying out viable undertakings involving inter-governmental co-operation. Yet even for such organizations there are complex operational problems which are not always easily resolved. The complexity is compounded when two or more UN agencies combine their efforts in regional projects of long-range duration.

Functional classification of projects

Regional projects have been sponsored by UN agencies when one or both of two sets of conditions prevail. Either the nature of the project itself requires inter-country action, or the organiza-

[73] During 1958, Unesco's outlays for major projects ran to nearly $1 million, and for the Participation programme about $1.75 million. In addition, a considerable portion of the funds appropriated for normal programme activities was spent on regional meetings, seminars, fellowships, and the like. UNICEF has not been included since it is not a specialized agency. If it were it would of course top the list.

[74] See, in this connection, *Administrative Aspects of United States Foreign Assistance Programs*, a study prepared by the Brookings Institution for the Special U.S. Senate Committee to Study the Foreign Aid Program, 85th Cong., 1st Sess. (Washington: G.P.O., March 1957).

tion of a project regionally promises to be more effective or more economical than a series of separate country-based undertakings would be.[75] In the first category are projects relating to the control of human and plant diseases and pests which sweep across national boundaries, as, for instance, malaria, the desert locust, and foot-and-mouth disease. In the second category three main types of projects are to be found. One common type has to do with training—by means of regional seminars, centres, and institutes—of administrative, scientific, technical, educational, and social welfare personnel from groups of countries 'with similar background and environmental conditions.' About half of all the regional projects launched by UN organizations in recent years have been of this kind. Another important group is focused on the economic or social development of an area (*e.g.*, a river valley) comprising neighbouring countries. Among notable examples are the Central American Economic Integration project and the plan for developing the Lower Mekong basin, both of which will be described later. Finally, there have been a number of projects in which one or more UN agencies have served as the catalytic or co-ordinating instrument for survey and research work in special fields, such as water resources, rice improvement, forestry, nutrition, co-operatives, or organization for economic planning.

By subject-matter, for the year 1958, some eighty-three regional projects financed wholly or partially from EPTA funds were distributed as follows:[76]

	Per cent.
Development plans, basic surveys, and research (largely UN)	23·8
Agricultural production (chiefly FAO)	20·7
Health services (primarily WHO)	17·2
Community development (various agencies)	16·4
All other (public utilities, industrial production, education, social services, etc.)	21·9

Roughly half of these projects were continuations from the preceding year. Most of the larger training centres and institutes had been under way for several years, though this of course

[75] Most of the observations made here on the advantages, nature, and kinds of regional projects are based on the excellent report of TAB to TAC: *Regional and Inter-Regional Projects*, UN Doc. E/TAC/66, 24 June 1957.

[76] *Annual Report of the TAB for 1958, op. cit.*, p. 79.

was not true of seminars and symposia, which usually last only a week or so.

Origins and volume of projects

As already suggested, the initiative for regional projects comes from various sources. During 1957 and 1958 around a third of the EPTA requests were submitted by individual governments (usually after informal consultation with their neighbours indicating an active interest). In 1957, forty countries served as hosts for such projects, in which a total of 132 countries and territories participated. Among the participants were thirty-four governments which had no EPTA 'country' programmes. Little over half of the 1957–58 requests resulted from recommendations made by inter-governmental bodies, including UN regional commissions and regional committees and conferences of specialized agencies. In some cases such recommendations were subsequently approved by the governing organs of the agency concerned. The remainder emanated from inter-governmental organizations outside the UN system, such as the Caribbean and South Pacific Commissions and the Organization of American States.

In addition to conducting regional projects under the aegis of EPTA, the UN and its affiliated agencies, as noted above, finance such undertakings from their regular budgets or special financial resources. Indeed, the aggregate outlays for regional projects from these sources are now substantially larger than from EPTA. For 1958, the totals ran as follows:[77]

EPTA-financed projects	$3,061,000
Projects otherwise financed	5,091,000

Almost two-thirds of the second group were WHO projects, Unesco and BTAO accounting for another 30 per cent. It goes without saying that regular programme projects originate within the agency concerned, either directly from the substantive divisions of their central secretariats or by way of regional or technical conferences and committees. In the case of BTAO,

[77] *Ibid.*, Annex VI. Figures for FAO regular programme projects were not reported, presumably because its budget does not identify expenditures on regional projects—apart from total programme expenditures in technical fields. Nor were regional health projects financed by PAHO included. If these two groups of projects were added, the aggregate figures would be considerably higher.

however, recommendations by ECOSOC, based on proposals from its Social and Population Commissions, have led to special regional allocations from the UN's regular budget for technical programmes. Certain projects draw their financing partly from EPTA and partly from regular budget funds, or the source of financing may occasionally be shifted during the course of a project's execution.

Geographically, for 1958 (a typical year), regional projects financed from *all* sources were distributed, in terms of dollar expenditure, as follows:[78]

	Per cent.
Latin America	33·5
Asia and the Far East	22·8
Middle East	11·2
Europe	8·5
Africa	5·2
Inter-regional	18·8

Projects listed as 'inter-regional' are those that include trainees from, or provide advisory services to, countries located in more than one of the five principal regions, as, for example, the Desert Locust project which, while centred in the Arabian Peninsula, co-ordinates national campaigns against this menace to agriculture throughout its invasion area—from West Africa to India. The proportionately high percentage of project expenditure for Latin America is attributable to the large number of co-operative undertakings in which Central American Governments are engaged. As Africa grows in importance as a development area, its share in regional projects is likely to increase while that of Europe, except possibly in the health field, may decline.

In TAB and TAC circles the question of how much of EPTA's annual resources should be allocated for regional projects has received recurring attention over the years. To reproduce here in detail the arguments for and against a fixed maximum percentage would be unnecessarily tedious. Suffice

[78] These percentages were derived from the TAB Report cited above. In the EPTA programme (Category I projects), as approved for 1959, regional projects were distributed by number as follows:

Asia and the Far East	36	Africa	7
Latin America	26	Europe	4
Middle East	17	Inter-regional	9

it to say that since 1955 the amount initially set aside for planning such projects has been limited to 10 per cent. of the total assumed planning targets for field operations. In actuality, however, the percentage of expenditure has in most years been considerably higher as a result of changes in project costs during the year, or the approval of second priority projects by the Executive Chairman of TAB from his contingency fund.[79]

At this point it is in order to mention that, under the regulations governing utilization of the new UN Special Fund, it may contribute to the financing of projects with a regional as well as a single-country base. Among the forty-four projects approved by the Fund's Governing Council by the end of 1959 were a few of a regional character that had previously received aid from EPTA funds.[80] It is possible that comprehensive surveys of regional development potentialities may become a significant aspect of the Fund's future operations.

In general, the attitudes of governments towards participation in regional projects have grown increasingly favourable over the years. At first there was some reluctance to do this because of a decided preference for straight country undertakings. Even though the latter continue to receive priority consideration, most governments now recognize the value of training projects conducted on a regional basis.

Virtually all of the specialized agencies have urged that the percentage of EPTA resources available for regional projects be increased. WHO and FAO, for reasons already suggested, attached special importance to such undertakings, and their governing organs from time to time adopted strongly worded resolutions to this effect.[81] ILO and Unesco favoured a more modest expansion of regional project allocations. BTAO, on the other hand, considered that the existing 10 per cent. limit should be maintained. However, TAB in 1957 recommended to TAC that the planning maximum should be raised to 12 per cent. This has since been the rule.

[79] The procedures by which TAB allocates EPTA resources for field projects will be explained in the next chapter (see pp. 371–375).

[80] *United Nations Review* (Feb. 1960), pp. 13–17, 24–28. Examples of such projects are presented later in this chapter. The Special Fund staff is reportedly sceptical of the feasibility of regional projects unless one government is willing to assume primary responsibility for the conduct of the project.

[81] See, for excerpts from these resolutions, E/TAC/66, 24 June 1957.

Administrative and financial arrangements

Upon approval of a regional project by the appropriate authority —TAB, so far as EPTA is concerned—agreements are made by the executing agency (or agencies) with the host and other participating governments specifying what their respective financial and administrative obligations shall be. It has sometimes been difficult to get firm commitments from the non-host governments. These commitments differ depending on the type of project, but for training centres and institutes the host government ordinarily agrees to provide counterpart administrative and technical personnel, physical facilities, and transportation within the country. The ratio of these counterpart contributions to the costs of EPTA assistance has been more than two to one for the majority of projects, 'without counting, however, the long-range capital investment made for them by the Governments.'[82] For 'fellows' attending regional training centres and seminars, 'the practice in most cases has been for the participating governments to pay one-half of the travel costs of the trainees from their home towns to the centres, and for the host countries to provide living accommodations and other facilities.'[83] Each government sending trainees continues payment of 'home' salaries during their absence from duty. Other costs, including compensation and travel of UN agency experts serving as instructors, and in some instances teaching materials or demonstrational equipment that must be imported, are met by the agency responsible for executing the project. The contribution of the participating governments to local subsistence costs for outside experts varies from partial to complete assumption of such payments while they are on service in each country involved in the project (teams of experts sometimes move from country to country to conduct short courses). Some governments have complained of the comparatively high counterpart expenditures and other local costs that they have had to assume for certain kinds of projects.

In a number of cases, where the donor agency did not carry out adequate reconnaissance in advance, project agreements have been concluded with host governments ill-prepared to fulfil

[82] *Annual Report of the TAB for 1957*, ECOSOC, O.R.: 26th Sess., 1958, Suppl. No. 5, p. 88, and *for 1958, op. cit.*, p. 79.

[83] UN Doc. E/TAC/66, 24 June 1957, p. 13.

their obligatons, *e.g.*, for providing suitable premises, equipment, and local services. It is a well-known fact that certain governments have aspired to serve as hosts for regional in lieu of exclusively national training centres or institutes mainly for prestige reasons.[84] In view of the sensitivities of participating governments, satisfactory joint financing arrangements have sometimes been hard to work out. The question of when the donor agency (or agencies) should begin to phase out, or terminate, assistance to projects that have been in operation for several years has also caused difficulty. Unhappy experiences in this respect recently prompted the Unesco General Conference to propose that, in the future, Unesco should limit the duration of its obligations by advance agreement, renewable if necessary, at the expiry of which the main financial responsibility would be transferred to the Member States concerned or to other institutions. The 1957 FAO Conference drew up a set of conditions that should henceforth govern agreements for regional projects, covering physical facilities and administrative services from the host government and providing assurance that the participating governments would pay annually over a fixed period of years sufficient funds to assure continuing operation of the project on a sound financial basis. The time required for a group of countries to find and select qualified trainees, with proficiency in the language of instruction, had unduly delayed the opening of some of the training institutes. These are some of the practical problems in inter-country undertakings that have to be met.

Regional projects are conducted under a variety of patterns. Some of these show real ingenuity on the part of the UN planners, for they often have no precedents to guide them. It has been necessary to learn by experience, sometimes painfully. The problem of co-ordinating the contributions of related organizations, in undertakings of an inter-agency character, has given rise to misunderstanding, if not friction, during the initial stages of certain projects. This has been particularly true of the larger training institutes, where differing agency educational philosophies and approaches have to be harmonized.

[84] For an example of this, the writer can draw from his own experience as co-director during 1954–55 of the TAA-sponsored Institute of Public Administration at Cairo. In its original request for this project, the Government of Egypt had strongly urged that the Institute should be open to civil servants from other Arab States. Following a preliminary survey of available resources and facilities, however, the Government was persuaded not to press this point—wisely as it turned out.

The status of the project director on the UN side (usually appointed by the principal agency) *vis-à-vis* members of the team from other agencies, has not always been made clear, thereby engendering intra-staff tension. Multiple supervision and reporting have in some cases led to confusion. When the device of 'co-directors' has been used—one representing the host government and the other designated by the chief UN organization—their working relations have required delicate adjustment. Such are inherent complexities with which project administrators have had to deal, and in the great majority of cases they have managed sooner or later to handle them reasonably well.

In the next section brief sketches of six important inter-agency programmes of a regional character are presented with a view to illustrating concretely different types of operational arrangements. Three of these programmes have an 'area development' character, one is designed to control the spread of a crop menace, and the other two are essentially for training purposes. Altogether, they involve the co-operation of the UN regional commissions, BTAO, and most of the specialized agencies, while in two cases project contributions have been received from organizations and groups outside the UN system.

Inter-Agency Regional Programmes: Case Histories

Central American Economic Integration

This is regarded as perhaps the most ambitious—as well as most successful—regional programme yet to be sponsored by ECLA. The programme dates from a resolution submitted by the delegations of the five Central American Governments to the 1951 session of the Commission (Costa Rica, El Salvador, Guatemala, Honduras, and Nicaragua). Under this resolution, as adopted, a Central American Economic Co-operation Committee was set up and preliminary studies were prepared by the ECLA secretariat looking towards 'the gradual and progressive integration of the Central American economies.' Concurrently, the Organization of Central American States established a standing Committee, composed of national Ministers of Economy, which became the policy-governing organ for the programme.[85]

[85] For a detailed account of this organization and related regional developments in Central America, see Norman J. Padelford, 'Cooperation in the Central American Region,' *International Organization* (Winter 1957).

In conjunction with the ECLA Committee, this inter-governmental group, which meets annually, considers types of basic surveys and technical services needed for the promotion of intra-regional trade; the development of transport, new industries, and agricultural resources; industrial training; the improvement of public administration; and related matters. The ECLA Committee operates through a series of sub-committees on specific problems.

At the operational level, activities within the Central American programme are co-ordinated by ECLA—through its sub-office at Mexico City. A Working Group, consisting of the Director of this office, the TAB Representative, and local representatives of the participating specialized agencies, translates resolutions of the Committee of Ministers into concrete proposals to be financed largely from EPTA funds. After formal authorization by the Committee, these proposals are consolidated into an inter-governmental request and sent to the TAB secretariat in New York. With the Report of the Working Party before it, TAB then takes action on the request by making available funds earmarked for regional projects allocations to BTAO and such other agencies as participate from year to year in the programme. These allocations are used to engage experts, award fellowships, and provide small amounts of equipment for specific studies, field surveys, and training arrangements. Among the specialized agencies taking part in the programme have been FAO, Unesco, and ILO.[86]

Most of the back-stopping for the technical assistance projects is provided by the ECLA office in Mexico City. Its professional staff prepares job descriptions, briefs experts, and reviews their reports and by frequent trips around the region keeps in touch with project operations. It is also responsible for the presentation of formal reports on the programme to the governments through the secretariat of the Committee of Ministers of Economy. On the other hand, each participating agency appoints its own experts, awards fellowships, and prepares final recommendations for government action. The latter, however,

[86] By 1957, nearly $3 million had been spent on the programme, distributed as follows: ECLA (for special studies and staff travel)—$850,000; EPTA (for administrative expenses, experts and fellowships)—$1,080,000; host governments (for buildings and other local costs)—$950,000. (Information supplied by courtesy of the Director of the Mexico City ECLA office.)

must be cleared by the ECLA office before they are submitted to national authorities. During the first few years, according to reliable testimony in Mexico City, some friction developed among the agencies over their respective shares in the programme, one or two allegedly seeking to 'perpetuate themselves' in as many projects as possible; but this situation appears to have improved.

By general admission, the results of the Central American Integration programme to date have been impressive. Possibly the most spectacular achievement was the conclusion, in June 1958, of a multilateral treaty setting up a free trade area for the region. A year later the treaty had gone into effect for three of the Central American countries (Guatemala, El Salvador, and Nicaragua), and the other two were expected to ratify shortly.[87] This action was heralded at the time as a first step towards the eventual realization of a common market for all of Latin America. Intensive work on the equalization of external tariffs is now under way and studies are being made of the prospects for new industries that will be opened up by the establishment of free trade throughout the region. To this end a Central American Industrial Initiatives Commission was recently created. This body, including representatives of private enterprise as well as of governments, holds semi-annual meetings for the purpose of facilitating the exchange of information on industrial schemes and planning technical and economic studies to promote their 'rationalized' development.

Two permanent institutions have emerged from the Central American programme. One of these is the Advanced School of Public Administration for Central America, set up in 1954 at San José (Costa Rica) to train senior government officials and thus to develop nuclear staffs for national training centres for intermediate and junior personnel.[88] BTAO has supplied most of the School's teaching faculty while a majority of the students have held fellowships from BTAO or Unesco—the latter also co-operating in conducting special courses on educational administration. By the middle of 1959, over 350 persons had attended the School. In accordance with a multilateral agreement signed by the five participating countries, the School's academic and administrative policies are determined by a

[87] *The New York Times*, 6 July 1959.

[88] For a detailed description of ESAPAC, see the *United Nations Review* (December 1958), pp. 51–53.

General Board consisting of one representative appointed by each government. The Director of the School has thus far been provided by BTAO.

The other permanent institution is the Central American Research Institute for Industry, which was inaugurated in 1956 at Guatemala City and which is governed similarly to the Advanced School of Public Administration for Central America. The Institute is divided into three technical departments for research, industrial services, and scientific documentation, respectively. It maintains close contact with the ECLA economics staff, as well as the Inter-American Institute of Agricultural Sciences (an OAS agency) located at Turrialba (Costa Rica). ILO assists 'in matters relating to productivity through its Productivity and Vocational Training Mission now established as a special project within the Central American Integration Programme.'[89] It is noteworthy that this Research Institute should have been chosen as the first regional project to receive financial aid (amounting to $900,000) from the new UN Special Fund in 1959.

Notwithstanding the unstable political situation in certain Central American countries, ECLA has been able to stimulate a degree of inter-governmental economic co-operation that would have been regarded as visionary a decade ago. The high quality of its professional staff, and the imaginative leadership provided by its Central American Committee, have combined to mobilize such resources as the UN system could offer for assistance towards the goal of economic integration.

Mediterranean Development

In its annual survey for 1953, the ECE secretariat drew attention to the retarded development of southern Europe and, at its session in the spring of 1954, the Commission decided to set up a special study group on this question. The idea for this particular project originated with the ECE and FAO secretariats and was formally proposed by the Mediterranean Forestry Sub-Commission of FAO, set up under the sponsorship of its Regional Forestry Commissions for Europe and for the Near East to help formulate a forest policy for the entire Mediterranean basin. The special ECE survey group recommended that FAO be

[89] UN Doc. E/TAC/L.178, 20 Nov. 1958.

requested to undertake a fundamental study of Mediterranean forestry problems. By agreement between the FAO Director-General and the Executive Secretary of ECE, the FAO Forestry Division at Rome then took the initiative in working out plans for this study, in co-operation with the ECE/FAO Timber Committee. As plans progressed, it was decided to broaden the scope of the study to include problems of land and water use generally. In the spring of 1956, FAO obtained from TAB a small allocation of funds to finance the designing of the project, and for this purpose engaged a group of outside consultants, assisted by the staffs of its own Forestry, Agriculture, and Economic divisions and by specialists seconded from ECE. On the basis of an interim report submitted by this group to the 1957 FAO Conference, the latter appropriated in the regular budget a substantial sum to support a series of country land use surveys over the ensuing two-year period, with the aid of other United Nations agencies and national authorities. Studies prepared previously by FAO on the situation in Greece, Iraq, Israel, Lebanon, Syria, and Turkey were used as models for surveys in Morocco, Tunisia, Spain, and Yugoslavia. These ten country studies 'would enable FAO to determine how and at what pace the other countries of the region can be covered.'[90] It is expected that EPTA funds will be made available to aid in covering the costs of such studies.

Within FAO headquarters this project is controlled by an Internal Policy Committee chaired by the Director-General and including the Deputy Director-General and directors of the participating divisions. At the working level there is a Steering Committee, headed by the Director of the Forestry Division. Team visits are being organized for each of the countries 'to study their development programmes' and 'establish contact with existing administrative machinery and personnel' for preparing national plans. A comprehensive report on the first three years of the project was submitted to the FAO Conference in the fall of 1959. This report proposed an ambitious programme of regional development over the next twenty years—embracing both land and water resources for agriculture, grazing, and forestry purposes.[91]

[90] *FAO Programme of Work for 1958 and 1959* (Rome: 1958), p. 23.
[91] Press Release FAO/1026, 6 Oct. 1959.

Although this whole undertaking was then still at a fairly early stage, it was hoped by FAO that it would eventually lead to concerted policy action by the Mediterranean Governments. In the short range, it should stimulate more realistic requests for technical assistance in the fields of forest, soil, and water resource use. Whether, however, there will eventually emerge some kind of Mediterranean Development Authority, as certain FAO officials envisage in their more optimistic moments, is highly doubtful in view of the persistent political cleavages in the region.

Desert Locust Control

For several years FAO has been engaged in continuing efforts to control the incidence of plant pests, notably the locust. Locust control campaigns have been carried on in two principal areas—Central America, against 'migratory' locusts, and the Arabian Peninsula, against the ruinous depredations of the 'desert' locust. As noted earlier in this chapter, the scope of the Desert Locust Control project has gradually been extended to cover East and West Africa and South-west Asia as well, and is now designated as an 'inter-regional' undertaking.

The Desert Locust programme got its initial impetus from a special International Conference on the Control of the Desert Locust convened by FAO at the suggestion of the British Government as far back as 1951. This Conference, *inter alia*, recommended the establishment of a permanent FAO Technical Advisory Committee on Locust Control, which was approved by the FAO Conference the same year. The membership of this Committee consists of locust technicians appointed by the following seven governments: France, India, Iran, Pakistan, the United Arab Republic, the United Kingdom, and the United States, with an observer from the Arab League. Since most of these governments have tended to send second-rate specialists to Committee meetings, FAO has not relied very much on its technical proposals. There is also a second Committee for organizational and administrative questions in which participate all countries liable to be attacked by the desert locust, and in addition, countries taking part in the international control efforts (e.g., the United Kingdom and the United States). The two Committees now hold their annual sessions more or less conjointly since there is considerable overlap of membership.

For the formulation of a long-term control programme FAO utilizes a staff working group of its own. Recently, for project-planning, an inter-agency group was set up with WHO and Unesco. The two latter organizations collaborate in the co-ordination of scientific studies of the habits of the locust. Out in the field there is a small office at Jeddah (in Saudi Arabia) which serves as a co-ordinating centre for the Arabian international campaign. At Addis Ababa a modest Regional East African Secretariat stimulates co-operative efforts in Ethiopia, Sudan, and the Somalilands. One FAO specialist is stationed permanently in Yemen to prod that government and obtain information. Field teams consisting principally of Saudi Arabians, Middle Easterners, and Pakistanis aid in applying control techniques. In 1958 an effort was under way to establish a West African regional office for the programme but FAO was reportedly experiencing difficulty in inducing France and the independent African States to agree concerning the proposal. At Rome the entire programme is supervised by a senior officer of the Plant Production Branch of the secretariat.

The costs to date of the international campaign against the desert locust plague have been met largely by special contributions, both in cash and in kind, from interested Member governments.[92] In 1958, the Executive Chairman of TAB allocated $90,000 from contingency funds for the project. The total costs of the Arabian campaign for 1958 and 1959 were estimated at $1,200,000, covering field staff, vehicles, bait, insecticides, exhaust sprayers, and power dusters.[93] In the fall of 1959, the Special Fund approved a contribution of approximately $2·5 million over a six-year period to this programme with a view to accelerating more effective international action—the largest contribution by SF to any individual project up to that time.[94]

The long-run objective of the Desert Control project, from FAO's point of view, is to prevent the locust scourge as far as this is scientifically and administratively possible. Jointly with Unesco, FAO is now conducting a study of the breeding

[92] Although not a Member of FAO, the Soviet Union has contributed 500 pounds of insecticides for use in the anti-locust campaign—presumably in view of the danger of its territory being invaded by this pest.

[93] *Report of the Fifth Session of the FAO Desert Control Committee* (Rome: June 1958), p. 31.

[94] The nineteen countries participating in the programme had pledged $1·37 million towards its support over this period.

grounds of the locust at different points in the desert across the wide arc from Morocco to India. In conjunction with the British Government, the FAO secretariat initiated in 1958 a monthly *International Desert Information Service*, somewhat on the order of WHO's quarantine intelligence service. In FAO circles the hope is that an autonomous International Locust Control Service can ultimately be established for Arabia, North Africa, and the Pakistan-Indian region.[95]

Development of the Lower Mekong Basin

One of the major rivers of Asia, the Mekong rises in Tibet and flows for over 2,500 miles south-eastward into the South China Sea. Its lower basin embraces large parts of Laos, Thailand, Cambodia, and South Viet-Nam. The Mekong has been 'an idle and destructive giant, its tremendous power as yet unharnessed.'[96] In 1951, the ECAFE secretariat, through its Bureau of Flood Control and Water Resources Development, initiated exploratory studies of a possible multi-purpose development programme for the Lower Mekong, covering flood control, irrigation, navigation, and water power. For some years ECAFE stood virtually alone in advocating such an ambitious undertaking. The UN Bureau of Economic Affairs at New York then evinced little interest in the idea, while TAA raised various objections to it. Gradually, however, these attitudes shifted towards active support of the proposal.

In 1956, ECAFE authorized its secretariat to make a more detailed survey, with special attention to feasible technical projects that might be of benefit to two or more of the riparian countries. A year earlier, the U.S. International Co-operation Administration, at the request of the four governments concerned, had financed a reconnaissance survey by a team of six American experts. This survey group came to conclusions more or less parallel to those of ECAFE, but with greater emphasis on the kinds of basic data and trained personnel essential to an effective long-range development programme.[97]

During the 1957 session of ECAFE, representatives of the

[95] Such arrangements already exist for Africa south of the Sahara and for Central and South America.

[96] 'Harnessing the Mighty Mekong: A United Nations Survey,' *United Nations Review* (March 1958).

[97] UN Doc. ECAFE/L.119, 22 Feb. 1957.

four governments, after considering the two survey reports, recommended the establishment of a permanent inter-governmental Committee for Co-ordination of Investigations of the Lower Mekong Basin. This recommendation was adopted by Member governments and later that year such a committee came into being. Composed of senior engineering officials, the Committee was given full power to prepare plans for co-ordinated research and field surveys and to make requests for financial and technical assistance to EPTA and bilateral aid programmes. The Committee was serviced exclusively by the ECAFE secretariat until early in 1959, when an Executive Agent (paid from EPTA funds) was appointed as its chief of staff with an office in ECAFE headquarters at Bangkok.[98] The Executive Agent, aided by two technical specialists, handles decisions on a day-to-day basis, subject to general approval by the Executive Secretary of ECAFE.

The Committee early agreed that an inter-governmental request should be submitted to TAB for a general engineering survey of the river and its tributaries. A survey mission for this purpose, organized by TAA, was headed by the American, Lieutenant-General Wheeler, engineering consultant to the World Bank but better known in United Nations circles for his outstanding success in directing Suez Canal clearance operations. Reporting in February 1958, the Wheeler Mission proposed a five-year programme of studies and investigations at an estimated cost of $5·7 million for first priority undertakings, and of $3·5 million for secondary operations.[99] Endorsing these recommendations as a basis for moving ahead, the Co-ordinating Committee asked that the Special Fund, when established, give preferential consideration to the realization of the first priority proposals of the Wheeler Mission. In December 1959 a grant of nearly $1·4 million was made by the Fund for a survey of four Mekong tributaries, with the UN as the executing agency for this four-year undertaking.

Pending receipt of funds adequate to finance the entire list of first-priority projects, the Co-ordinating Committee decided to concentrate at the outset on the establishment of hydrological stations and aerial mapping. To help support the study phases

[98] C. Hart Schaaf, appointed to this post, was formerly Deputy Executive Secretary of ECAFE, then RTAR in Israel, and later RTAR in the Philippines.
[99] UN Doc. E/CN.11/475, 24 Feb. 1958.

of these operations, TAB allocated in 1958 the sum of $200,000. For much of the engineering work it is anticipated that contracts will be made with United States firms in view of the extensive experience of the United States with river basin development, most notably through the Tennessee Valley Authority. An International Advisory Board has been set up to aid the Coordinating Committee in examining the qualifications of engineering firms and, later, in selecting appropriate sites for dams, barrages, navigation facilities, and hydro-electric installations.

The far-reaching potentialities of the Mekong scheme have motivated several governments, western as well as eastern, to make special contributions towards its initial costs. By early 1960, contributions had been received, or pledged, totalling nearly $5 million, from Australia, Canada, France, India, Iran, Japan, New Zealand, the Soviet Union, the United Kingdom, and the United States. The United States contribution, amounting to over $2 million, is being used primarily for training local personnel in hydrology and gathering hydrological data; the Canadian offer of $1·3 million has been earmarked for an aerial survey; India is providing some meteorological equipment; while the Soviet Union has indicated that it would be prepared to extend technical aid, either directly or through ECAFE, for the designing of power stations.

Within the UN family, various specialized agencies had by 1958 staked out their respective claims for sharing in the technical assistance aspects of the Mekong programme: WHO as to health and sanitation; WMO in connection with weather services; ILO for manpower surveys; Unesco for the study of water volume and salt infusion; and FAO with respect to land use, forestry, and fisheries possibilities. At that time FAO had in the field a team of EPTA-financed experts surveying agricultural priorities, the initiative for this survey being taken jointly by the FAO regional office at Bangkok and the Rome secretariat. The IAEA subsequently suggested the use of radioactive isotopes for hydrologic measuring.

The Mekong programme is of course still at the planning stage. At best it is not likely to reach the operational phase for some years. But progress to date in organizing the plan has been distinctly encouraging. Among UN-sponsored economic development activities it represents the first case where 'sovereign' governments in Asia have agreed to set up a permanent organization for the planning of a co-operative development programme which, if it is carried through, will require outside capital financing on a large scale.[100] Furthermore, the Mekong programme, although originally conceived by ECAFE and now modestly supported by EPTA and SF contributions, has already attracted substantial financial aid directly from ten national governments.[101] These are unique features. The designation of a senior UN official as executive agent for the inter-governmental organizations is a further novel arrangement. In the Mekong project, technical assistance is being utilized for the planning of a capital investment programme—precisely the kind of situation for which the UN Special Fund was envisaged.

Provided the project does not crash on the shoals of political conflict, it could lead to the creation of a TVA-like development authority, or corporation, for the Mekong basin, perhaps with a UN representative as a non-voting member of its board of directors. The economic consequences of the comprehensive development of the region, for the 17,000,000 persons who inhabit it, might be proportionately as beneficial as those of TVA for the latter's clientele—in terms of expanded food supply and enlarged resources for transport, industry, and social services. To quote C. V. Narasimhan, formerly Executive Secretary of ECAFE and now Associate Managing Director of SF at New York: 'If things go forward in the Mekong project as smoothly as they have gone till now, a real economic revolution will have begun in this part of South-east Asia.'[102]

The Andean Indian Programme

We now turn to an undertaking whose social objective is broadly similar to that of the Mekong River project but the *milieu* and processes of which are markedly different. This is the ILO-inspired programme for improving the conditions of life for some 10,000,000 Indians (descendants of the Incas) who

[100] In 1958 a meeting of the Co-ordinating Committee was actually held at Bangkok during a time when Thailand and Cambodia had broken off diplomatic relations over a border dispute. The Cambodian delegate was transported to Bangkok in a plane provided by the U.S. Operations Mission since there was at the time no direct commercial air communication with Phom-Penh.

[101] The riparian governments had pledged nearly $1 million from local funds. See 'Putting the Mighty Mekong to Work,' *United Nations Review* (March 1960).

[102] *United Nations Review* (March 1958).

inhabit the Altiplano (high Andean plateau) in Bolivia, Ecuador, and Peru, and who constitute from 50 to 80 per cent. of the population of these three South American countries. The origins of this project may be traced back to 1946, when ILO set up its Expert Committee on Indigenous Labour.[103] Three years later the ILO Conference of American States, at its fourth session, requested the ILO Governing Body to 'recommend that governments take steps to adopt legislation which would fit the real needs and the special problems of [their] indigenous populations.'[104] This action was soon followed by a request from the UN General Assembly to ECOSOC to study the situation in conjunction with interested specialized agencies. A year later the Council asked the Secretary-General to render expert assistance, with the collaboration of such agencies, to countries requesting it.[105] When the ILO Expert Committee met early in 1951, various resolutions pointing specifically towards the Andean region were adopted, one of them proposing the creation of an inter-agency working party to survey what might be done to raise living standards for the poverty-stricken aborigines of the Andean plateau. At the request of the three governments concerned, the Director-General of ILO asked TAB to allocate from EPTA funds a sum sufficient to cover the expenses of a team of experts for a field survey. Such an allocation was made in February 1952 and later that year an inter-agency mission left for South America.

Besides ILO, the following organizations were represented on the mission: UN, FAO, WHO, Unesco, and the OAS. After spending four months in the field, the mission submitted recommendations for an 'action programme' regional in scope and consisting of a limited number of 'localized' projects. The programme, which was to be of 'limited duration and self-liquidating' aimed at encouraging participation of the community itself. During 1953–54, the Governments of Bolivia, Ecuador, and Peru signed agreements with the UN, ILO, FAO, WHO, and Unesco committing the signatory governments and international agencies to collaboration in a technical assistance

[103] For a vividly written, balanced analysis of the development of this programme to 1956, see Agnese Nelms Lockwood, 'Indians of the Andes,' *International Conciliation*, No. 508 (May 1956). A more recent (official) account is contained in a 104-page illustrated booklet entitled *The Andean Programme* and issued by the ILO (Geneva: 1958).

[104] Lockwood, *op. cit.*, p. 361.

[105] ECOSOC Resolution 318 (XI), 24 July 1950.

programme along the lines advocated by the inter-agency mission. TAB requested ILO to assume primary responsibility for administering the programme; and with this in view the Deputy Director-General of ILO was designated to handle supervision of it at Geneva. ILO then proceeded to conclude agreements with the other agencies governing the status of their experts and providing that the latter might report to their own agency headquarters on purely technical matters but would be operationally responsible to the chief of the field project to which they were attached.

In 1954, two other steps were taken relating to the control and execution of the programme. First, TAB set up an Advisory Committee from its own membership to guide it in determining allocations of funds and in co-ordinating the programme. Second, a Director of the programme at the regional level was appointed by ILO, in consultation with the other agencies, and provided with a deputy and secretarial staff at Lima. To the regional Director was delegated responsibility for (1) negotiating project arrangements with the three governments, (2) drawing up provisional annual budgets for the programme, and (3) exercising general supervision over field projects. The Director, according to information conveyed to the writer during a visit to the Lima office in 1957, spends over half his time in the field—travelling over rugged, mountainous country by plane, train, truck, and jeep.

Sub-offices for the programme have been set up at La Paz and other project centres. Twice a year, at La Paz, a meeting is held, consisting of the regional Director, the project chiefs, and visiting personnel from the headquarters of the participating agencies, to review the progress of the programme as a whole. In 1957, ILO proposed that a regional inter-agency committee be established to co-operate with the regional Director in the preparation of working plans and yearly budget estimates, and in the evaluation of periodic reports from project chiefs and individual experts (all of whom are required to provide the regional director with copies of reports sent to headquarters).[106] This proposal was intended not only to facilitate co-ordination of action in the field but to relieve agency headquarters of having

[106] The regional committee was to be composed of the regional Director (as chairman) and representatives of the UN, WHO, FAO, and Unesco, perhaps with the country RTARs and the Director of the ILO Lima office as 'associate' members.

to make decisions on a lot of detailed matters. By late 1958 this idea had been accepted 'in principle' by the other agencies, but with some reservations on the part of certain organizations.

To date, the Andean programme, in terms of focus, content, and financing, has gone through one phase and is now entering a second. During the first phase the programme consisted of a limited number of community centres financed in part by funds allocated by TAB on a regional basis, and in part by contributions from the participating governments. Almost from the outset the Andean experiment so caught the imagination of worker (and to some extent employer) groups in advanced Western countries that substantial gifts of equipment and tools for its workshops were made from these sources.[107] Each project centre typically includes 'a carpentry shop, a metal work and mechanic shop, a recreation room for the community, a small dispensary and consulting room, and facilities for the Mission personnel.'[108] The projects are in the nature of small demonstration and pilot undertakings, designed to provide training in handicrafts and in the use of simple agricultural techniques, with some attention to better sanitation, housing, and elementary schooling for both children and adults. In certain areas assistance has been given in the construction of new villages (of sun-baked mud brick); in others, UN experts have carried on extension work in neighbouring villages. A number of graduates of the Unesco-sponsored Fundamental Educational Centre for Latin America, located at Patzcuaro, Mexico (see below), have been used as mission instructors.

Since the Andean Indians, 80 per cent. of whom are illiterate, use Indian dialects and do not speak Spanish, communication between them and the UN experts has had to be carried on mainly through interpreters supplied locally. At first many of the Indians exhibited considerable suspicion, even resistance, concerning the advent of 'foreigners' in their midst. When, for example, a health team visited one area to spray DDT against parasites, 'some of the Indians actually believed that the destruction of parasites by DDT would mean that their dogs and rabbits

[107] Up to 1958, donations valued at $200,000 had been received from labour and employer groups in the United States, Belgium, West Germany, Sweden, Denmark, and Norway. The Belgian Government had made a gift of antibiotics. ILO Doc. G.B. 138/T.A./D.1/2, Feb.-March 1958.

[108] Lockwood, *op. cit.*, p. 367.

would also be killed. To protect them, one woman hid hers so well in a sack that they suffocated.'[109] Bit by bit, however, an atmosphere of confidence and understanding was built up and most of the beneficiary groups are now said to be quite responsive.

In Bolivia, an experiment in relocation was launched in 1956. Some 250 carefully selected young Indians were brought down from the highlands to the fertile plains east of the Andes and resettled in the town of Cotoca, where their housing, health, and diet have been closely supervised. Only a few have chosen to return to their former homes, most of them having been able to adapt themselves fairly quickly to a new form of life. Yet it would be unrealistic to assume that migration on a large scale is feasible—if only because its costs would be prohibitive. But selective resettlement, if successful, might help to 'alleviate the overpopulation that is draining the often barren soil of the Altiplano . . . open the door for the younger and more ambitious campesinos to change their way of life . . . and provide colonists for the fertile, yet underpopulated areas' of the region.[110]

By 1957, ILO and the other participating agencies came to the conclusion that responsibility for running the project centres should gradually be transferred to the national administrations of the countries concerned, with the UN Andean Mission functioning primarily in an advisory capacity. During this second phase of the programme UN technical assistance is to become a part of each over-all country programme, as determined by the government with guidance from the RTAR. It was realized that differences in national administrative structures and processes would make the development of any genuinely regional organization extremely difficult. By this time, moreover, the three governments were beginning to display serious interest in carrying on the programme themselves, whereas their earlier inclination had been to 'let the international agencies do it.' The first five years of the programme had demonstrated, on a small scale, what might be done on a larger scale over the long pull. It was therefore proposed that programme emphasis should be shifted towards (1) integration with local and national institutions and increasing participation of each community in

[109] 'The People of the Andes,' UN *Technical Assistance Newsletter* (March 1959).
[110] *Ibid.*

its own improvement, and (2) the training of national administrative and technical personnel, local community leaders, and auxiliary workers.[111] Dire shortages of technicians, doctors, public health nurses, midwives, social workers, and rural teachers dictated the decision to concentrate on long-term training.

Under the most favourable conditions, it is probable that substantial aid from the UN system will be necessary for several years to come. There is now a strong urge to enlarge the scope of the programme, and Colombia has recently requested that its activities be extended to that country also. With this prospect in view, the ILO, in 1958, discussed with the four governments the desirability of applying jointly to the Special Fund for an annual appropriation of about $1 million over a six-year period, to be divided among them according to agreed proportions. An additional sum of $100,000 would be asked for the expenses of the regional office of the programme, which would be reorganized so as to cope with the expanded operations. The Special Fund, however, decided to confine its initial aid (totalling more than $1 million over a two- to three-year period) to the resettlement and agricultural and vocational teacher training phases of the programme. This contribution, moreover, is to be divided among the governments of Bolivia, Ecuador, and Peru.

It is too soon to appraise the over-all impact of the demonstrational phase of the Andean programme. On the one hand, it has been criticized in certain quarters for having attempted to apply techniques beyond the absorptive capacity of ignorant Indians. On the other hand, there is evidence that their receptivity has steadily increased year by year. So far the programme has been confined to laboratory experiments—a kind of miniature community development in action. The extent to which the Andean Indian can be 'integrated' into the life of the twentieth century will ultimately depend on how adequately and intelligently the national governments of this region carry forward what the UN system has initiated. The real test will be this: can they—will they—convert a unique 'pioneering venture' into sustained, co-ordinated national policy?

From the standpoint of administration, the Andean programme

[111] For a detailed explanation of the proposed new orientation of the programme, see the *Report to the Advisory Committee on the Andean Programme*, ILO Doc. AIP/AC/4, June 1958.

to date has encountered some of the same problems noted in connection with other inter-agency arrangements. Differences of agency approach—the ILO approach predominating—have at times produced disagreement within project teams. For the expert, as Mrs. Lockwood has discerningly observed, 'there is inevitably some sense of divided loyalty when, as in a program like the Andean Indian, he is recommended and paid by his agency, and yet is responsible to [a project chief], who in turn is responsible to ILO.'[112] Inter-agency co-ordination at the field level still leaves something to be desired, though this has noticeably improved in recent years. Looking ahead, the meshing of the programme's expanding regional machinery with three (or perhaps four) national administrative systems will call for wisdom and tolerance on the part of the operators on both sides.

Fundamental Education Centres

Closely related to the Andean Indian programme in social purpose is the work of Unesco in the field of fundamental education. Fundamental education, as the concept has evolved in Unesco, means something more than combating illiteracy for its own sake: implicit in the idea 'is its impact on poverty and disease as well as on ignorance . . . [it seeks to promote] greater individual and community capacity to develop roads and bridges, schools and clinics, cooperative markets and community centers.'[113] In order to further this multi-purpose goal, the United Nations, as indicated at the beginning of this chapter, has, particularly since the inauguration of EPTA, attempted to promote co-ordinated action by cognate agencies in what is now called 'community development.' Unesco's role within this functional complex is education, but such agencies as ILO, FAO, WHO, and the UN Bureau of Social Affairs also have significant contributions to make.

Unesco's field activities in fundamental education began as early as 1947, when a mission was sent to Haiti to explore ways in which the poverty-stricken people of the Marbial valley might be helped to raise their standards of living. From the vicissitudes of this mission important lessons were learned—not least

[112] *Op. cit.*, p. 427.
[113] Laves and Thomson, *op. cit.*, p. 148.

that the problems of such an area must be attacked on several fronts simultaneously for lasting impact to result. This experience set the pattern for Unesco's later efforts in fundamental education. These efforts, as Laves and Thomson have classified them, include (1) studies designed to identify the best methods and media, (2) assistance to governments in how to apply them, and (3) practical aid in the training of supervisors and field workers and in the preparation of suitable teaching materials.[114]

In connection with this third task, Unesco decided in 1951 to establish a world-wide network of six training and production centres organized regionally—one in Latin America, Africa, the Middle East, and India, and two in the Far East. This scheme originated with the then Director-General, Dr. Jaime Torres-Bodet, who had previously conducted a spectacularly successful campaign against illiteracy in his own country (Mexico) during his tenure as Minister of Education. The plan was to be developed over a twelve-year period. However, the heavy costs of carrying out such an ambitious programme proved too much for Unesco's regular budget; and when an appeal for funds from private sources (including the Ford Foundation) failed to materialize, the plan was reduced in scope, only two regional centres having come into being—one in Mexico for Latin America and the other in Egypt (now the U.A.R.) for the Arab States. A further reason for abandoning the idea of establishing centres in other regions of the world was the fear that their diversity of languages and cultures would complicate the problem of instruction.

The Latin American Centre (known by its Spanish initials as CREFAL) is located at Patzcuaro, a village overnight by train from Mexico City, where former President Cardenas of Mexico made available his imposing summer residence, along with adjacent buildings and grounds. By agreement, the Government of Mexico provided for new construction and additional land on which dormitories, workshops, and recreational facilities have been built; the Government also takes care of maintenance and repairs. For the Arab States Centre (ASFEC), located at

[114] *Ibid.*, pp. 149–57. Most of the comments on Unesco's regional Fundamental Education Centres presented below are based on the account given in the Laves-Thomson volume, along with observations made by the writer personally during visits to the Centres in 1955, 1957, and 1958.

Sirs-el-Layyan, a sizable dust-covered town in the Nile Delta an hour's ride by car from Cairo, the Government of Egypt agreed to provide buildings, office furniture, maintenance, some local transport, and local service staff.

Unesco negotiated understandings with TAA, ILO, FAO, and WHO by which they were to supply experts in their respective subject-matter fields for the instructional staffs of the two centres, as well as limited amounts of workshop equipment in certain cases. As regards CREFAL, the Organization of American States offered to produce reading materials adapted to its special needs. Each centre has a director and a deputy director, appointed by Unesco, and an international staff of some twenty to thirty persons, about half of whom are also Unesco employees. Agency experts at ASFEC are 'integrated' into the Centre community by living in the same dormitory.[115] At CREFAL they occupy a cluster of bungalows. The composition of the teaching staff at ASFEC has become increasingly 'regionalized' in recent years—perhaps prematurely so. Furthermore, its successive directors have all been of Egyptian nationality, one of whom, notoriously unsuited for such a post, was eventually forced to resign under unpleasant circumstances. The Director of CREFAL (down to 1959) had been a Mexican from the outset. The policy of using host country nationals as directors, reportedly resulting from political pressure, is now recognized as having been unfortunate.

For each Centre an inter-agency Advisory Committee has been established. This committee, which meets annually, is chaired by a Unesco representative (sent from Paris) and includes among its members the host country RTAR. On the CREFAL committee there is also a representative of OAS. These committees deal with budgets, staffing, and programme co-ordination, and make recommendations to the participating agencies. In the case of ASFEC, an Arab States Advisory Committee, consisting of the cultural attachés of the participating governments stationed at Cairo, reviews annually the progress and needs of the programme and submits requests to the agencies.

Originally, Unesco's share of the costs of the two Centres was financed entirely from its regular budget (including that of its

[115] At ASFEC, the WHO and ILO experts at first wanted exclusive use of their 'official' cars, but the Director insisted that they go into a common car pool along with those provided by Unesco. Neither TAA nor FAO supplied cars for its experts.

Exchange of Persons service for student fellowships). After EPTA got into full swing, however, a substantial (though still minor) part of these costs, relating to the compensation and international travel of experts, was shifted to the latter programme. For the biennium 1957–58, the total costs of the two Centres amounted to a little more than $1·5 million, of which 54 per cent. came from Unesco's regular budget; 30 per cent. from EPTA (including assistance provided by TAA and the other specialized agencies); 12 per cent. from the participating governments; and 4 per cent. from OAS (for CREFAL only).[116] It will be noted that Unesco still bears the major financing burden. In 1953, it tried to induce the governments to absorb more of the costs, especially for fellowships, but the effort failed. Later an approach was made to the United Nations in the hope that it might be willing to defray most of the administrative costs, if not to assume complete control, in connection with its community development programme. The UN Bureau of Social Affairs took the position that, while such a solution would be desirable in many ways, it would be difficult to persuade the Advisory Committee on Administrative and Budgetary Questions of the General Assembly to approve such a large addition to the budget of the Department of Economic and Social Affairs. As a *modus operandi*, at least until 1962, it was decided that the Centres should remain under Unesco supervision—which decision prompted one senior official at Paris to remark ruefully to the writer that 'Unesco was left holding the bag!'

The programmes of the two Centres, while differing in minor particulars, involve four main types of activities: (1) teacher training, (2) technical and experimental studies, (3) practical field work in nearby villages, and (4) the production of special materials for teaching illiterates, such as text-books, illustrated pamphlets, wall posters, filmstrips, and audio-visual aids. Each government is invited to nominate fixed quotas of trainees annually, the majority of whom have in fact been proposed by ministries of education. One of the senior Unesco-appointed members of the Centre staff makes a recruiting trip to the participating countries once a year. In the Arab States, a National Committee of Selection interviews each candidate

[116] These percentages are based on figures given in Unesco's *Proposed Programme and Budget for 1959–1960*, *op. cit.*, p. 32.

before deciding on nominations. At ASFEC a staff selection board discusses all proposed candidates before making the final selection. Their average age on admission has been around thirty. The nominating governments continue the salaries of trainees and pay their transportation to and from the International Centre. During his training course, each student receives from Unesco a monthly stipend sufficient to cover food, laundry, and incidentals.

Regular training programmes, lasting from about a year to eighteen months, are offered at two levels—an advanced course for university graduates and a more general course for trainees with only secondary school education. There are also a number of short courses, ordinarily of three months' duration, for specialists in agricultural extension work, public health nurses, rural social workers, and primary school teachers, and in the techniques of producing audio-visual materials. The regular courses embrace such subjects as rural education, community development, co-operatives and rural industries, rural housing, home economics, and literacy teaching. At ASFEC a pictorial projective test is now being given to each regular trainee on admission in order to discover his basic attitudes towards rural people. On the basis of these tests it is hoped to validate techniques which can be used in the selection of future trainees.

About midway in the training period teams of students do several months of 'laboratory' work in the surrounding villages, where they try to apply the methods and materials developed at the Centre. To make this field experience as life-like as possible, arrangements have been made for each student to live from time to time with a village household. On their return to the Centre (usually once a week) the student teams exchange views and report on their experience. The research division at ASFEC during 1958 conducted a systematic study of the attitudes of the villagers towards their community and its problems and their own role in community life, with a view to orienting the trainees as realistically as possible to community values and needs. In 1958, a sociologist from the United States was engaged by Unesco to devise simple measurement methods that might be used by CREFAL trainees in assessing the results of their field activities. One member of the inter-agency advisory committee for ASFEC observed to the writer that conditions in the 'practice' villages probably were no longer typical, due to the impact of ASFEC trainee teams over a period of years, and he thought that a new group of villages ought to be selected for field work.

By mid-1958, some 400 trainees from nineteen Latin American countries (together with a few even from the United States) had been graduated from CREFAL, and nearly 300 from ten Arab countries from ASFEC.[117] An appraisal of the two Centres made by an inter-agency team set up by ACC in 1955–56 revealed that most of the earlier graduates were then employed in positions involving use of their training.[118] One group held supervisory posts in fundamental education sections of ministries of education (or of Indian affairs in South America); others were rural school teachers or school inspectors; and some had positions in rural welfare units of ministries of health or of social affairs. One recent criticism is that the training programmes of the Centres have not been co-ordinated sufficiently closely with government needs. In some quarters it is believed that too much attention has been given to the development of 'grass roots' workers and not enough to the preparation of administrators and supervisors. On the other hand, it is argued that the greatest multiplier effect will come from training the 'trainers' of others (*e.g.*, rural school teachers). One of the weaknesses of the programme, in the view of the United Nations appraisal group, was that they had failed to develop any considerable number of specialists outside the field of education itself, thus not contributing to the broader goal of 'community development.' Since 1956, it is only fair to say, this aspect of the programme has received increasing emphasis.

Both Centres suffered from a number of administrative headaches during their earlier years. At CREFAL, in particular, the international staff was torn by factionalism, with the Mexicans 'cliqued' against the others, and the North Americans against the South Americans. Four members of the CREFAL Unesco staff were charged with having been members of Communist organizations, one of them resigning under pressure and the others being dismissed by Unesco. However, staff morale appears to have improved. There were also complications

[117] The students from the United States, at CREFAL, have been Puerto Ricans and American Indian teachers.

[118] The report of this appraisal may be found in Unesco Doc. 44 EX/7, 11 June 1956.

arising from WHO's insistence that its staff appointees should remain responsible to it both technically and administratively, and FAO also caused some trouble in this respect. But the situation was eventually cleared up and it is now understood that all agency appointees are responsible to the Centre director on both counts, even though they still report to their own agency on technical matters. In case of disagreement, the director has the final word. At ASFEC, staff members normally route their technical reports to the director, who retains one copy and sends the other on to headquarters with such comments as he cares to make; by exception, however, ILO appointees are instructed by Geneva to report directly to ILO headquarters, with a copy to the Centre director. It has taken time to weld an international multi-agency staff into a cohesive functioning group.

Communication between the Centres and Unesco headquarters has not always worked smoothly. Once a year a headquarters officer comes to each Centre for the meeting of the inter-agency advisory committee and there are brief, sporadic visits from other senior officials. The director reports semi-annually to the Unesco Department of Education on substantive matters and the administrative officer of each Centre directly to the appropriate headquarters unit on administrative and financial business. The financing of the Centres from various sources necessitates a complicated set of accounts, including monthly reports on EPTA expenditures to each of the participating agencies. At times Paris has failed to keep the Centres informed on changes of policy affecting their relations with governments. To cite but one instance of this: while on a recruiting tour, a senior official of CREFAL made commitments to various governments concerning the admission of trainees to a short course on audio-visual aids which had been planned. Paris then advised him that this course was to be transferred to the Participation programme and would be handled directly by the central secretariat. The CREFAL official wrote a strong letter in protest. Even so, headquarters instructed governments to send their nominations (for fellowships) to Paris instead of to CREFAL. In the confusion, however, most of them dispatched their nominations to CREFAL. Eventually the commitments were honoured but not without considerable misunderstanding all around.

The Centre Directors visit Paris only occasionally. The Deputy Director of CREFAL, during a five-year tour of duty as *de facto* internal manager of that Centre, was never called to Paris. After two or three years he began to feel isolated and asked to be transferred back to headquarters (where he had previously been stationed). Documents alone, he remarked to the writer, did not tell what was really happening in the Department of Education, what with its frequent changes of personnel and procedures.

Now that both of the Centres have survived their 'growing pains,' the question of their future status is under serious consideration by Unesco and the ACC. Unesco has intimated that it might terminate its financial and managerial support by the end of 1962, when the Centres will have been in operation for a full decade. In the UN and ACC *milieu* there is a growing feeling that ASFEC might well be handed over to the host government and run as a national institution, perhaps with provision for continuing certain services to other Arab countries. CREFAL, on the other hand, is not regarded as being ready yet for transfer to the Mexican Government. During 1959, a series of meetings, sponsored by the ACC Working Group on Community Development, were to discuss the long-range future of both Centres. Meanwhile, the term 'fundamental education' had fallen into disfavour. Partly because of pressure from the UN Bureau of Social Affairs and the Social Commission of ECOSOC, and partly because sensitive governments in the under-developed countries do not relish being singled out for a special kind of education, the 1958 Unesco General Conference adopted a resolution instructing the Director-General 'to take immediate steps to secure that a proper terminology which can be applied all over the world to be used by Unesco for all kinds of education of adults and young persons, and to discontinue as rapidly as possible the use of the term "fundamental education" in all official documents of Unesco.'[119] What the new all-inclusive label will be had not been revealed when this chapter was written.

[119] Unesco Doc. 10 C/Resolutions, 5 Jan. 1959.

9

PROGRAMMES AND PROJECTS AT THE COUNTRY LEVEL

Since its inauguration a decade ago, the Expanded Programme of Technical Assistance has exerted a marked influence on the procedures of field programming throughout the UN system. The primary objective of EPTA was—and still is—to help countries 'strengthen their national economies' by providing advisory, training, and operational services of specified kinds. It is the individual *country* that forms the basic component of its operations and the target towards which it is ultimately directed. This observation holds even for *regional* projects inasmuch as they are necessarily based on *inter*-governmental co-operation rather than on *supra*-national arrangements.

The chief purpose of the present chapter is to analyse the process by which country programmes are planned under the rules formulated by the Technical Assistance Board and approved by the Technical Assistance Committee on behalf of ECOSOC.[1] As suggested earlier in this study, this is a complex process by reason of the multi-agency structure of EPTA on the one hand and its special financing pattern on the other. The new Programme was launched on a largely uncharted sea, and its managers, in the light of operating experience, had to learn how to steer their course by improvisation.

Evolution of 'Expanded Programme' Guide-lines

The birth of EPTA dates from action taken by ECOSOC in August 1949, only a few months after the dramatic pronouncement of President Harry S. Truman's 'bold new program for making the benefits of our scientific advances and industrial progress available for the improvement and growth of underdeveloped areas.' Mr. Truman had emphasized that his 'Point

[1] The process by which UNICEF and the Special Fund arrive at decisions on project requests from individual governments, more or less independently of EPTA, is also briefly described in this chapter (see pp. 402–406, 411–417).

Four' should be carried forward 'as a co-operative enterprise in which all nations work together through the United Nations and its specialized agencies *wherever possible*' (italics added). Under the impetus of Point Four, ECOSOC, as early as March 1949, had requested the Secretary-General, through ACC, to prepare a comprehensive plan for a programme of technical assistance which would expand and supplement activities already being carried on by the UN and certain of the specialized agencies. To this end the Secretary-General organized a working group of experts representing the organizations concerned. The conclusions of this group were embodied in a bulky document which came to be known in Secretariat circles as the 'Grey Book' and which provided the basis for the Council's discussions the following summer.[2]

The experts had been able to arrive at a consensus only after prolonged and spirited argument. The main point at issue was where the locus of administration and financial control of the new programme should be lodged. The UN's position was that it should have centralized jurisdiction over programme policy and administration, with the understanding that projects would be farmed out to the various agencies for execution. This idea met with stiff resistance from the functional agencies, each of which wanted to have complete control over a fixed share of programme funds. The result was a compromise providing for the establishment of TAB as a 'confederative' organ with 'co-ordinative' functions, but with little or no operational authority.

ECOSOC accepted substantially without change the proposals of the experts. An omnibus resolution was adopted which set forth the guiding principles and organizational machinery for the new programme.[3] This resolution remains to this day its legislative 'Bible' although, as we shall see later, it has been amended in various particulars over the years. As TAB was originally constituted, the Secretary-General served as its *ex-officio* chairman, but since he was too busy to give personal attention to TAB the then Assistant Secretary-General for Economic Affairs usually deputized for his chief as *de facto* presiding officer. In effect, what this arrangement meant was

[2] See *Technical Assistance for Economic Development*, UN Doc. E/1327/Add. 1, May 1949.
[3] ECOSOC Resolution 222 (IX), 15 Aug. 1949.

that the United Nations would have dual representation on the Board inasmuch as the Director-General of TAA also participated in its meetings. Other than on procedural matters, TAB's actions were to be taken by 'general agreement.' In case a consensus could not be reached the issue might be referred to TAC for decision. But this almost never happened and the unanimity rule prevailed. According to the Council's enabling resolution, TAC was to examine each year's programme as proposed by TAB and submit to the full Council such recommendations as it deemed appropriate; receive reports on the progress of the programme; and review the 'working relationships between the participating organizations and the effectiveness of the methods of co-ordination' as necessary. In theory, TAB itself was a subsidiary body of ACC but the latter Committee, meeting only twice a year and having many other important matters to consider, tended during the first few years to allow TAB to go its own way.

The Secretary-General, after consultation with the other agencies, was authorized to designate an Executive Secretary for TAB, with power to convene its meetings, prepare its agenda and documentation, make studies, and direct the Board's central secretariat. This officer was also given responsibility for preparing the record of the Board's decisions and its annual report.

Under ECOSOC's original legislation, the financial contributions made by governments for EPTA were to be paid into a Special Account under the UN's fiscal administration. For the first fiscal year 85 per cent. of the total contributions received was to be transferred automatically to the participating organizations, in accordance with the following percentages: FAO, 29; UN, 23; WHO, 22; Unesco, 14, ILO, 11; and ICAO, 1. The remaining 15 per cent. and also all of any amount received in excess of $20,000,000, could be allotted by TAB itself, taking into account 'all relevant factors.' Although the basic percentage formula for allocation of funds to agencies continued to be applied until 1956, the proportion of funds automatically allocated was altered. Thus, for 1952 and 1953, this was reduced to 50 per cent. and then raised for 1954 and 1955 to 75 per cent. These variations reflected the pulling and hauling of advocates of centralization and its opponents.

The Programme Process

The early development of EPTA under the foregoing regulations revealed certain inherent shortcomings. As a central co-ordinating instrument TAB, lacking an independent executive head and as a body of officials responsible for the administration of technical assistance in their respective agencies, proved incapable of adjusting project requests to over-all economic development needs in the claimant countries. By automatically allotting funds to the administering agencies, one assumption had been that 'balanced development would have to be injected into the program of each country from the outside . . . and that agencies experienced with the problems of development would be able more readily to propose practical programs and establish priorities.'[4] But, as things worked out, agency vested interests and high-pressure salesmanship militated against the formulation of 'balanced' country programmes.

With the object of strengthening EPTA's machinery for programme co-ordination, the practice of appointing country representatives—prototype of the later RTAR—was begun as early as 1951. A year later TAB was provided with a full-time Executive Chairman. This officer, appointed by the Secretary-General, was empowered to make recommendations to TAB as to programme proposals and projects; to exercise continuing supervision over the implementation of the programme as a whole; and to review the adequacy of the co-ordination of activities financed from the Special EPTA Account.[5] He was also to convene and preside over meetings of the Board. It was further provided that decisions by TAB on programme matters should normally be taken by 'general agreement between the Executive Chairman and all members of the Board,' but when such general agreement could not be reached a recommendation by a majority of Board members, with the concurrence of the Chairman, would be considered as 'approved.' Failing this, the matter could be referred to TAC either by a majority of the Board members or by the Chairman. While the intent of this legislation clearly was to eliminate the potential 'veto' of individual Board members on the one hand, and to give the Chairman a suspensory veto power on the other, it appears to have made little difference in the Board's subsequent behaviour. When, on

[4] Arthur Goldschmidt, 'Program Planning and Development,' *The Annals* of the American Academy of Political and Social Science (May 1959).

[5] ECOSOC Resolution 433 (XIV), 11 June 1952.

general policy questions, divergencies of opinion develop within the Board, TAC is requested to settle the issue; but for specific programme matters decisions continue to be made by consensus after discussion. This has meant that agency interests ordinarily are accommodated on some generally acceptable compromise basis. To put it differently, there is a sufficient common area of agreement among members of 'the club' to enable them to 'co-ordinate themselves' without too much difficulty.[6]

In 1954, a major change in programming procedures was ordered by ECOSOC. On the initiative of the French delegation, it was then proposed (1) that automatic allocations of funds to agencies should be eliminated altogether and (2) that, beginning with the 1956 programme, each agency's share should be based on the total costs of requests for projects from the agency contained in annual country programmes to be drawn up by the claimant governments themselves, in consultation with the RTAR. The rationale of the French proposals was that most governments in the under-developed countries had reached a point where they could best determine their own programme priorities with the advice of the donor agencies as to the technical designing of specific projects. It was understood that the French proposals were intended to reduce autonomy in country programme-planning and, indirectly at least, to buttress the position of TAB and TAC with respect to over-all control.

Accordingly, most of the specialized agencies vigorously argued against acceptance of the new formula, each claiming that it was the best judge of its own programme, and fearing that by decentralizing country programme formulation to the national level its share of total programme funds would suffer. The further point was made by several agencies that it would be extremely difficult for them to plan and staff their respective EPTA operations without knowing in advance approximately the size of their annual allocations. With a view to meeting this objection, it was decided that each agency should receive not less than 85 per cent. of the total amount allocated to it during the current year. Another amendment of the French

[6] One senior officer of the TAB secretariat, in conversation with the writer, could not recall a single instance where TAB had come to a split decision on programme or project matters.

proposals provided that 5 per cent. of the estimated financial resources, after setting aside the expenses of the TAB secretariat and field offices and any necessary contribution to the Working Capital and Reserve Fund, should be retained by the Executive Chairman of TAB 'to meet any urgent needs that might arise during the implementation of the annual Programme.' Otherwise, the French proposals, though not without considerable misgiving by various Members, were adopted by ECOSOC without significant change.[7] The Working Capital and Reserve Fund, referred to above, had been instituted in 1951 for use in making advances to participating organizations pending the receipt of contributions from governments, and for facilitating the utilization of different currencies. The Fund was progressively built up to a level of $12 million, where it has been maintained for several years.

The accompanying diagram shows the principal steps involved in applying the 1954 country programming formula. The initial step, which takes place some fourteen months before the beginning of the programme year in question, is the establishment by TAB of the global 'pre-planning target' for programme operations based on the anticipated amount of contributions to EPTA to be made at the annual pledging conference. TAB then communicates to the participating organizations their respective 'gross and net planning shares' as rough guides to advance planning. The next step, completed by April, is the determination by TAB of tentative targets for country and regional programmes.

This is a highly involved operation. ECOSOC's basic legislation governing EPTA stipulates that due regard should be paid to needs of the claimant countries '*and to their geographic distribution*' (italics added). During the period 1950–58, assistance of some kind was received by as many as 140 countries and territories, distributed regionally as follows:[8]

[7] ECOSOC Resolution 542B (XVIII), 29 July 1954, and General Assembly Resolution 831 (IX), 26 Nov. 1954. One administrative feature of the French proposals failed of adoption, namely, than an 'Administrative Council,' to be elected by ECOSOC and consisting of representatives of twenty-one governments participating in EPTA, should replace TAC as the inter-governmental review organ. Some years later (1957), however, ECOSOC expanded the membership of TAC by adding six members from other governments with important interests in EPTA.

[8] *United Nations Review* (July 1959). In the programme as approved for 1960, Africa's share was increased to 15·7 per cent., with some diminution in the shares of Latin America and the Middle East.

TECHNICAL ASSISTANCE BOARD PROCEDURE
FOR PLANNING AND DEVELOPING THE PROGRAMME

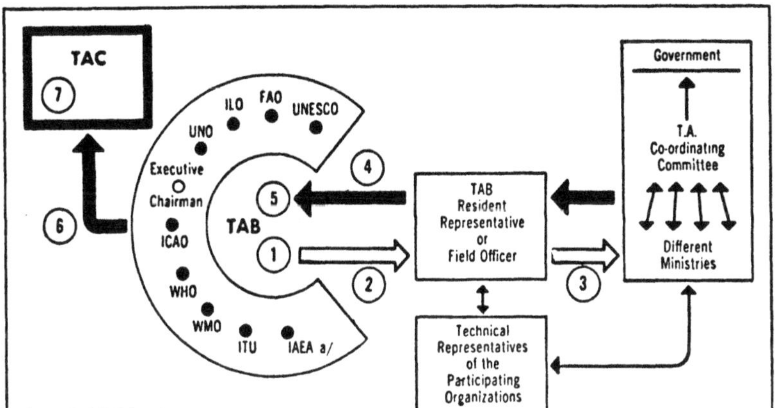

a/ International Atomic Energy Agency

EXPLANATORY NOTES

(1) **October-April:** (a) In October, TAB establishes planning target for the next year's field programme on the basis of probable contributions by governments.

(b) In April, TAB formulates target figures for country and regional programmes.

(2) **May:** Target figures communicated, via TAB Resident Representatives, to governments.

(3) **May-June:** Representatives of the Participating Organizations negotiate projects with the appropriate government ministries in each country. TAB Resident Representative assists in and co-ordinates programming discussions with the Government's Technical Assistance Co-ordinating Committee, which assigns project priorities and consolidates country programme request within target figure.

(4) **July:** Governments transmit programme requests to TAB, via Resident Representatives, with copies to Participating Organizations.

(5) **August:** TAB Secretariat examines and consolidates government requests in the light of Participating Organizations' cost estimates.

(6) **October:** TAB recommends over-all programme to Technical Assistance Committee.

(7) **November:** TAC reviews and approves the over-all programme and authorizes allocation of funds for its implementation to the Participating Organizations in proportion to their shares in the approved over-all programme

	Number of Territorial Units	*Percentage of Total Assistance*
Africa	35	9·5
Asia and the Far East ..	41	32·4
Europe	18	7·8
Latin America	35	27·2
Middle East	11	20·3
Inter-regional	—	2·8

Among the political units receiving assistance in 1958 were nearly fifty non-self-governing and trust territories, together with a number of other areas which had previously been in this category but had become independent. As the membership of the United Nations and the specialized agencies has expanded, the EPTA pie has necessarily been cut into more and more slices. Since the amount of annual contributions has remained fairly stable for some years, the programme shares of certain countries have had to be reduced in favour of newly independent and recently admitted States, especially in Africa—a decision naturally not relished by those countries suffering reductions. For 1958, the Board, faced with the announcement by the United States of its intention to reduce the percentage on which it would match other contributions, was obliged to apportion funds for the field programme on the basis of an anticipated amount some $800,000 less than that approved for the preceding year.

During the earlier years, TAB attempted to apply various objective criteria in allocating country programme shares, such as territorial size, population, national income per capita, health and education needs, and programme levels in neighbouring countries. While in principle this is still done, obligations already incurred in respect of *continuing* projects, together with the effect of the 85 per cent. rule governing agency allocations, allow little leeway for major adjustments. For these same reasons the pattern of distribution of funds by agencies has not altered materially from the automatic percentage formula adopted at the outset of EPTA.[9]

Within the target figure for each country, tentative 'sub-totals' are established for each participating agency, largely on the basis

[9] The shares of the UN, FAO, and WHO have declined slightly; that of Unesco has increased a bit; ILO's has remained constant; while ICAO's has gone up from 1 to around 4 per cent. WMO and ITU, which came into EPTA later, now receive approximately 1 per cent each. IAEA's share for 1960 was about 2 per cent.

of detailed information provided by agency headquarters. A TAB working party examines all the relevant data and the Board then approves Category I and II country planning targets, along with the agency 'sub-totals.'[10] This information is communicated to recipient governments by the TAB secretariat through the RTARs. The Category II programme consists of projects that may be proposed by governments up to about 50 per cent. of the Category I target figure, *i.e.*, of projects that may be financed from savings in Category I projects. This is a device for encouraging governments to establish over-all priorities in their programme formulations.

During the period from April through June, negotiations take place between national government ministries and representatives of the donor organizations *at the country level* concerning project requests to be inserted into the draft country programme. The RTAR assists in 'co-ordinating' such requests by discussions with the government's technical assistance co-ordinating unit (see below) and, as necessary, with individual ministries as well. The ramifications of these negotiations will be explored later in this chapter. Suffice it to note here that in July the country programme requests, along with detailed supporting data on special forms provided by the TAB secretariat, are transmitted by the governments to TAB headquarters through the RTAR, with copies to the participating agencies. On the basis of cost estimates for experts, supplies, and fellowships provided by the agencies, the TAB secretariat consolidates the Category I and II draft programmes and circulates them in revised form to the agencies for their information. In October, a TAB working party goes over the entire programme and transmits to the Board its recommendations, which are then reviewed by the Board itself. Finally, TAB submits its programme proposals to the Technical Assistance Committee meeting in November.

In examining the proposed programme, TAC limits itself to such broad policy considerations as over-all subject-matter priorities, programme trends, inter-relationships, and evaluation. It does not deal with country allocations; to do so might perhaps invite political log-rolling within the Committee. Subject to formal confirmation by ECOSOC and the General Assembly,

[10] TAB has also set up working groups on Administration and Finance and on Fellowships.

TAC's resolution approving the annual programme authorizes TAB to allocate funds to each of the participating organizations in proportion to its share in the global programme.

On occasion, the General Assembly has passed resolutions exhorting TAB to pay special attention, in its programme allocations, to the needs of specified countries or territories.[11] Although TAB obviously is obliged to take note of such resolutions, it has not hesitated to point out that to respond directly to them would create serious disturbance in the programme shares of other countries, especially when over-all programme reductions are necessary. Fortunately, this tendency towards policy intrusion by the Assembly has been rare. Nor has there been much interference, on programme matters, by the permanent delegations of Member States at UN headquarters. Now and then a delegation will contact the TAB secretariat in connection with some special request from its government for a project under the contingency fund, and occasionally delegation members discuss arrangements for country programmes with the staff of TAA. On the whole, however, the permanent delegations are poorly informed concerning their government's position as to EPTA.

The Programming Role of the RTAR

Let us now look more closely at what goes on at the country level during the negotiation of annual programmes. In this context the RTAR plays a key role. The theory of so-called 'balanced' country programming rests on a double assumption: (1) that recipient governments can and should correlate their technical assistance requests as closely as possible with their basic economic and social development needs; and (2) that the RTAR should do everything he can to facilitate this 'across-the-board' effort to bring project requests into some sort of ordered whole. Whether he performs this difficult function well or poorly depends primarily on his own personal capacities. Legally, his position is devoid of authority with respect *both* to the claimant government and to the UN agencies providing assistance. The situation, as a senior staff official of TAB recently observed, is

[11] Notably by Resolutions 1228, 1254, 1259, and 1303, adopted at its Thirteenth Session (1958), and Resolutions 1383 and 1415 at the following session.

somewhat analogous to an embassy in relation to the various functional departments in the government at home and to the personnel working in corresponding functional areas in the field. In the case of the Expanded Programme, however, the agencies concerned are autonomous bodies, and there is no supreme administrative authority to which an appeal could be taken.[12]

Only with respect to BTAO and Unesco, for which the RTAR himself serves as *de facto* field representative, does he have anything approaching 'line' authority. He is therefore forced back on his own personal resources in carrying out his principal function—that of programme co-ordination.

Administratively, the RTAR is responsible to the Executive Chairman of TAB, and it is from the latter that he receives his 'terms of reference' (in accordance with such general directives as are prescribed by TAB). As noted earlier in this study, these terms of reference, in so far as relations with the host government are concerned, are set forth in the standard letter to the government covering the RTAR's appointment. After the adoption of the new country programming formula, TAB attempted to define 'the working relations' of the RTARs with the field representatives of the participating UN organizations. This definition, contained in a communication sent to all RTARs in 1956, is in effect merely a set of suggestions for their guidance.[13] *Inter alia*, it makes the RTAR responsible for consultations with the designated co-ordinating unit of the claimant government in the drawing up of country programmes, as well as for 'co-ordinating consultations between governments and participating organizations.' The field representatives of the latter are enjoined to keep the RTAR informed of the progress of their 'technical' discussions with government ministries, which should be 'carried out through and in agreement with' the RTAR, who is also given responsibility for negotiating project agreements involving more than one agency. But the RTAR has no sanctions which he can apply to agencies failing to conform to these general instructions, part of which are susceptible to differing interpretations.

Broadly speaking, one can distinguish three types of RTARs in so far as their approach to country programme co-ordination is concerned. There are a small number who take vigorous

[12] In an unpublished paper presented by Laurence Michelmore to a panel of the American Political Science Association, New York, September 1957.

[13] UN Doc. TAB/CM/FIELD/110, 2 Aug. 1956.

initiatives—even to the point of trying to 'inspire' or 'mastermind' the programming operation. These are usually the more aggressive personalities. In certain country situations this approach has worked well, though not in all. It runs the risk of 'back-firing' since it may not only ruffle the feathers of specialized agency representatives but offend the sensitivities of the host government. Second, there is the 'passive' type of RTAR who allows the government and the agencies to work out their programme proposals pretty much on their own. This type ordinarily is content to assist in project execution by smoothing out difficulties encountered by the experts. Between these two extremes, which together account for only a minority of the total number of RTARs, are those who tactfully endeavour to influence programme focus and content by suggestion to the government and the participating agencies. This group, as one able RTAR aptly described it to the writer, tend to behave like 'constitutional monarchs'—by advising and mediating but not by imposing their views. Such a role conception calls for the subtle exercise of persuasion based on a thorough appreciation of the political, administrative, and financial limitations within which the national authorities have to manœuvre. It also assumes the development of mutual confidence between the RTAR, the government, and the participating agencies; the ability to view national problems sympathetically; tolerance and patience when things go wrong; skill in negotiation; and the capacity to appraise intelligently the feasibility (though not necessarily the technical design) of projects. Ideally, therefore, the RTAR should be a good diplomat, a person of sound political judgment, and an able administrator. Although few possess this package of qualifications in full, the more successful RTARs have measured up to such standards reasonably well. But there is no stereotyped pattern: the job is what the individual RTAR makes of it.

In a few cases the RTAR has, on request, become a *de facto* adviser to the government on economic policy. However, when this delicate task is assumed, care must be taken not to indulge in open criticism of high government policy, for this might undermine the RTAR's whole position, which, from a political standpoint, is inherently weak. On occasion, the RTAR may be called upon by the Executive Chairman of TAB to remind the host government of arrears in the payment of its contributions to the EPTA account—a *démarche* calling for considerable diplomatic finesse.[14]

Attitudes of the Specialized Agencies

Among the organizations participating in EPTA, only TAA welcomed the expanded role of the RTAR in country programme-planning at the time the revised formula went into effect. Most of the major specialized agencies then looked upon the new arrangement with a cold eye, certain of them evincing a disinclination to co-operate. This was notably the case with WHO and FAO and, to a somewhat lesser extent, ILO. Over the period from 1955 to early 1959, the writer had opportunity to sample agency viewpoints both at headquarters and in some fourteen countries scattered from South America to the Far East. From this sampling his conclusion is that the role of the agencies, contrary to the assumption that prevailed when country programming was inaugurated, has in some instances increased rather than diminished. There would appear to be two reasons for this: On the one hand, the agencies now feel that they must vigorously negotiate for as many projects as possible in order to protect their share in the total country programme, thus perpetuating a competitive situation. Paradoxically, as the former Director of the UN Bureau of Technical Assistance Operations (formerly TAA) recently noted, the role of the agencies has increased also because they 'are now more effective instruments for program planning. They have nearly ten years of experience behind them. Their staffs have worked intimately with their counterparts in many countries.'[15] Interestingly enough, this enhanced role of the agencies has gradually led to a more co-operative spirit on their part, though evidence of inter-agency competition for projects has by no means disappeared. The evolution of agency attitudes is summarized below.

To consider WHO first: at the outset the RTAR was viewed

[14] One RTAR, stationed in the Middle East, stated that he had sent several written reminders to the Foreign Office relative to the country's unpaid pledge. By other means he discovered that the Ministry of Finance had failed to release the funds through sheer bureaucratic inertia; whereupon he contacted a personal friend in the Foreign Office (an under-secretary) who assured him that he would give the matter his 'personal' attention and that the 'money would be forthcoming within a week'!

[15] Goldschmidt, *op. cit.*, p. 54.

by most WHO staff officials as 'an agent of TAB imperialism.' In the words of one senior officer at Geneva, 'the governments should do their own planning and co-ordination in direct contact with the UN and the other agencies'; the job of RTAR, he thought, was an almost impossible one and should be abandoned. This point of view was encountered in more extreme terms at the Washington regional office, which clearly resented the efforts of the RTARs to exercise 'authority' over health projects, thereby 'driving WHO-PASB into the ground.' The new programming procedures were regarded with distinct disfavour by regional directors in other parts of the world, one of whom complained that health would 'get only what was left after the other ministries carved out their share of the pie.' This attitude, also found in FAO, ILO, and even Unesco, reflects a common tendency to depreciate the position of the functional ministry concerned in the national administrative 'power' structure—whether it be health, agriculture, labour, or education. As late as 1957, in one region, WHO was reported as not recognizing the role of the RTAR in programme co-ordination; the regional office corresponded directly with national health authorities concerning projects without informing the RTAR. In another region, one RTAR observed that WHO tended to operate like a 'sovereign power' and that he was not consulted by the WHO staff prior to the submission of health proposals to the government's co-ordinating unit. Here the national health ministry was rated by the RTAR as being in a strong bargaining position.

In 1957, the Advisory Committee of the General Assembly, reporting on WHO's handling of EPTA, took occasion to note that WHO's regional structure had tended 'to diminish the Organization's dependence' on the RTARs. In this same report it was pointed out that the

> Director-General has previously expressed reservations with regard to the new procedures for country programming on the ground that, while these procedures would be suited to a large-scale programme of assistance with a significant impact on a country's planning for development, they merely give rise to avoidable complexities in a programme of relatively small size. The Director-General nevertheless assured the Committee that, inasmuch as the new procedures have been adopted, it would be unwise to change them frequently.[16]

[16] *First Report of the Advisory Committee on Administrative and Budgetary Questions*, UN Doc. A/3596, 9 July 1957.

As indicated in the preceding chapter, the fact that WHO plans its regular field programmes on a different time schedule from EPTA means that WHO field representatives ordinarily solicit from national health authorities EPTA project requests for two years ahead. One WHO regional officer in the Far East referred to difficulties that had arisen from confusion as to what 'co-operation with the RTARs' actually meant.

While there is still some resistance to the EPTA country-programming system at WHO's headquarters, its field staffs are now instructed to collaborate with the RTARs on programme matters. By and large, the situation at the country level has substantially improved since 1957. The relations between WHO field representatives and TAB country officers are in most cases much more friendly than formerly. Even so, it is not uncommon for WHO to negotiate project commitments in excess of its 'sub-total' within a country's planning target.[17]

In FAO's *milieu* a similar cluster of attitudes towards the new country programme formula may be detected. Initially, according to reliable authority, the FAO Director-General was 'dead set against it.' 'If you want to help FAO,' he is said to have told one RTAR during a briefing session at Rome, 'stay out of its bailiwick!' In more restrained language various senior officials, in 1955, voiced opposition to the new programming arrangements, largely on the ground that they were likely to accentuate intra-governmental antagonisms by reason of EPTA's small scale, thus becoming a nuisance. As late as 1957, the Advisory Committee of the UN General Assembly reported that from FAO's standpoint the new procedures were regarded as unnecessarily complex and labour-consuming.[18]

Out in the field the writer discovered the same inclination as in WHO to negotiate in excess of FAO country 'sub-totals.' In one important Latin-American country, the RTAR reported that the head of FAO's regional office would hold discussions with the Ministry of Agriculture concerning EPTA projects which resulted in what both the Ministry and FAO considered to be 'firm' commitments. This action placed the national

[17] One WHO regional Director, in communicating with a national Health Ministry, has suggested that he be informed of any projects that could not be recommended within the country's EPTA 'ceiling,' so that they might be included in the supplementary list of regular WHO projects.

[18] *Third Report of the Advisory Committee* . . ., UN Doc. 3598, 9 July 1957.

co-ordinating unit in an uneasy predicament in dealing with proposals that already had the endorsement of an international agency. When, as not infrequently happened, certain of the requests had to be rejected because of lack of money the situation became positively embarrassing. This RTAR later adopted the policy of advising each UN agency prior to its consultations with ministries what his recommendations as to agency shares were to be. In another Latin American country, the RTAR told of an instance where the FAO country representative had negotiated his 'programme' on the basis of instructions from Rome—only to receive different instructions from the FAO regional representative a little later. In this same country one FAO expert wrote a letter to the Minister of Agriculture expressing disappointment with the scope of the approved FAO programme. The letter was passed along to the Cabinet and the RTAR had to use all his tact to smooth over resentments. In still another area the FAO regional representative deplored the fact that FAO's proportion of country programme funds was declining in various countries, partly because other sectors of the economy were 'waking up,' but partly, also, because the RTARs were allegedly helping other UN organizations (notably TAA) in the bargaining process.

In Asia, a regional representative noted that FAO had lost ground in the competition for projects since most ministries of agriculture, surprisingly enough, were in a woefully weak bargaining position in comparison with other ministries.[19] In one large Asian country it appears that the FAO country representative would sit outside the door of the meeting of the national co-ordinating unit and brief the Minister of Agriculture when he presented his FAO project proposals, the purpose being, in the words of the former, 'to prevent undesirable changes in the programme already negotiated'! In two countries (Pakistan and the Philippines), where FAO has no local representative, the RTAR acted in this capacity. Even in one of these countries, however, FAO headquarters reportedly communicated at times with the Ministry of Agriculture on EPTA matters without informing the RTAR.

By 1958, FAO National Committees had been set up in

[19] The only Asian Members of the UN allocating more than 5 per cent. of their budgets to agriculture in 1958 were India and Japan.

fifty-three of the Organization's seventy-seven Member States. The idea for such Committees dates back to a recommendation of the Hot Springs Conference of 1943, where FAO itself was conceived. The Committees are advisory bodies intended 'to serve as focal points for national demonstration of interest and co-operation in the work of FAO.' Most of them are chaired by the Minister of Agriculture or his deputy and include representation of other government departments concerned with FAO's activities. In some of the Committees farm organizations and co-operatives are also represented, and occasionally the national legislature as well. Like the Unesco National Commissions, many of the FAO Committees are little more than paper creations, their activity being confined to preparing materials for the national delegation to the FAO Conference. In some cases, however, the more active Committees, provided with a small secretariat in the agricultural ministry, stimulate and screen requests for technical assistance. The FAO regional representatives have been instructed by Rome to encourage this role. Yet none of the Committees have become effective programme-planning instruments as envisaged by the theory underlying their creation and by statements made more recently by various delegations at FAO Conferences.

By 1958, the general attitude at FAO headquarters towards country programming had become distinctly more favourable than it was three years earlier. One senior official characterized the system as a 'revolving process' through which ideas from national agricultural services, FAO outposted officers, the FAO headquarters technical divisions, and the country RTARs were sifted and eventually harmonized. Frankly admitting that his views had changed, another official stressed the salutary effect of the new procedures on the kinds of project proposals that were being submitted: there were in his opinion fewer 'foolishly' conceived and 'fuzzy' requests. FAO field representatives, he went on to say, were now being directed to consult meticulously with the RTARs at all stages, and where the latter were 'disposed to co-operate' good results were being obtained. The 1957 FAO Conference deplored 'the harmful effects of the competition between the various agencies' and the consequent 'tendency for agencies to accept requests for projects whose viability might otherwise be questioned, were it not for the fact that a refusal to accept a particular request might lead to the corresponding amount of funds being transferred to some project in the field of interest of another agency.'

So far as ILO is concerned, initial scepticism regarding the revised programme procedures seems to have rested chiefly on serious doubts whether many governments in the under-developed areas would be capable of 'co-ordinating' their over-all technical assistance programmes on a priority basis. Even so, in the view of various Geneva officials, the new formula at least had the merit of forcing governments to take a broad look at their needs from year to year. One senior ILO officer was of the opinion that the country-programming idea should have been adopted at the outset of EPTA—before the pattern of fixed agency allocations 'got set.' By 1955, he felt, it was too late to alter this pattern. The head of one ILO field office argued that agency 'sub-totals' should not be communicated to governments since the latter tended to regard them as 'sacrosanct.' (This view, incidentally, was encountered among a number of RTARs and field officials of other specialized agencies.) Certain ILO officials stressed the fact that the organization had to deal not only with ministries of labour but with related government departments as well—which complicated its project-negotiating problem. Under the old system, moreover, it was possible for an agency to transfer project funds from one country to another during the course of the financial year; under the new, this would be much more difficult, with the consequence that governments would be tempted to spend money foolishly and quickly in order to avoid lapse of funds. This, unfortunately, has proved to be the case in various countries. Finally, the fear was expressed that the RTARs would find it hard to be 'objective' in passing on EPTA requests involving the specialized agencies in view of the fact that they would be acting as field representatives for TAA.

By and large, good relations now appear to exist between ILO field staffs and the RTARs. Yet ILO, like its sister agencies, does not refrain at times from negotiating over and beyond its country target. In one RTAR's experience, ILO had been 'notorious' in this respect, often negotiating up to the double of its sub-total. When the head of the ILO field office was taxed about this, he admitted that it should not be done but, with a shrug, commented, 'What can we do when all the rest do likewise?' Nevertheless, the RTARs, especially in countries where there is no local ILO office, are being increasingly drawn upon for advice and services.

Unesco's reactions to country programming were from the outset distinctly more sympathetic than in WHO, FAO, or ILO. In large measure this difference in attitude may be attributed to the fact that Unesco has no general field structure. Initially it may have tried to keep the RTARs out of the picture but perforce it soon found itself drawing upon them for local support services and, concomitantly, for aid in negotiating EPTA project agreements. After 1956, moreover, the Director-General decided to utilize the RTARs in connection with the local planning of the new Participation programme, to which reference was made earlier in this study; otherwise, as he pointed out to the ACC, Unesco would have to set up 'a separate and costly chain of command' from Paris to the field.[20] In those countries where Unesco 'chiefs of mission' are maintained, the latter also play an important part in project negotiation, but always in close collaboration with the RTAR. As regards natural science undertakings, the field science co-operation offices are consulted by Unesco headquarters from time to time on technical matters.

A further influence on programming at the national level is exerted by certain of the Unesco National Commissions. In those few countries where the Commissions have effective staffs, new projects are not infrequently instigated by them, or old projects examined as to whether United Nations assistance should be requested for another year. Once a year a representative of BMS makes a visit to each country during which he consults with government ministries, the Unesco National Commission (if any), the representatives of related UN agencies, and the RTAR, with respect to future requests.

Not even Unesco, however, has been immune to the temptation to encourage national ministries to ask for projects in excess of the agency sub-total. One justification for this that has been given on occasion is that some governments in the less developed countries do not understand the importance of education and science for national development, and that there is a tendency

[20] UN Doc. CO-ORD/S.R.22/4/Rev. 1, 14 July 1956.

for too little of the national resources to be used for 'educational' as distinct from strictly 'economic' development.

By and large, the evidence suggests that Unesco plays the game fairly with the RTARs and usually keeps its country programmes within its allotment.[21] When, for example, Unesco was recently faced with a 10 per cent. increase in aeroplane fares, it informed the RTARs that it would stay within its allotments by 'shaving' various projects a bit, instead of asking for additional funds.

Concerning ICAO only a word need be said. Its technical assistance operations are so specialized in character that the RTARs have given them little attention in the programme co-ordinating process.[22] In each country ICAO has only one project in operation at a given time, namely, civil aviation, though under this heading any of a variety of activities may be undertaken depending upon the state of development of the country. ICAO's principal objection to the revised programming system has been that it 'wastes time and money,' involving long field trips each year in order to negotiate projects with governments. The relations between the ICAO technical assistance missions and most RTARs, however, now appear to be quite satisfactory. Various ICAO regional directors, although having little directly to do with EPTA, indicated that they favoured country programming if only because it relieved them of responsibility for 'untangling knotty' project situations.

To sum up: while the field picture remains spotty, varying markedly from country to country, agency particularism has noticeably declined during the past few years. By over-bargaining, as one RTAR has noted, the specialized agencies are beginning to discover that they tend to 'cut their own throats.' When one agency 'misbehaves' in this regard, the government can 'under-cut' it the following years. Under the present arrangements many governments have the illusion of 'giving money to the agencies.' The latter, however, now accept reductions in their country programme shares with better grace than they did during the first year or so. They slowly are coming to realize that competitive bidding misleads national ministries,

[21] In one country visited by the writer the RTAR characterized Unesco as 'the most greedy' agency; in most of the others, however, it was praised as the 'most co-operative.'

[22] *Report of the Advisory Committee on Administrative and Budgetary Co-ordination between the United Nations and ICAO* . . ., UN Doc. A/3861, 20 Aug. 1958.

creates false expectations, and results in disappointments. Agency 'carpet-baggers,' to quote another RTAR, no longer try to 'build empires' as much as they used to and they are now more concerned with basic problems of project construction. The influence of the RTARs on programming has steadily grown in most countries. As of 1956, a former RTAR could testify that he had not been consulted by any of the participating organizations on 'any single project.'[23] Moreover, field experts during the earlier years were instructed by certain agencies not to provide the RTAR with copies of their periodic reports. Today such situations are highly exceptional.

The RTARs are now being consulted in advance by the TAB secretariat regarding proposed agency sub-totals. Several RTARs remarked to the writer that the sub-total pattern still made the agencies 'happy' but that otherwise there was not much point to it. In one case the RTAR has found it helpful to use the term 'guide-lines' rather than 'sub-totals' when discussing the country programme with the government. Still another RTAR favours confining the sub-total arrangement to successful continuing projects and letting the government distribute the rest of its country-planning allotment, with regard to the agencies, as it wishes. In 1959, TAB considered the suggestion that agency sub-totals be abolished but did not recommend that this be done for the present. In the Board's view, no doubt reflecting lingering agency opposition to the elimination of sub-totals, it would be difficult to establish equitably and soundly country totals

> except on the basis of the needs in the different fields which are known to the agencies. Since the country totals are in effect mainly based on the sum of the agency sub-totals, it [seemed] appropriate that governments should be informed of the latter as well as the former, in order to understand the basis of the Board's recommendations.[24]

Notwithstanding the Board's caution, there are growing signs that the days of the sub-total system are numbered.[25]

National Co-ordinating Machinery

'Balanced' country programming under TAB rules is a complicated process not only because of the geographic and functional

[23] D. Belloch, 'Bold New Programme,' *International Affairs* (January 1957).
[24] Report of TAB on *Country Programming Procedures*, UN Doc. E/TAC/84, 13 May 1959.
[25] See p. 542.

separatism of the participating UN agencies and the power relationships between them, but equally because of the widely divergent culture patterns and political and administrative systems of the recipient countries. Shifting party coalitions, changing combinations of powerful family groups, and fluctuating civil-military alliances produce unstable political control situations in many countries, ranging from authoritarian to more or less democratic in character. From the administrative standpoint, governments in the economically under-developed areas tend to consist of a loose congeries of competing units. Entrenched vested interests often intimidate the bureaucracy and block clear-cut decision-making. Career civil services based on professional merit are the exception and not the rule, and shortages of trained personnel make it extremely difficult for most governments, irrespective of other resources at their disposal, to construct and execute sound, comprehensive, and sustained programmes of economic development.

When the Expanded Programme of Technical Assistance was initiated, few governments in the less developed regions had any central economic planning or co-ordinating machinery worthy of the name. Whatever the other impacts of the 1954 country-programming formula, it is generally agreed that it has contributed importantly to the creation and improvement of such machinery. By 1958, according to TAB, some forty-two countries, accounting for about 80 per cent. of the global programme, maintained some kind of council, board, committee, office, or unit with co-ordinating functions.[26] In a number of instances the establishment of such arrangements was directly stimulated—or at least influenced—by the RTAR. Several countries, moreover, have sought technical assistance from the United Nations in the fields of public administration and economics to help them organize and staff their co-ordinating machinery.

It is not surprising that the forms and effectiveness of such machinery should vary widely. Most of the earlier co-ordinating schemes consisted of inter-ministerial committees, with a small staff usually provided by the Ministry of Foreign Affairs. Although this pattern still obtains in roughly one-third of the

[26] *Annual Report of the TAB for 1958*, ECOSOC, O.R.: 28th Sess., 1959, Suppl. No. 5, pp. 62–64. See also *Co-ordination at the National Level: Report of the Secretary-General*, UN Doc. E/3107, 6 May 1958.

forty-two countries covered by TAB's survey, the tendency in recent years has been to place the co-ordinating staff either in the Ministry of Finance or Planning or Economy, as the case may be, or to attach it to the office of the Chief Executive or to that of the National Development Council or Board where such exists. In a considerable number of countries, moreover, the inter-departmental committee device has been abandoned—or modified—with a view to minimizing 'log-rolling' by representatives of competing government departments. There has also been a discernible trend towards strengthening permanent staffing facilities for planning and co-ordination, though with few exceptions such staffs are still decidedly inadequate.

The functions of national co-ordinating units embrace several kinds of operations. All of them serve as the central channel of communication for EPTA and as the reviewing and approving organ for annual programme requests. In addition, about three-fourths are charged with following up on the execution of EPTA projects and with clearing candidates for fellowships. In the third place, the terms of reference of about the same number include similar functions relating to technical assistance programmes from sources other than the UN system.[27] With one exception all of the units handle the clearance of EPTA experts.

The working relationships between the RTARs and the national co-ordinating mechanisms range from exceedingly close and informal to rather limited and formal contacts. In certain countries the RTAR regularly sits with the committee or board (where this pattern is used) and participates in its discussions. In others, he attends only on invitation; and in still others not at all—because, as one RTAR frankly put it, 'they don't relish having foreigners in private meetings held inside the Foreign Office.' Some illustrations of specific national situations are presented below.

In Country A (Latin America), the Department of International Organizations and Conferences of the Foreign Ministry handles both policy and procedural matters relating to the UN system in general. One section of this Department is responsible for UN and OAS technical assistance. The small staff of this section assembles and submits project requests to an inter-

[27] The role of national co-ordinating units in inter-programme co-ordination is considered in Chap. 10 (pp. 427–441).

departmental committee on which ministerial directors at the technical level sit. When and as necessary the minister himself may come 'to battle' for his proposals, particularly when political implications are involved. Each project is in theory examined as to its value in relation to others, and priorities are determined after discussion by consensus. There is no formal voting. The Committee is chaired by the chief of the International Organizations Department as the most 'disinterested' member. The RTAR usually attends Committee meetings. In case of serious dispute the Foreign Minister himself may be called in to 'arbitrate.' According to reliable testimony, a good deal of log-rolling takes place in the committee, the more powerful ministries, and even bureaux within ministries, usually winning out. There is reportedly little follow-up or evaluation of the results of projects. A number of other Latin-American countries have substantially the same set-up.

In Country B (Middle East), national co-ordinating arrangements have gone through two stages. At the outset there was an inter-ministerial committee representing all of the claimant departments and agencies of the government. Within this committee, polite 'vote-trading' appears to have been the rule. The RTAR (in 1955) could not recall any project it had ever rejected. Largely at his suggestion the inter-ministerial committee was discontinued in 1956 and a Co-ordination Office established in the Ministry of National Planning. As of 1958, this Office was headed by a director and included in its professional staff were an economist, an engineer, and a social welfare specialist. The Office reports directly to the Minister of Planning. Within each subject-matter ministry there is a 'delegate' (usually an under-secretary) who serves as point of contact with the Office. In January, the Office requests all ministries to consider their EPTA needs and to fill out detailed requests not later than March. The Office staff makes a study of the requests, during the course of which it contacts each ministerial delegate in order to be sure that the ministry is equipped to 'receive' the project, *i.e.*, by providing counterparts, etc. At the next stage (from March to May) the Office sets provisional priorities on an A-B-C basis, including the relative amounts to be asked for experts, fellowships, and equipment. The draft programme document is then submitted to the RTAR with recommendations. Another month is spent in consultations with the ministries in the light of suggestions made by the RTAR on how to keep within the TAB country target. Cuts are explained to the ministries by the delegates, each minister, however, deciding what should be eliminated within the agency sub-total. If there is disagreement as to the amount, an appeal to the Minister of National Planning is possible. In June the annual programme, after being initialled by the Director of the Co-ordination Office and signed by the Minister of National Planning, is officially sent to the RTAR by way of the Minister of Foreign Affairs.

The purview of the National Co-ordination Office extends to all sources of foreign aid, including bilateral programmes. An attempt is made by the Office to relate project requests in their *ensemble* to national economic planning needs. The Minister of National Planning himself heads a cabinet-level National Planning Committee. This particular country, however, does not as yet have any over-all plan. Instead, there are 'sector' plans in different ministries, *e.g.*, a five-year industrialization plan over which the Ministry of Industry has charge and to which an important ILO project has been geared. TAA has provided advisory services for the National Planning Committee itself.

The Co-ordination Office plays an active role in project implementation, including the approval of job descriptions, the orientation of experts after arrival, and the administration of fellowships. On the whole, this national set-up seemed to be doing a reasonably effective job.

In Country C (also in the Middle East), the co-ordination of EPTA requests is closely meshed with the National Plan Organization. The latter, set up in 1949, has substantial revenues (from oil concessions) at its disposal for the financing of large-scale economic development undertakings. Within the Plan Organization there is an Economic Bureau, the senior staff of which includes twenty-two foreign experts financed by a Ford Foundation grant; and a Technical Bureau staffed by a group of specialists recruited (though not paid) by the International Bank. A team of United States experts, under an ICA contract, advises the Plan Organization on problems of administration and staffing generally.

For EPTA co-ordination purposes, there is a committee of

under-secretaries of the interested ministries which is chaired by the Managing Director of the Plan Organization. The Committee has a small staff (located in the Plan Organization) the head of which provides liaison with the various ministries. A series of subject-matter sub-committees have been set up to examine requests for assistance in their respective fields. The full Committee, which meets two or three times a year, formally approves the EPTA country programme. The RTAR (or his assistant) sits with the Committee and is treated in effect as a member. The programme as approved is submitted to him under the signature of the Managing Director of the Plan Organization.

This country has one of the largest EPTA programmes of any in the world. Very few changes, however, are now made in it from year to year because of (1) the large number of continuing projects and (2) the stabilized country-planning ceiling. Many of these projects are designed to provide assistance in the designing and execution of national development schemes financed through the Plan Organization, which are kept under review by its Economic Bureau. The various ministries report to the office of the EPTA Co-ordinating Committee on the work of UN agency experts attached to their services. This country (by 1958) was about half-way through its second seven-year plan. Thanks in large part to the vigorous initiative of the RTAR, EPTA assistance appears to be making a significant impact on the technical aspects of its over-all economic development planning.

Country D (in South Asia) offers another example of long-range national economic planning with which EPTA operations are closely related. As early as 1951, a staff unit for the co-ordination of certain types of foreign aid was set up. Five years later this unit was enlarged to cover the co-ordination of EPTA requests. Now located in the Department of Economic Affairs of the Ministry of Finance, it forms part of a Foreign Aid Division. The latter includes three branches—one for EPTA and the regular UN programme, the second for the Colombo Plan and small bilateral programmes, and the third for the U.S. aid programme. Each branch has a section officer and four staff assistants. The regular programmes of the UN specialized agencies are not handled by this Division reportedly because of pressures from various ministries to retain a direct channel with such agencies. The office of the Foreign Aid Division is physically located in the same building as the TAB office, an arrangement which makes it easy for the RTAR to maintain close informal contact with the Division's staff.

Originally, under this country's set-up, programme co-ordination was handled at the policy level by the National Planning Commission itself. But this task reportedly became so burdensome that it was decided to create a special Foreign Aid Committee. This body, chaired by the 'Joint Secretary' who also heads the Foreign Aid Division, consists of a technical officer designated by the Planning Commission, one officer of the Ministry of Education, and one or two staff officers of the Foreign Aid Division. The latter Division receives and processes requests for foreign aid under EPTA and handles the question of fellowships under all programmes. In this connection, a circular setting 'ground rules' and inviting proposals is sent annually to each claimant ministry and independent department of the government. These ground rules relate to the conditions and types of aid available. When the Foreign Aid Committee meets, it scrutinizes the compiled requests and determines priorities. While it may propose changes in UN agency shares, the distribution is in actuality based on an earmarking of funds in terms of prior experience and continuing needs. The economic development angle reportedly is kept to the fore in the Committee's deliberations. After the country programme is provisionally agreed to, it is referred to the Planning Commission for 'guidance' and 'formal' approval. The Chairman of the Committee then submits it to the RTAR, who normally does not attend Committee meetings.

The one weakness of this country's co-ordinating machinery, according to local UN opinion, lies in its permanent staff, which is held to lack experience for the task of effective programme analysis. The co-ordinating unit, moreover, occupies a relatively low position in the administrative hierarchy and thus sometimes fails to stand up to the demands of influential ministers. On one occasion, when the Minister of Health proposed requests well above WHO's sub-total, the head of the co-ordinating unit suggested to the RTAR that he ask the Minister to reduce his programme. 'No,' replied the RTAR, 'that's your job!' Broadly considered, however, this country's machinery works reasonably well.

The experience of Country E (Far East) illustrates a further variation in the national co-ordinating process. In this country there is a National Economic Council, dating back to 1935 but reorganized in 1946. This body consists of a permanent chairman and nine members representing the national legislature, the National Development Bank and the Central Bank, and the private economic sector (industry, labour, and so forth). The Council has three offices: (1) for National Planning, (2) for Statistical Co-ordination and Standards, and (3) for Foreign Aid Co-ordination. The last-named office, with a permanent staff of thirty to forty persons drawn from the civil service, has authority to deal with all forms of external aid. The staff, however, is divided into subject-matter units rather than by foreign aid sources. Project requests from the ministries are assembled and analysed by this staff, which takes the large United States ICA programme as the focal point from which to consider the UN and other smaller aid programmes. When a ministry submits proposals in excess of the UN agency sub-total concerned, the Director of the Foreign Aid Office holds an informal discussion with senior representatives of this and related ministries and endeavours to adjust the issue by general agreement. In effect the Office has the final say since there is no provision for appeal. The draft programme is referred to the National Planning Office for scrutiny in order to assure its correlation with the current national economic plan. The approved programme is then sent to the RTAR under the signature of the Chairman of the National Economic Council.

It is to be noted that in this set-up there is no inter-ministerial committee. The powerful position of the National Economic Council in the executive branch of the government gives it strong moral authority over individual ministries, which are under constant pressure to keep within their respective EPTA allotments. Every week or so the RTAR consults with the Foreign Aid Office concerning programme planning and execution. In June he circulates the draft programme to each EPTA expert for comment as to the advisability of project changes, extensions, and terminations, and in certain cases he has induced the government not to ask for further extensions.

The Foreign Aid Office serves as the channel for the clearance of all foreign experts and exercises surveillance over the conditions under which projects are implemented. It also keeps a central register of all former and current fellows and trainees studying abroad, and analyses the use of such training after their return.

In this country the combination of a well-staffed, high-level co-ordinating unit and an ingenious RTAR has facilitated an effective approach to the problem of programme planning. Among the countries visited by the writer it would rate high on all counts.

On the basis of on-the-spot inquiries in fourteen countries, the writer would hazard the generalization that the most effective job of programme co-ordination is being done where three conditions prevail: (1) the co-ordinating unit has a strong, permanent professional staff; (2) this is closely associated with the top-level economic planning organ (if any); and (3) the power of decision on programme requests is lodged either in a single high-level official or in a small executive group on which claimant ministries are not directly represented. Inter-departmental committees with such representation are prone to recommend a multiplicity of small projects without regard to relative needs or priorities, and are notably susceptible to log-rolling pressures from their more influential members. It would appear that the least appropriate place to locate the co-ordination staff unit is in the bureau of international organizations of the Foreign Ministry. Such a bureau is likely to be so swamped with UN documentation on all sorts of matters and with so much political and diplomatic business that it will have little time—or competence—to focus effectively on technical assistance problems.

As recent TAB reports indicate, efforts are being made in a considerable number of countries to improve their co-ordinative machinery, often with advice from the RTAR or from a UN advisory group. Of the forty-four countries surveyed in 1958, thirty-four had long-range development plans of a comprehensive or sectional character. Increasingly, their technical assistance projects were being integrated with these plans. Many countries whose economic planning is still at an early stage were showing 'a pronounced tendency to ask for technical assistance in the formulation of their development plans.'[28] It is in the economically least developed and newly independent states that co-ordinative arrangements tend to be most rudimentary. This, of course, is precisely what one would expect. It will take a long time for the governments of such countries to build up the administrative standards and develop the trained personnel requisite for an effective analysis of economic needs in relation to basic physical and human resources. In the meantime, EPTA country programming is helping to awaken many governments to a wider consciousness of how technical aid may best contribute towards a realization of long-range economic and social goals.[29]

Trends in the Content of the Expanded Programme

In terms of major functional fields, global EPTA expenditures have not varied significantly since the early years of the Programme. According to TAB's classificatoiy scheme, these fields range downward, by dollar volume, in the following order:

agricultural production (chiefly FAO)
health services (chiefly WHO)
basic surveys of resources and assistance in economic planning and public administration (UN, FAO, ILO, Unesco)
industrial production (UN, ILO)
auxiliary services to agriculture and industry (UN, FAO, ILO)
public utilities: power, transport, communications (UN, ICAO, ITU, WMO)
education (including fellowships) (Unesco, ILO, FAO, WHO, UN)
community development (UN, Unesco, FAO, WHO, ILO)
other social services (UN, Unesco, FAO, ILO)

The shares allotted to projects relating to health, community development, and various social services have declined a little since 1954, while those for agriculture and education have slightly

[28] *Annual Report of the TAB for 1958, op. cit.*, p. 67.

[29] Philip Glick relates how the RTAR in Brazil (June 1954) provided the government with its first 'comprehensive picture' of UN technical assistance activities in the country. Accordingly, the government then 'became critical of itself for having submitted thirty-nine requests, spread over a variety of fields, and each asking for a small amount of short-term assistance.' *The Administration of Technical Assistance, op. cit.*, p. 282.

deviated above and below the norm. One disconcerting feature in programme content is that the proportion of funds spent on what has been called 'institution-building' has not expanded over the years. This has accounted for well less than a third of total project outlays, and it was little greater in 1958 than four years earlier. Since 1952, only 10 to 15 per cent. of all EPTA experts have worked in the field of public administration.[30]

If the global programme is viewed in terms of objects of expenditure, one discovers that the proportion spent on fellowships and trainee grants has fairly steadily declined from around 20 per cent. (for 1950–51) to 13 per cent. (for 1958). As one RTAR has observed, fellowships tend to be 'the poor relations' of EPTA, largely because so many governments prefer to receive experts and supplies rather than to send their nationals abroad for training. Another factor in this situation has been the availability of substantial fellowship funds from non-UN sources. The proportion of project costs expended for experts has remained fairly constant—at 70 to 75 per cent.—the remainder (10 to 12 per cent.) being used for equipment and supplies.[31] In all, some 8,000 experts served on EPTA assignments during the decade from 1950 to 1959, and there were 14,000 fellowship awards. The *per capita* cost of an expert was of course several times higher than for a fellow. Recently, between 2,000 and 2,500 experts have been on field duty each year.[32]

Looked at from the standpoint of individual countries, programme size shows a wide variation. By dollar volume, the four largest programmes in 1958 were in India, the United Arab Republic, Indonesia, and Pakistan, in that order—total project costs ranging from $2·5 million down to roughly $1 million for each country. Below this group the volume declined progressively to only a few thousand dollars in the case of certain small countries and dependencies. In the following six countries over 100 experts (EPTA and regular programme) were on duty during this same year: India, 212; Iran, 141; Indonesia, 113; U.A.R., 109; Pakistan, 107; Libya, 107. For the rest the number

[30] This estimate is taken from Albert Lepawsky, 'Technical Assistance: A Challenge to Public Administration,' *Public Administration Review* (Winter 1956). The percentage has not noticeably changed since 1956.

[31] In one Latin American country, the RTAR explained its decided preference for equipment this way: The government thinks it has enough qualified technicians of its own and the bureaucracy fears that if technical assistance recommendations are put into effect the number of government jobs for nationals may be reduced.

[32] These figures do not include some 750 experts financed from regular budget funds.

scaled down to less than ten for some twenty countries and territories.

By forms of action, country programmes may be classified in various ways. Considered as 'instruments' for providing assistance, these include (1) demonstration and pilot undertakings; (2) survey missions preparatory to programme planning; (3) advisory missions (and individual advisory experts); (4) training facilities within the country (*e.g.*, new centres, institutes, workshops, aid to existing educational institutions); (5) fellowships for training and study abroad; and (6) operational missions.[33] During the earlier years of EPTA, the first two forms of assistance—demonstrations and broad surveys—were widely used. While this is still the case in many of the least developed and newer countries, there has been a discernible trend away from these two instruments and towards the provision of advisory services and of relatively long-term aid for training and research, the latter being regarded as having the largest 'multiplier effect.' This trend is noticeable in all of the major specialized agencies.

Although the operational mission as such has seldom been employed in EPTA, projects involving long-term advice to national administrations, as well as those where UN experts participate directly in the establishment of permanent training institutions, have led in perhaps a sixth of the cases to the assumption of quasi-operational responsibilities.[34] The line between advice and operations is often hard to draw. On the other hand, the UN system has not developed anything comparable to the *servicio* arrangement widely used in the U.S. bilateral programme in Latin America.[35] This is not because a multinational team is not capable of administering *jointly* with officials of the recipient government an operational service or institution.[36] It is due rather to two other factors: (1) the inability of the UN

[33] For an interesting comparison of the forms of technical assistance utilized by the UN system and by the U.S. Point Four programme, see Philip Glick, 'The Choice of Instruments for Technical Co-operation,' *The Annals* (May 1959).

[34] During 1957, 13 per cent. of the EPTA experts were engaged in quasi-executive functions or handling day-to-day administrative work. *Annual Report of the TAB for 1957.* ECOSOC. O.R.: 26th Sess., 1958, Suppl. No. 5, p. 79.

[35] For a description of the *servicio* arrangement, see Glick, 'The Choice of Instruments for Technical Co-operation,' *op. cit.*; for an official U.S. Government appraisal, see K. R. Iverson, 'The "Servicio" in Theory and Practice,' *Public Administration Review* (Autumn 1951).

[36] Wide use of the *servicio*, under multilateral auspices, might result in governmental units being administered by a variety of principles and procedures. Such arrangements might also be difficult to transfer to a ministry if the salary levels were higher than in other divisions of the ministry.

agencies to make binding project commitments for more than a year or two; and (2) the lack of substantial funds for equipment and supplies. 'Without joint financing,' observes Glick, 'there is no hope of winning acceptance of joint administrative control.' The new Special Fund may make such funds available —at any rate for permanent training and research institutions— while the recently inaugurated OPEX programme, as noted earlier, is designed to provide UN specialists for 'operational and executive' functions who are to be 'integrated' within the service of the beneficiary government.[37]

To date, the UN system has made virtually no use of the contract device for technical assistance, whether with universities or with private management and engineering firms. In the former TAA, informal co-operative arrangements with certain universities were entered into, but not long-term contracts.[38] The fact is that not many universities outside the Anglo-Saxon world are so organized as to be able to undertake overseas instructional or advisory assignments over a period of years. TAA has concluded contracts with seven or eight private firms— on the whole, with rather unhappy results. One example of this in a Far Eastern country turned out disastrously when the government discovered that the terms of the contract included a large sum for technical publications which the specialist, provided by a United States management concern, never received.[39] At first glance, use of private firms, especially for 'sensitive' assignments, seems attractive, but experience with such arrangements in the U.S. programme has shown that they may be more costly than the direct recruitment of experts by the donor organization. In an international programme such as that of the UN system, any extensive 'farming out' of projects to private concerns might provoke political objections from certain member governments. If no public agency is available, the Special Fund may enter into contracts with private institutions

[37] A United Nations technical assistance experiment in Bolivia, launched in 1949, served as a partial precedent for the OPEX idea. See Albert Lepawsky, 'The Bolivian Operation: New Trends in Technical Assistance,' *International Conciliation*, No. 479 (March 1952).

[38] As of 1958, ICA had some eighty contracts with American universities totalling $71 million—most of them for periods of three years or longer. UN Doc. A/4220, 25 Sept. 1959.

[39] There were other complications, *e.g.*, the specialist did not enjoy the same privileges and immunities as TAA experts on duty in the country, and thus carried two professional cards—one as an employee of the management firm and the other as UN consultant.

(management firms, research institutes) for the execution of projects. Or the UN agency, as 'executor,' may sub-contract out all or part of a project to a private or semi-private firm. This practice has not been discouraged by the Managing Director of the Fund.

Let us now turn our attention to the internal composition of country programmes from the viewpoint of the number, size, and duration of projects. In these respects, to be sure, the situation varies tremendously from country to country. Within the 1958 global programme, there were over 1,300 different projects distributed among more than 100 political units. The majority of these projects consisted of 'bits and pieces' in the sense that short-term advisory undertakings, involving only one or two or three experts, still outnumbered those of longer duration conducted by a project team. Recently, however, there has been a tendency to consolidate certain of these bits and pieces into more integrated arrangements, particularly in the fields of industry and public utilities. In several major countries a number of relatively large-scale inter-agency projects have come into being, notably in connection with 'regional development' programmes, *e.g.*, for the North-east and the Amazon Valley in Brazil, and for water and power development in East Pakistan.[40] Such undertakings have created administrative problems, to which we shall refer in Chapter 11, but they are symptomatic of a real effort to co-ordinate technical assistance operationally within a country.

One of the difficult problems facing EPTA administrators has been when to terminate assistance to projects that have been in operation for more than a year. From 70 to 75 per cent. of the total number of Category I projects now fall into this group.[41] For 1957 and 1958 about one-sixth had been under way for over four years. In certain countries, and for certain agencies, the proportion of continuing projects in the annual programme has at times run as high as 90 per cent. When this situation prevails there is little room for intra-programme adjustments or for the introduction of important new projects, the country programme

[40] For details, see Michael Louw, 'The United Nations Program in Brazil,' *The Annals* (May 1959); and Huntington Gilchrist, 'Technical Assistance from the United Nations—As Seen in Pakistan,' *International Organization* (Autumn 1959).

[41] For detailed analyses of 'continuing' projects, see *Annual Report of the TAB for 1957*, *op. cit.*, pp. 18–19, and *for 1958*, *op. cit.*, pp. 24–29.

thus tending to become 'frozen.' In this connection, however, it should be remembered that many projects are inherently of a long-term character, *e.g.*, integrated disease control programmes, national fundamental education centres, training and research institutes. In other cases, moreover, project labels are deceiving since significant changes may take place in the nature of a project without any change in its official title. Finally, it is necessary to ensure 'an orderly transfer of responsibility for such projects to the Governments concerned—for this transfer . . . may not only come too late [but] it may also come too soon, that is to say, before a country has been able to train the essential personnel to continue a project on its own account.'[42] For projects requiring substantial national budgetary outlays on a continuing basis the necessary revenues may not always be available. The basic question for EPTA, therefore, has been how to determine the *optimum* duration of assistance.

With a view to approaching this problem more intelligently, TAC recently proposed that tentative completion dates for new projects should be agreed upon with the recipient government when they are approved. Since 1957, this practice has been substantially followed by some of the participating organizations. When such action is not feasible, it has been suggested that a date be fixed by the government for a general review of the project, in consultation with the executing agency (or agencies). In its 1959 report to TAC on country-programming procedures, TAB proposed certain further steps: (1) that all new projects should be approved by the government through its national co-ordinating machinery 'for their full duration,' with assurance of such local support as necessary throughout; (2) that as far as possible a plan of operations for the entire period should be drawn up at the outset; and (3) that continuation of a project beyond the agreed terminal date should be subject to 'the same sort of action by the government co-ordinating machinery as is required in the case of a new project.'[43] In addition, TAB now urges governments, when requesting projects, to specify clearly their objectives and their relation to any long-term development plan and to assistance expected from sources other than the UN system. If such conditions were generally complied with

[42] *Annual Report of the TAB for 1958*, *op. cit.*, p. 24.
[43] UN Doc. E/TAC/84, previously cited.

by governments and donor organizations, not only would there be a sounder basis for coping with the continuing project dilemma, but the number of vaguely planned project requests would be greatly reduced.

UNICEF's Contribution to National Assistance Programmes

As already indicated, direct assistance to governments from the UN system not only includes the field activities financed from EPTA and from the regular budgets of the UN and certain of the specialized agencies, but also substantial contributions from UNICEF in the form of equipment and supplies to programmes designed primarily for children and mothers. The RTARs, for the most part, now take into account anticipated regular programme projects in connection with the formulation of country programmes and, as we have just seen, the national co-ordinating machinery in a growing number of countries is being charged with responsibility for correlating EPTA requests with undertakings to be aided from agency regular budget funds. The fact that regular programme field activities are not allocated by the respective agencies on the basis of country targets complicates this process. So far as UN assistance is concerned, it is comparatively easy for the RTAR to co-ordinate regular programme and EPTA requests in his capacity as BTAO's country representative, and, to a somewhat lesser extent, for Unesco as well. But for WHO's extensive regular programme the problem is a more difficult one because of the differing time-schedules for programme planning, as noted in the preceding chapter.

With respect to UNICEF-aided operations, the situation is equally complex by reason of the fact that UNICEF allocates its funds directly to field projects continuing over a period of years—without setting country-planning shares in advance. Between UNICEF field officials and government authorities, project discussions go on almost constantly on an informal basis. An attempt is made to assess the substance of a project before it reaches the stage of an official government request. Sometimes a 'feeler' may come through WHO or FAO, the two agencies that are required to approve the technical aspects of UNICEF projects before they are authorized by the UNICEF Executive

Board. As indicated in Chapter 6, this co-operative relationship is facilitated at the headquarters level by two joint policy committees (UNICEF-WHO and UNICEF-FAO), as well as by the assignment of WHO and FAO technical advisers to UNICEF's central secretariat.

At the country level, close working relations between UNICEF's field officers and those of the technical-advisory agencies are essential if operating plans for UNICEF projects are to be cleared expeditiously. With this in view, WHO, for example, has stationed at the UNICEF regional office in Bangkok a medical adviser for UNICEF programmes throughout WHO's Eastern Mediterranean, South-east Asia, and Western Pacific regions. This adviser, while directly responsible to Geneva on substantive and technical matters, is subject to guidance and instructions from the three WHO regional directors. He has two kinds of functions: first as a day-to-day operating adviser to UNICEF with respect to decisions about technical medical equipment, and so forth, and second, a liaison function, interpreting UNICEF's immediate concerns to WHO and interpreting WHO advice to UNICEF. It is his responsibility to clear agreements for UNICEF projects where WHO is technically concerned. By taking extensive field trips he attempts to visit each major UNICEF programme at least once a year. But since it is impossible for him to be everywhere at once, in such a vast expanse of territory, medical personnel on the staffs of the three WHO regional offices are also drawn into the picture. Even so, according to testimony of various UNICEF field representatives, it has sometimes been difficult to meet operating deadlines because of delays in obtaining clearance from WHO. In actuality, observed one RTAR to the writer, the amount of technical control exercised by WHO has now and again been more nominal than real.

For projects involving WHO's technical approval, UNICEF supplies apparatus, vehicles, drugs, vaccines, powdered milk, and so forth, while WHO provides such technical staff as may be necessary. In one Latin American country, the head of the PASB 'zone' office reportedly committed UNICEF to contributions towards a malaria control programme by so informing the Minister of Health without prior consultation with the UNICEF country representative. In another country (Middle

East), the UNICEF field representative complained of complications caused by the separate locations of the WHO and UNICEF regional offices, with both of which he had to deal. By and large, however, co-operation between UNICEF and WHO at the field level now seems to be working reasonably well.

In 1957, UNICEF decided to expand the scope of its operations in the field of nutrition. This action brought FAO into the picture as adviser on the economic aspects of such programmes, WHO providing scientific advice on diets. The new child nutrition programmes are aimed not only at increasing the quantity and the quality of milk production for school feeding and for use at maternal and child welfare centres, but at promoting a wide range of protective foods grown locally (*e.g.*, soya products, fish, poultry). In launching such programmes, the first step usually is

> for milk and dairy survey teams, consisting of representatives of FAO and UNICEF, to visit the country concerned. . . . If these surveys include recommendations for the provision of equipment for dairy plants and for the production of milk powder, etc., the agreements between the Governments, UNICEF and FAO require the recipient Government to include in its EPTA programme-request the provision of a dairy plant management adviser to supervise the installation and operation of the equipment, and a dairy production expert to develop hygienic milk production in the area.[44]

FAO supplies the dairy expert adviser, but UNICEF engages its own engineering staff to oversee the installation of equipment.[45] FAO, unlike WHO, exercises technical control over these programmes directly from Rome, instead of through its field offices. In one Far Eastern country the inauguration of a child nutrition programme was delayed on account of differences of opinion between FAO's Economics Division at Rome and the medical staff of the WHO regional office.

At the headquarters level, an inter-secretariat Working Group on Milk and Milk Products, representing all three agencies, was set up some years ago to re-examine national child nutrition programmes. Plans were then being made by their secretariats, together with that of Unesco, 'to develop and test prototype materials for nutrition education and extension work for rural populations with little or no literacy.'[46]

[44] *Annual Report of the TAB for 1958, op. cit.*, p. 43.

[45] UNICEF has also contributed equipment for the installation of new penicillin and DDT plants in a number of countries.

[46] Report by the Secretary-General on *Coordination between UNICEF and the Regular and Technical Assistance Programmes of the United Nations and the Specialized Agencies*, UN Doc. E/3109, 13 May 1958.

UNICEF has recently moved into the somewhat amorphous field of community development. Accordingly, it is being brought into close relationship with the UN Bureau of Social Affairs, the latter acting in some instances as a technical-advisory unit, along with WHO or FAO as appropriate. UNICEF's role in this field consists of providing demonstrational equipment, teaching materials, and operating supplies for the welfare aspects of rural community development programmes, including the training of village level multi-purpose workers and professional personnel. In order to expedite the planning of such operations, it has been agreed that the UNICEF regional and area directors should consult with the UN Social Welfare Advisers stationed at ECLA, ECAFE, and Beirut before submitting project proposals to the semiannual sessions of the UNICEF Executive Board for approval. The UN Bureau's staff at New York helps the central UNICEF secretariat to screen such proposals. In India, during 1958, a rural community development project, covering 200 villages, was being supplied by UNICEF with such things as gardening tools, powdered milk, and materials needed for increasing fisheries and poultry production. Another example of UNICEF aid to community development is the training of women village leaders in East Africa. Recently an agreement was reached by UNICEF and the Bureau of Social Affairs relative to the provision of social services for children.

With relatively large funds at its disposal, UNICEF supplements importantly what little EPTA is able to do on the supply side for undertakings emphasizing the welfare elements in economic development. During recent years, UNICEF's annual allocations have exceeded $22 million—as much as two-thirds of EPTA's global outlays—and, for 1959, were more than $28 million. Then over 55 million mothers and children in more than 100 countries and territories benefited from UNICEF aid to nutrition programmes and disease control campaigns, covering tuberculosis, yaws, leprosy, trachoma, malaria, and venereal disease. Additional millions were provided with services at maternal and child welfare centres and at hospitals equipped for training purposes with UNICEF's help. During 1959 it had 371 active programmes in operation. For every dollar allocated by UNICEF in that year, the recipient governments committed themselves to spend from $2.00 to $2.50 on the projects aided. In certain countries UNICEF's activities have exceeded in dollar terms the aggregate annual expenditures under EPTA.

In the opinion of a number of RTARs, UNICEF has sometimes dangled offers of equipment before governments which the latter find it hard to resist even though they may not be in a position to use the equipment effectively. Nor has UNICEF always made as thorough an analysis as it might have of the conditions under which its supplies could be used to best advantage. But there have probably been as many cases where UNICEF was brought into a project prematurely by ill-advised technical officers from other UN agencies.

The UNICEF programme has enormous popular appeal: it is the world-wide symbol of the UN as a humanitarian instrument. UNICEF gets things done—and with as much dispatch as possible given the inter-agency framework within which it is obliged to function. Logically, and on grounds of operating economy, a strong case could be made for completely incorporating UNICEF's activities into EPTA; but to do so might well mean the loss of millions of dollars now being offered for the sake of the world's under-privileged children.

Financial Support from Recipient Governments

Over and beyond the funds made available from EPTA, agency regular budgets, and UNICEF, certain recipient governments have received UN system assistance on what is called a 'payment basis.' Under this arrangement the government itself agrees to pay for experts recruited by the UN organizations from 'funds-in-trust' set up for this purpose. 'In most cases assistance of this type is given through self-contained project agreements that cut across calendar years. . . . However, available information indicates that the total of expenditures actually incurred [for 1958] on [such] technical assistance projects . . . was in the neighbourhood of $1·3 million.'[47] Of some twenty-one countries receiving assistance on the payment basis, Iran and Iraq (each with large oil revenues) accounted for over half the total. Currently Venezuela, another oil-producing country, is launching a substantial programme of this kind, and TAB has expressed

[47] *Annual Report of the TAB for 1958, op. cit.*, p. 29.

the hope that other countries may provide such funds as 'a useful adjunct' to regular UN programme and EPTA sources. Almost 90 per cent. of assistance on a payment basis has been channelled through FAO—the UN, ILO, Unesco, and ICAO making up the remainder.

A small portion of this category of assistance has been furnished by so-called 'third party' governments. Thus, for example, the Government of the Netherlands, in 1958, made a contribution to pay for experts of Dutch nationality who served in various countries under FAO and TAA auspices, while this Government jointly with that of New Zealand provided an appreciable amount towards the cost of a milk project administered by FAO in India. These contributions were in addition to their annual pledges to EPTA centrally.

Finally, it should be remembered that the local cost payments for EPTA projects made by most beneficiary governments constitute a significant addition to the funds provided directly by UN organizations. From 1954, when the current local costs plan was inaugurated, through 1958, such payments aggregated around $7·5 million, or about 5 per cent. of the total financial contributions from all governments to the central EPTA account.[48] Local cost payments per year almost quadrupled during this period. Nor do these figures include other expenditures by host governments on projects aided by EPTA, which in recent years have aggregated two to three times the total project allocations from EPTA. The 'self-help' principle on which EPTA is predicated appears to have worked.

TAB Country Programming in Transition

At the time these lines were written the TAB country-programming system had been in effect for only four full years. This is a short period on which to venture an assessment of its over-all impact. As we have already suggested, its most obvious effect has been to stimulate governments to consider their assistance needs in a broader context than hitherto—through the establishment and gradual strengthening of national co-ordinating

[48] These figures are derived from statistics given in the *Technical Assistance Newsletter* (June-July 1959). In 1959, ECOSOC decided to institute a simpler system for calculating 'local costs' on the basis of a percentage of the total costs of experts' services. See ECOSOC Resolution 736 (XXVIII), 30 July 1959.

machinery. To be sure, the situation in this regard still differs enormously from country to country. Programme construction is carried out much more realistically in countries with political stability and a reasonably well-developed administrative system than in those still inexperienced in economic development planning and lacking in trained administrative and technical personnel.

In most countries the aggregate contribution from the UN family of agencies represents only a very minor percentage of national outlays for economic and social development. The UN contribution, in other words, constitutes merely a 'fringe' programme. Furthermore, the determination of project priorities is influenced by agency competition under the 'sub-total' arrangement, and in part, especially for countries with weak co-ordinative machinery, by the pulling-and-hauling of entrenched departmental vested interests. Since 1956, the attempt to rate Category I project requests on a priority basis has been abandoned as not 'worth the trouble.' On the other hand, the number of poorly conceived and 'half-baked' project proposals, while still considerable, has noticeably declined in many countries. The country target system has tended to choke off at the source a goodly number of projects of this character. It seems clear that the most successful projects have on the whole been those where the UN experts remained on duty for at least two years. Contrariwise, the necessity of limiting binding project commitments to a year or less, because of the uncertainties of EPTA financing, has militated against the long-term planning of important undertakings for which a period of several years' duration is essential.

In 1958, the Economic and Social Council asked TAB to make a general study of the experience gained under the country-programming procedures with the object of exploring how they might be simplified and made more flexible.[49] We have already referred to two of the conclusions reached by TAB as a result of this study, relating to agency sub-totals and to continuing projects. In the one case, it will be recalled, the Board refrained from recommending any change; in the second, however, it proposed a number of constructive steps designed to facilitate a more effective handling of long-range projects. The Board

[49] ECOSOC Resolution 700 (XXVI), 31 July 1958.

considered a number of objectionable features of the country-programming system pointed out by certain of the specialized agencies, notably WHO and FAO. It was observed, for example, that EPTA planning procedures were 'more involved and time-consuming in relation to the amount of assistance received than those of most other aid programmes.'[50] In this connection, the argument was made that too little time was left for negotiations with governments between the determination of their Category I programme target and the submission of the consolidated country programme to TAB. Not infrequently projects were included in the programme without any prior discussion with the representatives of the appropriate UN agency. As a result of such haste, requests had sometimes been approved 'without adequate investigation' of the necessary technical conditions or local support. The budgeting of projects on an annual basis, moreover, often allowed inadequate time to recruit qualified experts and thus compelled the executing agency either to provide experts of lower qualifications or to advise the government that the project could not be carried out. Finally, objection was raised as to the regulations governing the obligation of funds in annual project budgets. Allocations for equipment sometimes lapsed for lack of time to draw up specification lists and place orders by the end of November.

In its report to TAC, the Board made a number of recommendations aimed at meeting some of these criticisms. Most importantly, it proposed that country programmes should henceforth be planned on a two-year basis, thus bringing EPTA into line with the biennial budgeting of regular programme activities in FAO and Unesco. Such a change, the Board noted, should permit a more thorough appraisal of proposed projects and also provide more time for the recruitment of suitable experts and the ordering of supplies and equipment. 'The compulsion for hasty decisions inevitable under the present procedure would disappear.' Further, it was believed that biennial planning would improve the technical soundness of major assistance projects. Under the proposed procedure, while TAC would approve a programme for a two-year period, TAB would submit to it a mid-period report on its progress,

[50] UN Doc. E/TAC/84, 13 May 1959. The comments on proposed country-programming improvements that follow are drawn mainly from this document.

with information on any substantial modifications that had been made. At its session at Geneva in the summer of 1959, ECOSOC approved the Board's recommendation 'as an experiment.'[51]

Although TAB did not propose any basic change in the sub-total system, it suggested that up to 5 per cent. of the total funds allocated to the field programme should be withheld from Category I country target figures at the planning stage, to be divided between the Executive Chairman's contingency fund and the participating agencies. The agency shares would be available to meet unforeseen meritorious requests of governments which might emerge after the biennial programme was approved. The Executive Chairman's share would be used mainly for providing additional assistance to newly independent countries 'whose over-all needs are seen during the programming season to be greater than had been anticipated when country totals were established.'

Two minor suggestions, intended to provide greater operational flexibility, were (1) that orders for supplies and equipment might be placed up to the end of the fiscal year instead of by 30 November, and (2) that in cases where an appointee to a fellowship was unable to use his fellowship award the nominating government might propose a qualified substitute, after the close of the financial year, subject to the condition that the same course of study is followed and the substitute is acceptable to the country (or countries) of study.

Finally, the Board gave considerable thought to how programme consultations at the country level might be better co-ordinated. Although it did not make any specific recommendation on this subject, it approved in principle the practice of holding 'round-table' discussions (where feasible) between the RTAR and representatives of the participating agencies—a procedure already being carried out in a few countries. Such discussions, in the Board's view, might usefully include representatives of UNICEF. Stress was also laid on the desirability of joint meetings of representatives of the different aid pro-

[51] ECOSOC Resolution 735 (XXVIII), 30 July 1959. The procedural implications of this action for the 1961–62 programme are spelled out in UN Doc. E/TAC/93, 13 Nov. 1959. Balances of allocations not obligated at the end of the first year of the biennium, for example, would carry over to the second year. Operational savings during the first year could be used the second year on the same country programme; transfers of such savings to another country, however, would require TAB approval.

grammes operating in a country, though it was realized that such meetings could properly be convened only by the government's national co-ordinating unit.

All in all, the foregoing recommendations, while moderate in character, reflect a reasoned effort to improve country programming without altering its general rationale. The position of the RTAR, with respect to the specialized agencies, remains constitutionally unchanged despite recent suggestions from various members of TAC that it should be strengthened. The RTAR's emerging role as adviser to the new Special Fund at the country level, however, is clearly enhancing his influence and prestige.

The future orientation of EPTA may in part depend upon how recipient governments react to the operational policies of the Special Fund, and to a lesser degree, perhaps, upon the impact of OPEX on the instrumentalities of technical assistance. From the financial point of view, the Special Fund now represents an alternative channel for which the contributions of governments may be earmarked, possibly with an adverse effect on EPTA's budgetary resources—unless aggregate contributions for technical assistance substantially expand.

Project Procedures under the Special Fund

The Special Fund, to which reference has already been made at several points in these pages, had been in operation less than eighteen months when this study went to press. Although, by the end of 1959, some forty-four projects had been approved by the Fund's Governing Council, only a few had got beyond the planning (or recruitment) stage at the time these lines were written. Nevertheless, it may be useful to describe briefly the procedures developed by the Fund's staff to date for considering project requests and arranging for the execution of approved undertakings.

Submission of project requests

Unlike the TAB system, the rules of the Special Fund permit the submission of project applications at any time during the year. Requests may be initiated either by individual governments, or by groups of governments, prepared to make firm financial commitments towards the local support of the project concerned. In countries where a TAB Resident Representative is stationed, project requests are sent to him and he then forwards them to the Managing Director at UN headquarters; in other countries requests are mailed directly to New York. The Fund staff has prepared a memorandum describing 'the form and content' of a request as a guide to national authorities.[52] Detailed information is sought concerning the location, duration, and dimensions (*e.g.*, number of experts, fellowships, equipment, of the project and the kind and amount of the government's contribution to its operations. In addition, 'the request should state what action is expected to follow the successful completion of the project,' with particular reference to likely sources of investment or other measures, legislative or administrative or both, which the government plans to take in order to ensure the project's permanent impact.

As the primary channel of communication between the requesting government and Special Fund headquarters, the RTAR is asked by the latter for a confidential opinion on local conditions and institutions, as well as on the proposed contribution to the project by the government. In this connection, the RTARs receive instructions from the Managing Director after clearance with the Executive Chairman of TAB. In some instances requesting governments have been given special aid in re-drafting or clarifying project applications by representatives of the UN agency which would presumably execute the project if approved. Any extra expense involved is reimbursed to the agency by the Fund.

Appraisal and selection of projects

All project requests that reasonably conform to the conditions laid down in the memorandum referred to above are appraised for technical soundness and administrative and financial arrangements by the headquarters staff of the Fund or, if and as necessary, by the UN Department of Economic and Social Affairs or the specialized agency with competence in the field of the project. In cases where professional expertise is lacking in any UN agency, temporary outside consultants may be engaged for

[52] UN Doc. SF/4, 11 Jan. 1960 (a revised version of an earlier memorandum dated 6 Feb. 1959).

this purpose. Investigations are frequently made on the spot through the RTAR's office or the country or regional office of the UN or specialized agency concerned.

In selecting projects for recommendation to the Governing Council, the Managing Director is guided generally by the following criteria:[53]

- concentration on relatively large projects
- relative urgency of the needs of requesting countries
- the prospect of early and tangible results
- technical, organizational and financial feasibility
- effective integration of projects into national development programmes
- no conditions of a political nature
- preference to projects lasting for more than one year—up to a maximum of five years
- early transfer of responsibilities to the assisted country

'Consideration is given to wide geographic distribution over a period of years.' What this means is that the Fund may not find it possible to ensure a wide geographic spread in a given year. In any event, decisions are made in terms of the merits of individual projects, and country targets are not fixed.

From the standpoint of substantive content, further selective criteria became necessary in view of the relative scarcity of financial resources as compared with the number of applications for aid. Accordingly, for the time being at least, the Managing Director does not support requests covering elementary, high school, or mass education, or the work of liberal arts colleges; nor will he consider favourably preliminary surface geological surveys. On the other hand, for example, the training of vocational school instructors, agricultural extension workers, and specialized vocational engineering and agricultural personnel falls within the Fund's current priority scheme, as do natural resources, manpower, and economic surveys and long-term technological research undertakings.[54]

When a project request is received which seems to fall within the province of EPTA, it is suggested to the government that

[53] Derived from UN Doc. SF/1, 1 Jan. 1959.

[54] See 'The United Nations Special Fund: From Concept to Reality,' *United Nations Review* (Feb. 1960). The writer was informed (April 1960) that the SF staff was then engaged in working out functional boundary lines with the specialized agencies (notably Unesco and ILO).

the request be referred to that Programme, especially if the financial dimensions of the project (otherwise meritorious) are too small for the Fund to consider. An appreciable number of requests approved during 1959 represented outgrowths of successful EPTA projects.

Once the Managing Director has decided in favour of a given project, he informs the government concerned that he is prepared to recommend it to the Governing Council provided the government agrees to provide *x* amount of 'counterpart' support of the project, together with 15 per cent. of the 'local costs' of experts. At the same time, the government is advised that the Director intends to designate such-and-such an agency to execute the undertaking. If the government's reply is satisfactory, the project goes into the list to be submitted to the Council.

Before coming to a final decision on pending projects, the Managing Director may, and presumably does, seek the advice of a 'Consultative Board,' consisting of the UN Secretary-General, the Executive Chairman of TAB, and the President of the International Bank (or their designated representatives). The establishment of such a Board was authorized by the General Assembly with a view to encouraging high-level liaison between the relevant operations of the Special Fund, EPTA, and the Bank.[55]

Twice a year, after the conclusion of the appraisal process, and taking into account the financial situation of the Fund, the Managing Director transmits his 'programme' recommendations to the Governing Council. The Governing Council does not attempt to perform a screening function. Instead, it has thus far approved without a vote all the projects recommended to it—as an expression of 'confidence in the judgment of the Managing Director,'[56] the Council's main task being to provide general policy guidance and review of the administration of the Fund.

Project execution

Approved projects are carried out, as far as possible, by the United Nations, by some specialized agency, or by the International Atomic Energy Agency, although the Managing

[55] GA Resolution 1240 (XIII), 14 Oct. 1958.
[56] 'The United Nations Special Fund: From Concept to Reality,' *op. cit.*

Director may, if necessary, contract for the services of other agencies, private firms, universities, research institutes, or individual specialists. All such arrangements involve the prior approval of the receiving government and of the executing agency. In order to expedite arrangements, the Fund staff has drafted 'standard' agreements (1) with governments and (2) with the UN agencies for signature in advance. A 'Plan of Operations,' in effect the project agreement, is prepared by the Fund staff within the general framework of the standard agreements. 'As a control document it provides the standards against which the three parties may measure the progress of the project; as an agreement, it embodies a detailed statement of the obligations of the three parties involved.'[57]

In all cases a single agency is made responsible for the execution of the project. It has the right, however, to 'sub-contract' out all or parts of a project to another agency (or agencies). The Fund staff, early in 1960, was operating by a rule of thumb that would limit an executing agency to receiving no more than 2 per cent. for equipment and 10 per cent. for expert recruitment costs to which SF projects give rise. Previously, certain specialized agencies had submitted percentages for overhead expenses that were considered much too high both by the Fund staff and by the Governing Council. At least one agency, on the other hand, had reportedly agreed to assume responsibility for projects without any additional cost to the Fund.

The actual execution of Fund projects by a UN agency involves operations similar to those explained earlier in this study with respect to other field programmes, such as recruitment, assignment, support services, equipment, supervision, and reporting. Appointment contracts, to be sure, may run for the duration of a Fund project, which may be as long as three to five years. One obvious source of recruitment will be current and former EPTA experts with outstanding performance records.

Characteristics of initially approved projects

By the close of 1959, the Special Fund had received 164 requests for assistance, totalling $161 million. Up to that time pledges to the SF amounted to not quite $60 million. As indicated

[57] UN Doc. SF/L.22, 4 Dec. 1959.

above, forty-four of these project requests were by then approved by the Council. They called for an aggregate cost to the SF of $32 million, to which the receiving governments promised to add $44 million in counterpart funds. These projects were distributed geographically as follows:[58]

Regions	*Number*	*Special Fund Contribution*
Africa	6	$3,198,820
Africa, Middle East and Asia .. (Regional Desert Locust Control)	1	2,492,700
Asia and Far East	11	10,012,850
The Americas	18	10,012,742
Europe	3	2,064,415
Middle East	5	4,128,990
Total	44	$31,910,517

By subject-matter the projects were divided into the following categories:

water, irrigation, power surveys	13
agriculture, livestock or soil surveys or institutes	7
fisheries	2
meteorology	3
mineral or geological surveys	3
industrial institutes research	3
vocational training	7
university technological training	5
general development surveys	1
Total	44

The projects ranged in duration from six months (an Argentine power survey) to six years, the average being three and a half years. The executing agencies were distributed by number of projects as indicated below:

FAO	17	Unesco	6
ILO	7	IBRD	4
UN	7	WMO	3

Over half of this list of projects were surveys designed to 'reveal natural wealth in the less developed countries concerned.' A second broad category 'aimed at a fuller utilization of human resources of the low-income countries.'[59] As noted in Chapter

[58] 'The United Nations Special Fund: From Concept to Reality,' *op. cit.*

[59] Paul G. Hoffman, *One Hundred Countries: One and One Quarter Billion People* (Washington: Albert D. and Mary Lasker Foundation, 1960), p. 42.

8, a few provided aid to large-scale regional undertakings originally sponsored by other UN programmes. The allocations to individual projects ranged from about $150,000 up to nearly $2·5 million. Since project budgets do not include an estimate for contingencies, the Governing Council authorized the Managing Director 'to increase the total amount allocated to any project by not more than 15 per cent., if in his opinion this was necessary to meet unforeseen contingencies.'[60]

No distinct project pattern had yet emerged. In certain requests, moreover, the 'pre-investment' possibilities were not easy to detect. There was some indication that the more requests a country presented, the more likely it was to get a project approved. In time, however, the Fund's managers should be able to develop rules that will eliminate such anomalies.

The Special Fund, all in all, appears to have got off to an auspicious start. Two major questions remained unanswered (1) could the RTAR offices and the executing agencies carry their extra responsibilities without adding to their staff resources?[61] and (2) should the Special Fund and EPTA remain *separate* operations—or be merged into a *single*, enlarged programme of aid to economic development? To these queries we shall return in our final chapter.

[60] UN Doc. SF/L.26, 22 Oct. 1959.

[61] At SF headquarters (as of the spring of 1960) one discovered some complaint over the slowness with which the UN and certain specialized agencies were getting SF projects 'off the ground.' On the average, a period of as long as six months was said to elapse between official approval of a project and the appearance of the project mission in the host country.

10

THE INTERRELATIONS OF UN AND OTHER AID PROGRAMMES

Earlier in this study various devices aimed at co-ordinating field programmes within the UN family of agencies were described. Complex though this problem be, it is but part of the wider task of how to correlate economic and technical assistance offered to under-developed countries from all sources, public and private. Short of the emergence of some global economic development authority with power to determine the objectives and content of national development programmes, and to direct the flow of aid, progress towards this goal can of course be realized only in piecemeal fashion—through informal arrangements for consultation and clearance at programme headquarters and, even more, at the country level. The purpose of the present chapter is to examine briefly the role of the UN system and of recipient governments in this evolving inter-programme co-ordinative process.

Proliferation of Sources of Aid

International assistance in the economic, social, and technical fields is now being provided by a labyrinth of public and private agencies, organizations, and groups. The number and variety of aid programmes has steadily proliferated during the 1950s. In their totality, these include public multilateral programmes on both a global (*e.g.*, UN system) and on a regional (*e.g.*, OAS) scale. Also, among the publicly sponsored programmes is the Colombo Plan, which operates in effect as a loose arrangement for clearing bilateral aid agreements with countries in South and South-east Asia. In addition, there are between fifteen and twenty straight bilateral programmes financed by individual national governments, ranging in size from those of the United States, the Soviet Union, the United Kingdom, and France, on down to the limited programmes of such small countries as the Netherlands, Norway, and Sweden. To a large extent the economic assistance offered by the United Kingdom, France, and Italy is designed for their own overseas territories or such territories formerly under their control.

Private assistance is channelled through philanthropic foundations and voluntary groups, religious and humanitarian. Notable among the former organizations are the Rockefeller, Ford, Asia, and Near East Foundations, and the Co-operative for American Remittances Abroad (CARE)—all financed by United States money. Voluntary international groups include the Red Cross, YMCA, the World Veterans Federation, the International Co-operative Alliance, the Agricultural Mission associated with the World Council of Churches, the American Friends Service Committee, and various orders of the Catholic Church.[1] Trade union organizations in certain countries also sponsor sporadic technical assistance activities abroad. It is proper to note that a considerable part of the aid provided by voluntary groups is of an emergency or relief character and thus does not call for co-ordination with aid activities related to the fundamental development of the receiving nation's economy.

According to a survey conducted by the UN Secretariat in 1958, the value of economic aid rendered to under-developed countries from major public sources averaged $2 billion net annually over the three-year period 1953–54 to 1956–57, and was at the rate of $2·5 billion net in 1956–57.[2] This total consists of the dollar value of loans, direct grants, technical services, and fellowships offered by fifteen donor countries, EPTA, UNICEF, UNKRA, UNRWA, and IBRD. It does not, however, cover technical aid provided under the regular budgets of the UN and the specialized agencies. Nor does it include the economic aid operations of Soviet bloc countries, which were estimated elsewhere at about $1·6 billion for the period 1955–58, largely in the form of easy credit arrangements for construction projects with the so-called 'uncommitted'

[1] For an excellent analysis of the overseas activities of United States voluntary groups, see Edwin A. Bock, *Fifty Years of Technical Assistance* (Chicago: Public Administration Clearing House, 1954); also, James G. Maddox, *Technical Assistance by Religious Agencies in Latin-America* (Univ. of Chicago Press, 1956). For the range of international fellowship programmes, both governmental and private, see Nicole J. Deney, 'Some Examples of International Scholarship and Fellowship Programmes,' in the Unesco *International Social Science Bulletin*, Vol. VIII, No. 4 (1957).

[2] Report by the Secretary-General on the *Economic Development of Under-Developed Countries*, UN Doc. E/3131, 3 June 1958.

countries of the Middle East and Asia (plus Yugoslavia).[3] In connection with such credit agreements, provision is usually made for 'Soviet style technical assistance, that is the hiring of specialized services by the contracting country. Most commonly, [Soviet] experts are used to assist in preliminary engineering surveys, to supervise construction, and to direct installation of equipment.'[4] During the first six months of 1958, it is estimated that there were some 2,800 Soviet bloc technicians who had assignments of a month or more in fifteen under-developed countries, all but 400 being concentrated in Afghanistan, Egypt, India, Indonesia, Syria, and Yemen. (During this same year a mere handful (fifty-two) of Soviet bloc experts were operating under EPTA sponsorship—chiefly in India.)

Since 1958, the trend in foreign economic aid has been upward. West Germany has joined the ranks of donor countries, while Japan and certain other countries have substantially increased their contributions. Concurrently, there has been continuing discussion in OEEC and European Common Market circles of the desirability of initiating special aid programmes for the under-developed countries of the non-Communist world.[5] Such programmes, if they materialize, are likely to take the form of 'soft' loans rather than of direct grants.

During 1959, moreover, the authorized capital stock of IBRD was doubled. Although none of the doubled subscriptions of Member countries was paid in cash, they all added to the amounts on which the Bank can call if needed to meet its obligations. Thus the Bank was given substantial reinforcement of its borrowing power in the investment markets of the world, most of its lendable funds being raised through Bank bond sales to private investors. Also, in 1959, on United States initiative, the Board of Governors of IBRD resolved to ask the Executive Directors of the Bank to draft a Charter for a new lending agency—the International Development Association—which, it was proposed, would be administered by the Bank, would have a capital stock of $1 billion, and would be authorized

[3] *The New York Times*, 22 March 1959.

[4] Waldenar S. Neilsen and Zoran S. Hodjera, 'Sino-Soviet Bloc Technical Assistance—Another Bilateral Approach,' *The Annals* of the American Academy of Political and Social Science (May 1959). For a more comprehensive study of Soviet aid, see Joseph S. Berliner, *Soviet Economic Aid* (New York: Praeger, 1958).

[5] At the time these lines were written, discussions were under way among various North Atlantic nations and Japan, under United States leadership, as to ways and means of increasing capital aid to the newer under-developed countries.

to make loans for economic development, widely defined, under more flexible terms than those of the World Bank itself. Finally, to serve Latin American needs, an Inter-American Development Bank, also with an initial capital stock of $1 billion, was being projected under the aegis of the Organization of American States.

So far as major lending operations within the non-Communist world are concerned, there is little question of overlap or duplication. Each lending institution, whether national or international, ordinarily appraises the resources, needs, and capacity to absorb further capital of the borrowing country, as well as the merits of the specific projects for which capital aid is sought, before a decision on the loan request is made. In Washington, informal consultation takes place between the IBRD staff and the U.S. Export-Import Bank and Development Loan Fund authorities as necessary.[6] The principal problem, from the standpoint of UN system field activities, concerns their substantive relations with the U.S. Point Four programme, with the Colombo Plan in South and South-east Asia, and with the OAS training projects in Latin America. Secondly, in a limited number of countries, there is the problem of keeping in touch with the overseas programmes of major private foundations.

The co-ordination of technical assistance may be said to have two objectives. On the negative side,

> the principal objective should be to avoid a competitive scramble among agencies operating in the same field or in closely related fields of activity. . . . On the positive side, over-all co-ordination should first of all aim at the development of balanced country and regional planning and execution, including criteria for determining project priorities. Second, a sustained effort should be made to correlate aid programmes with prospective sources of capital financing once the purely technological aspects of assistance are terminated.[7]

To what extent has progress been made towards these objectives? Available evidence would suggest that inter-programme competition, resulting in serious duplication, has almost disappeared since 1952, when the foregoing quotation was written.

[6] Through the National Advisory Council for Monetary and Financial Problems of the U.S. Government, the U.S. Director's attitude towards the lending policies of IBRD and IMF is co-ordinated with those of the U.S. foreign lending agencies.

[7] The quotation is from the author's study on *International Technical Assistance*, *op. cit.*, p. 121.

On the other hand, there has been considerably less progress towards the over-all planning of country aid programmes with a view to the pooling of programme resources from all sources for maximum effect.

Informational Exchange at Programme Headquarters

Inter-programme co-ordination, at the very least, involves the periodic exchange of information among headquarters staffs. Such exchange developed rather sporadically, but by 1954 it had become a regular feature of the relations of the TAB secretariat with its American counterpart—at first MSA, then FOA, and now ICA—in Washington. Conferences of the two staff groups alternated between Washington and New York, with a view to discussing programme trends, possibly overlaps, and common operational problems. For some years the draft UN programme has been sent annually to ICA/Washington for scrutiny, project by project. When the proposed UN programme is before TAC, the U.S. representative may reserve 'the United States position' with reference to any UN agency project suspected by ICA of overlapping, or conflicting, with a similar ICA undertaking. ICA headquarters, in the meantime, transmits to the directors of all U.S. Operations Missions a letter with a copy of the UN programme for the country concerned. Country desk officers at ICA headquarters sometimes attach comments or queries about specific projects. Each country mission director is asked to review in detail and resolve problems on the spot with the RTAR or UN agency representative as the case may be. When agreement cannot be reached—this rarely happens—the mission director is instructed to communicate with Washington—by cable if necessary—so that ICA headquarters may take up the matter with the TAB secretariat.[8]

Differences in the composition and time-table of ICA's annual programme have made it impracticable to submit the programme in advance of final approval to UN headquarters. In this connection alone, it must be remembered that the annual outlays for technical assistance alone by the United States Government are several times greater than total EPTA alloca-

[8] It should be noted that ICA has recognized WHO as the co-ordinating agency in the field of health and that the headquarters staffs of the two organizations consult together constantly as to their respective health programmes.

tions. Also, some of ICA's technical operations are tied in with capital financing through developmental grants. Be this as it may, the annual review of the draft EPTA programme by ICA, during recent years, has led to the conclusion that duplication in project requests between it and the ICA programme has all but disappeared.

As we shall see shortly, this improvement in co-ordination may be attributed partly to the enhanced role of the RTAR and partly to the impact of stronger national co-ordinating machinery in a growing number of countries. As early as 1952, the Executive Chairman of TAB initiated the issuance of procedural instructions to the RTARs and country liaison officers regarding co-operation with the field representatives of regional and bilateral programmes of technical assistance in their respective jurisdictions. Similar instructions were simultaneously sent by Washington to United States diplomatic and consular officers then having responsibility for U.S. economic and technical aid programmes. Three years later, in 1955, these instructions were strengthened on both sides—by emphasizing the importance of holding at least twice a year meetings of United Nations and United States field staffs for a systematic review of country programme objectives and trends. In cases where both ICA and EPTA were providing aid in closely related fields, it was suggested that advance discussion of the general content of the advice should take place so as to avoid conflicting recommendations on the same subject. To quote from the text of these instructions:

> If there are significant differences in conceptual approach or in methodology between the two programs, the UN and U.S. representatives should either (*a*) achieve common agreement among themselves . . . or (*b*) jointly present the two viewpoints to the host government so that it may decide whether it wishes to utilize two approaches (presumably in different geographic areas), to choose one, or to select elements of each. [Such differences, incidentally, have not always been easy to resolve in education and community development projects.]

Since 1955, ICA/Washington has repeated its co-ordinative instructions in even stronger terms.[9] In order to keep the U.S. field staffs acquainted with the progress of EPTA generally, ICA/Washington has from time to time distributed to the USOMs copies of relevant issues of the UN *Technical Assistance*

[9] See the *ICA Programming Process: Procedural Instructions* (Washington: G.P.O., 1959).

Newsletter. Conversely, during 1957, ICA prepared for the use of TAB and the UN agencies a special publication summarizing U.S. Point Four operations for the preceding and current years and those contemplated for 1958.

Contact with the Colombo Plan both by TAB and by the United States Government is maintained by the assignment of 'liaison' officers at its Bureau of Technical Co-operation at Colombo (Ceylon). Ordinarily, the RTAR for Ceylon serves in this capacity for TAB. In addition, both TAB and ICA are represented by observers at the meetings of the Colombo Plan Council for Technical Co-operation.[10] The Director of the Bureau frequently visits UN programmes in countries receiving Colombo Plan assistance. The Colombo Plan Council has taken the view that the co-ordination of requests for aid must be the ultimate responsibility of recipient governments. Even so, it has ventured to suggest as desirable such forms of co-operation with the UN and U.S. programmes as uniformity of treatment of experts and trainees; the briefing and orientation of one agency's expert by heads of mission and other staff of another agency; exchange of information on experts; mutual help in recruiting experts; and the collaboration of different agencies in building up institutions in Asia.

Within the Latin American region, relations between the UN system and the OAS, in the economic and social field, have had two aspects. One has concerned the relations of ECLA with the Inter-American Economic and Social Council; the other, the relations of EPTA with the OAS Technical Co-operation programme in which various inter-American agencies participate. At the outset of ECLA, the U.S. Government, which had originally opposed its creation, evinced considerable fear that its activities would duplicate those of the IA/ECOSOC. Indeed, in 1951, there reportedly was a move on the part of Washington for the consolidation of ECLA with the latter body. Once, however, it was realized that the Latin American republics were solidly in favour of continuing ECLA, this idea was abandoned. In the meantime, during the first session of

[10] The RTAR at Bangkok, for example, has represented the Executive Chairman of TAB at these meetings on a number of occasions. From 1950 through 1957, trainees from seventeen Colombo Plan countries totalled 5,622, while 792 experts had been negotiated for. *Report for 1956–57 by the Council for Technical Co-operation in South and South-East Asia* (London: H.M.S.O., 1957).

ECLA (1948), representatives of the two bodies had met and agreed on a rough division of labour between them, ECLA's work to be concerned especially with 'those extra-continental aspects of Latin American economic problems and with those arising from world economic maladjustment.'[11] At the time it was also decided that reports be exchanged between the two bodies and that ECLA's secretariat should co-ordinate its work with IA/ECOSOC 'through appropriate liaison.' To further such liaison a Committee on Co-ordination at the secretariat level was established in 1951. This working group, which meets twice a year, has facilitated staff consultation regarding the preparation of the annual economic surveys of Latin America. Over the years, for example, the two secretariats have also co-operated to achieve greater statistical uniformity and to avoid duplication in the collection of statistical data; on the training of statisticians; and on studies of Latin American trade, commodity problems (*e.g.*, coffee), and economic development programming.

At the working level there is no serious problem of substantive overlap or conflict. But at the inter-governmental level certain difficulties have persisted. These have stemmed primarily from the fact that individual governments are not co-ordinated internally so as to speak with the same voice in ECLA and in IA/ECOSOC. By reason of this, differing approaches to the trade problem have at times emerged. At the first session of the ECLA Trade Committee, in 1956, a proposal was adopted which led to a meeting of representatives of central banks as a first step towards the 'multilateralization' of trade in Latin America. A year later ECLA itself put forward the 'free regional market' idea. Meanwhile, in 1954, an Inter-American Conference of Ministers of Finance had requested a study of the same subject by the IA/ECOSOC secretariat. The report of this study, presented to the Inter-American Economic Conference of 1957 at Buenos Aires, advocated a somewhat different solution to the problem of trade and payments.[12]

Until 1958, the U.S. Government appeared to feel that ECLA placed too much emphasis on public as against private

[11] John S. Houston, *Latin America in the United Nations* (New York: Carnegie Endowment for International Peace, 1956), p. 228.

[12] The ECLA staff had no part in the planning for the Buenos Aires conference. It is to be noted that the views of the IMF with respect to payments arrangements were closer to the position of the IA/ECOSOC than to that of the ECLA secretariat.

investment; nor was the Washington Administration sympathetic towards the Latin American fondness for general economic planning which was so strikingly revealed at ECLA meetings. However, the demand for large-scale economic assistance from Latin American countries gathered such momentum that Washington executed a complete reversal of policy and gave its full support to the project for an Inter-American Development Bank (referred to above) emanating from the 'Committee of Twenty-One' which was set up by the Meeting of American Foreign Ministers in September 1958—a proposal that had been discussed for some years in ECLA circles.

In 1949, the IA/ECOSOC, animated by President Truman's Point Four proposal and with general encouragement from Washington, established a committee to prepare a technical assistance programme to be conducted by OAS and its affiliated agencies. It was decided that this programme, modest in scale, should be confined to training and research centres designed to meet regional needs. A Co-ordinating Committee on Technical Assistance was created in 1950 'to perform functions broadly comparable to those of its TAB counterpart' in EPTA.[13] The Secretary-General of OAS served as *ex officio* chairman of this Committee. Six years later, in 1956, the Committee was replaced by a Technical Co-operation Board with a full-time Executive Director, whose office (located in the Pan American Union) became the Board's secretariat.[14]

As early as August 1950, the TAB secretariat in New York initiated liaison arrangements with the Co-ordinating Committee staff in Washington. These arrangements provided for mutual reporting procedures, the interchange of requests for technical assistance from Latin American Governments, and reciprocal representation (without vote) at meetings of the two governing bodies. In view of the small scope and functional limitations of the OAS programme, it has been easy to avoid overlapping projects in the training field, particularly since the demand for such facilities is so much greater than the available resources.

[13] Sharp, *International Technical Assistance*, *op. cit.*, p. 108. Agencies participating in the OAS technical co-operation programme include (in addition to the Pan American Union) the Inter-American Indian Institute, the Inter-American Institute of Agricultural Sciences, the Inter-American Statistical Institute, the American International Institute for the Protection of Childhood, the Pan American Institute of Geography and History, and the Pan American Sanitary Bureau.

[14] See IA/ECOSOC Doc. ES-Res.29/56-E, approved 28 Sept. 1956.

During recent years plans have been under consideration for an expansion of OAS activities in the domain of technical assistance. The provision of 500 fellowships was recommended by the OAS Council in November 1957, while a year later this body decided to develop an intensive and large-scale programme of technical training, including assistance to universities and technical institutes in the American countries and the training of professional personnel for the staffing of national economic development activities. The 1959 OAS budget provides funds for an appreciable expansion in these directions, as well as for supplying direct advisory services to governments on request either from the Pan American Union staff or by consultants engaged on a temporary basis. If and as OAS broadens the scope of its technical assistance operations, the problem of correlating them with cognate activities sponsored by the UN and Unesco in the Latin American region will call for careful scrutiny by the programme planners on both sides.

In passing, a special word about UNICEF's liaison with other aid-granting organizations in the welfare domain is in order. So far as ICA is concerned, most of UNICEF's regional directors visit Washington once or twice a year to talk over country assistance programmes at the working level. At UNICEF headquarters there is a liaison office for non-governmental organizations which devotes full time to contact with such agencies. An NGO/UNICEF advisory committee has existed for many years, comprising virtually all of the major private welfare agencies active in the international field. This committee is represented at each UNICEF Executive Board meeting.

Co-operative Arrangements at the Country Level

Useful and desirable as liaison between programme headquarters staffs is, it does not—indeed it cannot—deal with the core of the problem of inter-programme co-ordination. Co-ordination at the centre must be supplemented, if not preceded, by co-ordination at the base. By the time project requests reach programme headquarters things may have gone too far for any fundamental alteration of country programmes. It is not enough to prevent duplication of project undertakings, but, as TAB has observed, there should be a positive attempt to enhance 'the value of projects through concerted effort to ensure the best timing of each action, and the most effective combination of assistance coming from different sources.'[15] This calls for the joint endeavours of the RTAR, programme field office staffs, project experts, and the recipient government's own co-ordinating machinery (if any).

For some years TAC has exhorted governments to improve the co-ordination of EPTA resources with other available programmes of economic and technical assistance. The representatives of many of the recipient countries, however, have been sensitive to any implication that the UN or any other outside group might interfere with their 'sovereign' right to determine their own aid-co-ordinating procedures. National economic development planning, in their view, is solely the responsibility of each government concerned. This reaction has prompted representatives of the donor governments, in TAC discussions, to stress time and again that they had no desire to 'dictate' what kind of national co-ordinating machinery should be established.[16]

According to TAB's survey for 1958, the functions of the co-ordinating machinery of thirty-one (out of forty-two) countries included other technical assistance programmes, bilateral and multilateral. This total, which at first glance is impressive, needs to be interpreted. In perhaps half of these thirty-one countries, such machinery is of so recent origin, or has so little authority, or is so poorly staffed, as not to be particularly effective. It is only in a relatively small number of countries that the role of national co-ordinative units in across-the-board programme co-ordination is a controlling one. In some of this group of countries the governments have developed 'a standard procedure under which all individual ministries are required to specify, in their requests for technical assistance, the relationship, if any, of an Expanded Programme project to the operating or planned projects under any other programmes.'[17]

For the majority of aid-receiving countries, however, the development of inter-programme co-ordination hinges upon the existence of informal co-operative attitudes and relationships between UN and other programme staffs within the country.

[15] Quoted in ECOSOC Resolution 659A (XXIV), 30 July 1957.
[16] For a typical illustration of such a clash of views within TAC, see UN Doc. E/TAC/142, 16 July 1957.
[17] *Annual Report of the TAB for 1956*, ECOSOC, O.R.: 24th Sess., 1957, Suppl. No. 5, p. 13.

It goes without saying that this differs widely from country to country in terms of relevant political, psychological, and administrative factors. No two situations are exactly alike. The development of good relationships depends largely on the initiative of the key officials concerned, in particular, the RTAR and USOM Director.

There is perhaps no better way to illuminate the ramifications of the problem than by looking at how it is conditioned in specific countries. The countries contained in the sample that follows (all of which were visited by the writer) are widely distributed geographically as well as by population, territorial size, administrative structure, and the dimensions of foreign aid received.

In Country A, a subtle blend of nationalism and pride has produced a marked sensitivity towards the acceptance of foreign aid from any 'official' source. Until quite recently, even the UN was visualized as being dominated by the United States and the colonial Powers. As the national image of the UN has grown more favourable, the reaction to taking UN aid has changed from a negative to a more positive one. Although the United States programme is now viewed somewhat more favourably than formerly, there is still a distinct preference for multilateral as against bilateral aid. The negativistic approach of the United States Ambassador of a few years ago, who reportedly was opposed to any form of technical aid outside the fields of health, agriculture, and education, accounted in part for the persistence of a critical attitude towards proposals for United States aid. On the other hand, the small size of the UN programme, its atomization into small lumps under different agencies, and lack of supplies and equipment, tended to militate in favour of the U.S. programme.

In this particular country there was an inter-agency committee for the co-ordination of UN programme requests, with a small staff located in the Foreign Ministry. While in theory this committee had jurisdiction over bilateral aid requests as well, it seldom extended its purview beyond the UN programme. Negotiations for U.S. Point Four aid were usually handled at a higher level (Ambassador with Minister of Foreign Affairs or President) in view of their 'diplomatic' implications.[18] There

[18] The USOM Director admitted to the writer that he would prefer to have his mission located physically outside the Embassy—in order, as it were, 'to divorce its operations from diplomacy.'

was no single organ for national economic planning, this function being dispersed among several agencies.

The relations between the RTAR and the USOM directorate appeared to be friendly and informal. From time to time the Director (or Deputy Director) of USOM and the RTAR lunched together to talk over 'what the country needed most.' Programme documents were being regularly exchanged. The RTAR remarked in the writer's presence that he regarded Point Four 'as his natural ally,' adding that he 'bent backward to co-operate.' In two fields an agreement had been reached for a division of functions between EPTA and the U.S. programme. One of these was industrial productivity, where it was decided that the ILO should work through the Ministry of Labour while the U.S. would deal directly with private industry. The second field had to do with industrial development, where it was agreed that TAA should be responsible for advising the central bank on the organization of economic research while Point Four would concern itself with the training of supervisors, managers, and technicians in co-operation with private firms and labour unions. The Labor attaché of the U.S. Embassy made it a practice to keep in close touch with local ILO office and project personnel. On his initiative it was proposed that the best trainees graduating from the ILO-aided Labour Institute should be sent to the United States (at its expense) for a three-month period in order to get a practical course on the application of safety methods. ILO reacted favourably to this offer of co-operation. On the other hand, the audio-visual specialist at USOM had offered to exchange instructional materials with a Unesco-sponsored Film Institute but had elicited no response.

In this country the most notable instance of inter-programme co-operation was the malaria eradication campaign, then being financed jointly by the host government, UNICEF, and PASB (which handled the U.S. Government's special contribution). On the group of international consultants set up to advise the Directing Council of the programme were representatives of WHO, UNICEF, and ICA (USOM). This group was also available to give guidance to the operating units of the programme. Interestingly enough, the only snag in running this programme, so far as foreign participation was concerned, reportedly had arisen from the failure of the local UNICEF and PASB offices to clear budget requests with each other on one occasion.

A large private United States foundation was carrying on an extensive research programme designed to increase agricultural production. The resident FAO experts working in similar fields had established close contacts with the scientific staff of the foundation's project, which was viewed most favourably by them and by the national Ministry of Agriculture.

To an outside observer what seemed to be most needed in this country was high-level advice and assistance on how it might better organize itself for long-range economic planning. Most of the technical projects under way appeared to be justifiable in and of themselves, but there was lacking any integrated attack on the basic problems of the economy. Five different economic planning agencies were said to have tried in vain to persuade the census bureau to adopt improved statistical methods. The unfortunate impact of extreme nationalism on the one side and of internal organizational competition on the other had hardly been conducive to a balanced utilization of foreign aid resources.

In Country B, the United States Government had been in the 'aid business' for many years and its chief of mission, by reason of his long period of service, had been able to build up a confidential relationship with many of the top government leaders. By contrast, the UN programme, still relatively new, had suffered from discontinuity in RTARs. As in Country A, there was a small, rather ineffective unit in the Foreign Office which was supposed to co-ordinate EPTA proposals. For U.S. Point Four matters, however, the Director of Foreign Commerce (at a higher hierarchical level) served as principal co-ordinator. On paper there existed an Economic Planning Commission but it virtually never met. The government at the time was in effect run by its three most powerful ministers (of Foreign Affairs, Finance, and Justice), backed by the army.

In this setting, it was customary for the national authorities to consult the Director of USOM prior to deciding whether to request expanded aid from the UN programme. Whenever there appeared to be potential competition between the U.S. and UN programmes the USOM Director would usually offer to withdraw in favour of the latter. He made it a point to keep in touch with the RTAR and UN agency directors frequently. Social contacts between the United States and UN project personnel were said to be friendly but irregular. By tacit agreement, the U.S. programme was directed towards 'grass roots' demonstration projects serving 'the greatest number of little people,' the UN programme tending to operate more centrally—with and through the upper level bureaucracy. The Director of USOM, while well impressed with the quality of the UN technicians, ventured the observation that they were becoming somewhat 'aggressive and expansionist.' The chief shortcoming in the UN programme, in his view, was that it tried to get results too quickly. (Parenthetically, the writer discovered in several countries a rather condescending attitude towards UN technical assistance activities on the part of certain U.S. mission personnel—an attitude compounded of misinformation and of being unduly impressed by the dollar dimensions of U.S. operations.)

In Country C, much larger in population and territorial size than the two preceding countries, U.S. technical co-operation outlays, at the time of the writer's visit, ran approximately $3 million a year—about six times higher than total EPTA expenditures. The latter included two relatively sizable regional programmes. There was also one small OAS-sponsored undertaking—the Pan American Training Centre for the Evaluation of Natural Resources, for which the operating agency was the Pan American Institute of Geography and History.

At the time, a National Committee under the Foreign Ministry and representing various subject-matter ministries, banks, and private ministries, was responsible for co-ordinating UN and OAS programme requests. This Committee had an Executive Director and a relatively good but small staff attached to the office of the Foreign Minister. Point Four negotiations were channelled through a completely separate high-level unit in the Ministry of Finance, the staff of which had benefited from Point Four training assistance.

For some years prior to the writer's visit, there had been difficulties in the relations of the RTAR and USOM. One of the directors of USOM, an ex-newspaper man and a political appointee, was said to have 'gummed up the works.' Point

Four, commented the RTAR, seemed to change its policy every six months. The successor to this USOM Director and the then U.S. Ambassador were reportedly 'at swords' points' much of the time. Then came a new USOM Director of a very different sort whose relations with his Embassy were excellent. He and the RTAR (who had not changed during this entire period) were said to get along famously together. Their practice was to lunch together privately once a month for frank discussion and interchange of information. According to certain of the USOM staff, the results of these meetings were not communicated to them—a procedure they were inclined to criticize.

However this may be, both men made much of the 'fine co-operative spirit' that then prevailed among U.S. and UN personnel. At the RTAR's request, for example, ICA had furnished an irrigation specialist for one of the regional projects under UN sponsorship. A joint ICA-Unesco staff committee had been established to work out a division of labour as between the basic elementary training, secondary education, and industrial training fields. The U.S. Labor Attaché was keeping in close touch with, and informally advising, ILO's industrial apprenticeship project. UNICEF was using ICA-aided health centres for the distribution of milk. A public health dentistry course was about to be organized by ICA jointly with PASB. ICA was handling the health aspects of an extensive river valley development project under a team of FAO and Unesco specialists. By mutual understanding, a division of function had been worked out between the U.S.-aided agricultural *servicio* and the FAO regional office, ICA agreeing not to 'invade' the field of forestry or fisheries. For an agricultural credit programme ICA was providing an extension adviser and FAO a rural credit expert. Before launching an irrigation project in another part of the country, ICA had consulted FAO and got its approval of a demonstration survey. These are illustrations of the possibilities of inter-programme co-operation on an *ad hoc* basis at an early stage of project development.

The real weakness in this country's arrangements, much as in Country A, was the absence of strong, integrated machinery for general economic planning and the assessment of technical assistance needs in relation thereto. Some 'sector' planning was being done by the Economic Development Bank and there was an Economic Council appointed by the President chiefly on a political basis. The latter body issued reports, largely of an academic character, but nothing happened since it had no actual contact with either the U.S. or UN aid programmes.

Country D is a small but relatively advanced nation whose requests for foreign technical aid have been comparatively modest. Shortly before the writer's visit, a new RTAR had arrived on the scene. It appeared that the USOM staff had found the previous holder of the post rather difficult to work with: he had taken little initiative towards co-operation. But the USOM staff was delighted with the new appointee, who was at once invited to attend a Point Four staff meeting. In this country, foreign aid was then handled by a large inter-departmental committee with which the RTAR sat. This committee dealt with all technical assistance requests, including Point Four. Decisions were reportedly reached only after long hours of wrangling and inter-ministerial bargaining. Nor was there any pretence at comprehensive economic development programming.

Even so, the U.S. and UN agency staffs had contrived informally to develop co-operative arrangements with a view to broadening the scope and improving the quality of a number of going projects. Only one instance of actual duplication came to the writer's attention. ICA and PASB had each proposed to provide a sanitary engineer on the optimistic assumption that a sanitary engineering division would be established in the Ministry of Health. Meanwhile, the Minister was forced to resign and nothing was done. Consequently, two foreign sanitary engineers found themselves with no counterparts. This situation, however, could hardly be charged to poor liaison between the two programmes. ICA had provided a number of lecturers for courses in Public Administration being conducted under TAA sponsorship at the Faculty of Economic Sciences, and six of the best graduates from these courses were being sent at ICA's expense to Puerto Rico for additional training. A U.S. public health administrator was acting as adviser to a PASB-UNICEF rural health centre, while the national Ministry of Health had set up a committee to co-ordinate WHO and Point Four health activities in the country.

In this country there were two OAS training projects. One of these—a Workshop on the Administration of Children's

Services—had just been terminated after five years of operation by the American International Institute for the Protection of Childhood. During the life of the Workshop a number of social welfare workers from other countries had participated while on fellowship appointments from the UN Bureau of Social Affairs in New York. The other OAS undertaking—on Technical Education for the Improvement of Agricultural and Rural Life—was being administered by a zonal office of the Inter-American Institute of Agricultural Sciences (headquarters in Costa Rica). The activities of this office were concerned mainly with training and demonstration work in the field of agricultural statistics and extension. It was responsible for organizing a series of twelve-week seminars for trainees in the five countries of the zone. In addition to the seven technicians attached to the office staff, FAO, Point Four, and the Rockefeller Foundation had all made available visiting specialists for instructional purposes. A number of FAO fellows had been assigned to attend the seminars. FAO had also given seed and fertilizers for one of the Institute's other field projects.

Country E, located in a different part of the world, has had a long tradition of using foreign advisers, both official and private. Accordingly, it has been inclined to accept foreign aid from any source and for any purpose consistent with its national foreign policy. EPTA runs one of its largest-scale operations in this country, while the U.S. Government maintains a substantial programme of technical projects and developmental loans.[19] The Ford Foundation had helped to initiate a variety of rural development undertakings. Several European Governments, Japan, and Pakistan offered fellowships in special fields on a bilateral basis. A long-range, multi-purpose river development project (covering an area bigger than that of TVA) was being handled by a United States private management firm on contract. The International Bank had made several loans to the government for its development programme.

For over ten years the government of this country has had an elaborately structured National Plan Organization, and it is now (1959) well into its second 'seven-year plan.' The co-ordinating unit for UN technical assistance is meshed with the Plan

[19] For 1958, the U.S. technical co-operation programme in this country exceeded in amount the global allocations from EPTA resources.

Organization and reports to its Managing Director. This arrangement facilitates top-level clearance of all significant foreign aid projects in relation to over-all plan priorities. The head of the co-ordinating unit checks other aid programmes in the course of scrutinizing annual requests to UN agencies in order to spot any obvious duplication.

At the staff level, within the three major aid-granting organizations (ICA, TAB, and Ford), there were excellent and close working relations. The RTAR kept in frequent contact with the Ford Foundation representative as well as with the USOM Director. The RTAR and the latter had arrived at a number of informal understandings regarding areas of operation for EPTA and ICA, respectively. Thus, for instance, it was agreed that the U.S. group in industrial development should focus on stimulating the private sector of the economy while TAA experts would concentrate on advising the technical staffs of the Ministry of Industries. In the agricultural field the United States would help to implant methodology for extension work and aid in forest management, grazing and watershed development; FAO, on the other hand, would assist with irrigation planning, soils surveys, milk production, cotton-breeding, and nutrition programmes. It was further understood that ICA should continue to handle major projects in public administration, TAA confining itself mainly to the operation of a clerical training centre. On the initiative of the chief of the Public Administration Division of USOM, an informal co-ordinative committee for this subject-matter area had been set up, including representation of USOM, the TAA clerical training centre, the ICA-supported Institute of Administrative Affairs (in the University), and the ICA-financed administrative division of the National Plan Organization. This committee met every Saturday to exchange experience and consider future needs. When the regional representative of the UN Bureau of Social Affairs visited the country, the RTAR advised against any UN action in the community development field, since this was already being activated by Point Four and the Ford Foundation.

Numerous instances of inter-programme participation in going projects were encountered, only a few of which can be cited here. The ICA-supported advisers to the Manpower Development Division of the Plan Organization were conducting an informal evaluation of an ILO-assisted Vocational Training Centre at the request of the ILO team leader, this service, incidentally, being performed without charge to ILO. The regional water development project mentioned above had not only stemmed from proposals made by an FAO survey mission in 1956, but FAO was later asked—and agreed—to supply to the contracting firm expert advisers on hydrology, irrigation, soil surveys, and fertilizers, whose salaries were reimbursed by the government out of 'funds-in-trust.' Point Four had provided nearly all of the equipment for the ICAO Training Centre at the municipal airport, and USOM staff specialists in aeronautics had helped the ICAO team with its installation.

The Ford-supported staff of the Economic Bureau of the Plan Organization was working closely with the TAA experts attached to the Ministry of Industries. The findings of these experts, according to the head of the Bureau, had frequently pointed to the need of legislation or revamped operating policies of vital interest to the long-range planners. The Bureau had also found useful the special knowledge of a visiting FAO agricultural economist.

All in all, this country presented an impressive case of inter-programme co-operation at the source. The combination of an experienced, well-staffed planning organization on the national side, with broad-gauged, resourceful staff personnel on the aid-granting side, had produced a favourable environment in which to circumvent the hurdles of agency separatism.

Country F, an equally important aid-receiving area, exemplifies the impact of reasonably effective procedures for the furtherance of inter-programme collaboration. The government of this country is said to have a bias in favour of multilateral as against bilateral technical aid because of a 'colonialism psychosis' which, although declining, still persists. Even so, this country has accepted large quantities of technical as well as direct grant and loan assistance from the United States and, recently, on a smaller scale from the Soviet Union. The Ford Foundation maintains in this country its largest overseas programme, embracing sizable rural community development, education, economic research, regional planning and public administration projects. On the multilateral side, the multifarious aid activities of the UN system aggregate more than twice as much in dollar terms than in any other recipient country. In addition, this country is the beneficiary of considerable aid through the Colombo Plan. Now about to enter its third 'five-year plan,' this country has a relatively strong National Planning Commission. The government channels all internal requests for foreign aid, regardless of source, through a foreign aid unit in the Ministry of Finance. Each year this unit circularizes all the central ministries, state government authorities, and the University Grants Commission as to the kinds and conditions of available aid, covering experts, trainee grants, and supplies. Within the co-ordinating unit, as noted in Chapter 9, there are three branches dealing with technical assistance—one for U.S. Point Four, another for EPTA, and a third for the Colombo Plan and small bilateral programmes. Separate branches are concerned with capital aid in its various forms. The Ford Foundation proposals are handled on still a different basis within the Department of Economic Affairs of the Ministry.

Both the RTAR and the USOM Director were in agreement that these co-ordinative arrangements were working fairly well so far as inter-programme relations were concerned. There was no problem of project overlap in a country whose staggering needs far exceeded available resources, domestic and foreign. Constant exchange of information takes place between the TAB office and USOM concerning programme preparation and implementation. Each year the RTAR sends a copy of the draft country programme to USOM for advance comment. There is frequent consultation between the functional division directors of USOM and their UN agency counterparts—in industry, agriculture, health, education, and labour. In the health field, an inter-agency co-ordinating committee composed of representatives of WHO, UNICEF, ICA, the Ford and Rockefeller Foundations, was established several years ago on WHO's initiative. WHO provides the secretary. In this committee, which now meets quarterly, current and future project proposals are discussed and recommendations made as to the most appropriate sources of foreign aid in terms of programme policy. Recently the committee proposed a new graduate nursing course, training facilities for young doctors, and a public health indoctrination programme, the groundwork for which was done by WHO, UNICEF, and the Ford Foundation. These proposals were subsequently forwarded by the national Ministry of Health to the Foreign Aid co-ordinating unit—following clearance with the Central Council of State Health Ministers.

ICA and ILO had co-operated on a number of undertakings. Thus, for an ILO-aided vocational training project ICA agreed to provide supplies and equipment after negotiations initiated by the head of the ILO branch office. In one case, however, there had been complications. In 1952, ILO had helped to set up a productivity centre in a large state capital. Five years later the Ministry of Commerce and Industry established a National Productivity Council with ICA aid. There apparently had been sketchy prior consultation with the National Planning Commission but none with the Minister of Labour, who reportedly was highly displeased. The earlier productivity centre appeared to be heading towards insignificance when the Minister of Commerce, realizing the trouble, sent a letter to the head of the local ILO office inviting him to become a member of the Governing Body of the new Productivity Council.[20] The latter agreed on condition that the training element be stressed, which the Governing Body then recognized. At the time of the writer's visit, ILO was shifting the focus of its aid to the new productivity project, although the provincial centre was still operating.

With regard to the Ford Foundation's programme, the local representative explained that it was his practice to consult USOM and the UN agencies concerned prior to formulating proposals for consideration at Foundation headquarters in New York. This practice, incidentally, is followed in all countries where there are sizable Ford Foundation economic and social programmes.[21] The rationale of the Foundation's overseas activities has been not to encroach upon functional areas appropriate for ICA or a UN agency to handle with the resources at

[20] He was of course a national of the host country.

[21] From 1950 to 1958, the Ford Foundation appropriated some $75 million for field programmes in under-developed countries, chiefly in the Middle East and Asia. In 1958, it made available $300,000 to the UN and FAO to help finance plans for 1960 censuses in Asian countries. In 1959, a team of thirteen American agricultural experts, recruited by the Ford Foundation at the request of the Government of India, reported on the possibilities of increasing food production by applying improved techniques. *The New York Times*, 21 April 1959. About a year later the Foundation appropriated $10·5 million for a pilot programme to demonstrate how India's food output might be expanded. *Ibid.*, 28 April 1960.

its disposal. As one Ford Foundation country representative put it, 'our task is to help plan and create new institutions.' This means the identification of urgent problems on which nothing is being done and then the application of wisdom in formulating and implementing feasible demonstration projects. Being non-governmental, a philanthropic foundation cannot be suspected of political motivations and it can operate as a truly disinterested party. In the country here under consideration, Ford Foundation teams had co-operated with ICA on community development programmes and with WHO on an environmental sanitation undertaking.

To sum up: the situation in Country F, while still a bit spotty, was conducive to co-operative inter-programme relationships. There was no serious problem of substantive overlap. The chief unresolved task seemed to be how to eliminate dead or dubious projects from public programmes already under way; but this problem reaches beyond programme co-ordination into matters of programme operation and evaluation to be considered in the next chapter.

Country G, the final case in our sample, although much smaller than the preceding one, has benefited from a very substantial flow of United States economic aid since its independence and now is utilizing a diversified programme of UN technical assistance of modest dimensions. Its national co-ordinating machinery, roughly similar in structure and functions to that of Country F, appeared to be staffed with somewhat more experienced personnel, who gave evidence of doing a first-rate job of screening project requests to all aid-granting agencies. During 1958 the co-ordination office had issued a report describing every project receiving, or due to receive, assistance from UN organizations, ICA, or Colombo Plan countries.

Relations between the former Resident Representative and USOM had reportedly not been too cordial. His successor, however, lost no time in cultivating the Point Four mission, the Director of which early invited him to attend a senior staff meeting with a view to explaining the UN programme. The two men sat down together and went over the programme, sections of which were submitted to USOM staff division heads for comment.

In general, contacts between UN and ICA project personnel,

while growing, appeared to be less close than in countries E and F. The public administration staff of USOM, for example, knew scarcely any of the UN experts in related fields. The head of an ICAO training centre volunteered the observation that an 'obstructionist' attitude towards ICAO seemed to exist in local ICA circles. Even so, ICA had agreed to supply some equipment for the training centre.

In the domain of health, WHO and ICA had apparently gone through a period of mutual criticism and working at cross purposes. The situation had improved—partly as a result of better briefing of ICA health personnel concerning WHO's role as the general co-ordinator of international health work. As in country F, there was an inter-programme co-ordinating committee for health, but it was said 'to be dying a natural death' because of the preference of the national health authorities for dealing directly with each donor agency.

On the other hand, the writer's attention was called to a good example of inter-programme co-operation in agriculture. On the initiative of an FAO expert on sampling and experimental design, the government had set up a committee on agricultural surveys, with this expert as chairman. One of his first decisions was to co-opt to the committee two ICA experts on statistics and agricultural economics. Moreover, a TAA industrial economist attached to the staff of the National Economic Council was co-operating closely with ICA experts serving the Industrial Development Centre. The ILO adviser on co-operative banking admitted that he had greatly profited from suggestions received from an ICA technician advising the Labour Education Centre. Another interesting case of co-operation at the working level was the establishment, on UNICEF's initiative, of a co-ordinating committee of 'supply' agencies representing UNICEF, ICA, and various voluntary groups. This committee met monthly to consider local distribution problems.

In this country, one could detect a distinct 'cooling-off' not only towards the acceptance of United States bilateral aid in particular, but towards the use of foreign technical advisers in general. In a number of fields (*e.g.*, public administration) the feeling was that there were enough trained local people to do the job on their own. Notwithstanding, the UN programme of assistance in this area is unlikely to diminish in volume in the immediate future if only because it consists chiefly of continuing projects.

UN Field Relations with Colombo Plan Operations

In three countries—Pakistan, Thailand, and the Philippines—the writer had opportunity to examine briefly the procedures by which Colombo Plan technical aid operations are governed and related to other aid programmes. The Colombo Plan has not found it necessary to develop any special machinery at the country level—if only because of the relatively small size of its programmes. Each donor country handles aid requests through its diplomatic mission in the recipient country, or, in the case of (British) Commonwealth Members, through the High Commissioner's office. Typically, one or two members of the mission staff are designated to deal with Colombo Plan matters.

To take a specific example: in Karachi, the Colombo Plan officer on the Canadian High Commissioner's staff is the local channel for the receipt of requests for aid. What actually happens is that the High Commissioner sends a letter to the Division of Economic Affairs of the Pakistan Government indicating the 'ceiling' tentatively set by Ottawa for Pakistan for the ensuing year. Meanwhile, his Colombo Plan officer scouts the ministries as to their needs and the types of requests they might properly submit. The Division of Economic Affairs, as the general co-ordinating unit for all foreign aid (except from the United States), screens the requests and sends those approved to the High Commissioner's office. The Colombo Plan officer, with the High Commissioner's approval, then selects the proposals to be authorized, and informal bilateral agreements are negotiated on the spot with the Pakistan authorities—usually through an exchange of letters—without the need of prior clearance by Ottawa.

There appeared to be a steady flow of information between the local Colombo Plan authorities—British and Australian as well as Canadian—and the USOM and TAB offices. All programmes were reported to be 'presenting a united front' to the government. There was no longer any effort to sell 'weak' projects, once rejected, to some other programme. Among examples of

Colombo Plan participation in UN-aided projects were the provision of machinery for a power house by Canada (in the FAO-assisted Ganges flood control project), and the financing by Australia of equipment for an ITU-aided telecommunications project. A training centre in West Pakistan for radio personnel (a part of this project) was being operated by Colombo Plan experts from the British post office. The Australian Government had paid for the travel of five Pakistan trainees to Australia to examine radio transmitters there.

The procedures employed by the United Kingdom and by Australia in Bangkok seemed to be equally informal, flexible and decentralized—with some variations as to detail. So far as the United Kingdom is concerned, there is no allocation by London of money to countries in advance, the appropriation being made in two lump sums—one for trainees and the other for experts and equipment. Aid requests from the Thai Government are sent to the British Embassy, where the First Secretary divides his time between Colombo Plan and ECAFE matters. It is his practice to circulate to the TAB office, USOM, and the Asia Foundation lists of past and current candidates for trainee grants under the Colombo Plan, and these offices reciprocate.[22] Complete clearance is thus possible during the two or three months necessary for processing candidacies. The First Secretary could recall only a few instances where the government had apparently tried to play off two countries against each other in the Colombo Plan. The appointment of trainees from among candidates nominated by the government is made by an Embassy selection committee, which interviews individuals. The government may be advised to withdraw candidates from time to time—without any reasons being given.

As regards Australia, Colombo Plan funds are earmarked in Canberra to countries based on the volume of pressures for assistance, nearby countries tending to be favoured slightly over the others (*e.g.*, Thailand). The Colombo Plan officer at the Australian Embassy circulated to the Thai Government co-ordinating unit a memorandum calling attention to available technical aid funds and pointing especially to certain fields that are likely to receive priority consideration by the donor government. Thus, in 1958, the Thai Government was

[22] There is only a handful of Colombo Plan experts in Thailand.

encouraged to ask for trainee grants relating to a lignite production project, which was then the only undertaking in Thailand receiving capital aid through the Colombo Plan.

The clearance of aid requests among programmes, in the opinion of the Australian Colombo Plan officer in Bangkok, did not present much of a problem. This was principally the business of the government itself. Inter-programme staff meetings were held from time to time and exchange of information regularly took place. UN experts, he noted, often approached Colombo Plan authorities for equipment, and he was favourably inclined towards giving equipment to 'effective' UN projects.

Both the British and Australian procedures provide for some inspection from London and Canberra, respectively. The Colombo Plan unit in the Commonwealth Relations Office at London has two scientific advisers who visit the receiving countries every six months, not only to examine the progress of Colombo Plan experts and the use to which equipment is being put, but to discuss with government officials desirable future projects. Field visits are made from time to time by staff members of the Colombo Plan Branch of the Australian Foreign Office and of the Commonwealth Education Office in Canberra for similar purpose.

Without repeating what are substantially the same procedures governing Colombo Plan operations in the Philippines, it is in order to note that there seemed to be more contact between the UN and Colombo Plan project personnel than between UN and Point Four experts. At the bimonthly meetings of UN agency experts held by the RTAR, moreover, questions were often raised as to the possibility of supplementing UN project resources with Colombo Plan equipment or trainee grants. The British Colombo Plan representative had recently spent several hours with the RTAR for the purpose of facilitating such arrangements. As illustrations of this *ad hoc* type of co-operation, a United Kingdom fellowship had been awarded in the economic development field in connection with a TAA economic survey project; two United Kingdom grants in meterology were made to buttress a WMO project; and a printing outfit was provided by the United Kingdom for a Unesco-aided scientific documentation centre.

A growing number of cases of Colombo Plan co-operation with EPTA activities have been reported by TAB in recent years. In India, for instance, WHO assistance to maternal and child health centres has been co-ordinated with that provided under the Colombo Plan. According to the FAO regional representative for Asia, Colombo Plan equipment (especially tractors) has been made available for FAO demonstration projects. It is his habit to suggest to ministries of agriculture that they explore Colombo Plan possibilities in view of the extremely limited amounts of money for equipment allocated to FAO under TAB rules. In India, UNICEF and the Colombo Plan have a kind of informal understanding as to the division of responsibilities for aiding in the construction and installation of dairies. Co-operative arrangements have been the more easy to work out by reason of the decentralized, non-bureaucratic administration of Colombo Plan operations.

INTER-PROGRAMME RELATIONS IN PERSPECTIVE

From the foregoing sample of inter-programme relations at the base, the significant factors in the co-ordinative process become clear. In descending order of importance, these include: (1) the kind of co-ordinative machinery developed within recipient governments; (2) the kind of relationships that exist among the heads of resident aid missions; and (3) the working relations of project personnel in cognate programme areas. For effective inter-programme co-ordination, from the planning through the operating and evaluative stage, sustained attention to the problem at all three of these levels is necessary. While the operating relationships of project personnel do not need to be formalized, they should be based on the realization that all programmes are—or should be—working towards the same goal—without excessive pride of authorship. Much depends on how well the operators in one programme become familiar with what is actually being done, or what is available, under the others. Ignorance, misinformation, or indifference is sometimes the cause of undue programme 'separateness' within a country.

In the better organized governments, the practice of 'shopping around' for foreign aid at the cheapest price has virtually disappeared. Where the national co-ordinating machinery is weak or non-existent, the task of developing mutually satisfactory programme relationships falls mainly on the resident programme heads, notably the RTAR and USOM Director.[23] Available evidence indicates that nearly all RTARs now regularly present their draft country programmes to the USOMs, but reciprocity is by no means complete. There is allegedly a difficulty here: the principle underlying TAB country programming is that it should conform as far as possible to what the government wants and draft country programmes are seldom modified by TAB headquarters—never by TAC; whereas the USOMs are obliged to operate under shifting policy directives from Washington. Action taken by a USOM in formulating a country programme is subject to change—often substantial change—both at ICA headquarters and by Congress. But this differential should not —and indeed in some countries it does not—prevent an informal examination by the RTAR of USOM's programme proposals to Washington.

With respect to programme operations, the growing extent to which the resources of different programmes are being put to joint use is one of the more encouraging features of over-all programme development. Here it is the experts on the job who are chiefly responsible for concrete proposals leading to 'other programme' participation in the projects to which they are assigned by their own agencies. The over-all picture for 1958, as reported by TAB, showed that approximately one-fourth of 949 EPTA projects reviewed in forty-four countries included some form of active co-operation with other programmes. Of the 219 projects in this category, 178 involved co-operation with other bilateral programmes (chiefly the United States), while there were 22 cases of co-operation with the Colombo Plan, 5 with OAS training projects, and 14 with non-governmental organizations.[24] The most common form of co-operation, as Mrs. Lockwood has noted in her study of Libya, has been for the United Nations to ask for 'logistical support' from the United States, and conversely, for the United States to draw upon the United Nations 'reservoir of experts.'[25] As already

[23] Incidentally, in some countries the RTAR has used the USOM as a means of bringing specialized agency staffs 'into line.'

[24] *Annual Report of the TAB for 1958*, ECOSOC, O.R.: 28th Sess., 1959, Suppl. No 5, p. 65.

[25] Agnese Nelms Lockwood, 'Libya—Building a Desert Economy,' *International Conciliation*, No. 521 (March 1957).

indicated in Chapter 8, there have been instances of regional projects (*e.g.*, Mekong River development) where several bilateral programmes have supplemented the efforts of several UN agencies in the same undertaking. A number of governments, according to TAB's findings, have emphasized that differing planning and operating procedures have tended 'to complicate the task of inter-programme co-ordination.' In a few cases, moreover, results reportedly fell below expectations on account of 'defective team-work and personality conflicts among experts' from co-operating programmes. Occasionally, each side apparently has claimed that 'the other has taken credit where it was not due.' This sort of situation, however, probably does not occur any more frequently than in inter-agency team projects involving the UN family alone.

On the whole, liaison at the field level would appear to be least satisfactory between UN agency activities and the smaller bilateral governmental programmes on the one side, and the diversified undertakings of various voluntary groups on the other. Aside from the case of such major private groups as the Ford, Rockefeller, and Asia Foundations, there is only sporadic contact (UNICEF excepted) with philanthropic religious, business, and educational institutions that engage in overseas welfare programmes. It would be helpful if some kind of general clearing-house arrangement could be set up by such private groups with a view to disseminating information to one another as well as to public agencies on the object, scope, and locale of their overseas programmes.

So far as the smaller public bilateral programmes are concerned, there is not likely to be any serious difficulty with donor governments from the non-Communist world. But where an under-developed country accepts technical aid from Communist countries, as well as from the UN and various 'free world' governments, the problem may become more complex. In such areas, of which there are only a few as yet, it may be more a question of how to identify clearly the objectives of the UN programme, in comparison with those of the Communist countries, than of attempting somehow to 'co-ordinate' the two types of action. Thus far, as noted earlier in this chapter, Soviet assistance has been provided on a project-by-project basis rather than in relation to general economic development planning in country terms. For the most part, Soviet technicians are sent into a country for relatively short periods to aid in inaugurating engineering and construction projects for which easy loan financing is being provided. These groups usually live together at one location and have little or no contact with foreign experts of other nationalities. Nor does the Soviet Government maintain special resident missions for aid administration in the capitals of the recipient countries. The negotiation of aid agreements apparently has often taken place during the visit of top Communist officials to the country concerned. Conceivably, to be sure, a shift in Soviet aid policy might improve the chances of UN-Soviet co-operation.[26] But here we enter the area of political speculation.

Much of the talk about the need of better inter-programme co-ordination has been predicated on the assumption that money is being wastefully spent on ill-conceived and over-lapping projects. So far as the UN system is concerned such an assumption would appear, by and large, no longer to be justified. The 'fringe' character of UN aid operations lends an air of unreality to glibly asserted claims of 'overspending' for purposes already being taken care of by other programmes (chiefly Point Four). 'The needs of most developing countries,' observed a senior ICA official recently, 'are so great that the basic problem is that of how best to use all available sources of help.'[27] It is not over-laps but gaps that seriously concern the managers of international economic and technical aid programmes.

[26] Not long ago the Government of Cambodia asked WHO's liaison officer at Phom-Penh to act as co-ordinator for all foreign aid in the health field, including that from WHO, the U.S., the U.S.S.R., Communist China, Poland, and Japan. Could this be a straw in the wind? Health is probably as neutral a subject as any for trans-ideological co-operation.

[27] Alvin Roseman, 'An American Aid Mission Director's View of Technical Cooperation,' *The Annals* (May 1959), p. 7.

11

PROGRAMME IMPACT AND EVALUATION

No more baffling problem confronts UN field programme administrators than that of evaluating the substantive impact of programme action on the recipient countries. There are several reasons why this should be the case. First of all, the diversity of projects—as to objective, type, size, and duration—is so great that it is virtually impossible to devise common criteria by which to test their effectiveness. Second, UN system assistance 'constitutes only a fraction of the total development activities taking place in a given country at a given time. . . . To attempt to isolate the contribution directly made by [EPTA and other programme] projects and to subject it to quantitative measurement would be an illusory operation.'[1] Third, the task of assembling relevant statistical and other data, often fragmentary and unreliable, for hundreds of separate projects in a hundred different countries and territories, would be an excessively costly and time-consuming undertaking. Finally, the results of technical assistance are to a large extent not susceptible of any exact measurement: they are frequently intangible and in many instances will yield dividends only gradually—over a period of many years or even decades.

Within these limitations, however, a considerable effort has been made during recent years to review UN field programmes in terms of the administrative and psychological conditions under which they are conducted. The main purpose of the present chapter is to examine how these factors have affected programme operation and follow-up. Already—in our discussions of the recruitment of experts, communication and back-stopping, project supervision, and programme making—we have dealt with certain aspects of this problem, and we shall endeavour not to repeat the essentials of these earlier chapters. In the pages that follow, our focus will be primarily on the governments and peoples who receive assistance—their basic attitudes towards

[1] *Annual Report of the TAB for 1958*, ECOSOC, O.R.: 28th Sess., 1959, Suppl. No. 5, p. 57.

it, the administrative support they provide for UN project personnel, the psychological *rapport* established between the donors and receivers, and the kinds of action that are taken to translate the recommendations of international advisers into permanent national policy or institutional arrangements.

Administrative Conditions of Project Implementation

In introducing this subject, it must be remembered that the multilateral aid programmes sponsored by the UN family of agencies are predicated on two fundamental propositions: (1) that aid should be provided 'as far as possible in the form' desired by the recipient governments, and (2) that it should not 'be a means of foreign economic and political interference in the internal affairs of the country concerned.'[2] These two conditions have on the one hand influenced the forms of assistance and, on the other, tended to limit its substantive impact. The motivations of governments requesting assistance have to be taken into account by programme managers, and the real motivations are sometimes veiled behind the officially professed reasons for seeking aid. In certain instances, it has turned out that governments have been primarily interested in obtaining an international subsidy for going economic or social programmes of their own—by using UN experts instead of already available national personnel. Not infrequently, moreover, powerful national officials have been known to ask for UN assistance with a view to enhancing their own prestige, or to strengthening their claims for larger budgetary support of their ministries or departments. Such administrative 'empire-builders' are to be found within the governmental power structure of all countries, whether economically advanced or under-developed. Or the pressures of local vested interests may prejudice the chances of effective project operations. In still other situations, foreign experts have been sought to cover up the failures of national programme-planning, the responsible politicians thus trying to shift the blame to foreign advisers.

> The experts investigate, make recommendations, and fly away. The Government is now free to carry out the experts' proposals, or to shelve them, as it wishes. Honor is satisfied. It would be quite false to describe such a technique as general, or perhaps predominant, but the foreign expert

[2] ECOSOC Resolution 222A (IX), 15 Aug. 1949, Annex I.

is no stranger to the role of stalking-horse or scapegoat in Asia today [nor, it might be added, in the Middle East and Latin America].[3]

Another kind of complication may arise when, during the interval between the formal approval of an assistance programme and its implementation, a change of political régime occurs, accompanied by an altered set of economic development priorities and resulting in failure to provide the necessary legislative or executive authorization for UN-aided projects. Or, as a former RTAR recently observed, the experts may arrive and find that the government has forgotten all about its original request for their services. Or a new group of senior officials, unsympathetic to the requests made by their predecessors, may place road-blocks in the path of the UN project advisers attached to their ministry. In Lebanon, during the civil disturbances of 1958, UN assistance operations had virtually to be suspended. Government employees were not at their desks, transportation became dangerous, and most UN experts were encouraged to take home leave, which in some cases was subsequently extended. While such political hazards as these may be exceptional, they are inherent in the setting of a world-wide voluntary programme of aid to States with widely varying degrees of political and administrative stability.

Operational Planning

Let us now look more closely at some of the administrative problems encountered in carrying out UN-aided projects within a country. As indicated in Chapter 9, it was not uncommon, during the earlier years of country programming, for project agreements to be negotiated in a hurry, with little attention to the development of a sound plan of operations, including the spelling out of the kinds and amounts of local support required for their effective implementation. Experts were not infrequently sent into isolated places without adequate back-stopping from the executing agency or the provision of essential local arrangements. In other cases, involving team participation in a large-scale undertaking likely to continue indefinitely, insufficient consideration was given to the scope, objectives, administrative setting, and budgetary requirements of the project. The project team would appear on the scene only to discover that nothing had

[3] Hugh Tinker, 'The Name and Nature of Foreign Aid,' *International Affairs* (Jan. 1959).

been done towards locating or equipping suitable premises for the undertaking. Months might pass before the necessary legislation was adopted, or administrative orders were issued, to implement such requirements. Where careful, on-the-spot reconnaissance surveys are conducted in advance of the formulation of a project request, the government bureaucracy may be dissuaded from generating an unrealistic project scheme, but even this does not always result in any clear stipulation of the local 'wherewithal' needed for its execution. All too many governments have not unnaturally miscalculated, in optimistic fashion, what is involved in the obligations they undertake under a project agreement, the terms of which have frequently been quite imprecise on these points.

While it would be an exaggeration to claim that vague and loosely structured project requests no longer find their way into approved country programmes, the situation in this respect has distinctly improved during recent years, especially in those countries where reasonably effective national co-ordinating machinery has been developed. Moreover, agency field representatives, when not too pressed by time, now give much more attention than formerly to project operating arrangements in their negotiations with national ministries. Many RTARs actively participate in the process of getting projects off on the right track—by putting experts into immediate touch with their counterparts and taking part personally in the initial discussion of project-planning with experts and counterparts.

Local administrative support

Notwithstanding the increasing proportion of well-planned projects, the quality and adequacy of local administrative support still leaves a great deal to be desired. Some projects, to be sure, call for more support than others. In certain cases counterparts may not be needed at all; on the other hand, where an expert is working in a number of different fields, he may require several counterparts, either on a full- or part-time basis. During 1957 and 1958, in the forty or so countries covered by TAB's evaluation surveys, about three-fourths of the total number of experts involved had national counterparts attached to them. For 14 per cent. of the projects with results rated as 'below expectation,' or which were prematurely terminated, failure to provide counterparts, or their provision 'too late,' was listed by the RTARs as a major cause of difficulty. Only a little over half of the counterparts supplied for surveys of physical, human, and economic resources were rated as 'satisfactory,' probably because comparatively few trained and experienced local persons were available for this type of activity. The proportion of satisfactory counterparts was appreciably higher for projects involving (1) the establishment of technical, administrative, and medical services, or (2) the introduction of improved techniques in industry and agriculture. In some of the latter cases, counterparts were obtained from private enterprise and institutions able to offer more attractive conditions of employment than governments. In India, the central Foreign Aid Co-ordinating Unit now requires each national ministry and state government to certify in advance that it will provide appropriate counterparts for technical assistance personnel.

It is not surprising that a substantial number of counterparts should have been regarded as lacking in minimum technical qualifications, for, as the TAB survey points out, 'the technical assistance given to a country tends to be in inverse ratio to the technical knowledge available in that country.'[4] But there are other reasons for dissatisfaction with counterparts, *e.g.*, the demoralizing conditions in many national civil services caused by political interference, promotion by seniority, insecurity of tenure, poor pay, or, in some instances, widespread corruption; frequent changes of counterparts during the course of a project; and the practice of holding two or more jobs concurrently.[5] In one case that came to the writer's attention, the national director of a TAA-aided project held at the time four other positions. In addition, he happened to be 'anti-foreign' and extremely sensitive to any criticism of the performance of the department to which the project was attached. In another country the local counterparts for a large-scale educational project had endeavoured to 'use' the UN experts with a view to furthering the political advancement of certain personally

[4] *Annual Report of the TAB for 1958, op. cit.*, p. 69.

[5] In one Middle Eastern country, some years ago, a TAA expert found it impossible to work with the highly opinionated Director-General of the Statistical Department of the Ministry of Finance, for which he had been designated as adviser. When the expert ventured to suggest that the Minister 'fire the fellow' the latter replied that it was 'politically impossible.' The expert, who threatened to resign, was nevertheless urged by the Minister to stay on.

ambitious officials. In this same country the national 'co-director' of a TAA-sponsored training institute adroitly exploited this position, which he held concurrently with a senior post in the Civil Service Commission, so as to smooth the way for a rank promotion in the ministry to which he was formerly attached and to which he later returned—and at the higher rank. These are examples of predicaments that can strain the patience—and poise—of an international adviser.

With regard to the kinds of working relationships that develop between UN experts and their local collaborators, an experienced Unesco field official has discerningly classified assistance projects in the following sense:[6] first, there is the 'new activity' type of project in which the recipient government has had no previous experience and for which the advice given by the expert is unlikely to be challenged by his counterpart. While this situation usually puts the expert in a privileged position, lack of trained local personnel and the problem of incorporating the new activity into existing administrative rules and regulations can give rise to difficulties. Second, there is the 'improvement' project where the recommendations of the expert may conflict with existing ideas and previous policy decisions may block or upset his plans for the prosecution of the project.

In the third place, one finds the 'sheltered' type of project, stemming from some important local personage who has a direct interest in its success and who will ordinarily assure the fullest possible local support and thus make the expert's task a relatively easy one. Next comes the 'foundling' project, which has become detached from its original sponsor and been transferred to another official who regards it 'without enthusiasm or even with aversion.' Here the expert may face a really tough problem and the survival of such an undertaking is seldom very promising. Or the key official through which a project must be implemented may actively oppose the changes it will introduce for fear his status will be jeopardized. This is the 'obstructed' type of project that is apt to give the expert even more trouble. Finally, there is the 'mistaken' project, where it turns out that the requesting ministry has in mind something quite different from what the executing agency has understood, or it does not con-

[6] In a contribution to *Link*, a quarterly bulletin formerly issued by Unesco for better mutual understanding between the secretariat and field experts (October 1957).

form to the conditions under which the agency is able to supply aid. In this case the results may be similarly disappointing, or occasionally the agency may, as a last resort, decide to withdraw its expert (or experts).

These various types of projects of course are not mutually exclusive; nor would all of the projects undertaken by different UN agencies necessarily fit into such a classification. But it does help one to visualize the sorts of operational situations with which foreign technicians have to grapple. From his own observations, the writer could cite a complicated state of affairs (of a somewhat different character) that may confront a project leader—where he finds himself caught between two 'feuding' government departments, each manœuvring to keep control of the project in its own hands and thus producing a frustrating impasse lasting for months.

Regardless of the kind or scale of project, failure of the government to provide appropriate clerical assistance, office or institutional facilities, local transportation, and translation services cannot help but handicap the work of international experts however technically qualified, culturally adjusted, or devoted to their tasks they may be. At best, in most countries, such administrative support is likely to be either inadequate or of very poor quality, or both. According to TAB's 1958 survey of over forty countries, less than two-thirds provided secretarial services and local transport even on a *minimum* basis, *i.e.*, at levels prevalent locally though below desirable standards.[7] The proportion for the preceding year was substantially lower. When secretarial assistance is non-existent, or clearly inadequate, much of the time of highly paid UN experts has to be spent on routine clerical duties. This is a chronic complaint. As indicated in Chapter 7, the RTAR's office, or occasionally an agency's local field office, may be able to provide some help in typing reports and correspondence, but seldom enough. On the whole, the executing agencies tend to turn a blind eye to administrative deficiencies of this sort, assuming that the host government somehow will handle matters.[8]

[7] *Annual Report of the TAB for 1958*, *op. cit.*, p. 70.

[8] On the other hand, it would both be contrary to the principles of EPTA regarding the participation of governments in the programme and would dissipate the already hard-pressed reserves if the agencies were to endeavour to provide such facilities on any fulsome scale. The necessity is often recognized, but realistically it is often difficult to fill in the gaps, except on an *ad hoc* basis, left by deficiencies in the government-provided facilities.

As regards local transport, most experts have to depend on getting a car from the government pool. Not infrequently they have found it necessary literally to beg for car rides to and from villages where demonstration projects are located. In one Asian country, an expert said that, after much difficulty, he had managed to get a car assigned to him for official use—only to have it 'pinched' by the Minister! A change of régime then took place and a car was at last made available. Increasingly, in a considerable number of countries, governments are now 'trying to make it attractive for experts to own cars by allowing duty-free imports and permitting re-sale at market prices.' But this is not a wholly satisfactory solution for experts with children who have to be transported to schools distant from their residence. As TAB has noted,

> it is not uncommon for an expert to lose several working days in an office for lack of transportation at a time when his presence would have been much more useful on some project in an outlying area, such as fundamental education, rural health development, or agricultural extension work.[9]

If space permitted, the writer could cite numerous instances that came to his notice where lack of essential local facilities had adversely affected the development of field projects. Suffice it to call attention to only three or four such situations by way of illustration. In one Asian country, a children's theatre project sponsored by Unesco's Participation programme failed to get off the ground for months because suitable premises were not provided by the government—as it was supposed to do under the project agreement. Meanwhile, a training centre for teachers had to be operated in a private house under most unsatisfactory conditions. Nor were any counterparts supplied for a long time. When the two experts sought an explanation, they reportedly 'got into hot water.' The difficulty apparently sprang from administrative confusion occasioned by the division of the Ministry of Education into two ministries, one part becoming the Ministry of Scientific Research and Culture. Although the older Ministry remained the official channel with Unesco, the new one was given responsibility for the project.

In one country, an expert in optical mechanics had to be withdrawn after eighteen months because no training facilities were provided by the government. Yet the executing agency,

[9] *Annual Report of the TAB for 1958, op. cit.*

in taking such action, refrained from apprising the government of the real reasons, leaving it with the supposition that the expert was going on home leave and that another government had requested his services. In another country, it was discovered that WHO had once spent some $25,000 on public health experts before any facilities were available for their work. A nursing school project sponsored by the same agency elsewhere had to wait for two years before hospital wards were equipped for student nurse training, and even then very poorly, despite provisions to this effect in the project agreement. The quarters in which the nursing school itself was housed were so filthy that it took three months to make them fit for human habitation. Equipment for instructional purposes was notoriously deficient; while the local administrative director appointed to the school was almost impossible to co-operate with—'you never knew where you stood with him,' remarked the able leader of the WHO team of nurse educators.

It is not intended to convey to the reader the impression that such situations as these are typical of the conditions under which projects are implemented. On the whole, the picture in the majority of countries in this respect is now fairly reassuring. One RTAR, for example, has contrived the expedient of having the requesting subject-matter minister, as well as the Minister of Finance, sign a special form stipulating their financial and staff commitments under each project agreement. In the Philippines, the government has set up a unique arrangement by which it allocates each year to the RTAR's account a substantial sum for 'Project Development Costs.' This may be drawn upon at his discretion to finance local services and equipment needed by going projects over and beyond the original allotments. Judicious use of this fund has made it possible to increase the efficiency of several important undertakings. In this country, incidentally, the amount expended by the government on local project support is virtually equal to the entire allocation of funds from EPTA.

There are now signs that some of the UN agencies are beginning to take a stronger line with governments that fail to live up to their project obligations. TAB's recent proposal (referred to in Chapter 9) that initial agreements should include specific commitments as to local support for the duration of a project represents an encouraging step in this direction. A further desirable move would be for TAB to draw up minimum acceptable standards for local services and equipment. Where it proves financially impossible for a government to meet such standards, the executing agency might frankly recognize the fact and itself assume responsibility for assuring them without delay—similar to what is done when a recipient government is relieved 'by waiver' of paying for the local subsistence of UN experts. Any additional outlays by the executing agency could be financed by reducing the assistance granted under other parts of the current annual programme. In certain instances it might be feasible to bill the government later for these costs in local currency. Alternatively, the extra outlays for local services and equipment might be regarded as a necessary part of the over-all operational cost of a project.

Intra-project co-ordination

In addition to the indices of improvement noted above, the RTAR in many countries is now taking an increasingly active part in smoothing out local administrative snarls. In these trouble-shooting operations he is frequently in a position to draw upon the national co-ordinating unit for support where its functions extend to project execution. Such support is particularly important in the case of inter-agency projects, or projects over which two or more national ministries share control. There have been a few instances where it was found advisable to designate a UN 'administrative co-ordinator' for large-scale undertakings involving the participation of several UN agencies and of several government departments. This kind of arrangement calls for constant surveillance if conflicts of jurisdiction are to be avoided. In one Latin American country, a regional development project ran into serious difficulties partly because the responsibilities of the co-ordinator were not clearly defined, and partly because of friction that developed between the national and regional institutions involved in the undertaking. The execution of this project was further complicated by the tendency of the regional representative of one of the specialized agencies to intervene in order 'to protect the rights of his agency.'

Arrangements between the principal agency and the other co-operating agencies have often been loosely worked out by agency headquarters—merely by an exchange of letters which does not sufficiently differentiate their respective financial and operational roles. As indicated in an earlier chapter, moreover, the ambiguous status of a project leader *vis-à-vis* the other members of the group has at times militated against unified team action, in single-agency as well as in multi-agency projects. An interesting illustration of this was discovered by the writer in connection with a large irrigation project where the team leader designated by FAO complained of having been given a 'heavy' responsibility but no authority with respect to the work of the other twenty experts in the team, some of whom reported to other technical divisions at Rome than the one to which he himself was responsible. When things went wrong, he had somehow 'to put the pieces together'; but under the circumstances this was not easy. In another country a senior TAA expert had apparently arrogated to himself the role of 'dean' of all the resident experts in the industrial and minerals field—an attitude they resented. In a third case, the team leader of a complex Unesco training and research project remarked that, although there were good personal relations among the associated experts, they did not constitute a 'coherent' group and were doing little 'corporate' work. Where situations of this kind exist, the RTAR may, and often does, inject his influence by calling together the project team and suggesting some acceptable *modus operandi*. It is only fair to add that most project teams manage to work together with little more strain than might be anticipated from such personality differences as inevitably exist in any professional group, whether of uni- or multi-national composition.

Cultural and Psychological Relationships

The execution of aid programmes is conditioned not only by local administrative arrangements but by the impact of various cultural and psychological forces. Certain of these have already been referred to in our observations on the working relations of project experts and their local counterparts.

Although it was not possible in the present study to examine intensively, country by country, how cultural resistances may subtly affect project operations, the reader should realize that they are encountered, in one degree or another, in virtually every host country. The wider the differences between its culture system and those cultures with which the visiting experts are familiar, the more difficult the problem of mutual adjustment and effective communication is apt to be. In this process, to be sure, language sometimes constitutes a serious barrier to understanding between the giving and receiving groups, particularly in non-Western countries. But misunderstanding, confusion, and even frustration may equally develop from the failure of the foreign technician to appreciate local attitudes towards change, or from differences in time-sense, work habits, and incentive patterns. Traditional ways of doing things, class and kinship structures, and religious beliefs may impede the acceptance, for example, of nutritional programmes or new farming devices. Or the rate at which administrative innovations may be injected into a civil service based on particularistic norms may turn out to be much slower than Western-oriented specialists originally anticipate.

In the Middle East and Asia, the inter-personal relationships of foreign advisers and host country officials 'are invariably overlaid with a formal politeness that often conceals what the official's real reaction is.'[10] The latter may give an affirmative response to some apparently reasonable request for action while knowing full well that he will not be able to carry out his promise. In certain Latin American countries the foreign expert discovers among government bureaucrats a kind of 'inferiority complex' that causes them instinctively to resent the intrusion of foreign advisers in their accustomed way of life. This sensitivity must be understood by the UN adviser if he is to gain the confidence of the officials with whom he is associated. Only by a deliberate determination to learn as well as to teach, and by humility, consideration, and patience, is it possible to break through this 'culture curtain.'[11] All of which underlines once again the vital importance of thorough cultural and sociological briefing and of relatively long-term projects.

Many Western experts appear to have been more concerned

[10] The quotation is from the author's monograph on 'Bureaucracy and Politics—Egyptian Model,' in William J. Siffin, ed., *Toward the Comparative Study of Public Administration* (Bloomington: Indiana Univ., 1957), p. 172.

[11] See Dorothy Lee, 'The Culture Curtain,' *The Annals* of the American Academy of Political and Social Science (May 1959).

with the cross-cultural transfer of modern techniques than with the development of less advanced methods carefully adapted to the receiving culture. The latter task is of course an exceedingly difficult one. There have reportedly been instances where WHO doctors have gone into countries with widespread illiteracy and the most rudimentary public health services and tried to impose the latest Western standards, not by a slow, gradual process, but immediately. Such professional 'fanaticism,' as one WHO headquarters official has called it, may backfire against the outside adviser. To quote a thoughtful critic of FAO's programme in Latin America,

> Usually the foreign technician must go through a period of trial, adaptation, re-trial, and re-adaptation before discovering, in co-operation with local technicians, what a real improvement under local conditions would be. . . . For the most part, technical co-operation must be a 'partnership-over-time-in-institutionalization'—not so much a technique as *a pattern of solving problems* within agriculture.[12]

Some of the most successful cases of cross-cultural adaptation, especially in pilot projects, have been those where teaching is done by the use of simple examples that lie within the native life experience. The more closely such demonstrations are related to the felt needs of local communities the more likely they are to take root.

The transfer of expertise in the social sciences seems even more difficult than in such technical fields as health or agriculture. This is probably because of the 'value elements' in modern sociology, economics, and public administration. In the last-named field, with which the writer happens to be most familiar, the expert from an advanced industrialized country is often inclined to assume that objectivity in personnel management can easily be infused into an essentially agrarian culture where personalized values are endemic. Or he may fail to consider that new administrative procedures can only be built into the traditional institutions of the recipient country. The distinction between 'line' and 'staff' functions in administration is hard to explain to officials accustomed to mixing up these two types of operations. The meagre results from certain of the earlier administrative survey missions may perhaps be traced to the notion that

[12] Arthur T. Mosher, *Technical Cooperation in Latin-American Agriculture* (Univ. of Chicago Press, 1957), p. 241.

comprehensive administrative reform is politically possible here and now—instead of through a gradual infiltration of ideas and processes over a decade or perhaps longer. It has not always been recognized that administrative change may threaten the position of entrenched groups in societies where over-staffed government bureaucracies are the refuge for the otherwise unemployed. Similarly, well-intentioned proposals for land reform can endanger the power or prestige of a strong land-owner class. Or improved educational and social services may be obstructed by a ruling *élite* fearful that the 'secularization' of the masses will make them less submissive and more susceptible to political propaganda against the upper classes.

These are merely a few examples of types of resistances to which UN project teams must accommodate themselves. As their experience has grown, many of them have become sophisticated concerning the realities of technical assistance. Experts with previous field assignments now move into another country with a much fuller awareness of the cultural limitations of their mission than was the case in the early 1950s. In this respect, UN multi-national teams have a distinct advantage over advisory groups hailing from the same cultural area. For example, a team of instructors for a UN-sponsored training institute is frequently able to provide advice, say, on educational or administrative methods, from different national sources and thus develop an eclectic approach to the peculiar problems of the host country. The outside adviser working alone can often be recruited from an area whose stage of development is not too far above that of the receiving country, or where special knowledge and experience exist on such subjects as tropical medicine, rice breeding, forest management, fisheries, literacy teaching, consumers' co-operatives, and rural community development. Technical know-how may be broadly diffused among the major industrial nations but none of them—whether it be the United States, Britain, France, Germany, or the U.S.S.R.—has a monopoly of all the skills and processes suitable for developing agrarian societies widely differentiated by climate, natural resources, political systems, and cultural patterns.

In 1958, according to TAB's survey, EPTA experts serving in some forty-four countries were, with few exceptions, rated by the RTARs and the host governments as having 'maintained a high standard of performance, both technically and in their capacity to adapt themselves to their respective environments.'[13] Of the total number (1,878), less than 2 per cent. had had to be withdrawn before the completion of their assignments. The proportion of withdrawals for the preceding year was roughly the same.

These figures, to be sure, probably give a somewhat optimistic index of the adjustability of the total group of experts to the *milieu* of their missions. For the premature termination of an assignment is ordinarily resorted to only in extreme cases. Most recipient governments are as reluctant to ask for the withdrawal of an expert as his agency is to take such action on its own initiative. Aside from developments beyond the control of the expert, ill-health, flagrant misbehaviour, and drastic changes in project plans constitute the chief causes for withdrawal.[14] Nor does the low percentage of withdrawals provide a reliable indication of the state of experts' morale. From private discussions with nearly 100 experts in fourteen countries, the writer gained the impression that the number of 'low morale' cases, while considerable, has been no greater than might reasonably be expected in any uprooted group of professionals working under varying degrees of frustration around the globe. As noted in Chapter 5, many experts are prone to complain about the treatment they receive from their agency or from the host government, concerning such matters as lack of secretarial service or local transport, difficulties in making travel arrangements, leaves-of-absence, delays in the payment of salary and allowances, or the right to import free of duty household appliances, motor-cars, drugs, tobacco, and liquor. But it does not follow from this 'complaint complex' that they have become basically disillusioned, disgruntled, or soured on the job. On the contrary, the vast majority, on being asked whether they regretted having accepted UN overseas employment, replied emphatically in the negative.

[13] *Annual Report of the TAB for 1958, op. cit.*, p. 71.

[14] For example, one specialized agency was obliged to dismiss an expert on community development in a Latin American country because he refused to submit regular reports to Geneva or to attend meetings with other experts in the capital of the country. In another case, an agency expert bypassed the RTAR by going directly to the Foreign Office in an effort to obtain permission to import his *third* air-conditioner (though he lived alone). He later ran over a child with his car and failed to stop. On recommendation by the RTAR, the appointing agency finally agreed to recall the expert even though his contract had only three months to run.

On one significant point, the behaviour of UN field experts appears to differ from that of United States Point Four personnel. By and large, the former, partly perhaps because they represent different nationalities, do not 'colonize' among themselves nearly so much as do those from the United States. UN groups stationed in non-Western capitals ordinarily do not live in 'a compound' but are scattered over town. Nor do they indulge in lavish entertaining as do their United States colleagues if only because their emoluments and perquisites are distinctly lower. In some places, there is comparatively little social life among the UN experts, although many RTARs now go out of their way to stimulate informal social contacts among experts from different countries. In India, the Soviet technicians reportedly have found it hard to get on with colleagues of other nationalities; some are said to have become restless and to want to go home. On the other hand, there seems to be considerably more social intercourse, in many countries, between UN groups and local people than is true of the United States colony. Contacts outside office hours, and at the family level, are easier to make by UN personnel who know the local language or have had previous experience in countries with closely related culture structures, than by those on their first overseas assignment—other things being equal. Since the proportion of the former is considerably greater in the UN multilateral than in the United States bilateral programme, it is natural that there should be more 'fraternization' in the one case than in the other. This situation, to be sure, varies widely from country to country, and in certain places the UN experts appear to be just as socially isolated from their hosts as are those from the United States—or the representatives of other Western national programmes.

THE ROLE OF PUBLICITY

The dissemination of information locally concerning the UN system in general, and its economic and social activities in particular, may help to create a favourable climate for programme reception and follow-up. Under the original legislation establishing EPTA, requesting governments were to agree 'to give publicity' to the programme within their territories. But the extent to which this is done differs tremendously from place to place. In the great majority of under-developed areas, public understanding of the objectives and work of the UN agencies is woefully meagre. Where widespread illiteracy prevails, such understanding is ordinarily confined to certain *élite* groups in the governmental and educational spheres, and some of these groups have only a fragmentary, or distorted, image of what the UN and associated organizations actually do outside the 'crisis' areas of 'peace and security.'

In this context, the local public often tends to confuse UN-sponsored technical assistance projects with similar undertakings under United States or other auspices. During his tour of duty in Egypt, for example, the writer and his UN colleagues were on several occasions labelled by the press as U.S. Point Four experts, despite all they could do in advance to make it clear that they were engaged in a UN-aided enterprise.[15] According to the testimony of various RTARs, similar misunderstandings have occurred in other countries.

Differing views exist (1) as to what kinds of UN-stimulated publicity may most effectively aid in dispelling confusion and misunderstanding and in building up local support for UN programmes, and (2) as to what the targets of such public information activity should be. While there appears to be general agreement that the available mass media should be used as channels for spreading information about UN programmes in a country, the coverage of these media is decidedly limited in agrarian societies where few can read and the telecommunications networks (radio and television) are still at an embryonic stage of development. In such situations other techniques, such as the dissemination of pictorial materials, mobile exhibits, mass demonstrations and specially adapted documentary films may be needed to supplement the printed or spoken word. UN experts themselves need to make better use of audio-visual devices within the projects for which they are responsible—as means of instructing farmers in improving agricultural practices, of training teachers, and of teaching illiterate groups the importance of personal hygiene and environmental sanitation. For the literate elements in the population there is the further problem of providing suitable printed materials in the local language (or

[15] 'Point Four' has become an all-embracing symbol throughout the Middle East and South Asia.

languages), and related to the native culture, for use in schools and by civic and professional groups—operations calling for trained staff, equipment, and money.

Another question on which opinions vary is whether the UN agencies should content themselves with distributing straight factual information, or undertake to 'sell' or 'glorify' UN programmes by means of propagandistic publicity. There are certain types of projects, *e.g.*, of an engineering or industrial character, which may not need any publicity, or for which elaborate publicity may even be harmful, particularly if it builds up expectations that cannot be fulfilled. On the other hand, projects in fields of health and agriculture, involving mass co-operation for their success, usually require carefully designed informational action in order to overcome traditional prejudices, customs, or superstitions.[16] In the latter category of projects are malaria eradication campaigns, child nutrition programmes, and efforts to introduce new seeds, fertilizers, and farm tools. Between these two extremes are a wide variety of 'institution-building' undertakings, affecting public administration and education, training, and research institutions, for which the chief informational targets clearly should be the politicians, administrators, educators, technicians, and scientists.

Local UN informational channels

There are three sets of instruments for UN informational action at the regional and country levels: (1) the UN Information Centres, maintained by OPI; (2) the TAB field offices; and (3) various specialized agency information services, operating chiefly through regional offices. By 1959, UN Information Centres had been established in some twenty-seven countries, only fourteen of which, however, were in the under-developed category.[17] Ten of the latter Centres have a regional coverage, notably those in Accra, Bangkok, Bogotá, Mexico City, New Delhi, and Teheran. At Bangkok and Santiago, the information unit serves the needs of ECAFE and ECLA, respectively, as well as OPI. Typically, as noted earlier in this study, the staffs

[16] During 1958, 'lack of support from people in the project area owing to the purpose of the project not being sufficiently understood' was listed as a major cause of results 'below expectations' in 3 per cent. of the projects so characterized. *Annual Report of the TAB for 1958, op. cit.*, p. 77.

[17] There were only four Centres in Latin America and two in all Africa. Of 57 professional officers on the staffs of the 27 UNICs, only 26 were assigned to the less developed areas.

of the UNICs are limited to two or three professional officers and an equally small number of locally recruited subordinate employees. Their budgets for travel within the country (or region) and for hospitality, photographic and radio supplies, and internal production are seldom adequate to meet the requirements of a balanced information programme. The load of administrative paperwork has often been so heavy that the staff has had little time for attention to ways and means of gearing its substantive activities to local conditions. Until very recently, OPI headquarters has tended to concentrate on administrative rather than policy directives to Centre directors.[18] Masses of UN documents would flow into the Centres but few were equipped with a trained librarian to keep them in manageable form for use by local readers (officials, professors, students).[19]

Within the limitations of their staff and material resources, the better Centres manage to arrange for reasonably adequate local press and radio publicity relating to UN technical assistance projects. All Centre directors are officially instructed to co-operate with the RTAR, and vice versa, in connection with the issuance of press releases on arrivals and departures of experts, holding press conferences on significant project developments, and planning radio broadcasts in which selected experts or visiting 'top brass' participate. Weekly newsletters are in some cases disseminated to the press and government information services throughout the area; in others, feature scripts are prepared for radio stations. In so far as UN and specialized agency documentary films are made available by the OPI Film Unit or agency headquarters—too few copies are ordinarily supplied—they are distributed to schools, student associations, civic groups, professional organizations, and rural centres. Some of these films are focused on specific country situations.[20] Each RTAR is expected to collaborate with the UNIC director

[18] See the *Report of the Expert Committee on United Nations Public Information*, UN Doc. A/3928, 20 Sept. 1958; also, for a critical assessment, see Richard N. Swift, 'The United Nations and Its Public,' *International Organization* (Winter 1960).

[19] At several Centres visited by the writer, UN documents had not been catalogued, and were piled on shelves and tables (in one case face down) in confused array. Some Centres also receive substantial quantities of material from specialized agencies which have no field office in the country concerned.

[20] See the *Annual Report of the TAB for 1958*, *op. cit.*, Annex XIII, for a list of such films produced during the period 1952–58. Some illustrative titles are: 'Afghanistan Moves Ahead'; 'A Village Awakens' (Greece); 'The Fishermen of Quintay' (Chile); 'Ethiopia Advances'; 'Water for the People' (Iraq, Central America); 'Challenge in the Desert' (Libya); and 'Miracle in Java.'

in building up lists for the dissemination of informational materials. Several UNIC directors have actively stimulated the organization of national 'associations for the UN' though in most countries such non-governmental organizations still are either non-existent or inactive.

In a number of areas, the relations between the RTAR's office and the UNIC have not been conducive to effective co-operation. One reason for this is that busy UNIC directors, provided with inadequate staff, have been inclined to focus their efforts on the political and diplomatic aspects of UN operations—to the neglect of the economic and social side of the picture. Some directors have seemed to be more interested in high protocol and in sponsoring receptions for visiting UN executives and the official *élites* of the national capital than in activating a dynamic informational programme stressing the 'grass roots' impact of health, agricultural, educational, and welfare projects. Also, there are RTARs who prefer to handle the informational job themselves, either because they feel that they are more intimately acquainted with project operations than the UNIC staff, or because they find that they can do the job as they view it with less loss of time and motion than by operating through UNIC channels.

In those under-developed countries in which no UNIC is located—the vast majority—the RTARs can count on only limited assistance from the regional UNIC staff, partly through visits of the director when he meets the local press, arranges for tape-recordings of experts' experiences, and collects material for stories to be placed in the local and regional press; and partly through the temporary assignment of an information officer from the Centre for the coverage of local projects. Conversely, in such areas, the RTARs often co-operate with the regional UNIC in the dissemination of more general United Nations material provided by it. Such inter-office co-operation is handicapped by distance, faulty communication, the cost of travel, and the preoccupation of certain UNIC directors with administrative matters. But the results should not be written off as worthless.

Many RTARs have themselves gone out of their way to cultivate close personal relations with the local press, and this has usually paid off in favourable coverage of EPTA. In certain countries, moreover, the RTAR has arranged for taped interviews with experts in the native languages, the tapes being sent to OPI and the duplicates used for internal publicity. One enterprising RTAR has utilized his periodic meetings with experts at project sites as a means of getting human interest stories into the press.

In recent years special emphasis has been given to the celebration of United Nations Day. Where the UNIC and RTAR have collaborated closely to this end, the occasion has provided an excellent opportunity to centre public attention on what the UN system is doing for the welfare of the people of the country. In some places arrangements have been made for the schools to set aside time for the discussion of UN problems, and students have prepared special essays on UN activities. At Bangkok, in 1958, an elaborate ceremony was held in front of the ECAFE building. After a speech by the Executive Secretary a balloon was released for each member country. The Thai Army produced 30,000 facsimiles of the UN flag, with a legend in Thai, which the Boy Scouts pasted on buses, taxis, and *samlors*. At Montevideo, in 1957, an exhibit was put on display in the centre of the city, including a set of attractive posters illustrating the technical assistance functions of each specialized agency. On one gigantic poster there was a world map showing the distribution of experts and fellows for each country. A press conference was held by the Executive Chairman of TAB (who happened to be on tour at the time) in front of the world map explaining EPTA. The Uruguayan press commented favourably and widely on the exhibition. In the Philippines, the UNIC constructed an ingenious diagram indicating all local UN agency offices and representatives, along with the names of the members of the Philippine Committee for ECAFE and of the Unesco National Commission. This diagram, which was placed in the entrance hall of the building where the TAB and UNIC offices were then located, reportedly had attracted much attention from local visitors.

At major field centres where agency regional offices are located, their staffs in some cases include an information unit. WHO, FAO, and UNICEF all maintain active regional information services.[21] These services devote most of their efforts to

[21] ILO, Unesco, and ICAO have no information staff stationed in the field. At their Paris office, IBRD and IFC share an information officer who distributes materials about their activities to countries in Europe.

publicizing meetings, seminars, and projects sponsored by their respective organizations. Such services are sometimes better equipped than the local UNICs with tape-recorders, photographic apparatus, and film supplies. On the other hand, they find it equally difficult to cover adequately vast regional areas because of the meagre travel funds at their disposal. For the dissemination of publicity, they tend to rely largely on periodic news memoranda to government ministries, the press, and professional groups—of doctors, nurses, welfare workers, teachers, and so forth. UNICEF produces special publications in English and Chinese for distribution in its Asian region, and from time to time provides tape-recorded speeches, film strips, and pictorial material. The WHO regional office at Manila distributes annually an illustrated brochure on the work of WHO in the Western Pacific and it recently prepared a pamphlet of suggestions for the celebration of World Health Day. The FAO regional information officer at Mexico City sends a monthly information bulletin by air mail to Latin American countries in Spanish (though not in Portuguese or French for lack of translation facilities).

Except at the regional centre itself, only spotty use appears to be made by agency informational services of the UNICs in the region, or vice versa. One WHO regional officer remarked that certain UNIC directors seemed to 'have chips on their shoulders' and were overly sensitive of their prerogatives allegedly as the 'personal representatives' of the UN Secretary-General. (Similar comments, incidentally, were made to the writer by a number of RTARs.) Co-operation between agency informational services and the UNICs seems to vary according to the interests and personalities of their chiefs. On the other hand, collaboration by the informational outposts of sister agencies appears to be steadily growing. WHO information officers, in particular, now work very closely with their UNICEF colleagues.

Improvement of field publicity

It is generally recognized that UN system public information at the country level could be improved. Obstacles to such improvement relate in part to budgets, in part to staffing and organization, and in part to the knotty problem of how to adapt informational materials to cultural diversities. These three obstacles are in considerable degree inter-dependent. With more money, more adequate staffing of field information units would be possible. With more adequate staff and equipment, it should be possible to produce more materials geared to regional needs and values. By better co-ordination of informational resources in the field, the over-all impact of informational efforts should become more effective, along with some economy in monetary expenditure.

The budgetary problem derives largely from the fact that few member countries in the UN family of agencies are information-minded. The concept of 'public relations,' as distinguished from controlled propaganda, is poorly understood except in the industrialized nations of the West. On the national delegations to organization conferences, moreover, specialists in communication are conspicuous by their absence. Among diplomats and treasury representatives the appropriation of money for informational purposes is all too often viewed as a means whereby the bureaucracy of the organization may expand in size and power. Each year, in the Fifth Committee of the UN General Assembly, no part of the budget is subject to more detailed, critical examination than that of the Office of Public Information. Similar reactions are to be found in the general conferences of agencies like WHO and FAO. Proposals for economy and retrenchment in public information expenditures are recurring themes in the recommendations of pre-conference budget review bodies, such as the Advisory Committee of the UN Assembly.

Following upon the Report of the Expert Committee on UN Public Information in 1958, various steps were proposed by the Secretary-General to strengthen the field operations of OPI.[22] In the main, his proposals involved the shifting of staff and funds (within OPI's over-all budget) from headquarters to the UNICs. Under his plan, additional officers in the radio and visual fields would be transferred or outposted to UNICs at major centres for varying periods. Also, a somewhat larger proportion of OPI's publications budget would be allocated for the local production, adaptation, and initiation of informational

[22] See his *Report on Public Information Activities of the United Nations*, UN Doc. A/4122, 16 June 1959.

materials, including 'originally written or regionally adapted pamphlets,' some of which would be prepared by outside writers engaged for this purpose—under the supervision of the UNIC director. A series of regional projects is now under way in which combined teams of radio and visual reporters visit certain areas to collect materials and produce programmes designed primarily for regional consumption. In Asia, for example, the All-India Radio has recently established a special unit which, in co-operation with the UN regional radio officer, is to produce not only scripts for use by UN headquarters but also programmes in the regional idiom. During 1959 the possibilities for similar regional radio production were being explored in Latin America. Feature stories of technical assistance, based on interviews with EPTA experts and local officials, are currently being disseminated on a world-wide scale by the UN Radio Division. Plans are in progress for on-the-spot radio and television coverage of various projects in Africa and Central America.

In addition, the Information Centres, both in the contributing and the receiving countries, are now given advance notice of the appointment of experts and their assignments. Releases based on interviews with outgoing or incoming experts, on feature stories relating to major projects, on headquarters activities in the field of technical assistance and the Special Fund, are all brought to the attention of UNICs in weekly 'Notes to Centres,' or where a particular region is especially concerned, by special notification. All Centre directors and RTARs are being urged to facilitate local recordings by experts, which are then integrated into short-wave programmes in many languages beamed from UN headquarters.

With a view towards better co-ordination of field information services, the Consultative Committee on Public Information (an inter-agency group subsidiary to ACC), at its meeting in March 1959, agreed on a number of measures looking towards the pooling, or common use, of information facilities and equipment at important field centres. The Committee recommended that there should be closer co-ordination in sales and distribution arrangements for UN and agency documentation, including the issuance of joint catalogues and the exchange of mailing lists. In addition, it was agreed that the UN Visual

Services (formerly Film) Board should undertake a number of joint productions in the film, filmstrip, television, and still-photographic fields covering UN and the specialized agency activities around the world. The chief information officers of the UN and the participating agencies further promised to combine their efforts in preparing an appropriate commemoration of 'a decade of technical assistance' in 1960. There was some discussion in the Consultative Committee of the feasibility of exchanging information personnel among the different agencies. While admitting the desirability of such exchange 'in principle,' the Committee felt that various administrative and procedural difficulties would limit its practicability.

In theory, a good case can be made for the establishment of a fully integrated information service covering the entire UN system at major field centres. There would be more effective and more economical utilization of existing staff and resources, and would make possible the development of joint reference libraries and documentation centres. The feasibility of any such step will depend on progress in the sharing of office premises and in inter-agency co-operation generally. In a considerable number of countries where UNICs cannot be maintained for budgetary reasons, the provision of an information officer for the TAB office would have much to commend it. With the backing he could get from an active regional UNIC, a locally recruited staff member, with some training in information, might in some cases be adequate for this purpose.

In the final analysis, given the apparent unwillingness of UN and specialized agency policy-control organs to support any considerable increase in appropriations for public information operations, national information services and the co-operation of private organizations will have to be largely relied upon to provide local publicity for UN-sponsored economic and social projects.[23] This being the case, it would appear not inappropriate for TAB to invite governments to request 'technical assistance' with a view to strengthening their own informational structures. To some extent this is already happening in the telecommunications field, but many governments could profit

[23] Note, in this connection, the exhortation to the Secretary-General, in General Assembly Resolution 1335 (XIII), 13 Dec. 1958, to enlist the co-operation of governments, privately owned mass media, NGOs, and educators in informing the peoples of the world about the UN and its activities.

from outside expert advice on how to utilize modern communications techniques for developing understanding of, and popular support for, economic development programmes in particular. The more widespread and more intelligent such understanding and support, the more likely (other factors remaining equal) will national authorities be disposed to translate sound project recommendations from UN sources into continuing policy and administration.

Action Follow-up on Country Projects

As already noted, the basic objective of technical assistance is to help governments and peoples help themselves. Technical assistance is not an end in itself but a means of providing ideas, methods, and skills which can be put to constructive use in the developing countries, both during and after the termination of project missions. The application of project recommendations may take various forms. For example, this may involve the adoption of legislative reform measures, the setting up of new institutions, the strengthening or reorganization of existing institutions, or the introduction of new techniques into general administrative, health, educational, or welfare services. Surveys of resources (human, water, soils, mineral) may call for the appropriation of funds for the building of dams, power plants, highways, port facilities, factories, hospitals, schools, and the like. Such funds may come from domestic capital formation or, more likely, partially or wholly from foreign grants or loans. So far as this category of operations is concerned, technical assistance ideally needs to be correlated with available investment sources and a country's capacity to absorb foreign capital—which is the *raison d'être* of the new Special Fund.

Formulation of project recommendations

A close relation exists between follow-up action by recipient governments and the care with which project recommendations are formulated. In the formal sense such recommendations consist of reports submitted to governments on an interim or final basis, or both. During the course of a project, moreover, advisory personnel may and frequently do transmit informal suggestions to their counterparts or to senior officials with whom they are associated. Accordingly, the impact of a project may begin to be felt well before the termination of UN assistance. The extent to which such suggestions take root tends to vary with the degree of mutual confidence that has been established between the outside experts and host country administrators.

As noted in Chapter 7, the preparation of formal reports on projects usually begins in the field—before the expert (or project team) leaves the country of assignment. In the ILO, for example, all advisory experts are instructed to prepare their final report in draft form and to submit it to the nearest field office 'in progressive sections' during the concluding weeks of their mission, in order 'to facilitate final review' on its completion.[24] A model report form is provided to the expert in advance. This form calls, in order, for a brief indication of the origin of the project, including the terms of reference of the mission; a description of the technical context of the project; a detailed statement of what was accomplished and of the difficulties encountered; and a summary of major findings, conclusions, and recommendations for further action by the government or by ILO, or both, with an estimate of the probable benefits from the recommendations. ILO experts are enjoined not to make 'far-reaching proposals which would require the government to undertake changes in all directions' at once; but to place emphasis on 'a few basic recommendations whose implementation is regarded as essential and feasible.'

Interim reports as necessary may be submitted to governments after clearance with the ILO field office. All final reports, on the other hand, must be approved by ILO headquarters. Ordinarily, the expert spends several days (or even weeks) in Geneva for consultation with the appropriate technical division regarding the content and tone of his report. He may be asked to re-write the report entirely, or merely to change certain portions of it. After approval by the Director-General, the Field Services Division processes the official text of the report, which is then formally transmitted to the government concerned in his name.

BTAO and the other assistance-granting entities follow more or less comparable procedures. In BTAO, for instance, the expert is asked to send three copies of his final report in draft

[24] See ILO's memorandum entitled *Information for Experts* (Dec. 1955).

form to headquarters about two months before the end of his assignment in order to ensure that the final report 'meets the wishes of the government and the requirements of BTAO.' While still in the field, however, the expert is instructed to transmit a copy of the draft report to national authorities with the notation that it 'has not been cleared with BTAO' and therefore does not necessarily reflect its official views.

Unesco experts are requested to discuss with the appropriate government officials their preliminary suggestions before the completion of their assignments 'in order to avoid misunderstandings' later. Two copies of all final reports are sent, through the chief of mission or head of project, to headquarters at the time that copies are submitted locally to government authorities and the RTAR. In the case of experts on survey (as distinguished from advisory) missions, the final report is submitted directly to Paris without a copy to the government, although it is expected that the expert will have discussed his recommendations with the government in the course of preparing the report. At Paris, the programme department concerned reviews the draft report and may propose changes in it. If a report is unduly critical of government policies, it may not be submitted to the government at all, but this occurs very rarely. This policy has been questioned by certain mission chiefs on the ground that the government should be aware of critical opinions. Criticisms that are thought to be insulting or destructive are of course eliminated from all reports with the consent of their authors.

Despite all the precautions taken to couch project reports in terms that will command attention from recipient governments, a good many reports are so long and detailed that they are often not read at all, or only by one or two officials. Another unfortunate tendency has been to include unrealistic proposals which have little hope of being considered seriously. So much time is consumed in editing and translating reports at agency headquarters that they may not reach the government for months after the departure of the expert or project team. More than one RTAR commented to the writer on the harmful effects of such delays: in the meantime the senior staff of a government department or institution may have changed, or the incentive to act may have been lost during the intervening period. In some cases, moreover, the recommendations contained in project reports do not appear to have been sufficiently integrated with cognate projects in the same country.

No final project report may be published without the consent of the government for which it is intended. Even in printed form, a report remains 'restricted' until permission to 'de-restrict' is granted.[25] The majority of experts' reports are eventually published under their own signature and are made available to other governments and UN organizations, as well as to individual administrators, scholars, technicians, and scientists on request. From a random sampling of published reports it is the writer's impression that good judgment has not always been exercised in deciding whether a report warrants publication. On the other hand, many published reports are not only of high quality but have significant implications for other countries confronted with similar problems.

Means of stimulating follow-up action by governments

It is inherent in the concept of UN technical assistance that 'efforts should be directed from the outset to enable the government concerned to take over full responsibility for the project as early as feasible and to continue it as a part of its own national development activities.'[26] What can the donor agencies do to stimulate such action? There is of course no way for them to force governments to carry on after the termination of projects. The only means at their disposal are facilitation and persuasion. On the negative side, they may in some cases resort to the threat of scaling down future assistance, but such a threat is not likely to have much effect on a government which for political reasons is disinclined to implement a particular project.[27] From the UN agency standpoint, moreover, the desire to have as many experts in the field as possible, in comparison with sister agencies, produces little incentive to threaten a reduction of assistance the following year.

[25] The TAB secretariat circulates from time to time lists of experts' reports which have been 'de-restricted' so far as the agencies participating in EPTA are concerned.

[26] *Annual Report of the TAB for 1958, op. cit.*, p. 77. Occasionally, the advice resulting from a project may be negative, which, if followed, might save the recipient government from making unwise expenditures.

[27] For a suggestion as to how such action might perhaps be made more effective, see Chap. 13 (p. 549).

Government attitudes towards incorporating project recommendations into legislative policy or administrative action may be influenced by changes in the domestic financial situation or in the balance of international payments, resistances from vested interests, internal strife, or the shift of control from one *élite* group to another.[28] In Lebanon, for example, a promising project for the setting up of a central statistical organization reached the report stage, and the recommendations in the form of a legislative bill were referred to the Minister of Economy and then to the Council of Ministers for action. The civil war of 1958 subsequently intervened and the project had to be abandoned for lack of money to finance it. Even so, something was achieved by way of improving statistical methods. In another country, where a new political régime recently came into power, there had previously been little follow-up on UN projects through sheer bureaucratic inertia, but the situation reportedly has since improved.

On the positive side, there are a number of devices the donor agency may employ to induce follow-up action. One such device, utilized especially by WHO, is to request governments to submit continuing reports for a period of years (after the withdrawal of assistance) on what they are doing, say, to carry on anti-disease campaigns initiated with the aid of WHO advisers. Another expedient is to write a letter to the national authorities shortly after the issuance of the final report on a project, asking them whether they agree with the findings, and if so, what they plan to do towards putting the recommendations into effect. A number of RTARs have utilized this expedient in connection with terminated UN projects.[29] On occasion, governments, in their replies, have pointed to certain aspects of the experts' proposals which UN headquarters conceded were impracticable.

A combination of this procedure with the promise of further assistance might be even more effective. For instance, the head of an agency, in transmitting the final report on a project to the

[28] The press of one Latin American country, commenting on UN technical assistance in 1957, reflected a not uncommon attitude: 'Nothing is said in technical assistance reports that has not already been said, repeated, advised, and planned by our own technicians.... Why have UN recommendations not been carried out? . . . It is because we do not want to do so.' (Author's translation.) *El País* (Montevideo), 29 July 1957.

[29] In one case, where a country had received aid from a number of UN statistical experts but had done nothing towards improving its statistical organization, the RTAR suggested an independent survey by a world-renowned specialist, who recommended that no further help be given the government unless it establish a career service for statistical personnel.

government, might ask it to let him know whether the recommendations are acceptable and will be implemented. At the same time, it could be intimated that a request for other forms of assistance would not be considered by the agency until and unless the government replied affirmatively as to its intention of carrying out the project recommendations. This procedure has apparently not been used nearly as widely as it might be with a view to inducing the application of project findings. Such findings, however, do in fact frequently lead to requests for additional assistance to strengthen a country's resources for long-term project implementation. The additional aid may take the form of providing experts in related fields or of fellowships for the advanced training of key staff personnel.

It is in order to note, also, that a good many informal recommendations made by UN experts are implemented bit by bit during the course of projects. This frequently happens with regard to training centres and administrative reform projects, where the introduction of new methods costs little or no money. Commenting on advisory assistance in the fiscal field, moreover, the present Director of BTAO has observed:

> Sometimes years elapse before a recommendation can be implemented. Normally, progress takes place in piece-meal fashion. Nobody can expect comprehensive and immediate implementation of a mission's recommendations. Partial implementation is the rule and is obviously fraught with certain dangers, particularly wherever public finance is involved.[30]

In a number of instances, developmental loans made by the International Bank may be traced to the influence of UN agency technical assistance recommendations, although relatively few of the latter have been thorough enough to provide a firm basis for determining capital financing needs. Conversely, many of the Bank's general survey missions have had an impact on the character of a country's technical assistance requests. Thus, for example, a UN expert was assigned 'to set up an income tax system in Nicaragua after the Bank's experts had advised on the basic legislation.'[31] In another case, a Bank 'ports' mission

[30] Henry Bloch, 'The Fiscal Advisory Functions of United Nations Technical Assistance,' *International Organization* (Spring 1957).

[31] *Ibid.* 'The Bank has now been organizing general survey and other advisory missions over a long enough time for some of the effects to be seen. In no case, of course, has a country adopted and implemented in full the recommendations. Nor was this to be expected. A report must first go through a process of selection, adaptation and assimilation by the country itself.' *The World Bank: Policies and Operations* (Washington: IBRD, June 1957), p. 83.

to India recommended a loan to Calcutta and Madras for port improvement and suggested to the Indian Government that a study be made of the feasibility of building a 'satellite' port at the former city. The Government then requested the UN to provide an expert for such a study, which was granted. An Institute of Science and Industrial Research in Ceylon, partially financed by BTAO, stemmed from a proposal made by a Bank mission.

As noted in Chapter 2, the International Monetary Fund dispatches to Member governments on request so-called 'consultation' missions on a confidential basis to provide advice on various aspects of fiscal and banking policy. These missions consist exclusively of personnel from the Fund's central staff and carry with them the full authority of the Fund. Any recommendations made by such a mission to a government are made in the name of the Fund. By the same token, the Fund is morally obliged, if the government follows the recommendations, to provide financial assistance where required to carry out the proposed programme. When Member governments have failed to carry out the recommendations, the Fund has withheld financial aid until the situation is corrected. This link between technical assistance, policy advice, and financial support is unique with the Fund. It has the effect of lending stature and weight to any technical adviser sent out by the Fund, whether of senior or junior rank.

It is interesting to consider whether the UN agencies are in a stronger or weaker position than the United States or other national governments sponsoring bilateral aid programmes, with respect to sanctions they can apply to recipient governments for project implementation. Testimony from the field on this point is decidedly mixed. The majority of RTARs with whom the writer raised the question were inclined to think that a powerful and rich 'sovereign' government like the United States was able to bring to bear much more decisive pressure than a UN agency if only because the former could dangle—or threaten to withdraw—large-scale offers of capital aid as an inducement to follow-up action on technical projects. Also, they felt, the United States was in a position to insist upon drastic reform measures as a condition for receiving such aid; whereas the UN had to rely chiefly on the force of suggestion or persuasion. Notwithstanding, some RTARs and agency field office directors were of the opinion that the close personal contacts established between UN project personnel and local people were conducive to a favourable atmosphere for long-term support of undertakings initiated with UN assistance. One RTAR strongly believed that any RTAR, if sufficiently skilful, ingenious, and persistent, could contrive reasonably effective sanctions to this end.

Over and beyond this aspect of the problem, reference was repeatedly made to the psychological advantage enjoyed by the UN programme by reason of its dissociation from any taint of 'colonialism' or 'imperialism'; no political, economic, or military strings were attached to it. Its purpose was not 'to win friends or gain allies.' There was no suspicion of a *quid pro quo* in a multilateral programme to which governments contribute as well as from which they receive aid. The UN programme, therefore, tends to be viewed as 'their own' and not as a foreign programme. There have been cases, moreover, where non-Western governments have been reluctant to accept United States aid because they do not want representatives of a powerful foreign government, however friendly, 'mixing' in sensitive policy decision areas, *e.g.*, taxation, trade, credit. This psychosis has carried over to the field of public administration with the result that certain governments have refused to take United States assistance even for training institutes. A government that cannot afford to face criticism that it is yielding to United States (or Soviet?) 'dictation' may be able to adopt recommendations from a multi-national group with much better grace. 'The International Bank,' as one discerning observer has recently noted, 'has proved again and again that the same American who would get nowhere operating out of an Embassy is able to become a trusted adviser in a newly developing country if he represents an agency of the United Nations.'[32]

TAB's recent annual surveys cite a growing number of cases where responsibility for projects benefiting from UN assistance has been successfully transferred to recipient governments. Such transfers include educational and training centres; various research undertakings; plant production, forestry, and fisheries

[32] Harlan Cleveland, in the Introduction to Commander Sir Robert G. A. Jackson's *The Case for an International Development Authority* (Syracuse Univ. Press, 1959), p. 10.

demonstration projects; TB and malaria control, nutritional, and maternal and child health campaigns; and projects for the improvement of administrative and technical services. In addition, there were a substantial number of projects where significant results had already been achieved and for which UN assistance was being steadily scaled down. Furthermore, in a considerable number of cases, there appeared to be a tendency for governments to cling to UN aid as long as possible. By their very nature, certain kinds of training enterprises require five to ten years' development before they are in shape to be turned over completely to the government—whether in public administration, vocational subjects, fundamental education, or civil aviation.

In one notable case, the Venezuelan Government, early in 1958, launched a 'crash' programme of administrative reform on the basis of a diagnostic survey conducted by a senior UN consultant. A National Commission on Public Administration (on the order of the U.S. Hoover Commission) was set up to implement his recommendations, and over a million dollars was allocated by the government to support its work. This represents the largest direct commitment, in money and man-power, so far made by any government to any EPTA project in the field of public administration. Three UN assistance experts are aiding the National Commission in planning and co-ordinating its programme of reform, with emphasis on developing appropriate Venezuelan institutions to carry on the work permanently, including the preparation of a civil service statute, the devising of a budget and accounting system, the establishment of machinery for 'organization and methods' studies, and the creation of a civil service training institute. This undertaking is cited as an example of how new methods and procedures along a broad front promise to be adopted progressively over a period of years, the net results of which it will not be possible to estimate for a long time after the termination of UN aid. The cumulative impact of such advisory operations is of course not susceptible of much, if any, quantitative evaluation—in contrast to projects designed to decrease the incidence of disease or infant mortality, or to expand agricultural productivity, where immediate results are measurable—and sometimes dramatic.

Fellowships and Special Training Programmes

In addition to on-the-spot field projects, the assistance programmes provided for governments through the UN family of agencies have, almost from the beginning, included funds for fellowships, scholarships, and trainee grants. Various fellowship schemes, sponsored by the UN, WHO, Unesco, and ILO, pre-dated the inauguration of EPTA and since then have been considerably expanded. Under EPTA, as indicated in Chapter 2, more than 14,000 fellowship awards were made during the period from 1950 through 1958 to nationals of some 130 countries and dependent territories; roughly three-fifths of this number were financed from the regular budgets of the UN and the affiliated agencies. This sizable army of men and women has pursued programmes of training in over 100 host nations, Europe and North America accounting for around two-thirds of the places of study. During 1958 alone, there were 3,500 awards, divided about evenly between EPTA and regular agency programmes. Among the latter, WHO has by far the largest programme, Unesco and the UN coming next in that order.

As noted in Chapter 9, in connection with country programme trends, the proportion of EPTA funds expended for fellowships has noticeably declined during recent years. This decline is at least in part attributable to the growing availability of national (and regional) centres and institutes for the training of administrators, technicians, and teachers at home. In the approved EPTA country programme allocations for 1959, however, the number of fellowships was considerably greater than for the preceding years, and TAB is now urging governments to take full advantage of fellowship opportunities in drawing up their annual programmes.[33] In the long run, the dividends from training programmes, whether at home or abroad, may be even more far-reaching than from advisory and demonstration projects. For the focus of these training schemes is on the development of personnel who will presumably have responsibility for planning and executing national economic and social welfare programmes over the next generation.

The success of any international fellowship programme

[33] *Report of TAC*, UN Doc. E/3191, 8 Dec. 1958.

depends mainly on two factors: (1) the care with which the grantees are selected in terms of personal potentials and suitability for particular types of training, and (2) how the training is utilized in the home countries after completion of the fellowship period. The planning and supervision of study programmes are probably of next importance.

Within the UN system, the rules governing the award and administration of fellowships are determined by each individual agency. At the same time, a conscious effort has been made to minimize duplication and over-lap among the granting organizations. To this end an inter-agency Technical Working Group on Fellowships was set up as early as 1949. This Group has made considerable progress towards the definition of common acceptable standards relating to language qualifications, the expenses to be borne by nominating governments, stipend rates, reporting procedures, and the like. Since the inception of EPTA, TAB has made use of constructive recommendations from this Group with a view to facilitating interchange of information of fellowship matters and the co-ordination of administrative arrangements. In this connection, the Exchange of Persons Service of Unesco has assembled and disseminated information on all available international fellowship programmes. Since 1948, this Service has published annually a handbook entitled *Study Abroad* which lists in detail opportunities for subsidized training under current international fellowship and exchange programmes. The Unesco secretariat has also conducted continuing studies of some of the complex problems involved in planning, financing, and implementing such programmes.

The selection process

Candidates for fellowships and grants financed from UN system funds are in all cases nominated by governments. National ministries and institutions constitute the official source of candidacies. Here the most difficult problem facing the granting organizations has been how to reduce to a minimum the tendency of governments to propose candidates on the basis of considerations not related to their personal qualifications for appointment. Favouritism and nepotism, rampant in the public services of many under-developed countries, have influenced, if not determined, the nomination of individuals clearly less well equipped for beneficial study abroad than other available persons. It has not been uncommon for national ministers to propose 'protégés,' political or personal, interested in having a pleasant 'junket' abroad.[34] Indeed, there have been instances where such persons, by adroit 'shopping around,' have managed to obtain a succession of lucrative travel grants. On the other hand, national ministers and senior administrators are often averse to releasing able subordinates who occupy key positions in important government services.

Various devices have been developed by granting agencies for the purpose of controlling these extraneous influences in the selection process. One such device, now widely utilized by BTAO and the major specialized agencies, has been to insist that fellowship candidacies be related as closely as possible to current assistance projects. Under this procedure the project leader, or an individual project expert, spots a promising candidate (or candidates). Frequently, the candidate is a local project counterpart who could profit from advanced training in his speciality in another country. Suggestions are informally conveyed to the employing ministry or institution that such a person be considered for a fellowship. The project expert may help to work out with the candidate a tentative programme of study—in what countries, at what level, what subjects, how long, and so forth. Where the project expert has gone at the matter conscientiously and with good judgment, this procedure has paid off handsomely.

A second safeguard, less consistently employed, is for the country or regional office, or mission chief of the appointing agency, or the TAB office, to interview candidates proposed by the government and, if not satisfied that they meet reasonable standards, or that they are adapted for a particular type of training, to suggest diplomatically to the government that other candidates be found.

In the third place, a number of governments have set up national selection committees to screen candidates in specified

[34] In one country, some years ago, the representative of the national Civil Service Commission on a selection committee for public administration fellowships (which included among its members two TAA experts) pressed for the acceptance of two candidates from the Commission's own staff who were clearly unqualified on every count for study abroad. It later developed that he had in effect promised them overseas 'junkets' as a personal favour.

fields, on which the local representative of the appointing agency is invited to sit. This has been done, for example, in some of the WHO and FAO regions, reportedly with good results. In a few countries candidates are screened by the Unesco National Commission, though not always very effectively. In one Latin American country, the Ministry of Education has established a fellowship clearance committee on which various granting organizations are represented, including the UN agencies, the U.S. Fulbright and Point Four units, and the British Council. This committee meets regularly to screen applications and keeps a register of awards and of the employment of 'returnees.' The national co-ordinating office in several countries now reviews all nominations for fellowships submitted by ministries and follows up on the performance of appointees while abroad so that they may be fitted into 'right jobs' on their return home. In order to discourage awards to the same candidate for the same purpose from a succession of sources, the application forms used by most of the UN agencies require the applicant to list all previous fellowships or study grants he has held or for which he has applied. Some of the larger TAB country offices, prodded by the TAB secretariat, are now engaged in building up a complete register of all current and former fellowship holders under the various UN programmes. This, of course, is a tedious and time-consuming operation, complicated by the need of extracting data from numerous government offices and by the insufficient staff available to most RTARs for the purpose.

The net effect of such procedures as the foregoing, while decidedly uneven, has been a considerable diminution of political interference in the selection process. What is still needed in most countries is a strong central unit (within their co-ordinating machinery) to develop objective criteria for appraising candidates proposed by ministries, and for the clearance and processing of applications for awards from *all* fund-granting organizations. Through such a unit an inventory of skills available in the country could be maintained and thus contribute to a sounder basis for determining in what fields and for what types of personnel foreign training is most urgently needed.

The final stage in the selection process, except in WHO, takes place at agency headquarters. Typically, nomination papers are transmitted to headquarters by the regional (or country) office concerned, or by the RTAR in the case of applications to agencies for which he serves as forwarding officer, with such confidential observations as may be appropriate, including statements from project experts and, occasionally, from other local sources of judgment. At agency headquarters there is usually a fellowship selection committee or unit which handles the nominations and obtains from the appropriate technical (or programme) division its advice as to proposed study plans, which must be approved formally by such division. Where the evidence is not convincing, headquarters may seek additional information from the field; or it may even suggest the withdrawal of a candidate by the nominating government, usually on the ground that the proposed study programme does not appear to fit a particular nominee. Any such step as this has to be taken with due regard for the sensitivities of the nominating government and is thus resorted to only rarely. In some cases a government will nominate more than one candidate for each allotted fellowship with an indication of its first choice, which may prove embarrassing if in the agency's judgment one of the other nominees seems to be better suited for appointment.

In WHO, the formal appointment of fellows for study within the region of origin is made by the regional office. If the proposed place of study is outside the region, the regional director sends the nomination with his comments to WHO headquarters, where the technical division concerned goes over the study plan. If it agrees with the proposed arrangements, the application is transmitted to the regional office in the region of study. In case of basic disagreement, headquarters communicates with the regional office of origin with a view to obtaining the nominating government's consent to the suggested changes. In rare instances a government may be advised to withdraw a candidate. Most of WHO's regular budget fellowships are now being awarded to public health administrators and medical scientists with at least two years' professional experience beyond their university training and usually with a year of previous graduate study abroad. Such awards to trained persons are often extended beyond the initial year to a second, third, fourth, or even fifth year. It is less difficult to place these advanced appointees in foreign schools of medicine or public health than in the case of more inexperienced grantees under EPTA.

Placement of fellows

Once appointed, fellowship holders are briefed either at agency headquarters or at the nearest field office (as in WHO), or both. Detailed arrangements for their course of study abroad are worked out by the fellowship unit of the appointing agency, in consultation with the substantive division concerned. In Europe, the National Technical Assistance Committees (referred to in Chapter 5) are frequently used by UN agencies in placing and advising fellows. In some instances, fellows may be assigned by special arrangement to a particular training programme. Thus, for example, TAA some years ago sent a group of senior revenue officials to the Harvard Law School International Programme in Taxation for advanced instruction. Similarly, a special course for inspectors (on UN study grants) was organized at the Board of Inland Revenue in London.[35] At present, BTAO is endeavouring to arrange for nuclei of fellows to study in the same institution or industry. Recently, moreover, the United Nations initiated an interesting experiment for the training of fellows in such fields as hydro-electric power, water development, mining, forestry, land management, and public administration. By arrangement with the University of British Columbia at Vancouver and a number of co-operating universities in north-western United States, a Regional Training Centre has been set up which combines special classroom instruction with guided field work. The idea underlying this experiment is to use the Pacific North-west, now undergoing rapid economic development, as a training laboratory for technicians from less developed areas. The experiment is being financed partly by the United Nations, partly by the University of British Columbia, and partly by the Government of Canada. Under the arrangement, fellows can be farmed out to other universities as well as to industries.

Two countries—Brazil and Denmark—now earmark half of their annual contribution to EPTA for special training and research institutions, seminars, and fellowship study within

[5] Bloch, *op. cit.*

their own borders.[36] The Brazilian arrangement, in particular, has given rise to financial and procedural complications which have necessitated extensive discussions between the TAB secretariat and the government for adjustment. During the past few years, fellows have been sent in considerable numbers to the Soviet Union and certain Eastern European countries. In many of these cases it has apparently been difficult to find out precisely where fellows are located and how they are being trained.

Utilization of study abroad

All agencies require periodic progress reports (ordinarily once a month) from fellows during the term of foreign study. Except in WHO, these reports are sent directly to agency headquarters. At the conclusion of the fellowship, each fellow submits a final report consisting of a summary of the course of study pursued, an analysis of the knowledge acquired, and comments on any difficulties he may have encountered. These reports are frequently useful in connection with the planning of future study programmes in similar fields. After their return home, fellows are instructed to submit one or more follow-up reports (covering a period of six months to two years) on the opportunities they have had to apply the experience derived from foreign study. According to the testimony of agency headquarters officials, this obligation is not always lived up to and the information in such reports as are received is often too vague to be of much value. A substantial number of former fellows 'get lost' so far as the appointing agency is concerned. Unesco, however, has maintained a directory of its fellows from the beginning, and as a means of keeping them in touch with the organization it distributes a periodic fellowship bulletin.

No very meaningful test of the impact of foreign study is possible without following the careers of returnees over a period of years. In nominating candidates, governments ordinarily assume an obligation to provide suitable employment for ex-fellows for a specified time (usually two to three years). But there is no legal sanction for such an obligation, which is in the nature of a 'gentleman's agreement.' Similarly, in accepting

[36] Certain UN agencies are reportedly planning to use Brazil as a major area of training for Africans.

a fellowship award, the grantee must agree to return to employment with his government. Here again, however, the sanction is only a moral one. Not infrequently ex-fellows accept more lucrative positions with private firms, which, to be sure, does not necessarily mean a loss to the country. The instability of government jobs has created a difficulty in some countries.

During recent years systematic surveys of the results of fellowship programmes have been undertaken by TAB and certain of the specialized agencies. In these evaluations answers to two basic questions have been sought: (1) in what kinds of employment are returned fellows engaged in relation to the objectives of the fellowship award? and (2) what special contributions are they making that might reasonably be attributed to their foreign study experience? WHO and Unesco have gone furthest in attempting to devise objective criteria for the conduct of such appraisals, and TAB has substantially followed the procedures of these two agencies in the annual surveys of EPTA fellowships it has conducted since 1956. The data for these various surveys have been obtained in part from ex-fellows' files at agency headquarters, in part by agency field officials, RTARs, and project experts through interview and observation on-the-spot, and in part from replies to detailed questionnaires sent directly to former fellows. Unesco is now planning to make studies of fellows in specific fields over a five-year period by appraising the extent to which they have been able to introduce new techniques at home (*e.g.*, modern library management methods by returned librarians). A special fellowship was recently made available by Unesco for the study of its own fellowship administration at headquarters.

The result of TAB's and WHO's most recent evaluations (conducted in 1958) were strikingly similar.[37] Each study revealed that roughly 90 per cent. of the sample (covering 1,271 ex-fellows in the case of TAB and 1,053 in the case of WHO) had completed their studies abroad, returned home, and accepted employment in their respective fields of study. Of the remaining 10 per cent., nearly half were employed in their home countries but in some other field, the others having failed to complete their fellowships, or to return home, or to obtain

[37] See the *Annual Report of the TAB for 1958, op. cit.*, pp. 73–75; and WHO Doc. A11/P-B/5, 2 April 1958.

employment. Of the 90 per cent. who had employment 'appropriate' to their studies, between one-third and two-fifths had received promotions or were carrying greater responsibility than before the fellowship period. From two-fifths to four-fifths were engaged in training operations; nearly half in introducing new methods; from a sixth to a fourth in establishing new services; and about a quarter in promoting or conducting research. A substantial number were engaged in two or more of these activities concurrently. The TAB survey cited numerous examples of former fellows who are now holding responsible positions in the national or local civil services of their governments—at the rank of director-general, director, deputy-director, or inspector of important administrative departments. Others were making significant contributions to national development programmes as officers of planning boards or managers of development corporations. A considerable number occupied educational posts as deans or professors of university faculties or research institutes.

Of the forty-three countries covered by the TAB review, nineteen were reported as having 'satisfactory' procedures for nominating fellowship candidates and thirteen as 'unsatisfactory.' Some fifteen countries appeared to be 'improving' their procedures. In thirteen countries, governments, through their national co-ordinating machinery, were beginning to keep detailed records of former EPTA fellows, with some assistance from RTAR. In a few countries ex-fellows have formed associations which meet periodically and with which the RTAR endeavours to keep in touch. Certain RTARs now follow the practice of calling together ex-fellows by fields of study for informal discussions of their activities, difficulties, and problems. TAB has recently suggested that each appointing agency should send advance notice to the RTAR of the probable dates of return of fellows and instruct them to contact the TAB office from time to time thereafter.

The foregoing developments, if and when extended to most countries to which fellowship awards are allocated, should provide a basis for reasonably complete, continuing surveys of the more obvious results of fellowship programmes. Supplementing such general surveys, case studies, based on social science techniques, need to be made with a view to discovering as accurately as possible the inter-relationship of such variables as the following: (1) eligibility requirements (including age, experience, and language qualifications); (2) methods of nomination and selection; (3) the duration of the fellowship; (4) types of study programmes (whether regular academic courses leading to a degree or certificate or special arrangements tailored to the needs of individuals or small groups. There is reason to believe, for example, that six months to a year (now the typical fellowship period) is too short a time for many grantees to learn anything of lasting value in a foreign country. Available evidence also suggests the desirability of more careful advance planning and of closer supervision of study programmes than has frequently been the case.

No international fellowship programme can be effectively conducted without constant attention to all these factors. Experience with fellowship schemes financed by large private foundations over many years has shown how tricky their administration is even when official sensitivities are not involved. In an inter-governmental programme the task of ensuring selection by merit is much more difficult. The UN Technical Working Group on Fellowships might usefully undertake to design, in collaboration with TAB and the appointing agencies, a number of intensive inquiries by qualified outside specialists. The costs of such studies could be shared by the agencies as a legitimate charge against fellowship administration. The findings, if taken seriously, might stimulate improved methods of selection, planning, supervision, and follow-up both by nominating governments and by the granting organizations.

Note on special training programmes

In addition to the general fellowship schemes described above, a number of special training programmes have been instituted by various UN organizations. Among these are a UN training programme for African government economists; the worker-trainee programme of the ILO, of which Yugoslavia has been the principal beneficiary; arrangements for the advanced training of young economists at the headquarters of certain of the UN regional economic commissions; a one-year study course, established at the International Monetary Fund in 1951, for specialists on fiscal and monetary problems nominated by

Member countries; and the Economic Development Institute, together with three other small training programmes, conducted by the International Bank. Space will permit a brief description only of the last-named arrangements by way of illustration.

The Economic Development Institute, begun in 1955 and supported in part during its first three years by grants from the Ford and Rockefeller Foundations, operates as a kind of staff college for senior officials responsible for the preparation and implementation of economic development plans in the Bank's less developed Member countries. The participants, limited to about twenty a year, must be nominated by their governments. Since there are always more nominations than can be taken care of with available funds and facilities, admission is on a competitive basis, the Bank endeavouring, as far as possible, to screen nominations in the field. The final selection is made by a committee of headquarters officials under the chairmanship of one of the Vice-Presidents of the Bank. The financing of training at the Institute is now shared by the governments sending students and the Bank itself.

The Institute, located in Washington, provides a six-month course including lectures, seminars, discussion groups, special job assignments, and occasional field trips. Instruction consists of a combination of theoretical and practical economics with special reference to economic growth and development. Student participants in the Institute are encouraged to undertake research on problems directly related to their future needs. When such studies are of sufficiently broad interest, they may be published for wider distribution. The Institute has a director and a small instructional staff on a full-time basis. This staff is assisted by temporary lecturers drawn from the Bank's own professional personnel and from other banks and universities.

In addition, the Bank maintains a six-month trainee programme for a small group of younger nationals from Member countries intended to acquaint them with the work of IBRD and its problems. Since 1950, there have also been a Public Finance programme 'tailored to fit the needs' of the individual trainee and a similar programme which may operate in various subject-matter fields. These last two arrangements, running from three to six months, are designed for middle and senior level officials.

According to Bank authorities, the graduates of all of these programmes have returned, enriched by the experience, to their home posts, to handle economic and fiscal policy-making at the national level.

The Continuing Task of Programme Appraisal

At the outset of this chapter reference was made to the difficulties of contriving feasible ways and means for an objective appraisal of programme impacts. To this complex problem much attention has been given by TAB and various individual agencies during recent years. As early as 1953, the WHO Executive Board initiated a study of certain WHO projects selected from all of its operating regions, and similar studies have been conducted by the WHO secretariat from time to time since then.[38] Concurrently, the International Labour Office undertook a series of detailed analyses of specific field projects in various countries, and in 1956 the Governing Body of ILO instructed the Office to submit annual progress reports on operational activities including an over-all evaluation.[39] These annual evaluations have been based on observations made by governments; reports received from field offices, RTARs, experts, and fellows; and frequent discussions with personnel connected in other ways with the execution of ILO's field programme.

In collaboration with TAB, Unesco sponsored in 1954 a special seminar at Geneva on 'Criteria and Techniques of Evaluation of Technical Assistance for Economic Development,' at which an effort was made to discover whether and how social science methods might be applied to the evaluative process.[40] Following upon the discussions at this meeting, a social scientist from the United States was engaged by Unesco to prepare a 'manual' on 'practical social science measurement techniques' for use by field workers in appraising the results of certain types of projects.[41] During 1958, an experiment was conducted

[38] See, in particular, the *Report on Programme Analysis and Evaluation*, in WHO, O.R.: No. 60, March 1955.

[39] Chapter V of the 1958 report on the *Administration of the Operational Programme*, ILO Doc. G.B.138/T.A/D.1/2, Feb.-March 1958.

[40] The report of this seminar was reproduced in the Unesco *International Social Science Bulletin*, Vol. VII, No. 3 (1955).

[41] This manual, by Dr. Samuel P. Hayes, Jr., was published during 1959 under the title, *Measuring the Results of Development Projects*.

at CREFAL to devise instruments for the use of its students in measuring the impact of their field work.[42] During 1959 a social science expert was sent by Unesco to South-east Asia to survey on-the-spot some of the results of community development action in that part of the world. At the conclusion of his trip a meeting of interviewers and social scientists was to be held to prepare a document for the guidance of future project personnel.

For UNICEF, WHO has prepared technical assessments of BCG vaccination, milk conservation, and maternal and child health campaigns in accordance with guide-lines laid down by UNICEF's programme evaluation unit at headquarters. Such assessments have been difficult to make because few governments have set up any appraisal systems of their own, and it has been necessary to utilize spotty check devices, with extensive reliance on the impressionistic attitudes of local doctors. On the other hand, UNICEF itself has carried on statistical analyses of unit costs of various types of field activities in relation to progress towards their targets. In these analyses comparisons have been made of per unit outlays by UNICEF and by recipient governments, as well as of the costs of different kinds of projects —with a good deal of precision.[43]

In 1957, the Public Administration Division of TAA convened in Geneva a working group for the purpose of reviewing its experience with eleven national and regional training institutes.[44] Participating in this meeting were TAA headquarters staff, current and former institute directors, representatives of the ILO and Unesco secretariats, and outside experts. This meeting produced some valuable commentary on the problems of operating training centres under differing conditions and a useful work paper was presented which listed specific questions that should be taken into account in appraising the results of any given institute. During the following year, a staff member of the Public Administration Division undertook a special evaluation of 'organization and methods' projects which was later examined by an expert working party in New

[42] A brief summary of this experiment appeared in the Unesco *International Social Science Bulletin*, Vol. XI, No. 2 (1959).

[43] See *Co-ordination between UNICEF and the Regular and Technical Assistance Programmes of the United Nations and the specialized agencies*, UN Doc. E/3109, 13 May 1958; also, recent 'General Progress Reports' of the Executive Director of UNICEF to his Executive Board.

[44] See *Training in Public Administration* (New York: United Nations, 1958).

York. One significant conclusion from this study was that improvements in administrative methods and techniques 'can only have a full effect if the machinery of government as a whole is well organized.'[45]

The foregoing are illustrations of efforts by various UN agencies to appraise their respective field programmes. With regard to EPTA in general, TAC was instructed by ECOSOC's original legislative resolution to carry out 'critical examinations of activities undertaken and results achieved' by the Programme. Following a preliminary report on the subject submitted by TAB to TAC in 1954, the latter set up a Working Group 'to go more fully into the whole question of Programme evaluation.' This Group decided that a comprehensive review (1) of technical assistance activities in six selected countries (Bolivia, Ceylon, Colombia, Iraq, Libya and Pakistan) should be made by the TAB secretariat after consultation with the participating agencies, and (2) of the fellowship programme as a whole—both reviews to cover the period from 1951 to 1954.[46] These reviews consisted mainly of a factual description of the results of some 200 projects and 5,000 fellowship awards. They did not purport to be a 'scientific' evaluation but rather provided 'the basic raw materials' for such purpose.

In the light of the two reviews and of replies to a questionnaire received from fifteen countries, TAC proposed in 1956 that a systematic evaluation of EPTA activities should henceforth be made a part of the annual TAB report.[47] These evaluations, covering the year 1956 and subsequently, have been based primarily on replies to a detailed questionnaire submitted by each RTAR to the TAB secretariat after informal consultation with recipient government authorities. As revised for 1958, the questionnaire included the following main headings: planning and programming; co-ordination; counterpart personnel; administrative support; appraisal of operations; regional and inter-regional projects; duration of projects; the use of experts (satisfaction or not, cases of withdrawal, follow-up on their work, and so forth); fellowships and training institutes; equipment and supplies; and efforts towards programme

[45] Report by the Secretary-General on *Technical Assistance in Public Administration*, UN Doc. E/3230, 3 April 1959.
[46] The results of the two reviews were reported in UN Doc. E/TAC/SC.1/R.1, 6 June 1955.
[47] UN Doc. E/2923, 8 Aug. 1956.

evaluation by the host government itself. For the first two evaluations, the RTAR was asked to submit a special report in January covering the preceding year. This arrangement, however, left the TAB secretariat with scarcely enough time to prepare its draft of the TAB annual report for review by the Board in March. It was also discovered that there was some duplication in the materials required for the RTAR's regular quarterly reports and the answers to the evaluation questionnaire. Accordingly, beginning with 1958, it was decided to utilize the RTAR's third quarterly report solely for submission of the evaluation materials, such report to reach TAB headquarters by the end of October. The new procedure not only allows more time for the analysis of country replies by the TAB staff in New York but appreciably reduces the volume of reporting by RTARs. The latter were advised by the TAB secretariat to maintain, on a day-to-day basis, brief but systematic records on individual projects and individual fellows, so as to facilitate the compilation of information for the evaluation questionnaire. The evaluation report is now classified as 'confidential' and copies are sent only to TAB headquarters and to the participating organizations and their appropriate regional offices (if any) for comment.

The annual evaluation, as presented in TAB's Report, deals not so much with the actual results achieved through EPTA activities as with 'those basic factors that make for sound programming and effective implementation, and thereby also for good end results.'[48] As might be expected, the key problem in making the country evaluations has been how to reduce to a minimum the element of subjectivity. The rationale of the EPTA evaluative process is that reactions from governments should be given first importance on the assumption that 'the consumer knows what he wants and what he is really getting' from technical assistance operations. This, however, ignores the fact that the desire to be polite and to give pleasure to the UN is sometimes a predominant consideration. Furthermore, many governments tend to speak with two voices—one in TAC meetings, as to the need of observing sound rules and regulations, and another in their co-ordinating units and ministries at home regarding actual project developments. Sometimes, when

[48] *Annual Report of the TAB for 1958, op. cit.*, p. 58.

projects go wrong, there may be almost a conspiracy of silence as to their shortcomings: ministers refrain from telling the legislative body for fear such revelations might reflect on themselves, while agency project personnel often do not like to admit anything that might become 'a black mark' on their records with the employing agency. In the view of certain RTARs and agency field directors, it is too much to hope for a thoroughly critical appraisal of projects by the interested parties—national authorities on the one side and agency experts on the other. Inevitably, according to this group, the tendency is for 'too rosy' a picture to emerge from the TAB type of annual survey.

There is no doubt that certain compromises have had to be made with 'objectivity,' given the limitations of an inter-governmental framework. It is also true that the attempt to rate projects as 'above or below expectations' involves a degree of subjectivity against which the RTAR, as the 'middleman' in the process, must always be on guard. A government agency, desirous of having a project continued for political or other reasons, may rate it more favourably than it deserves. Moreover, different RTARs employ varying standards and values in deciding how a project should be judged. Nor have all RTARs felt that they could be entirely outspoken concerning the deficiencies of administrative arrangements provided by host governments. On the other hand, an examination of a fair sample of country evaluation reports since 1956 reveals a growing tendency to introduce critical observations. The evaluation exercise is being taken much more seriously by most RTARs than was the case the first year.[49] Under present procedures, they have more time to collect information, to visit project sites, and to discuss operational problems with individual experts. Close contacts with projects have led to the identification of a 'common denominator' that the RTAR can often use in comparing their effectiveness. There appears to be less attempt at 'window-dressing' than formerly. In TAB's published report to TAC for 1958, there were many more frank admissions of weaknesses in project implementation than

[49] One RTAR in Latin America admitted that he had filled out the 1956 questionnaire while on an aeroplane trip—without any special consultation with government authorities or UN agency personnel: he knew all the answers, he said, by reason of having served in the area for several years.

two years earlier. From the standpoint of the RTAR, the annual evaluation exercise affords an excellent opportunity to take stock of the entire country programme; as one discerning RTAR expressed it, 'this is good discipline for ourselves.'

One potentially encouraging development, in a number of countries, has been the conduct of reviews of the country programme by the planning or co-ordinating machinery of the government itself. This is now being done in varying degree in Afghanistan, Argentina, India, Iran, Israel, Malaya, Nepal, the Philippines, and Yugoslavia. In Iran, for example, the Co-ordinating Unit receives copies of the experts' monthly reports and studies them with a view to eliciting from ministries further specific information regarding their work. The head of the unit sits down with the RTAR for a joint assessment of project operations for TAB purposes. In 1958, the Indian Government requested the United Nations to provide a team of outside specialists to undertake an evaluation of its far-reaching community development programme, towards which the United States, the Ford Foundation, and the United Nations have provided different kinds of assistance.

> The amount of care with which individual projects are analysed varies from country to country, depending largely on the quality of the planning and co-ordinating machinery. . . . In general, however, there is no doubt that under the country programming procedures, the annual programming exercise has steadily developed into a kind of comprehensive *built-in evaluation*.[60]

Evaluation is tending to become a continuing process, extending over the entire year.

Another development of some significance has been the recent establishment, or strengthening, of programme evaluation units at agency headquarters. In one form or another, WHO, FAO, ILO, Unesco, and UNICEF all maintain such units. Efforts are being made to improve the methodology of evaluation by experimentation with both quantitative and qualitative techniques. As already noted, the guide-lines for periodic reporting by project missions now stress the importance of a constant assessment of project trends and difficulties. The governing organs of the specialized agencies are giving increasing emphasis to the need of objective appraisals of field

[60] *Annual Report of the TAB for* 1958, *loc. cit.*

programmes.[51] In 1957, ECOSOC adopted a resolution requesting the United Nations and the specialized agencies to make an estimate of the probable scope, trend, and cost of their programmes in the economic, social, and human rights fields over the period 1959–64, followed by a consolidated report to the Council at its 1960 summer session.[52] FAO decided 'to combine this forward appraisal with an evaluation of its present programme,' while the 1958 Unesco General Conference laid down a series of criteria for appraising the organization's programmes during 1959. The Paris secretariat, meanwhile, prepared for ECOSOC a general appraisal of Unesco's entire programme during the twelve years of its existence.[53]

These over-all appraisals of programme trends must of course be distinguished from the type of annual survey conducted by TAB, where the main emphasis is on immediate project operations. To a considerable extent the TAB surveys are bound to become somewhat repetitive from year to year, 'leading substantially to the same conclusions,' in view of the stabilization of EPTA's dimensions. Accordingly, in 1959, TAB proposed to TAC that in the future each annual evaluation should concentrate on some specific theme or problem, instead of attempting an 'elaborate and omnibus type of review covering the entire ground.' Thus, for one year, special attention might be given to regional projects; for another year, to fellowships; and for subsequent years, to planning and co-ordinating machinery, or to the co-ordination of EPTA with non-UN aid programmes; and so on. After a four- or five-year cycle of such special appraisals, the general type of evaluation might be reverted to. These ideas received the endorsement of TAC.[54] During discussions in the Committee, several members felt that future evaluations should devote greater attention to detection of the causes of failure of projects, including the inclusion of information on projects that had suffered because of 'premature termination.' The proposed cyclical scheme should facilitate project evaluation 'in depth'—in contrast to the year-to-year piecemeal appraisals.

[51] In this connection, the Unesco General Conference, at its 1958 session, authorized the Director-General to study current developments in the techniques of social surveys and to organize pilot studies of evaluation techniques.

[52] ECOSOC Resolution 665C (XXIV), 1 Aug. 1957.

[53] For the findings of this survey, see Unesco Doc. 10C/10, 14 Aug. 1958.

[54] See the *Report of the Technical Assistance Committee*, UN Doc. E/3298, 29 July 1959.

Field programme evaluation will be a never-ending operation. Its sociological potentialities are far-reaching. There are basic questions that none of the evaluations thus far undertaken has touched. What, for example, has been the impact of technical assistance programmes on the attitudes of peoples around the world towards the UN system? How have its 'grass roots' operations affected the image of its goals and purposes in different culture areas? Studies of this kind, to be sure, would be difficult as well as expensive to conduct, and it is too much to expect—nor would it be appropriate for—the busy staffs of the UN family of agencies to undertake such research. But here lies a fascinating range of inquiry for social scientists which has scarcely been tapped.[55]

[55] For interesting suggestions as to how such studies might be designed, see Robert C. Angell, 'Discovering Paths to Peace,' in *The Nature of Conflict* (Paris: Unesco, 1957).

PART FOUR

RETROSPECT AND PROSPECT

12

THE OPERATIONAL BALANCE: HEADQUARTERS AND FIELD

This volume has endeavoured to portray the evolution of organizational and administrative arrangements through which the United Nations family of agencies is now conducting a nexus of economic and social programmes extending to the outer reaches of the world community. The central concern of the study has been the decade of experience beginning with the inauguration of the Expanded Programme of Technical Assistance in 1950.

The over-all framework within which UN agency administrators have had to operate is admittedly complicated, arising largely from organizational pluralism and the dispersion of policy controls among autonomous legislative bodies. In this setting, field programmes have emerged, or have been deliberately designed, both on a single agency and an inter-agency basis, followed recently by the Special Fund which combines centralized control with separate agency execution of projects. Financial support has been derived not only from the regular budgets of the UN and the associated agencies but from special voluntary contributions of various kinds. Funds have included currencies with differing degrees of convertibility, thus calling for skilful currency management.

Through experimentation, improvisation, and invention, programme administrators have managed to contrive operational procedures which, while still unnecessarily involved in some respects, work reasonably well. Noticeable progress towards a cohesive structure for programme implementation has been achieved. Many of the difficulties that persist are either inherent in the nature of the problem or stem from conditions imposed upon the operators by their 'masters'—the *ensemble* of Member States.

In fairness to the programme operators, it is only proper to note that these masters have tended to underestimate, partly by intent and partly through ignorance, the importance of supplying administrators with adequate operational tools. This 'economy complex' has been particularly evident with regard to appropriations for the improvement of field staff recruitment, for staff travel on official business, and for briefing and supporting services for field personnel. All of these operations cost money. Unfortunately, it has not been sufficiently recognized that, in proportion, as the quality of staff services improves, lost motion in project operations is likely eventually to decline and project effectiveness to increase—though it may be difficult to measure the latter in monetary terms. In the policy control organs, the tendency has been to regard all such items simply as 'overhead' costs (which, strictly speaking, they are), and then typically to conclude that these costs are already 'too high' —bureaucrats being what they are supposed to be in the 'Parkinsonian' sense! Government representatives seldom take cognizance of the fact that the *unit* costs of international administration are likely to be somewhat higher than for national administration because of the impact of the principle of geographic distribution on staff performance, the necessity of language interpretation and translation and the multilingual publication of documents, and disproportionately larger outlays for communication and transport.[1]

Agency heads, if anything, have been too timid in requesting—and pressing for—budgetary allocations sufficient to man and equip the instrumentalities essential for effective administration. Notwithstanding, every sign points to the fact, as Robert Asher has observed, that UN technical assistance 'is a notably more efficient operation than it was several years ago.'[2]

In the concluding section of this study it is proposed to focus attention on two of the most perplexing problems with which programme managers have been—indeed still are—confronted. The first of these relates to the internal administrative process

[1] Despite the fact that multilateral programmes have certain built-in overhead costs, there is evidence to show that the United Nations 'delivers' technical assistance at smaller administrative cost than the U.S. Point Four establishment. This appears to be explained by the fact that salaries, allowances, supporting administrative services, substantive back-stopping, evaluation procedures, and the preparation of justifications for legislative review involve proportionately lower levels of expenditures for the UN system than for the United States Government's overseas establishment.

[2] In his article on 'Economic Co-operation under UN Auspices,' *International Organization* (Summer 1958).

of individual agencies having responsibility for executing field programmes on a relatively sizable scale; more particularly, to the balance of controls as between headquarters and the field. The second problem is concerned with inter-agency relationships and the possibility of achieving more integrated programme-planning and implementation through the UN system as a whole. The present chapter will hazard some tentative generalizations on the first issue. In the final chapter an effort will be made to project discernible programme and organizational trends into the 1960s, pointing to the kind of role the UN system might most effectively play as an instrumentality for sharing the world's knowledge, skills and resources with its under-privileged peoples.

The Uses of Field Machinery

How to achieve a proper adjustment between centripetal and centrifugal pulls in programme-making and administration has been a recurring theme during the decade under survey. In this connection the establishment of permanent field machinery of some sort has been a pervasive development. No major organization has entirely escaped this tendency. Broadly, it has marked a shift of balance from clearing-house, research, and world policy-guidance activities towards the provision of direct aids and services to governments and peoples. The existence of such machinery, however, does not necessarily connote decentralization in the strict sense of the term. A field office, for example, may serve as an outpost of headquarters and even fortify central authority by providing it with a listening and contact point *vis-à-vis* governments. Decentralization involves something more than this, namely, the delegation to field units of powers of decision on administrative or substantive questions, or both. The real test of decentralization lies not so much in the work-load of an agency's field offices as in the frequency with which they decide matters themselves and how important such matters are.

In UN and specialized agency circles the concept of 'decentralization' has been employed in various ways at different times. For instance, it has been used to refer to the establishment (or extension) of field machinery *per se*, to the outposting of headquarters personnel to existing field units, to the devolution of decision-making authority as suggested above, or to varying combinations thereof. Once in operation, to be sure, agency field offices tend to acquire discretionary functions either by explicit delegation from the centre or by accretion through practice. In the UN system, as we have seen, the scope of such functions now ranges from the handling of relatively limited procedural matters relating to programme execution (*e.g.*, the Unesco field science co-operation offices) at one end of the scale, on to the over-all programme formulating and administering role of the WHO regional offices at the other end.[3] In FAO the trend appears to be towards a fuller use of field machinery for regional programme development, though without moving as far towards substantive decentralization as WHO. While the United Nations has no field establishment of its own for technical assistance *per se* (since the liquidation of the TAA Latin American outposting experiment), the TAB field offices perform for it various administrative and technical services not dissimilar to those provided by the field offices of certain specialized agencies. The secretariats of the UN regional commissions, which enjoy considerable discretion in connection with regional programme initiative, also advise certain categories of UN project experts on the technical side, along with some actual participation in operational projects.

It seems clear that as the international provision of direct services to governments grows in volume, diversity, and geographic spread, various types of decisions inevitably tend to be devolved upon field units. But what decisions and in what doses? Are there criteria that might help to determine the operational balance between headquarters and the periphery —and to adjust the balance as conditions change? Here we are dealing not with absolutes but with relatives: there can be no such thing as complete centralization or complete decentralization. 'Administrative arrangements may not cause or eliminate the maladjustments of centralization, but they can do much to augment or decrease their effect.'[4] What are the implications of a sound operational balance for headquarters organization, for

[3] Currently there is a move to devolve more authority upon the Unesco field science co-operation offices to implement programmes in the region, but covering natural science only.

[4] David B. Truman, *Administrative Decentralization* (Univ. of Chicago Press, 1940), p. 204.

field structure, and for the communications process by which the two are joined?

On some of these questions the evidence of this study is not conclusive. It was not always possible to examine case situations intensively enough to warrant firm generalizations. Accordingly, in the Appendix, the writer has ventured to suggest types of additional research that might confirm, refine, modify, or possibly invalidate some of the tentative hypotheses here put forward.[5]

THE PROS AND CONS OF DECENTRALIZATION

Stated broadly, the over-riding objective of any scheme of field organization would appear to be twofold: (1) to gear programme content as realistically as possible to programme end-use (governments, institutions, individuals), and (2) to facilitate programme implementation. The two facets of this over-all objective are closely interrelated. By maintaining an appropriate structure of adequately staffed field offices, an agency can presumably keep in more sustained and more relaxed touch with government officials and with the changing political and economic *milieu* than if it relies wholly on correspondence and relatively infrequent travel missions of headquarters staff. This is the more apt to be the case if field offices exercise a recognizable influence on the course of project construction and on the negotiation of project agreements. A strong regional office, moreover, can act as a 'transformer' of central policy decisions into regionally (and locally) understood values, and deal with governments on a more flexible basis than is usually possible for headquarters. The more such units are concerned with programme orientation, the more likely are host governments to develop a sense of identification with the agency's goals. As a by-product there may be a not unimportant educative impact.

On the side of programme implementation, the lodgement in field office staffs of definite responsibility for supervising, inspecting, and evaluating project operations can make for greater programme effectiveness than when these activities are handled primarily or wholly from headquarters. In addition, the devolution of authority to deal on the spot with staff

[5] See pp. 553-555.

complaints, arising out of the terms of their appointments, may contribute to staff morale and thus improve the quality of its performance. In so far as technical back-stopping can be provided at the field level, the less likely are project missions to acquire a sense of being isolated or forgotten. These generalizations, to be sure, rest on the assumption of well organized and properly staffed field offices at the professional level. A too thinly staffed office may be more of a nuisance than a help.

What is the other side of the coin? The more programme formulation is decentralized, the greater would appear to be the possibility of stressing regional claims at the expense of world needs and of diminishing the organization's role in setting general standards. If and as a large part of the professional staff of a programme-executing organization is deployed to field units, the leadership role of headquarters may be attenuated. Regional and local pressures may make themselves increasingly felt in the process by which the agency's total resources for operational activities are distributed. Political log-rolling is never entirely absent from decision-making even in a technical international agency, but it may have more scope where programme allocations are made largely in terms of geographic considerations.

From the standpoint of programme execution, the more discretion field units have in dealing with situations on a day-to-day basis, the more complex becomes the problem of ensuring that headquarters policy directives are actually carried out. Unless an effective system of staff rotation, reporting, and inspection is maintained, there may lurk the danger of subtle sabotage of central policy by field office bureaucracies.

Whatever the other arguments for or against extensive decentralization, there is fairly general agreement on one point—that it tends to involve higher administrative costs than a centralized system of field operations. This of course is as true of national as of international administrations. The wider the diversity of an agency's programme, the larger the number of professional personnel needed to staff field offices. Since there is not likely to be a corresponding reduction of such personnel at headquarters, some increase in total staff costs is probably unavoidable. Although such additional costs may to a certain extent be offset by smaller outlays for staff travel, the partial duplication of administrative and housekeeping services at the field level is likely to entail extra expenditure. The decentralization of accounting and personnel processing operations, for example, seems almost certain to result in higher unit costs than when such operations are concentrated at headquarters. Accordingly, the fetish for decentralization in certain Member government circles on the assumption of 'economy' would appear to rest on a shaky budgetary foundation.[6] However, as total programme resources available to the organization expand, the percentage outlays for field office expenses appear to decline perceptibly, the cost factor thus assuming diminishing importance.[7]

It is not to be implied from the above comparisons that the advantages and liabilities of decentralization can somehow be nicely weighed one against another as a basis for determining how much—or how little—of it a given agency would be advised to put into effect. Experience would suggest that pragmatism—not dogmatism—should be the guiding principle both for policy-controllers and for programme managers. The programme process in its entirety is an art rather than a science. Various patterns of action will inevitably evolve by trial and error. The delegation of responsibility to field units cannot wholly be detailed in rules, indispensable as basic procedural directives may be. Since programme situations never remain static, headquarters-field relationships need to be kept constantly under review. Moreover, the functional needs of different agencies are not necessarily the same: the case for regionalism in programming may be stronger in certain subject-matter areas than in others. Even so, it may help to clarify the

[6] No systematic study of the administrative costs of decentralization has ever been conducted by the WHO secretariat apparently for two reasons. One is the problem of devising criteria for such an inquiry. It would be relatively easy to isolate accounting costs, but any meaningful comparison of travel outlays would be extremely difficult to make. The second reason is doubt as to the utility of such a study. WHO's regional pattern is now firmly set in the *mores* of the organization and its Members. Even if it were shown that administrative costs were *x* per cent. higher than under an assumed centralized system, the claim of greater programme 'effectiveness' would undoubtedly be advanced to justify the continuance of regionalism—irrespective of any budgetary disadvantage. Director-General Chisholm, speaking before the Executive Board at its seventh session, admitted that 'the regionalization to which the Organization is committed is an extraordinarily expensive form of organization. Also, properly developed, properly used, it is an extremely efficient and effective form of organization.' WHO, O.R.: No. 46, Jan.-Feb. 1953, p. 158.

[7] In 1956, for instance, the administrative costs of WHO's regional offices amounted to 14·5 per cent. of the total regular budget; three years later they had declined to about 13 per cent.

problem if we try to differentiate the kinds of functions that would appear to call for predominantly centralized treatment from those that may advantageously be shared, in varying degrees, between headquarters and the field.

The Sharing of Functions Spatially

As a minimum, the following functions clearly must remain under essentially central control, even though in some instances field offices may usefully contribute to the decision-making process:

(1) *Substantive operations*

- the invention of new techniques and devices for the promotion of the purposes of the UN system in reference to economic and social development;
- the over-all planning, financing, and evaluation of agency field programmes;
- the stimulation and co-ordination of research of world-wide significance;
- the development of appropriate international standards;
- the provision of general clearing-house services for field missions, governments, and private groups;
- the organization of training arrangements on a world-wide scale.

(2) *Administrative and budgetary operations*

- the determination of agency-wide regulations governing personnel, budgeting, procurement, accounting, and auditing;
- the allotment of funds for field use;
- the management of currencies;
- the formulation of rules for reporting from the field.

At the opposite end of the spectrum, again as a minimum, would come the maintenance of a permanent field establishment geared to the volume and incidence of the agency's total field operations. Besides affording liaison with governments, this field structure should be in a position to provide briefing and technical support services for field personnel as far as budgetarily possible. It is of course recognized that for various highly specialized undertakings only headquarters will be able to supply technical briefing or substantive back-stopping. But the orientation of project missions to the cultural, political, economic and administrative environment with which they are to be confronted can ordinarily be provided more illuminatingly at the field level.

As regards field staffing, it is doubtful if the delegation to field office heads of the power to appoint or assign personnel in the professional categories is operationally wise. In terms of maintaining uniform standards, facilitating inter-regional transfers, and thus of promoting the long-term goal of a career field service, retention of control over appointments and assignments at headquarters (in consultation with regional officials as appropriate) would, on the whole, seem advisable. There would appear to be even more cogent reasons for leaving the authority to designate regional office heads in the hands of the agency's chief executive. The practice (as in WHO) of allowing inter-governmental regional committees to select the regional directors, with what amounts merely to a *pro forma* approval by the central Executive Board, may produce stress and strain that will undermine the authority of the Director-General.

Regional offices, on the other hand, may play an important role in the field recruitment process. A properly equipped (even if small) personnel unit, at the regional level, can provide valuable professional guidance to the technical specialists of the office in discovering and evaluating intra-regional talent for project appointments; similarly, in connection with the appraisal of government nominees for fellowship and trainee grants. Finally, as suggested earlier, field offices should be given wide discretion to deal with matters affecting the legal rights and duties of project as well as office staff, with headquarters concurrence or action required only in serious disciplinary or termination cases, or where substantial amounts of money are involved. Such delegation of authority serves to speed up decisions on a variety of annoying pay and status details and thereby helps to relieve staff anxieties.

In addition, a good case can be made for the delegation to field office heads of the power to determine internal organization and budgetary actions pertaining to their own offices (1) consistent with general financial and personnel regulations and (2) subject to *ex post facto* review by headquarters. While reasonable requests for allotment changes can usually be obtained from the central office without difficulty, this can involve considerable correspondence. The issuance of block allotments for field office purposes, within broad limits, would eliminate much of this extra paper work. Over and beyond being granted authority to make local purchases for office needs, the field office head, as is now the case in certain agencies, might well be allowed to buy project supplies when procurable from nearby points at reasonable prices; while project mission chiefs, with the approval of the agency field office, might usefully be authorized to purchase locally available items in emergencies even when the market price is higher than if ordered directly from abroad. Also, there would appear to be no strong reason against empowering an agency regional office director to authorize changes in project operational plans, within designated limits, so as to reduce the number of times headquarters approval of project alterations must be obtained in advance. Local administrative situations, involving the availability of counterparts and other support, often change after the negotiation of a project; or there may be a top-level reorganization that will require an adjustment of project arrangements. Some flexibility, by devolution to the regional director, would seem to be warranted.

Thus far, in discussing the functions of field organization, we have been concerned essentially with administrative and servicing operations. On these we have taken the view that the benefits of devolving fairly broad discretion upon field units are likely to out-weigh whatever disadvantages there may be. It is in order to add that in the case of relatively large field offices conformity with central norms probably may best be assured by assigning to such offices a trained administrative (or financial) officer with previous headquarters experience. This, as we have seen, is the practice with regard to WHO's regional offices and the UN regional commission secretariats. Similar arrangements might desirably be extended to other field offices serving major programme areas. The presence of a vigilant headquarters-oriented officer can help keep field office operations up to minimum standards of efficiency.

This brings us to the most controversial point of all: to what extent does it seem desirable to allow regional offices, regional inter-governmental bodies, or both, to influence programme-making in regional terms? A substantial gradation of impacts is possible in this connection. Are there any meaningful guide-lines that can be applied to the problem? Is there something inherent, for example, in health or in agriculture, that calls for regionalized treatment (as in WHO and to a lesser degree in FAO), in contrast to education (in Unesco) or to public administration (in the UN)?

While it can be argued that the basic problems of health or agriculture are more common to geographical groups of countries than, say, the problems of industrial or educational development, yet by the very nature of the UN system's aid programme concrete action must be geared to individual national governments—including most co-operative projects of a regional character.[8] This point is relevant even to multi-purpose river basin surveys (*e.g.*, the Mekong River). There is no evidence from the present study of any close relation between the degree of regional decentralization of programme formation in an agency and its inclination, or capacity, to devise effective regional (and inter-regional) projects.

Even granting as valid the assumption that programming in health and agriculture often may involve a distinct regional focus, it does not follow that FAO should go as far as WHO and adopt a policy which in effect gives to regionally-constituted bodies a decisive voice in determining programme content for their respective regions.[9] There were special historical and political reasons that led WHO initially to set up, and later to fortify the role of, regional offices and regional committees in programme construction. The traditions and pressures affecting FAO's orientation do not appear to be of the same order of magnitude. In FAO's case, the more limited (though growing) educational and advisory role played by a cluster of regional groups could potentially provide an adequate basis for keeping headquarters aware of evolving regional ideas, interests, and needs. Much the same comment could be made on the potentialities of the ILO regional conferences. The current trend in FAO towards linking its regional offices more closely

[8] Unesco, for example, rarely finds it possible to apply a common solution to the problems dealt with in its field programmes—even in neighbouring countries.

[9] In this connection, it is pertinent to recall that WHO's field programme operations are roughly 50 per cent. larger in dollar terms than are FAO's.

with the planning and management of regional meetings might perhaps be emulated by ILO.

Air navigation regionalism in ICAO presents unique features. Here geographical differences as to air traffic conditions have been sufficiently significant to warrant differentiated planning for air navigation facilities and services through regional channels. However, these channels—the regional air navigation meetings—are operationally regulated by ICAO's central Council and their proposals are intensively analysed by the Air Navigation Commission at Montreal before being referred to the Council for ultimate approval. This process is one of technical planning and does not involve the earmarking of funds to governments for direct aid projects. As regards field operations, ICAO's special problem seems to be how to relate more closely the existing regional office task of helping governments to implement regional air navigation plans with the planning and supervision of technical assistance projects financed from EPTA funds.

To sum up: what is being suggested here is that the role of regional offices in the programme process should be confined to technical guidance in project negotiation, co-operation with experts and government officials in the designing of project operational plans, continuing surveillance over project development, and aid to headquarters in following up and appraising project results. Where an organization finds it politically advisable to establish 'representative' regional bodies, the regional offices concerned can serve as conveyors of information and ideas to and from their meetings and assist headquarters in providing them with staff leadership. Over and beyond these functions, regional offices obviously have a major part to play in preparing, organizing, and conducting regional undertakings in the form of training and research seminars, symposia, and study tours. In different ways such activities are now being performed by the regional offices of WHO and FAO.

The UN regional commission secretariats sometimes play a significant part in the execution of regional (and even country) technical assistance projects. Moreover, they can and do co-operate with BTAO and the specialized agencies in sponsoring a variety of undertakings of regional interest. Unlike the WHO regional offices, however, each UN regional commission secretariat is under the direct control of an executive secretary appointed by the central head of the organization. This makes a subtle but important difference in its status *vis-à-vis* headquarters. While the regional commissions may make proposals for co-operative action by the governments of the region, the former are bound by basic programme directives issued by ECOSOC. Nor are the technical assistance activities of the United Nations itself planned primarily along regional lines.

The foregoing observations are intended to underline the complexity of adjusting headquarters-field relationships in inter-governmental agencies operating in different functional domains. While there are certain underlying postulates that should guide policy decisions generally, the patterns arrived at are bound to exhibit differences if only because of the impact of different traditions, administrative philosophies, styles of agency leadership, and clienteles. To seek complete inter-agency uniformity for its own sake would be a sterile endeavour. Even if the specialized agencies had at the outset been constituted as subordinate 'ministries' or 'departments' in a functionally integrated UN organization, the chances are that their field arrangements would have varied significantly—according to their particular functional requirements. Such, for example, is the picture to be found in the sprawling field organization of the United States Government, where different federal economic and social programmes are marked by varying degrees of policy and administrative devolution to divergent patterns of field areas and offices—often in partnership with the state governments.

Organizational Patterns at the Centre

However sensibly constructed the operational balance between headquarters and the field may be, it cannot be expected to yield maximum benefits unless its application is facilitated by an appropriate central organization, by a field structure tailored to the agency's programme needs, and by an adequate system of communication between headquarters and the field. Many of the operational dilemmas that plague administrators at the field level tend to mirror organizational and procedural difficulties at headquarters.

As for headquarters set-up, the first desideratum would appear to be the establishment of arrangements through which all field programmes, irrespective of the source of their financing, are reviewed and approved as parts of an integrated whole. As indicated in Chapters 6 and 8, the central secretariats of the major organizations involved in extensive field activities have been moving in this direction, albeit in different ways and at different rates, during recent years. What may be called 'programme cabinets' now function importantly in most cases as instruments for co-ordinating programme proposals emanating from the substantive divisions. This integrative policy-making process, as the Advisory Committee of the UN General Assembly has repeatedly observed, is complicated by differences in time schedules for the formulation and costing of programmes.

> For any given year, the Expanded Programme is planned on a firm basis, generally six to twelve months later than the regular programme; in some cases, where the regular programme is on a biennial basis [as in FAO and Unesco] the time gap is still longer in respect of the programmes for the second year of the biennial period.[10]

Nor can the requests from governments under the TAB country-programming system be entirely foreseen at the time the regular programme and budget document is drawn up. These difficulties might be mitigated, though not completely overcome, if the planning of country programmes under TAB rules could be undertaken on longer-than-a-single-year basis. As noted in Chapter 9, an experimental step in this direction was authorized by TAB during 1959 in the form of two-year planning. The element of uncertainty in EPTA programming would be still further reduced if requesting governments, as they are now

[10] UN Doc. A/4172, 25 Aug. 1959. Within the UN itself, regular programme and EPTA activities are now planned at the same time. In June 1959, the Secretary-General set up an Economic Policy Board consisting of the Under-Secretary for Economic and Social Affairs, the Commissioner of Technical Assistance, the then Under-Secretary for Public Administration, and the Director of Personnel, with himself as chairman and the Under-Secretary for Special Political Affairs as the 'executive member,' who was to act for the Secretary-General in the latter's absence. This Board was intended to aid in ensuring 'a flexible and co-ordinated approach' to requests for technical assistance, 'especially in the case of countries or areas with particular problems' in order that they may obtain 'maximum benefit from all available sources.' The Executive Chairman of TAB, the Managing Director of the Special Fund, and the Under-Secretary for Trusteeship and Information from Non-Self-Governing Territories were to attend meetings of the Board as appropriate (UN Press Release SG/822, 9 June 1959). This Board reportedly meets as occasion demands—about six to eight times a year—and deals with crisis situations as well as long-term policy trends. It could conceivably develop into an 'economic cabinet' for the Secretary-General—or lapse into non-use.

asked to do, would indicate at the outset tentative terminal dates for projects, along with operational plans for the full course of each new project. By assuming, as is the practice in WHO, an approximate level of EPTA funds for the budgetary period being planned for, it is possible for an agency not only to prepare a reasonably complete presentation of programme proposals from all budgetary sources, but to give particular attention to possibilities of inter-project consolidation.

The more integrated and better synchronized programme planning at agency headquarters becomes, the better equipped will field office staffs be to appraise the progress of current projects and judge the soundness of future project requests. By having available a full perspective on the agency's field operations and their interrelations, such staffs should be in a position to perform their negotiating tasks more intelligently and with greater discrimination.

Furthermore, and of equal importance for smooth central-field communication, there is the need of ensuring the closest possible working relations at headquarters between the subject-matter divisions and those units responsible for programme operations and servicing. In most of the UN agencies, the personnel, budgetary, fiscal, procurement, and accounting functions relating to EPTA are now being handled increasingly by the normal administrative services of the secretariat. This is a sensible trend, partly because it concentrates responsibility for such functions in the same units and partly, also, because this arrangement is economical in terms of the utilization of staff. On the other hand, the urge for economy clearly should not go to the point of taxing small staff groups beyond their capacity to handle expeditiously the extra servicing burden. Experience in certain agencies suggests that the provision of some additional staff, especially as regards personnel management, would give substantial returns.

A more crucial problem concerns the status and functions of the special unit serving as the principal channel for communication with recipient governments, field offices, and project missions. Some such unit now exists in the secretariats of all of the agencies with sizable field programmes. During the earlier years of EPTA, and in a few agencies to a certain extent even today, these units were criticized on two counts: (1) that they tended to become bottlenecks in handling communication flows from the field, and (2) that they were tempted to encroach upon the advisory and technical back-stopping prerogatives of the substantive divisions.

As for the first criticism, it is only fair to say that some of these operational units were not adequately staffed to process with dispatch the voluminous correspondence that pours in from the field. It should also be recognized that it took some time for these new special units to 'shake down' their internal procedures, and one or two are still far from being 'streamlined' in this regard. Part of the difficulty, however, has come from the slowness with which the administrative and substantive divisions at headquarters either act on matters referred to them by the special unit or return to the latter their comments for relay to the field. The institution of some kind of time-checking device in each special unit might help to speed up these intra-secretariat operations.

The second criticism reflects the difficulty of drawing a hard and fast line between the management and technical aspects of field programmes. More importantly, perhaps, it also reflects the existence of strain or friction between substantive and operational units. As experience has added to the sophistication of staff groups, this state of affairs has tended to disappear. Where, as recently at UN headquarters, the special operational unit (TAA) was merged for top-level control purposes with the major substantive department (ESA), improved teamwork between the two groups has been particularly evident. There is clearly no standard pattern for the solution of this problem. Staff attitudes and administrative leadership may in some situations be more important than organizational arrangements.

Somewhere in each central secretariat special responsibility needs to be lodged for ensuring that essential analysis and evaluation functions are performed for field programming. These functions include the analysis and classification of project reports and the development of criteria and techniques for appraising programme trends. Both of these operations involve continuing contracts with field offices. If handled imaginatively, each should aid significantly in improving the recruitment and briefing of experts, as well as future programme planning. For this purpose a small staff unit might usefully be attached either to the 'front office' of the organization (if a specialized agency) or to that of the Commissioner for Technical Assistance (in the UN). Since such a unit would need to 'ride herd' over various technical divisions where most of the spadework would have to be done, it should have a relatively high hierarchical status. On the other hand, it ought not to be given any direct administrative responsibilities. Its main job would be to think and study. Arrangements for the briefing and de-briefing of experts at headquarters, for example, should continue to be made by the special unit referred to above, in collaboration with the technical and administrative divisions concerned. In order to keep such a unit sensitized to operational developments, there should be a constant flow of staff into it from other headquarters divisions and from field assignments.

Rationalizing Agency Field Establishments

The pattern of organization relationships being adumbrated in this chapter is predicated on the assumption that, where field programme dimensions warrant, the maintenance of a suitable, permanent field structure can help to strengthen over-all programme execution. As demonstrated in Chapter 4, the galaxy of agencies constituting the UN family has evolved, in most cases piece by piece, criss-crossing networks of field offices. No two of these networks are exactly alike in terms of coverage, hierarchical contours, or location of offices. In some instances (notably FAO and UNICEF) there are offices at the regional, sub-regional (*i.e.*, zone or area), and country levels. In FAO, the 'zonal' offices (as in Latin America) are in practice responsible partly to the regional office and partly to Rome. ILO maintains two separate organizational structures in the field—its 'field' offices properly called and its older system of 'branch offices' and 'national correspondents,' the latter having little field programme responsibility. Unesco has established a number of field offices the functions of which are limited to the natural (and in two instances the social) science segment of its highly diversified field operations; in the Western hemisphere, by a curious circumstance, it has a 'regional' office at Havana in addition to a natural science co-operation office at Montevideo. UNICEF's two-layer hierarchy of field offices, while functionally unified, involves considerable duplicatory correspondence and reporting as between the base (single country or area offices) *and* the regional office *and* headquarters. In certain parts of the world, air communication between country offices and agency headquarters is just as quick as, if not quicker than, with the nearest regional office.

These are some of the differentials of agency field office patterns which have proliferated bit by bit as a result of political as well as operational reasons. Governments that want regional (or country) offices in their capitals for prestige purposes, or sometimes as a form of 'pork barrel,' exert pressures to this effect in the policy organs of the agency concerned. To the independent observer certain agency field office networks thus appear to have become operationally unwieldy. While a drastic overhauling of field machinery is probably neither politically nor administratively feasible, gradual adjustments are not out of the question. In so far as possible, in the interest of budgetary economy and the minimization of operational confusion, the field offices of an agency should form part of a single pyramid, with unbroken lines of responsibility upward from the base to the headquarters secretariat. It would seem wasteful to maintain field offices whose territorial coverage or delegated functions over-lap, or whose purview is confined to only one part of the agency's field activities—as is now to some extent the situation in ILO, Unesco, and ICAO. Where there is a cogent reason for establishing offices in between regional and country levels, their status in the hierarchical structure calls for careful definition if double reporting and double accounting are to be avoided. As a general proposition, the fewer the rungs on the territorial ladder, the less the chance of crossed lines.

Before setting up new field offices below the regional level, an agency would do well to consider possible alternatives. Where the areal coverage of a regional office is vast, and its programme volume is rapidly growing, it might be preferable to divide the region into two or more regions instead of adding hierarchically subordinate offices. Another possibility, in a different kind of situation, might be to arrange for more frequent visits of regional office staff to the area to be covered by the proposed new office. The cost of assigning additional staff to the existing regional office might in some cases prove to be less than of operating a separate, permanent office. In still another type of situation, where a TAB office is located in the area concerned, it might be possible to station a representative of the agency in the TAB office as a kind of 'functional attaché' and arrange for him to use on a shared basis the RTAR's servicing facilities. In the final chapter we shall consider further the potentialities of inter-agency utilization of the RTAR's administrative support services at the country level.

So far as the composition of the professional staff of agency regional offices is concerned, clearly no hard and fast rule can be laid down. The ratio of 'specialists' to 'generalists' will inevitably vary from one location to another, depending on the size of the region, the dimensions of the agency's total field operations in the region, and their subject-matter range. Here again a flexible balance should be sought, with due regard for the need of an able, experienced generalist, as head of the office, to keep the technicians working together as a well-knit team.

Communication and Control Channels

It is axiomatic that the effective working of any scheme of delegation to field units requires adequate and expeditious communication channels between headquarters and the field. At various junctures we have already referred to the importance of ensuring direct, unclogged lines of communication from field offices to headquarters, and vice versa, if administrative actions are to be handled without undue delay. The routing of correspondence from project personnel up the organizational hierarchy, however, calls for further comment here.

Where an agency maintains a well-run set of field offices, the volume of communication with headquarters on administrative and personal matters should be minimal. The settlement of such matters, one way or another, would usually take place at the nearest field office. Only in exceptional instances should it be necessary to clear with headquarters. When this happens the field office would ordinarily pursue the question with the appropriate headquarters service, attaching to its letter any explanatory statement the project expert might wish forwarded. It is of course assumed that the field office concerned would be so staffed as to be able to process such matters promptly—

likewise at headquarters. As far as possible, administrative support services should be provided for project personnel at the country level—whether through an agency field office located in the country of assignment or through the local TAB office (if any); the latter arrangement, incidentally, now obtains fairly generally for UN, Unesco, FAO, WMO, and ITU experts. Where experts are isolated in rural areas remote from any field office, special arrangements would have to be made, and in some instances the most practicable procedure might be to have such matters dealt with directly by headquarters.

How to channel communications relating to substantive questions presents a somewhat more complex problem. Two kinds of items are involved here: formal progress reports and informal letters of inquiry or explanation. Clearly, the guiding consideration should be a set of procedures that will minimize the amount of time the busy expert has to devote to reporting and letter-writing and that will facilitate prompt reply or action, as the case may be. By and large, there was a tendency during the early years of technical assistance to require excessive reporting in terms of frequency as well as subject-matter coverage. Moreover, hundreds of experts had virtually no clerical assistance then in the preparation of correspondence. Given these conditions, the reporting function often became annoyingly burdensome. In recent years most agencies have undertaken to simplify their reporting arrangements, while the provision of clerical help has improved considerably. These are both welcome trends.

How should formal reports be routed? On the assumption that project personnel are supplied with secretarial facilities, it is suggested that reports should be prepared in enough copies to allow for the deposit of one copy at the nearest field office of the employing agency, one copy at the TAB office (if any), and one at agency headquarters. In order to obviate the possibility of intermediate delays in transmission, the dispatch of all copies to their respective destinations should be made concurrently.

Under this procedure, any comments on the report that the regional director (or the expert's technical counterpart in the regional office) and the RTAR (or any of his professional staff) might desire to make would be sent directly to the expert or to agency headquarters, or to both, as appropriate. The expert would thus be likely to receive some sort of response to his reporting efforts with reasonable promptness instead of having to wait for several weeks or even months for a perfunctory reply from headquarters (as has sometimes been the situation in past years). The copy of the report sent to headquarters would be addressed to the special unit charged with the operational phases of field programmes. This unit, as suggested earlier, should immediately reproduce and distribute the report as a whole, or appropriate sections thereof, to the relevant substantive divisions for scrutiny and comment. The responsibility, however, for expediting a suitable reply to the author of the report should rest with the special unit. Should the reply involve a distinctly controversial point, or some action to be taken, headquarters might decide to forward a copy of its letter to the field office head so that, if necessary, the latter could initiate a discussion of the problem with the expert.

So far as informal letters to headquarters are concerned, use of the same channel (the operational unit) would appear desirable with a view to preventing crossed lines. However, in cases where an expert has previously established personal relations with the headquarters technical officer most competent to offer advice on a project, there is obviously a psychological advantage in allowing the expert to communicate directly with the officer on an informal basis, providing a copy of the letter and the reply is made available to the special operations unit for its file on the project. This is substantially how FAO headquarters operates its so-called 'godfather' back-stopping system, which on balance appears to have worked well.[11]

One aspect of field reporting that has led to some confusion concerns projects conducted by a team. Here difficulty has occasionally arisen from the failure of the sponsoring agency to define the responsibilities of the project leader in relation to the other members of the team. Instructions to the latter, moreover, have not always clearly indicated how and to whom they are to report. In principle, it would seem that individual project team members should be expected to report officially only to their project chief—normally by contributing a section

[11] UN practice also allows for direct correspondence between field experts and the substantive unit at headquarters.

to the leader's composite report. Yet there may be compelling reasons why project technicians, in certain highly complex or emerging spheres of activity, should be permitted to communicate directly with their counterparts at headquarters. Where there is no such counterpart (as is sometimes the case), the employment of outside specialists on a fee basis is probably the most economical way of ensuring competent technical judgment, both for the headquarters programme departments and for field missions. The IBRD has for many years utilized part-time consultants in this fashion with admirable results, and as indicated in Chapter 9, the Managing Director of the Special Fund plans to resort to this practice with respect to advice on project construction and appraisal when no UN organization is staffed for this purpose. The substantive units in the UN Department of Economic and Social Affairs also use consultants to handle projects for which there is no competent staff member.

Where team projects involve the participation of more than one UN agency, it is even more important that the lines of control should not become tangled. In this context all staff members clearly should route their technical reports (in two copies) to the project director, so that he may be kept informed of staff viewpoints, reactions, and proposals. Retaining one copy, the director would dispatch the other copy, with any comments he wished to make, to agency headquarters. Responsibility for running the project, both technically and administratively, should be firmly lodged in the director if the group is to function cohesively. In the case of relatively large, continuing projects, such as training institutions, a special policy-advisory mechanism in the form of an inter-agency committee may be useful (as noted in Chapter 8 in connection with regional undertakings). For sound administration, however, primary responsibility for the conduct of such enterprises should be centred in one of the participating organizations.

Finally, it may not be out of place to stress again the vital importance of maximizing the exchange of information laterally—particularly with regard to similar projects in different countries. Relatively few field missions are kept *au courant* of work being done in other places by persons with similar experience, responsibilities, and problems. While such exchange of experience is beginning to take place, it is still on a decidedly spotty basis. This remains perhaps the weakest link in the communications chain of most UN organizations. One of the continuing tasks of the proposed 'analysis and evaluation' unit might be to see to it that digests of selected project reports and records of oral *exposés* by returning experts are circulated to the current project missions concerned.[12]

Over and beyond the interchange of information relative to projects, more thought needs to be given to ways of tapping the reservoir of ideas of field personnel as a corporate group while they are still at the front line and their impressions are fresh. Here the emphasis should be on constructive suggestions rather than the opportunity merely to ventilate grievances. From time to time carefully selected groups of project experts might be assembled at agency field offices for closed-door discussions of their experience and reflections. Another procedure would be to conduct structured interviews with individual experts, or panels of experts, and make available the edited records to other field personnel as appropriate. Such devices, if built into briefing and back-stopping operations, might help substantially to enrich the fund of first-hand knowledge concerning the modalities of multinational field action. As Lord Salter has aptly observed, 'the wealth of advice from those who have had direct experience of assisting in development work in different parts of the world . . . urgently needs to be crystallized into doctrine, subject to constant review and modification, and then widely applied.'[13]

[12] To some extent this sort of thing is now being systematically developed in the UN Department of Economic and Social Affairs.

[13] In an article entitled 'The Economic Strategy of the West,' *Foreign Affairs* (July 1958).

13

THE ROAD AHEAD

The 1960s are likely to be a challenging period for the United Nations system in terms of its role as planner and dispenser of economic, social, and technical assistance to governments and peoples. As the decade opens there are visible signs in Western governmental circles of an acceptance of the view that such assistance, with enlarged dimensions, should be increasingly multilateralized one way or another. While in all probability the UN system will not, from the quantitative standpoint, become the principal instrumentality through which expanded public aid programmes are channelled, it may be in a position to exert a marked influence on the rationale and conditions of future aid operations. Even if only a fraction of additional aid should pass directly through UN hands, the Organization may be able, as Secretary-General Hammarskjold recently remarked, to help 'neutralize' the political impact of bilateral aid, thus, 'to some extent at least, overcoming the weaknesses inherent in bilateral aid.'[1]

In the broadest sense, the key task confronting major donor governments and international agencies alike will be that of devising policies and methods whereby admittedly inadequate technical and capital resources can be pooled for maximum impact on world economic and social growth. This is an extraordinarily complex problem, as much administrative as economic or financial. The UN system as presently constituted, and with such limited means as it now has at its disposal, cannot direct a massive attack on world poverty, disease, and ignorance. On the other hand, the UN family of organizations has acquired a storehouse of operational expertise from which valuable clues can be drawn for the future. The UN itself is now going through an evolving situation as a result of the establishment of the Special Fund and OPEX and their impact on the contours of technical aid. Together with the Special Fund, the newly created

[1] Press Conference at UN Headquarters, 18 Feb. 1960. Note to Correspondents, No. 2113, pp. 27–30.

International Development Association, as an affiliate of IBRD, bids fair to bring the UN into closer programming relationship with the international financial institutions in Washington than has hitherto been the case.[2] The more than doubling of the funds provided for technical assistance during 1960 (EPTA and SF), over the amount provided for EPTA two years earlier, is an encouraging if modest portent of stronger support from Member governments for the UN system's most popular type of activity.

The combined effect of these changes—and others that may be in the offing—on problems and processes of programme administration should have considerable significance. It is a nice question whether the UN agencies, from the standpoint of administrative effectiveness, benefited from having to start field operations on such a small scale. It is at least arguable that a better administrative job might have been done if the UN had been entrusted from the outset with operations more comparable in size to those of the former United Nations Relief and Rehabilitation Administration. The experience of this organization may suggest that the rather lukewarm and limited support which until recently has been given to technical assistance under UN auspices perforce made it seemingly less efficient in the administrative sense.[3] Whatever the validity of this view, there is little doubt that the allegedly high overhead costs of technical assistance operations have been due mainly to the small scale of the programme. Moreover, the constant realization of the terrific gap that exists between demonstrated need and available resources cannot help but have affected the morale of socially motivated field missions. The rapid emergence of an 'independent' Africa now confronts the UN system with a dramatic challenge—and opportunity—in this context.

This is by way of introducing the theme of the final chapter: how can the UN family of organizations *as a whole* be made a more effective instrumentality for the planning and execution of field programmes in the economic and social domain? Our exploration of this problem is predicated on two assumptions: (1) that in the foreseeable future it would be politically unrealistic

[2] The proposed Articles of Agreement for IDA are outlined in the U.S. Department of State *Bulletin* (29 Feb. 1960).

[3] The author is indebted for this thought to a senior official of UNICEF.

to anticipate any major alteration of the internal framework of the system—cumbersome though it may be; but (2) that it is entirely feasible to contrive adaptations of the structure and its processes so as to enhance their capacity to contribute to long-range programme goals.

The limitations of the existing framework stem largely from three situations:

1. the dispersion of programme controls through a series of more or less autonomous legislative bodies and administrative staffs, tied together rather tenuously by various co-ordinative devices;
2. a somewhat unevenly developed field establishment that has evolved as a natural consequence of agency particularism; and
3. the difficulties of following through from technical aid to national action in terms of policy, capital investment, processes, and institutions.

With a view to minimizing the shortcomings inherent in such a system, enlightened and vigorous leadership from agency heads, as well as from influential governments, will be indispensable. Certain things can be done by administrative directive; others will require budgetary or even legislative action. By and large, what is suggested below represents the continuation, or accentuation, of trends already discernible.

Towards Integration at the Centre

The term 'integration,' as employed here, does not imply the loss of functional identity, or of control over their own constitutional policies or regular budgets on the part of the specialized agencies. Each of them has a significant role to play in its own sphere and most of them have over the years acquired considerable skill and ingenuity in handling a growing variety of problems. Furthermore, it is important to remember that each of the major agencies has its own clientele inside Member countries—in some instances, as with agriculture, health, education, and labour, strongly organized—on which it can ordinarily count for sustained or even growing budgetary support. Were the functional agencies to be brought under a 'consolidated' budget controlled by the UN General Assembly, it is not unlikely that such support would have less impact on appropriations of funds than within the separate agency budgetary processes; and the aggregate resources available for functional activities might grow less rapidly than has characterized the major agency budgets during the past few years.[4]

At the same time, as the work of the specialized agencies has become more and more 'operational,' regardless of source of financing, the problem of co-ordinating over-all programme efforts has demanded closer attention. At the inter-governmental level, ECOSOC has recognized this by adopting a series of resolutions designed to encourage 'concerted action' by the UN and the agencies and concentration on programme priorities —with some success. Similarly, at the inter-secretariat level, ACC has been giving increasing thought to ways and means of improving the co-ordination of programme planning, and it is now playing a fairly active role with respect to the substantive orientation of EPTA. These moves towards more effective programme co-ordination among organizations have—or should have—equal relevance to the regular field programmes of the UN, WHO, Unesco, ILO, and IAEA, as well as UNICEF, most of which are not easily distinguishable from EPTA activities in purpose and substance.

The expanding range of action of ACC in programme matters has given rise to auxiliary inter-agency machinery which, as the Advisory Committee of the UN General Assembly has pointed out, tends to duplicate the organizational arrangements for EPTA in the form of TAB and its own working groups. While recognizing that TAB has over the years played a vitally important role in promoting agency co-operation in technical assistance, one could argue, from the strict administrative standpoint, that after a decade it has outlived much of its usefulness as an inter-agency co-ordinative mechanism. Today the central staff work for EPTA is performed by an able, experienced secretariat under the skilful leadership of the Executive Chairman. TAB's working members consist typically of the heads of the units concerned with technical assistance in their respective agency

[4] See Table 1, p. 38, for specialized agency budgetary trends in comparison with that of the United Nations. The approximate identity of UN and agency memberships, and the increasing similarity of contribution patterns to the regular budgets and to EPTA during recent years, would of course make budgetary consolidation a somewhat less involved matter than a decade ago. See UN Doc. A/4172, 25 Aug. 1959, para. 47.

headquarters. Although the Executive Chairman has the legal right to appeal to TAC against any decision by a majority of TAB with which he does not agree, this right is virtually never exercised, individual agency representatives often being able to dictate the collective compromise that becomes the accepted position. By reason of his own rich experience and intimate knowledge of the attitudes of governments, the Executive Chairman can, on occasion, exert considerable influence on TAB's decisions, but what tends to happen is agreement by low-level consensus. In this sort of 'club' setting, polite agency log-rolling has not been unknown.

Pursuing further the hypothesis of integration, a case may be made, in principle at least, for merging the operations of TAB and of the Special Fund. Indeed, for handling certain routine services, joint secretariat services are already in effect, while on the programme side the headquarters personnel of TAB and the Fund work closely together in adjacent offices.

As suggested in Chapter 9, the dividing line between these two forms of technical aid is more pragmatic than logical. The two programmes should in no way be regarded as competitive or as having different goals. To a considerable extent the Special Fund type of aid tends to complement various categories of assistance already being financed by EPTA. Each programme aims at contributing to the economic and social development of national communities. By concentrating under one rubric the appeal to governments for financial contributions, it might be easier to stimulate support, especially if some new and imaginative title for a combined programme were invented.[5] Financial consolidation, incidentally, would also simplify accounting procedures.

If the TAB and SF secretariats were fully integrated, there would appear to be no valid reason, on administrative grounds, for retaining two separate programme directors. Even under a single director, each of the two sets of operations might for a time retain its special identity—the one being focused on country programming TAB-style and the other on the support of somewhat larger and longer-term 'pre-investment' projects on

[5] In this connection, it is not without significance that the 1959 General Assembly expressed the wish that the term 'technical assistance' be replaced by the term 'technical co-operation' as a more appropriate description for all forms of technical aid activity. GA Resolution 1383/XIV, 20 Nov. 1959.

a selective basis. Sooner or later, however, it would doubtless seem only sensible to plan and implement both types of technical aid as a co-ordinated whole.

The logic of this set of assumptions would appear to call for the eventual disappearance of TAB as an inter-secretariat co-ordinative body. Direct and continuing cognizance of the points of view and interests of agencies participating in the merged programme could be maintained by 'seconding' agency specialists to the staff of the central programme director on a permanent or rotating basis or both. But all basic decisions of an operational character would be made by the director on his own responsibility, subject to such policy directives as were laid down by the inter-governmental organ by which the programme was controlled; and such decisions could be as swift and clear-cut as circumstances required.

Where would immediate inter-governmental control over a consolidated programme be lodged? This is a question with distinct political overtones, and the matter would doubtless be decided largely on political grounds. At present there are two control organs, each chosen by ECOSOC: one for EPTA, namely TAC, composed of the eighteen Members of ECOSOC itself and six others freely elected by that body; and the other the Governing Council of the Special Fund, consisting of eighteen members equally divided into two categories, one representing the 'more developed' and the other the 'less developed' countries, decisions on 'important' questions requiring a two-thirds majority of members present and voting. The latter body, in the light of its bipartite composition, would probably be more acceptable than the former to the beneficiaries of the programme. If a somewhat larger membership were deemed desirable, it would be a simple matter to increase it from eighteen to, say, the present size of TAC.

With a view to according recognition of specialized agency concerns in the over-all policy guidance of the merged programme, it might be worth considering the inclusion on the programme council of a representative of the executive body of each of the participating agencies. Such an arrangement would provide a kind of 'functional' representation at the inter-governmental level. Alternatively, in lieu of granting agency representatives full membership on the council, they might be given 'associate' member status, with right to participate in discussion but not to vote. Whatever the plan, it clearly should be in addition to the right of each agency to send staff observers to meetings of the programme council.

Within the context adumbrated above, the programme director would presumably be appointed by the Secretary-General, after consultation with his colleagues on ACC and subject to confirmation by the programme council. Under this arrangement there would be a direct line of responsibility from the director to the council with respect to general policy and operational matters, the Secretary-General, however, retaining the right to be consulted and to advise as appropriate. This right, as it were, would be exercised within the framework of ACC, which would continue to exercise its function of review and co-ordination of inter-programme relationships generally.

The writer is fully aware of the political difficulties of effecting in the immediate future a consolidation of the central structures of EPTA and the Special Fund. On the one hand, the vested interests of the specialized agencies in maintaining the existing EPTA model are such that any direct limitation of their administrative authority would be apt to meet with determined resistance. On the other hand, and perhaps more importantly, the under-developed countries would be apt to oppose vigorously any plan that threatened the separate identity of the Special Fund. It was at their behest that the Fund was set up as a distinct entity, since they hoped that as such it might stand a better chance of being expanded later into a SUNFED-type of programme, and many of them still appear to view the Special Fund as a forerunner of some sort of UN-operated capital development scheme. Not only has the Special Fund established a different operating pattern from that of EPTA, but it has thus far been able to retain final control over the allocation of its resources. Any premature attempt to merge the two programmes might run the risk of a compromise solution incorporating their less desirable features. Accordingly, the logic of administrative integration may have to yield for the time being to political realities surrounding UN system operations. Concurrently, it is possible that substantial re-allocation, or expansion, of UN resources for aids and services to governments might alter the administrative centre of gravity within the system in ways now only vaguely perceived. In any event, a progressively closer meshing of related field programme patterns should—and can—be developed on a pragmatic basis through inter-secretariat initiatives of various kinds.

In this evolving context, it would seem desirable that the working relationships of programme managers on the UN side, with those of the International Bank and its affiliates on the other, should be as fully interlocked as informal arrangements will allow.[6] The importance of such liaison, as noted in Chapter 9, was recognized by the General Assembly in 1958 in authorizing the establishment of a Consultative Board to advise the Managing Director of the Special Fund concerning programme proposals and project requests. The membership of this Board includes the Secretary-General, the Executive Chairman of TAB, and the President of IBRD. Representatives of the specialized agencies and of IAEA may be invited to meetings of the Board when projects mainly within their fields of activity are considered. This arrangement, still in its formative stage, has important potentialities for the development of continuing staff consultation between the United Nations and the nexus of intergovernmental financial institutions in Washington. One can envisage the creation of a 'preparatory committee,' somewhat on the order of the ACC, to handle the detailed tasks of analysis and of reviewing matters requiring the Board's attention. In view of the status of IDA, this new financing institution, as an affiliate of the Bank, will in effect be represented in the Board's deliberations. Out of such collaboration might eventually emerge an informal 'international economic development planning' group, drawn from the UN Department of Economic and Social Affairs, the TAB and SF secretariats (whether merged or not), and the IBRD-IFC-IDA staff. Such a group, by an agreed division of labour, might devise procedures for 'receiving and analyzing national development plans as they are issued by governments; for maintaining current records as to their fulfillment; and [possibly] for co-ordinating domestic, bilateral, and multilateral efforts to stimulate growth in a given area.'[7] In

[6] The fact that the Bank has agreed to act as executing agent for various Special Fund projects in the engineering field should help to pave the way towards closer UN-IBRD staff contacts in the field as well as at headquarters.

[7] Robert E. Asher, *et al.*, *The United Nations and Economic and Social Co-operation*, *op. cit.*, p. 235.

this way the UN system might gradually become the focal point of reference for all major international aid-granting programmes, including those sponsored by national governments (at least in the non-Communist world). While the UN would obviously not be in a position to impose any sort of supra-national control over outside programmes, its advice, if wisely formulated, would not lightly be disregarded.

For the past few years, informal meetings have been held—six to eight times a year—by a group of senior staff officials of the UN and of IBRD for the purpose of reviewing current and projected economic and financial developments of interest to each side, including loans and technical assistance projects. Since the advent of the Special Fund, the staff of IBRD is reported to have suggested to certain governments that they apply to the new Fund (instead of, for example, to the Bank itself) for assistance in conducting basic resources surveys preliminary, in some instances, to loan negotiations. Once IDA becomes a going concern, it may turn out that the Special Fund will do much of the technical preparatory work on loan requests outside the Bank's purview but which IDA might find it feasible to handle, particularly if, as Paul Hoffman has advocated, IDA's capital resources should be increased several times beyond the agreed initial figure.[8]

In this connection, the possibility that the UN itself may yet decide to create a capital-granting development fund should not be ignored, although the drive for this may lose momentum if IDA grows in resources and its lending policies are sufficiently liberal.[9] In the event that a modified 'SUNFED' should come into being, its management could without too much difficulty be grafted on the UN technical aid machinery in the interest of administrative simplicity and economy. Nor is it beyond the range of possibility, should support for the existing Special Fund increase, that its province may come to embrace modest capital grants for selected economic and social infra-structure projects, for example, in the newer countries of Africa and Asia. Under such conditions the transition from the

[8] See, in particular, the vividly written brochure by Mr. Hoffman entitled *One Hundred Countries: One and One Quarter Billion People*, *op. cit.*

[9] The old 'SUNFED' issue, under a slightly different caption, still remains on the agenda of ECOSOC and the General Assembly. See GA Resolution 1424 (XIV), 5 Dec. 1959.

pre-investment to the investment phase could be made smoothly and without interruption.

Towards Integration at the Country Level

The observations contained in the preceding pages are geared to two inter-related propositions: (1) an increasingly close integration of controls over UN system aid programmes should be encouraged by all practicable means, but (2) in the technical planning and execution of field projects individual agencies should continue to exercise a major function. Even so, as the dimensions of the Special Fund's operations expand, it seems clear that the tasks of the RTAR will grow in scope and volume.[10] The RTAR's co-ordinative, inspectional, and evaluative work for EPTA is now only one of his several obligations, what with the various kinds of services performed by his office for the SF, for OPEX, and for the support of field personnel of the UN, Unesco, FAO, WMO, ITU, and to some extent ILO, ICAO, IAEA, and UNICEF.[11] All signs point to a further proliferation of the RTAR's activities.

In the event that EPTA and the Special Fund were to be consolidated, and the merged programme placed under a single director responsible to a single inter-governmental programme council, it would probably be found desirable to lodge the power to appoint the RTAR with the programme director in agreement with the ACC. This procedure would allow the specialized agency heads to have a voice in the selection. On all matters relating to field programme operations, however, the RTAR would be responsible to the programme director. Since the RTAR in fact 'works for many masters' and performs a variety of functions, it would seem appropriate to change the title of the post to reflect more adequately his duties.

In any case, the growing importance of the RTAR in UN system field administration underscores the need of according the post a permanent career status as rapidly as possible. This should aid in attracting—and retaining—top-flight individuals for such

[10] According to reliable authority, some RTARs, during the latter part of 1959, were giving as much as half of their time to SF matters.

[11] As of early 1960, for example, 20 RTARs were acting as 'country representatives' for Unesco, 14 for FAO, 11 for ICAO, and 12 for IAEA—all on a continuing basis. In a number of countries the RTAR provides administrative support for UNICEF.

service. Fortunately, the trend is already in this direction: by 1960 nearly half of the incumbents held permanent appointments. In a number of countries, where programme operations are peculiarly difficult or are rapidly growing, the post should in the interest of equitable treatment be upgraded with regard to salary—a point now recognized in TAB circles. More urgent still is the need of providing allowances covering the removal of household effects and installation costs on reassignment to a new post. The financial burden imposed upon the RTAR, when he is transferred every three to five years, in establishing a new household on a scale appropriate to the inescapable representation requirements, has been little short of crushing in several instances. Also, representation allowances, as noted earlier in this study, are glaringly too low. Finally, it is clear that the geographic dimensions of the RTAR structure will need to be extended in the near future to various newly independent States where governmental personnel and administrative machinery are weakest.[12]

In Chapter 12, the view was advanced that maximum utilization should be made of the RTAR's office for operational purposes at the country level. Such utilization by the specialized agencies is now limited partly because of the maintenance of separate local offices in numerous countries. As suitable premises become available, the task of country programming might be handled in more unified fashion if small agency country offices were either converted into 'functional units' of the RTAR's staff, or failing this, physically located in the same building as the RTAR's office. While recognizing the practical obstacles involved in office consolidation, the writer is nevertheless of the opinion that real progress towards this goal, at the country level, should and can be registered during the coming decade. The pattern naturally will vary from centre to centre: in those cities where the RTAR's office is dwarfed by a regional commission secretariat or a large regional office of a specialized agency, this fact would have to be taken into account in determining the modalities of consolidation. But there are at most only six to eight centres where this is the situation.[13]

[12] During 1960, additional TAB offices were slated to be established in Guinea, the Republic of Korea, Nigeria, Saudi Arabia, Somalia, and the Syrian region of the U.A.R.

[13] Notably Mexico City, Santiago, New Delhi, Bangkok, Manila, and Addis Ababa.

A variety of arrangements may be necessary with regard to managing and financing 'pooled' services in different settings. Here again, however, generally acceptable procedures can be developed, given sufficient ingenuity on the part of office staffs.

Within the field structure of the UN itself, it may be found feasible to relate the local Information Centre more closely to the RTAR in certain countries. Already, in nine places where Information Centres exist, the RTAR's office processes their accounts, while in two cases information officers have been assigned by OPI to his office. In at least one country (India) the two offices (of TAB and UNIC) were (during 1960) to be consolidated as an experiment. Such arrangements elsewhere might help to gear the services of the UNICs more closely to the economic and social activities of the UN family in the area.

Somewhat similar developments affecting the country-level operations of UNICEF can be envisaged. In countries where the scale of such operations scarcely justifies the maintenance of a separate UNICEF office, local administrative support for UNICEF projects, including customs clearance of supplies and assistance to UNICEF officials on inspection trips, might be provided by the RTAR's staff. Depending on the situation, a UNICEF officer could be attached to the staff to help handle these matters.

That some administrative economy would result from office consolidation at the country level could, it is believed, be demonstrated by quantitative studies of selected country situations. More important than this, however, would be two other less tangible advantages: (1) greater convenience for host government officials in their dealings with the confusing array of UN organizations and programmes, and (2) the facilitation of informal contacts among the office and project staffs of different UN agencies. One of the striking impressions gained by an independent observer is the absence of a strong *esprit de corps* among UN agency field staffs in certain countries. Where they number as many as fifty and upwards, it frequently happens that individual project experts will serve out their term without coming to know more than a minor fraction of their colleagues from other agencies. If, for example, adequate facilities, including a modest social lounge as well as desk and conference room space, were made available at one central point, a more articulate awareness of belonging to and labouring for a single international family and for the same general goals should emerge. Field personnel might thus become less splintered by agency loyalties and the centrifugal effects of professional diversification be appreciably tempered. It is already manifest that in those relatively few places where this arrangement is approximated, inter-agency co-operation on projects at the field level tends to benefit.

There is little question that if the TAB field offices (or whatever they be called) are to perform effectively the multitude of services for which they are likely to be responsible during the years ahead, their staffs and facilities will need to be markedly strengthened. Most RTAR offices have been decidedly undermanned and poorly equipped, partly because they have had to depend too much on inefficient support services from host governments.[14] For almost half of the TAB offices operating in 1960, no internationally recruited staff was made available. As their work-load increases, this situation will become more critical. A subvention of $150,000 from the Special Fund for the 1960 TAB budget helped to ease the strain somewhat, but additional budgetary provision will be necessary for later years, not only to take care of urgent staff requirements in existing offices but to man the new offices that are set up.

In a limited number of countries the RTAR is now flanked by a 'deputy' or an 'assistant' at the middle- or upper-grade professional level. Such men, whose backgrounds vary greatly, are utilized in different ways—to oversee the administration of the office, to deal with designated aspects of programming, and so on. What is most lacking on the RTAR's staff, at any rate in those countries with sizable programmes, is a senior professional with considerable administrative experience and established competence in the economics of development, who can concentrate on the strategy of country programme-planning and evaluation. With a view to relieving the RTAR himself of innumerable 'drafting' chores, the provision of an intermediate grade officer to devote full time to the preparation of substantive and procedural reports is almost equally imperative.

[14] The current trend towards the payment of lump-sum grants by host governments, in lieu of furnishing local staff in kind, may make it possible to improve their quality here and there. See UN Doc. A/4269, 12 Nov. 1959, for further details.

In connection with the strengthening of the RTAR's staff facilities, the Special Fund's action in contributing towards the cost of operating TAB field offices offers a precedent for the sharing by the specialized agencies in the expenses of such offices in proportion to their use of space, service, supplies, and equipment. By inter-agency agreement, a formula could be worked out to cover the extra costs arising from the conversion of agency country offices into functional sections of an expanded RTAR's staff.

To recapitulate: the progressive integration of office arrangements at the country level should, on the one hand, tend to make the RTAR and his staff the local point of contact for governments on all general programme matters and, on the other hand, to centralize in one place administrative support services for project staffs, including briefing on local conditions. Except in those cities where large regional offices are located, the RTAR's office would serve as the principal symbol, locally, of the UN system's world welfare mission, and endeavour to create an increasingly favourable local climate for UN action—by employing all appropriate informational means at the disposal of the office.

As suggested in the preceding chapter, the specialized agencies would continue to maintain their own field establishments, chiefly at the regional level, in accordance with the needs of their over-all operational activities. But the role of this field machinery would be confined mainly to liaison and technical considerations—project planning, back-stopping, inspection, and evaluation. As at present, each agency would have the responsibility for executing technical assistance undertakings in its own field with respect to the management of experts, the provision of equipment and supplies, and the selection of fellows and trainees;[15] but at the country level all essential personnel, travel, budgetary, procurement, and accounting operations would, as far as practicable, be handled through the RTAR's office. Accordingly, agency offices at this level would gradually disappear from the scene as separate entities. If such a trend

[15] So far as the recruitment of project personnel is concerned, the development of *inter*-agency arrangements for clearance and field interviewing purposes might well be considered. The European National Committees (referred to in Chapter 5) are said to favour this. It is interesting to note that the UN recruitment services now in fact recruit appointees to all OPEX posts, though only after consultation with the appropriate specialized agency regarding appointments lying within its subject-matter province.

gained momentum, a considerable simplification of agency field apparatus should result.

Field Programming and Follow-through

The arrangements discussed above imply the introduction of greater flexibility into the field programme process than is now possible under EPTA regulations. Admittedly, a number of minor improvements in programme rules have been put into effect recently—in particular, the two-year planning experiment; but EPTA is still subject to widespread criticism on the ground that its limited resources are spread too thinly—among too many countries and territories around the globe. The majority of RTARs with whom the writer discussed this point were of the opinion that a serious effort should again be made to develop criteria according to which it would be possible to determine the allocation of EPTA resources with less regard for geographic distribution *per se*. As additional African territories attain their independence, the pressure to spread projects even more widely than at present is likely to increase, with the possibility of additional small, disparate undertakings—unless, in the meantime, substantially greater funds are forthcoming. It should not be impossible to construct an objective basis (relating need and capacity to use) for the distribution of funds. Such a formula should make it possible to exert a more decisive influence than hitherto on the orientation of country programmes, with a view to concentrating on 'strategic points in the economy' from the long-range developmental standpoint. At the same time, it would probably be necessary, for political reasons, to allow every requesting country to have at least a token part in the programme.

So long, however, as the agency 'sub-total' arrangement remains in effect, it will not be easy to adjust the subject-matter focus of going country programmes in terms of basic development priorities. In many cases, government ministries, faced with far greater needs for technical assistance than can be satisfied, have come to look upon their 'sub-totals' (even though intended to serve only as guide-lines) as their 'rightful pieces of the pie.' Under the sub-total system, given the meagre and relatively fixed aid resources available, priority programming has been largely a fiction. Such attention to priorities as has taken place has consisted of minor shifts in the amount of funds previously earmarked for individual agencies, resulting from inter-agency and inter-ministerial competition. Although such competition appears to be declining in countries with strong co-ordinating machinery, the case for discounting the sub-total arrangement altogether seems convincing: it is hardly compatible with the country-programming concept.

The rationale of the Special Fund's operation thus far has been quite different from that of EPTA. As noted in Chapter 9, the Fund has endeavoured, by a careful examination and assessment of individual country requests, to select projects for support on the basis of their 'pre-investment' potentialities, without being bound to observe the principle of geographic distribution in any firm sense. In determining whether to recommend support for a given project, the Fund's staff takes special account of its probable impact on the country's long-range economic growth; and in this connection the views of the government's top economic planning organs (if any) are elicited. A special effort is made to commit the government to support the project during its execution, and to undertake appropriate follow-up action.

Whether, as proposed earlier in this chapter, EPTA and the Special Fund should be merged or not, the RTAR's authority *vis-à-vis* field representatives of the specialized agencies should be re-defined in such a way as to prevent agency commitments on projects—even of an informal character—without the RTAR's prior knowledge and advice, and receiving governments should be so informed officially. What one would hope is that the local representatives of the agencies (including chiefs of mission), once housed in the RTAR's office, would become a 'programme team' working loyally together under the RTAR's leadership, notwithstanding the fact that on technical and miscellaneous matters members of the team would report to their respective agency headquarters. The RTAR would constitute the *de facto* chairman of the group.

A unified and enlarged programme, combining the best features of EPTA and the Special Fund, would allow substantially more leeway with regard to the kinds, dimensions, duration, staffing, and operational set-up of projects. On the whole, one would expect relatively fewer 'miniature' advisory projects, and probably a somewhat larger outlay for supplies and equipment in relation to that for experts.[16] There should be less danger of a sound project request falling between two stools, as, for example, a long-term training proposal the 'pre-investment' possibilities of which, however, are not readily apparent. The dovetailing of short-term diagnostic missions with long-term basic resources surveys or institutional projects would be facilitated. In one country, the focus of the programme over a five-year span might be mainly on the production in various ways of badly needed managerial and technical talent; in a second area, the number one priority could be the reorganization of the national administrative, budget and tax systems; in still a third, the expansion of health, educational, and welfare services; in a fourth, the improvement of agricultural production through land reform, irrigation, the introduction of better techniques, and the development of marketing schemes; and so on. Certain projects affecting a major sector of the economy might well be conceived in terms of a decade or longer.[17]

Since, in the final analysis, the wishes of the recipient government must be determinant, it should be a continuing obligation of the United Nations to do everything possible to infiltrate economic intelligence, technical know-how, and political wisdom into the processes through which these desires take concrete shape. To paraphrase one discerning RTAR, no programme is worth trying to implement without the sustained support of effective elements in the political and administrative framework of the government.

It follows from the foregoing that the RTAR (or equivalent officer) should serve as the key figure in respect of appraising programme proposals at the preliminary stage. On the basis of general guide-lines for programme planning supplied by programme headquarters, it would be his responsibility to attempt to inject meaningful criteria into governmental decisions on

[16] During 1959, the first year of the SF's operation, 35·4 per cent. of the dollar allocation for projects was for equipment, 42·9 per cent. for experts, 6·1 per cent. for fellowships, 6·9 per cent. for agency administrative costs, and 8·7 per cent. for miscellaneous items. UN Doc. SF/L.28, 13 April 1960.

[17] In this connection, it is of some significance that TAB is now considering the feasibility of what it calls 'project programming,' by which is meant the preparation and approval of projects for their entire anticipated duration, up to five years, even though funds would be allocated only to cover the parts falling within a given country-programming period. UN Doc. E/TAC/97, 20 May 1960.

project priorities. Provided a relationship of mutual confidence existed between the RTAR and the bureaucratic *élites* of the host government—and this would be indispensable—he should be able to exercise more effective initiative in respect of programme construction than has tended to be the case in past years.

In performing this complex task, the RTAR would draw heavily on his own 'programme officer' (if any) for over-all guidance. At the technical level the advice of his multi-agency professional team would be available at various stages of the process. In the case of continuing projects (some of which the RTAR might properly recommend for liquidation), as well as of fairly straightforward projects in well-established fields, no special investigation by the RTAR's office might be necessary. For a second category of requests, involving more complicated subject-matter or operational arrangements, the expertise of the organization that would presumably execute the project if approved could be utilized, whether through a regional office, directly from agency headquarters, or from its travelling central staff. There would remain a third group of projects, cutting across subject-matter lines or falling within highly specialized or newly emerging fields, that might require the judgment of outside consultants engaged for the purpose, or possibly a combination of UN agency specialists and independent experts. The RTAR, after tapping available local advice, would submit to programme headquarters his views as to whether an intensive inquiry should be made and under what auspices; the central programme director, in consultation with his own staff, would decide. In certain cases a request might be referred immediately to headquarters for its own independent investigation.

At periodic intervals—at least every two years—each RTAR would be required to submit to programme headquarters his recommendations for the next stage of the country programme. The dollar dimensions of such recommendations would be related to country targets previously set by the programme director. If and as the financing of the combined programme were put on a basis longer than a single year, country-planning targets might progressively cover longer periods.[18] Such targets,

[18] In EPTA, country-planning targets, beginning with the 1961–62 programme, are to be set for a two-year period.

however, would be regarded not as rigidly fixed totals but as little more than rough guide-lines subject to change by the programme director.

In fixing initially, and subsequently adjusting, country programme targets, the economic development 'general staff' at headquarters, referred to earlier in this chapter, would have an important advisory role. The programme director, in presenting to the programme council his periodic country programme proposals, should be authorized to recommend deletions and other modifications of the draft programmes submitted by the RTARs. Any government thus affected would be entitled to a general explanation of the reasons for such changes, certain of which might involve the reference back of project requests for further study and re-designing.

In addition to periodic general country programme formulations, it would obviously be desirable to empower the programme director to consider important projects of an urgent character—regional or country—at any time. The longer the interval for country programme-planning, the greater the justification of this arrangement. With this end in view, as well as to take care of any necessary extra allocations to going projects, a substantial fraction, say 20 to 25 per cent., of total project funds would need to be placed at the disposition of the programme director as a 'project reserve.'[19] Allocations from this reserve above a small fixed amount would of course require the approval of the programme council. This might be sought by a mailed-in vote in case no meeting of the council were scheduled for the immediate future.

In line with the foregoing ideas, programme rules setting maximum percentages for expenditures on supplies and equipment might usefully be relaxed. With two or three times as much money for project purposes as was until recently available to EPTA alone, there would appear to be no sound reason for rigidly limiting such outlays.

Nor would it seem desirable to impose a percentage ceiling on outlays for regional projects or programmes. Indications are

[19] TAC recommended in 1959 that a 5 per cent. planning reserve be created for EPTA 'when the financial situation permits.' UN Doc. E/TAC/93, 13 Nov. 1959. The Special Fund had not then decided whether to establish a reserve. This decision was deferred pending a decision whether project allocations might exceed actual pledges or not. UN Doc. SF/L.26, 22 Oct. 1959.

that resort to a regional base not only for training programmes but for industrial and commercial development planning will be increasingly characteristic of long-range economic programme efforts in Africa, Asia, and parts of Latin America during the years ahead. The UN economic commission secretariats bid fair to play significant roles in connection with certain types of technical assistance relating to regional plans, as already seen, for example, in the Central American Economic Integration Project.[20] The new Economic Commission for Africa, at its 1960 session, adopted a resolution requesting that all multilateral aid henceforth be planned in consultation with the Commission's secretariat.

As indicated earlier, approved projects, whether country or regional, would normally be executed by the UN, a specialized agency, or the IAEA. In the event no member of the UN family were equipped, or willing, to undertake the implementation of a given undertaking, the programme director, as is now possible under the Special Fund, should be empowered to contract for the services of non-UN organizations, including private management and engineering firms, research institutes, and universities. In order to keep the chain of command straight, however, full responsibility for carrying out a project should always be conferred on a single agency which, by sub-contracting, could, as need be, arrange for the participation of other agencies or groups.

Although the set-up outlined in the preceding pages refers primarily to across-the-board aid programmes financed by voluntary contributions, those agencies (notably WHO, Unesco, ILO, and IAEA) with assistance programmes financed out of their regular budgets should be encouraged to make use of the RTAR's office in connection with the implementation of projects under such programmes. While decisions as to programme construction would rest with each agency concerned, it should be required to keep the RTAR fully *au courant* of all project requests and the action taken on them. In turn, the RTAR, in scrutinizing EPTA-SF proposals, would be expected to bear in mind the kinds of assistance being rendered to the host country, not only by regular programmes of the agencies, but equally by all other major aid sources, including private and public entities outside the UN system. Working in conjunction with the

[20] See pp. 343–346.

national co-ordinative machinery, the RTAR's office might serve as a local clearing-house for up-to-date information on all types of foreign aid received by the government. The maintenance of such an inventory should facilitate the joint financing of projects involving two or more agencies or programmes. Periodic meetings of local representatives of aid-giving organizations, on the order of those already being held in various countries, might properly be convened on the initiative of the RTAR for exchange of experience.

A special word concerning UNICEF is in order here. The magic appeal of 'children' may justify its continuance as a separately financed activity, but there are sound reasons why UNICEF's project planning should be correlated as closely as possible with the welfare sector of national development programmes. Here again, as intimated earlier in this chapter, the RTAR can and should be instrumental in promoting more effective co-ordination of UNICEF undertakings with related WHO, FAO, and UN assistance work than has always been the case. The trend towards longer-term EPTA projects should aid in meshing UNICEF's contributions with those of cognate organizations.

The cumulative influence of introducing into field programming operations greater flexibility on the one hand, and closer integration on the other, should be salutary. During the earlier years, UN technical assistance was successful chiefly in transferring technical know-how in isolated, small-sized 'chunks,' sometimes with immediately spectacular results (*e.g.*, an increase in rice production or a decline in the incidence of trachoma). Typically, this was done through short-term demonstrational and advisory projects, some of which left a permanent impact on the life of the community. Gradually, quasi-operational, basic training, and institution-buttressing projects, of longer duration, emerged in programme planning. Now, under the Special Fund, this trend is being accentuated, with particular emphasis on the feasibility of linking certain categories of technical assistance with sources of capital investment. The policies of the International Development Association, if imaginatively conceived, may promote this linkage in ways only vaguely envisaged at present. Under IDA, long-term, low-interest loans may be made available, not only for national infra-structure purposes but to other international organizations and regional development authorities, while direct grants are not entirely ruled out after the initial five-year period.

The so-called pre-investment type of technical assistance, however, constitutes only one part—albeit an important one—of the diversified domain covered by the field activities of the UN and associated agencies. Among these are many projects that do not involve foreign capital financing for their conversion into permanent national policy or administration. Often all that is required is will and determination on the part of the national leadership not to allow the matured recommendations of project teams to fall on fallow ground once they bid their hosts good-bye. In Chapter 11, the point was made that international organizations of the UN type might take a firmer line with beneficiary governments concerning project carry-through. Technical assistance—henceforth to be known as technical co-operation—is a two-way street: the taxpayers of the major donor countries have a right to expect that the UN system will exhaust every reasonable means of minimizing the chance that their contributions will go down the drain. There of course is bound to be some wastage—from bad planning, or poor selection of experts, or local administrative road blocks, or the impact of unforeseen hazards, political and otherwise; but with experience the percentage of loss should steadily decline.

In the writer's view, governments which are unwilling to provide tolerable operating conditions for project teams, as specified in the project agreement, or which make no serious effort to implement project recommendations (provided these are sensible and constructive) should ordinarily not be regarded as immediately eligible for further aid from UN agency sources.

While it is true that a considerable number of governments have recently increased the amount of their contributions in local currency to project operations, there remains a substantial number of cases where no tangible follow-up takes place at the termination of admittedly successful projects. Except where it can be shown that failure to implement such projects was due to circumstances beyond a government's control, it would seem only reasonable that some sort of 'non-eligibility' rule be generally applied. Such a rule might be formulated by ACC for ECOSOC's consideration and, at least so far as EPTA and SF are concerned, adoption as legislation. If this initiative were taken, there is a strong probability that the specialized agencies would also conform in respect of their regular field programmes.

The writer would be the first to admit that any such rule would need to be applied with tact and understanding. Its utility would no doubt be chiefly as a threat. One of the continuing tasks of the RTAR's office should be to keep an up-to-date record, such as is now being done in various countries for fellowships, of the kinds of consequences that flow from completed UN-aid projects—over a decade or more. In his periodic evaluations of the programme for headquarters, the RTAR should give special attention to the host government's score on project follow-up. If aggregate programme resources expand over the coming years—as now seems likely—the UN family of agencies will have stronger bargaining power against 'backsliding' governments. There will be more to offer to—and more to withhold from—such governments. The International Bank, in its capacity as a multilateral lending institution, has demonstrated how it is possible to induce borrowing countries to adopt higher standards of performance than has tended to be the case with the United States bilateral aid programme. If approached tactfully, most beneficiary nations are inclined to accept guidance and tolerate direct pressures from international agencies.

There are subtle ways in which UN organizations can stimulate follow-up action by recipient governments. Thus far, as indicated in Chapter 11, their full potentialities have not been realized. In this connection, the development of more carefully designed and longer-term projects should produce a firmer impact on local values and *mores*, and thus tend to motivate governing *élites* to instigate legislative, budgetary, or administrative action. Should the OPEX pattern prove workable on any considerable scale, the occupancy of a variety of senior administrative and technical posts by UN-selected personnel may become a significant method of injecting new ideas, procedures, and standards into national and local public services. Finally, the top-level planning and co-ordinative machinery of a government, as it grows in sophistication, prestige, and authority, may be expected to smooth project carry-through by the operating ministries, services, and institutions concerned. There are encouraging indications that this is beginning to happen in the better organized governments. It is the newly independent and poorest nations that will require sustained, sympathetic 'nursing' by the United Nations community if they are to develop stable institutions and viable economies.

So comes to an end our survey of the conduct of economic and social programmes under UN system auspices. We have been dealing with the dynamics of international administration in an evolving policy context. By the time this volume appears in print certain of its suggestions for future action may no longer be entirely relevant because of intervening policy decisions beyond human prediction. Even so, the author ventures to hope that the attempt to describe and evaluate the operational experience of the 1950s may offer useful insights for the 1960s—both to the practitioner and to the investigator.

It is the writer's judgment that the UN nexus of organizations has demonstrated administrative capacity to plan and carry out world-wide field programmes with relatively high standards of performance. Such standards have been achieved against the backdrop of a loose-jointed institutional structure and of hybrid, uncertain budgetary arrangements. Despite this, the sense of working towards a common goal has come more and more to animate programme personnel—in the field possibly even more than at headquarters. To be sure, mistakes have been made along the way; here and there in the record one finds instances of ill-advised or foolish action; and there is still some evidence of bureaucratic pettiness in inter-agency relationships. On balance, however, responsible programme staffs have displayed an impressive inclination to improvise when necessary, to invent where improvisation is not enough, and to experiment with an open mind. Self-criticism, through the development of systematic evaluative techniques, has not infrequently led to the abandonment of questionable practices and the introduction of improved methods.

The United Nations system may be entering a new phase. Unless a nuclear disaster should beset the world, it seems probable that expanding responsibilities will be devolved upon the system in the domain of economic and social co-operation. Further extensions of international action may well require the creation of patterns of organization, control, and procedure substantially different from existing forms. Here again there will be opportunity for secretariat groups to utilize their innovating talents—as they did in preparing the original plans for EPTA, in exploring alternative possibilities for a SUNFED, in working out arrangements for the Special Fund, in launching the OPEX scheme, and in defining the functions of IDA; not to mention such special efforts as WHO's world-wide malaria eradication campaign, FAO's Mediterranean Development project, Unesco's Participation programme, the Lower Mekong River undertaking, and recent ventures into the community development field calling for the co-operation of various agencies. In building for the future, the UN Secretary-General recently observed, what should be sought is 'the optimum balance between a system with a large number of autonomous bodies and a system with a strong concentration of tasks within a lesser number of organizations. The way will have to be found by trial and error.'[21]

How well the UN system measures up operationally to the challenges ahead will depend equally on the kinds of operational support it receives from Member governments—support in the form of a less cumbersome framework; assurance of sustained financing for substantive programmes over longer periods than a year or two; and budgetary appropriations sufficient to attract and retain staff personnel personally and technically equipped to deal with trans-cultural situations. It is the governments, fully as much as the international bureaucrats, that hold the key to the future.

The United Nations Organization *in toto*, reflected a wise observer a few years ago, 'is only a slender taproot of a necessary world community. We do not know how soon, by what means, and through what tribulations it will achieve solid existence. But one thing is certain. We cannot hope to bind the world together as long as there are harsh discrepancies in the standards of living of its various parts. For the first time in history, through the United Nations, we have all accepted the principle of a common international responsibility for general conditions everywhere; and the rapid and varied growth of Technical Assistance proves that the taproot is drawing well.'[22]

[21] In an address delivered at the University of Chicago Law School, 1 May 1960. UN Press Release SG/910.

[22] David Mitrany, 'The International Technical Assistance Program,' *Proceedings* of the Academy of Political Science (January 1953).

APPENDIX

SUGGESTIONS FOR FURTHER RESEARCH

At various points in this volume reference was made to types of problems on which further research might produce valuable insights for programme operators. Not the least justification for a broad pioneer survey, such as the present one, is that it can provide a useful springboard for more intensive inquiries. Many of the assumptions of the present study, which were necessarily tentative, call for more systematic exploration than was possible within the limitations of time and money available to a single investigator. Indeed, the results of additional research might make it necessary to modify, or possibly to discard as unsound, some of his generalizations.

For convenience, the research proposals that follow are grouped under three main rubrics: (1) personnel problems, (2) headquarters-field relations, and (3) the programme process. For the most part they constitute topics involving the objective comparison of agency practices, or of operational situations on a sample basis, with a view to determining as far as possible the relative impact of key factors on each set of practices or situations. While some of this research, time permitting, could be done by UN staff groups themselves, much of it, by its very nature, would require contributions from independent social scientists for whom, to be sure, the sympathetic co-operation of official personnel would be indispensable. Not only are private scholars often able to bring a fresh point of view, but they can present their findings with a freedom ordinarily denied international officials. Ideally, such research should be conducted by multi-national teams. The study of certain of the problems here listed would obviously be time-consuming and expensive. Even so, the findings of discerningly designed studies of this kind might aid programme managers as well as contribute, cumulatively, to 'the development of a realistic theory of international administration that will not be "culture-bound." '[1]

Personnel Problems

1. Analyses of the recruitment of field personnel with the object of identifying the personal characteristics and types of experience that make for successful performance in trans-cultural operations. For example, what kinds of attitudes and motivations appear to contribute to effective adjustment? to disillusionment? to demoralization? These studies should take into account such variables as age range, family status, social origins, educational background, and previous experience. (See Harlan Cleveland, Gerard J. Mangone, and John Clarke Adams, *The Overseas Americans*, New

[1] See the author's article, 'The Study of International Administration: Retrospect and Prospect,' *World Politics* (Oct. 1958).

York, McGraw-Hill, 1960, for clues as to how such studies might be set up methodologically.)

2. Studies of the results of UN agency fellowship schemes in relation to eligibility requirements, techniques of selection, duration of the period of study, and types of study programmes.

3. Comparative studies of agency practices with regard to tenure, promotion, and rotation of field personnel, as they affect morale and performance.

4. Analyses of briefing and de-briefing procedures in UN organizations with continuing field programmes. In addition to an intensive examination of written materials, these studies should include depth interviews (*a*) of agency supervisory officials and (*b*) of field experts during, and after the termination of, their assignments.

Headquarters-Field Relations

5. Studies of the administrative costs of field programme operations in relation to programme size, geographic spread, and degree of decentralization of programme execution to field units. Under this heading it would be useful to compare centres where there are local specialized agency offices with centres where there is a TAB office but no other field unit. This should provide a means of determining how much duplication of services, equipment, local transport, and clerical staff is likely to occur within given operational dimensions, and the probable savings from office consolidation. It goes without saying that in so far as possible such studies should estimate the costs of project delays and break-downs because of lack of adequate field back-stopping, and indicate intangible losses arising from the frustrations of government officials and of experts, and so forth.

6. Studies of the communication process in cognate agencies designed (*a*) to show, through the use of statistical devices, trends in volume and tempo of different kinds of traffic through the organizational hierarchy and (*b*) to discover, by an intensive examination of procedures, the causes of delays, blockages, and crossed-lines.

7. A comparative assessment of the effectiveness of agency reporting systems in terms of the content, frequency, routing, and utilization of reports from the field.

The Programme Process

8. Studies of the operation of different patterns of national planning and co-ordinative machinery in relation to programme making and execution, with the aim of identifying significant trends and of discovering the most effective ways of aiding governments to improve their administrative processes for developmental purposes.

9. Comparative studies of different methods of project programming for economic and technical assistance, as illustrated by IBRD, EPTA, the Special Fund, UNICEF, and the U.S. Point Four programme.

10. Sample analyses of project follow-up in relation to a country's stage

of development and degree of political and administrative stability on the one hand, and to kinds of project instruments and recommendations on the other.

11. Studies, in selected culture areas, of the impact of UN field operations on 'grass root' attitudes towards the UN system and on the popular image of its goals and purposes.

12. Comparisons, in a representative sample of countries, of bilateral and UN multilateral aid programmes with reference to host country reactions, the adjustment of project experts, impact on national policies and institutions, and the like.

From the operational standpoint, certain of the studies proposed above could be combined, particularly if they were conducted on a group basis. Some might require larger-scale financing than could be managed from organization budgets. It would seem not inappropriate for ECOSOC, or the ACC, to take the initiative in defining the general terms of reference for a comprehensive research project covering these problems that appear to be the most urgent and important. If outside financing were felt to be necessary, the Secretary-General might be authorized to enlist support from a private foundation, and in any event to engage the services of an international team of social scientists suitably qualified by experience to design and carry out the inquiry. This arrangement would have the advantage of ensuring access to all relevant official personnel, unpublished materials, and non-confidential files. Whatever the procedure, it goes without saying that the investigators should be permitted to present their substantive findings frankly—on their own responsibility as independent scholars.

INDEX

Abbreviations are explained in the list on pages xiii—xiv

www.ingramcontent.com/pod-product-compliance
Ingram Content Group UK Ltd.
Pitfield, Milton Keynes, MK11 3LW, UK
UKHW020223290926
15470UKWH00001B/341

9 780313 203